Special Edition

Using

Visual C++ .NET

Kate Gregory

S0-ARM-125

que®

201 W. 103rd Street
Indianapolis, Indiana 46290

SPECIAL EDITION USING VISUAL C++ .NET

Copyright© 2002 by Que® Publishing

All rights reserved. No part of this book shall be reproduced, stored in a retrieval system, or transmitted by any means, electronic, mechanical, photocopying, recording, or otherwise, without written permission from the publisher. No patent liability is assumed with respect to the use of the information contained herein. Although every precaution has been taken in the preparation of this book, the publisher and author assume no responsibility for errors or omissions. Nor is any liability assumed for damages resulting from the use of the information contained herein.

International Standard Book Number: 0-7897-2466-9

Library of Congress Catalog Card Number: 2001096462

Printed in the United States of America

First Printing: April 2002

04 04 03 02   4 3 2 1

Trademarks

All terms mentioned in this book that are known to be trademarks or service marks have been appropriately capitalized. Que cannot attest to the accuracy of this information. Use of a term in this book should not be regarded as affecting the validity of any trademark or service mark.

Warning and Disclaimer

Every effort has been made to make this book as complete and as accurate as possible, but no warranty or fitness is implied. The information provided is on an "as is" basis. The author and the publisher shall have neither liability nor responsibility to any person or entity with respect to any loss or damages arising from the information contained in this book.

Publisher
David Culverwell

Executive Editor
Candy Hall

Acquisitions Editor
Michelle Newcomb

Development Editors
Katie Pendergast
Sarah Robbins

Managing Editor
Thomas Hayes

Project Editor
Tricia Liebig

Copy Editor
Margo Catts

Indexer
Rebecca Salerno

Proofreader
Jody Larsen

Technical Editor
Vincent Mayfield

Team Coordinator
Cindy Teeters

Media Developer
Michael Hunter

Interior Designer
Ruth Harvey

Cover Designer
Dan Armstrong
Ruth Harvey

Page Layout
D&G Limited, LLC

CONTENTS

ABOUT THE AUTHOR

Kate Gregory is a founding partner of Gregory Consulting Limited (www.gregcons.com), which has been providing consulting and development services throughout North America since 1986. Her experience with C++ stretches back to before Visual C++ existed—and she enthusiastically converted upon seeing the first release. Gregory Consulting develops software and Web sites, and specializes in combining the two to create active sites. The firm, which has grown to ten people, builds quality custom and off-the-shelf software components for Web pages and other applications, and consults on Internet and intranet topics for clients in government and small- to medium-sized firms.

Kate teaches and writes on a variety of related topics, including .NET, XML, C++, object-oriented techniques, and UML. She also speaks at conferences, including Microsoft Developer Days, on topics of interest to the Visual C++ community, and serves as the MSDN Regional Director for Toronto. (MSDN is an outreach program for developers who use Microsoft tools.) Her books for Que include *Using UseNet Newsgroups*, *Building Internet Applications with Visual C++*, and three previous editions of *Special Edition Using Visual C++*. She has also contributed to four other books for Que. Kate welcomes mail at kate@gregcons.com and provides updates and bonus chapters for this book at the usingvisualc.net Web site.

DEDICATION

To my children, Beth and Kevin, who keep me connected to the world away from the keyboard, and remind me every day how good it feels to learn new things.

ACKNOWLEDGMENTS

This is the fourth edition I have written of Special Edition Using Visual C++ and the largest of them all. To cover both the classic Windows programming model and the .NET model in a single book is quite a challenge. And as always, to do so while product features and release dates are changing as you write makes it a roller coaster ride. But I haven't been on that ride alone, and as I reach the end of it, I am pleased to have a little spot in the book to thank those who have shared the trip.

First, I must thank my family. My husband Brian is not only a trooper who can free my time for writing, but is also a sounding board and fellow geek who can stay up late discussing the merits of the session state service or other cool .NET features. My children, Beth and Kevin, who probably think it's normal to write books, have learned when I can be lured away from the keyboard and when I can't—and are looking forward to this book being over!

My Gregcons employees have all helped to make this book possible as well: shooting figures, testing code, finding bugs, and generally pitching in, not to mention putting up with my absences from the office. Hans Hesse deserves special mention for his cheerfulness in the face of hundreds of screenshots, and for having a commitment as strong as my own to accurate, working code in every chapter.

There's an army of editors, proofers, indexers, illustrators, and general saints who turn my Word documents into the book you hold in your hand. Many of the team members this time have been involved in other Que projects with me, and I know that I landed the "good ones" for this book. Special mention has to go to Michelle Newcomb, who stuck with me even after moving to another division, and moved heaven and earth to accommodate shifting timelines. Vince Mayfield, my technical editor, tested all the code and checked every figure to be sure you get a high-quality book. Thanks Vince!

Although I cheerfully share the credit for the accurate and educational aspects of this book, the mistakes and omissions I have to claim as mine alone. Please bring them to my attention (kate@gregcons.com) so that they can be corrected in subsequent printings and editions. I am as grateful as ever to readers who have done so in the past, and improved this book in the process.

TELL US WHAT YOU THINK!

As the reader of this book, *you* are our most important critic and commentator. We value your opinion and want to know what we're doing right, what we could do better, what areas you'd like to see us publish in, and any other words of wisdom you're willing to pass our way.

As a Publisher for Que, I welcome your comments. You can fax, email, or write me directly to let me know what you did or didn't like about this book—as well as what we can do to make our books stronger.

Please note that I cannot help you with technical problems related to the topic of this book, and that due to the high volume of mail I receive, I might not be able to reply to every message.

When you write, please be sure to include this book's title and author as well as your name and phone or fax number. I will carefully review your comments and share them with the author and editors who worked on the book.

Fax: 317-581-4666

E-mail: feedback@quepublishing.com

Mail: David Culverwell
Que
201 West 103rd Street
Indianapolis, IN 46290 USA

INTRODUCTION

Visual C++ .NET is a language, a variant of C++. You build Visual C++ applications with Visual Studio .NET, a powerful and complex tool for building two kinds of applications: 32-bit applications for various flavors of Windows (95, NT, 2000, XP, and so on) and .NET applications that run in the .NET runtime.

Visual Studio .NET is an amazing tool. With its code-generating wizards, it can produce the shell of a working Windows or .NET application in seconds. It comes with a class library called Microsoft Foundation Classes (MFC) that has become the industry standard class library for Windows software development in a variety of C++ compilers. The Base Class Library of classes that support .NET provides even more power and ease of use. The visual editing tools make layout of menus and dialogs a snap. The time you invest in learning to use this product will pay for itself on your first Windows or .NET programming project.

WHO SHOULD READ THIS BOOK?

This book teaches you how to use Visual C++ to build 32-bit Windows applications, including database applications, Internet applications, and applications that tap the power of COM. It also teaches you what .NET is all about, how to use Visual C++ to write .NET applications that use databases, the Internet, and more. You even learn how to mix and match COM and .NET technologies. That's a tall order, and to fit all that in a thousand pages, some things have to go. This book does not teach you the following:

- **The C++ programming language**. You should already be familiar with C++.
- **How to use Windows applications**. You should be a proficient Windows user, able to resize and move windows, double-click, and recognize familiar toolbar buttons, for example.
- **How to use Visual C++ as a C compiler**. If you already work in C, you can use Visual C++ as your compiler, but new developers should take the plunge into C++.
- **Windows programming without MFC**. This, too, is okay for those who know it, but not something to learn now that MFC exists.

You should read this book if you fit one of these categories:

- You know some C++ and some Windows programming techniques and are new to Visual C++. You will learn the product much more quickly than you would if you just tried writing programs.

- You've been working with previous versions of Visual C++. Many times users learn one way to do things and end up overlooking some of the newer productivity features.

- You want to create .NET applications but you don't want to move to C# or Visual Basic. You'll learn the basics of .NET, and how to use those basics from C++.

- You've been working with Visual C++ .NET for a while and are beginning to suspect you're doing things the hard way. Maybe you are.

- You work in Visual C++ .NET regularly, and you need to add a feature to your product. For Windows tasks such as Help, printing, and threading, or .NET tasks such as database access or security, you'll find a "hand up" to get started.

BEFORE YOU START READING

You need a copy of Visual C++ .NET and must have it installed. The installation process is simple and easy to follow, so it's not covered in this book.

Before you buy Visual C++ .NET, you need a modern Windows operating system: Windows 2000 or Windows XP. The Windows applications you'll create will run on older versions of Windows, but to get the full benefit of .NET, you should use XP or 2000. As for your screen, the bigger the better. The illustrations in this book were all prepared at a resolution of 800×600 and, as you will see, at times things become a little crowded. The sample code is all available on the Web, at `http://www.usingvisualc.net`, so following along will be simpler if you also have access to the Web.

Finally, you need to make a promise to yourself—that you will follow along in Visual C++ as you read this book, clicking and typing and trying things out. You don't need to type all the code if you don't want to: It's all on the Web site for you to look at. However, you should be ready to open the files and look at the code as you go.

WHAT THIS BOOK COVERS

A topic such as Windows and .NET programming in Visual C++ covers a lot of ground. This book contains 25 chapters and 4 reference appendixes (A to D). Be sure to look over the titles of the appendixes now and turn to them whenever you are unsure how to do something. They provide valuable references for the following:

- Appendix A, "Windows Programming Review and a Look Inside `CWnd`," covers the specifics of Windows programming that are now hidden from you by MFC classes such as `CWnd`.

- Appendix B, "XML Review," gives a quick summary of some important concepts in XML. XML is a notation for exchanging data between applications and much of .NET relies on it.
- Appendix C, "The Visual Studio User Interface, Menus, and Visual Studio," explains all the menus, toolbars, editing areas on the screens, shortcuts, and so on, that make up the highly complicated and richly powerful interface between you and Visual Studio.
- Appendix D, "Upgrading from Visual C++ 6," is for those of you who know what you want to do, but can't find the right menu item now.

Depending on your background and willingness to poke around in menus and the online help, you might just skim these appendixes once and never return, or you might fill them full of bookmarks and yellow stickies. Although they don't lead you through the sample applications, they will teach you a lot.

The main part of the book is in Chapters 1 through 25. Each chapter teaches you an important programming task or sometimes two closely related tasks, such as building a taskbar, adding Help to an application, or building an XML Web service. Detailed instructions show you how to build a working application, or several working applications, in each chapter.

The first chapter in this book explains what .NET is and what it's all about. If you're only interested in .NET, you'll want to skip the 14 chapters that follow, because they cover Windows programming. Then ten .NET chapters cover what you need to know to move to .NET. Here's a brief overview of some of the material that is covered and where you can find it.

WINDOWS APPLICATIONS

Windows applications are the kinds of applications you made with Visual C++ before .NET came along. They run on several different versions of Windows, including Windows 95 and Windows 98. Many C++ developers need to maintain these applications and will not be porting them to .NET immediately. With Visual C++, you don't have to—you can continue to develop those applications with Visual Studio .NET.

DIALOGS AND CONTROLS

What Windows program doesn't have a dialog box? An edit box? A button? Dialog boxes and controls are vital to Windows user interfaces, and all of them, even the simple button or piece of static text, are windows. The Win32 common controls enable you to take advantage of the learning time users have devoted to other programs and the programming time developers have put in on the operating system. They can then offer the same File Open dialog box as everybody else, the same hierarchical tree control, and so on. Learn more about all these controls in Chapters 3, "Interacting with Your Application" and 7, "Status Bars, Toolbars, and Common Controls."

Messages and Commands

Messages form the heart of Windows programming. Whenever anything happens on a Windows machine, such as a user clicking the mouse or pressing a key, a message is triggered and sent to one or more windows, which do something about it. Visual C++ makes it easy for you to write code that catches these messages and acts on them. Chapter 3 explains the concept of messages and how MFC and other aspects of Visual C++ enable you to deal with them.

The View/Document Paradigm

A paradigm is a model, a way of looking at things. The designers of MFC chose to design the framework based on the assumption that every program has something it wants to save in a file. That collection of information is referred to as the *document*. A *view* is one way of looking at a document. There are many advantages to separating the view and the document, explained further in Chapter 4, "Displaying Information." MFC provides classes from which to inherit your document class and your view class, so that common programming tasks such as implementing scrollbars are no longer your problem.

No matter how smart your Windows program is, if you can't tell the user what's going on by putting some words or pictures onscreen, no one will know what the program has done. Your view classes do a remarkable amount of the work automatically (one of the advantages of adopting the document/view paradigm), but at times you have to do the drawing yourself. You learn about drawing on the screen, device contexts, scrolling, and more in Chapter 4.

Printing on Paper and Saving on Disk

Adding printing capabilities to your program is sometimes the simplest thing in the world, because the code you use to draw onscreen can be reused to draw on paper. If more than one page of information is involved, though, things become tricky. Chapter 5, "Printing and Saving," explains all this, as well as mapping modes, headers and footers, and more.

Some good things are meant to be only temporary, such as the display of a calculator or an online chat window. However, most programs can save their documents to a file and open and load that file to re-create a document that has been stored. MFC simplifies this by using archives and extending the use of the stream I/O operators >> and <<. You learn all about reading and writing to files in Chapter 5.

The Component Object Model

COM was the best way to make components before .NET arrived. And there's no need to leave COM behind to embrace .NET—a COM component is a .NET object and a .NET object is a COM component. Learn how to make a COM component in Chapter 9, "Building COM+ Components with ATL." You can see how to mix and match .NET with COM in Chapter 23, "COM Interop."

THE INTERNET

Distributed computing, in which work is shared between two or more computers, is becoming more and more common. Programs need to talk to each other, people need to send messages across a LAN or around the world, and MFC has classes that support these kinds of communication. Although .NET brings the power of the Internet to every application, you can still tap that power from Windows applications. Chapter 10, "Internet Programming," shows how to use the WinInet classes or do your own sockets programming.

DATABASE ACCESS

Database programming keeps getting easier. With ODBC you call API functions that access a huge variety of database files—Oracle, DBase, an Excel spreadsheet, a plain text file, old legacy mainframe systems using SQL, whatever! You call a standard name function, and the API provided by the database vendor or a third party handles the translation. The details are in Chapter 11, "Database Programming."

ADVANCED WINDOWS MATERIAL

For developers who have mastered the basics, this book features some advanced chapters to move your programming skills forward. You will learn how to prevent memory leaks, find bottlenecks, and locate bugs in your code with the techniques discussed in Chapter 12, "Improving Your Application's Performance." Chapter 13, "Debugging," shows you how to find and correct bugs like a pro.

As user demands for high-performance software continue to multiply, developers must learn entirely new techniques to produce powerful applications that provide fast response times. For many developers, writing multithreaded applications is a vital technique. Learn about threading in Chapter 14, "Multitasking with Windows Threads." Chapter 15, "Special Win32 Application Types," introduces you to console applications, using and building your own DLLs, and Unicode.

.NET PROGRAMMING

What is .NET? It's so many things: a platform on which code can run, a library of powerful and useful classes, a cross-language development technique, a set of protocols for Web services, and much more. The second half of this book will move you into the world of .NET.

GETTING STARTED

Start with Chapter 1, ".NET Background," explains .NET and contrasts it to traditional Windows programming. It's your starting point for a journey to .NET. Your next stop is Chapter 16, "The Common Language Runtime." Here you'll learn how .NET applications run in the runtime, and about the tremendous functionality offered by the .NET Framework. In Chapter 17, "Getting Started with .NET," you'll begin to develop .NET code for yourself.

INTER-LANGUAGE DEVELOPMENT

Imagine calling VB code from C++, or C++ code from C#. Imagine doing it without having to do anything special to indicate you are crossing a language boundary. How about writing a Visual Basic class that actually inherits from a class written in C++—and debugging across languages, too. That's part of the promise of .NET. See it happen in Chapter 18, "Integrating with Visual Basic" and Chapter 19, "Integrating with C#."

MANAGED AND UNMANAGED CODE

After you've done a little .NET development, you're ready to understand what "managed" means for code and data. Chapter 20, "Managed and Unmanaged Code," explains what's going on and why it matters to you, the developer.

WEB SERVICES

XML Web services are a cross-vendor initiative that are likely to change the way we all develop software in this decade. To find out what they are and how simple it is to develop and use XML Web services with Visual C++, read Chapter 21, "Creating an XML Web Service."

DATABASE PROGRAMMING

Database programming in classic Windows applications has become pretty easy. On the .NET side, ADO.NET takes it to another level, easily handling disconnected programming and giving you full control over the way your data is handled. Read Chapter 22, "Database Access with ADO.NET," for more details.

COM INTEROP

Most development shops have a lot of time and effort invested in existing applications, and many of those applications express some of their functionality through COM. Of course you want to use your old COM objects from your new .NET applications. You may also want your COM applications to use some new .NET objects. No problem! In fact, it's actually easier to use a COM object from a .NET application than from a classic COM C++ application. Chapter 23, "COM Interop," shows you just how easy it is.

SECURITY

With .NET, code can come from anywhere—your hard drive, the LAN, or the Internet. Code can download and run without you even noticing. But if that code is malicious, don't you want to notice it run? The .NET Framework prevents access to local resources by remote code, to protect your system. Chapter 24, "Security and Policies," explains how it works and shows how to take control of your own machine.

CONVENTIONS USED IN THIS BOOK

One thing this book has plenty of is code. Sometimes you need to see only a line or two, so the code is mixed in with the text, like this:

```
int SomeFunction( int x, int y);
{
    return x+y;
}
```

You can tell the difference between code and regular text by the fonts used for each. Sometimes, you'll see a piece of code that's too large to mix in with the text: You will find an example in Listing 0.1.

LISTING 0.1

```
CHostDialog dialog(m_pMainWnd);
    if (dialog.DoModal() == IDOK)
    {
        AppSocket = new CSocket();
        if (AppSocket->Connect(dialog.m_hostname,119))
        {
            while (AppSocket->GetStatus() == CONNECTING)
            {
                YieldControl();
            }
            if (AppSocket->GetStatus() == CONNECTED)
            {
             CString response = AppSocket->GetLine();
                SocketAvailable = TRUE;
            }
        }
    }
    if (!SocketAvailable)
    {
        AfxMessageBox("Can't connect to server. Please
➡ quit.",MB_OK|MB_ICONSTOP);
    }
```

The character on the next-to-last line (➡) is called the *code continuation character*. It indicates a place where a line of code had to be broken to fit it on the page, but in reality the line doesn't break there. If you're typing code from the book, don't break the line there—keep going. If you're reading along in code that Visual C++ generated for you, don't be confused when the line doesn't break there.

Remember, the code is in the book so that you can understand what's going on, not for you to type it. All the code is on the companion Web site as well. Sometimes you will work your way through the development of an application and see several versions of a block of code as you go—the final version is on the Web site. You'll find the site by going to http://www.quepublishing.com or http://www.usingvisualc.net.

Tip

This is a Tip: A shortcut or an interesting feature you might want to know about.

Note

This is a Note: It explains a subtle but important point. Don't skip Notes, even if you're the kind who skips Tips.

Caution

This is a Caution, and it's serious. It warns you of the horrible consequences if you make a false step, so be sure to read all of these that you come across.

When a word is being defined or emphasized, it's in *italic*. The names of variables, functions, and C++ classes are all in `monospaced font`. Internet URLS and things you should type are also in `monospace`. Remember, no URL ends with punctuation, so ignore any comma or period after the URL.

TIME TO GET STARTED

That about wraps things up for the introduction. You've learned what you need to get started, including some advanced warning about the notations used throughout the book. Jump right in, learn all about writing Windows applications with MFC, or .NET applications with the .NET Framework, and then get started on some development of your own. Good luck and have fun!

.NET BACKGROUND

In this chapter

WHAT IS .NET?

Whether you're a seasoned Windows programmer with Visual C++, an Internet programmer who is watching the latest trends, or a new developer unclear on the differences between the various programming platforms, I bet there's one question you'll ask yourself as you get ready to use Visual Studio .NET: just what is .NET, anyway?

How Do You Say It? How Do You Search for It?

The character before the word "net" is pronounced "dot," so in circumstances where a . character doesn't belong (for example, as in the name of a mailing list or at the start of a file name), people often refer to "dot-net." If you want to do some Web searches to see what's new with .NET, you'll probably have the best luck searching for "dotnet" rather than ".NET"–after all, the word "net" appears on a lot of Web pages that have nothing to do with this new initiative.

Unfortunately, there's no single answer. Microsoft is using the .NET label on more than one product, but they all fit together into an initiative and a strategy. So .NET is:

- A platform on which code can run.
- A class library of code that can be used from any language.
- New versions of development tools such as Visual Studio.
- New versions of some development languages.
- A set of server products that facilitate .NET work.
- A new way of designing and creating applications that share work among components, even over the Internet.

The .NET platform doesn't run executables that run on Windows or other platforms. Instead the Common Language Runtime (CLR) executes .NET applications that have been compiled to MSIL (Microsoft Intermediate Language, also called just Intermediate Language, or IL). This "execution engine" converts MSIL to native code but also provides many other services, including memory management, security, and interaction between applications, such as when your code uses a COM object or calls code from a DLL. At the moment the .NET platform is implemented only on various flavors of Windows, but that in itself will save many developers headaches.

The .NET SDK (Software Development Kit) comes with Visual Studio .NET and includes the .NET classes, which are classes that can be used from any .NET language and that provide tremendous functionality to developers. Some of this functionality is also provided to pure Windows programmers in libraries such as MFC, and some of it wraps services you may have been using in COM or COM+, but much of it—such as working with XML or checking security authorization—is available only in .NET.

Visual Studio .NET is the newest version of Visual Studio, and it's really quite different from versions that came before. In the past, Visual Studio has been a bundle of related tools, each with its own user interface and its own strengths and weaknesses. Now, Visual Studio is a single product that can be used to write code in several different languages. Rather than having the Visual Basic way to connect code to a button and click, which is different from the Visual C++ way to do the same, now there is just the Visual Studio way. This means, of course, that some developers have extra learning to do. You might want to read Appendix C, "The Visual Studio User Interface" even if you think you know former versions of Visual Studio thoroughly. Appendix D, "Upgrading From Visual C++ 6," is also likely to be helpful for experienced Visual C++ programmers.

Some of the languages that ship with Visual Studio .NET have undergone changes to adapt to the .NET approach. Visual C++ has changed the least. A few keywords have been added that let C++ developers request specific .NET features or capabilities in code. Existing Visual C++ 6 projects should open and build in Visual Studio .NET without any changes at all. If you've heard a lot of rumors about .NET changing development languages, they were probably referring to Visual Basic, which has changed quite a bit. Visual C++ programmers have no worries on that score.

Figure 1.1 shows how the various .NET languages, XML Web services, XML, the .NET class library, and the CLR work together to create a .NET application.

Figure 1.1
The .NET initiative is much more than just a new compiler release.

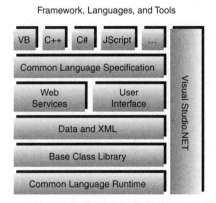

Framework, Languages, and Tools

Microsoft has labeled several server products with the .NET tag as well. These servers are

- Microsoft Application Center 2000
- Microsoft BizTalk Server 2000
- Microsoft Commerce Server 2000
- Microsoft Exchange 2000
- Microsoft Host Integration Server 2000
- Microsoft Internet Security and Acceleration Server 2000
- Microsoft Mobile Information 2001 Server
- Microsoft SQL Server 2000

Application Center is an add-on product for Windows 2000 Server that is designed for high-traffic, highly available Web sites. It simplifies deployment of a Web site across multiple servers. Because the hallmark of an Application Center is that it makes managing multiple servers as easy as managing a single server, developers shouldn't have to keep in mind that they are targeting an Application Center Web site.

BizTalk Server dramatically simplifies the work involved in exchanging XML documents between applications or between companies. BizTalk Server calls XML Web services or legacy COM objects to handle documents as they arrive. Much of the common work, such as maintaining document queues and routing incoming documents to the appropriate handler, is built into BizTalk Server and does not have to be hand coded each time. BizTalk Orchestration Designer is a Visio-like tool that can automate workflow, with many of the steps in the workflow involving a call to a COM object or .NET component.

Commerce Server is a set of tools for building e-commerce Web sites. Before you write your own shopping cart, customer tracker, or site traffic analyzer, be sure to see what Commerce Server has to offer.

Exchange is much more than an e-mail server; it provides collaboration tools as well. Many XML Web services hook into Exchange—for example, to schedule meetings.

Host Integration Server simplifies access to legacy systems such as DB2 for OS/390 and AS/400, file transfer for AS/400, AS/36, and VSAM, IMS transactions, and AS/400 data queues. You can work with legacy data as though it were available through ODBC, using familiar COM+ and MTS services.

Internet Security and Acceleration Server is a caching proxy server and firewall that keeps your enterprise protected and connected at the same time.

Mobile Information Server is for wireless providers such as cellular service providers and for enterprise intranets. It simplifies the task of synchronizing and serving information to wireless and mobile users, and brings .NET functionality to mobile devices.

SQL Server is Microsoft's high-end, scalable, and powerful database server. Plenty of XML and .NET support has been added to this version.

What's important about all these server products is that they can work together by exchanging a little XML, by calling each other's services, or by putting messages into queues. It is getting easier and easier to build a solution by gluing together existing components. Always check to be sure that you aren't reinventing the wheel before you start to code a .NET solution.

Overall, .NET has the potential to become a movement that encourages developers to offer applications over the Internet and consume such services. At the same time it offers a measure of platform independence (within the Windows family now, and perhaps other platforms later) and language independence. These developments will make the job of new programmers easier, but they leave old programmers with a lot of material to learn.

Useful Web Sites

A lot of information about .NET is on the Web, and not just at Microsoft's Web sites. Here are some sites you'll want to browse for samples, useful WXML Web services, and announcements:

- `http://www.usingvisualc.net`. The support site for this book. Here you'll find sample code, corrections, updates, and bonus chapters that just couldn't fit into the printed book.

- `http://msdn.microsoft.com/net`. Microsoft's hub for .NET developers.

- `http://discuss.develop.com/dotnet.html`. Searchable archives of the DevelopMentor dotnet discussion list. Check the dates on any article before relying on the information; this list has been in existence since, well before the first public beta version of Visual Studio.NET was released.

- `http://www.devx.com/dotnet/`. Links to articles, samples, and available XML Web services.

- `http://www.gotdotnet.com`. A site run by the .NET development team. It features samples and tutorials, many of which are contributed by non-Microsoft developers.

WHY WRITE AN XML WEB SERVICE?

The heart of .NET is the XML Web service. Perhaps you've seen a Microsoft presentation where cheerful people book doctors' appointments from their desktops or their cellular phones. Then they check the weather, order takeout food, and stroll off into the sunset. All these tasks are done with XML Web services, the presenter tells you, and they are all possible today.

The Internet is soon to be full of XML Web services, all free or inexpensive, and all easy to access. You can probably imagine why you would want to write an application that uses an XML Web service: to save programming. If your application needs to convert currencies, or get the latest weather forecast or sports results, an XML Web service that provides that functionality—already written—is a wonderful discovery. Your job as a programmer will be far easier, and your application will be more useful and popular. What's more, they are a cross-platform, cross-programming-language, cross-vendor solution: An XML Web service you write in Visual C++ might be used by some Perl code running on a Unix machine. You might write some Visual C++ code that uses an XML Web service written in Java and running on a kind of machine you've never heard of. As long as it's on the Internet, and meets the standards for an XML Web service, issues such as operating system and programming language are irrelevant.

But who are these angels who are writing and providing XML Web services? Why would you want to join them in providing functionality over the Internet for anyone to run and use? There are four good business reasons to provide an XML Web service:

- It's quite simple to charge for access to an XML Web service, so you could write and provide one as a money-making venture in its own right.

- A free XML Web service might drive business to your primary product or service.

- A private XML Web service could simplify the architecture of a multi-tier application that uses the Internet as infrastructure.

- Writing an XML Web service frees you from creating a visual user interface.

There are lots of ways to charge for access to an XML Web service. You might restrict access to subscribers only, and charge them a monthly fee. This would be a terrific way to distribute weather or traffic updates, for example. The information your XML Web service provides would be integrated into some other application to be displayed to the user.

Alternatively, you could charge a fee each time the XML Web service was used. Whether the user is identified by an IP address, or by a user ID passed into the XML Web service, it's still a simple matter to record who used the service and update a billing record. For example, you might sell access to currency exchange rates this way.

A free XML Web service might help you to sell more of your primary products and services. If health insurance companies use an XML Web service to book a doctor's appointments, an underutilized doctor gets more visits each day. If travel agents can use an XML Web service to make restaurant reservations, book a rental car, or reserve a hotel room, then those businesses all experience an increase in business, because they made it easy for the travel agent to drive customers to them.

It takes a lot of time and effort to create a Web site on which consumers can make their own restaurant reservations. You need exciting graphics, an intuitive user interface, and plenty of computing power and bandwidth so that the whole glitzy, high-graphics experience serves out quick as a wink to easily-bored consumers. Then you need to spend plenty of effort and money attracting consumers to your site and persuading them to make their own reservations. When you create an XML Web service, on the other hand, you don't need a graphical user interface at all! Your XML Web service is used by other applications—and they don't consume anywhere near the bandwidth that humans do, because they don't need graphics, instructions, or "Contact Us" pages. The only persuading needed is to those travel agents and other businesses that might want to make reservations electronically. Tell them how their applications can reach your XML Web service, and you're all set. That's awfully appealing.

That same simplicity of development appeals to businesses who don't want to expose a free XML Web service to the public. Using XML Web services as part of an intranet or extranet development project can save a great deal of time and effort. Your multi-tier applications can use the Internet for infrastructure while still running securely. A desktop application might call an XML Web service on a remote server to add a new record to a database, or to retrieve records that have changed recently—perhaps because consumers have been using the Web site to register for an event or to place an order.

Government agencies, universities, and other institutions are often obliged to make certain information publicly available. They, too, feel the pressure to add graphics and glitz to their presentation of this information. But budget pressures can mean that some information is not available at all. Making it available through an XML Web service delegates development of the user interface to others, while the institution focuses on providing the information alone, at the lowest possible cost. Many developers are currently "screen scraping" information from boring Web sites for use on more flashy sites. These developers will be thrilled when the information is available as an XML Web service.

WHAT ABOUT EXISTING MFC APPLICATIONS?

Does all this talk of XML Web services leave any room for the skills you had before the .NET initiative? Is COM dead? Is MFC dead? Is ATL dead? These are questions many developers are asking. The simple answer is no, these older technologies are not dead. Yes, old skills still have value. A few years ago, people used to ask me whether Java was going to kill C++. I always answered, "Did C++ kill Cobol?" Of course not. In the same way, .NET isn't going to kill traditional Windows-only programming.

One of the design goals for Visual C++ .NET was that it should be, to quote a member of the Microsoft development team, "a great upgrade" for those doing non-.NET Windows programming. This, by the way, was not a design goal for other parts of Visual Studio.NET, including Visual Basic.NET. If you're used to programming in MFC or ATL, you're going to be even more productive with those tools when you use Visual Studio.NET. None of the things you used to do has become harder or hidden. You don't have to learn .NET or XML or anything new to support your old applications, or make new ones that are a lot like the old ones.

There are still circumstances when MFC and other pre-.NET technologies are the right choice for your application. Consider using what .NET people are calling "native code" or "unmanaged code" if the following is true:

■ You have a large application that is working well and needs only minor enhancements. As the old saying goes, "If it ain't broke, don't fix it." That certainly applies to software. Maintain your application, and be glad you can mix and match managed and unmanaged code. You may be able to integrate your application into the .NET world someday, but you don't have to rewrite it to do so.

■ Your application is subject to availability constraints that forbid it from gathering information and functionality over the Internet through an XML Web service, and it may not expose any of its information as an XML Web service. Such an application has less to gain by embracing .NET.

■ You have demanding performance requirements. Unmanaged C++ code is faster than managed (.NET) MSIL code. There will be high-performance applications that never move to .NET, and others that will move later, when performance improves.

About half of this book covers traditional Windows programming, also called non-.NET programming, native code, and unmanaged code. Check these chapters:

■ Chapter 2, "Building Your First Windows Application," walks you through various kinds of applications you can create with Visual C++ .NET and introduces you to the MFC Application Wizard.

■ Chapter 3, "Interacting with Your Application," shows how to add a dialog box to gather information, and discusses the Windows messaging approach.

- Chapter 4, "Displaying Information," explains the MFC Document/View paradigm and demonstrates simple graphics and text techniques for the non-dialog portions of your application.

- Chapter 5, "Printing and Saving," walks you through these two essential foundations of a document-based Windows application.

- Chapter 6, "Building a Complete Application: ShowString," pulls together the work of the previous chapters, and adds menus to create a sample application on which you could base much of your Windows programming.

- Chapter 7, "Status Bars, Toolbars, and Common Controls," demonstrates adding richer touches to your user interface.

- Chapter 8, "Help, Property Pages, and Wizards," shows you how to explain yourself to your users and how to walk them through common procedures.

- Chapter 9, "Building COM+ Components with ATL," introduces the concepts of COM and creating a simple COM component.

- Chapter 10, "Internet Programming," covers "old-fashioned" Internet programming— that is, non.NET Internet programming, which can be remarkably simple.

- Chapter 11, "Database Programming," shows how to add data access to your applications.

- Chapter 12, "Improving Your Application's Performance," covers profiling, memory leaks, and other performance-related matters in traditional Windows programming.

- Chapter 13, "Debugging," introduces you to the powerful and useful Visual Studio debugger. Track down problems quickly with the techniques in this chapter.

- Chapter 14, "Multitasking with Windows Threads," shows how Windows threading is supported by MFC, and how your applications can do two things at once.

- Chapter 15, "Special Win32 Application Types," covers DLLs, console applications, NT or Windows 2000 services, and other unusual application types.

- Reference A, "Windows Programming Review and a Look Inside CWnd," is a look under the hood at the way Win32 programming works, and how MFC makes it simpler.

WHAT ABOUT COM DEVELOPERS?

A COM developer might do any of several things:

- Maintain an application that uses COM components.
- Write new applications that use COM components.
- Maintain one or more COM components.
- Write new COM components.

Many COM developers, of course, do more than one of these things. Nonetheless, it's handy to split the tasks up this way and examine the impact of .NET on each of the four activities.

If you maintain an application that uses COM components, you don't have to change anything. If you like, you can port the application to .NET and still use those same components from the .NET side. Or you can leave your application as a "classic COM" application even when the COM components you were using get re-released as .NET components. You can then use the .NET components just as you use COM components.

If you're writing a new application, you might be tempted to make it a .NET application. After all, a lot of neat services are available to a .NET application that will save you time and effort. But perhaps you're looking wistfully at a catalog full of COM components and thinking you can't make a .NET application and use existing COM components. No problem! A .NET application can talk to a COM component just as if it were a .NET component.

If you've written (and perhaps sold) one or more COM components, you might be worried about the task of porting them to .NET. There is no task. A COM component is a .NET component, or at least you can go around acting as if it were.

If you're writing a new component, you might hesitate to write it as a .NET component, in case the majority of your market doesn't move to .NET right away. You can hedge your bets and write it as a COM component, because it will behave as a .NET component anyway. But if the services available in .NET appeal to you, write it as a .NET component. Old code can use it as a COM component.

From the point of view of those who consume them, there is no difference between a COM component and a .NET component. They are interchangeable. This is the magic of "COM interop" and it was a major goal of the .NET team. COM has been a huge success, and there is a large installed base of COM components—and component consumers—that must be supported.

If you have spent a lot of time learning COM programming, and are comfortable and familiar with HRESULTS, GUIDs, QueryInterface and the like, you don't have to leave it all behind. But if COM programming has always intimidated you, all those existing components will be available to you from new .NET code. Alternatively, you can use .NET to create a component that will be available to the installed base of COM applications out in the world. You can even write a .NET component that extends an existing COM component.

For more about how easy it is to "mix and match" classic COM with .NET, read Chapter 23, "COM Interop."

WILL C++ BE THE RIGHT LANGUAGE FOR .NET?

There's a lot of coverage on Visual Basic.NET and how different it is from Visual Basic 6. There's a lot of coverage on C# and how new and exciting it is. Where does this leave Visual C++? Should C++ developers learn another language? Should new programmers skip C++ and go straight to another language? No way.

In previous versions of Visual Studio, the interface has been slightly different for each language. Visual Basic programmers might double-click to perform a common task (such as editing code associated with a dialog box control), whereas Visual C++ programmers were expected to choose something from a drop-down box, for example. Those days are gone. The Visual Studio user interface is the same no matter the language you use. In fact, on the Start, Programs menu, you don't choose a language as you used to. Compare Figure 1.2, the Visual Studio 6 menu choices, to Figure 1.3, the Visual Studio.NET choices.

Figure 1.2
Visual Studio 6.0 was a collection of related tools, one per language.

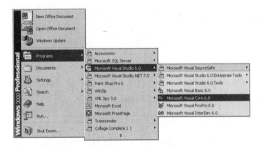

Figure 1.3
Visual Studio.NET is a single tool that works with many languages.

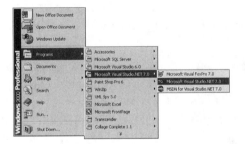

This new level of integration means that you can work with whatever language is right for you within Visual Studio. In fact, it's quite simple to mix languages within a single solution. When you use the Common Language Runtime, the services and functionality it offers are equally available to all languages. A Visual Basic 6 programmer couldn't use all the functionality of MFC, but had to wait for a Visual Basic library to be released. Now Visual Basic programmers, Visual C++ programmers, and programmers in every language supported in Visual Studio can use the functionality of the Common Language Runtime.

In fact, the languages you use in Visual Studio don't even have to be Microsoft languages. You can use Visual Studio to edit, run, and debug any language that can "hook in" to Visual Studio. Figure 1.4 shows Perl being debugged within Visual Studio.

With .NET, you can write a base class in Visual C++, inherit from it in Visual Basic, and use the class in a C# program. Your choice of language is almost entirely a matter of convenience, and of using what you already know. Why learn a new language if you're already familiar with one of the .NET languages?

Figure 1.4
Visual Studio.NET supports non-Microsoft languages, such as Perl.

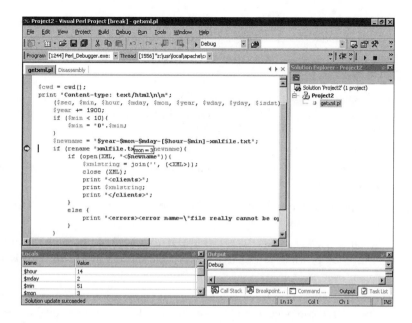

CH
1

There is, however, one exception, and it's one that's sure to warm the hearts of C++ programmers everywhere. Simply put, we can do things that other programmers can't. C++ code can be managed—which is to say a full participant in the .NET fun—or unmanaged. Unmanaged code is less portable, and doesn't get all the .NET goodies. The advantage is that it's much faster. For certain kinds of applications, where speed is everything, unmanaged C++ code using "classic" libraries, such as ATL, is going to be the development technique of choice.

WHAT SHOULD A NEW .NET PROGRAMMER LEARN?

If you're an old-time Visual C++ programmer (say from the year 2000 or earlier) and you want to get started with .NET, I'd recommend spending a little time in the Win32 half of this book. Run through a task you already know how to do. A lot of wizards have disappeared (and some others are just in hiding) and the way you connect parts of your application to code has changed quite a bit. Re-familiarize yourself with the Visual Studio user interface before you start to learn .NET. Appendix D, "Upgrading from Visual C++ 6," covers a lot of the ground for you. Save yourself some frustration and read it before you start to type code.

If you've never touched Visual Studio before, and you're not scheduled to maintain an existing MFC application, I encourage you to read the .NET half of this book first. Check these chapters:

- Chapter 16, "The Common Language Runtime," introduces you to the wonderful services offered to .NET programmers in all languages.

- Chapter 17, "Getting Started with .NET," walks you through the steps of creating the basic building block of .NET functionality, the .NET component.

- Chapter 18, "Integrating with Visual Basic," shows how to mix Visual C++ and Visual Basic.

- Chapter 19, "Integrating with C++," shows how to mix Visual C++ and Visual C#. (C# is the language, and has been submitted to a standards body. Visual C# is Microsoft's implementation of the language.)

- Chapter 20, "Managed and Unmanaged Code," explains the restrictions placed on managed code, and the benefits gained in return. It shows you when to use each and how to combine them.

- Chapter 21, "Creating an XML Web Service," shows you how to expose your functionality to the World Wide Web simply and easily.

- Chapter 22, "Database Access with ADO.NET," explores the latest of many ways Microsoft provides you to access data—and shows you why this one is a big improvement over previous data access techniques.

- Chapter 23, "COM Interop," gets into the nitty-gritty of making COM components into .NET components and vice versa. It's a lot easier than you'd expect.

- Chapter 24, "Security and Policies," explains how the .NET runtime can protect you from malicious code—and how to control the way security works in your applications.

The entire .NET initiative is built on XML. Does that mean you need to know XML to work with .NET? It most certainly does not. One of the big attractions of .NET is that it brings the benefits of XML to all kinds of programmers, whether they know XML or not.

However, if you do know a little bit about XML, you get even more benefit from .NET. For example, XML is ordinary, human-readable text, not a binary file. That means you can look at it with Notepad, or type some yourself with Notepad, rather than having to use a tool. If you can look at the XML your application is generating, you can debug more quickly and with a lot less pain. If XML is a mystery to you, be sure to read Reference B, "XML Review," which covers the highlights of XML from a .NET point of view.

FROM HERE

It's time to get started! If you can't wait to dive into .NET, head for Chapter 16, "The Common Language Runtime," to learn more about the .NET platform on which all managed applications run. On the other hand, if you want to stick with traditional Windows programming with MFC for the next little while, Chapter 2, "Building Your First Windows Application," will get you started. If you're an experienced Visual C++ user, try Appendix D, "Upgrading From Visual C++ 6." If you run into trouble after that, use the index to find the place in the first part of the book that covers the Windows programming topic that's bothering you. Good luck!

CHAPTER 2

BUILDING YOUR FIRST WINDOWS APPLICATION

In this chapter

CREATING A WINDOWS APPLICATION

Visual C++ doesn't just compile code; it generates code. You can create a Windows application based on the Microsoft Foundation Classes (MFC) in minutes with a tool called the MFC Application Wizard. In this chapter you'll learn how to tell the MFC Application Wizard to make a starter application for you with all the Windows boilerplate code you want. The MFC Application Wizard is a very effective tool. It copies into your application the code that almost all Windows applications require. After all, you aren't the first programmer to need an application with resizable edges, Minimize and Maximize buttons, a File menu with Open, Close, Print Setup, Print, and Exit options, are you?

With its wizards, the New Project dialog box can make many kinds of applications, but what most people want, at least at first, is an executable (.exe) program. The MFC Application Wizard is the tool for the job. Most people also want the MFC Application Wizard to produce boilerplate code—the classes, objects, and functions that have to be in every program. To create a program like this, choose File, New, and then Project. Select Visual C++ Projects as the Project Type, then select MFC Application as the Template as shown in Figure 2.1.

Tip

If you want to make a .NET application, jump ahead to Chapter 17, "Getting Started with .NET," this chapter and those that follow describe building classic Windows applications.

Figure 2.1
The Project Types and Templates list boxes of the New Project dialog box are where you choose the kind of application you want to build.

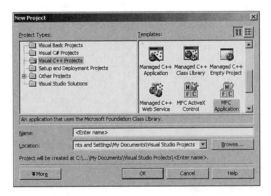

After choosing MFC Application as the Template from the list box on the right, fill in a project name and click OK. The MFC Application Wizard appears and presents you with a number of tabs to customize your application. At each tab, you can make decisions about what kind of application you want. At any time, you can change from one tab to another without losing any changes you may have made. You can press Cancel to abandon the whole process, Help for more details, or Finish to go ahead and create the application without changing any more options. The following sections explain each tab.

A MFC application uses MFC, the Microsoft Foundation Classes. You will learn more about MFC throughout this book.

DECIDING HOW MANY DOCUMENTS THE APPLICATION SUPPORTS

The first decision to communicate to the MFC Application Wizard (AppWizard) is the Application Type tab, as shown in Figure 2.2. You must choose whether your application should be SDI, MDI, dialog based, or have multiple top-level documents. The MFC Application Wizard generates different code and classes for each of these application types.

The four application types to choose from are as follows:

- A single document interface (SDI) application, such as Notepad, has only one document open at a time. When you choose File, Open, the currently open file is closed before the new one is opened.

- A multiple document interface (MDI) application, such as older versions of Excel or Word, can open many documents (typically files) at once. There is a Window menu and a Close item on the File menu. It's a quirk of MFC that if you plan to provide multiple views on a single document, you must build a MDI application.

- A dialog-based application, that comes with Windows, does not have a document at all. There are no menus. (If you'd like to see Character Map in action, it's usually in the Accessories folder, reached by clicking Start. You may need to install it by using Add/Remove Programs under Control Panel.)

- The multiple top-level document application type is new in this version of Visual C++. Office 2000 applications such as Excel or Word are examples of this type of application. Every document has its own window complete with menus, title bars, and toolbars. Figure 2.3 shows Microsoft Word 2000 with several open documents.

Figure 2.2
The first step in building a typical application with the MFC Application Wizard is choosing the interface.

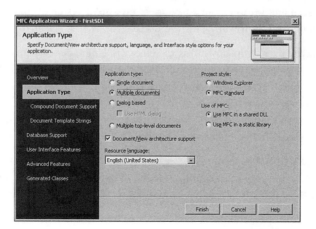

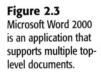

Figure 2.3
Microsoft Word 2000 is an application that supports multiple top-level documents.

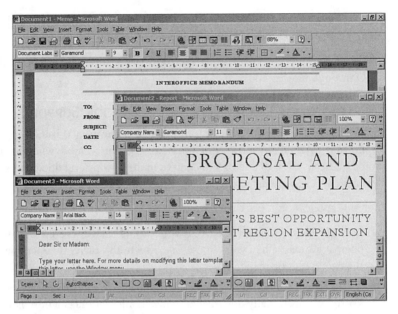

As you change the radio button selection, the picture on the top right of the dialog box changes to demonstrate how the application appears if you choose this type of application.

Dialog-based applications are quite different from MDI or SDI applications. Some of the MFC Application Wizard tabs and options are disabled when you're creating a dialog-based application. Dialog-based applications are presented in more detail later in the section, "Creating a Dialog-Based Application."

Beneath these choices is a check box where you can indicate whether you want support for the Document/View architecture. This framework for your applications is explained in Chapter 4, "Displaying Information." Experienced Visual C++ developers, especially those who are porting an application from another development system, might choose to turn off this support. In general, however, you should leave the option selected.

Lower on the screen is a drop-down box to select the language for your resources. If you have set your system language to anything other than the default, English (United States), make sure you set your resources to that language, too. If you don't, you will encounter unexpected behavior from Class View and Properties Window later. (Of course, if your application is for users who will have their language set to U.S. English, you might not have a choice. In that case, change your system language under the Control Panel.)

The Select Project Style group of radio boxes enable you to choose what kind of user interface you would like for your application. Choose Windows Explorer for a browser-style interface, or MFC standard for a more traditional interface.

The next question isn't as straightforward. Do you want the MFC library as a shared DLL or statically linked? A DLL (dynamic link library) is a collection of functions used by many different applications. Using a DLL makes your programs smaller but makes the installation a little more complex. Have you ever moved an executable to another directory, or another computer, only to find it won't run anymore because it's missing DLLs? If you statically link the MFC library into your application, it is larger, but it is easier to move and copy around.

If your users are likely to be developers themselves and own at least one other application that uses the MFC DLL or aren't intimidated by the need to install DLLs as well as the program itself, choose the shared DLL option. The smaller executable is convenient for all. What's more, if your users install a Windows update, often updated versions of MFC DLLs will be installed as part of that update. This can be very helpful. If your users are not developers, choose the statically linked option. It reduces the technical support issues you have to face with inexperienced users. If you write a good install program, you can feel more confident about using shared DLLs.

COMPOUND DOCUMENT SUPPORT

The third tab in the MFC Application Wizard is used to specify the amount of compound document support you want to include, as shown in Figure 2.4. Object linking and embedding (OLE) is a technology based on COM (the component object model) and is also referred to as compound document technology.

Figure 2.4
The third tab in the MFC Application Wizard is used to set the compound document support you need.

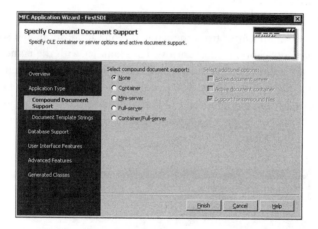

There are five choices for compound document support:

- If your application doesn't use documents made up of other objects, or create objects that might be useful in another application, choose None. For the purposes of this chapter, you should choose None.

- If you want your application to contain embedded or linked objects, such as Word documents or Excel worksheets, choose Container.

- If you want your application to serve objects that can be embedded in other applications, but it never needs to run as a standalone application, choose Mini-Server.

- If your application serves documents and also functions as a standalone application, choose Full-Server.

- If you want your application to have the capability to contain objects from other applications and also to serve its objects to other applications, choose Container/Full-Server.

If you choose to support compound documents, you can also support compound files. Compound files contain one or more objects and are saved in a special way so that you can change one of the objects without rewriting the whole file. This spares you a great deal of time. Check the check box labeled Support for Compound Files on the right side of the dialog box to enable support for compound documents.

In addition to compound files, you may also choose to support Active documents. Active documents are an extension of compound files. They allow each object to control how it is viewed and printed. If you want your application to have the capability to contain Active documents, check the check box labeled Active Document Container. If you want your application's documents to be used as Active documents, check the check box labeled Active Document Server. If your application will be an Active document server, you must specify a document File Extension on the next tab, Document Template Strings.

DOCUMENT TEMPLATE STRINGS

The Document Template Strings tab is shown in Figure 2.5. The MFC Application Wizard builds many names and prompts from the name of your application, and sometimes it needs to abbreviate your application name. Until you are familiar with the names the MFC Application Wizard builds, you should check them on this Document Template Strings dialog box and adjust them, if necessary. You can also change the mainframe caption, which appears in the title bar of your application. The file extension (if you choose one) is incorporated into filenames saved by your application and restricts the files initially displayed when the user chooses File, Open.

Figure 2.5
The fourth tab of the MFC Application Wizard enables you to adjust the ways names are abbreviated.

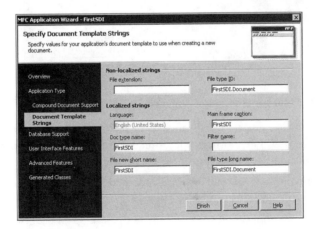

DATABASE SUPPORT

The next tab in the MFC Application Wizard deals with the level of database support, as shown in Figure 2.6.

Figure 2.6
The fifth tab in the MFC Application Wizard enables you to choose how much database support you want for your application.

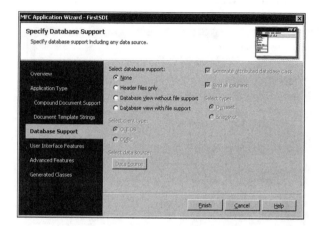

When building a database application, often you will choose to let the wizard generate a view class for you, derived from CRecordView, that's easy to use. This view will display database records with very little programming effort on your part. There are four choices for database support:

- If you aren't writing a database application, choose None.

- If you want to have access to a database but don't want to use the view and menu the wizard can provide, choose Header Files Only.

- If you want to derive your view from CRecordView and have a Record menu but don't need to save anything to the local hard drive, choose Database View Without File Support.

- If you want to support databases as in the preceding option but also need to save a document on disk (perhaps your application will save some user options), choose Database View With File Support.

If you choose to have a database view, you must specify a data source now. Click the Data Source button to set this up.

As you select different radio buttons, the picture on the top right of the dialog box changes to show you the results of your choice. As well, other options become enabled or grayed as you change the type of application to be created. You can learn more about these options in Chapter 11, "Database Programming."

SPECIFY USER INTERFACE FEATURES

The next tab in the MFC Application Wizard (see Figure 2.7) offers some of the interface appearance options for your application. This tab contains a number of independent check boxes. Check them if you want a feature; leave them unchecked if you don't.

Figure 2.7
The sixth tab of the MFC Application Wizard enables you to set some interface options.

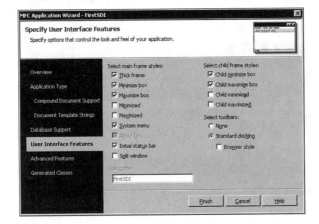

The first group of check boxes, **Select Main Frame Styles**, lists the properties you can set for frames. Frames hold windows; the system menu, title bar, minimize and maximize boxes, and window edges are all frame properties. The main frame holds your entire application. A MDI application has a number of MDI child frames—one for each document window—inside the main frame. You have the following options for modifying the main frame, and get the described results if the options are checked:

- **Thick Frame**. Your application will have a thick frame as its border that can be used to resize the window. Uncheck to prevent resizing.

- **Minimize Box**. Your application will have a Minimize box on the top right of the main window.

- **Maximize Box**. Your application will have a Maximize box on the top right of the main window.

- **Minimize**. Your application will be minimized automatically when you start it.

- **Maximize**. Your application will be maximized automatically when you start it.

- **System menu**. Your application will have an icon on the top left of the main window that opens the system menu when clicked.

- **About box**. The MFC Application Wizard will create a dialog box for you that contains information about your program, which can be customized. It also creates an option in the Help menu to display the dialog box. You can choose not to have an About box only if you are creating a dialog-based application.

- **Initial Status Bar**. AppWizard creates a status bar to display menu prompts and other messages. Later, you can write code to add indicators and other elements to this bar, as described in Chapter 7, "Status Bars, Toolbars, and Common Controls."
- **Split window**. Your application will have a splitter bar.

If you are creating a MDI application, you can also choose how you want your child windows to appear with the check boxes in the Select child frame styles group. This group includes the following check boxes, which produce the described results if they're checked:

- **Child Minimize Box**. Each of your child windows will have a minimize box in the top right corner.
- **Child Maximize Box**. Each of your child windows will have a maximize box in the top right corner.
- **Child Minimized**. Your child windows will be minimized when they are created.
- **Child Maximized**. Your child windows will be maximized when they are created.

Finally, you can choose whether you want your application to have a toolbar. Choose None to have no toolbar, and Standard Docking to have a toolbar that is fixed to the top of the screen. You can edit it to remove unwanted buttons or to add new ones linked to your menu items. To have a toolbar like those in new versions of Internet Explorer, check the Browser Style check box. Toolbars are discussed in more detail in Chapter 7.

ADVANCED FEATURES

The seventh tab of the MFC Application Wizard is the Advanced Features tab (see Figure 2.8). This tab enables you to choose extra features you would like to have in your application. The MFC Application Wizard generates all the code necessary for you to use these features, which you can then customize if you would like. As on the User Interface Features tab, check options you would like included in your application.

Figure 2.8
The seventh tab of the MFC Application Wizard governs the last few features your application might support.

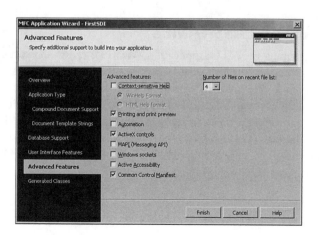

The following are the features the MFC Application Wizard can generate for you if you check the appropriate boxes:

- **Context-Sensitive Help**. Your Help menu will gain the Help Topics option. When this option is selected a window appears that has Contents, Index, and Find capabilities. The MFC Application Wizard generates the code needed to implement Help. This decision is hard to change later because quite a lot of code is added in different places when implementing context-sensitive help. If you choose to include context-sensitive help, you can then choose whether you use the classic WinHelp format or the HTML Help format. Chapter 8, "Help, Property Pages, and Wizards," describes Help implementation.

- **Printing and Print Preview**. Your application will have Print and Print Preview options on the File menu, and much of the code you need to implement printing will be generated by AppWizard. Chapter 5, "Printing and Saving," discusses the rest.

- **Automation**. If you want your application to surrender control to other applications through automation, check this check box.

- **ActiveX Controls**. If you want your application to use ActiveX controls, select this check box.

- **MAPI (Messaging API)**. Your application will be able to use the Messaging API to send a fax, e-mail, or other messages. Chapter 10, "Internet Programming," discusses the Messaging API.

- **Windows Sockets**. Your application will be able to access the Internet directly, using protocols such as FTP and HTTP (the World Wide Web protocol). Chapter 10 discusses sockets. You can produce Internet programs without enabling socket support if you use the WinInet classes, also discussed in Chapter 10.

You can also set how many files you want to appear on the recent file list for this application. Four is the standard number; change it only if you have good reason to do so.

FILENAMES AND CLASSNAMES

The final tab in running the MFC Application Wizard to create an executable Windows program enables you to confirm the classnames and the filenames that AppWizard creates for you, as shown in Figure 2.9. AppWizard uses the name of the project (FirstSDI in this example) to build the classnames and filenames. You should not need to change these names. If your application includes a view class, you can change the class from which it inherits; the default is CView, but many developers prefer to use another view, such as CScrollView or CEditView. The view classes are discussed in Chapter 4. Go back to the Overview tab after looking over this tab.

Figure 2.9
The final step of building a typical application with the MFC Application Wizard is to confirm filenames and classnames.

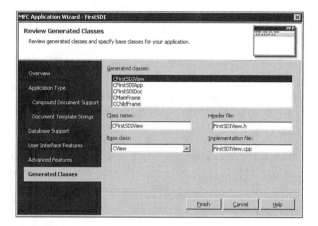

CREATING THE APPLICATION

On the Overview tab, the MFC Application Wizard shows you what is going to be created, as shown in Figure 2.10. If anything here is wrong, go back to the appropriate tab and make any necessary changes. Return to the Overview tab and review its contents again; click Finish to actually create the application. This takes a few minutes, which is hardly surprising because hundreds of code lines, menus, dialog boxes, help text, and bitmaps are being generated for you in as many as 20 files. Let it work.

Figure 2.10
You can see a summary of what the MFC Application Wizard is going to create for you by examining the Overview tab.

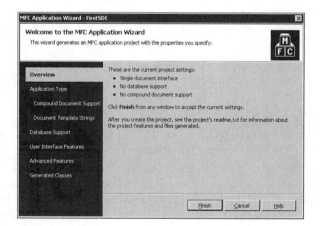

TRY IT YOURSELF

If you haven't started Visual Studio already, do so now. If you've never used it before, you may find the interface intimidating. There's a full explanation of all the areas, toolbars, menus, and shortcuts in Appendix C, "The Visual Studio User Interface, Menus, and Visual Studio."

Bring up the New Project dialog box by choosing File, New, then Project... From the New Project dialog box choose Visual C++ Projects as the project type and MFC Application as the template. In the dialog box, fill in a folder name where you would like to keep your applications; the MFC Application Wizard makes a new folder for each project. Fill in FirstSDI for the project name, then move through the MFC Application Wizard tabs. Choose an SDI application from the Application Type tab, but leave the other tabs unchanged. Now click Finish. When the MFC Application Wizard has created the project, choose Build, Build from the Visual Studio menu to compile and link the code.

When the build is complete, choose Debug, Start. You have a real, working Windows application, shown in Figure 2.11. Play around with it a little: Resize it, minimize it, maximize it.

Figure 2.11
Your first application looks like any full-fledged Windows application.

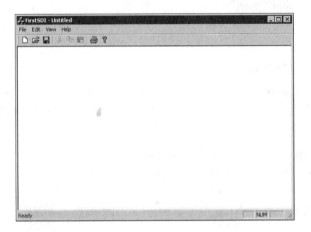

Try out the File menu by choosing File, Open; it brings up the familiar Windows File Open dialog box (though no matter what file you choose, nothing seems to happen); and then choose File, Exit to close the application. Execute the program again to continue exploring the capabilities that have been automatically generated for you. Move the mouse cursor over one of the toolbar buttons and pause; a ToolTip will appear, reminding you of the toolbar button's purpose. Click the Open button to confirm that it is connected to the File Open command you chose earlier. Open the View menu and click Toolbar to hide the toolbar; then choose View Toolbar again to restore it. Do the same thing with the status bar. Choose Help, About, and you'll see it even has an About box with its own name and the current year in the copyright date (see Figure 2.12).

Repeat these steps to create a MDI application called FirstMDI. The creation process differs only in the New Project dialog box, where you specify the project name, and the Application Type tab, where you choose a MDI application. Accept the defaults on all the other tabs, create the application, build it, and execute it. You'll see something similar to Figure 2.13: a MDI application with a single document open. Try out the same operations you tried with FirstSDI.

Figure 2.12
You even get an
About box in this
starter application.

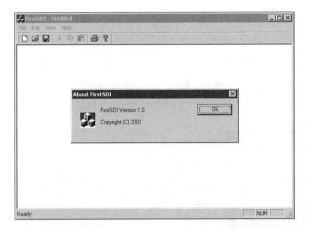

CH

2

Figure 2.13
An MDI application
can display a number
of documents at
once.

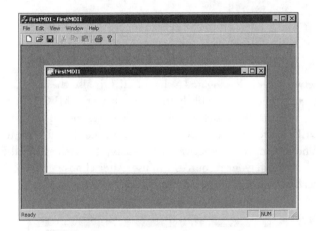

Choose File, New, and a second window, FirstMDI2, appears. Try minimizing, maximizing, and restoring these windows. Switch among them using the Window menu. All this functionality is yours from the MFC Application Wizard, and you don't have to write a single line of code to get it.

CREATING A DIALOG-BASED APPLICATION

A dialog-based application has no menus other than the system menu, and it cannot save or open a file. This makes it good for simple utilities such as the Windows Character Map. The MFC Application Wizard tabs are a little different for a dialog-based application, primarily because such applications can't have a document and therefore can't support database access or compound documents. To create a dialog-based application, call this application FirstDialog and start the MFC Application Wizard as you did for the SDI or MDI application. Go to the Application Type tab and choose a dialog-based application, as shown in

Figure 2.14. Don't select Use HTML Dialog. This choice lets you use HTML and DHTML to implement a Windows application, but it's not something you should try for your first dialog-based application.

Figure 2.14
To create a dialog-based application, specify your preference on the Application Type tab of the MFC Application Wizard.

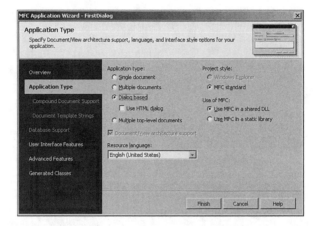

The decision between static linking and a shared DLL is also the same as for the SDI and MDI applications. If your users are likely to already have the MFC DLLs (because they are developers or because they have another product that uses the DLL) or if they won't mind installing the DLLs as well as your executable, go with the shared DLL to make a smaller executable file and a faster link. Otherwise, choose As a Statically Linked Library. You can also choose what language your resources will use. After choosing dialog-based, move down to the User Interface Features tab, shown in Figure 2.15.

Figure 2.15
The User Interface Features tab of the MFC Application Wizard enables you to choose the title of your dialog box as well as whether you would like an About box.

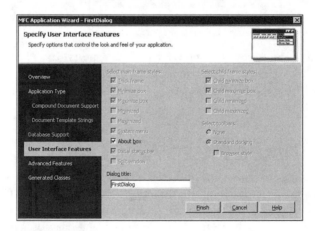

If you would like an About item on the system menu, select the About Box item. You can also specify a new title for the dialog box if you wish. Move on to the next tab, Advanced Features (shown in Figure 2.16).

Figure 2.16
The Advanced
Features tab involves
choosing Help, class
inheritance,
Automation, ActiveX,
and Sockets settings.

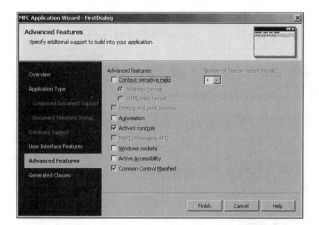

To have the MFC Application Wizard lay the framework for Help, select the Context-Sensitive Help option. If you choose to have Help, you can then choose whether you would like the traditional WinHelp format or the newer HTML Help format. If you want your application to surrender control to other applications through automation, select the Automation check box. If you want your application to contain ActiveX controls, select the ActiveX Controls check box. If you are planning to have this application work over the Internet with sockets, check the Windows Sockets box. (Dialog-based apps can't use MAPI because they have no document.) Move to the Generated Classes tab, shown in Figure 2.17.

Figure 2.17
The Generated
Classes tab for a
dialog-based appli-
cation gives you a
chance to adjust
filenames and
classnames.

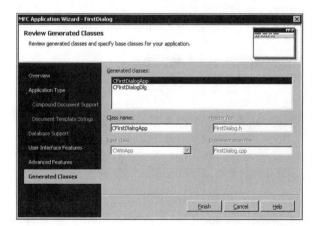

In this step you can change the names the MFC Application Wizard chooses for files and classes. This is rarely a good idea because it confuses people who maintain your code if the filenames can't be easily distinguished from the classnames and vice versa. If you realize after looking at this dialog box that you made a poor choice of project name, click Cancel, rename the project, then go through the MFC Application Wizard again. Return to the

CH

2

Overview tab to see the summary of the files and classes to be created as well as the options you chose to include; it should look similar to Figure 2.18.

Figure 2.18
The Overview tab of the MFC Application Wizard summarizes the files, classes, and options before creating them.

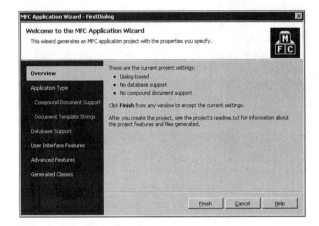

If any information in this dialog box isn't what you want, go back to the appropriate tab and change your choices. When the information is correct, click Finish and wait while the application is created.

To try it yourself, create an empty dialog-based application yourself, call it FirstDialog, and accept the defaults in each tab of the MFC Application Wizard. When it's complete, choose Build, Build to compile and link the application. Choose Debug, Run to see it in action. Figure 2.19 shows the empty dialog-based application running.

Figure 2.19
A starter dialog application includes a reminder of the work ahead of you.

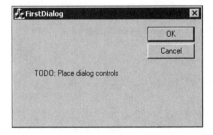

Clicking the OK or Cancel button, or the X in the top-right corner, makes the dialog box disappear. Clicking the system menu in the top-left corner gives you a choice of Move, Close, or About. Figure 2.20 shows the About box that was generated for you.

Figure 2.20
The same About box
is generated for SDI,
MDI, and dialog-
based applications.

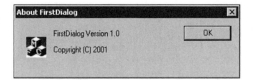

CREATING DLLs, CONSOLE APPLICATIONS, AND MORE

Although most people use the Visual C++ wizards to create an executable program, they can make many other kinds of projects. You choose File, New, and then Projects... as discussed at the start of this chapter, and choose Visual C++ Projects as the project type. Many of these templates create .NET projects, which are discussed in the second half of this book, starting in Chapter 16, "The Common Language Runtime."

CH

2

PROJECT TEMPLATES

Visual C++ project templates include:

- **ATL Project.** ATL is the Active Template Library, and it's used to write small ActiveX controls or COM components. Chapter 9, "Building COM+ Components with ATL," discusses the ActiveX Template Library.

- **ATL Server Project**. ATL server is a tool for writing very high-performance ISAPI extensions. It's discussed in Chapter 10.

- **ATL Server Web Service Project**. ATL Server can also be used for Web Services with extreme performance requirements.

- **Custom Wizard**. Perhaps you work in a large programming shop that builds many applications. Although the MFC Application Wizard saves a lot of time, your program-mers may spend a day or two at the start of each project pasting in your own *boilerplate*, which is material that is the same in every one of your projects. You may find it well worth your time to build a Custom AppWizard, which is a wizard of your very own that puts in your boilerplate as well as the standard MFC material. After you have done this, your application type is added to the list box on the left of the Projects tab of the New dialog box shown earlier in Figure 2.1.

- **Extended Stored Procedure**. If you work with stored procedures, you might be inter-ested in writing an extended stored procedure. It runs as compiled code on the database server and can use the Win32API.

- **Makefile Project**. If you want to create a project that is used with a different make util-ity than Visual Studio, choose this wizard from the left list in the Templates list box. No code is generated. If you don't know what a make utility is, don't worry—this wizard is for those who prefer to use a standalone tool to replace one portion of Visual Studio.

- **Managed C++ Application**. This is the basic .NET executable application. Learn more about it in Chapter 17.

- **Managed C++ Class Library**. This is how .NET programmers package up classes to be used by other projects. You'll see examples in Chapter 17.

- **Managed C++ Empty Project**. This .NET project type doesn't provide any starter files.

- **Managed C++ Web Service**. Learn more about this .NET project type in Chapter 21, "Creating an XML Web Service."

- **MFC ActiveX Control**. ActiveX controls are controls you write that can be used on a Visual C++ dialog, a Visual Basic form, or even a Web page. These controls are the 32-bit replacement for the VBX controls many developers were using to achieve intuitive interfaces or to avoid reinventing the wheel on every project.

- **MFC Application**. This is the project type that has been covered throughout this chapter.

- **MFC DLL**. If you want to collect a number of functions into a DLL, and these functions use MFC classes, choose this wizard. (If the functions don't use MFC, choose Win32 Project, then DLL as the application type, discussed a little later in this section.) Building a DLL is covered in Chapter 15, "Special Win32 Application Types."

- **MFC ISAPI Extension DLL**. ISAPI stands for Internet Server API and refers to functions you can call to interact with a running copy of Microsoft Internet Information Server, a World Wide Web server program that serves out Web pages in response to client requests. You can use this API to write DLLs used by programs that go far beyond browsing the Web to sophisticated automatic information retrieval. This process is discussed in Chapter 10.

- **Win32 Project**. This useful project type is discussed in the next section.

WIN32 PROJECT

There are times when you want to create a Windows application in Visual C++ that doesn't use MFC and doesn't start with the boilerplate code that the MFC Application Wizard produces for you. To create such an application, choose the Win32 Project template from the list on the right side in the New Project dialog box, fill in the name and folder for your project, and click OK. You can then choose what type of Win32 application you would like to create from the Application Settings tab. You have the following choices:

- **Win32 Console Application**. A console application looks very much like a DOS application, though it runs in a resizable window. (Console applications are 32-bit applications that won't run under DOS, however.) It has a strictly character-based interface with cursor keys rather than mouse movement. You use the Console API and character-based I/O functions such as `printf()` and `scanf()` to interact with the user. Some very rudimentary boilerplate code can be generated for you, or you can have just an empty project. Chapter 15 discusses building and using console applications.

- **Win32 Windows Application**. Choosing this option creates a bare Win32 application with a window. The Win32 Application Wizard generates all the code you need to create and display a bare window without using MFC.

- **DLL**. Choose to create a Win32 DLL if you would like to create a Dynamic Link Library without using MFC. The Win32 Application Wizard generates the minimum amount of code you need to have a functioning DLL.

- **Static Library**. Although most code you reuse is gathered into a DLL, you may prefer to use a static library because that means you don't have to distribute the DLL with your application. Choose this wizard from the list on the left side of the New Project Workspace dialog box to create a project file into which you can add object files to be linked into a static library, which is then linked into your applications.

Changing Your MFC Application Wizard Decisions

Running the MFC Application Wizard is a one-time task. Assuming you are making a typical application, you choose File, New, then Project; enter a name and folder; choose MFC Application; go through the tabs; create the application starter files; and then never touch the MFC Application Wizard again. However, what if you choose, for example, not to have online Help and later realize you should have included it?

The MFC Application Wizard, despite the name, isn't really magic. It pastes in bits and pieces of code you need, and you can paste in those very same bits yourself. Here's how to find out what you need to paste in.

1. Create a project with the same options you used in creating the project whose settings you want to change, and don't add any code to it.

2. In a different folder create a project with the same name and all the same settings, except the one thing you want to change (Context-Sensitive Help in this example).

3. Compare the files using WinDiff, which comes with Visual Studio.

Now you know what bits and pieces you need to add to your full-of-code project to implement the feature you forgot to ask AppWizard for.

Some developers, if they discover their mistake soon enough, find it quicker to create a new project with the desired features and then paste their own functions and resources from the partially built project into the new empty one. It's only a matter of taste, but after you go through either process for changing your mind, you probably will move a little more slowly through those MFC Application Wizard tabs.

Understanding the MFC Application Wizard's Code

The code generated by the MFC Application Wizard may not make sense to you right away, especially if you haven't written a C++ program before. You don't need to understand this code to write your own simple applications. Your programs will be better ones, though, if you know what they are doing, so a quick tour of the MFC Application Wizard's boilerplate code is a good idea. You'll see the core of an SDI application, a MDI application, and a dialog-based application.

You need the starter applications FirstSDI, FirstMDI, and FirstDialog, so if you didn't create them earlier, do so now. If you're unfamiliar with the Visual Studio interface, glance through Appendix C, to learn how to edit code and look at classes.

A SINGLE DOCUMENT INTERFACE APPLICATION

An SDI application has menus that the user uses to open one document at a time and work with that document. This section presents the code that is generated when you create an SDI application with no database or compound document support, with a toolbar, a status bar, Help, and with the MFC library as a shared DLL—in other words, when you accept all the MFC Application Wizard defaults other than the application type.

Five classes have been created for you. For the application FirstSDI, they are as follows:

- **CAboutDlg**. A dialog class for the About dialog box.
- **CFirstSDIApp**. A CWinApp class for the entire application.
- **CFirstSDIDoc**. A document class.
- **CFirstSDIView**. A view class.
- **CMainFrame**. A frame class.

Dialog classes are discussed in Chapter 3, "Interacting with Your Application." Document, view, and frame classes are discussed in Chapter 4. The header file for CFirstSDIApp is shown in Listing 2.1. The easiest way for you to see this code is to double-click on the classname, CFirstSDIApp, in the Class View pane. This opens the header file for the class in the Visual Studio editor.

LISTING 2.1   FirstSDI.h—MAIN HEADER FILE FOR THE FirstSDI APPLICATION

```
// FirstSDI.h : main header file for the FirstSDI application
//
#pragma once

#ifndef __AFXWIN_H__
    #error include 'stdafx.h' before including this file for PCH
#endif

#include "resource.h"       // main symbols


// CFirstSDIApp:
// See FirstSDI.cpp for the implementation of this class
//

class CFirstSDIApp : public CWinApp
{
```

LISTING 2.1   CONTINUED

```
public:
    CFirstSDIApp();


// Overrides
public:
    virtual BOOL InitInstance();

// Implementation
    afx_msg void OnAppAbout();
    DECLARE_MESSAGE_MAP()
};
```

This code is confusing at the beginning. The #pragma once is a clever form of *include guard-ing*. It guarantees that the file will never be compiled more than once in a single build. Including the same file more than once is quite likely in C++. Imagine that you define a class called Employee, and it uses a class called Manager. If the header files for both Employee and Manager include, for example, BigCorp.h, you get error messages from the compiler about "redefining" the symbols in BigCorp.h the second time it is included and compiled.

The actual meat of the file is the definition of the class CFirstSDIApp. This class inherits from CWinApp, a MFC class that provides most of the functionality you need. The MFC Application Wizard has generated some functions for this class that override the ones inher-ited from the base class. The section of code that begins //Overrides is for virtual function overrides. The next section of code is a message map and declares that there is a function called OnAppAbout. You can learn all about message maps in Chapter 3.

The MFC Application Wizard generated the code for the CFirstSDIApp constructor, InitInstance(), and OnAppAbout() in the file firstsdi.cpp. Here's the constructor, which ini-tializes a CFirstSDIApp object as it is created:

```
CFirstSDIApp::CFirstSDIApp()
{
    // TODO: add construction code here,
    // Place all significant initialization in InitInstance
}
```

This is a typical Microsoft constructor. Because constructors don't return values, there's no easy way to indicate that there has been a problem with the initialization. There are several ways to deal with this. Microsoft's approach is a two-stage initialization, with a separate ini-tializing function so that construction does no initialization. For an application, that func-tion is called InitInstance(), shown in Listing 2.2.

LISTING 2.2   CFirstSDIApp::InitInstance()

```
BOOL CFirstSDIApp::InitInstance()
{
    CWinApp::InitInstance();
```

LISTING 2.2   CONTINUED

```
// Initialize OLE libraries
if (!AfxOleInit())
{
    AfxMessageBox(IDP_OLE_INIT_FAILED);
    return FALSE;
}
AfxEnableControlContainer();
// Standard initialization
// If you are not using these features and wish to reduce the size
// of your final executable, you should remove from the following
// the specific initialization routines you do not need
// Change the registry key under which our settings are stored
// TODO: You should modify this string to be something appropriate
// such as the name of your company or organization
SetRegistryKey(_T("Local AppWizard-Generated Applications"));
LoadStdProfileSettings(4);  // Load standard INI file options (including MRU)
// Register the application's document templates.  Document templates
//  serve as the connection between documents, frame windows and views
CSingleDocTemplate* pDocTemplate;
pDocTemplate = new CSingleDocTemplate(
    IDR_MAINFRAME,
    RUNTIME_CLASS(CFirstSDIDoc),
    RUNTIME_CLASS(CMainFrame),          // main SDI frame window
    RUNTIME_CLASS(CFirstSDIView));
AddDocTemplate(pDocTemplate);
// Parse command line for standard shell commands, DDE, file open
CCommandLineInfo cmdInfo;
ParseCommandLine(cmdInfo);
// Dispatch commands specified on the command line.  Will return FALSE if
// app was launched with /RegServer, /Register, /Unregserver or /Unregister.
if (!ProcessShellCommand(cmdInfo))
    return FALSE;
// The one and only window has been initialized, so show and update it
m_pMainWnd->ShowWindow(SW_SHOW);
m_pMainWnd->UpdateWindow();
// call DragAcceptFiles only if there's a suffix
//  In an SDI app, this should occur after ProcessShellCommand
return TRUE;
}
```

InitInstance gets applications ready to go. The code you see here starts by initializing the OLE libraries, then enabling the application to contain ActiveX controls with a call to AfxEnableControlContainer(). It then sets up the Registry key under which this application will be registered. (The Registry is introduced in Chapter 5. If you've never heard of it, you can ignore it for now.)

InitInstance() goes on to register single document templates, which is what makes this an SDI application. Documents, views, frames, and document templates are all discussed in Chapter 4.

Following the comment about parsing the command line, InitInstance() sets up an empty CCommandLineInfo object to hold any parameters that may have been passed to the application when it was run, and it calls ParseCommandLine() to fill the object. Finally, it calls

`ProcessShellCommand()` to do whatever those parameters requested. This means your application can support command-line parameters to save users time and effort, without requiring any effort on your part. For example, if the user types at the command line `FirstSDI fooble`, the application starts and opens the file called fooble. The command-line parameters that `ProcessShellCommand()` supports are shown in Table 2.1.

TABLE 2.1 `ProcessShellCommand()`—SUPPORTED COMMAND-LINE PARAMETERS

Parameter	Action
None	Start application and open new file.
Filename	Start application and open file.
/p filename	Start application and print file to default printer.
/pt filename printer driver port	Start application and print file to the specified printer.
/dde	Start application and await DDE command.

If you would like to implement other behavior, make a class that inherits from `CCommandLineInfo` to hold the parsed command line; then override `CWinApp::ParseCommandLine()` and `CWinApp::ProcessShellCommand()` in your own app class.

You may already know that you can invoke many Windows programs from the command line; for example, typing `Notepad blah.txt` at a DOS prompt opens blah.txt in Notepad. Other command line options work, too, so typing `Notepad /p blah.txt` opens blah.txt in Notepad, prints it, and then closes Notepad.

That's the end of `InitInstance()`. It returns TRUE to indicate that the rest of the application should now run.

The message map in the header file indicates that the function `OnAppAbout()` handles a message. Which one? Here's the message map from the source file:

```
BEGIN_MESSAGE_MAP(CFirstSDIApp, CWinApp)
    ON_COMMAND(ID_APP_ABOUT, OnAppAbout)
    // Standard file based document commands
    ON_COMMAND(ID_FILE_NEW, CWinApp::OnFileNew)
    ON_COMMAND(ID_FILE_OPEN, CWinApp::OnFileOpen)
    // Standard print setup command
    ON_COMMAND(ID_FILE_PRINT_SETUP, CWinApp::OnFilePrintSetup)
END_MESSAGE_MAP()
```

This message map catches commands from menus, as discussed in Chapter 3. When the user chooses Help About, `CFirstSDIApp::OnAppAbout()` is called. When the user chooses File New, File Open, or File Print Setup, functions from `CWinApp` handle that work for you. (You would override those functions if you wanted to do something special for those menu choices.) `OnAppAbout()` looks like this:

```
void CFirstSDIApp::OnAppAbout()
{
    CAboutDlg aboutDlg;
    aboutDlg.DoModal();
}
```

CH

2

This code declares an object that is an instance of CAboutDlg, and calls its DoModal() function to display the dialog box onscreen. (Dialog classes and the DoModal() function are both covered in Chapter 3.) There's no need to handle OK or Cancel in any special way—this is just an About box.

OTHER FILES

If you selected Context-Sensitive Help, the MFC Application Wizard generates a .HPJ file and a number of .RTF files if you choose WinHelp, or an .HHP, .HHK, .HHC and a number of .HTM files if you chose HTML Help, to give some context-sensitive help. These files are discussed in Chapter 8 in the "Components of the Help System" section.

The MFC Application Wizard also generates a README.TXT file that explains what all the other files are and what classes have been created. Read this file if all the similar filenames become confusing.

A number of project files are also used to hold your settings and options, to speed build time by saving partial results, and to keep information about all your variables and functions. These files have extensions such as .ncb, .vcproj, .sln, and so on. You can safely ignore these files because you do not use them directly.

UNDERSTANDING A MULTIPLE DOCUMENT INTERFACE APPLICATION

A multiple document interface application also has menus, and it enables the user to have more than one document open at once. This section presents the code that is generated when you choose a MDI application with a toolbar, a status bar, Help, and the MFC library as a shared DLL, but with no database or compound document support. As with the SDI application, these are the defaults. The focus here is on what differs from the SDI application described in the preceding section.

Six classes have been created for you. For the application FirstMDI, they are

- CAboutDlg. A dialog class for the About dialog box.
- CChildFrame. A frame class for the child windows.
- CFirstMDIApp. A CWinApp class for the entire application.
- CFirstMDIDoc. A document class.
- CFirstMDIView. A view class.
- CMainFrame. A frame class for the main window.

The application class header is shown in Listing 2.3.

LISTING 2.3   FirstMDI.h—MAIN HEADER FILE FOR THE FirstMDI APPLICATION

```
// FirstMDI.h : main header file for the FirstMDI application
//
#pragma once
```

LISTING 2.3   CONTINUED

```
#ifndef __AFXWIN_H__
    #error include 'stdafx.h' before including this file for PCH
#endif

#include "resource.h"        // main symbols


// CFirstMDIApp:
// See FirstMDI.cpp for the implementation of this class
//

class CFirstMDIApp : public CWinApp
{
public:
    CFirstMDIApp();


// Overrides
public:
    virtual BOOL InitInstance();

// Implementation
    afx_msg void OnAppAbout();
    DECLARE_MESSAGE_MAP()
};
```

How does this differ from FirstSDI.h? Only in the classnames. The constructor is also the same as before. OnAppAbout() is just like the SDI version. How about InitInstance()? It is shown in Listing 2.4.

LISTING 2.4   CFirstMDIApp::InitInstance()

```
BOOL CFirstMDIApp::InitInstance()
{
    CWinApp::InitInstance();

    // Initialize OLE libraries
    if (!AfxOleInit())
    {
        AfxMessageBox(IDP_OLE_INIT_FAILED);
        return FALSE;
    }
    AfxEnableControlContainer();
    // Standard initialization
    // If you are not using these features and wish to reduce the size
    // of your final executable, you should remove from the following
    // the specific initialization routines you do not need
    // Change the registry key under which our settings are stored
    // TODO: You should modify this string to be something appropriate
    // such as the name of your company or organization
    SetRegistryKey(_T("Local AppWizard-Generated Applications"));
    LoadStdProfileSettings(4);  // Load standard INI file options (including MRU)
    // Register the application's document templates.  Document templates
```

LISTING 2.4 CONTINUED

```
//  serve as the connection between documents, frame windows and views
CMultiDocTemplate* pDocTemplate;
pDocTemplate = new CMultiDocTemplate(IDR_FirstMDITYPE,
    RUNTIME_CLASS(CFirstMDIDoc),
    RUNTIME_CLASS(CChildFrame), // custom MDI child frame
    RUNTIME_CLASS(CFirstMDIView));
AddDocTemplate(pDocTemplate);
// create main MDI Frame window
CMainFrame* pMainFrame = new CMainFrame;
if (!pMainFrame->LoadFrame(IDR_MAINFRAME))
    return FALSE;
m_pMainWnd = pMainFrame;
// call DragAcceptFiles only if there's a suffix
//  In an MDI app, this should occur immediately after setting m_pMainWnd
// Parse command line for standard shell commands, DDE, file open
CCommandLineInfo cmdInfo;
ParseCommandLine(cmdInfo);
// Dispatch commands specified on the command line.  Will return FALSE if
// app was launched with /RegServer, /Register, /Unregserver or /Unregister.
if (!ProcessShellCommand(cmdInfo))
    return FALSE;
// The main window has been initialized, so show and update it
pMainFrame->ShowWindow(m_nCmdShow);
pMainFrame->UpdateWindow();
return TRUE;
}
```

What's different here? Using WinDiff can help. WinDiff is a tool that comes with Visual Studio and is reached from the Tools menu. (If WinDiff isn't on your Tools menu, see the "Tools" section of Appendix D.) Using WinDiff to compare the FirstSDI and FirstMDI versions of InitInstance() confirms that, other than the classnames, the differences are

- The MDI application sets up a CMultiDocTemplate and the SDI application sets up a CSingleDocTemplate, as discussed in Chapter 4.

- The MDI application sets up a mainframe window and then shows it; the SDI application does not.

This shows a major advantage of the Document/View paradigm: It enables an enormous design decision to affect only a small amount of the code in your project and hides that decision as much as possible.

UNDERSTANDING THE COMPONENTS OF A DIALOG-BASED APPLICATION

Dialog-based applications are much simpler than SDI and MDI applications. Create one called FirstDialog, with an About box, no Help, no automation, ActiveX control support, no sockets, and MFC as a shared DLL. In other words, accept all the default options.

Three classes have been created for you for the application called FirstMDI:

- CAboutDlg. A dialog class for the About dialog box.
- CFirstDialogApp. A CWinApp class for the entire application.
- CFirstDialogDlg. A dialog class for the entire application.

The dialog classes are the subject of Chapter 3. Listing 2.5 shows the header file for CFirstDialogApp.

LISTING 2.5 DIALOG16.H—MAIN HEADER FILE

```
// FirstDialog.h : main header file for the PROJECT_NAME application
//

#pragma once

#ifndef __AFXWIN_H__
    #error include 'stdafx.h' before including this file for PCH
#endif

#include "resource.h"        // main symbols


// CFirstDialogApp:
// See FirstDialog.cpp for the implementation of this class
//

class CFirstDialogApp : public CWinApp
{
public:
    CFirstDialogApp();

// Overrides
    public:
    virtual BOOL InitInstance();

// Implementation

    DECLARE_MESSAGE_MAP()
};
```

CFirstDialogApp inherits from CWinApp, which provides most of the functionality. CWinApp has a constructor, which does nothing, as did the SDI and MDI constructors earlier in this chapter, and it overrides the virtual function InitInstance(), as shown in Listing 2.6.

LISTING 2.6 FIRSTDIALOG.CPP—CFirstDialogApp::InitInstance

```
BOOL CFirstDialogApp::InitInstance()
{
    CWinApp::InitInstance();

    AfxEnableControlContainer();
```

LISTING 2.6   CONTINUED

```
CFirstDialogDlg dlg;
m_pMainWnd = &dlg;
int nResponse = dlg.DoModal();
if (nResponse == IDOK)
{
    // TODO: Place code here to handle when the dialog is
    //  dismissed with OK
}
else if (nResponse == IDCANCEL)
{
    // TODO: Place code here to handle when the dialog is
    //  dismissed with Cancel
}

// Since the dialog has been closed, return FALSE so that we exit the
//  application, rather than start the application's message pump.
return FALSE;
}
```

This puts up the dialog box that is the entire application. To do that, the function declares an instance of CFirstDialogDlg, dlg, and then calls the DoModal() function of the dialog box, which displays the dialog box onscreen and returns IDOK if the user clicks OK, or IDCAN-CEL if the user clicks Cancel. (This process is discussed further in Chapter 3.) It's up to you to make that dialog box actually do something. Finally, InitInstance() returns FALSE because this is a dialog-based application and when the dialog box is closed, the application is ended. As you saw earlier for the SDI and MDI applications, InitInstance() usually returns TRUE to mean "Everything is fine; run the rest of the application" or FALSE to mean "Something went wrong while initializing." Because there is no "rest of the application," dialog-based apps always return FALSE from their InitInstance().

FROM HERE

The MFC Application Wizard gives you a lot of options and starts you down a lot of roads at once. This chapter explains InitInstance() and shows some of the code affected by the very first MFC Application Wizard decision: whether to have the MFC Application Wizard generate a dialog-based, SDI, or MDI application. Most of the other MFC Application Wizard decisions are about topics that take an entire chapter.

By now you know how to create applications that don't do much of anything. To make them do something, you need menus or dialog controls that give commands, and you need other dialog controls that gather more information. These are the subject of the next chapter, Chapter 3.

INTERACTING WITH YOUR APPLICATION

In this chapter

UNDERSTANDING DIALOG BOXES

Windows programs have a graphical user interface. In the long-ago days of DOS, programs would print a prompt onscreen and direct the user to enter whatever value the program needed. With Windows, however, most user input is obtained from dialog boxes. For example, a user can give the application details about a request by typing into edit boxes, choosing from list boxes, selecting radio buttons, checking or unchecking check boxes, and more. These components of a dialog box are called *controls*.

Chances are that your Windows application will have several dialog boxes, each designed to retrieve a specific type of information from your user. For each dialog box that appears onscreen, you need to develop two entities: a dialog resource and a dialog class.

The dialog resource is used to draw the dialog box and its controls onscreen. The class holds the values of the dialog box, and it is a member function of the class that causes the dialog box to be drawn onscreen. They work together to achieve the overall effect: making communication with the program easier for your user.

You build a dialog resource with the Resource Editor, adding controls to it and arranging them to make the control easy to use. Class Wizard then helps you to create a dialog class, typically derived from the MFC class CDialog, and to connect the resource to the class. Usually, each control on the dialog resource corresponds to one member variable in the class. To display the dialog box, you call a member function of the class. To set the control values to defaults before displaying the dialog box, or to determine the values of the controls after the user is finished with the box, you use the member variables of the class.

CREATING A DIALOG RESOURCE

The first step in adding a dialog box to your MFC application is creating the dialog resource, which acts as a sort of template for Windows. When Windows sees the dialog resource in your program, it uses the commands in the resource to construct the dialog box for you.

In this chapter you learn to work with dialog boxes by adding one to a simple application. Create an SDI application just as you did in Chapter 2, "Building Your First Windows Application," calling it simply SDI. You will create a dialog resource and a dialog class for the application, write code to display the dialog box, and write code to use the values entered by the user.

To create a dialog resource, first open the application. Choose Project, Add Resource from Visual Studio's menu bar. (If the Add Resource choice does not appear on the menu, choose View, Solution Explorer and ensure you have the SDI project selected, not the entire solution.) The Add Resource dialog box, shown in Figure 3.1, appears. Double-click Dialog in the Resource Type box. The dialog box editor appears, as shown in Figure 3.2.

Figure 3.1
Double-click Dialog on the Add Resource dialog box.

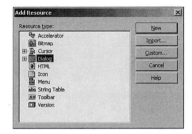

Figure 3.2
A brand new dialog box resource has a title, an OK button, and a Cancel button.

Bring up the Properties window for the new dialog box by choosing View, Properties Window. Change the caption to Sample Dialog, as shown in Figure 3.3.

Tip

You use the Properties window quite a lot as you work on this dialog box resource, but it can get in the way. You can set the window to auto-hide by clicking the pushpin in the upper left corner. A label appears, docked on the side of the screen. Hover over this label to make the window reappear.

The control toolbox shown at the far right of Figure 3.2 is used to add controls to the dialog resource. Dialog boxes are built and changed with a very visual WYSIWYG interface. If you need a button on your dialog box, you grab one from the control toolbox, drop it

Figure 3.3
Use the Properties window to change the title of the new dialog box.

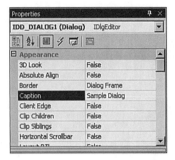

where you want it, and change the caption from Button1 to Lookup, or Connect, or whatever you want the button to read. All the familiar Windows controls are available for your dialog boxes, including

- **Static text**. Not really a control, this is used to label other controls such as edit boxes.
- **Edit box**. Single line or multiline, this is a place for users to type strings or numbers as input to the program. Read-only edit boxes are used to display text.
- **Button**. Every dialog box starts with OK and Cancel buttons, but you can add as many of your own as you want.
- **Check box**. You use this control to set options on or off; each option can be selected or deselected independently.
- **Radio button**. You use this to select only one of a number of related options. Selecting one button deselects the rest.
- **List box**. You use this box type to select one item from a list hardcoded into the dialog box or filled in by the program as the dialog box is created. The user cannot type in the selection area.
- **Combo box**. A combination of an edit box and a list box, this control enables users to select from a list or type their response, if the one they want isn't on the list.

The sample application in this chapter has a dialog box with a selection of controls on it, to demonstrate the way they are used.

DEFINING DIALOG BOX AND CONTROL IDS

Because dialog boxes are often unique to an application (with the exception of the common dialog boxes), you almost always create your own IDs for both the dialog box and the controls it contains. You can, if you want, accept the default IDs that the dialog box editor creates for you. However, these IDs are generic (for example, IDD_DIALOG1, IDC_EDIT1, IDC_RADIO1, and so on), so you'll probably want to change them to something more specific. In any case, as you can tell from the default IDs, a dialog box's ID usually begins with the prefix IDD, and control IDs usually begin with the prefix IDC. You change these IDs in the Properties window: Click the control (or the dialog box background to select the entire background), and choose View, Properties Window; then change the resource ID to a descriptive name that starts with IDD for a dialog and IDC for a control.

CREATING THE SAMPLE DIALOG BOX

Change the ID property of the dialog box to IDD_SDIDIALOG. This ID will be used later to associate this dialog resource with a dialog class.

Click the Edit Control button on the control toolbox, and then click in the upper left corner of the dialog box to place the edit control. If necessary, grab a moving handle and move it until it is in approximately the same place as the edit control in Figure 3.4. Normally, you would change the ID from Edit1, but for this sample leave it unchanged.

Figure 3.4
You can build a simple dialog box quickly in the Resource Editor.

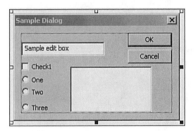

Add a check box and three radio buttons to the dialog box so that it resembles Figure 3.4. Change the captions on the radio buttons to One, Two, and Three. To align all these controls, click one of them, and then while holding down the Ctrl key, click each of the rest of them. Choose Format, Space Evenly, Across, and if necessary drag the stack of controls over with the mouse while they are all selected. Then choose Format, Space Evenly, Down, to adjust the vertical spacing. Alternatively, when the controls are selected, right-click and select Align Lefts or Align Tops.

The commands on the Format menu are also on the Dialog Editor toolbar, which appears docked at the top of your screen while you are using the Resource Editor. The toolbar symbols are repeated on the menu to help you learn which button is associated with each menu item.

Click the One radio button again and bring up the Properties window. Select True on the Group drop-down box. This indicates that this is the first of a group of buttons. When you select a radio button, all the other buttons in the group are deselected.

Add a list box to the dialog box, to the right of the radio buttons, and resize it to match Figure 3.4. With the list box highlighted, choose View, Properties Window. This brings up the Properties window, if it is not still pinned in place. Select the Sort drop-down box and select False. When Sort is set to True, the strings in your list box are automatically presented in alphabetical order. For this application, they should be presented in the order that they were added.

CH
3

WRITING A DIALOG CLASS

When the resource is complete, right-click somewhere in the dialog box and select Add Class from the context menu. This brings up the MFC Class Wizard. You can use this wizard to associate the new class with the dialog box you created. As shown in Figure 3.5, fill in the Class Name as CSdiDialog. Next choose CDialog from the Base Class drop-down box, then click Finish. The MFC Class Wizard creates a new class, prepares the source file (SdiDialog.cpp) and header file (SdiDialog.h), and adds them to your project.

Figure 3.5
Creating a dialog box class is simple with the MFC Class Wizard.

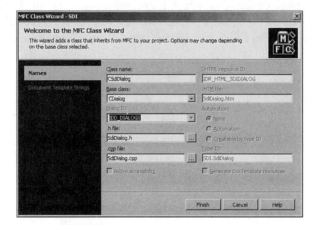

You can connect the dialog box controls to your code by adding member variables to your dialog class. To do this, choose View, Class View then select the CSdiDialog class. You can then either choose Add Variable from the Project menu, or right-click the class and choose Add, Add Variable from the Context menu. You can also right-click anywhere inside the dialog box and choose Variable... from the Context menu, but only after you have created a class for the dialog box.

You connect the dialog box controls to your code with the Add Member Variables Wizard, shown in Figure 3.6. A member variable in the new dialog box class can be connected to a control's value or to the control. This sample demonstrates both kinds of connection.

Click the Control Variable check box. This specifies that the member variable is to be connected to a control on the dialog box. Next, change the Control ID to IDC_CHECK1. Notice the Control Type changes to CHECK. Because a check box can be only selected or not selected, a simple Boolean variable can be used to contain its value. A full control class is not needed, so change the Category drop-down to Value rather than Control, and notice that the Variable type changes to BOOL, which holds the value True or False.

Enter the Variable Name as m_check, and change the Access to Public. Setting the Access to public signifies that any other classes or functions can use the variable. Enter a comment in the Comment field (such as "Sample Dialog check box value") to describe the purpose of the variable; the comment will be placed in the header file of the class at the point where the variable is defined. Finally click Finish to create the variable.

Figure 3.6
The Add Member
Variable Wizard con-
nects dialog box con-
trols to dialog box
class member
variables.

The following data types go with each control type:

- **Edit box.** Usually a string but also can be other data types, including int, float, and long
- **Check box.** BOOL
- **Radio button.** BOOL
- **List box.** String
- **Combo box.** String
- **Scrollbar.** int

Connect IDC_EDIT1 in the same way, to a member variable called m_edit of type CString
as a Value. Connect IDC_LIST1 as a Control to a member variable called m_listbox of type
CListBox. Connect IDC_RADIO1, the first of the group of radio buttons, as a Value to an
int member variable called m_radio. (You may have to type the word int in the Variable Type
box if it does not appear as an option.)

USING THE DIALOG CLASS

Now that you have your dialog resource built and your dialog class written, you can create
objects of that class within your program and display the associated dialog box element. The
first step is to decide what will cause the dialog box to display. Typically, it is a menu choice,
but because adding menu items and connecting them to code are not covered until Chapter
6, "Building a Complete Application: ShowString," you can simply have the dialog box display when the application starts running. To display the dialog box, you call the DoModal()
member function of the dialog class.

Modal and Modeless Dialog Boxes

Most of the dialog boxes you will code will be modal dialog boxes. A modal dialog box is on top of all the other
windows in the application: The user must deal with the dialog box and then close it before going on to other
work. An example of this is the dialog box that comes up when the user chooses File, Open in any Windows
application.

A modeless dialog box enables the user to click the underlying application and do some other work and then return to the dialog box. An example of this is the dialog box that comes up when the user chooses Edit, Find in many Windows applications.

Displaying a modeless dialog box is more difficult than displaying a modal one. The dialog object–the instance of the dialog class–must be managed carefully. Typically, it is created with new and destroyed with delete when the user closes the dialog box with Cancel or OK. You have to override a number of functions within the dialog class. In short, you should be familiar and comfortable with modal dialog boxes before you attempt to use a modeless dialog box.

ARRANGING TO DISPLAY THE DIALOG BOX

In Class View, expand the SDI item, and then expand CSDIApp. Double-click the InitInstance() member function. This function is called whenever the application starts. Scroll to the top of the file, and after the other #include statements, add this directive:

```
#include "sdidialog.h"
```

This ensures that the compiler knows what a CSdiDialog class is when it compiles this file. The sdidialog.h file was generated for you when you created the dialog box.

Double-click InitInstance() in the Class View again to bring the cursor to the beginning of the function. Scroll down to the end of the function, and just before the return at the end of the function, add the lines in Listing 3.1.

LISTING 3.1   SDI.CPP—LINES TO ADD AT THE END OF CSdiApp::InitInstance()

```
CSdiDialog dlg;
dlg.m_check = TRUE;
dlg.m_edit = "hi there";
CString msg;
if (dlg.DoModal() == IDOK)
{
    msg = "You clicked OK. ";
}
else
{
    msg = "You cancelled. ";
}
msg += "Edit box is: ";
msg += dlg.m_edit;
AfxMessageBox (msg);
```

ENTERING CODE

As you enter code into this file, you may want to take advantage of a feature that made its debut in Visual C++ 6.0: Intellisense. Covered in more detail in Reference D, Intellisense saves you the trouble of remembering all the member variables and functions of a class. If you type **dlg.** and then pause, a window appears, listing all the member variables and functions of the class CSdiDialog, including those it inherited from its base class. If you start to type the variable you want—for example, typing m_—the list will scroll to variables starting with m_. Use the arrow keys to select the one you want, and press Space or Tab to select it and continue typing code. You are sure to find this feature a great time saver. If the occasional pause as you type bothers you, Intellisense can be turned off by choosing Tools, Options and then clicking the General Item under Environment. Deselect the Enable auto-completion check box.

This code first creates an instance of the dialog box class. It sets the check box and edit box to simple default values. (The list box and radio buttons are a little more complex and are added later in this chapter, in "Using a List Box Control" and "Using Radio Buttons.") To make the dialog box display onscreen, the code calls its DoModal() function, which returns a number represented by IDOK if the user clicks OK and IDCANCEL if the user clicks Cancel. The code then builds a message and displays it with the AfxMessageBox() function.

The CString class has a number of useful member functions and operator overloads. As you see in this code, the += operator tacks characters onto the end of a string.

Build the project by choosing Build, Build or by clicking the Build button on the Build toolbar. Run the application by choosing Debug, Start. The dialog box displays with the default values you just coded, as shown in Figure 3.7. Change them, and click OK. You should get a message box telling you what you did, such as the one in Figure 3.8. Now the program sits there, ready to go, but because there is no more for it to do, you can close it by choosing File, Exit or by clicking the – in the top-right corner.

CH
3

Figure 3.7
Your application displays the dialog box when it first runs.

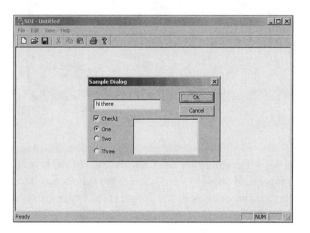

Run it again; change the contents of the edit box; and this time click Cancel on the dialog box. Notice in Figure 3.9 that the edit box is still reported as Hi There. This happens because MFC does not copy the control values into the member variables when the user clicks Cancel. Again, just close the application after the dialog box is gone.

Figure 3.8
After you click OK, the application echoes the contents of the edit control.

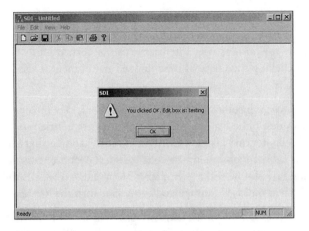

Figure 3.9
When you click Cancel, the application ignores any changes you made.

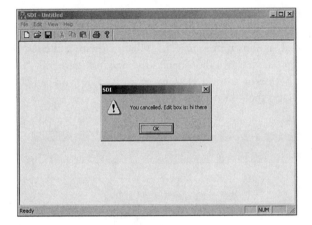

BEHIND THE SCENES

You may be wondering what's going on here. When you click OK on the dialog box, MFC arranges for a function called OnOK() to be called. This function is inherited from CDialog, the base class for CSdiDialog. Among other things, it calls a function called DoDataExchange(), which the MFC Class Wizard wrote for you. Here's how it looks at the moment:

```
void CSdiDialog::DoDataExchange(CDataExchange* pDX)
{
    DDX_Radio(pDX, IDC_RADIO1, m_radio);
    DDX_Control(pDX, IDC_LIST1, m_listbox);
    DDX_Text(pDX, IDC_EDIT1, m_edit);
    DDX_Check(pDX, IDC_CHECK1, m_check);

    CDialog::DoDataExchange(pDX);
}
```

The functions with names that start with DDX all perform data exchange: Their second parameter is the resource ID of a control, and the third parameter is a member variable in the associated dialog class. This is the way that the Add Member Variables Wizard connects the controls to member variables—by generating this code for you. Remember that the Add Member Variables Wizard also adds these variables to the dialog box class by generating code in the header file that declares them.

Thirty-four functions have names that begin with DDX: one for each type of data that might be exchanged between a dialog box and a class. Each has the type in its name. For example, DDX_Check is used to connect a check box to a BOOL member variable. DDX_Text is used to connect an edit box to a CString member variable. The Add Member Variables Wizard chooses the proper function name when you make the connection.

Some DDX functions are not generated by the Add Member Variables Wizard. For example, when you connect a list box as a Value, your only choice for type is CString. Choosing that causes Class Wizard to generate a call to DDX_LBString(), which connects the selected string in the list box to a CString member variable. In some cases the integer index into the list box might be more useful, and a DDX_LBIndex() function performs that exchange. You can add code to DoDataExchange() yourself to make this connection. If you do so, remember to add the member variable to the class as well. You can find the full list of DDX functions in the online documentation.

CH

3

USING A LIST BOX CONTROL

Dealing with the list box is more difficult because only while the dialog box is onscreen is the list box control a real window. You cannot call a member function of the list box control class unless the dialog box is onscreen. (This is true of any control that you access as a control rather than as a value.) This means that you must initialize the list box (fill it with strings) and use it (determine which string is selected) in functions that are called by MFC while the dialog box is onscreen.

When it's time to initialize the dialog box, just before it displays onscreen, a CDialog function named OnInitDialog() is called. Although the full explanation of what you are about to do has to wait until later in this chapter, follow the upcoming steps to add the function to your class.

1. In Class View, right-click CSdiDialog and choose Properties.

2. From the Properties window toolbar, click Overrides. (It's the green lozenge in the min-toolbar at the top of the Properties Window. You can hover over the buttons to have a pop-up tell you what they represent.) Some of the available functions that can be overridden are shown in Figure 3.10.

3. Click to the right of OnInitDialog, and a drop-down box will appear. Choose <Add> OnInitDialog, and the function will be created. The editor will open the file and scroll to OnInitDialog() so that you can edit it.

Figure 3.10
The list of available functions that can be overridden helps you override `OnInitDialog()`.

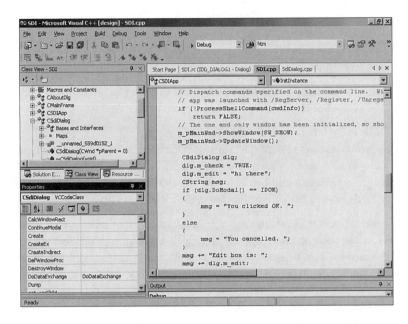

4. Remove the TODO comment and add calls to the member functions of the list box so that the function is as shown in Listing 3.2.

LISTING 3.2   SDIDIALOG.CPP—`CSdiDialog::OnInitDialog()`

```cpp
BOOL CSdiDialog::OnInitDialog()
{
    CDialog::OnInitDialog();

    m_listbox.AddString("First String");
    m_listbox.AddString("Second String");
    m_listbox.AddString("Yet Another String");
    m_listbox.AddString("String Number Four");
    m_listbox.SetCurSel(2);

    return TRUE;  // return TRUE unless you set the focus to a control
    // EXCEPTION: OCX Property Pages should return FALSE
}
```

This function starts by calling the base class version of `OnInitDialog()` to do whatever behind-the-scenes work MFC does when dialog boxes are initialized. Then it calls the list box member function `AddString()`, which, as you can probably guess, adds a string to the list box. The strings are displayed to the user in the order that they were added with `AddString()`. The final call is to `SetCurSel()`, which sets the current selection. As you see when you run this program, the index you pass to `SetCurSel()` is zero based, which means that item 2 is the third in the list, counting 0, 1, 2.

Usually, the strings of a list box are not hardcoded this way. To set them from elsewhere in your program, you have to add two things to the dialog box class: a `CStringArray` member variable and a function that adds strings to that array. The `OnInitDialog()` would use the array to fill the list box. Alternatively, you can use another one of MFC's collection classes or even fill the list box from a database. Database programming is covered in Chapter 11, "Database Programming."

Tip

If there is any other processing you would like to do just as the dialog box is being created and displayed, you can also add it to this OnInitDialog()function.

To have the message box display some indication of what was selected in the list box, you have to add another member variable to the dialog class. This member variable is set as the dialog box closes and can be accessed after it is closed. In Class View, right-click `CSdiDialog` and choose Add, Add Variable. Fill in the dialog box, as shown in Figure 3.11, and then click Finish. You have to manually fill in the Variable type as `CString`. This adds the declaration of the `CString` called `m_selected` to the header file for you. (If the list box allowed multiple selections, you would have to use a `CStringArray` to hold the list of selected items.) Strictly speaking, the variable should be private, and you should either add a public accessor function or make `CSdiApp::InitInstance()` a friend function to `CSdiDialog` to be truly object oriented. This example takes an excusable shortcut. The general rule still holds: Member variables should be private.

Figure 3.11
Add a `CString` to your class to hold the string that was selected in the list box.

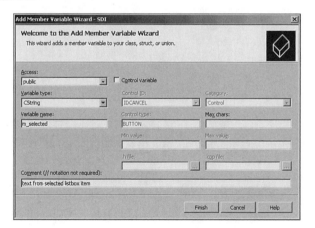

This new member variable is used to hold the string that the user selected. It is set when the user clicks OK or Cancel. To add a function that is called when the user clicks OK, follow these steps:

1. Right-click `CSdiDialog` in the Class View, and choose Properties.
2. From the Properties window toolbar, click the Overrides button.

3. In the drop-down box next to OnOK, choose <Add> OnOK. You are then shown the function name in the right column to remind you that you have overridden it. See Figure 3.12.

4. From the Solution Explorer double-click SdiDialog.cpp and scroll down to the OnOK() function. Edit it until it resembles Listing 3.3.

Figure 3.12
You have overridden OnOK.

LISTING 3.3 SDIDIALOG.CPP—CSdiDialog::OnOK()

```
void CSdiDialog::OnOK()
{
    int index = m_listbox.GetCurSel();
    if (index != LB_ERR)
    {
        m_listbox.GetText(index, m_selected);
    }
    else
    {
        m_selected = "";
    }

    CDialog::OnOK();
}
```

This code calls the list box member function GetCurSel(), which returns a constant represented by LB_ERR if there is no selection or if more than one string has been selected. Otherwise, it returns the zero-based index of the selected string. The GetText() member function fills m_selected with the string at position index. After filling this member variable, this function calls the base class OnOK() function to do the other processing required.

In a moment you will add lines to CSdiApp::InitInstance() to mention the selected string in the message box. Those lines execute whether the user clicks OK or Cancel, so you need to add a function to handle the user clicking Cancel. Simply follow the numbered steps for adding OnOK, except that you select OnCancel and choose <Add> OnCancel from its drop down box. The code, as shown in Listing 3.4, resets m_selected because the user canceled the dialog box.

LISTING 3.4 CONTINUED

```
void CSdiDialog::OnCancel()
{
    m_selected = "";
    CDialog::OnCancel();
}
```

Add these lines to `CSdiApp::InitInstance()` just before the call to `AfxMessageBox()`:

```
msg += ". List Selection: ";
msg += dlg.m_selected;
```

Build the application, run it, and test it. Does it work as you expect? Does it resemble Figure 3.13?

USING RADIO BUTTONS

You may have already noticed that when the dialog box first appears onscreen, the first radio buttons are automatically selected. You can arrange for the one you choose to be selected by default: Simply add two lines to `CSdiDialog::OnInitDialog()`. These lines set the second radio button and save the change to the dialog box:

```
m_radio = 1;
UpdateData(FALSE);
```

CH
3

Figure 3.13
Your application now displays strings in the list box.

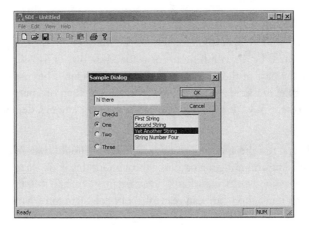

You may recall that `m_radio` is the member variable to which the group of radio buttons is connected. It is a zero-based index into the group of buttons, indicating which one is selected. Button 1 is the second button. The call to `UpdateData()` refreshes the dialog box controls with the member variable values. The parameter indicates the direction of transfer: `UpdateData(TRUE)` would refresh the member variables with the control values, wiping out the setting of `m_radio` you just made.

Unlike list boxes, a group of radio buttons can be accessed after the dialog box is no longer onscreen, so you don't need to add code to OnOK() or OnCancel(). However, you have a problem: how to convert the integer selection into a string to tack on the end of msg. There are ots of approaches, including the Format() function of CString, but in this case, because not many selections are possible, a switch statement is readable and quick. At the end of CSdiApp::InitInstance(), add the lines in Listing 3.5 just before the call to AfxMessageBox().

LISTING 3.5 SDIDIALOG.CPP—LINES TO ADD TO CSdiApp::InitInstance()

```
msg += "\r\n";
msg += "Radio Selection: ";

switch (dlg.m_radio)
{
case 0:
    msg += "0";
    break;
case 1:
    msg += "1";
    break;
case 2:
    msg += "2";
    break;
default:
    msg += "none";
    break;
}
```

The first new line adds two special characters to the message. Return, represented by \r, and New Line, represented by \n, combine to form the Windows end-of-line marker. This adds a line break after the part of the message you have built so far. The rest of msg appears on the second line of the message box. The switch statement is an ordinary piece of C++ code, which was also present in C. It executes one of the case statements, depending on the value of dlg.m_radio.

Once again, build and test the application. Any surprises? It should resemble Figure 3.14. You are going to be building and using dialog boxes throughout this book, so take the time to understand how this application works and what it does. You may want to step through it with the debugger and watch it in action. You can read all about debugging in Chapter 13, "Debugging."

UNDERSTANDING MESSAGE ROUTING

If there is one thing that sets Windows programming apart from other kinds of programming, it is messages. Most DOS programs, for example, relied on watching (sometimes called polling) possible sources of input, such as the keyboard or the mouse, to await input from them. A program that wasn't polling the mouse would not react to mouse input. In contrast, everything that happens in a Windows program is mediated by messages. A message is a way for the operating system to tell an application that something has happened—

Figure 3.14
Your application now selects Button Two by default.

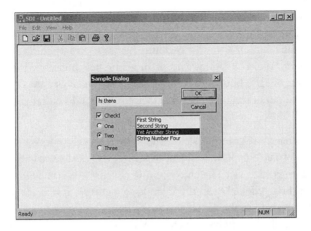

for example, the printer has become available, or the user has provided some input with the mouse or keyboard. A window (and every screen element is a window) can also send a message to another window, and typically most windows react to messages by passing a slightly different message along to another window. MFC has made it much easier to deal with messages, but you must understand what is going on beneath the surface. Messages are all referred to by their names, though the operating system uses integers to refer to them. An enormous list of #define statements connects names to numbers and enables Windows programmers to talk about WM_PAINT or WM_SIZE or whatever message they need to talk about. (The WM stands for Window Message.) An excerpt from that list is shown in Listing 3.6.

LISTING 3.6   EXCERPT FROM WINUSER.H—DEFINING MESSAGE NAMES

```
#define WM_SETFOCUS            0x0007
#define WM_KILLFOCUS           0x0008
#define WM_ENABLE              0x000A
#define WM_SETREDRAW           0x000B
#define WM_SETTEXT             0x000C
#define WM_GETTEXT             0x000D
#define WM_GETTEXTLENGTH       0x000E
#define WM_PAINT               0x000F
#define WM_CLOSE               0x0010
#define WM_QUERYENDSESSION     0x0011
#define WM_QUIT                0x0012
#define WM_QUERYOPEN           0x0013
#define WM_ERASEBKGND          0x0014
#define WM_SYSCOLORCHANGE      0x0015
#define WM_ENDSESSION          0x0016
```

As well as a name, a message knows what window it is for and can have up to two parameters. (Often, several different values are packed into these parameters, but that's another story.)

Different messages are handled by different parts of the operating system or your application. For example, when the user moves the mouse over a window, the window receives a WM_MOUSEMOVE message, which it almost certainly passes to the operating system to deal with. The operating system redraws the mouse cursor at the new location. When the left button is clicked over a button, the button (which is a window) receives a WM_LBUTTONDOWN message and handles it, often generating another message to the window that contains the button, saying, in effect, "I was clicked."

MFC has enabled many programmers to completely ignore low-level messages such as WM_MOUSEMOVE and WM_LBUTTONDOWN. Instead, programmers deal only with higher level messages that mean things such as "The third item in this list box has been selected" or "The Submit button has been clicked." All these kinds of messages move around in your code and the operating system code in the same way as the lower level messages. The only difference is what piece of code chooses to handle them. MFC makes it much simpler to announce, at the individual class's level, which messages each class can handle. The old C way, which is described in the next section, made those announcements at a higher level and interfered with the object-oriented approach to Windows programming, which involves hiding implementation details as much as possible inside objects.

UNDERSTANDING MESSAGE LOOPS

The heart of any Windows program is the message loop, typically contained in a WinMain() routine. The WinMain() routine is, like the main() in DOS or UNIX, the function the operating system calls when you run the program. You don't write any WinMain() routines because it is now hidden away in the code that AppWizard generates for you. Still, there is a WinMain(), just as there is in Windows C programs. Listing 3.7 shows a typical WinMain().

LISTING 3.7   TYPICAL WinMain() ROUTINE

```
int APIENTRY WinMain(HINSTANCE hInstance,
                HINSTANCE hPrevInstance,
                LPSTR lpCmdLine,
                int nCmdShow)
{

    MSG msg;
    if (! InitApplication (hInstance))
     return (FALSE);

    if (! InitInstance (hInstance, nCmdShow))
     return (FALSE);

    while (GetMessage (&msg, NULL, 0, 0)){
     TranslateMessage (&msg);
     DispatchMessage (&msg);
    }
    return (msg.wParam);
}
```

In a Windows C program such as this, InitApplication() typically calls RegisterWindow(), and InitInstance() typically calls CreateWindow(). (More details on this are in Appendix A, "Windows Programming Review and a Look Inside CWnd.") Then comes the message loop, the while loop that calls GetMessage(). The API function GetMessage() fills msg with a message destined for this application and almost always returns TRUE, so this loop runs over and over until the program is finished. The only thing that makes GetMessage() return FALSE is if the message it receives is WM_QUIT.

TranslateMessage() is an API function that streamlines dealing with keyboard messages. Most of the time, you don't need to know that "The A key just went down" or "The A key just went up," and so on. It's enough to know that "The user pressed A." TranslateMessage() deals with that. It catches the WM_KEYDOWN and WM_KEYUP messages and usually sends a WM_CHAR message in their place. Of course, with MFC, most of the time you don't care that the user pressed A. The user types into an edit box or similar control, and you can retrieve the entire string out of it later, when the user has clicked OK. Don't worry too much about TranslateMessage().

The API function DispatchMessage() calls the WndProc for the window that the message is headed for. The WndProc() function for a Windows C program is a huge switch statement with one case for each message the programmer planned to catch, such as the switch statement in Listing 3.8.

LISTING 3.8   TYPICAL WndProc() ROUTINE

```
LONG APIENTRY MainWndProc (HWND hWnd, // window handle
                    UINT message, // type of message
                    UINT wParam, // additional information
                    LONG lParam) // additional information
{

    switch (message) {
    case WM_MOUSEMOVE:
        //handle mouse movement
    break;

    case WM_LBUTTONDOWN:
        //handle left click
    break;

    case WM_RBUTTONDOWN:
        //handle right click
    break;

    case WM_PAINT:
        //repaint the window
    break;

    case WM_DESTROY: // message: window being destroyed
    PostQuitMessage (0);
    break;

    default:
```

CH
3

LISTING 3.8   CONTINUED

```
    return (DefWindowProc (hWnd, message, wParam, lParam));
    }

    return (0);
}
```

As you can imagine, these WndProcs become very long in a hurry. Program maintenance can be a nightmare. MFC solves this problem by keeping information about message processing close to the functions that handle the messages, freeing you from maintaining a giant switch statement that is all in one place. Read on to see how it's done.

READING MESSAGE MAPS

Message maps are part of the MFC approach to Windows programming. Rather than write a WinMain() function that sends messages to your WndProc, and then write a WndProc that checks which kind of message has arrived and then calls another of your functions, you just write the function that handles each kind of message, and you add a message map to your class that says, in effect, "I will handle this kind of message." The framework handles whatever routing is required to send that message to you.

Message maps come in two parts: one in the .h file for a class and one in the corresponding .cpp. Typically, they are generated by wizards, although in some circumstances you add entries yourself. Listing 3.9 shows the message map from the header file of one of the classes in a simple application called ShowString, presented in Chapter 6.

LISTING 3.9   MESSAGE MAP FROM SHOWSTRING.H

```
    afx_msg void OnAppAbout();

    DECLARE_MESSAGE_MAP()
```

This message map declares a function called OnAppAbout. DECLARE_MESSAGE_MAP() is a macro, expanded by the C++ compiler's preprocessor, that declares some variables and functions to set up some of this magic message catching.

The message map in the source file, as shown in Listing 3.10, is quite similar.

LISTING 3.10   MESSAGE MAP FROM CHAPTER 6'S SHOWSTRING.CPP

```
BEGIN_MESSAGE_MAP(CShowStringApp, CWinApp)

    ON_COMMAND(ID_APP_ABOUT, OnAppAbout)
    // Standard file based document commands
    ON_COMMAND(ID_FILE_NEW, CWinApp::OnFileNew)
    ON_COMMAND(ID_FILE_OPEN, CWinApp::OnFileOpen)
    // Standard print setup command
    ON_COMMAND(ID_FILE_PRINT_SETUP, CWinApp::OnFilePrintSetup)
END_MESSAGE_MAP()
```

MESSAGE MAP MACROS

BEGIN_MESSAGE_MAP and END_MESSAGE_MAP are macros that, like DECLARE_MESSAGE_MAP in the include file, declare some member variables and functions that the framework can use to navigate the maps of all the objects in the system. A number of macros are used in message maps, including the following:

- DECLARE_MESSAGE_MAP. Used in the include file to declare that a message map is in the source file.

- BEGIN MESSAGE MAP. Marks the beginning of a message map in the source file.

- END MESSAGE MAP. Marks the end of a message map in the source file.

- ON_COMMAND. Used to delegate the handling of a specific command to a member function of the class.

- ON_COMMAND_RANGE. Used to delegate the handling of a group of commands, expressed as a range of command IDs, to a single member function of the class.

- ON_CONTROL. Used to delegate the handling of a specific custom control notification message to a member function of the class.

- ON_CONTROL_RANGE. Used to delegate the handling of a group of custom control notification messages, expressed as a range of control IDs, to a single member function of the class.

- ON_MESSAGE. Used to delegate the handling of a user-defined message to a member function of the class.

- ON_REGISTERED_MESSAGE. Used to delegate the handling of a registered user-defined message to a member function of the class.

- ON_UPDATE_COMMAND_UI. Used to delegate the updating for a specific command to a member function of the class.

- ON_COMMAND_UPDATE_UI_RANGE. Used to delegate the updating for a group of commands, expressed as a range of command IDs, to a single member function of the class.

- ON_NOTIFY. Used to delegate the handling of a specific control-notification message with extra data to a member function of the class.

- ON_NOTIFY_RANGE. Used to delegate the handling of a group of control-notification messages with extra data, expressed as a range of child identifiers, to a single member function of the class. The controls that send these notifications are child windows of the window that catches them.

- ON_NOTIFY_EX. Used to delegate the handling of a specific control-notification message with extra data to a member function of the class that returns TRUE or FALSE to indicate whether the notification should be passed on to another object for further reaction.

- ON_NOTIFY_EX_RANGE. Used to delegate the handling of a group of control-notification messages with extra data, expressed as a range of child identifiers, to a

CH

3

single member function of the class that returns TRUE or FALSE to indicate whether the notification should be passed on to another object for further reaction. The controls that send these notifications are child windows of the window that catches them.

In addition to these, about 100 macros, one for each of the more common messages, direct a single specific message to a member function. For example, ON_CREATE delegates the WM_CREATE message to a function called OnCreate(). You cannot change the function names in these macros. Typically, these macros are added to your message map by Class View, as demonstrated in Chapter 6.

How Message Maps Work

The message maps presented in Listings 3.8 and 3.9 are for the CShowStringApp class of the ShowString application. This class handles application-level tasks such as opening a new file or displaying the About box. The entry added to the header file's message map can be read as "there is a function called OnAppAbout() that takes no parameters." The entry in the source file's map means "When an ID_APP_ABOUT command message arrives, call OnAppAbout()." It shouldn't be a big surprise that the OnAppAbout() member function displays the About box for the application.

If you don't mind thinking of all this as magic, it might be enough to know that adding the message map entry causes your code to run when the message is sent. But if you're wondering just how message maps really work, it's not too hard to understand. Every application has an object that inherits from CWinApp, and a member function called Run(). That function calls CWinThread::Run(), which is far longer than the simple WinMain() presented earlier but has the same message loop at its heart: call GetMessage(), call TranslateMessage(), call DispatchMessage(). Almost every window object uses the same old-style Windows class and the same WndProc, called AfxWndProc(). The WndProc, as you've already seen, knows the handle, hWnd, of the window the message is for. MFC keeps something called a handle map, which is a table of window handles and pointers to objects, and the framework uses this map to send a pointer to the C++ object, a CWnd*. Next, it calls WindowProc(), a virtual function of that object. Buttons or views might have different WindowProc() implementations, but through the magic of polymorphism, the correct function is called.

Polymorphism

Virtual functions and polymorphism are important C++ concepts for anyone working with MFC. They arise only when you are using pointers to objects and when the class of objects to which the pointers are pointing is derived from another class. Consider as an example a class called CDerived that is derived from a base class called CBase, with a member function called Function() that is declared in the base class and overridden in the derived class. There are now two functions: One has the full name CBase::Function(), and the other is CDerived::Function().

If your code has a pointer to a base object and sets that pointer equal to the address of the derived object, it can then call the function, as follows:

```
CDerived derivedobject;
CBase* basepointer;
basepointer = &derivedobject;
basepointer->Function();
```

In this case, `CBase::Function()` is called. However, there are times when that is not what you want, when you have to use a `CBase` pointer, but you really want `CDerived::Function()` to be called. To indicate this, in `CBase`, `Function()` is declared to be virtual. Think of it as an instruction to the compiler to override this function, if there is any way to do it.

When `Function()` is declared to be virtual in the base class, `CBase`, the code fragment above actually calls `CDerived::Function()`, as desired. That's polymorphism, and that shows up again and again with MFC classes. You use a pointer to a window, a `CWnd*`, that really points to a `CButton` or a `CView` or some other class derived from `CWnd`, and when a function such as `WindowProc()` is called, it is the derived function—`CButton::WindowProc()`, for example— that is called.

Note

You might wonder why the messages can't just be handled by virtual functions. This would make the virtual tables enormous, and slow the application too much. The message map system is a much faster approach.

`WindowProc()` calls `OnWndMsg()`, the C++ function that really handles messages. First, it checks to see whether this is a message, a command, or a notification. Assuming it's a message, it looks in the message map for the class, using the member variables and functions set up by DECLARE_MESSAGE_MAP, BEGIN_MESSAGE_MAP, and END_MESSAGE_MAP. Part of what those macros arrange is to enable access to the message map entries of the base class by the functions that search the message map of the derived class. That means that if a class inherits from `CView` and doesn't catch a message normally caught by `CView`, that message will still be caught by the same `CView` function as inherited by the derived class. This message map inheritance parallels the C++ inheritance but is independent of it and much more efficient than using virtual functions.

The bottom line: You add a message map entry, and when a message arrives, the functions called by the hidden message loop look in these tables to decide which of your objects, and which member function of the object, should handle the message. That's what's really going on behind the scenes.

MESSAGES CAUGHT BY MFC CODE

The other great advantage of MFC is that the classes already catch most of the common messages and do the right thing, without any coding on your part at all. For example, you don't need to catch the message that tells you that the user has chosen File, Save As—MFC classes catch it, put up the dialog box to obtain the new filename, handle all the behind-the-scenes work, and finally call one of your functions, which must be named `Serialize()`, to actually write out the document. (Chapter 5, "Printing and Saving" explains the Serialize() function.) You need only to add message map entries for behavior that is not common to all applications.

LEARNING HOW MFC CLASS WIZARD HELPS YOU CATCH MESSAGES

Message maps may not be simple to read, but they are simple to create if you use Class View. You create message maps in Visual C++ .NET by using the Class view and Properties window. This section shows you these tools for ShowString, rather than work you through creating a sample application.

THE CLASS VIEW WINDOW

The Class View window is displayed when you choose View, Class View or press Ctrl + Shift + C. Figure 3.15 shows the Class View window with the CSDIView class expanded. At the top of the window is a toolbar with two buttons. The first button allows you to choose how you would like to view the Class View items; the other allows you to create new folders in your project.

Figure 3.15
Class View contains all the information about a project's classes.

Below the toolbar is a tree of collapsing and expanding nodes that represent the classes, global functions and variables, macros and constants, as well as the folders you create. Under each node representing a class is nearly all the information that describes the class.

Double-clicking on a node takes you to its corresponding definition. For example, double-clicking the name of a class takes you to its header file, and puts the cursor right at the point where the class is first defined. Likewise, double-clicking a member variable or function takes you to the place it is defined. This enables you to quickly find and modify class data.

The first item under a class node is the Bases and Interfaces node. This node contains a list of the class's base classes and interfaces. Each of these nodes can in turn have base classes or interfaces. The Bases and Interfaces node makes it easy to view the class hierarchy associated with a class.

The next item is Available Overrides. This gives a list of all base class functions that have been declared virtual and can be overridden. Double-clicking one of the list items takes you to the function definition. Examples of functions that are usually overridden, are:

- `InitInstance()`. Overrides a virtual function in `CWinApp`, the base class for `CShowStringApp`, and is labeled with a V (for virtual function) in the list.

- `OnAppAbout()`. Catches the `ID_APP_ABOUT` command and is labeled with a W (for Windows message) in the list.

Below Available Overrides is Maps, which contains MESSAGE. MESSAGE lists all the messages that have handling functions in the class (the corresponding functions are listed later). When a message handling function is added to the class, here's what happens:

- A skeleton function is added to the bottom of the source file for the application.

- An entry to the message map is added in the source file.

- An entry to the message map is added in the include file.

- The list of messages and member functions in the Class View is updated.

Finally, Class View shows a list of all the class's member variables and member functions. Double-clicking one of these items takes you to the place in the file in which it is defined. This makes it easy to modify class members.

Right-clicking on one of the tree nodes brings up a useful context menu. To add a class to the project, right-click the name of the project, then choose Add, Add Class. To add a member variable or member function to a class, right-click the class, then choose Add, and then Add Variable or Add Function respectively.

THE MESSAGES BUTTON IN THE PROPERTIES WINDOW

In Visual C++ .NET, a new way of catching messages was added. Rather than using Class Wizard as in Visual C++ 6, Visual C++ .NET uses an interface similar to the Properties table in previous versions of Visual Basic. To get to the table of messages, select a class in Class View, choose Properties Window from the View menu, and then click the Messages button in the Properties window toolbar. Figure 3.16 shows the Properties window with the Messages button clicked. (It's between the yellow lightning bolt and the green lozenge.)

CH

3

Figure 3.16
The Messages button on the Properties window is the new way to catch messages.

On the left side of the messages table is a list of all the messages that can have handler functions in the selected class. On the right side of the messages table is a list of drop-down boxes. You can use the drop-down boxes to easily add or delete message-handling functions. To add a function, choose <Add> "function name" (the function name is chosen for you), and to delete a function choose <Delete> "function name" from the drop-down box. Notice you can add a function only if one is not already defined, and you cannot delete a non-existing function. A message area at the bottom of the window reminds you of the purpose of each function.

WHICH CLASS SHOULD CATCH THE MESSAGE?

The only tricky part of message maps and message handling is deciding which class should catch the message. That's a decision you can't make until you understand all the different message and command targets that make up a typical application. The choice is usually one of the following:

- The active view
- The document associated with the active view
- The frame window that holds the active view
- The application object

Views, documents, and frames are discussed in Chapter 4, "Displaying Information."

RECOGNIZING MESSAGES

There are almost 900 Windows messages, so you won't find a list of them all in this chapter. Usually, you arrange to catch messages with Class View and are presented with a much shorter list that is appropriate for the class with which you are catching messages. Not every kind of window can receive every kind of message. For example, only classes that inherit from CListBox receive list box messages such as LB_SETSEL, which directs the list box to move the highlight to a specific list item. The first component of a message name indicates the kind of window this message is destined for, or coming from. These window types are listed in Table 3.1.

TABLE 3.1 WINDOWS MESSAGE PREFIXES AND WINDOW TYPES

Prefix	Window Type
ABM, ABN	Appbar
ACM, ACN	Animation control
BM, BN	Button
CB, CBN	Combo box
CDM, CDN	Common dialog box
CPL	Control Panel application
DBT	Any application (device change message)
DL	Drag list box
DM	Dialog box
EM, EN	Edit box
FM, FMEVENT	File Manager
HDM, HDN	Header control
Prefix	Window Type
HKM	HotKey control
IMC, IMN	IME window
LB, LBN	List box
LVM, LVN	List view
NM	Any parent window (notification message)
PBM	Progress bar
PBT	Any application (battery power broadcast)
PSM, PSN	Property sheet
SB	Status bar
SBM	Scrollbar
STM, STN	Static control
TB, TBN	Toolbar
TBM	Track bar
TCM, TCN	Tab control
TTM, TTN	ToolTip
TVM, TVN	Tree view
UDM	Up Down control
WM	Generic window

CH

3

What's the difference between, say, a BM message and a BN message? A BM message is a message to a button, such as "Act as though you were just clicked." A BN message is a notification from a button to the window that owns it, such as "I was clicked." The same pattern holds for all the prefixes that end with M or N in the preceding table.

Sometimes the message prefix does not end with M; for example CB is the prefix for a message to a combo box, whereas CBN is the prefix for a notification from a combo box to the window that owns it. Another example is CB_SETCURSEL, which is a message to a combo box directing it to select one of its strings, whereas CBN_SELCHANGE is a message sent from a combo box, notifying its parent that the user has changed which string is selected.

UNDERSTANDING COMMANDS

What is a command? It is a special type of message. Windows generates a command whenever a user chooses a menu item, clicks a button, or otherwise tells the system to do something. In older versions of Windows, both menu choices and button clicks generated a WM_COMMAND message; these days you receive a WM_COMMAND for a menu choice and a WM_NOTIFY for a control notification such as button click or list box selection. Commands and notifications are passed around by the operating system just like any other message, until they get into the top of OnWndMsg(). At that point, Windows message passing stops and MFC command routing starts.

Command messages all have, as their first parameter, the resource ID of the menu item that was chosen or the button that was clicked. These resource IDs are assigned according to a standard pattern—for example, the menu item File, Save has the resource ID ID_FILE_SAVE.

Command routing is the mechanism OnWndMsg() uses to send commands (or notifications) to objects that can't receive messages. Only objects that inherit from CWnd can receive messages, but all objects that inherit from CCmdTarget, including CWnd and CDocument, can receive commands and notifications. That means a class that inherits from CDocument can have a message map. It won't have any entries for messages, only for commands and notifications, but it's still a message map.

How do the commands and notifications get to the class, though? By command routing. (This becomes messy, so if you don't want the inner details, skip this paragraph and the next.) OnWndMsg() calls CWnd::OnCommand() or CWnd::OnNotify(). The OnCommand() function checks all sorts of petty stuff (such as whether this menu item was grayed after the user selected it but before this piece of code started to execute) and then calls OnCmdMsg(). The OnNotify() function checks different conditions and then it, too, calls OnCmdMsg(). The OnCmdMsg() function is virtual, which means that different command targets have different implementations. The implementation for a frame window sends the command to the views and documents it contains.

This is how something that started out as a message can end up being handled by a member function of an object that isn't a window and therefore can't really catch messages.

Should you care about this? Even if you don't care how it all happens, you should care that you can arrange for the right class to handle whatever happens within your application. If the user resizes the window, a WM_SIZE message is sent, and you may have to rescale an image or do some other work inside your view. If the user chooses a menu item, a command is generated, and that means your document can handle it if that's more appropriate. You see examples of these decisions at work in Chapter 4.

Understanding Command Updates

This under-the-hood tour of how MFC connects user actions such as window resizing or menu choices to your code is almost finished. All that's left is to handle the graying of menus and buttons, a process called *command updating*.

Imagine you are designing an operating system, and you know it's a good idea to have some menu items grayed to show they can't be used right now. You can go about implementing this in two ways.

First, you can have a huge table with one entry for every menu item and a flag to indicate whether it's available. Whenever you have to display the menu, you can quickly check the table. Whenever the program does anything that makes the item available or unavailable, it updates the table. This is called the *continuous-update* approach.

The other way is not to have a table but to check all the conditions just before your program displays the menu. This is called the *update-on-demand* approach and is the approach taken in Windows. In the old C way of checking whether each menu option should be grayed the system sent a WM_INITMENUPOPUP message, which means "I'm about to display a menu." The giant switch in the WndProc caught that message and quickly enabled or disabled each menu item. This wasn't very object-oriented, though. In an object-oriented program, different pieces of information are stored in different objects and aren't generally made available to the entire program.

When it comes to updating menus, different objects know whether each item should be grayed. For example, the document knows whether it has been modified since it was last saved, so it can decide whether File, Save should be grayed. However, only the view knows whether some text is currently highlighted; therefore, it can decide whether Edit, Cut and Edit, Copy should be grayed. This means that the job of updating these menus should be parceled out to various objects within the application rather than handled within the WndProc.

The MFC approach is to use a little object called a CCmdUI, a command user interface, and give this object to whoever catches a CN_UPDATE_COMMAND_UI message. You catch those messages by adding (or getting Class View to add) an ON_UPDATE_COMMAND_UI macro in your message map. If you want to know what's going on behind the scenes, it's this: The operating system still sends WM_INITMENUPOPUP; then the MFC base classes such as CFrameWnd take over. They make a CCmdUI, set its member variables to correspond to the first menu item, and call one of that object's own member functions, DoUpdate(). Then, DoUpdate() sends out the CN_COMMAND_UPDATE_UI message with a pointer to this CCmdUI object as the

CCmdUI object the handlers use. The same CCmdUI object is then reset to correspond to the second menu item, and so on, until the entire menu is ready to be displayed. The CCmdUI object is also used to gray and ungray buttons and other controls in a slightly different context.

CCmdUI has the following member functions:

- Enable(). Takes a TRUE or FALSE (defaults to TRUE). This grays the user interface item if FALSE and makes it available if TRUE.
- SetCheck(). Checks or unchecks the item.
- SetRadio(). Checks or unchecks the item as part of a group of radio buttons, only one of which can be set at any time.
- SetText(). Sets the menu text or button text, if this is a button.
- DoUpdate(). Generates the message.

Determining which member function you want to use is usually simple. Here is a shortened version of the message map from an object called CWhoisView, a class derived from CFormView that is showing information to a user. This form view contains several Edit boxes, and the user may want to paste text into one of them. The message map contains an entry to catch the update for the ID_EDIT_PASTE command, as follows:

```
BEGIN_MESSAGE_MAP(CWhoisView, CFormView)
    ...
    ON_UPDATE_COMMAND_UI(ID_EDIT_PASTE, OnUpdateEditPaste)
    ...
END_MESSAGE_MAP()
```

The function that catches the update, OnUpdateEditPaste(), looks like this:

```
void CWhoisView::OnUpdateEditPaste(CCmdUI* pCmdUI)
{
 pCmdUI->Enable(::IsClipboardFormatAvailable(CF_TEXT));
}
```

This calls the API function ::IsClipboardFormatAvailable(), to see whether text is in the Clipboard. Other applications may be able to paste in images or other nontext Clipboard contents, but this application cannot and therefore grays the menu item if no text is available to paste. Most command update functions look just like this: They call Enable() with a parameter that is a call to a function that returns TRUE or FALSE, or perhaps a simple logical expression. Command update handlers must be fast because five to ten of them must run between the moment the user clicks to request that a menu be displayed and the moment before the menu is actually displayed.

LEARNING HOW VISUAL STUDIO HELPS YOU CATCH COMMANDS AND COMMAND UPDATES

Visual Studio helps with commands and command updates just as with messages. Clicking the Events button (it looks like a lightning bolt) from the Properties window toolbar (with a class selected in Class View) brings up a list of the resource IDs of every resource (menu, toolbar, dialog box controls, and so on) that can generate a command or message that can be caught in the class. If you expand one of the resource ID items, you see a list of commands, command updates, and messages associated with the resource, as shown in Figure 3.17.

Figure 3.17
The Events button on the Properties window enables you to catch or update commands.

Only two messages are associated with each menu resource ID: COMMAND and UPDATE_COMMAND_UI. The COMMAND message enables you to add a function to handle user button clicks or selections of menu options—that is, to catch the command. The UPDATE_COMMAND_UI message enables you to add a function to set the state of the menu item, button, or other control just as the operating system is about to display it—that is, to update the command.

Handler functions that catch or update a command are done the same way on the Events table as messages are done on the Messages table, or Overrides are done on the Overrides table. There is a regular pattern to the names, and experienced MFC programmers come to count on function names that follow that pattern. Command handler functions, like message handlers, have names that start with On. Typically, the remainder of the function name is formed by removing the ID and the underscores from the resource ID and capitalizing each word. Command update handlers have names that start with OnUpdate and use the same conventions for the remainder of the function name. For example, the function that catches ID_APP_EXIT should be called OnAppExit(), and the function that updates ID_APP_EXIT is called OnUpdateAppExit().

Not every command needs an update handler. The framework does some very nice work graying and ungraying for you automatically. Say you have a menu item—Network, Send— whose command is caught by the document. When no document is open, this menu item is grayed by the framework, without any coding on your part. For many commands, it's enough that an object exists that can handle them, and no special updating is necessary. For others, you may want to check that something is selected or highlighted or that no errors are present before you make certain commands available. That's when you use command updating.

FROM HERE

In this chapter you have seen how to build a dialog box so that your application can obtain information from the user. You've seen how to build the dialog resource in the Visual Studio Resource Editor, and how to connect that resource to a dialog class. You've seen how to get the values the user enters on a dialog box.

This chapter has also provided a behind-the-scenes look at Windows messages, and the MFC message map mechanism that routes messages to your code. You've also learned about commands and command updating.

With these basics behind you it's time to make your applications a little more interesting. A dialog box isn't the only way to communicate with your users, after all. The next chapter, "Displaying Information" introduces you to the concepts of documents and views, and shows how to display information in a document's view.

CHAPTER 4

DISPLAYING INFORMATION

In this chapter

UNDERSTANDING THE DOCUMENT CLASS

When you generate your source code with the MFC Application Wizard, you get an application featuring all the bells and whistles of a commercial 32-bit Windows application, including a toolbar, a status bar, ToolTips, menus, and even an About dialog box. However, in spite of all those features, the application really doesn't do anything useful. To create an application that does more than look pretty on your desktop, you need to modify the code that the MFC Application Wizard generates. This task can be easy or complex, depending on how you want your application to look and act.

Probably the most important set of modifications are those related to the document—the information the user can save from your application and restore later—and to the view—the way that information is presented to the user. MFC's document/view architecture separates an application's data from the way the user actually views and manipulates that data. Simply, the document object is responsible for storing, loading, and saving the data, whereas the view object (which is just another type of window) enables the user to see the data onscreen and to edit that data in a way that is appropriate to the application. In this chapter, you learn how MFC's document/view architecture works.

SDI and MDI applications created with the MFC Application Wizard are document/view applications. That means that the MFC Application Wizard generates a class for you derived from CDocument, and delegates certain tasks to this new document class. It also creates a view class derived from CView and delegates other tasks to your new view class. This section looks through the MFC Application Wizard starter application to see what you get.

Choose File, New, then Project... Fill in the project name as App1 and fill in an appropriate directory for the project files. Choose Visual C++ Projects from the Project Types box, and then choose MFC Application from the Templates box.

Navigate through the tabs on the left side of the dialog box, changing the settings as follows:

Application Type. Choose Multiple Documents for the application type.

Advanced Features. Deselect all check boxes except Printing and Print Preview.

After looking at the Overview tab to see a summary of the project settings, click Finish to create the project. Expand the App1 classes in Class View, and you see that six classes have been created: CAboutDlg, CApp1App, CApp1Doc, CApp1View, CChildFrame, and CMainframe. The document class, CApp1Doc, is where you will keep your application's information.

CApp1Doc represents a document; it holds the application's document data. You add storage for the document by adding data members to the CApp1Doc class. To see how this works, look at Listing 4.1, which shows the header file AppWizard creates for the CApp1Doc class.

LISTING 4.1 APP1DOC.H—THE HEADER FILE FOR THE CApp1Doc CLASS

```
// App1Doc.h : interface of the CApp1Doc class
//
```

LISTING 4.1   CONTINUED

```
#pragma once

class CApp1Doc : public CDocument
{
protected: // create from serialization only
   CApp1Doc();
   DECLARE_DYNCREATE(CApp1Doc)

// Attributes
public:

// Operations
public:

// Overrides
   public:
   virtual BOOL OnNewDocument();
   virtual void Serialize(CArchive& ar);

// Implementation
public:
   virtual ~CApp1Doc();
#ifdef _DEBUG
   virtual void AssertValid() const;
   virtual void Dump(CDumpContext& dc) const;
#endif

protected:

// Generated message map functions
protected:
   DECLARE_MESSAGE_MAP()
};
```

CH
4

Tip

If you're curious about the line at the top of this file, `#pragma once`, it's a compiler directive that keeps this file from being included multiple times. Multiple inclusions can be common in large projects, and this simple directive, generated for you by the MFC Application Wizard, can save a lot of frustration.

Near the top of the listing, you can see the class declaration's Attributes section, which is followed by the `public` keyword. This is where you declare the data members that are to hold your application's data. A little later in this chapter, you will create an application that stores an array of CPoint objects. That array will be declared as a member of the document class like this:

```
// Attributes
public:
   CPoint points[100];
```

CPoint

CPoint is an MFC class that encapsulates the information relevant to a point on the screen, most importantly the x and y coordinates of the point.

Notice also in the class's header file that the CApp1Doc class includes two virtual member functions called OnNewDocument() and Serialize(). MFC calls the OnNewDocument() function whenever the user selects the File, New command (or its toolbar equivalent, if a New button has been implemented in the application). You can use this function to initialize your document's data. In an SDI application, which has only a single document open at any time, the open document is closed and a new blank document is loaded into the same object; in an MDI application, which can have multiple documents open, a blank document is opened in addition to the documents that are already open. The Serialize() member function is where the document class loads and saves its data. This is discussed in Chapter 5, "Printing and Saving."

UNDERSTANDING THE VIEW CLASS

The view class displays the data stored in the document object and enables the user to modify this data. The view object keeps a pointer to the document object, which it uses to access the document's member variables in order to display or modify them. Listing 4.2 is the header file for CApp1View, as generated by the MFC Application Wizard.

Most MFC programmers add public member variables to their documents to make it easy for the view class to access them. A more object-oriented approach is to add private or protected member variables, and then add public functions to get or change the values of these variables.

LISTING 4.2   APP1VIEW.H—THE HEADER FILE FOR THE CApp1View CLASS

```
// App1View.h : interface of the CApp1View class
//


#pragma once


class CApp1View : public CView
{
protected: // create from serialization only
   CApp1View();
   DECLARE_DYNCREATE(CApp1View)

// Attributes
public:
   CApp1Doc* GetDocument() const;

// Operations
public:
```

LISTING 4.2 CONTINUED

```
// Overrides
   public:
   virtual void OnDraw(CDC* pDC);  // overridden to draw this view
virtual BOOL PreCreateWindow(CREATESTRUCT& cs);
protected:
   virtual BOOL OnPreparePrinting(CPrintInfo* pInfo);
   virtual void OnBeginPrinting(CDC* pDC, CPrintInfo* pInfo);
   virtual void OnEndPrinting(CDC* pDC, CPrintInfo* pInfo);

// Implementation
public:
   virtual ~CApp1View();
#ifdef _DEBUG
   virtual void AssertValid() const;
   virtual void Dump(CDumpContext& dc) const;
#endif

protected:

// Generated message map functions
protected:
   DECLARE_MESSAGE_MAP()
};

#ifndef _DEBUG  // debug version in App1View.cpp
inline CApp1Doc* CApp1View::GetDocument() const
   { return (CApp1Doc*)m_pDocument; }
#endif
```

CH

4

Near the top of the listing, you can see the class's public attributes, where it declares the GetDocument() function as returning a pointer to a CApp1Doc object. Anywhere in the view class that you need to access the document's data, you can call GetDocument() to obtain a pointer to the document. For example, to add a CPoint object to the aforementioned array of CPoint objects stored as the document's data, you might use the following line:

```
GetDocument()->m_points[x] = point;
```

You also can do this a little differently, by storing the pointer returned by GetDocument() in a local pointer variable and then using that pointer variable to access the document's data, like this:

```
pDoc = GetDocument();
pDoc->m_points[x] = point;
```

The second version is more convenient when you need to use the document pointer in several places in the function.

In release versions of your program, the GetDocument() function is inline, which means there is no performance advantage to saving the pointer this way, but it does improve readability. Inline functions are expanded into your code like macros, but offer type checking and other advantages.

Notice that the view class, like the document class, overrides a number of virtual functions from its base class. As you'll soon see, the OnDraw() function, which is the most important of these virtual functions, is where you paint your window's display. As for the other functions, MFC calls PreCreateWindow() before the window element (that is, the actual Windows window) is created and attached to the MFC window class, giving you a chance to modify the window's attributes (such as size and position). These two functions are discussed in more detail later in this chapter. OnPreparePrinting() is used to modify the Print dialog box before it displays for the user; the OnBeginPrinting() function gives you a chance to create GDI objects such as pens and brushes that you need to handle the print job; and OnEndPrinting() is where you can destroy any objects you might have created in OnBeginPrinting(). These three functions are discussed in Chapter 5.

When you first start using an application framework such as MFC, it's easy to get confused about the difference between an object instantiated from an MFC class and the Windows element it represents. For example, when you create an MFC frame-window object, you're actually creating two things: the MFC object that has member functions and member variables, and a Windows window that you can manipulate using the functions of the MFC object. The window element is associated with the MFC class, but is also an entity unto itself.

CREATING THE RECTANGLES APPLICATION

Now that you've had an introduction to documents and views, a little hands-on experience should help you better understand how these classes work. In the steps that follow, you build the Rectangles application, which demonstrates the manipulation of documents and views. When you first run this application, it draws an empty window. Wherever you click in the window, a small rectangle is drawn. You can resize the window, or minimize and restore it, and the rectangles are redrawn at all the coordinates where you clicked, because Rectangles keeps an array of coordinate points in the document and uses that array in the view.

First, use the MFC Application Wizard to create the basic files for the Rectangles program, selecting these options:

- Set the Project Type to Visual C++ Project, and then choose the MFC Application template. Name the project Rectangles. Click OK.
- On the Application Type tab, select Single Document Interface.
- On the Advanced Features tab, turn off all application features except Printing and Print Preview.

(The MFC Application Wizard is first discussed in Chapter 2, "Building Your First Windows Application.") When you're finished, go back to the Overview tab; it should look like Figure 4.1. Click the Finish button to create the project files.

Now that you have a starter application, it's time to add code to the document and view classes to create an application that actually does something. This application draws rectangles in the view and saves the coordinates of the rectangles in the document.

Figure 4.1
When you create an SDI application with the MFC Application Wizard, the overview summarizes your settings.

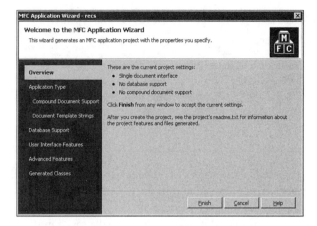

Follow these steps to add the code that modifies the document class to handle the application's data, which is an array of CPoint objects that determine where rectangles should be drawn in the view window:

1. Open the Class View window by choosing View, Class View.

2. Expand the Recs classes by clicking the + sign before them.

3. Right-click the CRecsDoc class and choose Add, Add Variable...from the shortcut menu that appears.

4. Fill in the Add Member Variable Wizard. For Variable Type, enter **CPoint[100]**. For Variable Name, enter **m_points**. Make sure Public is selected in the Access drop-down box. Click Finish.

5. Again, right-click the CRecsDoc class and choose Add, Add Variable....

6. For Variable Type, enter int. For Variable Name, enter **m_pointIndex**. Make sure public is selected in the Access drop-down box. Click Finish.

7. Click the + next to CRecsDoc in Class View to see the member variables and functions. The two member variables you added are now listed.

The m_points[] array holds the locations of rectangles displayed in the view window. The m_pointIndex data member holds the index of the next empty element of the array.

Now you need to get these variables initialized to appropriate values and use them to draw the view. MFC applications that use the document/view paradigm initialize document data in a function called OnNewDocument(), which is called automatically when the application first runs and again whenever the user chooses File, New.

The list of member variables and functions of CRecsDoc should still be displayed in Class View. Double-click OnNewDocument() in that list to edit the code. Using Listing 4.3 as a guide, remove the comments left by AppWizard and initialize m_pointIndex to zero.

CH

4

LISTING 4.3   RECSDOC.CPP—CRecsDoc::OnNewDocument()

```
BOOL CRecsDoc::OnNewDocument()
{
    if (!CDocument::OnNewDocument())
        return FALSE;

    m_pointIndex = 0;

    return TRUE;
}
```

There is no need to initialize the array of points because the index into the array will be used to ensure no code tries to use an uninitialized element of the array. At this point your modifications to the document class are complete. As you'll see in Chapter 5, you can make a few simple changes if you want this information actually saved in the document. To focus on views in this chapter, however, you will not be making those changes to the Recs application.

Now turn your attention to the view class. It uses the document data to draw rectangles onscreen. A full discussion of the way that drawing works must wait until later in this chapter, in the section "Understanding Device Contexts." For now it is enough to know that the OnDraw() function of your view class does the drawing. Expand the CRecsView class in ClassView and double-click OnDraw(). Using Listing 4.4 as a guide, remove the comments left by AppWizard and add code to draw a rectangle at each point in the array.

LISTING 4.4   RECSVIEW.CPP—CRecsView::OnDraw()

```
void CRecsView::OnDraw(CDC* pDC)
{
    CRecsDoc* pDoc = GetDocument();
    ASSERT_VALID(pDoc);

    int pointIndex = pDoc->m_pointIndex;

    for (int i=0; i<pointIndex; ++i)
    {
        int x = pDoc->m_points[i].x;
        int y = pDoc->m_points[i].y;
        pDC->Rectangle(x, y, x+20, y+20);
    }
}
```

Your modifications to the starter application generated by the MFC Application Wizard are almost complete. You have added member variables to the document, initialized those variables in the document's constructor and OnNewDocument() function, and used those variables in the view's OnDraw() function. All that remains is to enable the user to add points to the array. As discussed in Chapter 3, "Interacting with Your Application," you catch the mouse message with Class View and the Properties window and then add code to the message handler. Follow these steps:

1. Choose View, Class View. The Class View window appears.

2. Select CRecsView, then choose View, Properties Window. Then, click the Messages button on the Properties window toolbar. In the drop-down box next to WM_LBUTTONDOWN in the Messages table choose <Add> OnLButtonDown to add the message-response function to the class. Whenever the application receives a WM_LBUTTONDOWN message, it will call OnLButtonDown().

3. The editor will open the appropriate file and scroll to the function you just added. Add the code shown in Listing 4.5 to the function.

LISTING 4.5   RECSVIEW.CPP—CRecsView::OnLButtonDown()

```
void CRecsView::OnLButtonDown(UINT nFlags, CPoint point)
{
    CRecsDoc *pDoc = GetDocument();

    // don't go past the end of the 100 points allocated
    if (pDoc->m_pointIndex == 100)
        return;

    //store the click location
    pDoc->m_points[pDoc->m_pointIndex] = point;
    pDoc->m_pointIndex++;

    pDoc->SetModifiedFlag();
    Invalidate();

    CView::OnLButtonDown(nFlags, point);
}
```

The new OnLButtonDown() adds a point to the document's point array each time the user clicks the left mouse button over the view window. It increments m_pointIndex so that the next click goes into the point on the array after this one.

The call to SetModifiedFlag() marks this document as modified, or "dirty." MFC automatically prompts the user to save any dirty files on exit. (The details are found in Chapter 5.) Any code you write that changes any document variables should call SetModifiedFlag().

Tip

Earlier in this chapter you were reminded that private member variables and public access functions in the document have some advantages. One such advantage is that any document member function that changes a variable can also call SetModifiedFlag(), thus guaranteeing no programmer will forget it.

Finally, the call to Invalidate() causes MFC to call the OnDraw() function, so that the window's display will be redrawn with the new data. The Invalidate() function takes a single parameter (with the default value TRUE) that determines whether the background should

CH
4

be erased before it calls OnDraw(). On rare occasions you may choose to call Invalidate(FALSE) so that OnDraw() draws over whatever was already onscreen.

Finally, a call to the base class OnLButtonDown() takes care of the rest of the work involved in handling a mouse click.

You've now finished creating the complete application. Click the toolbar's Start button, or choose Build, Build Solution, to compile and link the application. After you have the Rectangles application compiled and linked, run it by choosing Debug, Start. When you do, you see the application's main window. Place your mouse pointer over the window's client area and click. A rectangle appears. Go ahead and keep clicking. You can place up to 100 rectangles in the window (see Figure 4.2).

Figure 4.2
The Rectangles application draws rectangles wherever you click.

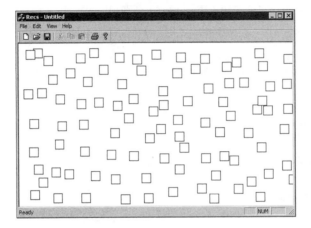

OTHER VIEW CLASSES

The view classes generated by AppWizard in this chapter's sample applications have been derived from MFC's CView class. In some cases, however, it is to your advantage to derive your view class from one of the other MFC view classes derived from CView. These additional classes provide your view window with special capabilities such as scrolling and text editing. Table 4.1 lists the various view classes along with their descriptions.

TABLE 4.1   VIEW CLASSES

Class	Description
CView	The base view class from which the specialized view classes are derived.
CScrollView	A view class that provides scrolling capabilities.
CEditView	A view class that provides basic text editing features.
CRichEditView	A view class that uses the RichEdit control to provide more sophisticated text editing capabilities.

TABLE 4.1   CONTINUED

Class	Description
CFormView	A view class that implements a form-like window that uses a dialog box resource.
CHtmlView	A view class that can display HTML, with all the capabilities of Microsoft Internet Explorer.
CListView	A view class that displays a ListView control in its window.
CTreeView	A view class that displays a TreeView control in its window.
CRecordView	A view class that can display database records along with controls for navigating the database.
CDaoRecordView	Same as CRecordView, except used with the DAO database classes.
COleDBRecordView	Same as CRecordView, except used with the OLE DB database classes.
CCtrlView	A base class from which view classes that implement 32-bit Windows common controls (such as the ListView, TreeView, and RichEdit controls) are derived.

To use one of these classes, substitute the desired class for the CView class in the application's project. When you use the MFC Application Wizard to generate your project, you can specify the view class you want on the Generated Classes tab, as shown in Figure 4.3. Then you can use the specific class's member functions to control the view window. Later in this chapter, you use the CScrollView class to implement a scrolling view.

Figure 4.3
You can use the MFC Application Wizard to select your application's base view class.

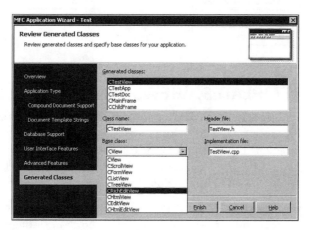

A CEditView object gives you all the features of a Windows edit control in your view window. Using this class, you can handle various editing and printing tasks, including Find and Replace. You can retrieve or set the current printer font by calling the GetPrinterFont() or

`SetPrinterFont()` member function or get the currently selected text by calling `GetSelectedText()`. Moreover, the `FindText()` member function locates a given text string, and `OnReplaceAll()` replaces all occurrences of a given text string with another string.

The `CRichEditView` class adds many features to an edit view, including paragraph formatting (such as centered, right-aligned, and bulleted text), character attributes (including underlined, bold, and italic), and the capability to set margins, fonts, and paper size. As you might have guessed, the `CRichEditView` class features a rich set of methods you can use to control your application's view object.

Figure 4.4 shows how the view classes fit into MFC's class hierarchy. Describing these various view classes fully is beyond the scope of this chapter. However, you can find plenty of information about them in your Visual Studio online documentation.

Figure 4.4
The view classes all trace their ancestry back to `CView`.

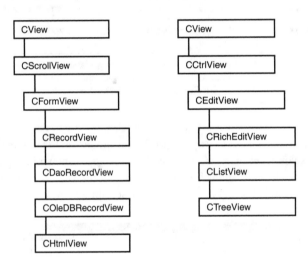

DOCUMENT TEMPLATES, VIEWS, AND FRAME WINDOWS

Because you've been working with MFC Application Wizard-generated applications in this chapter, you've taken for granted a lot of what goes on in the background of an MFC document/view program. That is, much of the code that enables the frame window (your application's main window), the document, and the view window to work together is automatically generated by the MFC Application Wizard and manipulated by MFC.

For example, if you look at the `InitInstance()` method of the Rectangles application's `CRecsApp` class, you see (among other things) the lines shown in Listing 4.6.

LISTING 4.6   RECS.CPP—INITIALIZING AN APPLICATION'S DOCUMENT

```
CSingleDocTemplate* pDocTemplate;
pDocTemplate = new CSingleDocTemplate(
    IDR_MAINFRAME,
    RUNTIME_CLASS(CRecsDoc),
```

LISTING 4.6   CONTINUED

```
      RUNTIME_CLASS(CMainFrame),
      RUNTIME_CLASS(CRecsView));
AddDocTemplate(pDocTemplate);
```

In Listing 4.6, you discover one secret that makes the document/view system work. In that code, the program creates a document-template object. These document templates have nothing to do with C++ templates. A document template is an older concept, named before C++ templates were implemented by Microsoft, that pulls together the following objects:

- A resource ID identifying a menu resource—IDR_MAINFRAME in this case
- A document class—CRecsDoc in this case
- A frame window class—always CMainFrame
- A view class—CRecsView in this case

Notice that you are not passing an object or a pointer to an object. You are passing the name of the class to a macro called RUNTIME_CLASS. It enables the framework to create instances of a class at runtime, which the application object must be able to do in a program that uses the document/view architecture. For this macro to work, the classes that will be created dynamically must be declared and implemented as such. To do this, the class must have the DECLARE_DYNCREATE macro in its declaration (in the header file) and the IMPLEMENT_DYNCREATE macro in its implementation. The MFC Application Wizard takes care of this for you.

For example, if you look at the header file for the Rectangles application's CMainFrame class, you see the following line near the top of the class's declaration:

```
DECLARE_DYNCREATE(CMainFrame)
```

As you can see, the DECLARE_DYNCREATE macro requires the class's name as its single argument.

Now, if you look near the top of CMainFrame's implementation file (MAINFRM.CPP), you see this line:

```
IMPLEMENT_DYNCREATE(CMainFrame, CFrameWnd)
```

The IMPLEMENT_DYNCREATE macro requires as arguments the name of the class and the name of the base class.

If you explore the application's source code further, you find that the document and view classes also contain the DECLARE_DYNCREATE and IMPLEMENT_DYNCREATE macros.

If you haven't heard of frame windows before, you should know that they contain all the windows involved in an application—this means control bars as well as views. They also route messages and commands to views and documents, as discussed in Chapter 3.

CH
4

The last line in Listing 4.6 calls AddDocTemplate() to pass the object on to the application object, CRecsApp, which keeps a list of documents. The AddDocTemplate() function adds this document to this list and uses the document template to create the document object, the frame, and the view window.

Because this is a Single Document Interface, a single document template (CSingleDocTemplate) is created. Multiple Document Interface applications use one CMultiDocTemplate object for each kind of document they support. For example, a spreadsheet program might have two kinds of documents: tables and graphs. Each would have its own view and its own set of menus. Two instances of CMultiDocTemplate would be created in InitInstance(), each pulling together the menu, document, and view that belong together. If you've ever seen the menus in a program change as you switched from one view or document to another, you know how you can achieve the same effect: Simply associate them with different menu resource IDs as you build the document templates.

UNDERSTANDING DEVICE CONTEXTS

Most applications need to display some type of data in their windows. Windows is a device-independent operating system, so you don't interact with devices directly; you do so indirectly instead through something called a *device context* (DC).

This device independence ensures that your programs run on all popular devices. In most cases, Windows handles devices for you through the device drivers that users have installed on the system. These device drivers intercept the data that the application needs to display and then translates the data appropriately for the device on which it is to appear, whether that's a screen, a printer, or some other output device.

A system with a VGA monitor may display data with fewer colors than a system with a Super VGA monitor. Likewise, a system with a monochrome monitor displays the data in only a single color. High-resolution monitors can display more data than lower-resolution monitors. The device drivers take the display requirements and fine-tune them to the device on which the data is to actually appear. And it's a data structure known as a device context that links the application to the device's driver.

A device context (DC) is an object that holds the attributes of a window's drawing surface, including the currently selected pen, brush, and font that will be used to draw on the screen. Unlike an artist, who can have many brushes and pens with which to work, a DC can use only a single pen, brush, or font at a time. If you want to use a pen that draws wider lines, for example, you need to create the new pen and then replace the DC's old pen with the new one. Similarly, if you want to fill shapes with a red brush, you must create the brush and select it into the DC.

A window's *client area* is a versatile surface that can display anything a Windows program can draw. The client area can display any type of data because everything displayed in a window—whether it be text, spreadsheet data, a bitmap, or any other type of data—is displayed graphically. MFC helps you display data by encapsulating Windows' GDI functions and objects into its DC classes.

INTRODUCING THE PAINT1 APPLICATION

In this chapter, you build the Paint1 application, which demonstrates fonts, pens, and brushes. Paint1 uses the document/view paradigm discussed earlier in this chapter and the view handles displaying the data. When run, the application displays text in several different fonts. When the user clicks, it displays lines drawn with several different pens. After another click, it displays boxes filled with a variety of brushes.

The first step in creating Paint1 is to build an empty shell with the MFC Application Wizard, as first discussed in Chapter 1. Choose File, New, Project, then select the Visual C++ Projects option in the list box. As shown in Figure 4.5, fill in the project name as Paint1 and fill in an appropriate directory for the project files. Make sure that MFC Application is selected. Click OK.

Figure 4.5
Start an MFC
Application Wizard
project workspace
called Paint1.

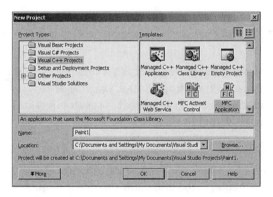

CH

4

Move through the MFC Application Wizard tabs; change the settings as follows; and then click Finish.

> **Application Type.** Choose Single Document for the application type.

> **Advanced Features.** Deselect all check boxes except Printing and Print Preview.

Now that you have a starter application, it's time to add code to demonstrate some ways an MFC program can display data onscreen.

Tip

Your starter application has menus, but you will ignore them completely. It would be quite a bit of work to remove them; just pretend they aren't there.

BUILDING THE PAINT1 APPLICATION

To build the Paint1 application, you first need to understand how painting and drawing work in an MFC program. Then you can set up the skeleton code to handle user clicks and the three different kinds of display. Finally, you fill in the code for each kind of display in turn.

PAINTING IN AN MFC PROGRAM

In Chapter 3 you learned about message maps and how to tell MFC which functions to call when it receives messages from Windows. One important message that every Windows program with a window must handle is WM_PAINT. Windows sends the WM_PAINT message to an application's window when the window needs to be redrawn. Several events cause Windows to send a WM_PAINT message:

- When users run the program: The application's window receives a WM_PAINT message almost immediately after the program is run, to ensure that the appropriate data is displayed from the very start.

- When the window has been resized or has recently been uncovered (fully or partially) by another window: Part of the window that wasn't visible before is now onscreen and must be updated.

- When a program indirectly sends itself a WM_PAINT message by invalidating its client area: This capability ensures that an application can change its window's contents almost any time it wants. For example, a word processor might invalidate its window after users paste some text from the Clipboard.

When you studied message maps, you learned to convert a message name to a message map macro and function name. You now know, for example, that the message map macro for a WM_PAINT message is ON_WM_PAINT(). You also know that the matching message map function should be called OnPaint(). This is another case where MFC has already done most of the work of matching a Windows message with its message-response function. (If all this message-map stuff sounds unfamiliar, you might want to review Chapter 3.)

You might guess that your next step is to catch the WM_PAINT message or to override the OnPaint() function that your view class inherited from CView, but you won't do that. Listing 4.7 shows the code for CView::OnPaint(). As you can see, WM_PAINT is already caught and handled for you.

LISTING 4.7   CView::OnPaint()

```
void CView::OnPaint()
{
    // standard paint routine
    CPaintDC dc(this);
    OnPrepareDC(&dc);
    OnDraw(&dc);
}
```

CPaintDC is a special class for managing paint DCs—device contexts used only in responses to WM_PAINT messages. An object of the CPaintDC class does more than just create a DC; it also calls the BeginPaint() Windows API function in the class's constructor and calls EndPaint() in its destructor. When a program responds to WM_PAINT messages, calls to BeginPaint() and EndPaint() are required. The CPaintDC class handles this requirement without your having to get involved in all the messy details. As you can see, the CPaintDC constructor takes a single argument, which is a pointer to the window for which you're creating the DC. This pointer points to the current view, so it's passed to the constructor to make a DC for the current view.

The OnPrepareDC() function is a CView function that prepares a DC for use. You'll learn more about it in Chapter 5.

The OnDraw() function does the actual work of visually representing the document. In most cases you will write the OnDraw() code for your application and never touch OnPaint(). In the example in this chapter, editing only the OnDraw() function is involved.

SWITCHING THE DISPLAY

The design for Paint1 states that when you click the application's window, the window's display changes. This seemingly magical feat is actually easy to accomplish. You just add a member variable to the view to store what kind of display is being done and then change it when users click the window. In other words, the program routes WM_LBUTTONDOWN messages to the OnLButtonDown() message-response function, which sets the m_display flag as appropriate.

First, add the member variable. You must add it by hand rather than through the shortcut menu because the type is not a normal type. Open Paint1View.h from the Solution Explorer and add these lines after the //Attributes comment:

```
protected:
    enum {Fonts, Pens, Brushes} m_Display;
```

This is an anonymous or unnamed enum. Switch to Class View, expand the classes, expand CPaint1View, and then double-click the constructor CPaint1View(). Add the following line of code in place of the TODO comment:

```
m_Display = Fonts;
```

This initializes the display selector to the font demonstration. You use the display selector in the OnDraw() function called by CView::OnPaint().

AppWizard has created CPaint1View::OnDraw(), but it doesn't do anything at the moment. Double-click the function name in Class View and add the code in Listing 4.8 to the function, removing the TODO comment left by AppWizard.

LISTING 4.8 CPaint1View::OnDraw()

```
void CPaint1View::OnDraw(CDC* pDC)
{
    CPaint1Doc* pDoc = GetDocument();
    ASSERT_VALID(pDoc);

    switch (m_Display)
    {
        case Fonts:
            ShowFonts(pDC);
            break;
        case Pens:
            ShowPens(pDC);
            break;
        case Brushes:
            ShowBrushes(pDC);
            break;
    }
}
```

You will write the three functions ShowFonts(), ShowPens(), and ShowBrushes() in upcoming sections of this chapter. Each function uses the same DC pointer that was passed to OnDraw() by OnPaint(). Add them to the class now by following these steps:

1. Right-click the CPaint1View class in ClassView and select Add, Add Function.

2. Enter **void** for the Return Type.

3. Enter **ShowFonts** for the Function name.

4. Add the parameter type of **CDC*** and parameter name of **pDC**.

5. Change the access to Protected. Click Finish.

6. Repeat steps 1 through 4 for ShowPens(CDC* pDC) and ShowBrushes(CDC* pDC).

The last step in arranging for the display to switch is to catch left mouse clicks and write code in the message handler to change m_display.

Select the CPaint1View class in the Class view. In the Properties window, click the Messages toolbar button. Select WM_LBUTTONDOWN from the list, click the dropdown box, and select Add OnLButtonDown. Visual Studio adds a function called OnLButtonDown() to the view and adds entries to the message map so that this function is called whenever users click the left mouse button over this view.

The editor will scroll to edit the function you just created. Add the code shown in Listing 4.9.

LISTING 4.9 CPaint1View::OnLButtonDown()

```
void CPaint1View::OnLButtonDown(UINT nFlags, CPoint point)
{
    if (m_Display == Fonts)
        m_Display = Pens;
```

LISTING 4.9   CONTINUED

```
    else if (m_Display == Pens)
        m_Display = Brushes;
    else
        m_Display = Fonts;

    Invalidate();

    CView::OnLButtonDown(nFlags, point);
}
```

When the user clicks a left mouse button, m_display is set to the next display type in the series. Of course, just changing the value of m_display doesn't accomplish much; the program still needs to redraw the contents of its window. The call to Invalidate() tells Windows that the whole window needs to be repainted. This causes Windows to generate a WM_PAINT message for the window, which means that eventually OnDraw() will be called and the view will be redrawn as a font, pen, or brush demonstration.

USING FONTS

Changing the font used in a view is a technique you'll want to use in various situations. It's not as simple as you might think because you can never be sure that any given font is actually installed on the user's machine. You set up a structure that holds information about the font you want, attempt to create it, and then work with the font you actually have, which might not be the font you asked for.

CH
4

A Windows font is described in the LOGFONT structure outlined in Table 4.2. The LOGFONT structure uses 14 fields to hold a complete description of the font. Many fields can be set to 0 or the default values, depending on the program's needs.

TABLE 4.2   LOGFONT FIELDS AND THEIR DESCRIPTIONS

Field	Description
lfHeight	Font height in logical units
lfWidth	Font width in logical units
lfEscapement	Angle at which to draw the text
lfOrientation	Character tilt in tenths of a degree
lfWeight	Font weight
lfItalic	A nonzero value indicates italics
lfUnderline	A nonzero value indicates an underlined font
lfStrikeOut	A nonzero value indicates a strikethrough font
lfCharSet	Font character set

TABLE 4.2   CONTINUED

Class	Description
lfOutPrecision	How to match requested font to actual font
lfClipPrecision	How to clip characters that run over clip area
lfQuality	Print quality of the font
lfPitchAndFamily	Pitch and font family
lfFaceName	Typeface name

Some terms in Table 4.2 need a little explanation. The first is *logical units*. How high is a font with a height of 8 logical units, for example? The meaning of a logical unit depends on the *mapping mode* you're using, as shown in Table 4.3. The default mapping mode is MM_TEXT, which means that one logical unit is equal to 1 pixel. Mapping modes are discussed in more detail in Chapter 5.

TABLE 4.3   MAPPING MODES

Mode	Unit
MM_HIENGLISH	0.001 inch
MM_HIMETRIC	0.01 millimeter
MM_ISOTROPIC	Arbitrary
MM_LOENGLISH	0.01 inch
MM_LOMETRIC	0.1 millimeter
MM_TEXT	Device pixel
MM_TWIPS	1/1440 inch

Escapement refers to writing text along an angled line. *Orientation* refers to writing angled text along a flat line. The *font weight* refers to the thickness of the letters. A number of constants have been defined for use in this field: FW_DONTCARE, FW_THIN, FW_EXTRALIGHT, FW_ULTRALIGHT, FW_LIGHT, FW_NORMAL, FW_REGULAR, FW_MEDIUM, FW_SEMIBOLD, FW_DEMIBOLD, FW_BOLD, FW_EXTRABOLD, FW_ULTRABOLD, FW_BLACK, and FW_HEAVY. Not all fonts are available in all weights. Four character sets are available (ANSI_CHARSET, OEM_CHARSET, SYMBOL_CHARSET, and UNICODE_CHARSET), but for writing English text you'll almost always use ANSI_CHARSET. The last field in the LOGFONT structure is the face name, such as Courier or Helvetica.

Listing 4.10 shows the code you need to add to the empty ShowFonts() function you created earlier.

LISTING 4.10   CPaint1View::ShowFonts()

```
void CPaint1View::ShowFonts(CDC * pDC)
{
    // Initialize a LOGFONT structure for the fonts.
    LOGFONT logFont;
    logFont.lfHeight = 8;
    logFont.lfWidth = 0;
    logFont.lfEscapement = 0;
    logFont.lfOrientation = 0;
    logFont.lfWeight = FW_NORMAL;
    logFont.lfItalic = 0;
    logFont.lfUnderline = 0;
    logFont.lfStrikeOut = 0;
    logFont.lfCharSet = ANSI_CHARSET;
    logFont.lfOutPrecision = OUT_DEFAULT_PRECIS;
    logFont.lfClipPrecision = CLIP_DEFAULT_PRECIS;
    logFont.lfQuality = PROOF_QUALITY;
    logFont.lfPitchAndFamily = VARIABLE_PITCH | FF_ROMAN;
    strcpy(logFont.lfFaceName, "Times New Roman");

// Initialize the position of text in the window.
    int position = 0;

    // Create and display eight example fonts.
    for (int x=0; x<8; ++x)
    {
        // Set the new font's height.
        logFont.lfHeight = 16 + (x * 8);

        // Create a new font and select it into the DC.
        CFont font;
        font.CreateFontIndirect(&logFont);
        CFont* oldFont = pDC->SelectObject(&font);

        // Print text with the new font.
        position += logFont.lfHeight;
        pDC->TextOut(20, position, "A sample font.");

        // Restore the old font to the DC.
        pDC->SelectObject(oldFont);
    }
}
```

The ShowFonts() function starts by setting up a Times Roman font 8 pixels high, with a width that best matches the height, and all other attributes set to normal defaults.

To show the many fonts displayed in its window, the Paint1 application creates its fonts in a for loop, modifying the value of the LOGFONT structure's lfHeight member each time through the loop, using the loop variable x to calculate the new font height:

```
logFont.lfHeight = 16 + (x * 8);
```

Because x starts at 0, the first font created in the loop is 16 pixels high. Each time through the loop, the new font is 8 pixels higher than the preceding one.

After setting the font's height, the program creates a CFont object and calls its CreateFontIndirect() function, which attempts to create a CFont object corresponding to the LOGFONT you created. It changes the LOGFONT to describe the CFont that was actually created, given the fonts installed on the user's machine.

After ShowFonts() calls CreateFontIndirect(), the CFont object is associated with a Windows font. Now you can select it into the DC. Selecting objects into device contexts is a crucial concept in Windows output programming. You can't use any graphical object, such as a font, directly; instead, you select it into the DC and then use the DC. You always save a pointer to the old object that was in the DC (the pointer is returned from the SelectObject() call) and use it to restore the device context by selecting the old object again when you're finished. The same function, SelectObject(), is used to select various objects into a device context: the font you're using in this section, a pen, a brush, or a number of other drawing objects.

After selecting the new font into the DC, you can use the font to draw text onscreen. The local variable position holds the vertical position in the window at which the next line of text should be printed. This position depends on the height of the current font. After all, if there's not enough space between the lines, the larger fonts overlap the smaller ones. When Windows created the new font, it stored the font's height (most likely the height that you requested, but maybe not) in the LOGFONT structure's lfHeight member. By adding the value stored in lfHeight, the program can determine the next position at which to display the line of text. To make the text appear onscreen, ShowFonts() calls TextOut().

The TextOut() function's first two arguments are the X and Y coordinates at which to print the text. The third argument is the text to print. Having printed the text, you restore the old font to the DC.

Build the application and run it. It should resemble Figure 4.6. If you click the window, it goes blank because the ShowPens() routine doesn't draw anything. Click again and it's still blank, this time because the ShowBrushes() routine doesn't draw anything. Click a third time and you are back to the fonts screen.

Figure 4.6
The font display
shows different types
of text output.

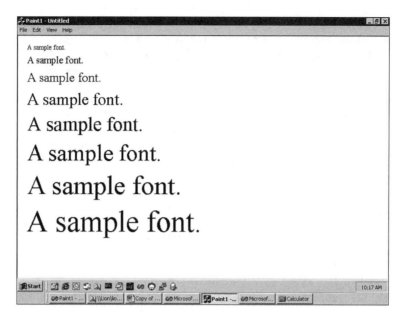

SIZING AND POSITIONING THE WINDOW

As you can see in Figure 4.6, Paint1 doesn't display eight different fonts at 800×600 screen settings—only seven can fit in the window. To correct this, you need to set the size of the window a little larger than the Windows default. In an MFC program, you do this in the mainframe class `PreCreateWindow()` function. This is called for you just before the mainframe window is created. The mainframe window surrounds the entire application and governs the size of the view.

The `PreCreateWindow()` function takes one parameter: a reference to a `CREATESTRUCT` structure. The `CREATESTRUCT` structure contains essential information about the window that's about to be created, as shown in Listing 4.11.

LISTING 4.11   THE CREATESTRUCT STRUCTURE

```
typedef struct tagCREATESTRUCT {
    LPVOID    lpCreateParams;
    HANDLE    hInstance;
    HMENU     hMenu;
    HWND      hwndParent;
    int       cy;
    int       cx;
    int       y;
    int       x;
    LONG      style;
    LPCSTR    lpszName;
    LPCSTR    lpszClass;
    DWORD     dwExStyle;
} CREATESTRUCT;
```

Of special interest to MFC programmers are the cx, cy, x, and y members of this structure. By changing cx and cy, you can set the window width and height, respectively. Similarly, modifying x and y changes the window's position. By overriding PreCreateWindow(), you have a chance to fiddle with the CREATESTRUCT structure before Windows uses it to create the window.

The MFC Application Wizard created a CMainFrame::PreCreateWindow() function. Expand CMainFrame in ClassView, double-click PreCreateWindow() to edit it, and edit it so that it resembles Listing 4.12. This sets the application's height and width. It also prevents users from resizing the application by using the bitwise and operator (&) to turn off the WS_SIZE-BOX style bit.

LISTING 4.12   CMainFrame::PreCreateWindow()

```
BOOL CMainFrame::PreCreateWindow(CREATESTRUCT& cs)
{
    cs.cx = 440;
    cs.cy = 480;

    cs.style &= ~WS_SIZEBOX;

    return CFrameWnd::PreCreateWindow(cs);
}
```

It's important that after your own code in PreCreateWindow(), you call the base class's PreCreateWindow(). Failure to do this leaves you without a valid window because MFC never gets a chance to pass the CREATESTRUCT structure on to Windows, so Windows never creates your window. When overriding member functions, you usually need to call the base class's version.

Build and run Paint1 to confirm that all eight fonts fit in the application's window. Now you're ready to demonstrate pens.

USING PENS

You'll be pleased to know that pens are much easier to deal with than fonts, mostly because you don't have to fool around with complicated data structures such as LOGFONT. In fact, to create a pen, you need to supply only the pen's line style, thickness, and color. The Paint1 application's ShowPens() function displays in its window the lines drawn by different pens created within a for loop. Listing 4.13 shows the code.

LISTING 4.13   CPaint1View::ShowPens()

```
void CPaint1View::ShowPens(CDC * pDC)
{
    // Initialize the line position.
    int position = 10;
```

LISTING 4.13 CONTINUED

```
    // Draw sixteen lines in the window.
    for (int x=0; x<16; ++x)
    {
        // Create a new pen and select it into the DC.
        CPen pen(PS_SOLID, x*2+1, RGB(0, 0, 255));
        CPen* oldPen = pDC->SelectObject(&pen);

        // Draw a line with the new pen.
        position +=  x * 2 + 10;
        pDC->MoveTo(20, position);
        pDC->LineTo(400, position);

        // Restore the old pen to the DC.
        pDC->SelectObject(oldPen);
    }
}
```

Within the loop, ShowPens() first creates a custom pen. The constructor takes three parameters. The first is the line's style, which is one of the styles listed in Table 4.4. (You can draw only solid lines with different thicknesses. If you specify a pattern and a thickness greater than 1 pixel, the pattern is ignored and a solid line is drawn.) The second argument is the line thickness, which increases each time through the loop. The third argument is the line's color. The RGB macro takes three values for the red, green, and blue color components and converts them to a valid Windows color reference. The values for the red, green, and blue color components can be anything from 0 to 255—the higher the value, the brighter that color component. The code shown in Listing 4.13 creates a bright blue pen. If all the color values were 0, the pen would be black; if the color values were all 255, the pen would be white.

TABLE 4.4 PEN STYLES

Style	Description
PS_DASH	A pen that draws dashed lines.
PS_DASHDOT	A pen that draws dash-dot patterned lines.
PS_DASHDOTDOT	A pen that draws dash-dot-dot patterned lines.
PS_DOT	A pen that draws dotted lines.
PS_INSIDEFRAME	A pen that's used with shapes, in which the line's thickness must not extend outside the shape's frame.
PS_NULL	A pen that draws invisible lines.
PS_SOLID	A pen that draws solid lines.

CH
4

If you want to control the style of a line's end points or create your own custom patterns for pens, you can use the alternative CPen constructor, which requires a few more arguments than the CPen constructor described in this section. To learn how to use this alternative constructor, look up CPen in your Visual C++ online documentation.

After creating the new pen, ShowPens() selects it into the DC, saving the pointer to the old pen. The MoveTo() function moves the pen to an X,Y coordinate without drawing as it moves; the LineTo() function moves the pen while drawing. The style, thickness, and color of the pen are used to draw the line. Finally, you select the old pen back into the DC.

There are a number of line drawing functions other than LineTo(), including Arc(), ArcTo(), AngleArc(), and PolyDraw().

Build and run Paint1 again. When the font display appears, click the window. You will see a pen display similar to the one in Figure 4.7.

Figure 4.7
The pen display shows the effect of setting line thickness.

USING BRUSHES

A pen draws a line of a specified thickness onscreen. A brush fills a shape onscreen. You can create solid and patterned brushes and even brushes from bitmaps that contain your own custom fill patterns. Paint1 displays both patterned and solid rectangles in the ShowBrushes() function, shown in Listing 4.14.

LISTING 4.14 CPaint1View::ShowBrushes()

```
void CPaint1View::ShowBrushes(CDC * pDC)
{
    // Initialize the rectangle position.
    int position = 0;
```

LISTING 4.14 CONTINUED

```cpp
    // Select pen to use for rectangle borders.
    CPen pen(PS_SOLID, 5, RGB(255, 0, 0));
    CPen* oldPen = pDC->SelectObject(&pen);

    // Draw seven rectangles.
    for (int x=0; x<7; ++x)
    {
        CBrush* brush;

        // Create a solid or hatched brush.
        if (x == 6)
            brush = new CBrush(RGB(0,255,0));
        else
            brush = new CBrush(x, RGB(0,160,0));

        // Select the new brush into the DC.
        CBrush* oldBrush = pDC->SelectObject(brush);

        // Draw the rectangle.
        position += 50;
        pDC->Rectangle(20, position, 400, position + 40);

        // Restore the DC and delete the brush.
        pDC->SelectObject(oldBrush);
        delete brush;
    }
// Restore the old pen to the DC.
    pDC->SelectObject(oldPen);
}
```

CH

4

The rectangles painted with the various brushes in this routine are all drawn with a border.
To arrange this, create a pen (the pen identified in Listing 4.14 is solid, 5 pixels thick, and
bright red) and select it into the DC. It will be used to border the rectangles without any
further work on your part. Like ShowFonts() and ShowPens(), this routine creates its graphical objects within a for loop. Unlike those two functions, ShowBrushes() creates a graphical
object (in this routine, a brush) with a call to new. This enables you to call the one-argument
constructor, which creates a solid brush, or the two-argument constructor, which creates a
hatched brush.

In Listing 4.14, the first argument to the two-argument constructor is just the loop variable,
x. Usually, you don't want to show all the hatch patterns but want to select a specific one.
Use one of these constants for the hatch style:

- HS_HORIZONTAL. Horizontal

- HS_VERTICAL. Vertical

- HS_CROSS. Horizontal and vertical

- HS_FDIAGONAL. Forward diagonal

- **HS_BDIAGONAL**. Backward diagonal
- **HS_DIAGCROSS**. Diagonal in both directions

In a pattern that should be familiar by now, ShowBrushes() selects the brush into the DC, determines the position at which to work, uses the brush by calling Rectangle(), and then restores the old brush. When the loop is complete, the old pen is restored as well.

The Rectangle() function is just one of the shape-drawing functions that you can call. Rectangle() takes as arguments the coordinates of the rectangle's upper left and lower right corners. Some others of interest are Chord(), DrawFocusRect(), Ellipse(), Pie(), Polygon(), PolyPolygon(), Polyline(), and RoundRect().

Tip

RoundRect() draws a rectangle with rounded corners, not a round rectangle. If you want to draw a circle, it's just a special case of Ellipse(), in the same way that a square is a special case of Rectangle().

Again, build and run Paint1. Click twice, and you can see the demonstration of brushes, as shown in Figure 4.8.

Figure 4.8
The brushes display shows several patterns inside thick-bordered rectangles.

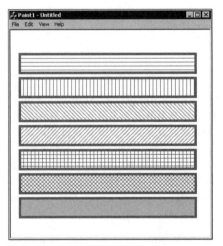

Remember the call to Invalidate() in CPaint1View::OnLButtonDown()? The Invalidate() function actually takes a Boolean argument with a default value of TRUE. This argument tells Windows whether to erase the window's background. If you use FALSE for this argument, the background isn't erased. In Figure 4.9, you can see what happens to the Paint1 application if Invalidate() is called with an argument of FALSE.

Figure 4.9
Without erasing the background, the Paint1 application's windows appear messy.

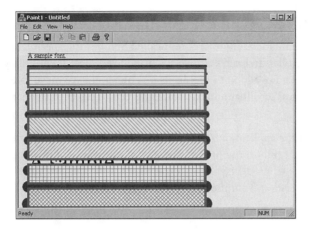

SCROLLING WINDOWS

In most applications, if a document is too large to completely fit within a window, you can view portions of it and scroll through it a bit at a time. If you want to enable users to view portions of a large document, you must create scrolling windows.

Adding scrollbars to an application from scratch is a complicated task. Luckily for Visual C++ programmers, MFC handles many of the details involved in scrolling windows over documents. If you use the document/view architecture and derive your view window from MFC's `CScrollView` class, you have scrolling capabilities almost for free.

If you create your application with the MFC Application Wizard, you can specify on the Generated Classes tab that you want to use `CScrollView` as the base class for your view class, as shown in Figure 4.10.

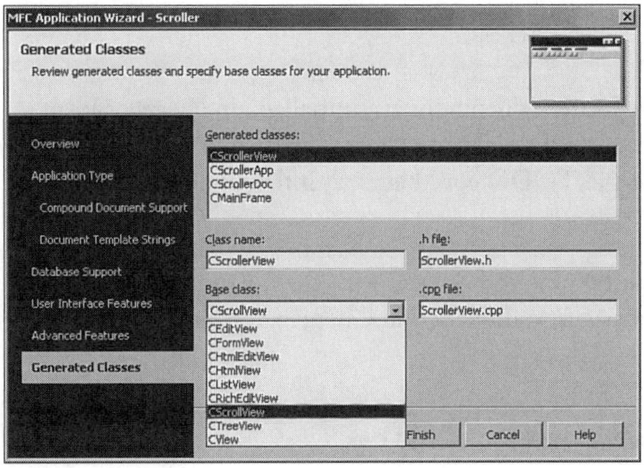

CH
4

Figure 4.10
You can create a scrolling window for your application.

BUILDING THE SCROLLER APPLICATION

In this section, you build a sample program called Scroller to experiment with a scrolling window. When Scroller first runs, it displays five lines of text. Each time you click the window, five lines of text are added to the display. When you have more lines of text than fit in the window, a vertical scrollbar appears, enabling you to scroll to the parts of the documents that you can't see.

As usual, building the application starts with the MFC Application Wizard. Choose File, New, then Project.... Fill in the project name as Scroller and fill in an appropriate directory for the project files. Choose Visual C++ Projects from the Project Types box, and then choose MFC Application from the Templates box.

Navigate through the tabs on the left side of the dialog box, changing the settings as follows:

> **Application Type**. Choose Single Document for the application type.
>
> **Advanced Features**. Deselect all check boxes except Printing and Print Preview.
>
> **User Interface Features**. Deselect System Menu and Initial Status Bar.
>
> **Generated Classes**. Select CScrollView from the Base Class drop-down box, as in Figure 4.10.

This application generates very simple lines of text. You need to keep track of only the number of lines in the scrolling view at the moment. To do this, add a variable to the document class by following these steps:

1. In ClassView, expand the classes and right-click CScrollerDoc.

2. Choose Add Variable from the shortcut menu.

3. Fill in **int** as the variable type.

4. Fill in **m_NumLines** as the variable name.

5. Select Public for the Access.

Variables associated with a document are initialized in OnNewDocument(), as discussed earlier in this chapter. In ClassView, expand CScrollerDoc and double-click OnNewDocument() to expand it. Replace the TODO comments with this line of code:

```
m_NumLines = 5;
```

To arrange for this variable to be saved with the document and restored when the document is loaded, you serialize it as discussed in Chapter 5. Edit CScrollerDoc::Serialize() as shown in Listing 4.15.

LISTING 4.15   CScrollerDoc::Serialize()

```
void CScrollerDoc::Serialize(CArchive& ar)
{
    if (ar.IsStoring())
```

LISTING 4.15   CONTINUED

```
    {
        ar << m_NumLines;
    }
    else
    {
        ar >> m_NumLines;
    }
}
```

Now all you need to do is use m_NumLines to draw the appropriate number of lines. Expand the view class, CScrollerView, in ClassView and double-click OnDraw(). Edit it until it's the same as Listing 4.16. This is very similar to the ShowFonts() code from the Paint1 application earlier in this chapter.

LISTING 4.16   CScrollerView::OnDraw()

```
void CScrollerView::OnDraw(CDC* pDC)
{
    CScrollerDoc* pDoc = GetDocument();
    ASSERT_VALID(pDoc);

    // Get the number of lines from the document.
    int numLines = pDoc->m_NumLines;

    // Initialize a LOGFONT structure for the fonts.
    LOGFONT logFont;
    logFont.lfHeight = 24;
    logFont.lfWidth = 0;
    logFont.lfEscapement = 0;
    logFont.lfOrientation = 0;
    logFont.lfWeight = FW_NORMAL;
    logFont.lfItalic = 0;
    logFont.lfUnderline = 0;
    logFont.lfStrikeOut = 0;
    logFont.lfCharSet = ANSI_CHARSET;
    logFont.lfOutPrecision = OUT_DEFAULT_PRECIS;
    logFont.lfClipPrecision = CLIP_DEFAULT_PRECIS;
    logFont.lfQuality = PROOF_QUALITY;
    logFont.lfPitchAndFamily = VARIABLE_PITCH | FF_ROMAN;
    strcpy(logFont.lfFaceName, "Times New Roman");

    // Create a new font and select it into the DC.
    CFont* font = new CFont();
    font->CreateFontIndirect(&logFont);
    CFont* oldFont = pDC->SelectObject(font);

    // Initialize the position of text in the window.
    int position = 0;

    // Create and display eight example lines.
    for (int x=0; x<numLines; ++x)
    {
```

CH
4

LISTING 4.16   CONTINUED

```
        // Create the string to display.
        char s[25];
        wsprintf(s, "This is line #%d", x+1);

        // Print text with the new font.
        pDC->TextOut(20, position, s);
        position += logFont.lfHeight;
    }

    // Restore the old font to the DC, and
    // delete the font the program created.
    pDC->SelectObject(oldFont);
    delete font;
}
```

Build and run the Scroller application. You will see a display similar to that in Figure 4.11. No scrollbars appear because all the lines fit in the window.

Figure 4.11
At first, the Scroller application displays five lines of text and no scrollbars.

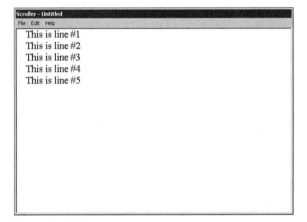

```
Scroller - Untitled
File   Edit   Help
    This is line #1
    This is line #2
    This is line #3
    This is line #4
    This is line #5
```

ADDING CODE TO INCREASE LINES

To increase the number of lines whenever users click the window, you need to add a message handler to handle left mouse clicks and then write the code for the handler. Right-click CScrollerView in Class View and choose Properties. In the Properties window choose the Messages button, then click to the right of WM_LBUTTONDOWN to add a handler. Edit the code: Listing 4.17 shows the completed handler. It simply increases the number of lines and calls Invalidate() to force a redraw. Like so many message handlers, it finishes by passing the work on to the base class version of this function.

LISTING 4.17   CScrollerView::OnLButtonDown()

```
void CScrollerView::OnLButtonDown(UINT nFlags, CPoint point)
{
    CScrollerDoc* pDoc = GetDocument();
    ASSERT_VALID(pDoc);

    // Increase number of lines to display.
    pDoc->m_NumLines += 5;

    // Redraw the window.
    Invalidate();

    CScrollerView::OnLButtonDown(nFlags, point);
}
```

ADDING CODE TO DECREASE LINES

So that you can watch scrollbars disappear as well as appear, why not implement a way for users to decrease the number of lines in the window? If left-clicking increases the number of lines, it makes sense that right-clicking would decrease it. Add a handler for WM_RBUTTONDOWN just as you did for WM_LBUTTONDOWN, and edit it until it's just like Listing 4.18. This function decreases the number of lines, but ensures that the number of lines is never negative.

LISTING 4.18   CScrollerView::OnRButtonDown()

```
void CScrollerView::OnRButtonDown(UINT nFlags, CPoint point)
{
    CScrollerDoc* pDoc = GetDocument();
    ASSERT_VALID(pDoc);

    // Decrease number of lines to display.
    pDoc->m_NumLines -= 5;

    if (pDoc->m_NumLines < 0)
    {
        pDoc->m_NumLines = 0;
    }

    // Redraw the window.
    Invalidate();

    CScrollView::OnRButtonDown(nFlags, point);
}
```

If you build and run Scroller now and click the window, you can increase the number of lines, but scrollbars don't appear. You need to add some lines to OnDraw() to make that happen. Before you do, review the way that scrollbars work. You can click three places on a vertical scrollbar: on the thumb (some people call it the elevator), above the thumb, or below it.

Clicking the thumb does nothing, but you can click and hold to drag it up or down. Clicking above it moves you one page (one screen) up within the data. Clicking below it moves you one page down. What's more, the size of the thumb is a visual representation of the size of a page in proportion to the entire document. Clicking the up arrow at the top of the scrollbar moves you up one line in the document; clicking the down arrow at the bottom moves you down one line.

What all this means is that the code that draws the scrollbar and handles the clicks needs to know the size of the entire document, the page size, and the line size. You don't have to write code to draw scrollbars or to handle clicks on the scrollbar, but you do have to pass along some information about the size of the document and the current view. The lines of code you need to add to OnDraw() are in Listing 4.19; add them after the for loop and before the old font is selected back into the DC.

LISTING 4.19 LINES TO ADD TO OnDraw()

```
// Calculate the document size.
CSize docSize(100, numLines*logFont.lfHeight);

// Calculate the page size.
   CRect rect;
GetClientRect(&rect);
CSize pageSize(rect.right, rect.bottom);

// Calculate the line size.
CSize lineSize(0, logFont.lfHeight);

// Adjust the scrollers.
SetScrollSizes(MM_TEXT, docSize, pageSize, lineSize);
```

This new code determines the document, page, and line sizes. The document size is the width and height of the screen area that could hold the entire document. This is calculated by using the number of lines in the entire document and the height of a line. (CSize is an MFC class created especially for storing the widths and heights of objects.) The page size is the size of the client rectangle of this view, and the line size is the height of the font. By setting the horizontal component of the line size to 0, you prevent horizontal scrolling.

To implement scrolling, pass these three sizes to SetScrollSizes(), which takes the mapping mode, document size, page size, and line size. MFC sets the scrollbars properly for any document and handles user interaction with the scrollbars.

Build and run Scroller again and generate some more lines. You should see a scrollbar like the one in Figure 4.12. Add even more lines and to see the thumb shrink as the document size grows. Finally, resize the application horizontally so that the text doesn't all fit. Notice how no horizontal scrollbars appear, because you set the horizontal line size to 0.

Figure 4.12
After displaying more lines than fit in the window, the vertical scrollbar appears.

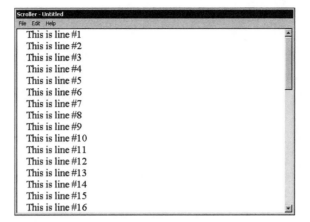

FROM HERE

Now that you know how to keep information in a document, and how to display that information on the screen by drawing or by writing text, you can interact with your users. You can draw on the techniques in Chapter 3 to gather information on a dialog box, then display that information to the user with a view. You can even create a view that scrolls automatically.

But the Windows applications you've seen so far in this book are just transitory: they can ask the user questions, and show the user information, but there's no way for that information to last. In the next chapter, "Printing and Saving," you learn about two ways to make information more permanent.

CH
4

CHAPTER 5

Printing and Saving

In this chapter

UNDERSTANDING BASIC PRINTING AND PRINT PREVIEW WITH MFC

If you brought together 10 Windows programmers and asked them what part of creating Windows applications they thought was the hardest, probably at least half of them would choose printing documents. Although the device-independent nature of Windows makes it easier for users to get peripherals to work properly, programmers must take up some of the slack by programming all devices in a general way. At one time, printing from a Windows application was a nightmare that only the most experienced programmers could handle. Now, however, thanks to application frameworks such as MFC, the job of printing documents from a Windows application is much simpler.

MFC handles so much of the printing task for you that, when it comes to simple one-page documents, you have little to do on your own. To see what I mean, follow these steps to create a basic MFC application that supports printing and print preview:

1. Choose File, New; select Visual C++ Projects, then double-click the MFC Application icon to start a new application called Print1 (see Figure 5.1).

Figure 5.1
Start a solution called Print1.

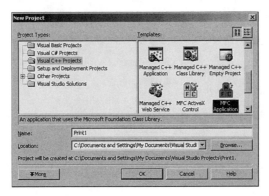

2. Give the new project the following settings in the MFC Application Wizard.
   - **Application Type**. Select Single Document.
   - **Advanced Features**. Turn off all application features except Printing and Print Preview.
3. Click Finish.
4. Expand the classes in the Class View, expand CPrint1View, double-click the OnDraw() function, and add the following line of code to it, right after the comment "TODO: add draw code for native data here":
   ```
   pDC->Rectangle(20, 20, 220, 220);
   ```

You've seen the Rectangle() function twice already: in the Recs app and the Paint1 app of Chapter 4, "Displaying Information." Adding this function call to the OnDraw() function of an MFC program's view class causes the program to draw a rectangle. This one is 200 pixels by 200 pixels, located 20 pixels down from the top of the view and 20 pixels from the left edge and reaches to a point 220 pixels from the top and 220 pixels from the left.

The declaration of this function has the pDC argument commented out, as follows:

```
void CPrint1View::OnDraw(CDC* /*pDC*/)
```

For the line of code you just added to work, you need to use this variable, so remove the comment characters to make the line resemble this one:

```
void CPrint1View::OnDraw(CDC* pDC)
```

Tip

If you haven't read Chapter 4 and aren't comfortable with device contexts, go back and read it now. Also, if you aren't comfortable with the document/view paradigm, you should read it, too. In this chapter, you override a number of virtual functions in your view class and work extensively with device contexts.

Believe it or not, you've just created a fully print-capable application that can display its data (a rectangle) not only in its main window but also in a print preview window and on the printer. To run the Print1 application, first compile and link the source code by choosing Build, Build Solution. Then, choose Debug, Start to run the program. The window shown in Figure 5.2 appears. This window contains the application's output data, which is a rectangle. Next, choose File, Print Preview. You see the Print Preview window, which displays the document as it will appear if you print it (see Figure 5.3). You will probably notice that the rectangle is a lot smaller in the Print Preview than it was in the application itself. You'll see how to fix that a little later in this chapter. Go ahead and print the document (choose File, Print). These commands have been implemented for you because you chose support for printing and print preview when you created this application with AppWizard.

CH
5

Figure 5.2
Print1 displays a rectangle when you first run it.

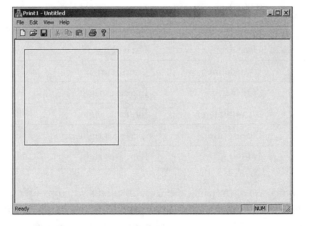

Figure 5.3
ThePrint1 application automatically handles print previewing, thanks to the MFC Application Wizard.

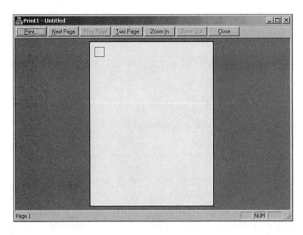

SCALING

One thing you may notice about the printed document and the one displayed onscreen is that, although the screen version of the rectangle takes up a fairly large portion of the application's window, the printed version is tiny. That's because the pixels onscreen and the dots on your printer are different sizes. Although the rectangle is 200 dots square in both cases, the smaller printer dots yield a rectangle that appears smaller. This is how the default Windows MM_TEXT graphics mapping mode works. If you want to scale the printed image to a specific size, you might want to choose a different mapping mode. Table 5.1 lists the mapping modes from which you can choose.

TABLE 5.1 MAPPING MODES

Mode	Unit	X	Y
MM_HIENGLISH	0.001 inch	Increases right	Increases up
MM_HIMETRIC	0.01 millimeter	Increases right	Increases up
MM_ISOTROPIC	User-defined	User-defined	User-defined
MM_ANISOTROPIC	User-defined	User-defined	User-defined
MM_LOENGLISH	0.01 inch	Increases right	Increases up
MM_LOMETRIC	0.1 millimeter	Increases right	Increases up
MM_TEXT	Device pixel	Increases right	Increases down
MM_TWIPS	1/1440 inch	Increases right	Increases up

Working with graphics in MM_TEXT mode causes problems when printers and screens can accommodate a different number of pixels per page. A better mapping mode for working with graphics is MM_LOENGLISH, which uses a hundredth of an inch, rather than a dot or pixel, as a unit of measure. To change the Print1 application so that it uses the MM_LOENGLISH mapping mode, replace the line you added to the OnDraw() function with the following two lines:

```
pDC->SetMapMode(MM_LOENGLISH);
pDC->Rectangle(20, -20, 220, -220);
```

The first line sets the mapping mode for the device context. The second line uses the new coordinate system to draw the rectangle. Why the negative values? If you look at MM_LOENGLISH in Table 5.1, you see that although X coordinates increase to the right as you expect, Y coordinates increase upward rather than downward. Moreover, the default coordinates for the window are located in the lower right quadrant of the Cartesian coordinate system, as shown in Figure 5.4. Figure 5.5 shows the print preview window when the application uses the MM_LOENGLISH mapping mode. When you print the document, the rectangle is exactly 2 inches square because a unit is now 1/100 of an inch and the rectangle is 200 units square.

Figure 5.4
The MM_LOENGLISH mapping mode's default coordinates derive from the Cartesian coordinate system.

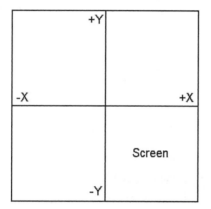

Figure 5.5
The rectangle to be printed matches the rectangle onscreen when you use MM_LOENGLISH as your mapping mode.

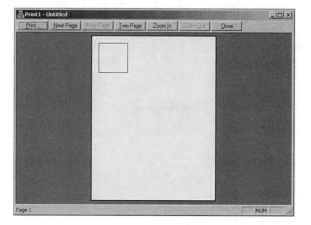

CH
5

PRINTING MULTIPLE PAGES

When your application's document is as simple as Print1's, adding printing and print previewing capabilities to the application is virtually automatic, because the document is only a single page and requires no pagination. No matter what you draw in the document window (except bitmaps), MFC handles all the printing tasks for you. Your view's OnDraw() function is used for drawing onscreen, printing to the printer, and drawing the print preview screen. Things become more complex, however, when you have larger documents that require pagination or some other special handling, such as headers and footers.

To get an idea of the problems with which you're faced with a more complex document, modify Print1 so that it prints lots of rectangles—so many that they can't fit on a single page. This gives you an opportunity to deal with pagination. And just to make things more interesting, add a member variable to the document class to hold the number of rectangles to be drawn, and enable the users to increase or decrease the number of rectangles by left- or right-clicking. Follow these steps:

1. Expand CPrint1Doc in ClassView, right-click it, and choose Add, Add Variable from the shortcut menu. The variable type is int, the variable name is m_numRects, and the access should be public. This variable holds the number of rectangles to display.

2. Double-click the CPrint1Doc constructor and change it from this:

   CPrint1Doc::CPrint1Doc(): m_numRects(0)

   to this:

   CPrint1Doc::CPrint1Doc(): m_numRects(5)

   This line arranges to display five rectangles in a brand new document.

3. Use the Properties window to catch mouse clicks by adding an OnLButtonDown() function to the view class (see Figure 5.6). Click on CPrint1View in the Class View, then click the Messages button, and click next to WM_LBUTTONDOWN to add the function.

4. The editor opens the code file for you and scrolls to the OnLButtonDown() function. Edit it so that it resembles Listing 5.1. Now the number of rectangles to be displayed increases each time users click the left mouse button.

LISTING 5.1   PRINT1VIEW.CPP—CPrint1View::OnLButtonDown()

```
void CPrint1View::OnLButtonDown(UINT nFlags, CPoint point)
{
    CPrint1Doc* pDoc = GetDocument();
    ASSERT_VALID(pDoc);

    pDoc->m_numRects++;
    Invalidate();

    CView::OnLButtonDown(nFlags, point);
}
```

Figure 5.6
Catch mouse clicks in the view class.

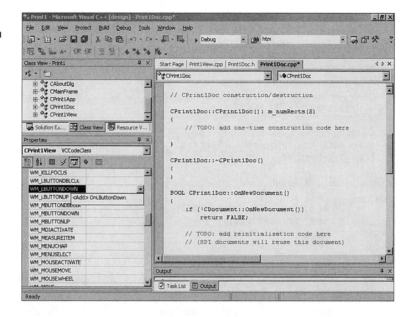

5. Use the Properties window to add an OnRButtonDown() function, as you added OnLButtonDown.

6. Edit the OnRButtonDown() function so that it resembles Listing 5.2. Now the number of rectangles to be displayed decreases each time users right-click.

LISTING 5.2   PRINT1VIEW.CPP—CPrint1View::OnRButtonDown()

```cpp
void CPrint1View::OnRButtonDown(UINT nFlags, CPoint point)
{
    CPrint1Doc* pDoc = GetDocument();
    ASSERT_VALID(pDoc);

    if (pDoc->m_numRects > 0)
    {
        pDoc->m_numRects--;
        Invalidate();
    }

    CView::OnRButtonDown(nFlags, point);
}
```

---

7. Rewrite the view's OnDraw() to draw many rectangles (refer to Listing 5.3). Print1 now draws the selected number of rectangles one below the other, which may cause the document to span multiple pages. It also displays the number of rectangles that have been added to the document.

CH

5

LISTING 5.3   PRINT1VIEW.CPP—CPrint1View::OnDraw()

```cpp
void CPrint1View::OnDraw(CDC* pDC)
{
    CPrint1Doc* pDoc = GetDocument();
    ASSERT_VALID(pDoc);

    pDC->SetMapMode(MM_LOENGLISH);

    CString s;
    s.Format("%d", pDoc->m_numRects);
    pDC->TextOut(300, -100, s);

    for (int x=0; x<pDoc->m_numRects; ++x)
    {
        pDC->Rectangle(20, -(20+x*200),
            200, -(200+x*200));
    }
}
```

When you run the application now, you see the window shown in Figure 5.7. The window not only displays the rectangles but also displays the rectangle count so that you can see how many rectangles you've requested. When you choose File, Print Preview, you see the print preview window. Click the Two Page button to see the window shown in Figure 5.8. The five rectangles display properly on the first page, with the second page blank.

Figure 5.7
Print1 now displays multiple rectangles.

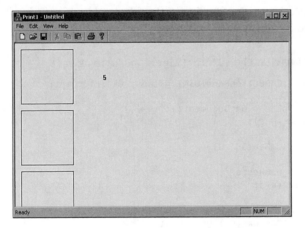

Now, click Close on the print preview to go back to the application's main window, and click inside it three times to add three more rectangles. Right-click to remove one. (The rectangle count displayed in the window should be seven.) After you add the rectangles, choose File, Print Preview again to see the two-page print preview window. Figure 5.9 shows what you see. The program hasn't a clue how to print or preview the additional page. The sixth rectangle runs off the bottom of the first page, and nothing appears on the second page.

Figure 5.8
Five rectangles are previewed properly; they will print on a single page.

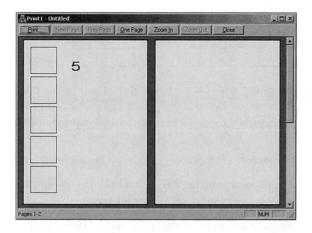

Figure 5.9
Seven rectangles do not yet appear correctly on multiple pages.

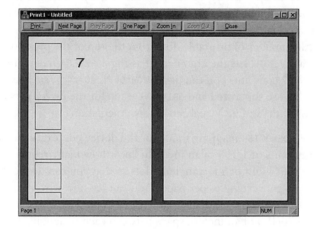

CH
5

The first step in correcting this behavior is to tell MFC how many pages to print (or preview) by calling the SetMaxPage() function in the view class's OnBeginPrinting() function. The MFC Application Wizard gives you a skeleton OnBeginPrinting() that does nothing. In the Class view, expand CPrint1View, then double-click OnBeginPrinting(). Modify it so that it resembles Listing 5.4.

LISTING 5.4   PRINT1VIEW.CPP—CPrint1View::OnBeginPrinting()

```
void CPrint1View::OnBeginPrinting(CDC* pDC, CPrintInfo* pInfo)
{
    CPrint1Doc* pDoc = GetDocument();
    ASSERT_VALID(pDoc);

    int pageHeight = pDC->GetDeviceCaps(VERTRES);
    int logPixelsY = pDC->GetDeviceCaps(LOGPIXELSY);
    int rectHeight = (int)(2.2 * logPixelsY);
    int numPages = pDoc->m_numRects * rectHeight / pageHeight + 1;
```

LISTING 5.4   CONTINUED

```
    pInfo->SetMaxPage(numPages);
}
```

OnBeginPrinting() takes two parameters: a pointer to the printer device context and a pointer to a CPrintInfo object. Because the default version of OnBeginPrinting() doesn't refer to these two pointers, the parameter names are commented out as follows to avoid compilation warnings:

```
void CPrint1View::OnBeginPrinting(CDC* /*pDC*/ , CPrintInfo* /*pInfo*/)
```

However, to set the page count, you need to access both the CDC and CPrintInfo objects, so your first task is to uncomment the function's parameters.

Now you need to get some information about the device context (which, in this case, is a printer device context). Specifically, you need to know the page height (in single dots) and the number of dots per inch. You obtain the page height with a call to GetDeviceCaps(), which gives you information about the capabilities of the device context. You ask for the vertical resolution (the number of printable dots from the top of the page to the bottom) by passing the constant VERTRES as the argument. Passing HORZRES gives you the horizontal resolution. There are 29 constants you can pass to GetDeviceCaps(), such as NUMFONTS for the number of fonts that are supported and DRIVERVERSION for the driver version number. For a complete list, consult the online Visual Studio documentation.

Print1 uses the MM_LOENGLISH mapping mode for the device context, which means that the printer output uses units of 1/100 of an inch. To know how many rectangles fit on a page, you have to know the height of a rectangle in dots so that you can divide dots per page by dots per rectangle to get rectangles per page. (You can see now why your application must know all about your document to calculate the page count.) You know that each rectangle is 2 inches high with 20/100 of an inch of space between each rectangle. The total distance from the start of one rectangle to the start of the next, then, is 2.2 inches. The call to GetDeviceCaps() with an argument of LOGPIXELSY gives the dots per inch of this printer; multiplying by 2.2 gives the dots per rectangle.

You now have all the information you need to calculate the number of pages needed to fit the requested number of rectangles. You pass that number to SetMaxPage(), and the new OnBeginPrinting() function is complete.

Again, build and run the program. Increase the number of rectangles to seven by clicking twice in the main window. Now choose File, Print Preview and look at the two-page print preview window (see Figure 5.10). Whoops! You obviously still have a problem somewhere. Although the application is previewing two pages, as it should with seven rectangles, it's printing exactly the same thing on both pages. Obviously, page two should take up where page one left off, rather than redisplay the same data from the beginning. There's still some work to do.

Figure 5.10
The Print1 application still doesn't display multiple pages correctly.

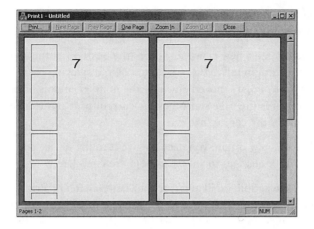

SETTING THE ORIGIN

To get the second and subsequent pages to print properly, you have to change where MFC believes the top of the page to be. Currently, MFC just draws the pages exactly as you told it to do in `CPrint1View::OnDraw()`, which displays all seven rectangles from the top of the page to the bottom. To tell MFC where the new top of the page should be, you first need to override the view class's `OnPrepareDC()` function.

Bring up ClassView and choose `CPrint1View`, then switch to the Properties window. Select the Overrides icon in the Properties window. Click `OnPrepareDC` in the Properties window, and then click <Add> in the drop-down box. A function is created for you; add the code shown in Listing 5.5 to this function.

LISTING 5.5   PRINT1VIEW.CPP—CPrint1View::OnPrepareDC()

```cpp
void CPrint1View::OnPrepareDC(CDC* pDC, CPrintInfo* pInfo)
{
    if (pDC->IsPrinting())
    {
        int pageHeight = pDC->GetDeviceCaps(VERTRES);
        int originY = pageHeight * (pInfo->m_nCurPage - 1);
        pDC->SetViewportOrg(0, -originY);
    }

    CView::OnPrepareDC(pDC, pInfo);
}
```

CH

5

The MFC framework calls `OnPrepareDC()` just before it displays data onscreen or before it prints the data to the printer. (One strength of the device context approach to screen display is that the same code can often be used for display and printing.) If the application is about to display data, you (probably) don't want to change the default processing performed by `OnPrepareDC()`. So, you must check whether the application is printing data by calling `IsPrinting()`, a member function of the device context class.

If the application is printing, you must determine which part of the data belongs on the current page. You need the height in dots of a printed page, so you call GetDeviceCaps() again.

Next, you must determine a new viewport origin (the position of the coordinates 0,0) for the display. Changing the origin tells MFC where to begin displaying data. For page one, the origin is zero; for page two, it's moved down by the number of dots on a page. In general, the vertical component is the page size times the current page minus one. The page number is a member variable of the CPrintInfo class.

After you calculate the new origin, you need to give it to the device context by calling SetViewportOrg(). Your changes to OnPrepareDC() are complete.

To see your changes in action, build and run your new version of Print1. When the program's main window appears, click twice in the window to add two rectangles to the display. (The displayed rectangle count should be seven.) Again, choose File, Print Preview and look at the two-page print preview window (see Figure 5.11). Now the program previews the document correctly. If you print the document, it will look the same in hard copy as it does in the preview.

Figure 5.11
Print1 finally previews and prints properly.

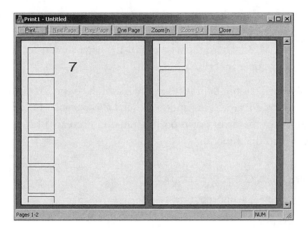

MFC AND PRINTING

Now you've seen MFC's printing and print preview support in action. As you added more functionality to the Print1 application, you modified several member functions that were overridden in the view class, including OnDraw(), OnBeginPrinting(), and OnPrepareDC(). These functions are important to the printing and print preview processes. However, other functions also enable you to add even more printing power to your applications. Table 5.2 describes the functions important to the printing process.

To print a document, MFC calls the functions listed in Table 5.2 in a specific order. First it calls OnPreparePrinting(), which calls DoPreparePrinting(), as shown in Listing 5.6. DoPreparePrinting() is responsible for displaying the Print dialog box and creating the printer DC.

TABLE 5.2 PRINTING FUNCTIONS OF A VIEW CLASS

Function	Description
OnBeginPrinting()	Override this function to create resources, such as fonts, that you need for printing the document. You also set the maximum page count here.
OnDraw()	This function serves triple duty, displaying data in a frame window, a print preview window, or on the printer, depending on the device context sent as the function's parameter.
OnEndPrinting()	Override this function to release resources created in OnBeginPrinting().
OnPrepareDC()	Override this function to modify the device context used to display or print the document. You can, for example, handle pagination here.
OnPreparePrinting()	Override this function to provide a maximum page count for the document. If you don't set the page count here, you should set it in OnBeginPrinting().
OnPrint()	Override this function to provide additional printing services, such as printing headers and footers, not provided in OnDraw().

LISTING 5.6 PRINT1VIEW.CPP—CPrint1View::OnPreparePrinting() AS GENERATED BY THE MFC APPLICATION WIZARD

```
BOOL CPrint1View::OnPreparePrinting(CPrintInfo* pInfo)
{
    // default preparation
    return DoPreparePrinting(pInfo);
}
```

As you can see, OnPreparePrinting() receives as a parameter a pointer to a CPrintInfo object. By using this object, you can obtain information about the print job as well as initialize attributes such as the maximum page number. Table 5.3 describes the most useful data and function members of the CPrintInfo class.

CH
5

TABLE 5.3 MEMBERS OF THE CPrintInfo CLASS

Member	Description
SetMaxPage()	Sets the document's maximum page number.
SetMinPage()	Sets the document's minimum page number.
GetFromPage()	Gets the number of the first page that users select for printing.
GetMaxPage()	Gets the document's maximum page number, which may be changed in OnBeginPrinting().
GetMinPage()	Gets the document's minimum page number, which may be changed in OnBeginPrinting().
GetToPage()	Gets the number of the last page users select for printing.

TABLE 5.3   CONTINUED

`m_bContinuePrinting`	Controls the printing process. Setting the flag to FALSE ends the print job.
`m_bDirect`	Indicates whether the document is being directly printed.
`m_bPreview`	Indicates whether the document is in print preview.
`m_nCurPage`	Holds the current number of the page being printed.
`m_nNumPreviewPages`	Holds the number of pages (1 or 2) being displayed in print preview.
`m_pPD`	Holds a pointer to the print job's `CPrintDialog` object.
`m_rectDraw`	Holds a rectangle that defines the usable area for the current page.
`m_strPageDesc`	Holds a page-number format string.

When the `DoPreparePrinting()` function displays the Print dialog box, users can set the value of many data members of the `CPrintInfo` class. Your program then can use or set any of these values. Usually, you'll at least call `SetMaxPage()`, which sets the document's maximum page number, before `DoPreparePrinting()` so that the maximum page number displays in the Print dialog box. If you can't determine the number of pages until you calculate a page length based on the selected printer, you have to wait until you have a printer DC for the printer.

After `OnPreparePrinting()`, MFC calls `OnBeginPrinting()`, which is not only another place to set the maximum page count but also the place to create resources, such as fonts, that you need to complete the print job. `OnPreparePrinting()` receives as parameters a pointer to the printer DC and a pointer to the associated `CPrintInfo` object.

Next, MFC calls `OnPrepareDC()` for the first page in the document. This is the beginning of a print loop that's executed once for each page in the document. `OnPrepareDC()` is the place to control what part of the whole document prints on the current page. As you saw previously, you handle this task by setting the document's viewport origin.

After `OnPrepareDC()`, MFC calls `OnPrint()` to print the actual page. Normally, `OnPrint()` calls `OnDraw()` with the printer DC, which automatically directs `OnDraw()`'s output to the printer rather than onscreen. You can override `OnPrint()` to control how the document is printed. You can print headers and footers in `OnPrint()` and then call the base class's version (which in turn calls `OnDraw()`) to print the body of the document, as demonstrated in Listing 5.7. (The footer appears below the body, even though `PrintFooter()` is called before `OnPrint()`—don't worry.) To prevent the base class version from overwriting your header and footer area, restrict the printable area by setting the `m_rectDraw` member of the `CPrintInfo` object to a rectangle that doesn't overlap the header or footer.

LISTING 5.7 POSSIBLE `OnPrint()` WITH HEADERS AND FOOTERS

```
void CPrint1View::OnPrint(CDC* pDC, CPrintInfo* pInfo)
{
    // Call local functions to print a header and footer.
    PrintHeader();
    PrintFooter();

    CView::OnPrint(pDC, pInfo);
}
```

Alternatively, you can remove `OnDraw()` from the print loop entirely by doing your own printing in `OnPrint()` and not calling `OnDraw()` at all (see Listing 5.8).

LISTING 5.8 POSSIBLE `OnPrint()` WITHOUT `OnDraw()`

```
void CPrint1View::OnPrint(CDC* pDC, CPrintInfo* pInfo)
{
    // Call local functions to print a header and footer.
    PrintHeader();
    PrintFooter();

    // Call a local function to print the body of the document.
    PrintDocument();
}
```

As long as there are more pages to print, MFC continues to call `OnPrepareDC()` and `OnPrint()` for each page in the document. After the last page is printed, MFC calls `OnEndPrinting()`, where you can destroy any resources you created in `OnBeginPrinting()`. Figure 5.12 summarizes the entire printing process.

Figure 5.12
MFC calls various member functions during the printing process.

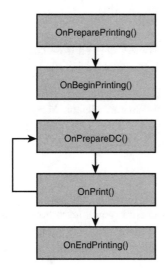

Сн

5

UNDERSTANDING SAVING AND PERSISTENCE

One of the most important things a program must do is save users' data after that data is changed in some way. Without the capability to save edited data, the work a user performs with an application exists only as long as the application is running, vanishing the instant the user exits the application. Not a good way to get work done! In many cases, especially when you use the MFC Application Wizard to create an application, Visual Studio provides much of the code necessary to save and load data. However, in some cases—most notably when you create your own object types—you have to do a little extra work to keep your users' files up to date.

When you're writing an application, you deal with a lot of different object types. Some data objects might be simple types, such as integers and characters. Other objects might be instances of classes, such as strings from the CString class or even objects created from your own custom classes. When you use objects in applications that must create, save, and load documents, you need a way to save and load the state of those objects so that you can re-create them exactly as users left them at the end of the last session.

An object's capability to save and load its state is called *persistence*. Almost all MFC classes are persistent because they're derived directly or indirectly from MFC's CObject class, which provides the basic functionality for saving and loading an object's state. The following section reviews how MFC makes a document object persistent.

EXAMINING THE FILE DEMO APPLICATION

When you use Visual Studio's MFC Application Wizard to create a program, you get an application that uses document and view classes to organize, edit, and display its data. As discussed in Chapter 4, the document object, derived from the CDocument class, is responsible for holding the application's data during a session and for saving and loading the data so that the document persists from one session to another.

In this chapter, you'll build the File Demo application, which demonstrates the basic techniques behind saving and loading data of an object derived from CDocument. File Demo's document is a single string containing a short message, which the view displays.

Three menu items are relevant in the File Demo application. When the program first begins, the message is automatically set to the string "Default Message." Users change this message by choosing Edit, Change Message. The File, Save menu option saves the document, as you'd expect, and File, Open reloads it from disk.

A REVIEW OF DOCUMENT CLASSES

Anyone who's written a program has experienced saving and opening files—object persistence, from the user's point of view. In this chapter you'll learn how persistence works. Although you had some experience with document classes in Chapter 4, you'll now review the basic concepts with an eye toward extending those concepts to your own custom classes.

When working with an application created by the MFC Application Wizard, you enable your document to save and load its state by following these steps:

1. Define the member variables that hold the document's data.

2. Initialize the member variables in the document class's `OnNewDocument()` member function.

3. Display the current document in the view class's `OnDraw()` member function.

4. Provide member functions in the view class that enable users to edit the document.

5. Add to the document class's `Serialize()` member function the code needed to save and load the data that the document comprises.

When your application can handle multiple documents, you need to do a little extra work to be sure that you use, change, or save the correct document. Luckily, most of that work is taken care of by MFC.

BUILDING THE FILEDEMO APPLICATION

To build the FileDemo application, start by using the MFC Application Wizard to create an SDI application. All the other choices should be left at their default values, so click Finish after selecting SDI and making sure that Document/View support is selected.

Double-click `CFileDemoDoc` in ClassView to edit the header file for the document class. In the Attributes section add a `CString` member variable called `m_message`, so that the Attributes section looks like this:

```
// Attributes
public:
    CString m_message;
```

In this case, the document's storage is nothing more than a single string object. Usually, your document's storage needs are much more complex. This single string, however, is enough to demonstrate the basics of a persistent document.

Tip

It's very common for MFC programmers to use public variables in their documents, rather than a private variable with public access functions. It makes it a little simpler to write the code in the view class that will access the document variables. It will, however, make future enhancements a little more work.

This string, like all the document's data, must be initialized. The `OnNewDocument()` member function is the place to do it. Expand `CFileDemoDoc` in the Class View and double-click `OnNewDocument()` to edit it. Add a line of code to initialize the string so that the function looks like Listing 5.9. You should remove the TODO comments because you've already done what they were reminding you to do.

CH

5

LISTING 5.9 INITIALIZING THE DOCUMENT'S DATA

```
BOOL CFileDemoDoc::OnNewDocument()
{
    if (!CDocument::OnNewDocument())
        return FALSE;

    m_message = "Default Message";

    return TRUE;
}
```

With the document class's m_message data member initialized, the application can display the data in the view window. You just need to edit the view class's OnDraw() function (see Listing 5.10). Expand CFileDemoView in ClassView and double-click OnDraw() to edit it. Again, you're just adding one line of code and removing the TODO comment. Don't forget to uncomment the pDC parameter.

LISTING 5.10 DISPLAYING THE DOCUMENT'S DATA

```
void CFileDemoView::OnDraw(CDC* pDC)
{
    CFileDemoDoc* pDoc = GetDocument();
    ASSERT_VALID(pDoc);

    pDC->TextOut(20, 20, pDoc->m_message);
}
```

Getting information onscreen, using device contexts, and the TextOut() function are all discussed in Chapter 4.

Build File Demo now, to make sure there are no typos, and run it. You should see Default Message appear onscreen, as in Figure 5.13.

Figure 5.13
The FileDemo application displays a string stored in the document.

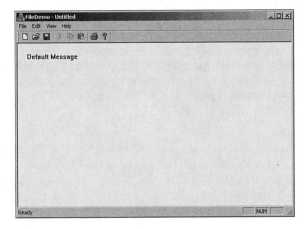

Now you need to enable users to change the string—that is, to edit the application's document. In theory, the application should display a dialog box in which the user can enter any desired string at all. For this example, you're just going to have the Edit, Change Message menu option assign the string a different, hard-coded value. ShowString, the subject of Chapter 6, "Building a Complete Application: ShowString," shows how to create a dialog box such as the one File Demo might use.

Click the Resource tab to switch to the Resource View, expand the resources, expand Menus, and double-click IDR_MAINFRAME to edit it. Click once on the Edit item in the menu you are editing to drop it down. Click the item marked Type Here at the end of the list and type **Change &Message**, as in Figure 5.14, which adds another item to the menu.

Figure 5.14
Add an item to the Edit menu for the user to change the message.

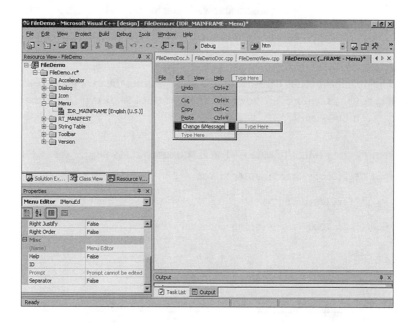

In ClassView, select CFileDemoView to make the connection between this menu item and your code. In the Properties window, click the Events icon and scroll until you see ID_EDIT_CHANGEMESSAGE. Click the + to expand it, then click COMMAND and choose <Add> OnEditChangemessage.Edit OnEditchangemessage() to match Listing 5.11.

LISTING 5.11   CHANGING THE DOCUMENT'S DATA

```
void CFileDemoView::OnEditChangemessage()
{
    CTime now = CTime::GetCurrentTime();
    CString changetime = now.Format("Changed at %B %d %H:%M:%S");
    GetDocument()->m_message = changetime;
    GetDocument()->SetModifiedFlag();
    Invalidate();
}
```

This function, which responds to the application's Edit, Change Message command, builds a string from the current date and time and transfers it to the document's m_message member variable. The call to the document class's SetModifiedFlag() function notifies the object that its contents have been changed. The application warns about exiting with unsaved changes as long as you remember to call SetModifiedFlag() everywhere there might be a change to the data. Finally, this code forces a redraw of the screen by calling Invalidate(), as discussed in Chapter 4.

Tip

If m_message were a private member variable of the document class, you could have a public SetMessage() function that called SetModifiedFlag() and be guaranteed no programmer would ever forget to call it. That's one of the advantages of writing truly object-oriented programs.

The document class's Serialize() function handles the saving and loading of the document's data. Listing 5.12 shows the empty shell of Serialize() generated by the MFC Application Wizard.

LISTING 5.12   FILEVIEW.CPP—THE DOCUMENT CLASS Serialize() FUNCTION

```
void CFileDoc::Serialize(CArchive& ar)
{
    if (ar.IsStoring())
    {
        // TODO: add storing code here
    }
    else
    {
        // TODO: add loading code here
    }
}
```

Because the CString class (of which m_message is an object) defines the >> and << operators for transferring strings to and from an archive, it's a simple task to save and load the document class's data. Add this line where the comment reminds you to add storing code:

```
ar << m_message;
```

Add this similar line where the loading code belongs:

```
ar >> m_message;
```

The << operator sends the CString m_message to the archive; the >> operator fills m_message from the archive. As long as all the document's member variables are simple data types such as integers or characters, or MFC classes such as CString with these operators already defined, it's easy to save and load the data. The operators are defined for these simple data types:

SimpleData

- BYTE
- WORD
- int
- LONG
- DWORD
- float
- double

Build File Demo and run it. Choose Edit, Change Message, and you should see the new string onscreen, as shown in Figure 5.15. Choose File, Save, and enter a filename you can remember. Now change the message again. Choose File, New, and you'll be warned about saving your current changes first, as in Figure 5.16. Choose File, Open, and browse to your file, or just find your filename toward the bottom of the File menu to re-open it, and you'll see that File Demo can indeed save and reload a string.

Figure 5.15
File Demo changes the string on command.

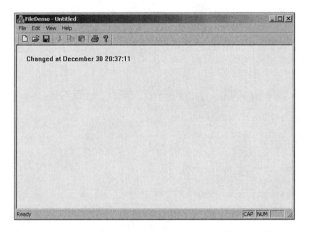

Figure 5.16
Your users will never lose unsaved data again.

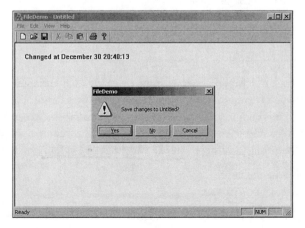

CH
5

Note

If you change the file, save it, change it again, and re-open the very same file, File Demo will not ask you to Revert to Saved Document? as some applications do. Instead, it will bail out of the File Open process partway through and leave you with your most recent changes. This behavior is built in to MFC. If the name of the file you are opening matches the name of the file that is already open, you will not revert to the saved document. That's why the instructions earlier had you choose File, New after saving and before re-opening your test file.

CREATING A PERSISTENT CLASS

What if you've created your own custom class for holding the elements of a document? How can you make an object of this class persistent? You find the answers to these questions in this section.

Suppose that you now want to enhance the File Demo application so that it contains its data in a custom class called CMessages. The member variable is now called m_messages and is an instance of CMessages. This class holds three CString objects, each of which must be saved and loaded for the application to work correctly. One way to arrange this is to save and load each individual string, as shown in Listing 5.13.

LISTING 5.13   ONE POSSIBLE WAY TO SAVE THE NEW CLASS'S STRINGS

```
void CFileDoc::Serialize(CArchive& ar)
{
    if (ar.IsStoring())
    {
        ar << m_messages.m_message1;
        ar << m_messages.m_message2;
        ar << m_messages.m_message3;
    }
    else
    {
        ar >> m_messages.m_message1;
        ar >> m_messages.m_message2;
        ar >> m_messages.m_message3;
    }
}
```

You can write the code in Listing 5.13 only if the three member variables of the CMessages class are public and if you know the implementation of the class itself. Later, if the class is changed in any way, this code also has to be changed. It's more object oriented to delegate the work of storing and loading to the CMessages class itself. This requires some preparation, but it's worth it. The following basic steps create a class that can serialize its member variables:

1. Derive the class from CObject.
2. Place the DECLARE_SERIAL() macro in the class declaration.
3. Place the IMPLEMENT_SERIAL() macro in the class implementation.

4. Override the `Serialize()` function in the class.

5. Provide an empty, default constructor for the class.

In the following section, you build an application that creates persistent objects in just this way.

THE MULTISTRING APPLICATION

The next sample application, MultiString, demonstrates the steps you take to create a class from which you can create persistent objects. It will have an Edit, Change Messages command that changes all three strings. Like File Demo, it will save and reload the document when the user chooses File, Save, or File, Open.

Build an SDI application called MultiString just as you built FileDemo. Add a member variable to the document, as before, so that the Attributes section of MultiStringDoc.h reads

```
// Attributes
public:
    CMessages m_messages;
```

The next step is to write the `CMessages` class.

LOOKING AT THE CMessages CLASS

Before you can understand how the document class manages to save and load its contents successfully, you have to understand how the `CMessages` class, of which the document class's `m_messages` data member is an object, works. As you work with this class, you will see how to implement the preceding five steps for creating a persistent class.

To create the `CMessages` class, use the ClassView. Right-click the project MultiString, choose Add, Add Class, then choose Generic C++ Class from the Generic category, as shown in Figure 5.17. Click Open and the Generic C++ Class Wizard, shown in Figure 5.18, appears. Name the class `CMessages`, enter `CObject` as the base class and leave the Access for the base class as Public.

CH
5

Figure 5.17
Create a new class to hold the messages.

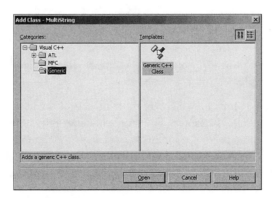

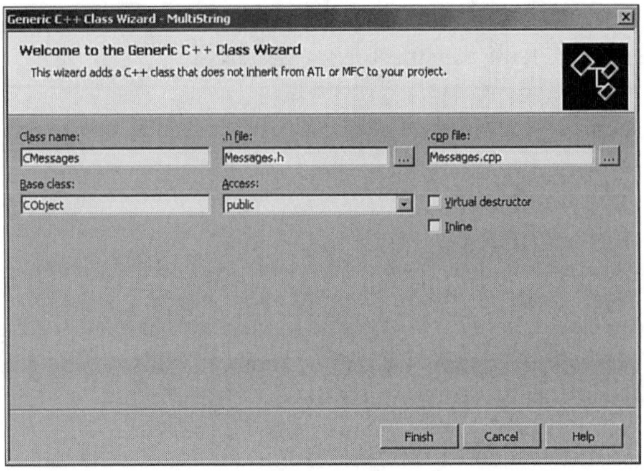

Figure 5.18
The new class is
called `CMessages`
and inherits from
`Cobject`.

This creates two files: messages.h for the header and messages.cpp for the code. It also adds some very simple code to these files for you. Switch back to editing Multistringdoc.h (you can use the tabs across the top of the editing area for this, or use the ClassView and double-click `CMultiStringDoc`) and add this line before the class definition:

```
#include "Messages.h"
```

This ensures that the compiler knows about the `CMessages` class when it compiles the document class. You can build the project now if you want to be sure you haven't forgotten anything.

Now switch back to Messages.h and add these lines inside the class definition:

```
    DECLARE_SERIAL(CMessages)

protected:
    CString m_message1;
    CString m_message2;
    CString m_message3;

public:
    void SetMessage(UINT msgNum, CString msg);
    CString GetMessage(UINT msgNum);
    void Serialize(CArchive& ar);
```

The DECLARE_SERIAL( ) macro provides the additional function and member variable declarations needed to implement object persistence.

Next come the class's data members, which are three objects of the `CString` class. Notice that they are protected member variables. The public member functions are next. `SetMessage()`, whose arguments are the index of the string to set and the string's new value, changes a data member. `GetMessage()` is the complementary function, enabling a program to retrieve the current value of any of the strings. Its single argument is the number of the string to retrieve.

Finally, the class overrides the `Serialize()` function, where all the data saving and loading takes place. The `Serialize()` function is the heart of a persistent object, with each persistent class implementing it in a different way. Listing 5.14 shows the code for each of these new member functions. Add it to messages.cpp.

LISTING 5.14   MESSAGES.CPP—THE `CMessages` CLASS IMPLEMENTATION FILE

```cpp
void CMessages::SetMessage(UINT msgNum, CString msg)
{
    switch (msgNum)
    {
    case 1:
        m_message1 = msg;
        break;

    case 2:
        m_message2 = msg;
        break;

    case 3:
        m_message3 = msg;
        break;
    }
}

CString CMessages::GetMessage(UINT msgNum)
{
    switch (msgNum)
    {
        case 1:
            return m_message1;
        case 2:
            return m_message2;
        case 3:
            return m_message3;
        default:
            return "";
    }
}

void CMessages::Serialize(CArchive& ar)
{
    CObject::Serialize(ar);

    if (ar.IsStoring())
    {
        ar << m_message1 << m_message2 << m_message3;
    }
    else
    {
        ar >> m_message1 >> m_message2 >> m_message3;
    }
}
```

CH

5

There's nothing tricky about the SetMessage() and GetMessage() functions, which perform their assigned tasks precisely. The Serialize() function, however, may inspire a couple of questions. First, note that the first line of the body of the function calls the base class's Serialize() function. This is a standard practice for many functions that override functions of a base class. In this case, the call to CObject::Serialize() doesn't do much because the CObject class's Serialize() function is empty. Still, calling the base class's Serialize() function is a good habit to get into because you may not always be working with classes derived directly from CObject.

After calling the base class's version of the function, Serialize() saves and loads its data in much the same way that a document object does. Because the data members that must be serialized are CString objects, the program can use the >> and << operators to write the strings to the disk.

Toward the top of messages.cpp, after the include statements, add this line:

```
IMPLEMENT_SERIAL(CMessages, CObject, 0)
```

The IMPLEMENT_SERIAL() macro is a partner to the DECLARE_SERIAL() macro, providing implementation for the functions that give the class its persistent capabilities. The macro's three arguments are the name of the class, the name of the immediate base class, and a schema number, which is like a version number. In most cases, you use 0 or 1 for the schema number.

USING THE CMessages CLASS IN THE PROGRAM

Now that CMessages is defined and implemented, member functions of the MultiString document and view classes can work with it. First, expand CMultiStringDoc and double-click OnNewDocument() to edit it. Add these lines in place of the TODO comments.

```
m_messages.SetMessage(1, "Default Message 1");
m_messages.SetMessage(2, "Default Message 2");
m_messages.SetMessage(3, "Default Message 3");
```

Because the document class can't directly access the data object's protected data members, it initializes each string by calling the CMessages class's SetMessage() member function.

Expand CMultiStringView and double-click OnDraw() to edit it. Here's how it should look when you're finished:

```
void CMultiStringView::OnDraw(CDC* pDC)
{
    CMultiStringDoc* pDoc = GetDocument();
    ASSERT_VALID(pDoc);

    pDC->TextOut(20, 20, pDoc->m_messages.GetMessage(1));
    pDC->TextOut(20, 40, pDoc->m_messages.GetMessage(2));
    pDC->TextOut(20, 60, pDoc->m_messages.GetMessage(3));
}
```

As you did for File Demo, add a "Change Messages" item to the Edit menu. Connect it to a view function called OnEditChangemessages. This function changes the data by calling the

CMessages object's member functions, as shown in Listing 5.15. The view class's OnDraw() function also calls the GetMessage() member function to access the CMessages class's strings.

LISTING 5.15   EDITING THE DATA STRINGS

```
void CMultiStringView::OnEditChangemessages()
{
    CMultiStringDoc* pDoc = GetDocument();
    CTime now = CTime::GetCurrentTime();
    CString changetime = now.Format("Changed at %B %d %H:%M:%S");

    pDoc->m_messages.SetMessage(1, CString("String 1 ") + changetime);
    pDoc->m_messages.SetMessage(2, CString("String 2 ") + changetime);
    pDoc->m_messages.SetMessage(3, CString("String 3 ") + changetime);
    pDoc->SetModifiedFlag();
    Invalidate();

}
```

Notice the call to the document's SetModifiedFlag() function, to ensure the user will be prompted to save these changes.

All that remains is to write the document class's Serialize() function, where the m_messages data object is serialized out to disk. You just delegate the work to the data object's own Serialize() function, as in Listing 5.16.

LISTING 5.16   SERIALIZING THE DATA OBJECT

```
void CMultiStringDoc::Serialize(CArchive& ar)
{
    m_messages.Serialize(ar);
    if (ar.IsStoring())
    {
    }
    else
    {
    }
}
```

As you can see, after serializing the m_messages data object, not much is left to do in the document class's Serialize() function. Notice that the call to m_messages.Serialize() passes the archive object as its single parameter. Build MultiString now and test it as you tested File Demo. It should do everything you expect.

READING AND WRITING FILES DIRECTLY

Although using MFC's built-in serialization capabilities is a handy way to save and load data, sometimes you need more control over the file-handling process. For example, you might need to deal with your files nonsequentially, something the Serialize() function and its associated CArchive object can't handle because they use stream I/O. In this case, you can

CH
5

handle files almost exactly as they're handled by non-Windows programmers: creating, reading, and writing files directly. Even when you need to dig down to this level of file handling, MFC offers help. Specifically, you can use the CFile class and its derived classes to handle files directly.

THE CFile CLASS

MFC's CFile class encapsulates all the functions you need to handle any type of file. Whether you want to perform common sequential data saving and loading or construct a random-access file, the CFile class gets you there. Using the CFile class is a lot like handling files the old-fashioned C-style way, except that the class hides some of the busywork details from you so that you can get the job done quickly and easily. For example, you can open a file for reading with only a single line of code. Table 5.4 shows the CFile class's member functions and their descriptions.

TABLE 5.4   MEMBER FUNCTIONS OF THE CFile CLASS

Function	Description
CFile	Creates the CFile object. If passed a filename, it opens the file.
Destructor	Cleans up a CFile object that's going out of scope. If the file is open, it closes that file.
Abort()	Immediately closes the file with no regard for errors.
Close()	Closes the file.
Duplicate()	Creates a duplicate file object.
Flush()	Flushes data from the stream.
GetFileName()	Gets the file's filename.
GetFilePath()	Gets the file's full path.
GetFileTitle()	Gets the file's title (the filename without the extension).
GetLength()	Gets the file's length.
GetPosition()	Gets the current position within the file.
GetStatus()	Gets the file's status.
LockRange()	Locks a portion of the file.
Open()	Opens the file.
Read()	Reads data from the file.
Remove()	Deletes a file.
Rename()	Renames the file.
Seek()	Sets the position within the file.
SeekToBegin()	Sets the position to the beginning of the file.
SeekToEnd()	Sets the position to the end of the file.

TABLE 5.4   CONTINUED

Function	Description
SetFilePath()	Sets the file's path.
SetLength()	Sets the file's length.
SetStatus()	Sets the file's status.
UnlockRange()	Unlocks a portion of the file.
Write()	Writes data to the file.

As you can see from Table 5.4, the CFile class offers plenty of file-handling power. This section demonstrates how to call a few of the CFile class's member functions. However, most of the other functions are just as easy to use.

Here's a sample snippet of code that creates and opens a file, writes a string to it, and then gathers some information about the file:

```
// Create the file.
CFile file("TESTFILE.TXT", CFile::modeCreate | CFile::modeWrite);

// Write data to the file.
CString message("Hello file!");
int length = message.GetLength();
file.Write((LPCTSTR)message, length);

// Obtain information about the file.
CString filePath = file.GetFilePath();
int fileLength = file.GetLength();
```

Notice that you don't have to explicitly open the file when you pass a filename to the constructor, whose arguments are the name of the file and the file access mode flags. You can use several flags at a time simply by combining their values with the or (|) operator, as in the little snippet you just read. These flags, which describe how to open the file and specify the types of valid operations, are defined as part of the CFile class and are described in Table 5.5.

CH
5

TABLE 5.5   THE FILE MODE FLAGS

Flag	Description
CFile::modeCreate	Creates a new file or truncates an existing file to length 0.
CFile::modeNoInherit	Disallows inheritance by a child process.
CFile::modeNoTruncate	When a file is being created, doesn't truncate the file if it already exists.
CFile::modeRead	Allows read operations only.
CFile::modeReadWrite	Allows both read and write operations.
CFile::modeWrite	Allows write operations only.
CFile::shareCompat	Allows other processes to open the file.

TABLE 5.5 CONTINUED	
Flag	**Description**
CFile::shareDenyNone	Allows other processes read or write operations on the file.
CFile::shareDenyRead	Disallows read operations by other processes.
CFile::shareDenyWrite	Disallows write operations by other processes.
CFile::shareExclusive	Denies all access to other processes.
CFile::typeBinary	Sets binary mode for the file.
CFile::typeText	Sets text mode for the file.
CFile::Write()	takes a pointer to the buffer containing the data to write and the number of bytes to write.

Notice the LPCTSTR casting operator in the call to Write(). This operator is defined by the CString class and extracts the string from the class.

One other thing about the code snippet: There is no call to Close()—the CFile destructor closes the file automatically when file goes out of scope.

Reading from a file isn't much different from writing to one:

```
// Open the file.
CFile file("TESTFILE.TXT", CFile::modeRead);

// Read data from the file.
char s[81];
int bytesRead = file.Read(s, 80);
s[bytesRead] = 0;
CString message = s;
```

This time the file is opened by the CFile::modeRead flag, which opens the file for read operations only, after which the code creates a character buffer and calls the file object's Read() member function to read data into the buffer. The Read() function's two arguments are the buffer's address and the number of bytes to read. The function returns the number of bytes actually read, which in this case is almost always less than the 80 requested. By using the number of bytes read, the program can add a 0 to the end of the character data, thus creating a standard C-style string that can be used to set a CString variable.

The code snippets you've just seen use a hard-coded filename. To get filenames from your user with little effort, be sure to look up the MFC class CFileDialog in the online help. It's simple to use and adds a very nice touch to your programs.

CREATING YOUR OWN CArchive OBJECTS

Although you can use CFile objects to read from and write to files, you can also go a step further and create your own CArchive object and use it exactly as you use the CArchive object in the `Serialize()` function. This enables you to take advantage of serialize functions already written for other objects, passing them a reference to your own archive object.

To create an archive, create a `CFile` object and pass it to the `CArchive` constructor. For example, if you plan to write out objects to a file through an archive, create the archive as follows:

```
CFile file("FILENAME.EXT", CFile::modeWrite);
CArchive ar(&file, CArchive::store);
```

After creating the archive object, you can use it just like the archive objects that MFC creates for you. For example, you can call `Serialize()` yourself and pass the archive to it. Because you created the archive with the `CArchive::store` flag, any calls to `IsStoring()` return TRUE, and the code that dumps objects to the archive executes. When you're finished with the archive object, you can close the archive and the file this way:

```
ar.Close();
file.Close();
```

If the objects go out of scope soon after you're finished with them, you can safely omit the calls to `Close()` because both `CArchive` and `CFile` have `Close()` calls in the destructor.

USING THE REGISTRY

In the early days of Windows programming, applications saved settings and options in initialization files, typically with the .INI extension. The days of huge WIN.INI files or myriad private .INI files are now gone—when an application wants to store information about itself, it does so by using a centralized system Registry. Although the Registry makes sharing information between processes easier, it can make things more confusing for programmers. In this section, you uncover some of the mysteries of the Registry and learn how to manage it in your applications.

CH
5

Tip

.NET applications don't use the Registry. This makes moving them from one computer to another much simpler. But the Registry isn't going anywhere; classic Windows applications will continue to use it.

HOW THE REGISTRY IS SET UP

Unlike .INI files, which are plain text files that can be edited with any text editor, the Registry contains binary and ASCII information that can be edited only by using the Registry Editor or special API function calls created specifically for managing the Registry. If you've ever used the Registry Editor to browse your system's Registry, you know that it contains a huge amount of information that's organized into a tree structure. Figure 5.19 shows how the Registry appears when you first run the Registry Editor. (On Windows 95, you can find the Registry Editor, REGEDIT.EXE, in your main Windows folder, or you can run it from the Start menu by choosing Run, typing **regedit**, and then clicking OK.

Under Windows NT, Windows 2000, and Windows XP, it's REGEDT32.EXE, so choose Run from the Start menu and type **regedt32**.)

Figure 5.19
The Registry Editor displays the Registry.

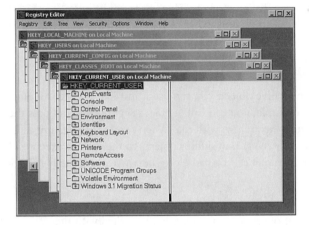

The far left window lists the Registry's predefined keys. The plus marks next to the keys in the tree indicate that you can open the keys and view more detailed information associated with them. Keys can have subkeys, and subkeys themselves can have subkeys. Any key or subkey may or may not have a value associated with it. If you explore deep enough in the hierarchy, you see a list of values in the far right window. In Figure 5.20, you can see the values associated with the current user's screen appearance. To see these values yourself, browse from HKEY_CURRENT_USER to Control Panel to Appearance to Schemes, and you can see the desktop schemes installed on your system.

Figure 5.20
The Registry is structured as a tree containing a huge amount of information.

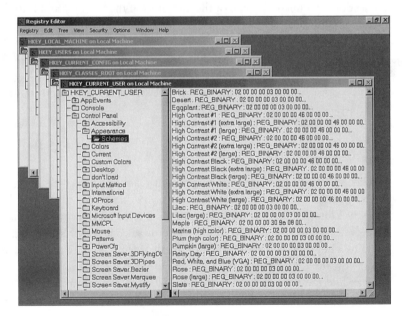

THE PREDEFINED KEYS

To know where things are stored in the Registry, you need to know about the predefined keys and what they mean. From Figure 5.19, you can see that the six predefined keys are

- HKEY_CLASSES_ROOT

- HKEY_CURRENT_USER

- HKEY_LOCAL_MACHINE

- HKEY_USERS

- HKEY_CURRENT_CONFIG

- HKEY_DYN_DATA

The HKEY_CLASSES_ROOT key holds document types and properties, as well as class information about the various applications installed on the machine. For example, if you explored this key on your system, you'd probably find an entry for the .DOC file extension, under which you'd find entries for the applications that can handle this type of document (see Figure 5.21).

Figure 5.21
The HKEY_CLASSES_ROOT key holds document and extension information, such as these entries for the .doc extension.

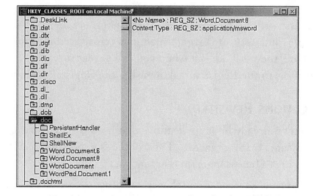

The HKEY_CURRENT_USER key contains all the system settings the current user has established, including color schemes, printers, and program groups. The HKEY_LOCAL_MACHINE key, on the other hand, contains status information about the computer, and the HKEY_USERS key organizes information about each user of the system, as well as the default configuration. Finally, the HKEY_CURRENT_CONFIG key holds information about the hardware configuration, and the HKEY_DYN_DATA key contains information about dynamic Registry data, which is data that changes frequently. (You may not always see this key on your system.)

USING THE REGISTRY IN AN MFC APPLICATION

Now that you know a little about the Registry, let me say that it would take an entire book to explain how to fully access and use it. As you may imagine, the Win32 API features many

CH
5

functions for manipulating the Registry. If you're going to use those functions, you had better know what you're doing! Invalid Registry settings can crash your machine, make it unbootable, and perhaps force you to reinstall Windows to recover.

However, you can easily use the Registry with your MFC applications to store information that the application needs from one session to another. To make this task as easy as possible, MFC provides the CWinApp class with the SetRegistryKey() member function, which creates (or opens) a key entry in the Registry for your application. All you have to do is supply a key name (usually a company name) for the function to use, as follows:

```
SetRegistryKey("MyCoolCompany");
```

You should call SetRegistryKey() in the application class's InitInstance() member function, which is called once at program startup.

After you call SetRegistryKey(), your application can create the subkeys and values it needs by calling one of two functions. The WriteProfileString() function adds string values to the Registry, and the WriteProfileInt() function adds integer values to the Registry. To get values from the Registry, you can use the GetProfileString() and GetProfileInt() functions. (You also can use RegSetValueEx() and RegQueryValueEx() to set and retrieve Registry values.)

When they were first written, the WriteProfileString(), WriteProfileInt(), GetProfileString(), and GetProfileInt() functions transferred information to and from an .INI file. Used alone, they still do. But when you call SetRegistryKey() first, MFC reroutes these profile functions to the Registry, making using the Registry an almost painless process.

THE SAMPLE APPLICATIONS REVISITED

In this chapter, you've already built applications that used the Registry. Here's an excerpt from CMultiStringApp::InitInstance(). This code was generated by MFC Application Wizard and is also in CFileDemoApp::InitInstance().

```
// Change the registry key under which our settings are stored.
// You should modify this string to be something appropriate
// such as the name of your company or organization.
SetRegistryKey(_T("Local AppWizardGenerated Applications"));

LoadStdProfileSettings();  // Load standard INI file options (including MRU)
```

MRU stands for Most Recently Used and refers to the list of files that appears on the File menu after you open files with an application. Figure 5.22 shows the Registry Editor displaying the key that stores this information, HKEY_CURRENT_USER\Software\Local AppWizard -Generated Applications\MultiString\Recent File List. In the foreground, MultiString's File menu shows the single entry in the MRU list.

Figure 5.22
The most recently used files list is stored in the Registry automatically.

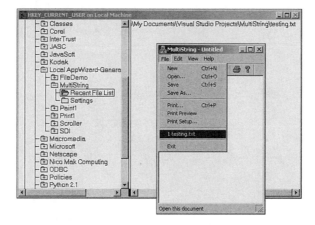

FROM HERE

This chapter showed you how to create applications that produce and hold information with a longer lifetime than one run of your application. A user might run your application, print something from it, then close the application. It's no longer running, but the printout is on the user's desk and still of use to someone. Or a user might run the application, save a document, and run the application again a week later to pick up working on that document in the same spot. The techniques you've met in this chapter are vital to almost every Windows application in existence.

In the next chapter, "Building a Complete Application: ShowString," you pull together a number of Windows programming techniques covered in these early chapters. You also learn how to use menus in a Windows application. The result is an application that showcases the skills every Windows developer needs: displaying, saving, and printing information; using dialog boxes and menus to interact with a user; and enabling a user to customize the appearance of an application.

CH
5

BUILDING A COMPLETE APPLICATION: SHOWSTRING

In this chapter

BUILDING AN APPLICATION THAT DISPLAYS A STRING

In this chapter you pull together the concepts demonstrated in previous chapters to create an application that really does something. You add a menu, a menu item, a dialog box, and persistence to an application that draws output based on user settings.

The sample application you will build is very much like the traditional "Hello, world!" of C programming. It displays a text string in the main window. The document (what you save in a file) contains the string and a few settings. There is a new menu item to bring up a dialog box to change the string and the settings, which control the string's appearance. This sample application is deliberately simple, and its chief purpose is to present the concepts of adding menu items and dialog boxes as clearly as possible. So, bring up Visual Studio and follow along.

CREATING AN EMPTY SHELL WITH APPWIZARD

First, use the MFC Application Wizard to create the starter application. (Chapter 2, "Building Your First Windows Application," covers the MFC Application Wizard and creating starter applications.) Choose File, New, Projects. Select a MFC Application, name the project ShowString so that your classnames will match those shown throughout this chapter, and click OK.

On the Application Type tab of the MFC Application Wizard, it doesn't matter much whether you choose SDI or MDI, but MDI will enable you to see for yourself how little effort is required to have multiple documents open at once. So, keep MDI.

The ShowString application needs no database support, no compound document support, and has a standard user interface, so skip ahead to the Advanced Features tab. Select Context-Sensitive Help, and select the HTML Help format. Leave the rest of the defaults. The generated classnames and filenames are all fine, so go back to the Overview tab, as shown in Figure 6.1. Confirm the settings and click Finish.

Figure 6.1
The Overview tab of the MFC Application Wizard summarizes the design choices for ShowString.

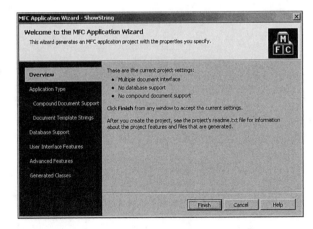

DISPLAYING A STRING

The ShowString application displays a string that will be kept in the document. You need to add a member variable to the document class, CShowStringDoc, and add loading and saving code to the Serialize() function. You can initialize the string by adding code to OnNewDocument() for the document, and to actually display it, override OnDraw() for the view. Documents and views are introduced in Chapter 4, "Displaying Information."

MEMBER VARIABLE AND SERIALIZATION

Add a private variable to the document and a public function to get the value by adding these lines to ShowStringDoc.h:

```
private:
    CString string;
public:
    CString GetString() {return string;}
```

The inline function gives other parts of your application a copy of the string to use whenever necessary but makes it impossible for other parts to change the string.

Next, change the skeleton CShowStringDoc::Serialize() function provided by AppWizard to look like Listing 6.1. (Expand CShowStringDoc in Class View and double-click Serialize() to edit the code.) Because you used the MFC CString class, the archive has the operators << and >> already defined, so this is a simple function to write. It fills the archive from the string when you are saving the document and fills the string from the archive when you are loading the document from a file. Chapter 5, "Printing and Saving," introduces serialization.

LISTING 6.1 SHOWSTRINGDOC.CPP—CShowStringDoc::Serialize()

```
void CShowStringDoc::Serialize(CArchive& ar)
{
    if (ar.IsStoring())
    {
        ar << string;
    }
    else
    {
        ar >> string;
    }
}
```

CH
6

INITIALIZING THE STRING

Whenever a new document is created, you want your application to initialize string to "Hello, world!" A new document is created when the user chooses File, New. This message is caught by CShowStringApp (the message map is shown in Listing 6.2, you can see it yourself by scrolling toward the top of ShowString.cpp) and handled by CWinApp::OnFileNew(). (Message maps and message handlers are discussed in Chapter 3, "Interacting with Your

Application.") Starter applications generated by the MFC Application Wizard call `OnFileNew()` to create a blank document when they run. `OnFileNew()` calls the document's `OnNewDocument()`, which actually initializes the member variables of the document.

LISTING 6.2   SHOWSTRING.CPP—MESSAGE MAP

```
BEGIN_MESSAGE_MAP(CShowStringApp, CWinApp)
    ON_COMMAND(ID_APP_ABOUT, OnAppAbout)
    // Standard file based document commands
    ON_COMMAND(ID_FILE_NEW, CWinApp::OnFileNew)
    ON_COMMAND(ID_FILE_OPEN, CWinApp::OnFileOpen)
    // Standard print setup command
    ON_COMMAND(ID_FILE_PRINT_SETUP, CWinApp::OnFilePrintSetup)
END_MESSAGE_MAP()
```

The MFC Application Wizard gives you this simple `OnNewDocument()`:

```
BOOL CShowStringDoc::OnNewDocument()
{
    if (!CDocument::OnNewDocument())
        return FALSE;

    // TODO: add reinitialization code here
    // (SDI documents will reuse this document)

    return TRUE;
}
```

To edit it, double-click `OnNewDocument()` in the ClassView window—you may have to expand `CShowStringDoc` first. Take away the comments and add this line in their place:

```
string = "Hello, world!";
```

(What else could it say, after all?) Leave the call to `CDocument::OnNewDocument()` because that handles all other work involved in making a new document.

GETTING THE STRING ONSCREEN

As you learned in Chapter 4, a view's `OnDraw()` function is called whenever that view needs to be drawn, such as when your application is first started, resized, or restored, or when a window that had been covering it is taken away. The MFC Application Wizard has provided a skeleton version for you:

```
void CShowStringView::OnDraw(CDC* pDC)
{
    CShowStringDoc* pDoc = GetDocument();
    ASSERT_VALID(pDoc);

    // TODO: add draw code for native data here
}
```

To edit this function, expand `CShowStringView` in the ClassView and then double-click `OnDraw()`. `OnDraw()` takes a pointer to a device context, as discussed in Chapter 4. The device context class, CDC, has a member function called DrawText() that draws text onscreen. It is declared as follows:

```
int DrawText( const CString& str, LPRECT lpRect, UINT nFormat )
```

The CString to be passed to this function is going to be the string from the document class, which can be accessed as pDoc->GetString(). The lpRect is the client rectangle of the view, returned by GetClientRect(). Finally, nFormat is the way the string should display; for example, DT_CENTER means that the text should be centered from left to right within the view. DT_VCENTER means that the text should be centered up and down, but this works only for single lines of text that are identified with DT_SINGLELINE. Multiple format flags can be combined with a bitwise or, |, so DT_CENTER|DT_VCENTER|DT_SINGLELINE is the nFormat that you want. The drawing code to be added to CShowStringView::OnDraw() looks like this:

```
CRect rect;
GetClientRect(&rect);
pDC->DrawText(pDoc->GetString(), &rect, DT_CENTER|DT_VCENTER|DT_SINGLELINE);
```

This sets up a CRect and passes its address to GetClientRect(), which sets the CRect to the client area of the view. DrawText() draws the document's string in the rectangle, centered vertically and horizontally.

At this point, the application should display the string properly. Build and execute it, and you will see something like Figure 6.2. You have a lot of functionality—menus, toolbars, status bar, and so on—but nothing that any other Windows application doesn't have, yet. Starting with the next section, that changes.

Figure 6.2
ShowString starts simply, with the usual greeting.

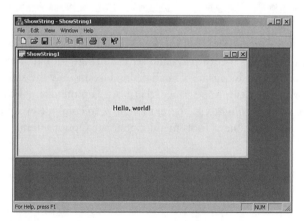

BUILDING THE SHOWSTRING MENUS

The MFC Application Wizard created two menus for you, shown in the Resource View window in Figure 6.3. (To show both at once, I used a horizontal tab group: you can learn more about tab groups in Appendix C, "The Visual Studio User Interface, Menus, and Visual Studio." The menu names are shortened on the tabs: IDR_ShowStringTYPE is above IDR_MAINFRAME.) IDR_MAINFRAME is the menu shown when no file is open; IDR_SHOWSTRINGTYPE is the menu shown when a ShowString document is open. Notice that IDR_MAINFRAME has no Window menus and that the File menu is much shorter than the one on the IDR_SHOWSTRINGTYPE menu, with only New, Open, Print Setup, Recent files, Close, and Exit items.

Figure 6.3
The MFC Application Wizard creates two menus for ShowString.

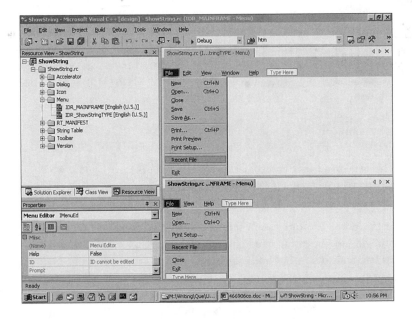

You are going to add a menu item to ShowString, so the first decision is where to add it. The user can edit the string that displays and set the string's format. You could add a Value item to the Edit menu that brings up a small dialog box for only the string, and then create a Format menu with one item, Appearance, that brings up the dialog box to set the appearance. The choice you are going to see here, though, is to combine everything into one dialog box and then put it on a new Tools menu, under the Options item.

> **Tip**
>
> You may have noticed already that more and more Windows applications are standardizing Tools, Options as the place for miscellaneous settings.

Do you need to add the item to both menus? No. When there is no document open, there is nowhere to save the changes made with this dialog box. So only IDR_SHOWSTRING-TYPE needs to have a menu added. Open the menu by double-clicking it in the Resource View window. At the far right of the menu, after Help, is an empty menu with Type Here in faint text. Click it and type **&Tools**. The Properties Window appears, and the Caption box contains &Tools. The menu at the end becomes the Tools menu, with an empty item underneath it; another empty menu then appears to the right of the Tools menu, as shown in Figure 6.4.

Figure 6.4
Adding the Tools menu is easy in the Resource View window.

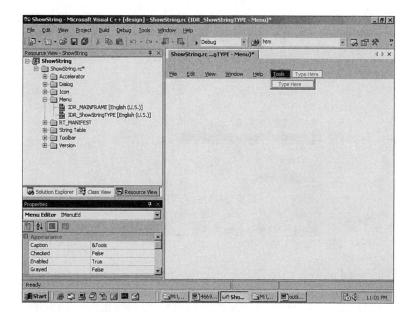

Click the new Tools menu and drag it between the View and Window menus, corresponding to the position of Tools in products such as Visual Studio and Microsoft Word. Next, click the empty sub-item that says Type Here. The Properties Window changes to show the blank properties of this item; enter &Options and the Properties Window reflects your changes, as shown in Figure 6.5.

The & in the Caption edit box precedes the letter that serves as the mnemonic key for selecting that menu with the keyboard (for example, Alt+T in the case of Tools). This letter appears underlined in the menu. No further work is required on your part. You can opt to select a different mnemonic key by moving the & so that it precedes a different letter in the menu or menu item name (for example, T&ools changes the key from T to o). You should not use the same mnemonic letter for two menus or for two items on the same menu.

All menu items have a resource ID, and this resource ID is the way the menu items are connected to your code. Visual Studio chooses a good one for you, but it doesn't appear right away in the Properties Window. Click some other menu item, and then click Options again; you see that the resource ID is ID_TOOLS_OPTIONS. Alternatively, press Enter when you are finished, and the highlight moves down to the empty menu item below Options. Press the up-arrow cursor key to return the highlight to the Options item.

CH
6

Figure 6.5
The menu command Tools, Options controls everything that ShowString does.

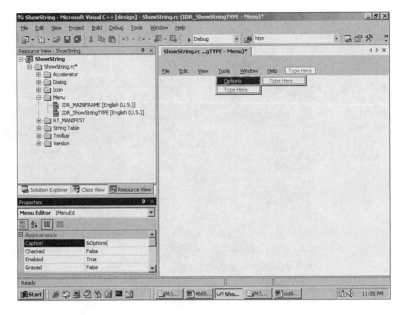

You should provide a sensible prompt for your menu item. The prompt is shown on the status bar when the user pauses the mouse over the menu item or moves the highlight over it with the cursor. After the resource ID has been assigned, you can add a prompt in the Properties Window. I chose Change String and Appearance for my prompt.

If you'd like to provide an accelerator, such as the Ctrl+C for Edit, Copy that the system provides, this is a good time to do it. Click the + next to Accelerator in the Resource View window and then double-click IDR_MAINFRAME, the only Accelerator table in this application. At a glance, you can see what key combinations are already in use. Ctrl+O is already taken, but Ctrl+T is available. To connect Ctrl+T to Tools, Options, follow these steps:

1. Click the empty line at the bottom of the Accelerator table. If you have closed the Properties Window, bring it back by choosing View, Properties Window. (Alternatively, double-click the empty line to bring up the Properties Window.)

2. Click next to ID to bring up a drop-down list box and choose ID_TOOLS_OPTIONS from the list, which is in alphabetical order. (There are a lot of entries before ID_TOOLS_OPTIONS; drag the elevator down to almost the bottom of the list or start typing the resource ID—by the time you type ID_TO, the highlight will be in the right place.)

3. Type T in the Key box; then make sure that the Control box is set to True and that the Alt and Shift boxes are set to False. (Watch the highlight in the main pane on the right as you do this: after you type T the accelerator is presumed complete and you may find yourself editing a new one without noticing.)

4. Click another line in the Accelerator table to save the changes.

Figure 6.6 shows the Properties Window for this accelerator again as it appears after you click the newly entered line.

Figure 6.6
Keyboard accelerators are connected to resource IDs.

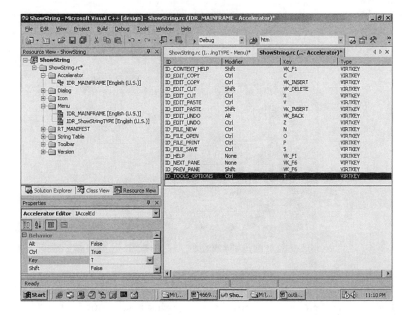

What happens when the user chooses this new menu item, Tools, Options? A dialog box is displayed. So, tempting as it may be to start connecting this menu to code, it makes more sense to build the dialog box first.

BUILDING THE SHOWSTRING DIALOG BOXES

Chapter 2 introduces dialog boxes. This section builds on that background. ShowString is going to have two custom dialog boxes: one brought up by Tools, Options and also an About dialog box. An About dialog box has been provided by the MFC Application Wizard, but it needs to be changed a little; you build the Options dialog box from scratch.

SHOWSTRING'S ABOUT DIALOG BOX

Figure 6.7 shows the About dialog box that the MFC Application Wizard makes for you; it contains the application name and the current year. To view the About dialog box for ShowString, open the Resource View window, expand the Dialogs list by clicking the + icon next to the word Dialogs, and then double-click IDD_ABOUTBOX to bring up the About dialog box resource.

CH
6

Figure 6.7
The MFC Application Wizard makes an About dialog box for you.

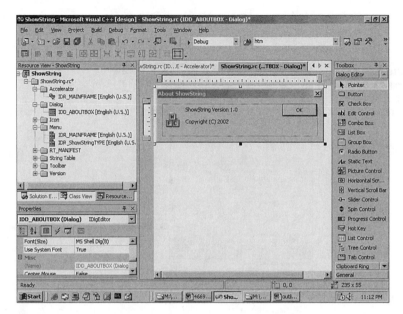

You might want to add a company name to your About dialog box. Here's how to add Que Books, as an example. Click the line of text that reads Copyright 2002, and it appears surrounded by a selection box. Bring up the Properties Window, if it isn't up. Edit the caption to add Que Books at the end; the changes are reflected immediately in the dialog box.

Tip

If the rulers you see in Figure 6.7 don't appear when you open IDD_ABOUTBOX in Developer Studio, you can turn them on by choosing Format, Guide Settings and then selecting the Rulers and Guides radio button in the top half of the Guide Settings dialog box.

I decided to add a text string to remind users what book this application is from. Here's how to do that:

1. Size the dialog box a little taller by clicking the whole dialog box to select it, clicking the sizing square in the middle of the bottom border, and dragging the bottom border down a little. (This visual editing is what gave Visual C++ its name when it first came out.)

2. In the floating toolbar called Toolbox, click the button labeled Static Text to get a static text control, which means a piece of text that the user cannot change, perfect for labels such as this. Click within the dialog box under the other text to insert the static text there.

3. In the Properties window, change the caption from Static to Using Visual C++ .NET. The box automatically resizes to fit the text.

4. Hold down the Ctrl key and click the other two static text lines in the dialog box. Choose Format, Align, Lefts, which aligns the edges of the three selected controls. The one you select last stays still, and the others move to align with it.

5. Choose Format, Space Evenly, Down. These menu options can save you a great deal of dragging, squinting at the screen, and then dragging again.

The About dialog box will resemble Figure 6.8. Click the Test Dialog button at the leftmost end of the Dialog Editor toolbar (the button looks like a little dialog box with a red exclamation mark on it) to preview the way your dialog box will look in to the user.

Figure 6.8
In a matter of minutes, you can customize your About dialog box.

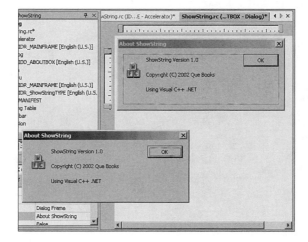

SHOWSTRING'S OPTIONS DIALOG BOX

The Options dialog box is simple to build. First, make a new dialog box by choosing Project, Add Resource, and then double-clicking Dialog. An empty dialog box called Dialog1 appears, with an OK button and a Cancel button, as shown in Figure 6.9.

Figure 6.9
A new dialog box always has OK and Cancel buttons.

CH

6

Next, follow these steps to convert the empty dialog box into the Options dialog box:

1. Use the Properties window to change the ID to IDD_OPTIONS and the caption to Options.

2. In the floating toolbar called Controls, click the button labeled Edit Control to get an edit box in which the user can enter the new value for the string. Click inside the dialog box to place the control and then change the ID to IDC_OPTIONS_STRING. (Control IDs should all start with IDC and then mention the name of their dialog box and an identifier that is unique to that dialog box.)

3. Drag the sizing squares to resize the edit box to make it as wide as possible.

4. Add a static label above the edit box and change that caption to String.

You will revisit this dialog box later, when adding the appearance capabilities, but for now it's ready to be connected. It will look like Figure 6.10.

Figure 6.10
The Options dialog box is the place to change the string.

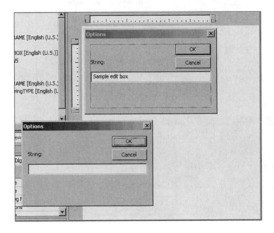

MAKING THE MENU WORK

When the user chooses Tools, Options, the Options dialog box should display. You use the Properties Window to arrange for one of your functions to be called when the item is chosen, and then you write the function, which creates an object of your dialog class and then displays it.

THE DIALOG CLASS

To create a class for your dialog box, right-click somewhere on your dialog box (not on a control) and choose Add Class to bring up the the MFC Class Wizard, shown in Figure 6.11.

Fill in the dialog box as follows:

1. Choose a sensible name for the class, one that starts with C and contains the word Dialog; this example uses COptionsDialog.

2. Choose CDialog as the base class. This MFC class provides basic dialog functionality.

3. Set the dialog ID to IDD_OPTIONS.

4. Click Finish to create the class.

Figure 6.11
The dialog class inherits from `CDialog`.

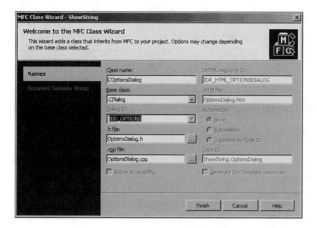

Now that the class has been created, you can add its member variables. On the Class View window, right-click the `COptionsDialog` class and choose Add, Add Variable. Connect IDC_OPTIONS_STRING to a public `CString` called `m_string`, just as you connected controls to member variables of the dialog box class in Chapter 2. Click Finish to add the variable.

Perhaps you're curious about what code was created for you when the Class Wizard made the class. The header file is shown in Listing 6.3.

LISTING 6.3   OPTIONSDIALOG.H—HEADER FILE FOR `COptionsDialog`

```cpp
#pragma once


// COptionsDialog dialog

class COptionsDialog : public CDialog
{
   DECLARE_DYNAMIC(COptionsDialog)

public:
   COptionsDialog(CWnd* pParent = NULL);   // standard constructor
   virtual ~COptionsDialog();

// Dialog Data
   enum { IDD = IDD_OPTIONS };

   // string edit box value
   CString m_string;

protected:
   virtual void DoDataExchange(CDataExchange* pDX);   // DDX/DDV support

   DECLARE_MESSAGE_MAP()
};
```

Сн

6

There are some macros here to help with message mapping, but there is only one member variable, m_string; one constructor; one destructor; and one member function, DoDataExchange(), which gets the control value into the member variable, or vice versa. The source file isn't much longer; it's shown in Listing 6.4.

LISTING 6.4   OPTIONSDIALOG.CPP—IMPLEMENTATION FILE FOR COptionsDialog

```
// OptionsDialog.cpp : implementation file
//

#include "stdafx.h"
#include "ShowString.h"
#include "OptionsDialog.h"


// COptionsDialog dialog

IMPLEMENT_DYNAMIC(COptionsDialog, CDialog)
COptionsDialog::COptionsDialog(CWnd* pParent /*=NULL*/)
  : CDialog(COptionsDialog::IDD, pParent)
    , m_string(_T(""))
{
}

COptionsDialog::~COptionsDialog()
{
}

void COptionsDialog::DoDataExchange(CDataExchange* pDX)
{
    CDialog::DoDataExchange(pDX);
    DDX_Text(pDX, IDC_OPTIONS_STRING, m_string);
}


BEGIN_MESSAGE_MAP(COptionsDialog, CDialog)
END_MESSAGE_MAP()


// COptionsDialog message handlers
```

The DoDataExchange() function calls DDX_Text() to transfer data from the control with the resource ID IDC_OPTIONS_STRING to the member variable m_string, or vice versa. Finally, there is an empty message map because COptionsDialog doesn't catch any messages.

CATCHING THE MESSAGE

The next step in building ShowString is to catch the command message sent when the user chooses Tools, Options. ShowString has seven classes: CAboutDlg, CChildFrame, CMainFrame,

`COptionsDialog`, `CShowStringApp`, `CShowStringDoc`, and `CShowStringView`. Which one should catch the command? The string and the options are saved in the document and displayed in the view, so one of those two classes should handle the changing of the string. The document owns the private variable and does not let the view change the string unless you implement a public function to set the string. So, it makes the most sense to have the document catch the command.

To catch the message, follow these steps:

1. Click the `CShowStringDoc` class in the Class View.
2. Open the Properties Window and click the Events button.
3. Expand the ID_TOOLS_OPTIONS item.
4. Click COMMAND, and choose <Add> OnToolsOptions from the drop-down box that appears.

Now you need to edit the generated code. What happened to `CShowStringDoc` when you arranged for the `ID_TOOLS_OPTIONS` command to be caught? The new message map in the header file looks like this:

```
// Generated message map functions
protected:
   DECLARE_MESSAGE_MAP()
public:
   afx_msg void OnToolsOptions(void);
```

The preceding code just declares the function. In the source file, the message map has changed to this:

```
BEGIN_MESSAGE_MAP(CShowStringDoc, CDocument)
   ON_COMMAND(ID_TOOLS_OPTIONS, OnToolsOptions)
END_MESSAGE_MAP()
```

This arranges for `OnToolsOptions()` to be called when the command `ID_TOOLS_OPTIONS` is sent. You also get a skeleton for `OnToolsOptions()`:

```
void CShowStringDoc::OnToolsOptions(void)
{
    // TODO: Add your command handler code here
}
```

CH
6

MAKING THE DIALOG BOX WORK

OnToolsOptions() should initialize and display the dialog box and then do something with the value that the user provided. (This process was first discussed in Chapter 2.) You have already connected the edit box to a member variable, m_string, of the dialog box class. Your code should initialize this member variable before displaying the dialog box and use it afterwards.

OnToolsOptions() displays the dialog box. Add the following code to the empty function that was generated for you when you arranged for the command to be caught by the CShowStringDoc class:

```
void CShowStringDoc::OnToolsOptions(void)
{
    COptionsDialog dlg;
    dlg.m_string = string;
    if (dlg.DoModal() == IDOK)
    {
        string = dlg.m_string;
        SetModifiedFlag();
        UpdateAllViews(NULL);
    }

}
```

This code fills the member variable of the dialog box with the document's member variable (the Add Member Variable Wizard added m_string as a public member variable of COptionsDialog, so that the document can change it) and then calls DoModal() to bring up the dialog box. If the user clicks OK, the member variable of the document changes, the modified flag is set (so that the user is prompted to save the document on exit), and the view is asked to redraw itself with a call to UpdateAllViews(). For this to compile, of course, the compiler must know what a COptionsDialog is, so add this line at the beginning of ShowStringDoc.cpp:

```
#include "OptionsDialog.h"
```

At this point, you can build the application and run it. Choose Tools, Options, and change the string. Click OK and you see the new string in the view. Exit the application; you are asked whether to save the file. Save it, restart the application, and open the file again. The default "Hello, world!" document remains open, and the changed document is opened as well, displaying the changed string. The application works, as you can see in Figure 6.12. (The windows are resized so that they both fit in the figure.)

Figure 6.12
ShowString can change the string, save it to a file, and reload it.

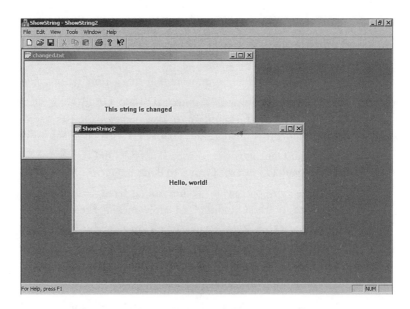

ADDING APPEARANCE OPTIONS TO THE OPTIONS DIALOG BOX

ShowString doesn't have much to do—just demonstrate menus and dialog boxes. However, the only dialog box control that ShowString uses is an edit box. In this section, you add a set of radio buttons and check boxes to change the way the string is drawn in the view.

CHANGING THE OPTIONS DIALOG BOX

It is quite simple to incorporate a full-fledged Font dialog box into an application, but the example in this section is going to do something much simpler. A group of radio buttons will give the user a choice of several colors. One check box will enable the user to specify that the text should be centered horizontally, and another that the text be centered vertically. Because these are check boxes, the text can be either, neither, or both.

Open the IDD_OPTIONS dialog box by double-clicking it in the Resource View window, and then add the radio buttons by following these steps:

1. Stretch the dialog box taller to make room for the new controls.
2. Click the radio button in the Toolbox, and then click the Options dialog box to drop the control onto the dialog box surface.

CH
6

3. Choose View, Properties to bring up the Properties window.

4. Change the ID of this first radio button to IDC_OPTIONS_BLACK, and change the caption to &Black.

5. Set the Group item to True to indicate that this is the first of a group of radio buttons.

6. Add another radio button with resource ID IDC_OPTIONS_RED and &Red as the caption. Do not set the Group item to True, because the Red radio button doesn't start a new group but is part of the group that starts with the Black radio button.

7. Add a third radio button with resource ID IDC_OPTIONS_GREEN and &Green as the caption. Again, do not set Group to True.

8. Drag the three radio buttons into a horizontal arrangement, and select all three by clicking on one and then holding Ctrl while clicking the other two.

9. Choose Format, Align, Bottoms (to even them up).

10. Choose Format, Space Evenly, Across to space the controls across the dialog box.

Next, add the check boxes by following these steps:

1. Click the Check Box in the Toolbox and then click the Options dialog box, dropping a check box onto it.

2. Change the resource ID of this check box to IDC_OPTIONS_HORIZCENTER and the caption to Center &Horizontally.

3. Set the Group item to True to indicate the start of a new group after the radio buttons.

4. Drop another check box onto the dialog box as in step 1 and give it the resource ID IDC_OPTIONS_VERTCENTER and the caption Center &Vertically.

5. Arrange the check boxes under the radio buttons.

6. Click the Group box on the Toolbox, and then click and drag a Group box around the radio buttons. Change the caption to **Text Color**.

7. Move the OK and Cancel buttons down to the bottom of the dialog box.

8. Select each horizontal group of controls and use Format, Center in Dialog, Horizontal, to make things neater.

9. Choose Edit, Select All, and then drag all the controls up toward the top of the dialog box. Shrink the dialog box to fit around the new controls. It should now resemble Figure 6.13.

Finally, set the tab order by choosing Format, Tab Order and then clicking the controls, in this order:

1. IDC_OPTIONS_STRING

2. IDC_OPTIONS_BLACK

3. IDC_OPTIONS_RED

4. IDC_OPTIONS_GREEN

5. IDC_OPTIONS_HORIZCENTER

6. IDC_OPTIONS_VERTCENTER

7. IDOK

8. IDCANCEL

Then click away from the dialog box to leave the two static text controls as positions 9 and 10.

Figure 6.13
The Options dialog box for ShowString has been expanded.

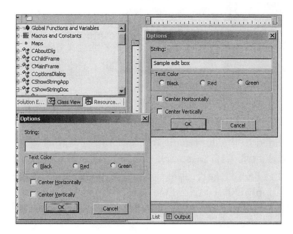

ADDING MEMBER VARIABLES TO THE DIALOG BOX CLASS

Having added controls to the dialog box, you need to add corresponding member variables to the `COptionsDialog` class. In the Class View, right-click `COptionsDialog` and choose Add, Add Variable to add member variables for each control. Add the following variables:

- `m_color`. To hold the radio button selection.
- `m_horizcenter`. To hold the check box value for horizontal centering.
- `m_vertcenter`. To hold the check box value for vertical centering.

The check boxes are connected to BOOL variables; these member variables are TRUE if the box is selected and FALSE if it isn't. The radio buttons are handled differently. Only the first—the one with the Group box set to True in its Properties dialog box—is connected to a member variable. That integer is a zero-based index that indicates which button is selected. In other words, when the Black button is selected, `m_color` is 0; when Red is selected, m color is 1; and when Green is selected, `m_color` is 2. Figure 6.14 shows the `m_color` member variable being created.

CH
6

Figure 6.14
Member variables in the dialog box class are connected to individual controls or the group of radio buttons.

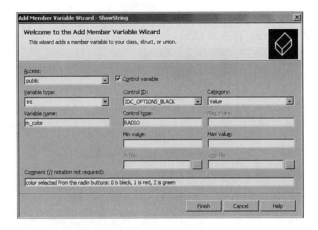

ADDING MEMBER VARIABLES TO THE DOCUMENT

The variables to be added to the document are the same ones that were added to the dialog box. You add them to the `CShowStringDoc` class definition in the header file, to `OnNewDocument()`, and to `Serialize()`. Add the lines in Listing 6.5 at the top of the `CShowStringDoc` definition in ShowStringDoc.h, replacing the previous definition of string and `GetString()`. Make sure that the variables are private and the functions are public.

LISTING 6.5   SHOWSTRINGDOC.H—`CShowStringDoc` MEMBER VARIABLES

```
private:
    CString string;
    int     color;
    BOOL horizcenter;
    BOOL vertcenter;
public:
    CString GetString() {return string;}
    int     GetColor() {return color;}
    BOOL GetHorizcenter() {return horizcenter;}
    BOOL GetVertcenter() {return vertcenter;}
```

As with string, these are private variables with public get functions but no set functions. All these options should be serialized; the new `Serialize()` function is shown in Listing 6.6. Change your copy by double-clicking the function name in Class View and adding the new code.

LISTING 6.6   SHOWSTRINGDOC.CPP—`Serialize()`

```
void CShowStringDoc::Serialize(CArchive& ar)
{
    if (ar.IsStoring())
    {
        ar << string;
        ar << color;
```

LISTING 6.6   CONTINUED

```
        ar << horizcenter;
        ar << vertcenter;
    }
    else
    {
        ar >> string;
        ar >> color;
        ar >> horizcenter;
        ar >> vertcenter;
    }
}
```

Finally, you need to initialize these variables in OnNewDocument(). What are good defaults for these new member variables? Black text, centered in both directions, was the old behavior, and it makes sense to use it as the default. The new OnNewDocument() looks like this:

```
BOOL CShowStringDoc::OnNewDocument()
{
    if (!CDocument::OnNewDocument())
        return FALSE;

    string = "Hello, world!";
    color = 0;      //black
    horizcenter = TRUE;
    vertcenter = TRUE;

    return TRUE;
}
```

Of course, at the moment, users cannot change these member variables from the defaults. To enable the user to change the variables, you have to change the function that handles the dialog box.

CHANGING ONTOOLSOPTIONS()

The OnToolsOptions() function sets the values of the dialog box member variables from the document member variables and then displays the dialog box. If the user clicks OK, the document member variables are set from the dialog box member variables and the view is redrawn. Having just added three member variables to the dialog box and the document, you have three lines to add before the dialog box displays and then three more to add in the block that's called after OK is clicked. The new OnToolsOptions() is as follows:

```
void CShowStringDoc::OnToolsOptions()
{
    COptionsDialog dlg;
    dlg.m_string = string;
    dlg.m_color = color;
    dlg.m_horizcenter = horizcenter;
    dlg.m_vertcenter = vertcenter;

    if (dlg.DoModal() == IDOK)
    {
```

CH

6

```
        string = dlg.m_string;
        color = dlg.m_color;
        horizcenter = dlg.m_horizcenter;
        vertcenter = dlg.m_vertcenter;
        SetModifiedFlag();
        UpdateAllViews(NULL);
    }

}
```

What happens when the user opens the dialog box and changes the value of a control, say, by deselecting Center Horizontally? The framework—through Dialog Data Exchange (DDX)—changes the value of `COptionsDialog::m_horizcenter` to FALSE. This code in `OnToolsOptions()` changes the value of `CShowStringDoc::horizcenter` to FALSE. When the user saves the document, `Serialize()` saves `horizcenter`. This is all good, but none of this code actually changes the way the view is drawn. That involves `OnDraw()`.

CHANGING OnDraw()

The single call to `DrawText()` in `OnDraw()` becomes a little more complex now. The document member variables are used to set the view's appearance. Edit `OnDraw()` by expanding `CShowStringView` in the Class View window and double-clicking `OnDraw()`.

The color is set with `CDC::SetTextColor()` before the call to `DrawText()`. You should always save the old text color and restore it when you are finished. The parameter to `SetTextColor()` is a COLORREF, and you can directly specify combinations of red, green, and blue as hex numbers in the form 0x00bbggrr, so that, for example, 0x000000FF is bright red. Most people prefer to use the RGB macro, which takes hex numbers from 0x0 to 0xFF, specifying the amount of each color; bright red is RGB(0xFF,0,0), for instance. Before the call to `DrawText()`, add these lines:

```
COLORREF oldcolor;
switch (pDoc->GetColor())
{
case 0:
    oldcolor = pDC->SetTextColor(RGB(0,0,0)); //black
    break;
case 1:
    oldcolor = pDC->SetTextColor(RGB(0xFF,0,0)); //red
    break;
case 2:
    oldcolor = pDC->SetTextColor(RGB(0,0xFF,0)); //green
    break;
}
```

Add this line after the call to DrawText():

```
pDC->SetTextColor(oldcolor);
```

There are two approaches to setting the centering flags. The brute-force way is to list the four possibilities (neither, horizontal, vertical, and both) and have a different `DrawText()` statement for each. If you were to add other settings, this would quickly become unworkable.

It's better to set up an integer to hold the DrawText() flags and OR in each flag, if appropriate. Before the call to DrawText(), add these lines:

```
int DTflags = 0;
if (pDoc->GetHorizcenter())
{
    DTflags |= DT_CENTER;
}
if (pDoc->GetVertcenter())
{
    DTflags |= (DT_VCENTER|DT_SINGLELINE);
}
```

The call to DrawText() now uses the DTflags variable:

```
pDC->DrawText(pDoc->GetString(), &rect, DTflags);
```

Now the settings from the dialog box have made their way to the dialog box class, to the document, and finally to the view, to actually affect the appearance of the text string. Build and execute ShowString and then try it. Any surprises? Be sure to change the text, experiment with various combinations of the centering options, and try all three colors.

From Here

If you've been following along with all the sample applications since the start of the book, you've seen most of the basics of Windows programming up to this point. You know how to work with menus and dialog boxes, how to draw text and simple pictures on the screen, and how to print and save a document. But lots more power is available to Windows programmers, and you're ready to start discovering it!

Chapter 7, "Status Bars, Toolbars, and Common Controls," gets you started on intuitive and efficient user interface components with a minimum of programming. You don't need to write a lot of code to add some very useful features to your interface. Chapter 8, "Help, Property Pages, and Wizards," shows how to use your application itself to train your users. ShowString turns up again in that chapter as a sample application to which Help is added.

CH
6

STATUS BARS, TOOLBARS, AND COMMON CONTROLS

In this chapter

WORKING WITH TOOLBARS

Building a good user interface is half the battle of programming a Windows application. Luckily, Visual C++ and the MFC Application Wizard supply an amazing amount of help in creating an application that supports all the expected user-interface elements, including menus, dialog boxes, toolbars, and status bars. Menus and dialog boxes are covered in Chapters 3, "Interacting with Your Application," and 6, "Building a Complete Application: ShowString." In this chapter, you learn how to get the most out of toolbars, status bars, and a variety of useful controls for your dialog boxes.

The buttons on a toolbar correspond to commands, just as the items on a menu do. Although you can add a toolbar to your application with the MFC Application Wizard, you still need to use a little programming polish to make things just right. Every application is different and the MFC Application Wizard can create only the most generally useful toolbar for most applications. When you create your own toolbars, you will probably want to add or delete buttons to support your application's unique command set.

For example, when you create a standard MFC Application Wizard application with a toolbar, the wizard creates the toolbar shown in Figure 7.1. This toolbar provides buttons for the commonly used commands in the File and Edit menus, as well as a button for displaying the About dialog box. What if your application doesn't support these commands? It's up to you to modify the default toolbar to fit your application.

Figure 7.1
The default toolbar provides buttons for commonly used commands.

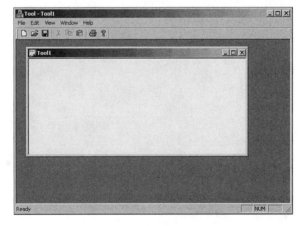

DELETING TOOLBAR BUTTONS

Create a multiple document interface application with a toolbar by choosing File, New, Project; choosing the MFC Application template from the Visual C++ Projects project type; naming the application Tool; and accepting the defaults on every tab. The MFC Application Wizard provides a docking toolbar by default. Build and run the application, and you should see a toolbar of your own, just like the one in Figure 7.1.

Before moving on, play with this toolbar a little. On the View menu, you can toggle whether the toolbar is displayed. Turn it off and then on again. Now click and hold on the toolbar between buttons and pull it down into the working area of your application. Let it go, and it's a floating palette. Drag it around and drop it at the bottom of the application or one of the sides—it docks against any side of the main window. Watch the tracking rectangle change shape to show you it will dock if you drop it. Drag it back off again so that it's floating and close it by clicking the small x in the upper right corner. Bring it back with the View menu and notice that it comes back to where you left it. All this functionality is yours free from the MFC Application Wizard and MFC.

The first step in modifying the toolbar is to delete buttons you no longer need. To do this, first select the Resource View tab to display your application's resources, then click on the + next to Tool.rc. Click the + next to Toolbar and double-click the IDR_MAINFRAME toolbar resource to edit it, as shown in Figure 7.2.

Figure 7.2
Use the toolbar editor to customize your application's toolbar.

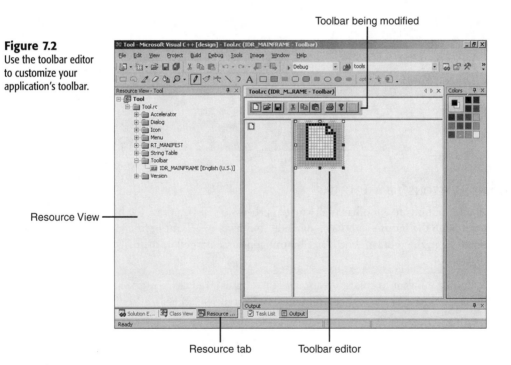

After you have the toolbar editor on the screen, deleting buttons is as easy as dragging the unwanted buttons from the toolbar. Place your mouse pointer on the button, hold down the left mouse button, and drag the unwanted button away from the toolbar. When you release the mouse button, the toolbar button disappears. In the Tool application, delete all the buttons except the Help button with a yellow question mark. Figure 7.3 shows the edited toolbar with only the Help button remaining. The single blank button template is only a

CH
7

starting point for the next button you want to create. If you leave it blank, it doesn't appear in the final toolbar.

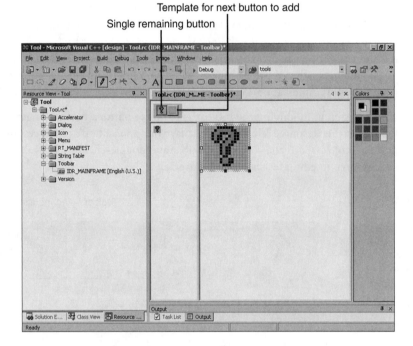

Figure 7.3
This edited toolbar has only a single button left (not counting the blank button template).

ADDING BUTTONS TO A TOOLBAR

Adding buttons to a toolbar is a two-step process: First you draw the button's icon, and then you match the button with its command. To draw a new button, first click the blank button template in the toolbar. The blank button appears enlarged in the edit window, as shown in Figure 7.4.

Suppose you want to create a command that draws a red circle in the application's window. To enhance the user interface, this command should be accessible from both the menu and the toolbar.

Draw a red circle on the blank button with the Filled Ellipse tool, and you've created the button's icon. Open the Properties window and give the button an appropriate ID, such as ID_DRAW_CIRCLE in this case.

Now you need to define the button's description and ToolTip. The description appears in the application's status bar. In this case, a description of "Draws a red circle in the window" might be good. The ToolTip appears whenever the user leaves the mouse pointer over the button for a second or two, acting as a reminder of the button's purpose. A ToolTip of Circle would be appropriate for the Circle button. Type these two text strings into the Prompt box. The description comes first, followed by the newline character (\n) and the ToolTip, as shown in Figure 7.5.

Figure 7.4
Click the button template to open it in the button editor.

Button template   Button editor

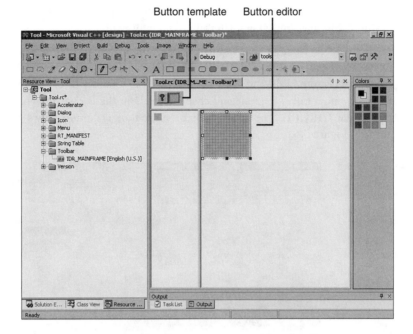

Figure 7.5
After drawing the button, specify its properties.

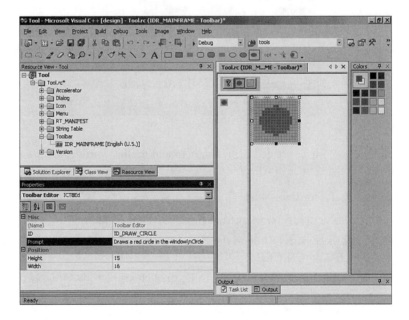

Toolbar buttons generally duplicate menu items. This provides the user with a quicker way of accessing commonly used commands. If you give a toolbar button and a menu item the same ID, the same command is generated when the toolbar button is clicked or the menu

CH

7

item is chosen. This enables you to create one event handler function to handle the user clicking the toolbar button and choosing the menu item.

Create the menu item for the command. Open the Resource View window, expand Tool.rc and Menu, then double-click IDR_ToolTYPE. Add a top-level menu called &Draw and place it between the Edit and View menus just as in Chapter 6. Under the Draw menu, create a menu item called &Circle and change the ID in the Properties window to ID_DRAW_CIRCLE. The prompt you gave the toolbar button shows up automatically, as shown in Figure 7.6.

Figure 7.6
Connecting menu items and toolbar buttons is as simple as changing the ID.

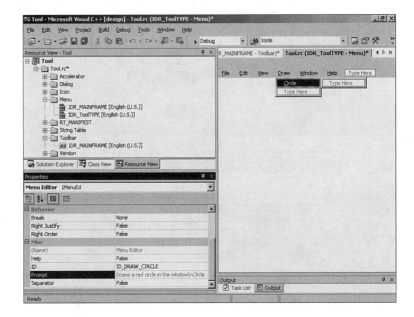

Now that you have created the menu item and toolbar button, you are ready to assign an event handler just as in Chapter 6.

To do this, follow these steps:

1. Select the CToolView class from the Class View window.

2. Click the Events button in the Properties window and expand the item labeled ID_DRAW_CIRCLE.

3. Select the box named COMMAND, then choose <Add> OnDrawCircle from the drop-down box that appears to add the event handler function, as shown in Figure 7.7.

Figure 7.7
You can use the Properties window to handle events from your toolbar buttons.

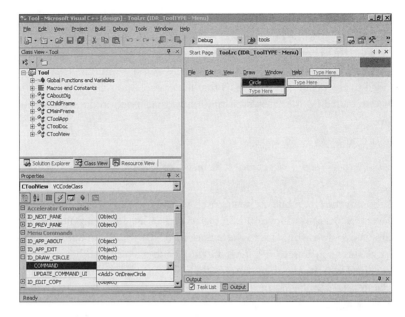

Note

If you haven't defined an event handler function for a toolbar button, or if there is no instance of the class that catches the message, MFC disables the button when you run the application. For example, if the message is caught by the document or view in an MDI application and there is no open document, the button is disabled. The same is true for menu commands. In fact, for all intents and purposes, toolbar buttons are menu commands.

If you compile and run the application now, you will see the window shown in Figure 7.8. In the figure, you can see the new toolbar button, as well as its ToolTip and description line. The toolbar looks sparse in this example, but you can add as many buttons as you like.

Figure 7.8
The new toolbar button shows its ToolTip and description.

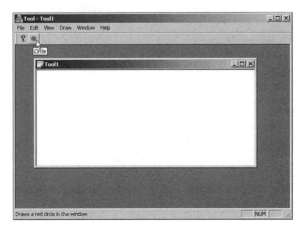

You can create as many buttons as you need; just follow the same procedure for each. After you have created the buttons, you're finished with the toolbar resources and ready to write the code that responds to the buttons. For example, in the preceding example, a circle button was added to the toolbar, and a message-response function, called OnDrawCircle(), was added to the program. MFC calls that message-response function whenever the user clicks the associated button. However, right now, that function doesn't do anything. It looks like this:

```
void CToolView::OnDrawCircle()
{
    // TODO: Add your command handler code here
}
```

Although the circle button is supposed to draw a red circle in the window, you can see that the OnDrawCircle() function is going to need a little help accomplishing that task. Add the lines shown in Listing 7.1 to the function so that the circle button does what it's supposed to do, as shown in Figure 7.9. This drawing code makes a brush, selects it into the DC, draws an ellipse with it, and then restores the old brush. The details of drawing are discussed in Chapter 4, "Displaying Information."

Figure 7.9
After code is added to OnDrawCircle(), the new toolbar button actually does something.

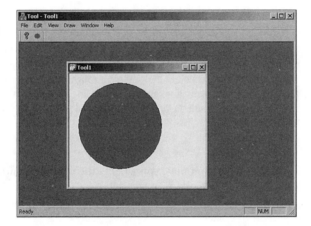

LISTING 7.1 CToolView::OnDrawCircle()

```
void CToolView::OnCircle()
{
    CClientDC clientDC(this);
    CBrush newBrush(RGB(255,0,0));
    CBrush* oldBrush = clientDC.SelectObject(&newBrush);
    clientDC.Ellipse(20, 20, 200, 200);
    clientDC.SelectObject(oldBrush);
}
```

THE CToolBar CLASS'S MEMBER FUNCTIONS

In most cases, after you have created your toolbar resource and associated its buttons with the appropriate command IDs, you don't need to bother any more with the toolbar. The code generated by AppWizard creates the toolbar for you, and MFC takes care of calling the buttons' response functions for you. However, at times you might want to change the toolbar's default behavior or appearance in some way. In those cases, you can call on the CToolBar class's member functions, which are listed in Table 7.1, along with their descriptions. The toolbar is accessible from the CMainFrame class as the m_wndToolBar member variable. Usually, you change the toolbar behavior in CMainFrame::OnCreate().

TABLE 7.1   MEMBER FUNCTIONS OF THE CToolBar CLASS

Function	Description
CommandToIndex()	Obtains the index of a button, given its ID.
Create()	Creates the toolbar.
GetButtonInfo()	Obtains information about a button.
GetButtonStyle()	Obtains a button's style.
GetButtonText()	Obtains a button's text label.
GetItemID()	Obtains the ID of a button, given its index.
GetItemRect()	Obtains an item's display rectangle, given its index.
GetToolBarCtrl()	Obtains a reference to the CToolBarCtrl object represented by the CToolBar object.
LoadBitmap()	Loads the toolbar's button images.
LoadToolBar()	Loads a toolbar resource.
SetBitmap()	Sets a new toolbar button bitmap.
SetButtonInfo()	Sets a button's ID, style, and image number.
SetButtons()	Sets the IDs for the toolbar buttons.
SetButtonStyle()	Sets a button's style.
SetButtonText()	Sets a button's text label.
SetHeight()	Sets the toolbar's height.
SetSizes()	Sets the button sizes.

Normally, you don't need to call the toolbar's methods, but you can achieve some unusual results when you do, such as the extra high toolbar shown in Figure 7.10. (The buttons are the same size, but the toolbar window is bigger.) This toolbar resulted from a call to the toolbar object's SetHeight() member function. The CToolBar class's member functions enable you to perform this sort of toolbar trickery, but use them with great caution.

Figure 7.10
You can use a toolbar object's member functions to change how the toolbar looks and acts.

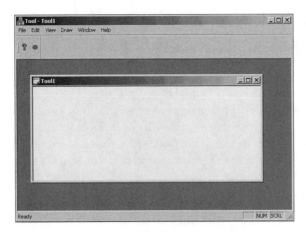

WORKING WITH STATUS BARS

Status bars are mostly benign objects that sit at the bottom of your application's window, doing whatever MFC instructs them to do. This consists of displaying command descriptions and the status of various keys on the keyboard, including the Caps Lock and Scroll Lock keys. In fact, status bars are so mundane from the programmer's point of view (at least they are in an MFC Application Wizard-generated application) that they aren't even represented by a resource that you can edit like a toolbar. When the MFC Application Wizard generates your application, there's not much left for you to do.

Or is there? A status bar, just like a toolbar, must reflect the interface needs of your specific application. For that reason, the `CStatusBar` class features a set of methods with which you can customize the status bar's appearance and operation. Table 7.2 lists the methods along with brief descriptions.

TABLE 7.2   METHODS OF THE `CStatusBar` CLASS

Method	Description
`CommandToIndex()`	Obtains an indicator's index, given its ID.
`Create()`	Creates the status bar.
`GetItemID()`	Obtains an indicator's ID, given its index.
`GetItemRect()`	Obtains an item's display rectangle, given its index.
`GetPaneInfo()`	Obtains information about an indicator.
`GetPaneStyle()`	Obtains an indicator's style.
`GetPaneText()`	Obtains an indicator's text.
`GetStatusBarCtrl()`	Obtains a reference to the `CStatusBarCtrl` object represented by the `CStatusBar` object.
`SetIndicators()`	Sets the indicators' IDs.

TABLE 7.2 CONTINUED

Method	Description
SetPaneInfo()	Sets the indicators' IDs, widths, and styles.
SetPaneStyle()	Sets an indicator's style.
SetPaneText()	Sets an indicator's text.

When you create a status bar as part of an application generated by the MFC Application Wizard, you see a window similar to that shown in Figure 7.11. (To make your own, create a project called Status and accept all the defaults, as you did for the Tool application.) The status bar has several parts, called panes, that display certain information about the status of the application and the system. These panes, which are marked in Figure 7.11, include indicators for the Caps Lock, Num Lock, and Scroll Lock keys, as well as a message area for showing status text and command descriptions. To see a command description, place your mouse pointer over a button on the toolbar (see Figure 7.12).

Figure 7.11
The default MFC status bar contains a number of informative panes.

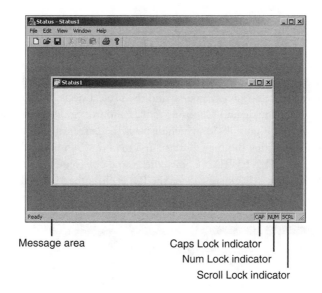

Message area

Caps Lock indicator

Num Lock indicator

Scroll Lock indicator

The most common way to customize a status bar is to add new panes. To add a pane to a status bar, complete these steps:

1. Create a command ID for the new pane.
2. Create a default string for the pane.
3. Add the pane's command ID to the status bar's indicators array.
4. Create a command-update handler for the pane.

The following sections cover these steps in detail.

CH
7

ToolTip

Figure 7.12
The message area is mainly used for command descriptions.

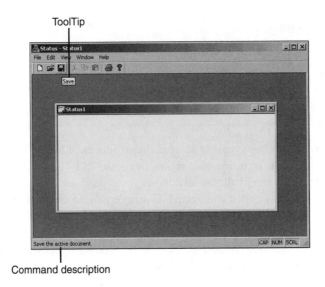

Command description

CREATING A NEW COMMAND ID

This step is easy, thanks to Visual C++'s symbol browser. To add the command ID, start by choosing Edit, Resource Symbols. (If the Resource Symbols option doesn't appear on the edit menu, switch to the Resource View, expand the project node, click on Status.rc, and then choose the Edit menu again.) Choosing Edit, Resource Symbols displays the Resource Symbols dialog box (see Figure 7.13), which displays the currently defined symbols for your application's resources. Click the New button, and the New Symbol dialog box appears. Type the new ID, **ID_MYNEWPANE**, into the Name box (see Figure 7.14). Usually, you can accept the Value that MFC suggests for the ID, such as the 101 in this example. The numerical value doesn't matter, as long as it's different from other IDs in use.

Figure 7.13
Use the Resource Symbols dialog box to add new command IDs to your application.

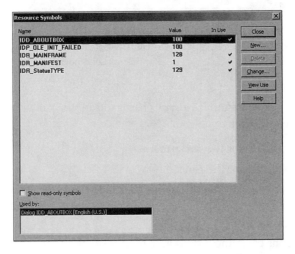

Figure 7.14
Type the new ID's name and value into the New Symbol dialog box.

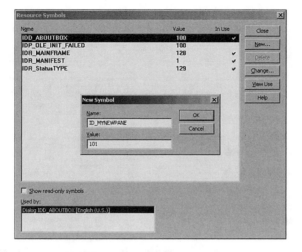

Click the OK and Close buttons to finalize your selections, and your new command ID is defined.

CREATING THE DEFAULT STRING

You have now defined a resource ID, but it isn't being used. To represent a status bar pane, the ID must have a default string defined for it. To define the string, first go to the Resource View window and double-click the String Table resource to open it in the String Table editor.

Now, click the very last line in the string table (it is blank) and a new ID appears. Click that ID and change it to ID_MYNEWPANE. In the Properties Window on the lower left, change the Caption to **Default String** (see Figure 9.15).

ADDING THE ID TO THE INDICATORS ARRAY

When MFC constructs your status bar, it uses an array of IDs to determine which panes to display and where to display them. This array of IDs is passed as an argument to the status bar's SetIndicators() member function, which is called in the CMainFrame class's OnCreate() function. You find this array of IDs shown near the top of the MainFrm.cpp file:

```
static UINT indicators[] =
{
    ID_SEPARATOR,           // status line indicator
    ID_INDICATOR_CAPS,
    ID_INDICATOR_NUM,
    ID_INDICATOR_SCRL,
};
```

CH
7

Figure 7.15
Define the new pane's default string in the string table.

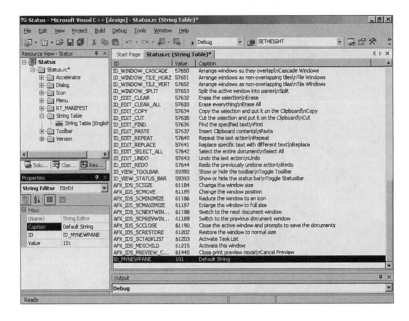

One way to reach these lines in the source code editor is to open the Class View window, expand `CMainFrame`, double-click `OnCreate()`, and scroll up one page. Alternatively, you could use Solution Explorer to open MainFrm.cpp and scroll down to this code.

To add your new pane to the array, type the pane's ID into the array at the position in which you want it to appear in the status bar, followed by a comma. (The first pane, ID_SEPARA-TOR, should always remain in the first position.) The indicator array with the new pane added should read as follows:

```
static UINT indicators[] =
{
    ID_SEPARATOR,            // status line indicator
    ID_MYNEWPANE,
    ID_INDICATOR_CAPS,
    ID_INDICATOR_NUM,
    ID_INDICATOR_SCRL,
};
```

CREATING THE PANE'S COMMAND-UPDATE HANDLER

MFC doesn't automatically enable new panes when it creates the status bar. Instead, you must create a command-update handler for the new pane and enable the pane yourself. (You first learned about command-update handlers in Chapter 3. Also, for most applications, the string displayed in the pane is calculated on the fly; the default string you defined in an earlier step is only a placeholder.

Normally, you use the Properties window to arrange for messages to be caught, but it doesn't help you catch status bar messages. You must add the handler entries to the message map yourself and then add the code for the handler. You add entries to the header file before the DECLARE_MESSAGE_MAP() macro, and to the map in the source file. Double-click CMainFrame in the Class View window to open the header file, and scroll to the bottom. Edit the message map so that it resembles Listing 7.2. When you write your own applications, you will use a variety of function names to update status bar panes, but the rest of the declaration will always be the same.

LISTING 7.2   MAINFRM.H—MESSAGE MAP

```
// Generated message map functions
protected:
    afx_msg int OnCreate(LPCREATESTRUCT lpCreateStruct);
    void OnUpdateMyNewPane(CCmdUI *pCmdUI);
    DECLARE_MESSAGE_MAP()
};
```

Next, you add the handler to the source message map to associate the command ID with the handler. Open any CMainFrame function and scroll upward until you find the message map, then edit it so that it looks like the code that follows:

```
BEGIN_MESSAGE_MAP(CMainFrame, CMDIFrameWnd)
    ON_WM_CREATE()
    ON_UPDATE_COMMAND_UI(ID_MYNEWPANE, OnUpdateMyNewPane)
END_MESSAGE_MAP()
```

You have now arranged for the CMainFrame member function OnUpdateMyNewPane() to be called whenever the status bar pane ID_MYNEWPANE needs to be updated.

Now you're ready to write the new command-update handler. In the handler, you enable the new pane and set its contents. Listing 7.3 shows the command-update handler for the new pane; add this code to mainfrm.cpp. As you can see, it uses a member variable called m_paneString. Update handlers should be very quick because the system calls them whenever it refreshes the display. The job of making sure that m_paneString holds the correct string should be tackled in a function that is called less often.

Command update handlers are discussed in Chapter 3 in the "Messages and Commands" section.

LISTING 7.3   CMainFrame::OnUpdateMyNewPane()

```
void CMainFrame::OnUpdateMyNewPane(CCmdUI *pCmdUI)
{
    pCmdUI->Enable();
    pCmdUI->SetText(m_paneString);
}
```

CH

7

Setting the Status Bar's Appearance

To add the last touch to your status bar demonstration application, you need a way
to set m_paneString.

The value you entered in the string table is only to assure Visual Studio that the resource ID
you created is in use. Right-click CMainFrame in the Class View window and choose Add,
Add Variable, to add m_paneString as a private member variable. The type should be
CString. To initialize it, double-click the CMainFrame constructor in Class View to edit it,
and change this line:

```
CMainFrame::CMainFrame(): m_paneString(_T(""))
```

To this:

```
CMainFrame::CMainFrame(): m_paneString(_T("Default String"))
```

To set up the status bar for the first time, add these lines to CMainFrame::OnCreate(), just
before the return statement:

```
CClientDC dc(this);
SIZE size = dc.GetTextExtent(m_paneString);
int index = m_wndStatusBar.CommandToIndex(ID_MYNEWPANE);
m_wndStatusBar.SetPaneInfo(index,ID_MYNEWPANE, SBPS_POPOUT, size.cx);
```

These lines set the text string and the size of the pane. You set the size of the pane with a
call to SetPaneInfo(), which needs the index of the pane and the new size.
CommandToIndex() obtains the index of the pane, and GetTextExtent() obtains the size. As a
nice touch, the call to SetPaneInfo() uses the SBPS_POPOUT style to create a pane that
seems to stick out from the status bar, rather than be indented.

The user changes the string by making a menu selection. Open the IDR_StatusTYPE menu
in the resource editor and add a top-level menu called &Tools between the View and
Window menu, and a menu item under it called &Change String. (Working with menus is
discussed for the first time in Chapter 6.) Let Visual Studio assign it the resource ID
ID_TOOLS_CHANGESTRING.

Use the Properties window to add an event handler for the Change String menu item in the
CMainFrame class.

Add a new dialog box resource into the application and change the ID to IDD_PANEDIA-
LOG. The caption should be Change Pane String. Add a single edit box, stretched the full
width of the dialog box, and leave the ID as IDC_EDIT1. Add a static text item just above
the edit box with the caption New String:.

Create a new class for the dialog box by right-clicking on some empty space within the dialog box and choosing Add Class. Set the class name to CPaneDlg, the base class to CDialog,
the dialog ID to IDD_PANEDIALOG, and then click Finish.

Add a variable to the CPaneDlg class called m_paneString. Keep the access set to Public,
check the Control Variable check box, set the Control ID to IDC_EDIT1, select the Value
drop-down box, and finally add a meaningful comment to make your code more clear.

Adding dialog boxes to applications and associating them with classes are discussed in more depth in several earlier chapters, including Chapters 3 and 6.

Switch to the Class View window, expand CMainFrame, and double-click OnToolsChangestring() to edit it so that it resembles the following:

```
void CMainFrame::OnToolsChangestring(void)

{
    CPaneDlg dialog(this);
    dialog.m_paneString = m_paneString;

    int result = dialog.DoModal();

    if (result == IDOK)
    {
        m_paneString = dialog.m_paneString;
        CClientDC dc(this);
        SIZE size = dc.GetTextExtent(m_paneString);
        int index = m_wndStatusBar.CommandToIndex(ID_MYNEWPANE);
        m_wndStatusBar.SetPaneInfo(index,
            ID_MYNEWPANE, SBPS_POPOUT, size.cx);
    }
}
```

This code displays the dialog box, and, if the user exits the dialog box by clicking OK, it changes the text string and resets the size of the pane. The code is very similar to the lines you added to OnCreate(). Scroll up to the top of MainFrm.cpp and add this line:

```
#include "panedlg.h"
```

This tells the compiler what the CPaneDlg class is. Build and run the Status application, and you should see the window shown in Figure 7.16. As you can see, the status bar contains an extra panel displaying the text "Default String." Notice the popped-out appearance of this pane. If you choose Tools, Change String, a dialog box appears into which you can type a new string for the panel. When you exit the dialog box via the OK button, the text appears in the new panel, and the panel resizes itself to accommodate the new string (see Figure 7.17).

Figure 7.16
The Status Bar Demo application shows how to add and manage a status bar pane.

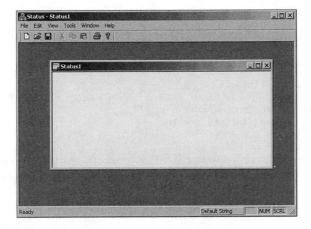

CH

7

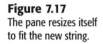

Figure 7.17
The pane resizes itself to fit the new string.

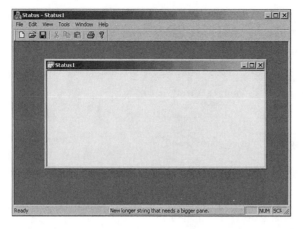

WORKING WITH REBARS

Rebars are toolbars that contain controls other than toolbar buttons. It was possible to add other controls to normal toolbars in the past, but difficult. With rebars, it's simple.

Start by using the MFC Application Wizard to make a project called ReBar and accept all the defaults on each tab. When the project is generated, double-click `CMainFrame` in the Class View window to edit the header file. This frame holds the open documents and is where a classic toolbar goes. The rebar for this sample goes here, too. Add the rebar as a public member variable:

```
CReBar m_rebar;
```

In this sample application, you add a check box to the bar, but you can add any kind of control at all. A check box, a radio button, and a command button (like the OK or Cancel button on a dialog box) are all represented by the `CButton` class, with slightly different styles. Add the check box to the header file right after the rebar, like this:

```
CButton m_check;
```

You saw in the preceding section that an application's toolbar is created and initialized in the `OnCreate()` function of the mainframe class. The same is true for rebars. Expand `CMainFrame` in the Class View window, and double-click `OnCreate()` to edit it. Add these lines just before the final return statement:

```
if (!m_rebar.Create(this) )
{
    TRACE0("Failed to create rebar\n");
    return -1;      // fail to create
}
```

The check box control needs a resource ID. When you create a control with the dialog editor, the name you give the control is automatically associated with a number. This control will be created in code, so you have to specify the resource ID yourself, as you did for the new pane in the status bar earlier in this chapter. Open the Resource View window, select

ReBar.rc, then choose Edit, Resource Symbols.... Choose New, then type the name IDC_CHECK and accept the number suggested. This adds a line to resource.h, defining IDC_CHECK, and assures you that other controls will not reuse this resource ID.

Back in CMainFrame::OnCreate(), add these lines to create the check box (note the styles carefully):

```
if (!m_check.Create("Check Here",
      WS_CHILD|WS_VISIBLE|BS_AUTOCHECKBOX,
      CRect(0,0,20,20), this, IDC_CHECK)  )
{
   TRACE0("Failed to create checkbox\n");
   return -1;        // fail to create
}
```

Finally, add these lines to add a band containing the check box control to the rebar:

```
m_rebar.AddBar(&m_check, "On The Bar", NULL,
               RBBS_BREAK | RBBS_GRIPPERALWAYS);
```

AddBar() takes four parameters: a pointer to the control that will be added, some text to put next to it, a pointer to a bitmap that is to be used for the background image on the rebar, and a rebar style, made by combining any of these style flags:

- RBBS_BREAK puts the band on a new line, even if there's room for it at the end of an existing line.
- RBBS_CHILDEDGE puts the band against a child window of the frame.
- RBBS_FIXEDBMP prevents the bitmap from being moved if the user resizes the band.
- RBBS_FIXEDSIZE prevents the user from resizing the band.
- RBBS_GRIPPERALWAYS guarantees sizing wrinkles are present.
- RBBS_HIDDEN hides the band.
- RBBS_NOGRIPPER suppresses sizing wrinkles.
- RBBS_NOVERT hides the band when the rebar is vertical.
- RBBS_VARIABLEHEIGHT enables the rebar to resize the band.

At this point, you can build the project and run it. You should see your rebar, as in Figure 7.18. The checkbox works in that you can select and deselect it, but nothing happens when you do.

To react when the user clicks the button, you need to catch the message and do something based on the message. The simplest thing to do is change what is drawn in the view's OnDraw(), which means that the view should catch the message. Double-click CReBarView in the Class View window to edit the header file, and scroll to the message map. Just before the line DECLARE_MESSAGE_MAP, add this line:

```
afx_msg void OnClick();
```

CH

7

Figure 7.18
The rebar contains a check box.

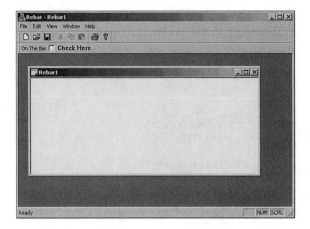

Expand CReBarView in the Class View window and double-click OnDraw(), which you will edit in a moment. After it, add this function:

```
void CReBarView::OnClick()
{
    Invalidate();
}
```

This causes the view to redraw whenever the user selects or deselects the checkbox. Scroll up in the file until you find the message map, and add (after the three entries related to printing) this line:

```
ON_BN_CLICKED(IDC_CHECK, OnClick)
```

At the top of the file, after the other include statements, add this one:

```
#include "mainFrm.h"
```

Now add these lines to OnDraw() in place of the TODO comment:

```
CString message;
if ( ((CMainFrame*)(AfxGetApp()->m_pMainWnd))->m_check.GetCheck())
    message = "The box is checked.";
else
    message = "The box is not checked.";
pDC->TextOut(20,20,message);
```

Don't forget to uncomment the pDC parameter to OnDraw(). The *if* statement obtains a pointer to the main window, casts it to a CMainFrame*, and asks the checkbox whether it is selected. Then the message is set appropriately.

Build the project and run it. As you select and deselect the checkbox, you should see the message change, as in Figure 7.19.

Figure 7.19
Clicking the check
box changes the view.

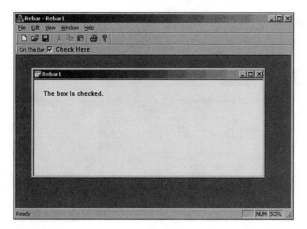

COMMON CONTROLS

As a Windows user, you're accustomed to seeing controls such as buttons, list boxes, menus, and edit boxes. As Windows developed, however, Microsoft noticed that developers routinely create other types of controls in their programs: toolbars, status bars, progress bars, tree views, and others. To make life easier for Windows programmers, Microsoft included these popular controls as part of the operating environment of Windows 95 (as well as later versions of Windows NT, Windows 98, Windows 2000, and Windows XP). Now Windows programmers no longer need to create their own versions of these controls from scratch. The following sections introduce you to many of the 32-bit Windows common controls.

This sample program is called Common. It demonstrates nine of the Windows common controls: the progress bar, slider, up-down, list view, tree view, rich edit, IP address, date picker, and month calendar controls, all of which are shown in Figure 7.20. In the following sections, you learn the basics of creating and using these controls in your own applications.

To make Common, create a new project with the MFC Application Wizard and name it Common. Choose a single-document interface (SDI) application in the Application Type tab. In the Generated Classes tab, choose CScrollView as the base class for your application's view class, CCommonView. This ensures that users can see all the controls in the view, even if they have to scroll to do so. Click Finish to complete the process.

The controls themselves are declared as data members of the view class. Double-click CCommonView in the Class View window to edit the header file and add the lines in Listing 7.4 in the Attributes section. As you can see, the progress bar is an object of the CProgressCtrl class. It's discussed in the next section, and the other controls are discussed in later sections of this chapter.

Ch

7

Figure 7.20
The Common sample application demonstrates nine 32-bit Windows common controls.

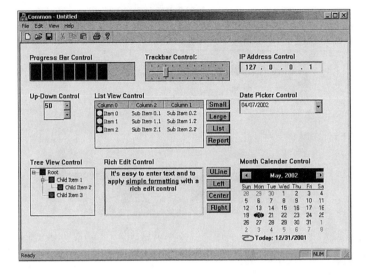

LISTING 7.4 COMMONVIEW.H—DECLARING THE CONTROLS

```
protected:
    //Progress Bar
    CProgressCtrl m_progressBar;

    //Trackbar or Slider
    CSliderCtrl m_trackbar;
    BOOL m_timer;

    // Up-Down or Spinner
    CSpinButtonCtrl m_upDown;
    CEdit m_buddyEdit;

    // List View
    CListCtrl m_listView;
    CImageList m_smallImageList;
    CImageList m_largeImageList;
    CButton m_smallButton;
    CButton m_largeButton;
    CButton m_listButton;
    CButton m_reportButton;

    // Tree View
    CTreeCtrl m_treeView;
    CImageList m_treeImageList;

    // Rich Edit
    CRichEditCtrl m_richEdit;
    CButton m_boldButton;
    CButton m_leftButton;
    CButton m_centerButton;
    CButton m_rightButton;
    // IP Address
    CIPAddressCtrl m_ipaddress;
```

LISTING 7.4   CONTINUED

```
    // Date Picker
    CDateTimeCtrl m_date;
    // Month Calendar
CMonthCalCtrl m_month;
```

Expand the CCommonView class. Double-click CCommonView::OnDraw() in Class View and replace the TODO comment with these lines:

```
pDC->TextOut(20, 22, "Progress Bar Control");
pDC->TextOut(270, 22, "Trackbar Control:");
pDC->TextOut(20, 102, "Up-Down Control");
pDC->TextOut(160, 102, "List View Control");
pDC->TextOut(20, 240, "Tree View Control");
pDC->TextOut(180, 240, "Rich Edit Control");
pDC->TextOut(470, 22, "IP Address Control");
pDC->TextOut(470, 102, "Date Picker Control");
pDC->TextOut(470, 240, "Month Calendar Control");
```

(As always when editing OnDraw() for the first time, remember to uncomment the pDC parameter.) These lines label the controls that you will add to CCommonView in this chapter.

THE PROGRESS BAR CONTROL

The common control that's probably easiest to use is the progress bar, which is nothing more than a rectangle that slowly fills in with colored blocks. The more colored blocks that are filled in, the closer the task is to being complete. When the progress bar is completely filled in, the task associated with the progress bar is also complete. You might use a progress bar to show the status of a sorting operation or to give the user visual feedback about a large file that's being loaded.

CREATING THE PROGRESS BAR

Before you can use a progress bar, you must create it. Often in an MFC program, the controls are created as part of a dialog box. However, Common displays its controls in the application's main window, which is the view of this single-document interface (SDI) application. Documents and views are introduced in Chapter 4. All the controls are created in the view class OnCreate() function, which responds to the WM_CREATE Windows message. To set up this message handler function, right-click CCommonView in the Class View window and choose Properties. In the Properties window, click the Messages button, and then scroll down and click the box labeled WM_CREATE. When you click the box a drop-down box appears alongside. From the drop-down box, choose <Add> OnCreate. Add this line in place of the TODO comment:

```
CreateProgressBar();
```

That function doesn't exist yet. To create it, right-click CCommonView in Class View again and this time choose Add, Add Function. Enter void for the Return type and enter CreateProgressBar for the Function name. Leave the access as Public. Click Finish to add the function; then edit it to resemble the following:

CH

7

```
void CCommonView::CreateProgressBar(void)
{
    m_progressBar.Create(WS_CHILD | WS_VISIBLE | WS_BORDER,
        CRect(20, 40, 250, 80), this, IDC_PROGRESSBAR);

    m_progressBar.SetRange(1, 100);
    m_progressBar.SetStep(10);
    m_progressBar.SetPos(50);
    m_timer = FALSE;

}
```

CreateProgressBar() first creates the progress bar control by calling the control's Create() function. This function's four arguments are the control's style flags, the control's size (as a CRect object), a pointer to the control's parent window, and the control's ID. The resource ID, IDC_PROGRESSBAR, has to be added by hand. To add resource symbols to your own applications, select Common.rc from the Resource View window, choose Edit, Resource Symbols, and then click the New button. Type in the resource ID Name **IDC_PROGRESSBAR**, and accept the default value Visual Studio provides.

The style constants are the same constants that you use for creating any type of window. (A control is nothing more than a special kind of window, after all.) In this case, you need at least the following:

- WS_CHILD. Indicates that the control is a child window.
- WS_VISIBLE. Ensures that the user can see the control.

The WS_BORDER is a nice addition because it adds a dark border around the control, setting it off from the rest of the window.

INITIALIZING THE PROGRESS BAR

To initialize the control, CCommonView::CreateProgressBar() calls SetRange(), SetStep(), and SetPos(). Because the range and the step rate are related, a control with a range of 1–10 and a step rate of 1 works almost identically to a control with a range of 1–100 and a step rate of 10.

When this sample application starts, the progress bar is already half filled with colored blocks. That's because CreateProgressBar() calls SetPos() with the value of 50, which is the midpoint of the control's range. (This is purely for aesthetic reasons. Usually a progress bar begins its life empty.)

MANIPULATING THE PROGRESS BAR

Normally you update a progress bar as a long task moves toward completion. In this sample, you will fake it by using a timer. When the user clicks in the background of the view, start a timer that generates WM_TIMER messages periodically. Catch these messages and advance the progress bar by following these steps:

1. Open the Class View window, then right-click the CCommonView class and choose Properties.

2. From the Properties window, click the Messages button.

3. Scroll down the list and select the WM_LBUTTONDOWN message, then choose <Add> OnLButtonDown from the drop-down box that appears. Expand the CCommonView class in the Class View window and double-click OnLButtonDown() to edit the code.

4. Edit OnLButtonDown() so that it looks like this:

```
void CCommonView::OnLButtonDown(UINT nFlags, CPoint point)
{
    if (m_timer)
    {
        KillTimer(1);
        m_timer = FALSE;
    }
    else
    {
        SetTimer(1, 500, NULL);
        m_timer = TRUE;
    }

    CScrollView::OnLButtonDown(nFlags, point);
}
```

This code enables users to turn the timer on or off with a click. The parameter of 500 in the SetTimer call is the number of milliseconds between WM_TIMER messages: This timer sends a message every half second.

5. In case a timer is still going when the view closes, you should override OnDestroy() to kill the timer. Right-click CCommonView in the Class View window yet again and choose Properties. Click the Messages button, then select WM_DESTROY and choose <Add> OnDestroy. Replace the TODO comment in the function with this line:

```
KillTimer(1);
```

6. Now, catch the timer messages. Open the Properties window for the CCommonView class and, as before, add a message handler function, this time for the WM_TIMER message. Replace the TODO comment in the function with this line:

```
m_progressBar.StepIt();
```

The StepIt() function increments the progress bar control's value by the step rate, causing new blocks to be displayed in the control as the control's value setting counts upward. When the control reaches its maximum, it automatically starts over.

Note

Notice that no CProgressCtrl member functions control the size or number of blocks that fit into the control. These attributes are indirectly controlled by the size of the control.

Сн

7

Build Common and execute it to see the progress bar in action. Be sure to try stopping the timer as well as starting it.

THE SLIDER CONTROL

Many times in a program you might need the user to enter a value within a specific range. For this sort of task, you can use MFC's CSliderCtrl class to create a slider (also called trackbar) control. For example, suppose you need the user to enter a percentage. In this case, you want the user to enter values only in the range of 0–100. Other values would be invalid and could cause problems in your program.

By using the slider control, you can force the user to enter a value in the specified range. Although the user can accidentally enter a wrong value (a value that doesn't accomplish what the user wants to do), there is no way to enter an invalid value (one that brings your program crashing down like a stone wall in an earthquake).

For a percentage, you create a slider control with a minimum value of 0 and a maximum value of 100. Moreover, to make the control easier to position, you might want to place tick marks at each setting that's a multiple of 10, providing 11 tick marks in all (including the one at 0). Common creates exactly this type of slider.

To use a slider, the user clicks the slider's slot. This moves the slider forward or backward, and often the selected value appears near the control. When a slider has the focus, the user can also control it with the Up and Down arrow keys and the Page Up and Page Down keys.

CREATING THE TRACKBAR

You are going to need a resource symbol for the trackbar control, so just as you did for the progress bar, open the Resource View window, select Common.rc, choose Edit, Resource Symbols, and click New. Enter **IDC_TRACKBAR** for the resource ID Name and accept the suggested value. In CCommonView::OnCreate(), add a call to CreateTrackBar(). Then add the new member function as you added CreateProgressBar() and type in the following code:

```
void CCommonView::CreateTrackBar(void)
{
    m_trackbar.Create(WS_CHILD | WS_VISIBLE | WS_BORDER |
        TBS_AUTOTICKS | TBS_BOTH | TBS_HORZ,
        CRect(270, 40, 450, 80), this, IDC_TRACKBAR);
    m_trackbar.SetRange(0, 100, TRUE);
    m_trackbar.SetTicFreq(10);
    m_trackbar.SetLineSize(1);
    m_trackbar.SetPageSize(10);
}
```

As with the progress bar, the first step is to create the slider control by calling its Create() member function. This function's four arguments are the control's style flags, the control's size (as a CRect object), a pointer to the control's parent window, and the control's ID. The style constants include the same constants that you would use for creating any type of window, with the addition of special styles used with sliders. Table 7.3 lists these special styles.

TABLE 7.3   SLIDER STYLES

Style	Description
TBS_AUTOTICKS	Enables the slider to automatically draw its tick marks.
TBS_BOTH	Draws tick marks on both sides of the slider.
TBS_BOTTOM	Draws tick marks on the bottom of a horizontal slider.
TBS_ENABLESELRANGE	Enables a slider to display a subrange of values.
TBS_HORZ	Draws the slider horizontally.
TBS_LEFT	Draws tick marks on the left side of a vertical slider.
TBS_NOTICKS	Draws a slider with no tick marks.
TBS_RIGHT	Draws tick marks on the right side of a vertical slider.
TBS_TOP	Draws tick marks on the top of a horizontal slider.
TBS_VERT	Draws a vertical slider.

INITIALIZING THE TRACKBAR

Usually, when you create a slider control, you want to set the control's range and tick frequency. If the user is going to use the control from the keyboard, you also need to set the control's line and page size—the amount that it moves in response to arrow keys or to page up and down keys. In Common, the program initializes the trackbar with calls to SetRange(), SetTicFreq(), SetLineSize(), and SetPageSize(), as you saw earlier. The call to SetRange() sets the trackbar's minimum and maximum values to 0 and 100. The arguments are the minimum value, the maximum value, and a Boolean value indicating whether the slider should redraw itself after setting the range. Notice that the tick frequency and page size are then set to be the same. This isn't absolutely required, but it's a very good idea. Most people assume that the tick marks indicate the size of a page, and you will confuse your users if the tick marks are more or less than a page apart.

A number of other functions can change the size of your slider, the size of the thumb, the current selection, and more. You can find all the details in the online documentation.

MANIPULATING THE SLIDER

A slider is really just a special scrollbar control. When the user moves the slider, the control generates WM_HSCROLL messages, which you will arrange for a function to catch. Open the Properties window for the CCommonView class, click the Messages button, then add a message handler function for the WM_HSCROLL message. Type in the following code:

```
void CCommonView::OnHScroll(UINT nSBCode, UINT nPos, CScrollBar* pScrollBar)
{
    CSliderCtrl* slider = (CSliderCtrl*)pScrollBar;
    int position = slider->GetPos();
    CString s;
    s.Format("%d   ", position);
    CClientDC clientDC(this);
```

```
            clientDC.TextOut(390, 22, s);
            CScrollView::OnHScroll(nSBCode, nPos, pScrollBar);
}
```

Looking at this code, you see that the control itself doesn't display the current position as a number nearby; it's the OnHScroll() function that displays the number. Here's how it works:

1. The OnHScroll() function's fourth parameter is a pointer to the scroll object that generated the WM_HSCROLL message.

2. The function first casts this pointer to a CSliderCtrl pointer; then it gets the current position of the trackbar's slider by calling the CSliderCtrl member function GetPos().

3. After the program has the slider's position, it converts the integer to a string and displays that string in the window with TextOut().

To learn how to make text appear onscreen, refer to Chapter 4 Before moving on to the next control, build Common and test it. Click around on the slider and watch the number change.

Tip

If you have Windows set to Large Fonts (perhaps because you have a high screen resolution), the current slider value might not be displayed in quite the right place because the string "Trackbar Control" takes up more space on the screen with large fonts. If this happens, simply change the TextOut call to write the current slider value a little farther to the right.

THE UP-DOWN CONTROL

The trackbar control isn't the only way you can get a value in a predetermined range from the user. If you don't need the trackbar for visual feedback, you can use an up-down control, which is little more than a couple of arrows that the user clicks to increase or decrease the control's setting. Typically, an edit control next to the up-down control, called a *buddy edit control* or just a *buddy control*, displays the value to the user.

In the Common application, you can change the setting of the up-down control by clicking either of its arrows. When you do, the value in the attached edit box changes, indicating the up-down control's current setting. After the control has the focus, you can also change its value by pressing your keyboard's Up and Down arrow keys.

CREATING THE UP-DOWN CONTROL

Add another function call to CCommonView::OnCreate(), this time calling CreateUpDownCtrl(). Add the member function and the code in Listing 7.5. Also add resource symbols for IDC_BUDDYEDIT and IDC_UPDOWN.

LISTING 7.5   COMMONVIEW.CPP—CCommonView::CreateUpDownCtrl()

```
void CCommonView::CreateUpDownCtrl()(void)
{
    m_buddyEdit.Create(WS_CHILD | WS_VISIBLE | WS_BORDER,
        CRect(50, 120, 110, 160), this, IDC_BUDDYEDIT);
    m_upDown.Create(WS_CHILD | WS_VISIBLE | WS_BORDER |
        UDS_ALIGNRIGHT | UDS_SETBUDDYINT | UDS_ARROWKEYS,
        CRect(0, 0, 0, 0), this, IDC_UPDOWN);
    m_upDown.SetBuddy(&m_buddyEdit);
    m_upDown.SetRange(1, 100);
    m_upDown.SetPos(50);
}
```

The program creates the up-down control by first creating the associated buddy control to which the up-down control communicates its current value. In most cases, including this one, the buddy control is an edit box, created by calling the CEdit class's Create() member function. This function's four arguments are the control's style flags, the control's size, a pointer to the control's parent window, and the control's ID. If you recall the control declarations, m_buddyEdit is an object of the CEdit class.

Now that the program has created the buddy control, it can create the up-down control in much the same way, by calling the object's Create() member function. As you can probably guess by now, this function's four arguments are the control's style flags, the control's size, a pointer to the control's parent window, and the control's ID. As with most controls, the style constants include the same constants that you use for creating any type of window. The CSpinButtonCtrl class, of which m_upDown is an object, however, defines special styles to be used with up-down controls. Table 7.4 lists these special styles.

TABLE 7.4   UP-DOWN CONTROL STYLES

Styles	Description
UDS_ALIGNLEFT	Places the up-down control on the left edge of the buddy control.
UDS_ALIGNRIGHT	Places the up-down control on the right edge of the buddy control.
UDS_ARROWKEYS	Enables the user to change the control's values by using the keyboard's Up and Down arrow keys.
UDS_AUTOBUDDY	Makes the preceding window the buddy control.
UDS_HORZ	Creates a horizontal up-down control.
UDS_NOTHOUSANDS	Eliminates separators between each set of three digits.
UDS_SETBUDDYINT	Displays the control's value in the buddy control.
UDS_WRAP	Causes the control's value to wrap around to its minimum when the maximum is reached, and vice versa.

This sample application establishes the up-down control with calls to SetBuddy(), SetRange(), and SetPos(). Thanks to the UDS_SETBUDDYINT flag passed to Create()

CH

7

and the call to the control's `SetBuddy()` member function, Common doesn't need to do anything else for the control's value to appear on the screen. The control automatically handles its buddy. Try building and testing now.

You might want up-down controls that move faster or slower than in this sample or that use hex numbers rather than base-10 numbers. Look at the member functions of this control in the online documentation, and you can see how to do that.

THE IMAGE LIST CONTROL

Often you need to use images that are related in some way. For example, your application might have a toolbar with many command buttons, each of which uses a bitmap for its icon. In a case like this, it would be great to have some sort of program object that could not only hold the bitmaps but also organize them so that they can be accessed easily. That's exactly what an image list control does for you—it stores a list of related images. You can use the images any way that you see fit in your program. Several common controls rely on image lists. These controls include the following:

- List view controls
- Tree view controls
- Property pages
- Toolbars

You will undoubtedly come up with many other uses for image lists. You might, for example, have an animation sequence that you'd like to display in a window. An image list is the perfect storage place for the frames that make up an animation, because you can easily access any frame just by using an index.

If the word "index" makes you think of arrays, you're beginning to understand how an image list stores images. An image list is very similar to an array that holds pictures rather than integers or floating-point numbers. Just as with an array, you initialize each "element" of an image list and thereafter can access any part of the "array" by using an index.

You don't, however, see an image list control in your running application in the same way that you can see a status bar or a progress bar control. An image list (again, similar to an array) is only a storage structure for pictures. You can display the images stored in an image list, but you can't display the image list itself. Figure 7.21 shows how an image list is organized.

Figure 7.21
An image list is much like an array of pictures.

Picture 1   Picture 2   Picture 3   Picture 4   Picture 5

CREATING THE IMAGE LIST

In the Common application, image lists are used with the list view and tree view controls, so the image lists for the controls are created in the `CreateListView()` and `CreateTreeView()` local member functions called from `CCommonView::OnCreate()`. Just as with the other controls, add calls to these functions to `OnCreate()` and then add the functions to the class. You will see the full code for those functions shortly, but because they are long, this section presents only the parts that are relevant to the image list.

A list view uses two image lists: one for small images and the other for large ones. The member variables for these lists have already been added to the class, so start coding `CreateListView()` with a call to each list's `Create()` member function, like this:

```
m_smallImageList.Create(16, 16, FALSE, 1, 0);
m_largeImageList.Create(32, 32, FALSE, 1, 0);
```

The `Create()` function's five arguments are

- The width of the pictures in the control.
- The height of the pictures.
- A Boolean value indicating whether the images contain a mask.
- The number of images initially in the list.
- The number of images by which the list can dynamically grow.

This last value is 0 to indicate that the list is not to grow during runtime. The `Create()` function is overloaded in the `CImageList` class so you can create image lists in various ways. You can find the other versions of `Create()` in your online documentation.

INITIALIZING THE IMAGE LIST

After you create an image list, you can add images to it. After all, an empty image list isn't of much use. The easiest way to add the images is to include the images as part of your application's resource file and load them from there. Add these four lines to `CreateListView()` to fill each list with images:

```
HICON hIcon = ::LoadIcon (AfxGetResourceHandle(),
    MAKEINTRESOURCE(IDI_ICON1));
m_smallImageList.Add(hIcon);
hIcon = ::LoadIcon (AfxGetResourceHandle(),
    MAKEINTRESOURCE(IDI_ICON2));
m_largeImageList.Add(hIcon);
```

Here the program first gets a handle to the icon. Then it adds the icon to the image list by calling the image list's `Add()` member function. (In this case, the list includes only one icon. In other applications, you might have a list of large icons for folders, text files, and so on, as well as another list of small icons for the same purposes.) To create the first icon, choose Project, Add Resource, and double-click Icon. Then edit the new blank icon in the Resource Editor. (It is automatically called IDI_ICON1.) From the Image menu, choose New Image Type, and then choose 16×16,256 colors in the dialog box that appears; click OK. You can

CH
7

spend a long time making a beautiful icon or, for the sake of this demonstration, just quickly fill in the whole grid with black and then put a white circle on it with the Ellipse tool. Add another icon, IDI_ICON2, and leave it as 32×32. Draw the same symbol on this icon.

You can use many member functions to manipulate an object of the CImageList class, adjusting colors, removing images, and much more. The online documentation provides more details on these member functions.

You can write the first few lines of CreateTreeView() now. It uses one image list that starts with three images. Here's the code to add:

```
m_treeImageList.Create(13, 13, FALSE, 3, 0);
HICON hIcon = ::LoadIcon(AfxGetResourceHandle(),
    MAKEINTRESOURCE(IDI_ICON3));
m_treeImageList.Add(hIcon);
hIcon = ::LoadIcon(AfxGetResourceHandle(),
    MAKEINTRESOURCE(IDI_ICON4));
m_treeImageList.Add(hIcon);
hIcon = ::LoadIcon(AfxGetResourceHandle(),
    MAKEINTRESOURCE(IDI_ICON5));
m_treeImageList.Add(hIcon);
```

Create IDI_ICON3, IDI_ICON4, and IDI_ICON5 the same way you did the first two icons. All three are 32×32. Draw circles as before, but use a different color for each icon so you can tell them apart. If you leave the background the same murky green you started with, rather than fill it with black, the circles appear on a transparent background—a nice effect.

THE LIST VIEW CONTROL

A list view control simplifies the job of building an application that works with lists of objects and organizes those objects in such a way that the program's user can easily determine each object's attributes. For example, consider a group of files on a disk. Each file is a separate object associated with a number of attributes, including the file's name, size, and the most recent modification date. When you explore a folder, you see files either as icons in a window or as a table of entries, each entry showing the attributes associated with the files. You have full control over the way that the file objects are displayed, including which attributes are shown and which are unlisted. The common controls include something called a *list view control*, so you can organize lists in exactly the same way. If you'd like to see an example of a full-fledged list view control, open the Windows Explorer (see Figure 7.22). The right side of the window shows how the list view control can organize objects in a window. (The left side of the window contains a tree view control, which you will learn about later in this chapter in the section titled "The Tree View Control.") In the figure, the list view is currently set to the report view, in which each object in the list receives its own line, showing not only the object's name but also the attributes associated with that object.

The user can change the way objects are organized in a list view control. Figure 7.23, for example, shows the list view portion of the Explorer set to the large-icon setting, and Figure 7.24 shows the small-icon setting, which enables the user to see more objects (in this case, files) in the window. With a list view control, the user can edit the names of objects in the list and in the report view users can also sort objects, based on data displayed in a particular column.

Figure 7.22
Windows Explorer uses a list view control to organize file information.

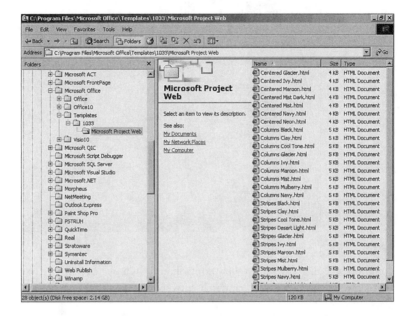

Figure 7.23
Here's Explorer's list view control set to large icons.

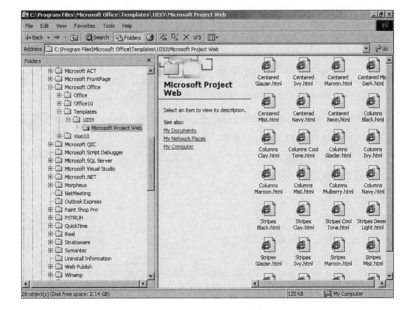

Figure 7.24
Here's Explorer's list view control set to small icons.

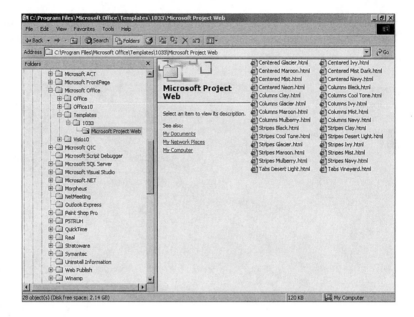

Common will also sport a list view control, although not as fancy as Explorer's. You will add a list view and some buttons to switch between the small-icon, large-icon, list, and report views.

CREATING THE LIST VIEW

How does all this happen? Well, it does require more work than the progress bar, trackbar, or up-down controls (it could hardly take less). You will write the rest of CreateListView(), which performs the following steps:

1. Creates and fills the image list controls
2. Creates the list view control itself
3. Associates the image lists with the list view
4. Creates the columns
5. Sets up the columns
6. Creates the items
7. Sets up the items
8. Creates the buttons

After creating the image lists, CreateListView() goes on to create the list view control by calling the class's Create() member function, as usual. Add these lines to CreateListView():

```
// Create the List View control.
    m_listView.Create(WS_VISIBLE | WS_CHILD | WS_BORDER |
        LVS_REPORT | LVS_NOSORTHEADER | LVS_EDITLABELS,
        CRect(160, 120, 394, 220), this, IDC_LISTVIEW);
```

The CListCtrl class, of which m_listView is an object, defines special styles to be used with list view controls. Table 7.5 lists these special styles and their descriptions.

TABLE 7.5   LIST VIEW STYLES

Style	Description
LVS_ALIGNLEFT	Left-aligns items in the large-icon and small-icon views.
LVS_ALIGNTOP	Top-aligns items in the large-icon and small-icon views.
LVS_AUTOARRANGE	Automatically arranges items in the large-icon and small-icon views.
LVS_EDITLABELS	Enables the user to edit item labels.
LVS_ICON	Sets the control to the large-icon view.
LVS_LIST	Sets the control to the list view.
LVS_NOCOLUMNHEADER	Shows no column headers in report view.
LVS_NOITEMDATA	Stores only the state of each item.
LVS_NOLABELWRAP	Disallows multiple-line item labels.
LVS_NOSCROLL	Turns off scrolling.
LVS_NOSORTHEADER	Turns off the button appearance of column headers.
LVS_OWNERDRAWFIXED	Enables owner-drawn items in report view.
LVS_REPORT	Sets the control to the report view.
LVS_SHAREIMAGELISTS	Prevents the control from destroying its image lists when the control no longer needs them.
LVS_SINGLESEL	Disallows multiple selection of items.
LVS_SMALLICON	Sets the control to the small-icon view.
LVS_SORTASCENDING	Sorts items in ascending order.
LVS_SORTDESCENDING	Sorts items in descending order.

The third task in CreateListView() is to associate the control with its image lists with two calls to SetImageList(). Add these lines to CreateListView():

```
m_listView.SetImageList(&m_smallImageList, LVSIL_SMALL);
m_listView.SetImageList(&m_largeImageList, LVSIL_NORMAL);
```

This function takes two parameters: a pointer to the image list and a flag indicating how the list is to be used. Three constants are defined for this flag: LVSIL_SMALL (which indicates that the list contains small icons), LVSIL_NORMAL (large icons), and LVSIL_STATE (state images). The SetImageList() function returns a pointer to the previously set image list, if any.

CREATING THE LIST VIEW'S COLUMNS

The fourth task is to create the columns for the control's report view. You need one main column for the item itself and one column for each sub-item associated with an item. For

CH

7

example, in Explorer's list view, the main column holds file and folder names. Each additional column holds the sub-items for each item, such as the file's size, type, and modification date. To create a column, you must first declare a LV_COLUMN structure. You use this structure to pass information to and from the system. After you add the column to the control with InsertColumn(), you can use the structure to create and insert another column. Listing 7.6 shows the LV_COLUMN structure.

LISTING 7.6   THE LV_COLUMN STRUCTURE, DEFINED BY MFC

```
typedef struct _LV_COLUMN
{
    UINT mask;          // Flags indicating valid fields
    int fmt;            // Column alignment
    int cx;             // Column width
    LPSTR pszText;      // Address of string buffer
    int cchTextMax;     // Size of the buffer
    int iSubItem;       // Subitem index for this column
} LV_COLUMN;
```

The mask member of the structure tells the system which members of the structure to use and which to ignore. The flags you can use are

- LVCF_FMT. fmt is valid.

- LVCF_SUBITEM. iSubItem is valid.

- LVCF_TEXT. pszText is valid.

- LVCF_WIDTH. cx is valid.

The fmt member denotes the column's alignment and can be LVCFMT_CENTER, LVCFMT_LEFT, or LVCFMT_RIGHT. The alignment determines how the column's label and items are positioned in the column.

Note

The first column, which contains the main items, is always aligned to the left. The other columns in the report view can be aligned however you like.

The cx field specifies the width of each column, whereas pszText is the address of a string buffer. When you're using the structure to create a column (you also can use this structure to obtain information about a column), this string buffer contains the column's label. The cchTextMax member denotes the size of the string buffer and is valid only when you're using the structure to retrieve information about a column.

CreateListView() creates a temporary LV_COLUMN structure, sets the elements, and then inserts it into the list view as column 0, the main column. This process is repeated for the other two columns. Add these lines to CreateListView():

```
// Create the columns.
    LV_COLUMN lvColumn;
```

```
lvColumn.mask = LVCF_FMT | LVCF_WIDTH | LVCF_TEXT | LVCF_SUBITEM;
lvColumn.fmt = LVCFMT_CENTER;
lvColumn.cx = 75;

lvColumn.iSubItem = 0;
lvColumn.pszText = "Column 0";
m_listView.InsertColumn(0, &lvColumn);
lvColumn.iSubItem = 1;
lvColumn.pszText = "Column 1";
m_listView.InsertColumn(1, &lvColumn);
lvColumn.iSubItem = 2;
lvColumn.pszText = "Column 2";
m_listView.InsertColumn(1, &lvColumn);
```

CREATING THE LIST VIEW'S ITEMS

The fifth task in CreateListView() is to create the items that will be listed in the columns when the control is in its report view. Creating items is not unlike creating columns. As with columns, Visual C++ defines a structure that you must initialize and pass to the function that creates the items. This structure is called LV_ITEM and is defined as shown in Listing 7.7.

LISTING 7.7   THE LV_ITEM STRUCTURE, DEFINED BY MFC

```
typedef struct _LV_ITEM
{
    UINT    mask;          // Flags indicating valid fields
    int     iItem;         // Item index
    int     iSubItem;      // Sub-item index
    UINT    state;         // Item's current state
    UINT    stateMask;     // Valid item states.
    LPSTR   pszText;       // Address of string buffer
    int     cchTextMax;    // Size of string buffer
    int     iImage;        // Image index for this item
    LPARAM  lParam;        // Additional information as a 32-bit value
} LV_ITEM;
```

In the LV_ITEM structure, the mask member specifies the other members of the structure that are valid. The flags you can use are

- LVIF_IMAGE. iImage is valid.

- LVIF_PARAM. lParam is valid.

- LVIF_STATE. state is valid.

- LVIF_TEXT. pszText is valid.

The iItem member is the index of the item, which you can think of as the row number in Report View (although the items' position can change when they're sorted). Each item has a unique index. The iSubItem member is the index of the sub-item, if this structure is defining a sub-item. You can think of this value as the number of the column in which the item will appear. For example, if you're defining the main item (the first column), this value should be 0.

The state and stateMask members hold the item's current state and its valid states, which can be one or more of the following:

- LVIS_CUT. The item is selected for cut and paste.
- LVIS_DROPHILITED. The item is a highlighted drop target.
- LVIS_FOCUSED. The item has the focus.
- LVIS_SELECTED. The item is selected.

The pszText member is the address of a string buffer. When you use the LV_ITEM structure to create an item, the string buffer contains the item's text. When you are obtaining information about the item, pszText is the buffer where the information will be stored, and cchTextMax is the size of the buffer. If pszText is set to LPSTR_TEXTCALLBACK, the item uses the callback mechanism. Finally, the iImage member is the index of the item's icon in the small-icon and large-icon image lists. If set to I_IMAGECALLBACK, the iImage member indicates that the item uses the callback mechanism.

CreateListView() creates a temporary LV_ITEM structure, sets the elements, and then inserts it into the list view as item 0. Two calls to SetItemText() add sub-items to this item so that each column has some text in it, and the whole process is repeated for two other items. Add these lines:

```
// Create the items.
    LV_ITEM lvItem;
    lvItem.mask = LVIF_TEXT | LVIF_IMAGE | LVIF_STATE;
    lvItem.state = 0;
    lvItem.stateMask = 0;
    lvItem.iImage = 0;

    lvItem.iItem = 0;
    lvItem.iSubItem = 0;
    lvItem.pszText = "Item 0";
    m_listView.InsertItem(&lvItem);
    m_listView.SetItemText(0, 1, "Sub Item 0.1");
    m_listView.SetItemText(0, 2, "Sub Item 0.2");

    lvItem.iItem = 1;
    lvItem.iSubItem = 0;
    lvItem.pszText = "Item 1";
    m_listView.InsertItem(&lvItem);
    m_listView.SetItemText(1, 1, "Sub Item 1.1");
    m_listView.SetItemText(1, 2, "Sub Item 1.2");

    lvItem.iItem = 2;
    lvItem.iSubItem = 0;
    lvItem.pszText = "Item 2";
    m_listView.InsertItem(&lvItem);
    m_listView.SetItemText(2, 1, "Sub Item 2.1");
    m_listView.SetItemText(2, 2, "Sub Item 2.2");
```

Now you have created a list view with three columns and three items. Normally the values wouldn't be hard-coded, as these were, but instead would be filled in with values calculated by the program.

MANIPULATING THE LIST VIEW

You can set a list view control to four different types of views: small icon, large icon, list, and report. In Explorer, for example, the toolbar features buttons that you can click to change the view, or you can select the view from the View menu. Although Common doesn't have a snazzy toolbar like Explorer's, it will include four buttons (labeled Small, Large, List, and Report) that you can click to change the view. Those buttons are created as the sixth step in CreateListView(). Add these lines to complete the function:

```
// Create the view-control buttons.
    m_smallButton.Create("Small", WS_VISIBLE | WS_CHILD | WS_BORDER,
        CRect(400, 120, 450, 140), this, IDC_LISTVIEW_SMALL);
    m_largeButton.Create("Large", WS_VISIBLE | WS_CHILD | WS_BORDER,
        CRect(400, 145, 450, 165), this, IDC_LISTVIEW_LARGE);
    m_listButton.Create("List", WS_VISIBLE | WS_CHILD | WS_BORDER,
        CRect(400, 170, 450, 190), this, IDC_LISTVIEW_LIST);
    m_reportButton.Create("Report", WS_VISIBLE | WS_CHILD | WS_BORDER,
        CRect(400, 195, 450, 215), this, IDC_LISTVIEW_REPORT);
```

If you're using large fonts, these buttons need to be more than 50 pixels wide. This code creates each button from position 400 to 450—make the second number larger to widen the buttons.

Add the following lines in CommonView.h, just after the DECLARE_MESSAGE_MAP() macro, to declare the handlers for each of these buttons.

```
    afx_msg void OnSmall();
    afx_msg void OnLarge();
    afx_msg void OnList();
    afx_msg void OnReport();
```

Edit the message map in CommonView.cpp as follows to associate the messages with the functions:

```
BEGIN_MESSAGE_MAP(CCommonView, CScrollView)
    // Standard printing commands
    ON_COMMAND(ID_FILE_PRINT, CScrollView::OnFilePrint)
    ON_COMMAND(ID_FILE_PRINT_DIRECT, CScrollView::OnFilePrint)
    ON_COMMAND(ID_FILE_PRINT_PREVIEW, CScrollView::OnFilePrintPreview)
    ON_WM_CREATE()
    ON_WM_LBUTTONDOWN()
    ON_WM_DESTROY()
    ON_WM_TIMER()
    ON_WM_HSCROLL()
    ON_COMMAND(IDC_LISTVIEW_SMALL, OnSmall)
    ON_COMMAND(IDC_LISTVIEW_LARGE, OnLarge)
    ON_COMMAND(IDC_LISTVIEW_LIST, OnList)
    ON_COMMAND(IDC_LISTVIEW_REPORT, OnReport)
END_MESSAGE_MAP()
```

Open the Resource View window and select Common.rc, and then choose Edit, Resource Symbols to bring up the Resource Symbols dialog box. Click New to add new IDs for each of the following constants referred to in this new code:

- IDC_LISTVIEW

- IDC_LISTVIEW_SMALL

Сн

7

- `IDC_LISTVIEW_LARGE`

- `IDC_LISTVIEW_LIST`

- `IDC_LISTVIEW_REPORT`

The four handlers each call `SetWindowLong()`, which sets a window's attribute. Its arguments are the window's handle, a flag that specifies the value to be changed, and the new value. For example, passing `GWL_STYLE` as the second value means that the window's style should be changed to the style given in the third argument. Changing the list view control's style (for example, to `LVS_SMALLICON`) changes the type of view that it displays. With that in mind, add the four handler functions to the bottom of CommonView.cpp:

```
void CCommonView::OnSmall()
{
   SetWindowLong(m_listView.m_hWnd, GWL_STYLE,
      WS_VISIBLE | WS_CHILD | WS_BORDER |
      LVS_SMALLICON | LVS_EDITLABELS);
}

void CCommonView::OnLarge()
{
   SetWindowLong(m_listView.m_hWnd, GWL_STYLE,
      WS_VISIBLE | WS_CHILD | WS_BORDER |
      LVS_ICON | LVS_EDITLABELS);
}

void CCommonView::OnList()
{
   SetWindowLong(m_listView.m_hWnd, GWL_STYLE,
      WS_VISIBLE | WS_CHILD | WS_BORDER |
      LVS_LIST | LVS_EDITLABELS);
}

void CCommonView::OnReport()
{
   SetWindowLong(m_listView.m_hWnd, GWL_STYLE,
      WS_VISIBLE | WS_CHILD | WS_BORDER |
      LVS_REPORT | LVS_EDITLABELS);
}
```

In addition to changing the view, you can program a number of other features for your list view controls. When the user does something with the control, Windows sends a `WM_NOTIFY` message to the parent window. A list view control sends the following notifications most often:

- `LVN_COLUMNCLICK`. Indicates that the user clicked a column header.

- `LVN_BEGINLABELEDIT`. Indicates that the user is about to edit an item's label.

- `LVN_ENDLABELEDIT`. Indicates that the user is ending the label-editing process.

Why not have Common enable editing of the first column in this list view? You start by overriding the virtual function `OnNotify()` that was inherited by `CCommonView` from

CScrollView. Open the Properties window for the CCommonView class and click the Overrides button. Scroll down the list, select the OnNotify box, then choose <Add> OnNotify from the drop-down box that appears. Add these lines of code at the beginning of the function, replacing the TODO comment:

```
LV_DISPINFO* lv_dispInfo = (LV_DISPINFO*) lParam;

    if (lv_dispInfo->hdr.code == LVN_BEGINLABELEDIT)
    {
        CEdit* pEdit = m_listView.GetEditControl();
        // Manipulate edit control here.
    }
    else if (lv_dispInfo->hdr.code == LVN_ENDLABELEDIT)
    {
        if ((lv_dispInfo->item.pszText != NULL) &&
            (lv_dispInfo->item.iItem != -1))
        {
            m_listView.SetItemText(lv_dispInfo->item.iItem,
                0, lv_dispInfo->item.pszText);
        }
    }
```

The three parameters OnNotify() receives are the message's WPARAM and LPARAM values and a pointer to a result code. In the case of a WM_NOTIFY message coming from a list view control, the WPARAM is the list view control's ID. If the WM_NOTIFY message is the LVN_BEGINLABELEDIT or LVN_ENDLABELEDIT notification, the LPARAM is a pointer to an LV_DISPINFO structure, which itself contains NMHDR and LV_ITEM structures. You use the information in these structures to manipulate the item that the user is trying to edit.

If the notification is LVN_BEGINLABELEDIT, your program can do whatever pre-editing initialization it needs to do, usually by calling GetEditControl() and then working with the pointer returned to you. This sample application shows you only how to get that pointer.

When handling label editing, the other notification to watch out for is LVN_ENDLABELEDIT, which means that the user has finished editing the label, by either typing the new label or canceling the editing process. If the user has canceled the process, the LV_DISPINFO structure's item.pszText member will be NULL, or the item.iItem member will be –1. In this case, you need do nothing more than ignore the notification. If, however, the user completes the editing process, the program must copy the new label to the item's text, which OnNotify() does with a call to SetItemText(). The CListCtrl object's SetItemText() member function requires three arguments: the item index, the sub-item index, and the new text.

At this point you can build Common again and test it. Click each of the four buttons to change the view style. Also, try editing one of the labels in the first column of the list view.

Figure 7.20 already showed you the report view for this list view. Figure 7.25 shows the application's list view control displaying small icons, and Figure 7.26 shows the large icons. (Some controls in these figures were not implemented when the figure was shot.)

CH
7

Figure 7.25

Here's the sample application's list view control set to small icons.

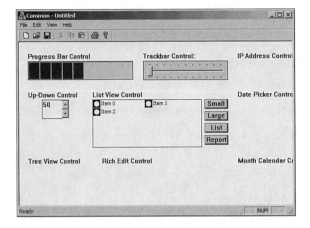

Figure 7.26

Here's the sample application's list view control set to large icons.

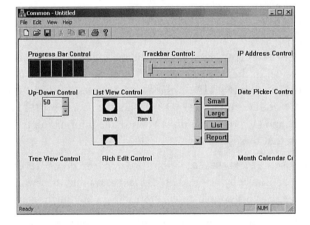

You can do a lot of other things with a list view control. A little time invested in exploring and experimenting can save you a lot of time writing your user interface.

THE TREE VIEW CONTROL

In the preceding section, you learned how to use the list view control to organize the display of many items in a window. The list view control enables you to display items both as objects in a window and objects in a report organized into columns. Often, however, the data you'd like to organize for your application's user is best placed in a hierarchical view. That is, elements of the data are shown as they relate to one other. A good example of a hierarchical display is the directory tree used by Windows to display directories and the files that they contain.

MFC provides this functionality in the CTreeCtrl class. This versatile control displays data in various ways, all the while retaining the hierarchical relationship between the data objects in the view.

If you'd like to see an example of a tree view control, revisit Windows Explorer (see Figures 7.22, 7.23, and 7.24 earlier in this chapter). The left side of the window shows how the tree view control organizes objects in a window. (The right side of the window contains a list view control, which you learned about in the preceding section). In the figure, the tree view displays not only the storage devices on the computer but also the directories and files stored on those devices. The tree clearly shows the hierarchical relationship between the devices, directories, and files, and it enables the user to open and close branches on the tree to explore different levels.

CREATING THE TREE VIEW

Tree views are a little simpler than list views. You will write the rest of `CreateTreeView()`, which follows these steps:

1. Creates an image list
2. Creates the tree view itself
3. Associates the image list with the list view
4. Creates the root item
5. Creates child items

Creating the image list, creating the tree control, and associating the control with the image list are very similar to the steps completed for the image list. You've already written the code to create the image list, so add these lines to `CreateTreeView()`:

```
// Create the Tree View control.
    m_treeView.Create(WS_VISIBLE | WS_CHILD | WS_BORDER |
        TVS_HASLINES | TVS_LINESATROOT | TVS_HASBUTTONS |
        TVS_EDITLABELS, CRect(20, 260, 160, 360), this,
        IDC_TREEVIEW);
    m_treeView.SetImageList(&m_treeImageList, TVSIL_NORMAL);
```

Remember to add a resource ID for `IDC_TREEVIEW`. The `CTreeCtrl` class, of which `m_treeView` is an object, defines special styles to be used with tree view controls. Table 7.6 lists these special styles.

TABLE 7.6   TREE VIEW CONTROL STYLES

Style	Description
TVS_DISABLEDRAGDROP	Disables drag-and-drop operations.
TVS_EDITLABELS	Enables the user to edit labels.
TVS_HASBUTTONS	Gives each parent item a button.
TVS_HASLINES	Adds lines between items in the tree.
TVS_LINESATROOT	Adds a line between the root and child items.
TVS_SHOWSELALWAYS	Forces a selected item to stay selected when losing focus.

CH

7

TABLE 7.6 CONTINUED

Style	Description
TVS_NOTOOLTIPS	Suppresses ToolTips for the tree items.
TVS_SINGLEEXPAND	Expands or collapses tree items with a single click rather than a double click.

CREATING THE TREE VIEW'S ITEMS

Creating items for a tree view control is much like creating items for a list view control. As with the list view, MFC defines a structure that you must initialize and pass to the function that creates the items. This structure is called TVITEM and is defined in Listing 7.8.

LISTING 7.8 THE TVITEM STRUCTURE, DEFINED BY MFC

```
typedef struct _TVITEM
{
    UINT        mask;
    HTREEITEM   hItem;
    UINT        state;
    UINT        stateMask;
    LPSTR       pszText;
    int         cchTextMax;
    int         iImage;
    int         iSelectedImage;
    int         cChildren;
    LPARAM      lParam;
} TV_ITEM;
```

In the TVITEM structure, the mask member specifies the other structure members that are valid. The flags you can use are as follows:

- TVIF_CHILDREN. cChildren is valid.
- TVIF_HANDLE. hItem is valid.
- TVIF_IMAGE. iImage is valid.
- TVIF_PARAM. lParam is valid.
- TVIF_SELECTEDIMAGE. iSelectedImage is valid.
- TVIF_STATE. state and stateMask are valid.
- TVIF_TEXT. pszText and cchTextMax are valid.

The hItem member is the handle of the item, whereas the state and stateMask members hold the item's current state and its valid states, which can be one or more of TVIS_BOLD, TVIS_CUT, TVIS_DROPHILITED, TVIS_EXPANDED, TVIS_EXPANDEDONCE, TVIS_FOCUSED, TVIS_OVER-LAYMASK, TVIS_SELECTED, TVIS_STATEIMAGEMASK, and TVIS_USERMASK.

The pszText member is the address of a string buffer. When you are using the TVITEM structure to create an item, the string buffer contains the item's text. When you are using the structure to obtain information about the item, it stores the information in the pszText buffer; cchTextMax is the size of the buffer. If pszText is set to LPSTR_TEXTCALLBACK, the item uses the callback mechanism. Finally, the iImage member is the index of the item's icon in the image list. If set to I_IMAGECALLBACK, the iImage member indicates that the item uses the callback mechanism.

The iSelectedImage member is the index of the icon in the image list that represents the item when the item is selected. As with iImage, if this member is set to I_IMAGECALLBACK, the iSelectedImage member indicates that the item uses the callback mechanism. Finally, cChildren specifies whether any child items are associated with the item.

In addition to the TVITEM structure, you must initialize a TVINSERTSTRUCT structure that holds information about how to insert the new structure into the tree view control. That structure is declared in Listing 7.9.

LISTING 7.9 THE TVINSERTSTRUCT STRUCTURE, DEFINED BY MFC

```
typedef struct tagTVINSERTSTRUCT {
    HTREEITEM hParent;
    HTREEITEM hInsertAfter;
#if (_WIN32_IE >= 0x0400)
    union
    {
        TVITEMEX itemex;
        TVITEM item;
    } DUMMYUNIONNAME;
#else
    TVITEM item;
#endif
} TVINSERTSTRUCT, FAR *LPTVINSERTSTRUCT;
```

In this structure, hParent is the handle to the parent tree view item. A value of NULL or TVI_ROOT specifies that the item should be placed at the root of the tree. The hInsertAfter member specifies the handle of the item after which this new item should be inserted. It can also be one of the flags TVI_FIRST (beginning of the list), TVI_LAST (end of the list), or TVI_SORT (alphabetical order). Finally, the item member is the TVITEM structure containing information about the item to be inserted into the tree.

Common first initializes the TVITEM structure for the root item (the first item in the tree). Add these lines:

```
// Create the root item.
    TVITEM tvItem;
    tvItem.mask =
        TVIF_TEXT | TVIF_IMAGE | TVIF_SELECTEDIMAGE;
    tvItem.pszText = "Root";
    tvItem.cchTextMax = 4;
    tvItem.iImage = 0;
    tvItem.iSelectedImage = 0;
    TVINSERTSTRUCT tvInsert;
    tvInsert.hParent = TVI_ROOT;
    tvInsert.hInsertAfter = TVI_FIRST;
```

CH

7

```
    tvInsert.item = tvItem;
    HTREEITEM hRoot = m_treeView.InsertItem(&tvInsert);
```

The CTreeCtrl member function InsertItem() inserts the item into the tree view control. Its single argument is the address of the TVINSERTSTRUCT structure.

CreateTreeView() then inserts the remaining items into the tree view control. Add these lines to insert some hard-coded sample items into the tree view:

```
// Create the first child item.
    tvItem.pszText = "Child Item 1";
    tvItem.cchTextMax = 12;
    tvItem.iImage = 1;
    tvItem.iSelectedImage = 1;
    tvInsert.hParent = hRoot;
    tvInsert.hInsertAfter = TVI_FIRST;
    tvInsert.item = tvItem;
    HTREEITEM hChildItem = m_treeView.InsertItem(&tvInsert);

    // Create a child of the first child item.
    tvItem.pszText = "Child Item 2";
    tvItem.cchTextMax = 12;
    tvItem.iImage = 2;
    tvItem.iSelectedImage = 2;
    tvInsert.hParent = hChildItem;
    tvInsert.hInsertAfter = TVI_FIRST;
    tvInsert.item = tvItem;
    m_treeView.InsertItem(&tvInsert);

    // Create another child of the root item.
    tvItem.pszText = "Child Item 3";
    tvItem.cchTextMax = 12;
    tvItem.iImage = 1;
    tvItem.iSelectedImage = 1;
    tvInsert.hParent = hRoot;
    tvInsert.hInsertAfter = TVI_LAST;
    tvInsert.item = tvItem;
    m_treeView.InsertItem(&tvInsert);
```

MANIPULATING THE TREE VIEW

Just as with the list view control, you can edit the labels of the items in Common's tree view. Also, like the list view control, this process works because the tree view sends WM_NOTIFY messages that trigger a call to the program's OnNotify() function.

OnNotify() handles the tree-view notifications in almost exactly the same way as the list view notifications. The only difference is in the names of the structures used. Add these lines to OnNotify() before the return statement:

```
TV_DISPINFO* tv_dispInfo = (TV_DISPINFO*) lParam;

    if (tv_dispInfo->hdr.code == TVN_BEGINLABELEDIT)
    {
        CEdit* pEdit = m_treeView.GetEditControl();
        // Manipulate edit control here.
    }
```

```
    else if (tv_dispInfo->hdr.code == TVN_ENDLABELEDIT)
{
    if (tv_dispInfo->item.pszText != NULL)
    {
        m_treeView.SetItemText(tv_dispInfo->item.hItem,
            tv_dispInfo->item.pszText);
    }
}
```

The tree view control sends a number of other notification messages, including TVN_
BEGINDRAG, TVN_BEGINLABELEDIT, TVN_BEGINRDRAG, TVN_DELETEITEM, TVN_ENDLABELEDIT,
TVN_GETDISPINFO, TVN_GETINFOTIP, TVN_ITEMEXPANDED, TVN_ITEMEXPANDING, TVN_KEYDOWN,
TVN_SELCHANGED, TVN_SELCHANGING, TVN_SETDISPINFO, and TVN_SINGLEEXPAND. Check your
Visual C++ online documentation for more information about handling these notification
messages.

Now is a good time to again build and test Common. Be sure to try expanding and collapsing the levels of the tree and editing a label. If you can't see all the control, maximize the
application and adjust your screen resolution if you can. The application scrolls eventually,
but not just yet.

THE RICH EDIT CONTROL

If you took all the energy expended on writing text-editing software and you concentrated
that energy on other, less mundane programming problems, computer science would probably be a decade ahead of where it is now. Although that might be an exaggeration, it is true
that when it comes to text editors, a huge amount of effort has been dedicated to reinventing the wheel. Wouldn't it be great to have one piece of text-editing code that all programmers could use as the starting point for their own custom text editors?

With MFC's CRichEditCtrl control, you get a huge jump on any text-editing functionality
that you need to install in your applications. The rich edit control is capable of handling
fonts, paragraph styles, text color, and other types of tasks that are traditionally found in text
editors. In fact, a rich edit control (named for the fact that it handles text in Rich Text
Format) provides a solid starting point for any text-editing tasks that your application must
handle. Your users can

- Type text.
- Edit text, using cut-and-paste and sophisticated drag-and-drop operations.
- Set text attributes such as font, point size, and color.
- Apply underline, bold, italic, strikethrough, superscript, and subscript properties to text.
- Format text, using various alignments and bulleted lists.
- Lock text from further editing.
- Save and load files.

CH
7

As you can see, a rich edit control is powerful. It is, in fact, almost a complete word-processor-in-a-box that you can plug into your program and use immediately. Of course, because a rich edit control offers so many features, there's a lot to learn. This section gives you a quick introduction to creating and manipulating a rich edit control.

CREATING THE RICH EDIT CONTROL

Add a call to CreateRichEdit() to the view class's OnCreate() function and then add the function to the class. Add resource IDs for IDC_RICHEDIT, IDC_RICHEDIT_ULINE, IDC_RICHEDIT_LEFT, IDC_RICHEDIT_CENTER, and IDC_RICHEDIT_RIGHT. Edit the new function, CreateRichEdit(), so that it looks like this:

```
void CCommonView::CreateRichEdit()
{
    m_richEdit.Create(WS_CHILD | WS_VISIBLE | WS_BORDER |
        ES_AUTOVSCROLL | ES_MULTILINE,
        CRect(180, 260, 393, 360), this, IDC_RICHEDIT);

    m_boldButton.Create("ULine", WS_VISIBLE | WS_CHILD | WS_BORDER,
        CRect(400, 260, 450, 280), this, IDC_RICHEDIT_ULINE);
    m_leftButton.Create("Left", WS_VISIBLE | WS_CHILD | WS_BORDER,
        CRect(400, 285, 450, 305), this, IDC_RICHEDIT_LEFT);
    m_centerButton.Create("Center", WS_VISIBLE | WS_CHILD | WS_BORDER,
        CRect(400, 310, 450, 330), this, IDC_RICHEDIT_CENTER);
    m_rightButton.Create("Right", WS_VISIBLE | WS_CHILD | WS_BORDER,
        CRect(400, 335, 450, 355), this, IDC_RICHEDIT_RIGHT);
}
```

As usual, things start with a call to the control's Create() member function. The style constants include the same constants that you would use for creating any type of window, with the addition of special styles used with rich edit controls. Table 7.7 lists these special styles.

TABLE 7.7 RICH EDIT STYLES

Style	Description
ES_AUTOHSCROLL	Automatically scrolls horizontally.
ES_AUTOVSCROLL	Automatically scrolls vertically.
ES_CENTER	Centers text.
ES_LEFT	Left-aligns text.
ES_LOWERCASE	Lowercases all text.
ES_MULTILINE	Enables multiple lines.
ES_NOHIDESEL	Doesn't hide selected text when losing the focus.
ES_OEMCONVERT	Converts from ANSI characters to OEM characters and back to ANSI.
ES_PASSWORD	Displays characters as asterisks.
ES_READONLY	Disables editing in the control.
ES_RIGHT	Right-aligns text.

Style	Description
TABLE 7.7 CONTINUED	
ES_UPPERCASE	Uppercases all text.
ES_WANTRETURN	Inserts return characters into text when Enter is pressed.

INITIALIZING THE RICH EDIT CONTROL

The rich edit control is perfectly usable as soon as it is created. Member functions manipulate the control extensively, formatting and selecting text, enabling and disabling many control features, and more. As always, check your online documentation for all the details on these member functions.

MANIPULATING THE RICH EDIT CONTROL

This sample application shows you the basics of using the rich edit control by setting character attributes and paragraph formats. When you include a rich edit control in an application, you will probably want to give the user some control over its contents. For this reason, you usually create menu and toolbar commands for selecting the various options that you want to support in the application. In Common, the user can click four buttons to control the rich edit control.

You've already added the code to create these buttons. Add lines just after the DECLARE_MESSAGE_MAP() macro in the header file to declare the handlers:

```
afx_msg void OnULine();
afx_msg void OnLeft();
afx_msg void OnCenter();
afx_msg void OnRight();
```

Similarly, add these lines to the message map in the source file:

```
ON_COMMAND(IDC_RICHEDIT_ULINE, OnULine)
ON_COMMAND(IDC_RICHEDIT_LEFT, OnLeft)
ON_COMMAND(IDC_RICHEDIT_CENTER, OnCenter)
ON_COMMAND(IDC_RICHEDIT_RIGHT, OnRight)
```

Each of these functions is simple. Add them each to CommonView.cpp. The OnULine() function looks like this:

```
void CCommonView::OnULine()
{
    CHARFORMAT charFormat;
    charFormat.cbSize = sizeof(CHARFORMAT);
    charFormat.dwMask = CFM_UNDERLINE;
    m_richEdit.GetSelectionCharFormat(charFormat);

    if (charFormat.dwEffects & CFM_UNDERLINE)
        charFormat.dwEffects = 0;
    else
        charFormat.dwEffects = CFE_UNDERLINE;
```

CH

7

```
    m_richEdit.SetSelectionCharFormat(charFormat);
    m_richEdit.SetFocus();
}
```

OnULine() creates and initializes a CHARFORMAT structure, which holds information about character formatting and is declared in Listing 7.10.

LISTING 7.10   THE CHARFORMAT STRUCTURE, DEFINED BY MFC

```
typedef struct _charformat
{
    UINT      cbSize;
    _WPAD     _wPad1;
    DWORD     dwMask;
    DWORD     dwEffects;
    LONG      yHeight;
    LONG      yOffset;
    COLORREF  crTextColor;
    BYTE      bCharSet;
    BYTE      bPitchAndFamily;
    TCHAR     szFaceName[LF_FACESIZE];
    _WPAD     _wPad2;
} CHARFORMAT;
```

In a CHARFORMAT structure, cbSize is the size of the structure. The dwMask member indicates which members of the structure are valid (can be a combination of CFM_BOLD, CFM_CHARSET, CFM_COLOR, CFM_FACE, CFM_ITALIC, CFM_OFFSET, CFM_PROTECTED, CFM_SIZE, CFM_STRIKEOUT, and CFM_UNDERLINE). The dwEffects member is the character effects (can be a combination of CFE_AUTOCOLOR, CFE_BOLD, CFE_ITALIC, CFE_STRIKEOUT, CFE_UNDERLINE, and CFE_PROTECTED). The yHeight member is the character height, and yOffset is the character baseline offset (for super- and subscript characters). The crTextColor member is the text color. bCharSet is the character set value (see the ifCharSet member of the LOGFONT structure). The bPitchAndFamily member is the font pitch and family, and szFaceName is the font name.

After initializing the CHARFORMAT structure, as needed, to toggle underlining, OnULine() calls the control's GetSelectionCharFormat() member function. This function, whose single argument is a reference to the CHARFORMAT structure, fills the character format structure. OnULine() checks the dwEffects member of the structure to determine whether to turn underlining on or off. The bitwise and operator, &, is used to test a single bit of the variable.

Finally, after setting the character format, OnULine() returns the focus to the rich edit control. By clicking a button, the user has removed the focus from the rich edit control. You don't want to force the user to keep switching back manually to the control after every button click, so you call the control's SetFocus() member function.

Common also enables the user to switch between the three types of paragraph alignment. Accomplishing this is similar to setting up toggling between character formats. Listing 7.11 shows the three functions—OnLeft(), OnRight(), and OnCenter()—that handle the alignment commands. Add the code for these functions to CommonView.cpp. As you can see, the main difference is the use of the PARAFORMAT structure rather than CHARFORMAT and the call to SetParaFormat() rather than SetSelectionCharFormat().

LISTING 7.11   COMMONVIEW.CPP—CHANGING PARAGRAPH FORMATS

```cpp
void CCommonView::OnLeft()
{
    PARAFORMAT paraFormat;
    paraFormat.cbSize = sizeof(PARAFORMAT);
    paraFormat.dwMask = PFM_ALIGNMENT;
    paraFormat.wAlignment = PFA_LEFT;
    m_richEdit.SetParaFormat(paraFormat);
    m_richEdit.SetFocus();
}
void CCommonView::OnCenter()
{
    PARAFORMAT paraFormat;
    paraFormat.cbSize = sizeof(PARAFORMAT);
    paraFormat.dwMask = PFM_ALIGNMENT;
    paraFormat.wAlignment = PFA_CENTER;
    m_richEdit.SetParaFormat(paraFormat);
    m_richEdit.SetFocus();
}
void CCommonView::OnRight()
{
    PARAFORMAT paraFormat;
    paraFormat.cbSize = sizeof(PARAFORMAT);
    paraFormat.dwMask = PFM_ALIGNMENT;
    paraFormat.wAlignment = PFA_RIGHT;
    m_richEdit.SetParaFormat(paraFormat);
    m_richEdit.SetFocus();
}
```

After adding all that code, it's time to build and test again. First, click in the text box to give it the focus. Then, start typing. Want to try out character attributes? Click the ULine button to add underlining to either selected text or the next text you type. To try out paragraph formatting, click the Left, Center, or Right button to specify paragraph alignment. (Again, if you're using large text, adjust the button size if the labels don't fit.) Figure 7.27 shows the rich edit control with some different character and paragraph styles used.

IP ADDRESS CONTROL

If you're writing an Internet-aware program, you might have already wondered how you're going to validate certain kinds of input from your users. One thing you could ask for is an IP address, like this one:

`205.210.40.1`

IP addresses always have four parts, separated by dots, and each part is always a number between 1 and 255. The IP address picker guarantees that the user gives you information that meets this format.

Figure 7.27
A rich edit control is almost a complete word processor.

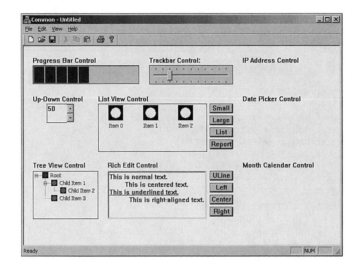

To try it out, add yet another line to OnCreate(), this time a call to CreateIPAddress(). Add the function to the class. The code is really simple; just add a call to Create():

```
void CCommonView::CreateIPAddress()(void)
{
    m_ipaddress.Create(WS_CHILD | WS_VISIBLE | WS_BORDER,
        CRect(470,40,650,65), this, IDC_IPADDRESS);
}
```

Remember to add a resource ID for IDC_IPADDRESS. No special styles are related to this simple control. It includes some useful member functions to get, set, clear, or otherwise manipulate the address. Check them out in the online documentation.

Build and run Common, and try entering numbers or letters into the parts of the field. Notice how the control quietly fixes bad values (enter 999 into one part, for example) and how it moves you along from part to part as you enter the third digit or type a dot. It's a simple control, but if you need to obtain IP addresses from the user, this is the only way to fly.

THE DATE PICKER CONTROL

How many different applications ask users for dates? It can be annoying to have to type a date according to some preset format. Many users prefer to click on a calendar to select a day. Others find this very slow and would rather type the date, especially if they're merely changing an existing date. The date picker control, in the MFC class CDateTimeCtrl, gives your users the best of both worlds.

Start, as usual, by adding a call to CreateDatePicker() to CCommonView::OnCreate() and then adding the function to the class. Add the resource ID for IDC_DATE. Like the IP Address control, the date picker needs only to be created. Add this code to CommonView.cpp:

```
void CCommonView::CreateDatePicker()(void)
{
```

```
    m_date.Create(WS_CHILD | WS_VISIBLE | DTS_SHORTDATEFORMAT,
        CRect(470,120,650,150), this, IDC_DATE);
}
```

The `CDateTimeCtrl` class, of which `m_date` is an object, defines special styles to be used with date picker controls. Table 7.8 lists these special styles.

TABLE 7.8   DATE PICKER CONTROL STYLES

Style	Description
DTS_APPCANPARSE	Instructs the date control to give more control to your application while the user edits dates.
DTS_LONGDATEFORMAT	After the date is picked, displays it as in Monday, May 20, 2002, or whatever your locale has defined for long dates.
DTS_RIGHTALIGN	Aligns the calendar with the right edge of the control. (If you don't specify this style, it aligns with the left edge.)
DTS_SHOWNONE	A date is optional: A check box indicates that a date has been selected.
DTS_SHORTDATEFORMAT	After the date is picked, displays it as in 5/20/02 or whatever your locale has defined for short dates.
DTS_TIMEFORMAT	Displays the time as well as the date.
DTS_UPDOWN	Uses an up-down control rather than a calendar for picking.

You might use a number of member functions to set colors and fonts for this control, but the most important function is `GetTime()`, which gets you the date and time entered by the user. It fills in a `COleDateTime` or `CTime` object, or a `SYSTEMTIME` structure, which you can access by individual members. Here's the declaration of `SYSTEMTIME`:

```
typedef struct _SYSTEMTIME {
  WORD wYear;
  WORD wMonth;
  WORD wDayOfWeek;
  WORD wDay;
  WORD wHour;
  WORD wMinute;
  WORD wSecond;
  WORD wMilliseconds;
} SYSTEMTIME;
```

If you want to do anything with this date, you're probably going to find it easier to work with as a `CTime` object.

For now, you probably just want to see how easy it is to use the control, so build and test Common yet again. Click the drop-down box next to the short date, and you will see how the date picker got its name. Choose a date and see the short date change. Edit the date and then drop the month down again, and you will see that the highlight has moved to the day you entered. Notice, also, that today's date is circled on the month part of this control.

CH

7

This month calendar is a control of its own. One is created by the date picker, but you will create another one in the next section.

MONTH CALENDAR CONTROL

The month calendar control used by the date picker is compact and neat. Putting one into Common is very simple. Add a call to CreateMonth() to CCommonView::OnCreate() and add the function to the class. Add a resource ID for IDC_MONTH, too; then add the code for CreateMonth(). Here it is:

```
void CCommonView::CreateMonth()(void)
{
   m_month.Create(WS_CHILD | WS_VISIBLE | DTS_SHORTDATEFORMAT,
      CRect(470,260,650,420), this, IDC_MONTH);
}
```

You can use many of the DTS_ styles when creating your month calendar control. In addition, the CMonthCalCtrl class, of which m_month is an object, defines special styles to be used with month calendar controls. Table 7.9 lists these special styles.

TABLE 7.9 MONTH CALENDAR CONTROL STYLES

Style	Description
MCS_DAYSTATE	Instructs the control to send MCN_GETDAYSTATE messages to the application so that special days (such as holidays) can be displayed in bold.
MCS_MULTISELECT	Enables the user to choose a range of dates.
MCS_NOTODAY	Suppresses the Today date at the bottom of the control. The user can display today's date by clicking the word Today.
MCS_NOTODAY_CIRCLE	Suppresses the circling of today's date.
MCS_WEEKNUMBERS	Numbers each week in the year from 1 to 52 and displays the numbers at the left of the calendar.

A number of member functions enable you to customize the control, setting the colors, fonts, and whether weeks start on Sunday or Monday. You are most likely to be interested in GetCurSel(), which fills a COleDateTime, CTime, or LPSYSTEMTIME with the currently selected date.

Build and test Common again and really exercise the month control this time. (Make the window larger if you can't see the whole control.) Try moving from month to month. If you're a long way from today's date, click the Today down at the bottom to return quickly. This is a handy control and should find a home in many of your applications.

SCROLLING THE VIEW

After adding all these controls, you might find that they don't all fit in the window. As Figure 7.28 shows, no scrollbars appear, even though CCommonView inherits from CScrollView. You need to set the scroll sizes for scrolling to work properly.

Figure 7.28
Although the view
inherits from
CScrollView, scroll
bars aren't automatic.

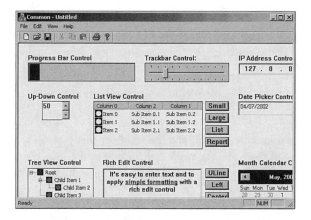

Expand CCommonView and double-click OnInitialUpdate() in Class View. Edit it so that it looks like this:

```
void CCommonView::OnInitialUpdate()
{
        CScrollView::OnInitialUpdate();

        CSize sizeTotal;
        sizeTotal.cx = 700;
        sizeTotal.cy = 500;

        SetScrollSizes(MM_TEXT, sizeTotal);
}
```

The last control you added, the month calendar, ran from the coordinates (470, 260) to (650, 420). This code states that the entire document is 700—500 pixels, so it leaves a nice white margin between that last control and the edge of the view. When the displayed window is less than 700×500, you get scrollbars. When it's larger, you don't. The call to SetScrollSizes() takes care of all the work involved in making scrollbars: sizing them to represent the proportion of the document that is displayed and dealing with the user's scrollbar clicks. Try it yourself—build Common one more time and experiment with resizing it and scrolling around. (The scrollbars weren't there before because the OnInitialUpdate() generated by the MFC Application Wizard stated that the app was 100×100 pixels, which wouldn't require scrollbars.)

So, what's going on? Vertical scrolling is fine, but horizontal scrolling blows up your application, right? You could use the techniques described in Chapter 13, "Debugging," to find the cause. The problem is in OnHScroll(), which assumed that any horizontal scrolling was related to the slider control and acted accordingly. Edit that function so that it looks like this:

```
void CCommonView::OnHScroll(UINT nSBCode, UINT nPos, CScrollBar* pScrollBar)
{
    CSliderCtrl* slider = (CSliderCtrl*)pScrollBar;
    if (slider == &m_trackbar)
    {
```

CH

7

```
        int position = slider->GetPos();
        CString s;
        s.Format("%d   ", position);
        CClientDC clientDC(this);
        clientDC.TextOut(390, 22, s);
    }

    CScrollView::OnHScroll(nSBCode, nPos, pScrollBar);
}
```

Now the slider code is executed only when the scrollbar that was clicked is the one kept in m_trackbar. The rest of the time, the work is delegated to the base class. For the last time, build and test Common—everything should be perfect now. Figure 7.29 shows the scrollbars in place.

Figure 7.29
A few changes to the view's
`OnInitialUpdate`
`()` gets you scrollbars.

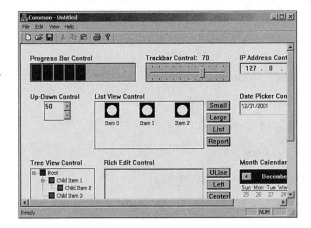

FROM HERE

In this chapter you have seen how to add a lot of flourish to your application with very little work. The MFC library has plenty of support for toolbars, status bars, and specialized controls from which you can build a user interface. This gives you more time to concentrate on the parts of your application that make it special.

Why not continue to make your application consistent with other Windows applications by adding Help, Wizards, and Property Pages to your project? These special dialogs inform your users about how to use your product, or ease their way through a set of steps. You can discover how to implement them in the next chapter, "Help, Property Pages, and Wizards."

If the IP Address Control presented in this chapter has gotten you thinking of an Internet side to your application, you'll want to read Chapter 10, "Internet Programming."

CHAPTER 8

HELP, PROPERTY PAGES, AND WIZARDS

In this chapter

ONLINE HELP

Too many programmers entirely neglect online Help. Even those who add Help to an application tend to leave it to the end of a project, and when the inevitable time squeeze comes, guess what? There's no time to write the Help text or make the software adjustments that arrange for that text to display when the user requests Help. Many programmers do this because they believe implementing Help is really hard. With Visual C++, though, it's a lot easier than you might anticipate. Visual C++ even writes some of your Help text for you! In this chapter you're going to add Help, after the fact, to the ShowString application built in Chapter 6, "Building a Complete Application: ShowString."

DIFFERENT KINDS OF HELP

This section presents four different questions you might ask yourself while developing Help:

- How does the user invoke it? (Getting Help)
- How does it look onscreen? (Presenting Help)
- What sort of answers does the user want? (Using Help)
- How does the developer implement it in code? (Programming Help)

None of these questions has a single answer. There are at least nine different ways for a user to invoke Help, three standard Help appearances, and three different programming tasks you must implement to display Help. These different ways of looking at Help can help you understand why the implementation involves a number of different techniques, which can be confusing at first.

GETTING HELP

The first decision in creating Help for your application is how the user is going to invoke it. There are a number of ways to open Help:

- By choosing an item from the Help menu, such as Help, Contents (choosing What's This? or About doesn't open Help immediately).
- By pressing the F1 key.
- By clicking the Help button on a dialog box.
- By clicking a What's This? button on a toolbar and then clicking something else.
- By choosing What's This? from the Help menu (the System menu for dialog box-based applications) and then clicking something.
- By clicking a Question button on a dialog box and then clicking part of the dialog box.
- By right-clicking something and choosing What's This? from the pop-up menu.
- In some older applications, by pressing Shift+F1 and then clicking something.
- Outside the application completely, by double-clicking the CHM file.

For the first three actions in this list, the user does one thing (chooses a menu item, presses F1, or clicks a button), and Help appears immediately. For the next five actions, there are two steps: typically, one click to go into Help mode (more formally called What's This? mode) and another to indicate which Help is required. Users generally divide Help into single-step Help and two-step Help, accordingly.

Presenting Help

The next question to ask is, "How does it look onscreen?" You can display Help in several ways:

- **Help Topics dialog box.** As shown in Figure 8.1, this dialog box enables users to scroll through an index, look at a table of contents, find a word within the Help text, or quickly open a favorite Help topic. (To open this dialog box in Windows, choose Start, Help.)

Figure 8.1
HTML Help is the new standard for Help.

The Help Topics dialog box enables users to search the Help text or go through the contents or index with Find.

- **Pop-up windows.** As shown in Figure 8.2, pop-up windows are relatively small and don't have buttons or menus. They disappear when you click outside them, cannot be resized or moved, and are perfect for a definition or quick explanation. To re-create Figure 8.2, right-click the MC button on the Windows calculator and choose What's This?

Figure 8.2
A pop-up Help topic window gives the user far less control and should be used for only short explanations.

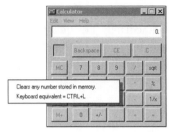

USING HELP

The next question to ask in developing Help is what sort of answers will the user want. In the book *Microsoft Windows User Experience* (Microsoft Press, 1999), Microsoft categorizes Help in this way and lists these kinds of Help:

- Contextual user assistance answers questions such as "What does this button do?" or "What does this setting mean?"

- Task-oriented Help explains how to accomplish a certain task, such as printing a document. (It often contains numbered steps.)

- Reference Help looks up function parameters, font names, or other material that expert users need to refer to from time to time.

- Wizards walk a user through a complicated task, just as the MFC Application Wizard walks you through creating an application.

These categories describe the content of the material presented to the user. Although these content descriptions are important to a Help designer and writer, they're not very useful from a programming point of view.

> **Tip**
>
> *Microsoft Windows User Experience* is provided with the MSDN CDs included with Visual Studio. In Visual Studio, choose Help, Contents. On the Contents tab of Help, expand the MSDN Library item, then the User Interface Design and Development item. Beneath that, expand the Windows User Interface item, then the Books item, then the Windows User Experience item. The book is divided into sections. Expand the Design Specification and Guidelines section, and beneath that the User Assistance section. Here you can find a number of pages of Help guidelines.

PROGRAMMING HELP

The final aspect of Help, and perhaps the most important question to a developer, is how to implement it in code. Three Windows messages are sent when the user invokes Help:

- WM_COMMAND
- WM_HELP
- WM_CONTEXTMENU

> **Note**
>
> Windows messages are discussed in Chapter 3, "Interacting with your Application."

When the user chooses a Help item from a menu or clicks the Help button on a dialog box, the system sends a WM_COMMAND message, as usual. To display the associated Help, you catch these messages and call the WinHelp system.

When the user right-clicks an element of your application, a WM_CONTEXTMENU message is sent. Your application catches the message and builds a shortcut menu on the spot. Because in most cases you want a shortcut menu with only one item on it—What's This?—you can use a pre-built menu with only that item and delegate the display of that menu to the Help system (more on this later in the "Programming for Context Help" section).

When the user opens Help in any other way, the framework handles most of it. You don't write code to catch the message that puts the application into What's This? mode; you don't write code to change the cursor; and you don't write the code that deals with clicks while in that mode. Your code catches a WM_HELP message that identifies the control, dialog box, or menu for which Help is required, and provides that Help. Whether the user pressed F1 or went into What's This? mode and clicked the item doesn't matter. In fact, you can't tell from within your application how the user invoked Help.

The WM_HELP and WM_CONTEXTMENU messages are handled almost identically, so from the point of view of the developer, there are two kinds of help: *command help* and *context help*. Each is discussed later in this chapter in the "Programming for Command Help" and "Programming for Context Help" sections, but keep in mind that there's no relationship between this split (between command and context help) and the split between one-step and two-step Help that users think of.

COMPONENTS OF THE HELP SYSTEM

As you might expect, a large number of files interact to make online Help work. The final product, which you deliver to your user, is the Help file, with the .hlp extension. It is built from component files. In Table 8.1, *appname* refers to the name of your application's .exe file. If only an extension appears in the filename column, there might be more than one file with a variety of names. The component files produced by the MFC Application Wizard are displayed in Table 8.1.

TABLE 8.1   HELP COMPONENT FILES

FileName	Description
.h	These Header files define resource IDs and Help topic IDs for use within your C++ code.
.hm	These Help Mapping files define Help topic IDs. The appname.hm file is generated every time you build your application—don't change it yourself.

TABLE 8.1	HELP COMPONENT FILES
HTMLDefines.h	This Header file define resource IDs and Help topic IDs for use within your C++ code.
.htm	These HTML files contain the Help text for each Help topic.
appname.hhc	You use this contents file to define the elements in the contents list. (Unlike older versions of Help, you don't need to distribute this file.)
appname.hhk	You use this index file to define the elements in your Help's index. (Unlike older versions of Help, you don't need to distribute this file.)
appname.hhp	The HTML Help Project file ties the preceding files together to produce, when compiled, a .chm file.

Help topic IDs are the connection between your Help text and the Help system. Your program uses a name such as HID_FILE_OPEN, for example, to direct the Help system to display a Help topic. The system looks for this Help topic ID in the Help file, which is compiled from the .htm files, including the file that contains your Help text for HID_FILE_OPEN. These topic IDs have to be defined twice: once for use by the Help system and once for use by your program. When the Help system displays a topic or the Help Topics dialog box, it takes over displaying other Help topics as the user requests them, with no work on your part.

HELP SUPPORT FROM THE APPLICATION WIZARD

When you build an MDI application (no database or OLE support) with the MFC Application Wizard and choose the Context-Sensitive Help option (on the Advanced Features tab), here is what you find:

- Message map entries are added to catch the commands ID_HELP_FINDER, ID_HELP, ID_CONTEXT_HELP, and ID_DEFAULT_HELP. No code is added to handle these; they are passed to CMDIFrameWnd member functions.
- A What's This? button is added to the toolbar.
- A Help Topics item is added to the Help menu for both of the menus the MFC Application Wizard provides: the one used when a file is open and the smaller one used when no files are open.
- Accelerators for F1 (ID_HELP) and Shift+F1 (ID_CONTEXT_HELP) are added.
- The default message in the status bar is changed from Ready to For Help, Press F1.
- A status bar prompt is added, to be displayed while in What's This? mode: Select an Object on Which to Get Help.
- Status bar prompts are added for the Help menu and its items.
- Help topic files (afx*.htm) for standard menu items, such as File Open or Edit Paste, are copied into the project. Extra topic files are also generated based on your choices in the MFC Application Wizard.

- An image file, containing an image of a standard bullet, is copied into the project. You can change this file or add new images as needed.

The task of implementing Help for an application breaks down into four steps:

1. You must plan your Help. Do you intend to provide reference material only, task-oriented instructions only, or both? To what extent will you supplement these with context pop-ups?

2. You must provide the programming hooks that will result in the display of the Help topics you have designed. This is done differently for command and context Help, as you will see in the sections that follow.

3. You must build the .htm files with the Help topic IDs and text to explain your application. If you have designed the Help system well and truly understand your application, this should be simple, though time-consuming.

4. You must ensure that your table of contents presents your Help topics in a logical structure.

Note

On large projects, often a technical writer rather than a programmer writes the Help text. This requires careful coordination. For example, you have to provide topic IDs to the Help writer, and you might have to explain some functions so that they can be described accurately in the Help. You have to work closely together throughout a project and respect each other's area of expertise.

PLANNING YOUR HELP APPROACH

Developing Help is like developing your software: You shouldn't do it without a plan. Strictly speaking, you shouldn't do it last. A famous experiment decades ago split a programming class into two groups. One group was required to hand in a completed user manual for a program before writing the program, the other to finish the program before writing the manual. The group who wrote the manual first produced better programs: They noticed design errors early, before the errors were carved in code, and they found writing programs much easier as well.

If your application is of any size, the work involved in developing a Help system for it would fill a book. In this section, there is room for only a few basic guidelines.

At the end of your planning process, you should have a list of Help topics and the primary way they will be reached. The topics you plan are likely to include the following:

- A page or so of Help on each menu item, reached by getting into What's This? mode and clicking the item (or by pressing F1 on a highlighted menu item).

- A page, reachable from the Contents, that lists all the menus and their menu items, with links to the pages for those items.

- A page, reachable from the Contents, for each major task that a user might perform with the application. This includes examples or tutorials.
- Context Help for the controls on all dialog boxes.

Although that might seem like a lot of work, remember that all the boilerplate resources have been documented already in the material provided by the MFC Application Wizard. This includes menu items, common dialog boxes, and more.

After you have a complete list of material and have identified the primary way each page is to be reached, think about links between pages (for example, the Application Wizard-supplied Help for File, Open mentions using File, New and vice versa) and pop-up definitions for jargon and keywords.

PLANNING HELP FOR SHOWSTRING

To demonstrate Help planning, this section plans Help for ShowString, the application introduced in Chapter 6. This simple application displays a string that the user can set. The string can be centered vertically or horizontally, and it can be black, green, or red. A new menu (Tools) with one item (Options) opens a dialog box on which the user can set all these options at once. The Help tasks you need to tackle include the following:

- Adding an Understanding Centering topic to the Help menu and writing it
- Defining Help IDs for topics you plan to explain
- Adding a Question button to the Options dialog box
- Writing code to display command and context help properly
- Changing the MFC Application Wizard's placeholder strings to ShowString or other strings specific to this application
- Adding a topic about the Tools menu and the Options item
- Adding a topic about each control on the Options dialog box
- Changing the text supplied by the MFC Application Wizard and displayed when the user requests context Help about the view
- Adjusting the Contents to point to the new pages

PROGRAMMING FOR COMMAND HELP

Command Help is simple, from a developer's point of view. (Of course, you probably still have to write the explanations, so don't relax too much.) As you've seen, the MFC Application Wizard added the Help Topics menu item and the message map entries to catch it, and the MFC class CMDIFrameWnd has the member function to process it, so you have no work to do for that. However, if you choose to add another menu item to your Help menu, you do so just as you do any other menu, using the Resource View window. Then, have your application class, CShowStringApp, catch the message.

Say, for example, that ShowString should have an item named Understanding Centering on the Help menu. Here's how to make that happen:

1. Open ShowString, either your own copy from working along with Chapter 6 or a copy you have downloaded from the book's Web site, in Visual Studio.

2. Open the IDR_MAINFRAME menu by switching to the Resource View window, expanding Menus, and double-clicking IDR_MAINFRAME. Add the Understanding Centering item to the Help menu (just below Help Topics) and let Developer Studio assign it the resource ID ID_HELP_UNDERSTANDINGCENTERING. (This is one occasion when a slightly shorter resource ID wouldn't hurt, but this chapter presents it with the longer ID.)

3. Add the item to the other menu, IDR_SHOWSTTYPE, as well. Use the same resource ID.

4. Use the Properties window to arrange for CShowStringApp to catch this message, as discussed in Chapter 6. Add the code for the new function, which looks like this:

```
void CShowStringApp::OnHelpUnderstandingcentering()
{
    HtmlHelp(HID_CENTERING);
}
```

This code fires up the Help system, passing it the Help topic ID HID_CENTERING. For this to compile, that Help topic ID has to be known to the compiler.

5. This information is going to be needed in more than one file, so create a new header file to hold it named helpmap.h. In the Solution Explorer window, right-click the HTML Help Files folder and choose Add, Add New Item. Select Header File and enter helpmap.h for the name, then click Open.

6. In the new file, type this line:

```
#define HID_CENTERING 0x01
```

The Help topic IDs in the range 0x0000 to 0xFFFF are reserved for user-defined Help topics, so 0x01 is a fine choice.

7. In ShowString.h add this line:

```
#include "helpmap.h"
```

Now the C++ compiler is happy, but when this runs, the call to HtmlHelp() isn't going to find the topic that explains centering. You need to add a help mapping entry.

8. In the Solution Explorer, under HTML Help files, find and double-click the Help project file, ShowString.hhp. Modify the map section (at almost the very bottom of the file) so it looks like this:

```
[MAP]
#include HTMLDefines.h
#include ..\helpmap.h
```

Now, both the Help system and the compiler know about this new Help topic ID. Later in this chapter, in the Writing Help Text section, you will see how to add a section that explains centering and connect it to this Help topic ID.

The other common use of command Help is to add a Help button to a dialog box that gives an overview of the dialog box. This used to be standard behavior but is now recommended only for large dialog boxes, especially those with complex interactions between the various controls. For simple boxes, the What's This? Help is a better choice, because the information comes up in a small pop-up rather than an entire page of explanations. To add a Help button to a dialog, follow the same steps you followed to add the menu item Help, Understanding Centering, but add a button to a dialog rather than an item to a menu. You wouldn't create a new .h file; add the button's Help topic ID to helpmap.h, which continues to grow in the following section.

PROGRAMMING FOR CONTEXT HELP

Your first task in arranging for context Help is to get a Question button onto the Options dialog box, because the MFC Application Wizard already added one to the toolbar. Open the Options dialog box and then view its properties. From the Properties window, set the Context Help property to true, as shown in Figure 8.3.

Figure 8.3
Turn on context help on the Options dialog box of ShowString.

As mentioned earlier, two messages are relevant to context Help: WM_HELPINFO when a user clicks something while in What's This? mode, and WM_CONTEXTMENU when a user right-clicks something. You need to arrange for your dialog box class, COptionsDialog, to catch these messages. Open the Properties window for the class and add command message handler functions for WM_HELPINFO and WM_CONTEXTMENU. This will add functions called OnHelpInfo() and OnContextMenu() to the class.

The next step is to write these functions. They both need to use a table to connect resource IDs to Help topic IDs. To create this table, add these lines at the beginning of OptionsDialog.cpp, after the comment block that reads // COptionsDialog dialog:

```
static DWORD aHelpIDs[] =
{
    IDC_OPTIONS_STRING, HIDD_OPTIONS_STRING,
    IDC_OPTIONS_BLACK, HIDD_OPTIONS_BLACK,
    IDC_OPTIONS_RED, HIDD_OPTIONS_RED,
    IDC_OPTIONS_GREEN, HIDD_OPTIONS_GREEN,
    IDC_OPTIONS_HORIZCENTER, HIDD_OPTIONS_HORIZCENTER,
```

```
    IDC_OPTIONS_VERTCENTER, HIDD_OPTIONS_VERTCENTER,
    IDOK, HIDD_OPTIONS_OK,
    IDCANCEL, HIDD_OPTIONS_CANCEL,
    0, 0
};
```

The Help system uses this array (you pass the address to the `HtmlHelp()` function) to connect resource IDs and Help topic IDs. The compiler, however, has never heard of `HIDD_OPTIONS_STRING`, so add this `include` statement to OptionsDialog.h before the definition of the `COptionsDialog` class:

```
#include "helpmap.h"
```

Add these lines to helpmap.h:

```
#define HIDD_OPTIONS_STRING       0x02
#define HIDD_OPTIONS_BLACK        0x03
#define HIDD_OPTIONS_RED         0x04
#define HIDD_OPTIONS_GREEN        0x05
#define HIDD_OPTIONS_HORIZCENTER      0x06
#define HIDD_OPTIONS_VERTCENTER      0x07
#define HIDD_OPTIONS_OK     0x08
#define HIDD_OPTIONS_CANCEL       0x09
```

The numbers are chosen arbitrarily. Now, after the two functions are written, the compiler will be happy because all these constants are defined. The Help system will also "know" these Help IDs. The stage is set; all that remains is to add the code for the functions at the end of OptionsDialog.cpp. Here's what `OnHelpInfo()` looks like:

```
BOOL COptionsDialog::OnHelpInfo(HELPINFO *pHelpInfo)
{
    if (pHelpInfo->iContextType == HELPINFO_WINDOW) // must be for a control
    {

    CString filename = AfxGetApp()->m_pszHelpFilePath;
    filename += "::/ctrlhlp.txt";           // the file that contains the
                                            // pop-up text

    return ::HtmlHelp(
                (HWND)pHelpInfo->hItemHandle,
                filename,
                HH_TP_HELP_WM_HELP,
                (DWORD_PTR)aHelpIDs) != NULL;
    }
    return TRUE;
}
```

This function calls the SDK `HtmlHelp()` function and passes the handle to the control, the path to the Help file, the command `HELP_WM_HELP` to request a context-sensitive pop-up Help topic, and the table of resource IDs and Help topic IDs built earlier. There's no other work for your function to do after kicking `HtmlHelp()` into action.

So that the compiler will recognize the `HtmlHelp()` function, add this line to the top of OptionsDialog.cpp:

```
#include <htmlhelp.h>
```

So that the linker can find the code for the `HtmlHelp()` function, add a dependency to the project. Click the project in the Solution Explorer and choose Project, Properties. In the left column, click Linker. Beneath Linker click General. In the Additional Library Directories box, enter the path to htmlhelp.lib, as in Figure 8.4. (Use the Search option from the Start menu if you aren't sure where this file is on your system.) On the left beneath Linker, click Input. Click next to Additional Dependencies and type **htmlhelp.lib**. Click OK.

Figure 8.4
Show Visual Studio where to find the library file that contains the `HtmlHelp()` function.

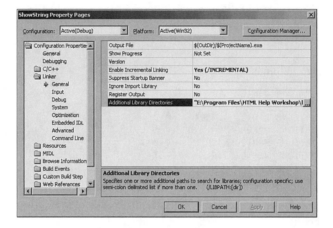

Tip

If you've never seen the `::` scope resolution operator used without a class name before it, it means "call the function that isn't in any class," and in Windows programming, that generally means the SDK function. These functions, which have been available since before MFC existed, are used only occasionally by MFC programmers.

Note

The second parameter of this call to `HtmlHelp()` directs the Help system to put up a certain style of Help window. `HELP_WM_HELP` gives you a pop-up menu, as does `HELP_WM_CONTEXTMENU`. `HELP_CONTEXT` produces an ordinary Help window, which can be resized and moved, and enables Help navigation. `HELP_FINDER` opens the Help Topics dialog box. `HELP_CONTENTS` and `HELP_INDEX` are obsolete and should be replaced with `HELP_FINDER` if you maintain code that uses them.

`OnContextMenu()` is even simpler. Add this code at the end of OptionsDialog.cpp:

```
void COptionsDialog::OnContextMenu(CWnd *pWnd, CPoint /*point*/)
{

    CString filename = AfxGetApp()->m_pszHelpFilePath;
    filename += "::/ctrlhlp.txt";            // the file that contains the
                                             // pop-up text

    ::HtmlHelp(
```

```
pWnd->GetSafeHwnd(),
        filename,
        HH_TP_HELP_CONTEXTMENU,
        (DWORD_PTR)aHelpIDs);
}
```

This function doesn't need to check that the right-click is on a control as `OnHelpInfo()` did, so it just calls the SDK `HtmlHelp()`. `HtmlHelp()` takes care of displaying the shortcut menu with only a What's This? item and then displays Help when that item is chosen. To check your typing, build the project by choosing Build, Build. There's not much point in testing it, though; the application wizard stuff is sure to work, and without Help content connected to those topics, none of the code you just added can succeed in displaying content.

Writing Help Text

HTML Help is the standard Help system for Windows applications. Using HTML for writing Help has many advantages:

- HTML can be written in any text editor. There's one built in to Visual Studio, but you are free to use whatever you like.

- You can include images (in formats supported by browsers, such as GIF and JPEG), Java applets, ActiveX controls, and any browser-supported scripting languages.

- You can use regular HTML links to link one topic to another or to other resources, such as online Web pages.

- Writing HTML is usually quite familiar to most programmers.

HTML Help content consists of a series of HTML files for the topics and specially formatted HTML files for the index and contents. Figure 8.5 shows Visual Studio's design view of a topic file generated by an application wizard. If you'd rather work with the raw HTML tags, switch to the HTML view using the tabs at the bottom of the editing area.

Figure 8.5
Help text, such as this boilerplate provided by the MFC Application Wizard, can be edited in any HTML editor.

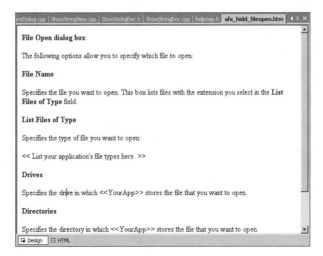

The topic HTML files can be formatted as you like, though they must be valid HTML, and it makes sense for you to stick with a format that will be familiar to most users. For the HTML Help ActiveX control to create contents and index pages, appname.hhc and appname.hhk (where *appname* is the name of your application) files must be formatted correctly.

Listing 8.1 shows the MFC Application Wizard-generated HTML Help contents file.

LISTING 8.1   THE HTML HELP CONTENTS FILE GENERATED BY THE MFC APPLICATION WIZARD.

```html
<!DOCTYPE HTML PUBLIC "-//IETF//DTD HTML//EN">
<HTML>
<HEAD>
<meta name="GENERATOR" content="Microsoft&reg; HTML Help Workshop 4.1">
<!-- Sitemap 1.0 -->
</HEAD><BODY>
<UL>
   <LI> <OBJECT type="text/sitemap">
           <param name="Name" value="&lt;&lt;YourApp&gt;&gt; Help Index">
           <param name="Local" value="main_index.htm">
           </OBJECT>
   <LI> <OBJECT type="text/sitemap">
           <param name="Name" value="Menus">
           </OBJECT>
   <UL>
           <LI> <OBJECT type="text/sitemap">
                   <param name="Name" value="File menu commands">
                   <param name="Local" value="menu_file.htm">
                   </OBJECT>
           <LI> <OBJECT type="text/sitemap">
                   <param name="Name" value="Edit menu commands">
                   <param name="Local" value="menu_edit.htm">
                   </OBJECT>
           <LI> <OBJECT type="text/sitemap">
                   <param name="Name" value="View menu commands">
                   <param name="Local" value="menu_view.htm">
                   </OBJECT>
           <LI> <OBJECT type="text/sitemap">
                   <param name="Name" value="Window menu commands">
                   <param name="Local" value="menu_window.htm">
                   </OBJECT>
           <LI> <OBJECT type="text/sitemap">
                   <param name="Name" value="Help menu commands">
                   <param name="Local" value="menu_help.htm">
                   </OBJECT>
   </UL>
   <LI> <OBJECT type="text/sitemap">
           <param name="Name" value="status bar">
           <param name="Local" value="afx_hidw_status_bar.htm">
           </OBJECT>
   <LI> <OBJECT type="text/sitemap">
           <param name="Name" value="toolbar">
           <param name="Local" value="afx_hidw_toolbar.htm">
           </OBJECT>
</UL>
</BODY></HTML>
```

When you edit this file later, you must keep to this layout:

- All the content topics are list items (`<LI>` tags) in an unordered list.
- Each list item has an `<OBJECT>` tag with the type attribute set to `text/sitemap`. This object creates the nodes in the contents tree.
- Each object has two `<PARAM>` tags, one named `Name` for the topic name and one named `Local` for the path to the topic .htm file.
- If a topic is the parent of other topics, then it has an unordered list of its own immediately after the `<OBJECT>` tag, as the `"Menus"` item does in Listing 8.1.

HTML Help's rendering of this file is shown in Figure 8.6. Notice how the nested HTML lists result in books that contain subtopics.

If you open the index file generated by the MFC Application Wizard (ShowString.hhk), you will notice that it contains only the bare shell of an HTML file, but if you open the compiled HTML Help file and look at the index you will notice several entries. This is because there are two ways to list items in the index.

Figure 8.6
The HTML Help viewer displays the contents HTML file as a tree of topics.

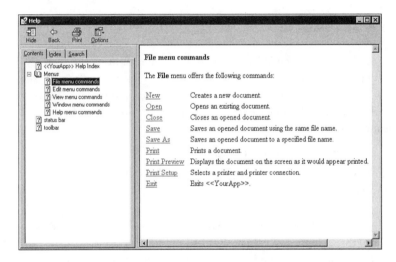

The first way to add items to the index is to add keywords as index entries in the topic files; the MFC Application Wizard added items this way. For example, here is the code generated to associate the File Close topic file with the `"files: managing"` keyword:

```
<OBJECT TYPE="application/x-oleobject" CLSID="clsid: 1e2a7bd0-dab9-11d0-b93a-
➥00c04fc99f9e">
    <PARAM NAME="Keyword" VALUE="files: managing">
</OBJECT>
```

You can add multiple keywords to a single topic by adding another `Keyword` parameter to the object with a different topic keyword as the value. Several topics can be associated with the same keyword. In this case the keyword is listed only once in the index and generates a pop-up menu with links to all the topics that are associated with the with the keyword.

The second way to add items to the index is to modify the index file directly. When you're hand-editing Help, this is the simpler of the two approaches. The structure of this file is almost identical to that of the contents file, but you have three <PARAM> tags for each object: the keyword of the index item, the title of the element, and the path to the topic file.

Writing HTML Help content is simple, which lets you focus on writing useful Help text.

CHANGING PLACEHOLDER STRINGS

To change the placeholder strings left behind by the MFC Application Wizard in the boiler-plate Help files, use the Replace in Files feature, which will change most of them at once. Follow these steps:

1. Choose Edit, Find and Replace, Replace in Files.
2. Enter <<YourApp>> in the Find What box and **ShowString** in the Replace With box. Set the Look In box to Current Project and the Files Types box to `*.*`.
3. Click Replace All.

The MFC Application Wizard sometimes creates more topics than are necessary for the Help project. This is the case for ShowString. ShowString does not support pasting from the clipboard, for example. Users will be confused if they see Help describing a feature not implemented in the application, so it is best to remove these files and any links to them. To remove the files you would follow these steps:

1. Remove any references to the files from the Help project file, ShowString.hhp.
2. Use Edit, Find to find any links to the files and delete them and any corresponding text.
3. Delete the files from the project and disk.

In addition to the extra files, the MFC Application Wizard leaves a lot of other placeholder strings throughout the Help project. All these strings start with << and end with >>, which in HTML are << and >> respectively. The messages contained within the delimiters describe what action should be taken at that point in the file. For example, some messages tell you to delete some text if a certain condition applies; others tell you to add a description of your application.

In a real application you would remove the unnecessary files and search through the generated Help files and replace the placeholders with the appropriate text. Because ShowString is only an example application, we will skip these steps.

ADDING TOPICS

It is more than likely that your application will require more Help topics than those generated by the MFC Application Wizard. Adding topics using HTML Help is very simple.

This section shows how to add new topics for the Tools menu, modify an existing topic to reflect the new menu, and add pop-up messages to the context help on the Options dialog.

To create a new topic, you must create the HTML topic file and add it to the Help project. The simplest way to do this is to copy an existing topic file, change the name, and update the content. Here's what to do:

1. Use Windows Explorer to make a copy of menu_edit.htm and rename it to menu_tools.htm.

2. Add this file to your project in the HTML Help Topics folder: right-click the folder and choose Add, Add Existing Item. Browse to the file and click Open.

3. Open the file in Visual Studio and update the content. Find all the instances of Edit in the file and replace them with **Tools**.

4. Delete all but one row of the table describing the menu items.

5. Change the link text from Cut to **Options** and change the description to **Changes string, color, and centering**.

Figure 8.7 shows the way menu_tools.htm looks after these changes.

6. Change the title of the page. With the menu_tools.htm file active in Visual Studio, choose View, Property Pages. Change the page title to **(Tools menu commands)**.

Figure 8.7
Change the menu_tools.htm file to explain the new menu item.

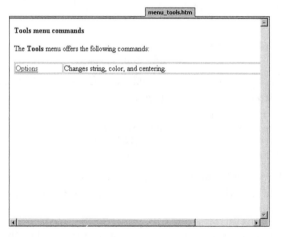

7. Change the link so that it points to the details on the Options command rather than the Cut command. Right-click the link text and choose Properties. Change the link from hid_edit_cut.htm to hid_tools_options.htm, as shown in Figure 8.8. This file doesn't exist yet, but it will be created soon.

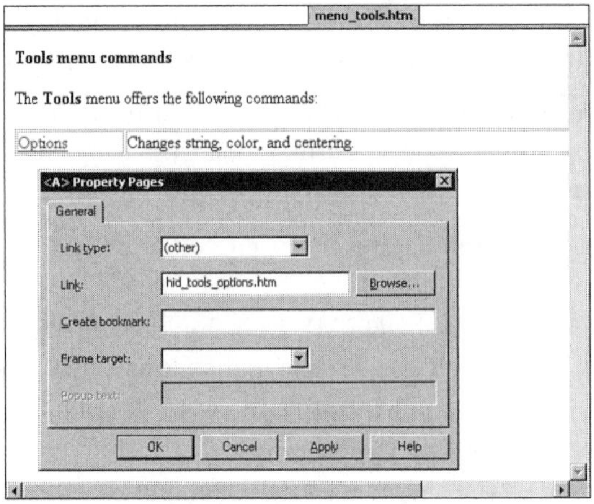

Figure 8.8
Update the link so it
refers to the correct
page.

8. The main index page of the Help project has references to the menus, so a link to the Tools menu should be added there as well. Open the file main_index.htm and add a link to the menu_tools.htm file below the View menu link.

9. There is no more work to do on the menu_tools.htm file, so save and close it. The next step is to add this file to the Help project. Open the application's Help project file, ShowString.hhp, and add this line to the end of the [FILES] section:

```
menu_tools.htm
```

10. Add this line to the end of the [ALIAS] section:

```
menu_tools                      = menu_tools.htm
```

11. Now the topic must be added to the contents file. Open ShowString.hhc and add these lines below the list item for the View menu:

```
<LI> <OBJECT type="text/sitemap">
<param name="Name" value="Tools menu commands">
      <param name="Local" value="menu_tools.htm">
      </OBJECT>
```

That is all that needs to be done for this topic. Menus typically aren't associated with keywords, so don't include any. Menus are also not usually included in the index, so don't add this topic to the index.

You can test the changes by recompiling the Help project (right-click the HTML Help project file in the Solution Explorer and choose Compile) and running your application. Open Help and expand the Menus book in the contents pane. Your topic is there, and if you click a topic title the viewer displays the appropriate file. There's a problem, though: if you click the Options link you are greeted with an error. The steps presented earlier created the topic file for the Tools menu, but not for the commands in that menu. In ShowString, the only command is the Options command. Follow these steps to create the topic for the Options command:

1. Copy an topic file and rename it hid_tools_options.htm. (It's easiest if you copy a file that is similar to one you are creating, such as hid_edit_cut.htm.) Add this file to the project under the HTML Help Topics folder.

2. Change the title of the page and update the content to match Figure 8.9. Do a Find and Replace on the file to replace all instances of hid_edit_cut with hid_tools_options.

3. Add this line to the [FILES] section of the HTML Help project file, ShowString.hhp:

```
hid_tools_options.htm
```

Add this line to the [ALIAS] section of the HTML Help project file:

```
hid_tools_options = hid_tools_options.htm
```

Figure 8.9
Write Help content for the Tools, Options menu item.

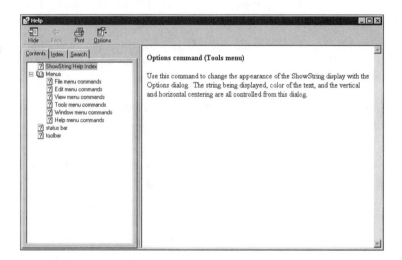

Compile your Help project and run your application. Test the changes by running Help. Now, close Help and click the What's This? button. Choose Options from the Tools and your Help topic for that command appears. You may be wondering how the application knows to associate the Options command with the topic file. Unlike the Understanding Centering command, you didn't define the Help ID anywhere. The MFC wizards take care of this: when the Options command was created, a new Help ID (identical to the menu ID with the prefix "H") was generated and stored in the file HTMLDefines.h in the hlp directory of your project. This file contains nearly all the Help IDs that are used in your application.

All that's left is to write the content for the context help on the Options dialog. To do this, create a new text file in the HTML Help Files folder of your project called ctrlhlp.txt. Add the following lines to the file:

```
.topic 2
Enter the string to display in the view.
.topic 3
Display the string in a black font.
```

```
.topic 4
Display the string in a red font.
.topic 5
Display the string in a green font.
.topic 6
Center the string horizontally in the window.
.topic 7
Center the string vertically in the window.
.topic 8
Close the dialog and apply the changes to the string.
.topic 9
Close the dialog, but don't apply any changes to the string.
```

This file is used to map pop-up text with a Help Topic ID. Notice that the topic numbers correspond to the Help Topic IDs that were assigned to the dialog's controls.

The next step is to add this file to the Help project. In ShowString.hhp, add this line to the end of the [FILES] section and the [TEXT POPUPS] section:

```
ctrlhlp.txt
```

This makes sure that the new text file gets compiled and the pop-up messages get associated with the Help Topic IDs.

The context help for the Options dialog is now complete. Build your application (the Help project is compiled automatically), and then run it. Open the Options dialog by choosing Options from the Tools menu. Notice the What's This? button added to the dialog's title bar. Click What's This? and then click a control; your context help pop-up appears. You can get the same result by right-clicking a control.

Explore each of the controls to be sure you have entered the correct text. Figure 8.10 shows the context Help for the String edit box. A more sophisticated application would implement a right-click context menu, like the one you get when you right-click in Visual Studio's text editor, but that is beyond the scope of this chapter.

Figure 8.10
Display Help for a dialog box control by clicking the Question button in the upper right corner and then clicking a control.

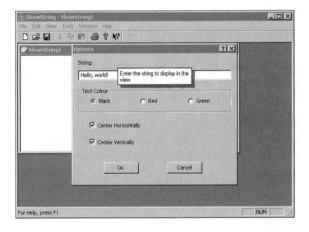

You still need to create a topic file for the Understanding Centering option on the Help menu. Make another copy of the Edit Cut topic file, rename it to hid_help_understanding-centering.htm, and add it to the project. Now make the following changes:

1. Change the title and headline of the document to Understanding Centering.

2. Replace the text with a short explanation of centering, like this:

   ShowString can center the displayed string within the view. The two options, Center Horizontally and Center Vertically, can be set independently on the Options dialog box, reached by choosing the Options item on the Tools menu. Text that is not centered horizontally is displayed at the left edge of the window. Text that is not centered vertically is displayed at the top of the window.

3. Add links from the word Tools to the menu_tools topic and from the word Options to the hid_tools_options topic, as before.

4. Change the HTML anchor in this page from hid_edit_cut to hid_help_understanding-centering.

5. Add the keyword "centering" to this topic. To do this, add this code after the BODY tag in the HTML:

   ```
           <OBJECT TYPE="application/x-oleobject" CLASSID="clsid:1e2a7bd0-dab9-
   11d0-b93a-00c04fc99f9e" VIEWASTEXT>
                   <PARAM NAME="Keyword" Value="centering">
           </OBJECT>
   ```

6. Add this line to the [FILES] section of the HTML Help project file:

   ```
   hid_help_understandingcentering.htm
   ```

   And this line to the [ALIAS] section:

   ```
   HID_CENTERING = hid_help_understandingcentering.htm
   ```

Test this change in the usual way, and when you choose Help, Understanding Centering from the ShowString menus, you should see something like Figure 8.11. Try following the links; you can use the Back button to return to the centering topic.

Figure 8.11
Display a teaching Help topic by choosing it from the Help menu.

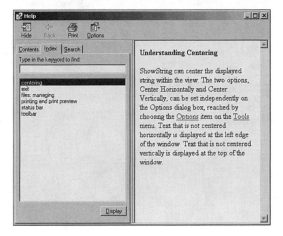

CHANGING THE HOW TO MODIFY THE DOCUMENT TOPIC

The MFC Application Wizard already provided a How to Modify the Document topic, in the file hidr_doc1type.htm, which needs to be edited to explain how ShowString works. It displays when the user selects the view area for context Help. Replace the text with a much shorter explanation that tells the user to choose Tools, Options. Add a link to both the Tools Menu Commands topic and the Options command topic. The link to the Tools Menu Commands topic is menu_tools.htm, and the link to the Options command topic is hid_tools_options.htm.

Ready to test again? Compile the Help project file, and execute ShowString; then click the What's This? button on the toolbar and click in the main view. Your new How to Modify Text entry should display.

ADJUSTMENTS TO THE CONTENTS

This tiny application is almost entirely documented now. You need to add the Understanding Centering topic to the Contents. Because a keyword was added to the HTML topic file, it is already listed in the index. The easiest way to tackle the Contents is with Help Workshop. Open the HTML Help Workshop from the Start menu by choosing Start, Programs, HTML Help Workshop, HTML Help Workshop. Open the HTML Help project file for the ShowString application, ShowString.hhp. Switch to the Contents pane and you can see that the Tools menu command entry is already there.

Add the Understanding Centering topic under a heading named Displaying a String. To add the heading, click the Insert a Heading button (the book icon) on the left side of the window. Set the title to Displaying a String, as shown in Figure 8.12. Click OK to add the entry. The new entry is added at the bottom of the list of headings on the left side of the window. Use the arrow buttons on the far left of the screen to move the Menu heading to bottom of the list and the Displaying a String heading beneath that.

Figure 8.12
Add entries to the Contents tab with Help Workshop's Edit Contents Tab Entry dialog box.

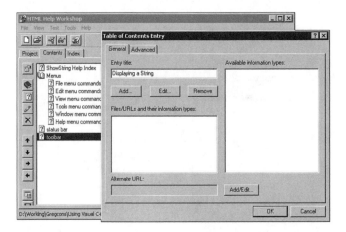

Select the Displaying a String heading and then click the Insert a Page button. Set the entry title to Understanding Centering. Associate this entry with a topic file by clicking the Add button beneath the entry title box and choosing Understanding Centering from the HTML Titles list. Click OK on the Path or URL dialog and then the Table of Contents Entry dialog.

You can view the changes that were made to the Help project by compiling and then viewing it. Both actions can be done directly from the HTML Help Workshop. Choose File, Compile to compile the project, and then choose View, Compiled File to view the resulting Help file. If you prefer, you can browse to the Showstring.chm file in the hlp folder of the ShowString project folder, and double-click it. You see something like Figure 8.13.

Figure 8.13
After compiling the help project, you can display the new table of contents by double-clicking the CHM file.

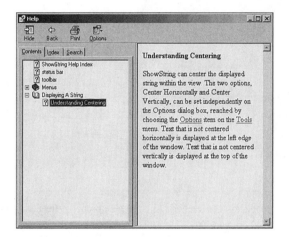

While you have the Help dialog box open, click the Index tab. If it looks a little sparse, you can always go back to the topic files and add more, as described earlier.
You can edit the files in the project by choosing them from the Projects pane of the HTML Help Workshop.

Now the Help file for this application is complete, and you've arranged for the relevant sections of the file to be displayed when the user requests online Help. You can apply these concepts to your own application, and never again deliver an undocumented product.

CREATING THE PROPERTY SHEET DEMO APPLICATION

One of the most useful types of graphical objects is the tabbed dialog box, also known as a property sheet. A property sheet is a dialog box with two or more pages. Windows is loaded with property sheets, which organize the many options that users can modify. You flip the pages by clicking labeled tabs at the top of the dialog box. Using such dialog boxes to organize complex groups of options enables users to more easily find the information and settings they need. As you've probably guessed, MFC supports property sheets, with the classes CPropertySheet and CPropertyPage.

Similar to property sheets are wizards, which use buttons rather than tabs to move from one page to another. You've seen a lot of wizards, too. These special types of dialog boxes guide users step by step through complicated processes.

Finding a sample property sheet is as easy as finding sand at the beach. Just click virtually any Properties command or bring up an Options dialog in most applications. For example, Figure 8.14 shows the dialog box that you see when you choose Tools, Customize from within Visual C++. This property sheet contains three pages in all, each covering different areas that can be customized.

Figure 8.14
The Customize properties sheet contains several tabbed pages.

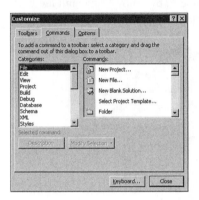

> **Note**
>
> Many people forget the difference between a property sheet and a property page. A property sheet is a window that contains property pages. Property pages are windows that hold controls. They appear on the property sheet.

As you can see, property sheets are a great way to organize many types of related options. Gone are the days of dialog boxes so jam-packed with options that you needed a college-level course just to figure them out. In the following sections, you'll learn to program your own tabbed property sheets by using MFC's `CPropertySheet` and `CPropertyPage` classes. You're about to build the Property Sheet Demo application, which demonstrates the creation and manipulation of property sheets. Follow the steps in the following sections to create the basic application, modify its resources, and set up the classes that are required.

CREATING THE BASIC FILES

First, use the MFC Application Wizard to create a new application called Props. Accept all the defaults: just click Finish on the MFC Application Wizard.

EDITING THE RESOURCES

Now you'll edit the resources in the application generated for you by the MFC Application Wizard, adding a menu item that brings up a property sheet. Follow these steps:

1. Open the Resource View window by choosing View, Resource View.

2. Open the application's main menu in the menu editor by double-clicking IDR_PropsTYPE under the Menu node in the Resource View window.

3. Select the blank menu item at the end of the File menu, and change the caption to &Property Sheet.... Then use your mouse to drag the new command above the New command so that it's the first command in the File menu (see Figure 8.15).

Figure 8.15
Add a Property Sheet command to the File menu.

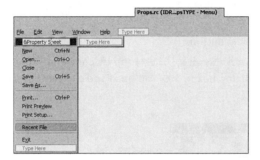

4. Click the + next to Dialog in the Resource View window. Double-click the IDD_ABOUTBOX dialog box ID to bring up the dialog box editor.

5. Add **Que Books** to the end of the copyright string.

6. Add a third static string with the text **Special Edition Using Visual C++.NET**, so that your About box resembles the one in Figure 8.16. Close the dialog box editor.

Figure 8.16
The finished About box looks like this.

ADDING NEW RESOURCES

Now that you have the application's basic resources the way you want them, it's time to add the resources that define the application's property sheet. This means creating dialog box resources for each page in the property sheet. Follow these steps:

1. Add a new dialog to the application by choosing Add Resource... from the Project menu and then double-clicking Dialog. The new dialog box, IDD_DIALOG1, appears in the dialog box editor. This dialog box, when set up properly, will represent the first page of the property sheet.

2. Delete the OK and Cancel buttons.

3. If the Properties window isn't visible, bring it up by choosing View, Properties Window. Change the ID of the dialog box to IDD_PAGE1DLG and the caption to Page 1 (see Figure 8.17).

Figure 8.17
Change the caption
and resource ID of
the new dialog box.

4. Change the Style of the dialog box to Child and set the Border to Thin.

   The Child style is necessary because the property page will be a child window of the property sheet. The property sheet itself will provide the container for the property pages.

5. Add an Edit box to the property page, as shown in Figure 8.18. In most applications, you would change the resource ID from IDC_EDIT1, but for this demonstration application, leave it unchanged.

6. Create a second property page by following steps 1 through 5 again. For this property page, use the ID IDD_PAGE2DLG, a caption of Page 2, and add a check box rather than an edit control (see Figure 8.19).

Figure 8.18
A property page can hold whatever controls you like.

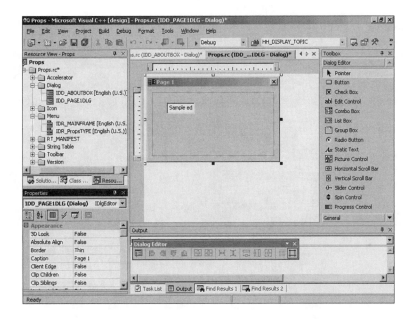

ASSOCIATING YOUR RESOURCES WITH CLASSES

You now have all your resources created. Next, associate your two new property page resources with C++ classes so that you can control them in your program. You also need a class for your property sheet, which will hold the property pages that you've created. Follow these steps to create the new classes:

1. Edit the Page 1 dialog and then double-click it. If you prefer, choose Project, Add Class from the menu bar. The MFC Class Wizard appears.

2. In the Class name box, type **CPage1**. In the Base Class box, select CPropertyPage. (Don't accidentally select CPropertySheet.) Then click Finish to create the class.

   You've now associated the property page with an object of the CPropertyPage class, which means that you can use the object to manipulate the property page as needed. The CPropertyPage class is especially important when you learn about wizards.

3. Select the CPage1 class in the Class View window and choose Project, Add Variable....

4. Name the new member variable m_edit. Check the Control variable check box and set the Category to Value, as shown in Figure 8.20, and then click OK. The MFC Class Wizard adds the member variable, which will hold the value of the property page's control, to the new CPage1 class. Click Finish to add the variable.

Figure 8.19
The second property page looks like this.

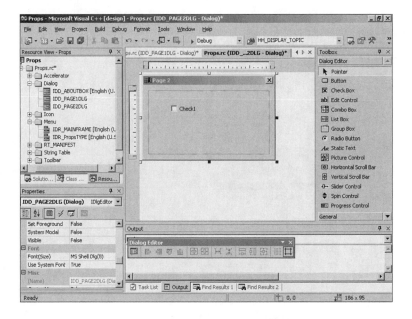

Figure 8.20
The MFC Class Wizard makes it easy to connect controls on a dialog box to member variables of the class representing the dialog box.

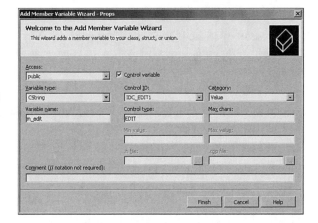

5. Follow steps 1 through 4 for the second property sheet. Name the class CPage2 and add a Boolean member variable called m_check for the IDC_CHECK1 control, as shown in Figure 8.21.

CREATING A PROPERTY SHEET CLASS

At this point, you've done all the resource editing and don't need to have so many windows open. Choose Window, Close All Documents. (If you're prompted to save your changes, answer Yes.) You'll now create a property sheet class that displays the property pages already created. Follow these steps:

1. Choose Project, Add Class... and double-click the MFC Class template. The MFC Class Wizard appears.

2. In the class name box, type **CPropSheet**, and then select CPropertySheet in the Base Class box. Click Finish to create the class.

Figure 8.21
The second property page needs a Boolean member variable called m_checkbox.

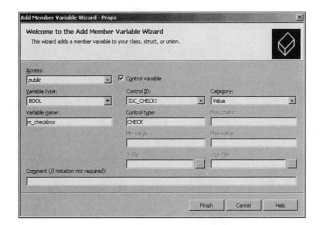

Now you have three new classes—CPage1, CPage2, and CPropSheet—in your program. The first two classes are derived from MFC's CPropertyPage class, and the third is derived from CPropertySheet. Although the MFC Class Wizard has created the basic source-code files for these new classes, you still have to add code to the classes to make them work the way you want. Follow these steps to complete the Property Sheet Demo application:

1. Open the Class View window and expand the Props classes.

2. Double-click CPropSheet to open the header file for your property sheet class, if it is not open already.

3. Add the following lines near the middle of the file, right before the CPropSheet class declaration:
```
#include "page1.h"
#include "page2.h"
```

These lines give the CPropSheet class access to the CPage1 and CPage2 classes so that the property sheet can declare member variables of these property page classes.

4. Add the following lines to the CPropSheet class at the end of the public section:
```
CPage1 m_page1;
CPage2 m_page2;
```

These lines declare the class's data members, which are the property pages that will be displayed in the property sheet.

5. Expand the `CPropSheet` class in the Class View window, and double-click the first constructor, `CPropSheet`. Add these lines to it:

```
AddPage(&m_page1);
AddPage(&m_page2);
```

This adds the two property pages to the property sheet whenever the sheet is constructed.

6. The second constructor is directly below the first; add the same lines there.

7. Double-click `CPropsView` in the Class View window to edit the header file, and add the following lines to the `//Attributes` section, right after the `CPropsDoc* GetDocument();;` line

```
protected:
    CString m_edit;
    BOOL m_check;
```

These lines declare two data members of the view class to hold the selections users make in the property sheet.

8. Add the following lines to the `CPropsView` constructor:

```
m_edit = "Default";
m_check = FALSE;
```

These lines initialize the class's data members.

9. Edit `CPropsView::OnDraw()` so that it resembles Listing 8.2. The new code displays the current selections from the property sheet. At the start of the program, the default values are displayed.

LISTING 8.2 `CPropsView::OnDraw()`

```
void CPropsView::OnDraw(CDC* pDC)
{
    CPropsDoc* pDoc = GetDocument();
    ASSERT_VALID(pDoc);

    pDC->TextOut(20, 20, m_edit);
    if (m_check)
        pDC->TextOut(20, 50, "TRUE");
    else
        pDC->TextOut(20, 50, "FALSE");
}
```

10. At the top of PropsView.cpp, after the `#include` of props.h, add another include statement:

```
#include "propsheet.h"
```

11. Bring up the Properties window for the `CPropsheetView` class, click the Events button, expand `ID_FILE_PROPERTYSHEET`, which is the ID of the new item you added to the File menu. In the drop-down box next to `COMMAND`, select <Add>OnFilePropertysheet, as shown in Figure 8.22.

Figure 8.22
Use the Properties
window to add the
OnFilePropertysh
eet() member
function.

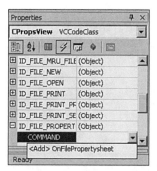

12. Edit the OnFilePropertysheet() function, and add the lines shown in Listing 8.3.

LISTING 8.3   CPropsView:: OnFilePropertysheet ()

```
void CPropsView::OnFilePropertysheet()
{
    CPropSheet propSheet("Property Sheet", this, 0);
    propSheet.m_page1.m_edit = m_edit;
    propSheet.m_page2.m_checkbox = m_check;
    int result = propSheet.DoModal();
    if (result == IDOK)
    {
        m_edit = propSheet.m_page1.m_edit;
        m_check = propSheet.m_page2.m_checkbox;
        Invalidate();
    }
}
```

The code segment in Listing 8.3 creates an instance of the CPropSheet class and sets the member variables of each of its pages. It uses the familiar DoModal function discussed in Chapter 3 to display the sheet. If users click OK, it updates the view member variables to reflect the changes made on each page and forces a redraw with a call to Invalidate().

RUNNING THE PROPERTY SHEET DEMO APPLICATION

You've finished the complete application. Click the Build button on the Build toolbar (or choose Build, Build) to compile and link the application. Run it by choosing Debug, Start, or by clicking the Execute button on the Build toolbar. When you do, you see the window shown in Figure 8.23.

As you can see, the window displays two values: the default values for the controls in the application's property sheet. You can use the property sheet to change these values. Choose File, Property Sheet; the property sheet appears (see Figure 8.24). The property sheet contains two pages, each of which holds a single control. When you change the settings of these controls and click the property sheet's OK button, the application's window displays the new values. Try it!

Figure 8.23
When it first starts, the Property Sheet Demo application displays default values for the property sheet's controls.

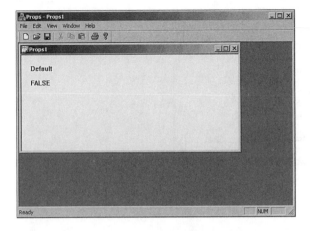

Figure 8.24
The application's property sheet contains two pages.

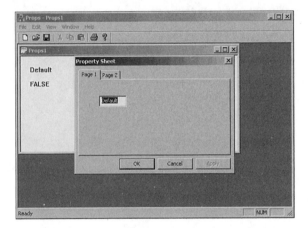

ADDING PROPERTY SHEETS TO YOUR APPLICATIONS

To add a property sheet to one of your own applications, you follow steps very similar to those you followed in the preceding section to create the demo application:

1. Create a dialog box resource for each page in the property sheet. These resources should have the Child and Thin styles and should have no system menu.

2. Associate each property page resource with an object of the CPropertyPage class. You can do this easily with the MFC Class Wizard. Connect controls on the property page to members of the class you create.

3. Create a class for the property sheet, deriving the class from MFC's CPropertySheet class. You can generate this class by using the MFC Class Wizard.

4. In the property sheet class, add member variables for each page you'll be adding to the property sheet. These member variables must be instances of the property page classes that you created in Step 2.

5. In the property sheet's constructor, call `AddPage()` for each page in the property sheet.

6. To display the property sheet, call the property sheet's constructor and then call the property sheet's `DoModal()` member function, just as you would with a dialog box.

After you write your application and define the resources and classes that represent the property sheet (or sheets—you can have more than one), you need a way to enable users to display the property sheet when it's needed. In Property Sheet Demo, this is done by associating a menu item with an event handler function. However you handle the command to display the property sheet, the process of creating the property sheet is the same. First, you must call the property sheet class's constructor, which Property Sheet Demo does like this:

```
CPropSheet propSheet("Property Sheet", this, 0);
```

Here, the program creates an instance of the `CPropSheet` class. This instance (or object) is called `propSheet`. The three arguments are the property sheet's title string, a pointer to the parent window (which, in this case, is the view window), and the zero-based index of the first page to display. Because the property pages are created in the property sheet's constructor, creating the property sheet also creates the property pages.

After you create the property sheet object, you can initialize the data members that hold the values of the property page's controls, which Property Sheet Demo does like this:

```
propSheet.m_page1.m_edit = m_edit;
propSheet.m_page2.m_checkbox = m_check;
```

Now it's time to display the property sheet, which you do just as though it were a dialog box, by calling the property sheet's `DoModal()` member function:

```
int result = propSheet.DoModal();
```

`DoModal()` doesn't take any arguments, but it does return a value indicating which button users clicked to exit the property sheet. In a property sheet or dialog box, you'll usually want to process the information entered into the controls only if users click OK, which is indicated by a return value of `IDOK`. If users exit the property sheet by clicking the Cancel button, the changes are ignored and the view or document member variables aren't updated.

CHANGING PROPERTY SHEETS TO WIZARDS

Here's a piece of information that surprises most people: A wizard is just a special property sheet. Rather than tabbed pages on each sheet that enable users to fill in the information in any order or to skip certain pages entirely, a wizard has Back, Next, and Finish buttons to move users through a process in a certain order. This forced sequence makes wizards terrific for guiding your application's users through the steps needed to complete a complex task. You can create your own wizards suited to whatever application you want to build. In the remainder of this chapter, you'll learn to create wizards and see how easy it is to convert a property sheet to a wizard.

RUNNING THE WIZARD DEMO APPLICATION

This section shows you the Wizard Demo application, which is built in much the same way as the Property Sheet Demo application that you created earlier in this chapter. This chapter doesn't present step-by-step instructions for building Wizard Demo. You can build it yourself if you want, using the general steps presented earlier in the chapter and the code snippets shown here.

When you run the Wizard Demo application, the main window appears, looking very much like the Property Sheet Demo main window. The File menu now includes a Wizard item; choosing File Wizard brings up the wizard shown in Figure 8.25.

Figure 8.25
The Wizard Demo application displays a wizard rather than a property sheet.

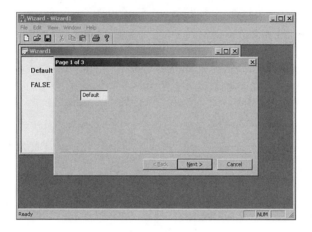

The wizard isn't too fancy, but it does demonstrate what you need to know to program more complex wizards. As you can see, this wizard has three pages. On the first page is an edit control and three buttons: Back, Next, and Cancel. The Back button is disabled because there's no previous page to go back to. The Cancel button enables users to dismiss the wizard at any time, canceling whatever process the wizard was guiding users through. The Next button causes the next page in the wizard to appear.

You can change whatever is displayed in the edit control, if you like. However, the magic really starts when you click the Next button, which displays Page 2 of the wizard (see Figure 8.26). Page 2 contains a check box and the Back, Next, and Cancel buttons. Now the Back button is enabled, so you can return to Page 1 if you want to. Go ahead and click the Back button. The wizard tells you that the check box must be checked (see Figure 8.27). As you'll soon see, this feature of a wizard enables you to verify the contents of a specific page before allowing users to leave the page.

Figure 8.26
In Page 2 of the wizard, the Back button is enabled.

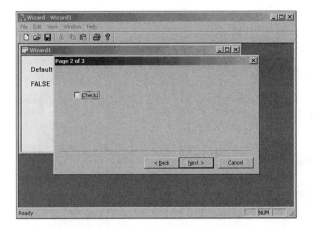

Figure 8.27
You must select the check box before the wizard will let you leave Page 2.

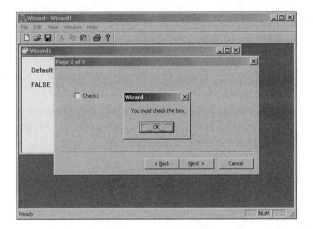

After checking the check box, you can click the Back button to move back to Page 1 or click Next to advance to Page 3. Assuming that you advance to Page 3, you see the display shown in Figure 8.28. Here, the Next button has changed to the Finish button because you are on the wizard's last page. If you click the Finish button, the wizard disappears, and the view is updated with the values you entered.

CREATING WIZARD PAGES

As far as your application's resources go, you create wizard pages exactly as you create property sheet pages: by creating dialog boxes and changing the dialog box styles. The dialog titles—Page 1 of 3, Page 2 of 3, and Page 3 of 3—are hard-coded onto each dialog box. You associate each dialog box resource with an object of the CPropertyPage class. Then, to take control of the pages in your wizard and keep track of what users are doing with the wizard, you override the OnSetActive(), OnWizardBack(), OnWizardNext(), and OnWizardFinish() functions of your property page classes. Read on to see how to do this.

Figure 8.28
This is the last page of the Wizard Demo Application's wizard.

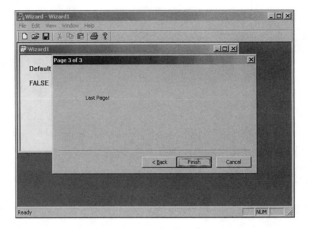

DISPLAYING A WIZARD

The File, Wizard command is caught by CWizView's OnFileWizard() function. It's very similar to the OnFilePropertysheet() function in the Property Sheet demo, as you can see from Listing 8.4. The first difference is the call to SetWizardMode() before the call to DoModal(). This function call tells MFC that it should display the property sheet as a wizard rather than as a conventional property sheet. The only other difference is that users arrange for property sheet changes to be accepted by clicking Finish, not OK, so this code checks for ID_WIZFINISH rather than IDOK as a return from DoModal().

LISTING 8.4 CWizardView::OnFileWizard()

```
void CWizardView::OnFileWizard()
{
    CWizSheet wizSheet("Sample Wizard", this, 0);
    wizSheet.m_page1.m_edit = m_edit;
    wizSheet.m_page2.m_check = m_check;
    wizSheet.SetWizardMode();
    int result = wizSheet.DoModal();
    if (result == ID_WIZFINISH)
    {
        m_edit = wizSheet.m_page1.m_edit;
        m_check = wizSheet.m_page2.m_check;
        Invalidate();
    }
}
```

SETTING THE WIZARD'S BUTTONS

MFC calls the OnSetActive() member function immediately upon displaying a specific page of the wizard. So, when the program displays Page 1 of the wizard, the CPage1 class's OnSetActive() function is called. Add code to this function that makes the wizard behave as you want. CPage1::OnSetActive() looks like Listing 8.5.

CH

8

> **LISTING 8.5**   CPage1::OnSetActive()

```
BOOL CPage1::OnSetActive()
{
    CPropertySheet* parent = (CPropertySheet*)GetParent();
    parent->SetWizardButtons(PSWIZB_NEXT);
    return CPropertyPage::OnSetActive();
}
```

You override the OnSetActive() function by opening the Properties window for the class, and then clicking the Overrides button. On the drop-down box beside OnSetActive, choose <Add> OnSetActive.

OnSetActive() first gets a pointer to the wizard's property sheet window, which is the page's parent window. Then the program calls the wizard's SetWizardButtons() function, which determines the state of the wizard's buttons. SetWizardButtons() takes a single argument, which is a set of flags indicating how the page should display its buttons. These flags are PSWIZB_BACK, PSWIZB_NEXT, PSWIZB_FINISH, and PSWIZB_DISABLEDFINISH. Because the call to SetWizardButtons() in Listing 8.5 includes only the PSWIZB_NEXT flag, only the Next button in the page is enabled.

Because the CPage2 class represents Page 2 of the wizard, its call to SetWizardButtons() enables the Back and Next buttons by combining the appropriate flags with the bitwise or operator (|), like this:

```
parent->SetWizardButtons(PSWIZB_BACK | PSWIZB_NEXT);
```

Because Page 3 of the wizard is the last page, the CPage3 class calls SetWizardButtons() like this:

```
parent->SetWizardButtons(PSWIZB_BACK | PSWIZB_FINISH);
```

This set of flags enables the Back button and provides a Finish button rather than a Next button.

Responding to the Wizard's Buttons

In the simplest case, MFC takes care of everything that needs to be done to flip from one wizard page to the next. That is, when users click a button, MFC springs into action and performs the Back, Next, Finish, or Cancel command. However, you'll often want to perform some action of your own when users click a button. For example, you may want to verify that the information that users entered into the currently displayed page is correct. If there's a problem with the data, you can force users to fix it before they move on.

To respond to the wizard's buttons, you override the OnWizardBack(), OnWizardNext(), and OnWizardFinish() member functions. Again, use the Events pane on the Properties window to do this. When users click a wizard button, MFC calls the matching function, which does whatever is needed to process that page. For example, the wizard in the Wizard Demo application doesn't let you leave Page 2 until you've checked the check box. This is accomplished with the overrides shown in Listing 8.6.

LISTING 8.6   RESPONDING TO WIZARD BUTTONS

```
LRESULT CPage2::OnWizardBack()
{
    CButton *checkBox = (CButton*)GetDlgItem(IDC_CHECK1);
    if (!checkBox->GetCheck())
    {
        MessageBox("You must check the box.");
        return -1;
    }
    return CPropertyPage::OnWizardBack();
}

LRESULT CPage2::OnWizardNext()
{
    UpdateData();
    if (!m_check)
    {
        MessageBox("You must check the box.");
        return -1;
    }
    return CPropertyPage::OnWizardNext();
}
```

These functions demonstrate two ways to examine the check box on Page 2. OnWizardBack() gets a pointer to the page's check box by calling the GetDlgItem() function. With the pointer in hand, the program can call the check box class's GetCheck() function, which returns a 1 if the check box is checked. OnWizardNext() calls UpdateData() to fill all the CPage2 member variables with values from the dialog box controls, and then looks at m_check. In both functions, if the box isn't checked, the program displays a message box and returns –1 from the function. Returning –1 tells MFC to ignore the button click and not change pages. As you can see, it is simple to arrange for different conditions to leave the page in the Back or Next direction.

FROM HERE

All developers like to believe that their applications are easy to use. I've been told many a time "it's obvious and intuitive" what to click or type somewhere. And for many of us, if we have a nagging suspicion that parts of our application may actually require a little work from our users, we don't really mind. "After all," developers have told me, "because of the amazing things you can do with this product, people don't mind having to do a little learning." But the truth is, people do mind. And they might just choose another product (or another developer, anyway) if your product is too hard to learn and too hard to use.

In this chapter you've seen how to write Help that will explain your product to your users. You've seen how to use property sheets to simplify the task of providing a lot of information at once. And you've learned how to write a wizard to walk your user through a specific task. These techniques will go a long way toward making your applications popular with your users.

In the next chapter, "Building COM+ Components with ATL," you will be looking at a very different kind of coding. Using COM components is a terrific way to reuse code across projects.

CH
8

BUILDING COM+ COMPONENTS WITH ATL

In this chapter

FUNDAMENTAL COM CONCEPTS

This chapter covers the theory and concepts of the Component Object Model (COM) and the extensions to COM known as COM+. Most new programmers have found COM (and the related technologies, ActiveX and OLE) intimidating. However, if you think of COM as a way to use code already written and tested by someone else, and as a way to save yourself the trouble of reinventing the wheel, you'll see why it's worth learning. Visual Studio and ATL, the Active Template Library, make COM and COM+ much easier to understand and implement by doing much of the groundwork for you.

WHAT IS COM?

COM is a binary standard for Windows objects. That means that objects can execute the executable code (in a DLL or EXE) that describes another object. Even if two objects were written in different languages, they can interact with the COM standard.

Note

> Because the code in a DLL executes in the same process as the calling code, using DLL is the fastest way for applications to communicate. When two separate applications communicate through COM, function calls from one application to another must be marshaled: COM gathers up all the parameters and invokes the function itself. A standalone server (EXE) is therefore slower than an in-process server (DLL).

How do they interact? Through an interface. A COM interface is a collection of functions, or really just function names. It's a C++ class with no data, only pure virtual functions. Your objects provide code for the functions. Other programs get to your code by calling these functions. All COM objects must have an interface named IUnknown (and most have many more, all with names that start with I, the prefix for interfaces).

The IUnknown interface has only one purpose: finding other interfaces. It has a function called QueryInterface() that takes an interface ID and returns a pointer to that interface for this object. All the other interfaces inherit from IUnknown, so they have a QueryInterface() too, and you have to write the code—or you would if there was no ATL. The full declaration of IUnknown is shown in Listing 9.1. The macros take care of some of the work of declaring an interface and aren't discussed here. Three functions are declared: QueryInterface(), AddRef(), and Release(). These latter two functions are used to keep track of which applications are using an interface. All interfaces inherit all three functions, and the developer of the interface must implement them.

LISTING 9.1 Iunknown—DEFINED IN \PROGRAM FILES\MICROSOFT VISUAL STUDIO.NET\VC7\INCLUDE\UNKNWN.H

```
MIDL_INTERFACE("00000000-0000-0000-C000-000000000046")
    IUnknown
    {
    public:
```

LISTING 9.1   CONTINUED

```
BEGIN_INTERFACE
virtual HRESULT STDMETHODCALLTYPE QueryInterface(
    /* [in] */ REFIID riid,
    /* [iid_is][out] */ void __RPC_FAR *__RPC_FAR *ppvObject) = 0;

virtual ULONG STDMETHODCALLTYPE AddRef( void) = 0;

virtual ULONG STDMETHODCALLTYPE Release( void) = 0;

template <class Q>
HRESULT STDMETHODCALLTYPE QueryInterface(Q** pp)
{
    return QueryInterface(__uuidof(Q), (void**)pp);
}

END_INTERFACE
};
```

COM provides services to programmers. For example, you don't need to locate a component to execute a function within it. If the component is properly registered, COM can find it and load it for you. COM also handles any marshaling or other preparation that is required for you to call a COM component's functions. Figure 9.1 illustrates the way you can think of COM facilitating these interactions. (If the component is in-process, as an ActiveX control is, the client speaks directly to the component without having to go through the runtime.)

Figure 9.1
The COM runtime handles all the work of finding, loading, and communicating with a component.

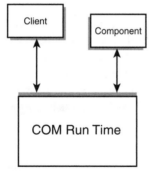

COM is the underlying technology that supports a variety of ways for programs to integrate and to share work. One of the technologies it supports is Automation, formerly called OLE Automation, which enables one program to call another program's methods.

WHAT IS AUTOMATION?

An Automation server lets other applications tell it what to do. It exposes functions and data, called methods and properties. For example, Microsoft Excel is an Automation server, and programs written in Visual C++ or Visual Basic can call Excel functions and set properties

CH
9

such as column widths. That means you don't need to write a scripting language for your application any more. If you expose all the functions and properties of your application, any programming language that can control an Automation server can be a scripting language for your application. Your users may already know your scripting language. They essentially will have no learning curve for writing macros to automate your application (although they will need to learn the names of the methods and properties you expose).

The important thing to know about interacting with automation is that one program is always in control, calling the methods or changing the properties of the other running application. The application in control is called an *Automation controller*. The application that exposes methods and functions is called an *Automation server*. Excel, Word, and other members of the Microsoft Office suite are Automation servers, and your programs can use these applications' functions to really save you coding time.

For example, imagine being able to use the function like the Word menu item Format, Change Case calls to convert the blocks of text your application uses to all uppercase, all lowercase, sentence case (the first letter of the first word in each sentence is uppercase, the rest are not), or title case (the first letter of every word is uppercase; the rest are not).

Generally speaking, an Automation server has a purpose beyond the services it offers to whatever Automation controllers are interested. For example, Word and Excel are both standalone products with millions of users. If you want to write some code that will offer services to other applications, yet not be used as a standalone executable, you probably want to write an ActiveX control.

WHAT ARE ACTIVEX CONTROLS?

ActiveX controls are tiny little Automation servers that load in-process. This means they are remarkably fast. They were originally called OLE Custom Controls and were designed to replace VBX controls—16-bit controls written for use in Visual Basic and Visual C++. (There are a number of good technical reasons why the VBX technology could not be extended to the 32-bit world.) Because OLE Custom Controls were traditionally kept in files with the extension .OCX, many people referred to an OLE Custom Control as an OCX control or just an OCX.

The original purpose of VBX controls was to enable programmers to provide unusual interface controls to their users. Controls that looked like gas gauges or volume knobs became easy to develop. But almost immediately, VBX programmers moved beyond simple controls to modules that involved significant amounts of calculation and processing. In the same way, many ActiveX controls are far more than just controls; they are components that can be used to build powerful applications quickly and easily.

Because controls are little Automation servers, they need to be used by an Automation controller, but the terminology is too confusing if there are controls and controllers, so we say that ActiveX controls are used by container applications. Visual Studio and Internet Explorer are container applications, as are many members of the Office suite and many non-Microsoft products.

In addition to properties and methods, ActiveX controls have *events*. To be specific, a control is said to *fire* an event, and it does so when there is something of which the container needs to be aware. For example, when the user clicks a portion of the control, the control deals with it, perhaps changing its appearance or making a calculation, but it may also need to pass on word of that click to the container application so that a file can be opened or some other container action can be performed.

It's usual, when working with COM technologies, to have a copy of the server application running on the same machine as the client or controller application. But it's not mandatory that you do so. To use COM over a network, you turn to a closely related technology: DCOM, or Distributed COM.

What Is DCOM?

The *D* in DCOM stands for *Distributed*. In a nutshell, DCOM enables you to treat code running on another computer just as though it were running on your computer. DCOM handles the issues of finding that code, marshaling parameters to the calls and returns from the calls, and handling the communications between the two computers, just as COM handles those issues when the component is on the same machine as your code. Figure 9.2 illustrates this idea.

Figure 9.2
DCOM makes distributed component programming as simple as single-machine component programming.

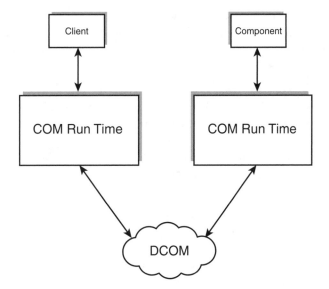

DCOM was designed to be a seamless evolution of COM and to work in much the same way that COM does. The idea was that programmers wouldn't have to do anything different when developing an application that used distributed components, or when developing distributed components, than they were doing when using plain old COM. And by and large the technology of DCOM works just that way.

There's a problem, though: When you write a component to be used on a single desktop, you don't need to worry about scalability and availability very much at all. In all likelihood, only one application will interact with the component at a time. Perhaps a handful of applications will interact with a very popular component, such as an XML parser. What's more, if the computer on which the component is installed has gone down, so has the computer on which the component-using code is installed, so availability isn't really an issue, either.

Things are quite different when the component and the component-using code are on different computers. Hundreds or thousands, even millions, of client computers could be running code that relies on the component. How can you make sure that your component can handle that kind of load? What happens if the connection between the component and the code that is using it is lost, or one of the computers goes down, or the connection to a database server is lost? These questions are ones that distributed programmers must face, and they are tough ones. The toolsets to help distributed programmers with these issues go beyond COM and DCOM. Microsoft Transaction Server (MTS) and Microsoft Message Queues (MSMQ) are two tools that were developed to help with these issues. You can learn more about them later in this chapter, in a section called "The Plus in COM+."

ATL, THE ACTIVE TEMPLATE LIBRARY

Working in COM can be intimidating when you first start, but parts of it move quickly from intimidating to boring. For example, every COM component must implement IUnknown. That's not hard after you have done it once—in fact, the code for IUnknown is the same in every COM component. So each project can start with a copy-and-paste session in which you bring over all the code that will be identical to this project. Yuck!

Both the intimidation and the boredom can be lessened dramatically with a library of some kind. Library code can provide the starting point or backbone for your project. If you don't know how to write that code, the library provides a reassuring starting point. If you know how to write the code and have written it many times before, the library spares you the pain of copying it from an old project into a new one.

In the past, MFC has served as the library in question. If you're writing a desktop application with a nice, rich user interface, you're probably using MFC anyway. Rich COM support was added to MFC many releases ago. But when developers started to build ActiveX controls, things changed. Often these controls had no visual interface at all, or had a very lightweight interface. The size of the final control started to be important, especially if a user was expected to download the control over the Internet before running it. Developers began to reject the MFC library for these lightweight controls, because it is simply enormous. Yet rejecting MFC meant writing COM code by hand.

This was the motivation behind ATL, the Active Template Library. It provides implementations for "stock" interfaces and makes it simple to build small, lightweight, fast COM components and controls. As you can probably tell from the name, it's a library of templates, whereas MFC is a library of classes. That means that you use the library code slightly differently. Even if you're not an experienced template user, you'll find ATL quite straightforward.

WHAT'S NEW IN ATL FOR .NET?

ATL was first released as a product after Visual C++ 4.0 had shipped. Versions 1.0, 1.1, and 2.0 of ATL were released through the Web. Version 2.1 shipped with Visual C++ 5, and version 3.0 shipped with Visual C++ 6. Now with Visual Studio .NET you get ATL 7.0—the intervening version numbers were skipped.

In previous versions of Visual Studio, there was an unspoken assumption that all Visual C++ programmers were MFC programmers. Plenty of useful classes were available in MFC only. Because ATL programmers don't use MFC, they faced the challenge of doing their own string manipulations, for example. No more. A number of useful classes have been moved from MFC so that they can be used in an ATL project with no MFC dependencies. These include:

- `CString`
- `CPoint`
- `CRect`
- `CSize`
- `CImage`

ATL now supports windowless ActiveX controls. A windowless control relies on its container to provide all the services that a window provides—such as catching messages and delivering notifications. Creating a window for the control to use consumes some execution time, so being able to rely on the container makes your control faster—and your code smaller. In addition, a windowless control can have transparent areas and can be a shape other than a rectangle.

If you've tried using the Standard Template Library (STL) in an ATL project in the past, you may have noticed that some of the types in an ATL project can't be used in the STL collection classes. (Often, using a template requires that certain operators be overloaded, for example.) ATL 7.0 includes simple collections: `CAtlArray`, `CAtlList`, `CAtlMap`, `CRBMap`, and `CRBMultiMap`. Rather than rely on functionality in the type you are collecting, these templates rely on companion classes called *traits*. For example, to declare an array of strings, use this line of code:

```
CAtlArray<CString, CStringElementTraits<CString>> array;
```

A SAMPLE ATL COMPONENT

ATL components should be simple and small. Typically they encapsulate business rules as part of a multi-tiered design. For demonstration purposes, a simple validation rule will do, such as for the format of a phone number. The component will have one method, `ValidatePhoneNumber()`, that takes a string as an input parameter and gives back two output parameters: an error code and an error message.

To create the component, you first create a project, and then add a component to it. Open Visual Studio and choose File, New, Project. Select Visual C++ projects and then ATL Project, as in Figure 9.3. Name the project PhoneFormat.

Figure 9.3
Create an ATL project.

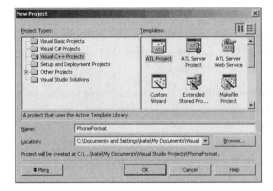

The ATL Project Wizard includes only one tab other than the Overview. The default settings, shown in Figure 9.4, are suitable for this project. Creating a DLL means that the component will be in-process with its client, for fastest possible execution. Click Finish to create the project.

Figure 9.4
Accept the ATL Project Wizard defaults.

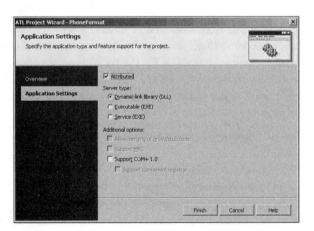

The next step is to add a component to the project. Right-click the PhoneFormat project in Class View and choose Add, Add Class. Expand the Visual C++ node and select ATL underneath it. Select ATL Simple Object, as in Figure 9.5, and click Open.

On the ATL Simple Object Wizard's Names tab, enter a short name of PhoneNumber. All the other boxes will fill themselves in as you type. Click the Options tab to look at the default options. As you can see in Figure 9.6, you have tremendous control over the behavior of the component. These default values are fine for this project, so just click Finish after looking them over.

Figure 9.5
Add an ATL Simple Object to your project.

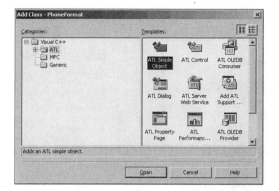

Figure 9.6
The Options tab of the Simple Object Wizard governs threading, aggregation, interfaces, and more.

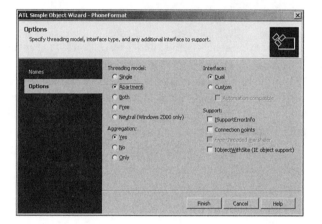

The Wizard gave this object a simple interface called IPhoneNumber. You need to add a method, ValidatePhoneNumber(), to the interface. Expand CPhoneNumber in the Class View and then expand Bases and Interfaces underneath that. Right-click IPhoneNumber and choose Add, Add Method.

The Add Method Wizard appears. Fill in the method name, ValidatePhoneNumber. Then add the parameters one at a time. First, the input string: Select the In check box, choose a type of BSTR (the string type for COM programming), and a name of Number. Click Add. Next, the first output parameter: Choose a type of BYTE*, then you can select the Out check box, enter a name of pError and click Add. For the last parameter, choose a type of BSTR*, select the Out check box, enter a name of pErrorString, and click Add. The completed dialog should resemble Figure 9.7. Click Finish.

Tip

Until you have chosen a type that is a pointer, such as BSTR* or BYTE*, the Out and Retval check boxes cannot be selected.

Figure 9.7
Add the method and
its three parameters.

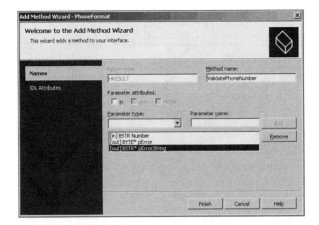

In the Class View, find `ValidatePhoneNumber` underneath `CPhoneNumber` and double-click it to edit the code. There are lots of ways you can validate that a string is in a certain format. Because this an ATL project, it makes sense to use the ATL regular expressions class, `CAtlRegExp`. Listing 9.2 shows the code for `ValidatePhoneNumber()`. Enter this code into the implementation file and build the project. Don't forget to add the `#include` statement so that the ATL Regular Expressions header is used.

LISTING 9.2   ValidatePhoneNumber

```
#include <atlrx.h>

// CPhoneNumber

STDMETHODIMP CPhoneNumber::ValidatePhoneNumber(BSTR Number, BYTE* pError, BSTR*
pErrorString)
{
   USES_CONVERSION;

   CAtlRegExp<> regexp;
   CAtlREMatchContext<> Context; //companion for match

   char* number = W2A(Number);
   regexp.Parse( "\\([0-9][0-9][0-9]\\) [0-9][0-9][0-9]-[0-9][0-9][0-9][0-9]" ); //
➥(800) 555-1212
   if (regexp.Match( number , &Context ))
   {
          *pError = 0;
          *pErrorString = SysAllocString(L"OK");

   }
   else
   {
```

LISTING 9.2 CONTINUED

```
        *pError = 1;
        *pErrorString = SysAllocString(L"Bad Format");
    }


    return S_OK;
}
```

Most of what's going on here is pretty obvious, but the way COM handles strings is not obvious at all. This function takes a BSTR—a binary string. The Match() function takes a C-style string: a char*. To convert between them, you can use the W2A macro. The macro USES_CONVERSION that you see at the top of the function defines it. A BSTR always uses wide characters, whereas an ordinary char* string uses ASCII characters—hence the macro name, W2A for wide-to-ASCII.

This code returns the two output parameters by de-referencing the pointers passed into the function. The error code is simple: This function is given a BYTE* and you can simply de-reference it, writing *pError=0 or *pError=1 as appropriate. The BSTR* is more difficult: You can't simply assign a literal string to the BSTR. The function SysAllocString takes care of allocating the memory in which the string is to be held while it is returned to the calling program. The L macro converts an ordinary quoted string to wide characters.

The component is complete. Just build it and fix any errors.

TESTING THE SIMPLE ATL COMPONENT

COM objects such as the phone number validator don't have a user interface. You test them by putting together a quick application with a very simple user interface. For this component, a dialog-based application with a text box for entering phone numbers will work well. The application creates an instance of the COM component you built with ATL, and uses it to validate the number that is entered. There are just a few steps to building the test project:

- Create an empty project
- Create a dialog box
- Connect the fields on the dialog box to variables
- Connect the button on the dialog box to a function
- Code the function
- Adjust the structure of the application and add COM support

CREATE AN EMPTY PROJECT

In Visual Studio, choose File, Close Solution, to close the PhoneFormat solution. Choose File, New, Project, to bring up the New Project dialog. Select Visual C++ Projects on the left, and MFC Application on the right. Name the application PhoneTest, as shown in Figure 9.8.

Figure 9.8
Create an MFC application to test the ATL component.

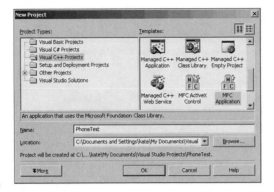

On the Application Type tab of the MFC Application Wizard, select Dialog Based. The other defaults are all okay for this application, so after flipping through the other tabs for a quick look, click Finish.

CREATE A DIALOG

> **Tip**
>
> The instructions that follow assume you have experience creating and editing a dialog in the Resource View. If not, you can find more details on the process in Chapter 3, "Interacting with Your Application."

In the Resource View, double-click IDD_PHONETEST_DIALOG to edit the main dialog of the application. Delete the static label with the TODO instruction. Click the OK button and choose View, Properties Window, if it is not already displayed. Using the Properties Window, change the ID of the button to ID_VALIDATE and the caption to Validate. Change the caption on the Cancel button to Close, but leave its ID unchanged.

Add an Edit Control and change its name to IDC_NUMBER. Put a static label before it, captioned **Number to Validate:**.

Add two static controls, one with the ID IDC_ERROR and the other with the ID IDC_MESSAGE, between the edit box and the two buttons. Change the caption of each of these to an empty string, and lengthen IDC_MESSAGE so that it can accommodate an error message.

Click in the background of the dialog (away from all the controls) to select the dialog itself, then drag the bottom of the dialog upwards to make a smaller dialog. The completed dialog should resemble Figure 9.9.

Figure 9.9
Build a simple dialog to exercise the `ValidatePhoneNumber()` method.

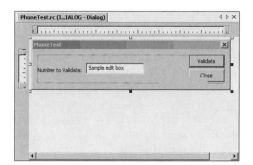

CONNECT THE FIELDS ON THE DIALOG BOX TO VARIABLES

Right-click the edit box, IDC_NUMBER, and choose Add Variable. This brings up the Add Member Variable Wizard. Leave the Control Variable check box selected, and from the drop-down box at the far right, choose Value rather than the default Control. This changes the Variable Type to `CString`. Enter **Number** for the Variable Name and click Finish. If you switch to the Class View and expand `CPhoneTestDlg`, you can see the new member variable.

In the same way, connect the static label called IDC_ERROR to a member variable called `Error` and connect IDC_MESSAGE to `Message`.

CONNECT THE BUTTON ON THE DIALOG BOX TO A FUNCTION

Click the Validate button on the dialog box. At the top of the Properties window is a toolbar. Find the Event button (it looks like a lightning strike) and click it. Click to the right of BN_CLICKED and a drop-down box appears. Drop it down and choose the only entry, `<Add> OnBnClickedValidate`. The function name appears in the Class View underneath `CPhoneTestDlg` and you are switched to editing the function.

CODE THE FUNCTION

When the button is clicked, the test code calls the `ValidatePhoneNumber()` method of the `IPhoneNumber` interface, as implemented in the `CPhoneNumber` class developed earlier in this chapter. Your coding effort will be substantially less if you use the `#import` directive. The `#import` directive enables you to treat a COM component as though it were an ordinary C++ object.

Open the source code for `CPhoneTestDlg`, and scroll to the top of the file. After the `#include` statements that are already there, add this line:

```
#import "..\PhoneFormat\Debug\PhoneFormat.dll" no_namespace
```

Tip

If you get any errors when you compile that refer to this line, make sure the path to PhoneFormat.dll is correct for your machine. (The .. in this line ensures that as long as the PhoneFormat and PhoneTest project folders are both under the same folder, this line will work.) Don't move the DLL; change the `#import` directive if necessary.

Edit OnBnClickedValidate() so that it looks like Listing 9.3.

LISTING 9.3   CPhoneTestDlg::OnBnClickedValidate()—VALIDATING THE ENTRY

```
void CPhoneTestDlg::OnBnClickedValidate()
{
    USES_CONVERSION;
    UpdateData();
    _bstr_t number = Number;
    unsigned char errorcode = 0;
    BSTR errormessage;
    try
    {
            IPhoneNumberPtr phone("PhoneFormat.PhoneNumber");
            phone->ValidatePhoneNumber(number, &errorcode, &errormessage);
            Error.Format("%u", errorcode);
            Message = W2A(errormessage);
    }
    catch (_com_error e)
    {
            Error.Format("%u", 99);
            Message = e.ErrorMessage();
    }
    UpdateData(false);
}
```

This function, like ValidatePhoneNumber(), uses the USES_CONVERSION macro to define some simple conversion macros. The call to UpdateData() moves the value the user typed in the edit box into the member variable, Number. Because ValidatePhoneNumber() takes a BSTR, this code creates a _bstr_t variable to pass in. The _bstr_t type encapsulates a BSTR with easy-to-use constructors that call SysAllocString for you, if required.

The actual COM call is wrapped in a try block in case anything goes wrong, such as the COM component being unavailable. Thanks to the #import directive, creating an instance of the COM component and calling its methods looks just like creating an ordinary C++ object. If you were wondering how to decide what string to pass into the IPhoneNumberPtr, it's the progid (short for program ID) of the COM component: the name of the project, a dot, and the name of the class you added into the project—PhoneFormat.PhoneNumber, in this case. In cases where you don't write the COM component you are using, expect to be told the progid.

> **Tip**
>
> If you haven't seen the Format method of the CString class before, it's an easy way to convert a number to a string. The %u for the first parameter indicates that you want the number treated as a simple unsigned number.

After the call to ValidatePhoneNumber(), this code sets the member variables associated with the two static controls, then calls UpdateData(false) to send the new values to the dialog.

Build the project at this point to make sure you don't have any errors, but it's not quite ready to run.

ADJUST THE STRUCTURE OF THE APPLICATION AND ADD COM SUPPORT

In the Class View, expand CPhoneTestApp and double-click OnInitInstance to edit it. Most dialog-based applications respond differently when the dialog is dismissed with OK than when it is dismissed with Cancel. This one does not need to, so the code can be quite a bit simpler. Find and remove these lines:

```
INT_PTR nResponse = dlg.DoModal();
if (nResponse == IDOK)
{
   // TODO: Place code here to handle when the dialog is
   //  dismissed with OK
}
else if (nResponse == IDCANCEL)
{
   // TODO: Place code here to handle when the dialog is
   //  dismissed with Cancel
}
```

In their place, add this single line:

```
dlg.DoModal();
```

(Because you changed the ID of the Validate button from IDOK to ID_VALIDATE, clicking it doesn't dismiss the dialog.) To activate COM support for this application, add this line at the very beginning of InitInstance():

```
::CoInitialize(NULL);
```

To clean up your COM work before returning from InitInstance(), add this line after the call to DoModal() and before the return statement:

```
::CoUninitialize();
```

Now, build the project again. It's ready to run. Enter a good phone number, and as you see in Figure 9.10, and you see an error code of 0 and a message of OK. Enter a bad one, as in Figure 9.11, and you see an error code of 1 and a message of Bad format.

CH

9

Figure 9.10
Valid phone numbers get a thumbs-up.

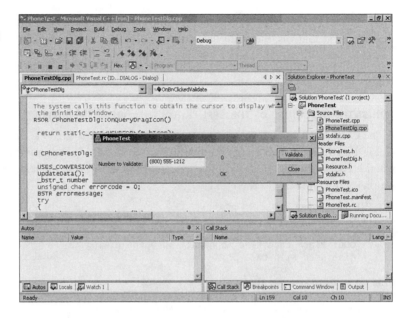

Figure 9.11
If the format is wrong, the COM component lets you know.

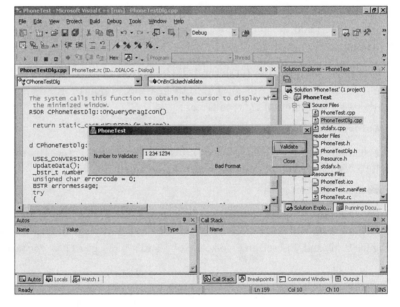

DEBUGGING A COM APPLICATION

If your COM component doesn't behave as you expect, you need to debug it. There's really nothing special about the process in this case, even though some of the code is not in the solution you have open. Here's how to step from OnBnClickedValidate() into ValidatePhoneNumber():

1. Put a breakpoint on the line in `OnBnClickedValidate()` that calls `ValidatePhoneNumber()`.

2. Start the application by choosing Debug, Start Debugging. When the dialog appears, enter a phone number.

3. Control stops when it reaches your breakpoint. Click the Step Into button on the Debug toolbar, or press F11.

4. The debugger first steps into a `bstr_t` copy constructor that is making a copy of the number. Press Shift+F11 or click Step Out to leave this constructor.

5. Step into the function call once again and notice that control is inside the overload of operator `->` for the smart COM pointer that the `#import` directive created. Step out of this function also.

6. Step into the call for a third time and notice that the smart COM pointer's code for `ValidatePhoneNumber()` is actually calling a function called `raw_ValidatePhoneNumber()`. Step over (F10) once, then Step into the call to `raw_ValidatePhoneNumber()`.

7. You'll find yourself in the code for another operator overload. Step out.

8. Step in one more time and—presto! You're in the code you wrote for `ValidatePhoneNumber()`. Now that you're here, try setting a breakpoint. That saves you having to step in and out so much on the way to the relevant code.

After you have a breakpoint in the COM component from inside your test solution, you should find it pretty simple to watch the component at work and understand any errors. Even if you stop debugging and start up again, your breakpoint will still be in place.

THE PLUS IN COM+

At the heart of COM+ is COM, the basic binary standard for interoperability in Windows. COM is language-independent: A component written in Visual Basic may be used in a Visual C++ application, for example. To make this possible requires a language-independent way to describe an interface. The COM solution to this problem is called Interface Definition Language, or IDL. If you look in the project folder for the PhoneFormat component, you can find a file called _PhoneFormat.idl, generated by Visual C++, that describes the component.

When you build the component, you create a DLL that includes the executable code for the `CPhoneNumber` class. You also create a type library, _PhoneFormat.tlb in this case, that describes your type—your COM component—to the COM framework. These parts of your component are pure COM.

As mentioned earlier in this chapter, DCOM consists of a number of services that were added to COM to support remote and distributed components. MTS was added around DCOM and COM, providing runtime services including transaction services, role-based security, and resource pooling. Most recently, COM, DCOM, and MTS were gathered together as COM+, and even more features—such as load balancing, object pooling, queued components and events—were added. Figure 9.12 shows how functionality and features have been layered onto COM over the years. It's important to realize that even when you're using all the bells and whistles of COM+, you are still using COM.

Figure 9.12
COM technologies have grown over time.

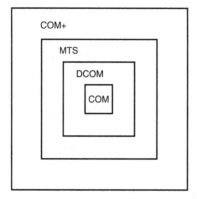

TRANSACTIONS

Many applications support the concept of a transaction. For example, if I am going to transfer money from one bank account to another, perhaps I plan to withdraw from one account and then deposit to the other. Either both will succeed or both will fail—I don't want a circumstance where the withdrawal worked, so some of my money is gone, but the deposit failed. And of course the bank doesn't want a circumstance where the deposit worked, so I have more money, but the withdrawal failed. To prevent this, the deposit and the withdrawal are gathered together into a transaction. If something goes wrong, you _roll back_ the transaction, undoing all of it. If everything works, you _commit_ the transaction, ensuring it cannot be rolled back.

Transaction support usually requires deliberate coding inside your application or component. You call a function to indicate that a transaction is starting, and call other functions to commit or abort (roll back) the transaction. With COM+, you can use _attributes_ to indicate that you are using transactions. This makes for much easier coding. In fact, an administrator or privileged user can even change transaction use with a deployment tool without recompiling your code. The support comes from the COM+ runtime, and your component need only ask for it.

ROLE-BASED SECURITY

Most applications need to perform some sort of authorization. For example, an order-taking application might allow any user to add an order, but only selected users to cancel an order after it has been taken. How will your code make this determination? There are several approaches:

- Keep a list of user accounts in code, and whenever users are added or removed, change and recompile your code.

- Create new accounts (such as Clerk and Manager) with new passwords, keep them in code, and expect users to sign in to just this application. From time to time, change the passwords and recompile the code.

- Create a database of user accounts and privilege levels, and look users up in the database to authorize actions. Changes to the database don't mandate that the code be recompiled.

This last option is clearly much more attractive (and secure) than the first two. But why should every developer do this work from scratch, when so many applications will need almost identical code? In COM+ role-based security, code can ask "Is this user a manager?" An administrator can maintain the list of users and roles with a deployment tool, and the code need never be recompiled to handle users being added, removed, or changed.

RESOURCE POOLING

Many applications start small and then grow. You add functionality, you add power, and eventually you move one of the components onto a server where more applications can leverage its abilities. Everything is going well until you realize—your application doesn't scale properly.

For example, imagine that your component needs to connect to a database. Many developers know that getting that connection carries a cost, so they get it once, store it inside the object, and use it as required. That's fine when only one or two connections will ever be consumed. But it's terrible when hundreds or thousands are needed—especially when most of those are sitting unused in a component that's inactive for a few moments or longer.

The runtime services of COM+ make it simple to pool resources such as database connections—or even execution threads—for maximum scalability. This is generally done transparently, behind the scenes, without extra effort for the programmer. That's always good news.

OBJECT POOLING

Imagine you are writing some sort of online order system, and you have objects in your server-side component such as Customer and Order. Whenever a new customer logs in to your Web site, you create a Customer object. Whenever that customer starts to place an order, you create an Order object to hold the items the customer is ordering, calculate totals, and so on.

When you start to handle hundreds or thousands of customers, you're going to notice that it's taking time to create and destroy these objects within the COM+ runtime. You can improve your performance dramatically if you let the runtime _de-activate_ an Customer object when it's no longer needed, and later _activate_ it to be used for a different customer. In fact, there's no need to wait until the customer leaves the Web site to de-activate the Customer object. If your customer is taking a minute or two to read a Web page and decide what to order, the runtime can de-activate the Customer object, activate it for some other part of the system to use for a different customer, and then activate it (or some other waiting Customer object) when this human customer finally decides what to order. This is all transparent to your code, as long as your object meets certain criteria that enable it to be pooled.

There's a certain amount of overhead associated with object pooling. For your savings to outweigh this overhead, some initialization or cleanup should be the same for all the object's instances. The initialization or cleanup that is specific to one instance (one human customer in our example) should be as little as possible.

QUEUED COMPONENTS

Microsoft Message Queuing (MSMQ) is a part of COM+ that simplifies messaging between applications, components, or tiers. One piece of code packages up a message, hands it to MSMQ, and then lets the runtime take it from there. MSMQ deals with finding the recipient, keeping the message in a queue if the recipient is offline at the moment, even sending confirmations and notifications to the sender. This means that distributed applications can work without requiring constant connectivity for all computers involved in an application—and without requiring a lot of extra code to support offline work.

COM+ Queued Components are the lowest-effort way to take advantage of MSMQ from within a COM+ application. A queued component cannot have functions that return values or change output parameters, because the methods may actually be called from a queued message, and there may be no caller to whom a reply can be sent. You add an attribute to your interface that marks this as a queued component, and the runtime takes care of making a queue and watching for messages to arrive in it. If you thought you couldn't build an application that supported working offline, look into Queued Components—you probably can use them to good effect.

EVENTS

COM+ events add a *publish-and-subscribe* aspect to your applications. Components that care about a specific action (a new user has been added, an order has been placed, a shipment has arrived) register themselves with the runtime as subscribers to specific named events. Other components may later publish those events. The publishers have no idea how many components are subscribed to a particular event, and no way to reach those subscribers. The publisher simply provides the event to the runtime. The runtime has the list of subscribers, and gets notification them by calling a specific method from (of course) a COM interface that each subscriber must implement.

Combining events with MSMQ gives you tremendous power and flexibility, keeping your application connected and working even when at times some of the computers are removed from the network. When connectivity is re-established, the waiting notifications are delivered, and processing continues as though the system were always connected.

FROM HERE

COM and COM+ are powerful technologies. If you're interested in ways to reuse code at the component level, and you're writing Windows applications, they have a lot to offer. Now that you grasp these concepts, you might want to learn more about .NET, an even more powerful way to reuse code at the component level. Chapter 1, ".NET Background," can give you a taste for that. Chapter 17, "Getting Started with .NET," shows you how to build a simple .NET object that works very much like a COM component.

For programmers who maintain existing COM applications or have a library of COM components they rely on, moving to .NET sounds like leaving behind the work that's already been done. But that's not the case at all. You see, a .NET object can be used just like a COM component. And your COM components can be used in .NET applications just as though they were .NET objects. You can see how simple it is in Chapter 23, "COM Interop."

If you're not ready to stop reading about Windows programming just yet, you could consider adding the power of the Internet to your applications using one of the many technologies introduced in Chapter 10, "Internet Programming."

CH
9

INTERNET PROGRAMMING

In this chapter

USING WINDOWS SOCKETS

Your applications can communicate with other applications through a network like the Internet in a number of ways. This chapter introduces you to the concepts involved with these programming techniques and develops applications to reinforce them. You'll learn about sockets programming with the Winsock libraries, MAPI programming, writing an ISAPI filter, and developing Web Services with ATL Server.

Before the Microsoft Windows operating system even existed, the Internet existed. As it grew, it became the largest TCP/IP network in the world. The early sites were UNIX machines, and a set of conventions called Berkeley sockets (released in 1981) became the standard for TCP/IP communication between UNIX machines on the Internet. Other operating systems implemented TCP/IP communications, too, which contributed immensely to the Internet's growth. On Windows, things were becoming messy, with a wide variety of proprietary implementations of TCP/IP. Then in the early 1990's a group of more than 20 vendors banded together to create the Winsock specification.

The Winsock specification defines the interface to a DLL, typically called WINSOCK.DLL or WSOCK32.DLL. Vendors write the code for the functions themselves. Applications can call the functions, confident that each function's name, parameter meaning, and final behavior are the same no matter which DLL is installed on the machine. For example, the DLLs included with Windows 98 and Windows 2000 are not the same at all, but a 32-bit Winsock application can run unchanged on either platform, calling the Winsock functions in the appropriate DLL.

An important concept in sockets programming is a socket's port. Every Internet site has a numeric address called an IP address, typically written as four numbers separated by dots: 198.53.145.3, for example. Programs running on that machine are all willing to talk, by using sockets, to other machines. But, if a request arrives at 198.53.145.3, which program should handle it?

Requests arrive at the machine, carrying a port number—a number that indicates for which program the request is intended. Some port numbers are reserved for standard uses; for example, Web servers traditionally use port 80 to listen for Web document requests from client programs such as Netscape Navigator or Microsoft Internet Explorer.

Most socket work is connection-based: Two programs form a connection with a socket at each end and then send and receive data along the connection. Some applications prefer to send the data without a connection, but there is no guarantee that this data will arrive. The classic example is a time server that regularly sends out the current time to every machine near it without waiting until it is asked. The delay in establishing a connection might make the time sent through the connection outdated, so it makes sense in this case to use a connectionless approach.

WINSOCK IN MFC

The MFC library that comes with Visual C++ has two classes that simplify working with sockets: CAsyncSocket and CSocket (which inherits from CAsyncSocket). These classes handle the API calls for you, including the startup and cleanup calls that would otherwise be easy to forget.

Windows programming is asynchronous: lots of different things happen at the same time. In older versions of Windows, if one part of an application was stuck in a loop or otherwise hung up, the entire application—and sometimes the entire operating system—would stick or hang with it. This is obviously something to avoid at all costs. Yet a socket call—perhaps a call to read some information through a TCP/IP connection to another site on the Internet—might take a long time to complete. (A function that is waiting to send or receive information on a socket is said to be *blocking*.) There are three ways around this problem:

- Put the function that might block in a thread of its own (see Chapter 14, "Multitasking with Windows Threads" for more information). The thread blocks, but the rest of the application carries on.
- Have the function return immediately after making the request, and have another function check regularly (poll the socket) to see whether the request has completed.
- Have the function return immediately, and send a Windows message when the request has completed.

The first option was not available when sockets programming was first brought to Windows, and the second is inefficient under Windows. Most Winsock programming adopts the third option. The class CAsyncSocket implements this approach. For example, to send a string across a connected socket to another Internet site, you call that socket's Send() function. Send() doesn't necessarily send any data at all; it tries to, but if the socket isn't ready and waiting, Send() just returns. When the socket is ready, a message is sent to the socket window, which catches it and sends the data across. This is called *asynchronous Winsock programming*.

> **Note**
>
> Winsock programming isn't a simple topic; entire books have been written on it. If you decide that sockets programming is the way to go, building standard programs is a good way to learn the process.

CAsyncSocket

The CAsyncSocket class is a wrapper class for the asynchronous Winsock calls. It has a number of useful functions that facilitate using the Winsock API. Table 10.1 lists the CAsyncSocket member functions and responsibilities.

TABLE 10.1 CAsyncSocket **MEMBER FUNCTIONS**

Method Name	Description
Accept	Handles an incoming connection on a listening socket, filling a new socket with the address information.
AsyncSelect	Requests that a Windows message be sent when a socket is ready.
Attach	Attaches a socket handle to a CAsyncSocket instance so that the instance can form a connection to another machine.
Bind	Associates an address with a socket.
Close	Closes the socket.
Connect	Connects the socket to a remote address and port.
Create	Completes the initialization process begun by the constructor.
Detach	Detaches a previously attached socket handle.
FromHandle	Returns a pointer to the CAsyncSocket attached to the handle passed to FromHandle().
GetLastError	Returns the error code of the socket. After an operation fails, call GetLastError to find out why.
GetPeerName	Finds the IP address and port number of the remote socket to which the calling object socket is connected, or fills a socket address structure with that information.
GetSockName	Returns the IP address and port number of this socket, or fills a socket address structure with that information.
GetSockOpt	Returns the currently set socket options.
IOCtl	Sets the socket mode, most commonly to blocking or non-blocking.
Listen	Instructs a socket to watch for incoming connections.
OnAccept	Handles the Windows message generated when a socket has an incoming connection to accept (often overridden by derived classes).
OnClose	Handles the Windows message generated when a socket closes (often overridden by derived classes).
OnConnect	Handles the Windows message generated when a socket becomes connected or a connection attempt ends in failure (often overridden by derived classes).
OnOutOfBandData	Handles the Windows message generated when a socket has urgent, out-of-band data ready to read.
OnReceive	Handles the Windows message generated when a socket has data that can be read with Receive() (often overridden by derived classes).

TABLE 10.1 CONTINUED

Method Name	Description
OnSend	Handles the Windows message generated when a socket is ready to accept data that can be sent with Send() (often overridden by derived classes).
Receive	Reads data from the remote socket to which this socket is connected.
ReceiveFrom	Reads a datagram from a connectionless remote socket.
Send	Sends data to the remote socket to which this socket is connected.
SendTo	Sends a datagram without a connection.
SetSockOpt	Sets socket options.
ShutDown	Keeps the socket open but prevents any further Send() or Receive() calls.

If you use the CAsyncSocket class, you'll have to fill the socket address structures yourself, and many developers would rather save themselves a lot of this work. In that case, CSocket is a better socket class.

CSocket

CSocket inherits from CAsyncSocket and has all the functions listed for CAsyncSocket. Table 10.2 describes the new methods added and the virtual methods overridden in the derived CSocket class.

TABLE 10.2 CSocket METHODS

Method Name	Description
Attach	Attaches a socket handle to a CAsyncSocket instance so that the instance can form a connection to another machine.
Create	Completes the initialization after the constructor constructs a blank socket.
FromHandle	Returns a pointer to the CSocket attached to the handle passed to FromHandle().
IsBlocking	Returns TRUE if the socket is blocking at the moment, waiting for something to happen.
CancelBlockingCall	Cancels whatever request had left the socket blocking.
OnMessagePending	Handles the Windows messages generated for other parts of your application while the socket is blocking (often overridden by derived classes).

In many cases, socket programming is no longer necessary because the WinInet classes, ISAPI programming, and ASP are bringing more and more power to Internet programmers. If you're the kind of person who enjoys seeing what's under the hood, or wants an easy way

CH

10

to add functionality to an existing program, sockets are worth exploring. Take a look through the online help for good socket examples.

USING THE MESSAGING API (MAPI)

The most popular networking feature in most offices is electronic mail. You could add code to your application to generate the right commands over a socket to transmit a mail message, but it's more simple to build on the work of others.

WHAT IS MAPI?

MAPI is a way of pulling applications that need to send and receive messages (messaging applications) together with applications that know how to send and receive messages (messaging services and service providers), to decrease the workload of all the developers involved. Figure 10.1 shows the scope of MAPI. Note that the word "messaging" covers far more than just electronic mail: A MAPI service can send a fax or voice mail message rather than an electronic mail message. If your application uses MAPI, the messaging services, such as e-mail clients that the user has installed, carry out the work of sending the messages that your application generates.

Figure 10.1
The Messaging API includes applications that need messaging and those that provide it.

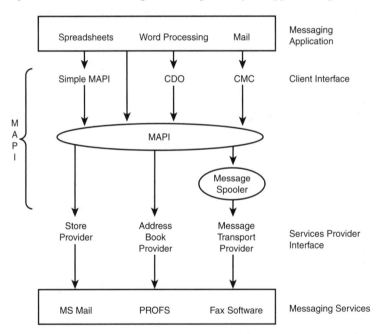

The extent to which an application uses messaging varies widely:

- Some applications can send a message, but sending messages isn't really what the application is about. For example, a word processor is fundamentally about entering and formatting text and then printing or saving that text. If the word processor can also send the text in a message, fine, but that's incidental. Such applications are said to be *messaging-aware* and typically use just the tip of the MAPI functionality.

- Some applications are useful without being capable of sending messages, but they are far more useful in an environment where messages can be sent. For example, a personal scheduler program can manage one person's To Do list whether messaging is enabled or not. If it is enabled, a number of workgroup and client-contact features—such as sending e-mail to confirm an appointment—become available. Such applications are said to be *messaging-enabled* and use some, but not all, of the MAPI features.

- Finally, some applications are all about messaging. Without messaging, these applications are useless. They are said to be *messaging-based*, and they use all of MAPI's functionality.

ADDING MAPI SUPPORT TO AN APPLICATION

On the file menu of many applications is a Send item that uses MAPI to send the document. (One motivation for this is to meet Windows logo requirements.) If your application has a document, being able to send it by e-mail to someone else is a useful feature.

To add this feature to your applications, it's best to think of it before you create the empty shell with the MFC Application Wizard. If you are planning ahead, use the following list to plan all the work you have to do to add this feature:

1. On the Advanced Features tab of the MFC Application Wizard, select the MAPI (Messaging API) checkbox.

That's it! The menu item is added, and message maps and functions are generated to catch the menu item and call functions that use your `Serialize()` function to send the document through MAPI. Figure 10.2 shows an application called MAPIDemo that is just an MFC Application Wizard empty shell.

CH
10

Figure 10.2
The MFC Application Wizard adds the Send item to the File menu, as well as the code that handles the item.

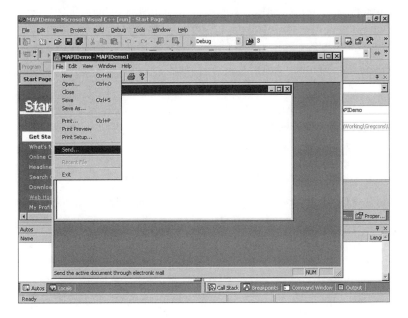

No additional code was added to this application, beyond the code generated by AppWizard, and the Send item is on the File menu, as you can see. If you choose this menu item, your MAPI mail client is launched to send the message. Figures 10.2 and 10.3 were captured on a machine with Microsoft Outlook installed, and so it is Microsoft Outlook that is launched, as shown in Figure 10.3. (If you have a different MAPI mail client installed, such as Lotus Notes, that client will launch.) The message contains the current document, and it is up to you to fill in the recipient, the subject, and any text you want to send with the document.

Figure 10.3

Microsoft Outlook is launched so that the user can fill in the rest of the e-mail message around the document that is being sent.

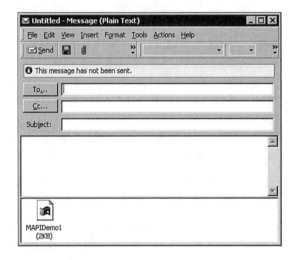

If the Send item doesn't appear on your menu, make sure that you have a MAPI client installed. Microsoft Outlook is an easy-to-get MAPI client. The `OnUpdateFileSendMail()` function removes the menu item Send from the menu if no MAPI client is registered on your computer.

If you didn't request MAPI support from the MFC Application Wizard when you built your application, here are the steps to manually add the Send item to your application:

1. Add the Send item to the File menu. Use a resource ID of `ID_FILE_SEND_MAIL`. The prompt is supplied for you.

2. Add these two lines to the document's message map:
   ```
   ON_COMMAND(ID_FILE_SEND_MAIL, OnFileSendMail)
   ON_UPDATE_COMMAND_UI(ID_FILE_SEND_MAIL, OnUpdateFileSendMail)
   ```

Adding the mail support to your application manually isn't much harder than asking the MFC Application Wizard to do it.

ADVANCED USE OF MAPI

If you want MAPI to do more than just send your document, such as build and send an e-mail message yourself, things do become more complex. There are four kinds of MAPI client interfaces:

- Simple MAPI, an older API not recommended for use in new applications.
- Common Messaging Calls (CMC), a simple API for messaging-aware and messaging-enabled applications.
- MAPI, a set of interfaces and a full-featured API for messaging-based applications.
- Collaboration Data Objects (CDO), an API with somewhat fewer features than Extended MAPI but ideal for use with Visual C++.

CMC, MAPI, and CDO are discussed in the sections that follow.

COMMON MESSAGING CALLS

The CMC API has only ten functions. That makes it easy to learn, yet those functions, described in the following list, pack enough punch to get the job done:

- `cmc_logon()` connects to a mail server and identifies the user.
- `cmc_logoff()` disconnects from a mail server.
- `cmc_send()` sends a message.
- `cmc_send_documents()` sends one or more files.
- `cmc_list()` lists the messages in the user's mailbox.
- `cmc_read()` reads a message from the user's mailbox.
- `cmc_act_on()` saves or deletes a message.
- `cmc_look_up()` resolves names and addresses.
- `cmc_query_configuration()` reports what mail server is being used.
- `cmc_free()` frees any memory allocated by other functions.

The header file XCMC.H declares a number of structures that hold the information passed to these functions. For example, recipient information is kept in this structure:

```
/*RECIPIENT*/
typedef struct {
    CMC_string              name;
    CMC_enum                name_type;
    CMC_string              address;
    CMC_enum                role;
    CMC_flags               recip_flags;
    CMC_extension FAR       *recip_extensions;
} CMC_recipient;
```

You could fill this structure with the recipient's name and address by using a standard dialog box or by hard-coding the entries, as in Listing 10.1.

LISTING 10.1   FILLING A CMC_recipient STRUCTURE

```
CMC_recipient recipient = {
    "Kate Gregory",
    CMC_TYPE_INDIVIDUAL,
    "SMTP:kate@gregcons.com",
    CMC_ROLE_TO,
    CMC_RECIP_LAST_ELEMENT,
    NULL };
```

The type, role, and flags use one of the predefined values shown in Listing 10.2. These values are defined in xcmc.h, which is usually in c:\Program Files\Microsoft Visual Studio .NET\Vc7\PlatformSDK\Include.

LISTING 10.2   (EXCERPT FROM INCLUDE\XCMC.H) COMMAND DEFINITIONS

```
/* NAME TYPES */
#define CMC_TYPE_UNKNOWN              ((CMC_enum) 0)
#define CMC_TYPE_INDIVIDUAL           ((CMC_enum) 1)
#define CMC_TYPE_GROUP                ((CMC_enum) 2)

/* ROLES */
#define CMC_ROLE_TO                   ((CMC_enum) 0)
#define CMC_ROLE_CC                   ((CMC_enum) 1)
#define CMC_ROLE_BCC                  ((CMC_enum) 2)
#define CMC_ROLE_ORIGINATOR           ((CMC_enum) 3)
#define CMC_ROLE_AUTHORIZING_USER     ((CMC_enum) 4)

/* RECIPIENT FLAGS */
#define CMC_RECIP_IGNORE              ((CMC_flags) 1)
#define CMC_RECIP_LIST_TRUNCATED      ((CMC_flags) 2)
#define CMC_RECIP_LAST_ELEMENT        ((CMC_flags) 0x80000000)
```

There is a message structure to fill in to create a message. You can hard-code the values, as in the recipient example of Listing 10.1, or present the user with a dialog box to enter the message details. Then your code would fill the structure using the values from the dialog box. This structure includes a pointer to the recipient structure you have already filled. Your program then calls cmc_logon(), cmc_send(), and cmc_logoff() to complete the process.

MAPI

The MAPI client interface is based on COM, the Component Object Model. Messages, recipients, and many other entities are defined as objects rather than as C structures. There are far more object types in MAPI than there are structure types in CMC. Access to these objects is through COM interfaces. The objects expose properties, methods, and events.

COLLABORATION DATA OBJECTS

If you understand the COM concept of Automation, you will easily understand CDO. Your application must be an Automation client, however, and building such a client is beyond the scope of this chapter. Visual Basic applications and scripting languages typically use

Automation, though it can also be used from a Visual C++ program. Your program would set up objects and then set their exposed properties (for example, the subject line of a message object) and invoke their exposed methods (for example, the Send() method of a message object).

The objects used in CDO include the following:

- Session
- Message
- Recipient
- Attachment

The messaging system of the CDO library was formerly known as Active Messaging. A detailed reference of these objects, as well as their properties and methods, can be found in MSDN under Messaging and Collaboration, Collaboration Data Objects, CDO CDO 1.2.1.

USING INTERNET SERVER API (ISAPI) CLASSES

ISAPI is used to enhance and extend the capabilities of your HTTP (World Wide Web) server. ISAPI developers produce extensions and filters. Extensions are DLLs a user invokes from a Web page in much the same way as CGI (common gateway interface) applications are invoked from a Web page. Filters are DLLs that run with the server and examine or change the data going to and from the server. For example, a filter might redirect requests for one file to a new location.

Note

For the ISAPI extensions and filters that you write to be useful, your Web pages must be kept on a server that is running an ISAPI-compliant server such as the Microsoft IIS Server. You must have permission to install DLLs onto the server, and, for an ISAPI filter, you must be able to change the Registry on the server. If your Web pages are kept on a machine administered by your Internet service provider (ISP), you will probably not be able to use ISAPI to bring more power to your Web pages. You may choose to move your pages to a dedicated server (a powerful Intel machine running Windows 2000 Server, or Advanced Server and Microsoft IIS is a good combination) so that you can use ISAPI, but this involves considerable expense. Make sure that you understand the constraints of your current Web server before embarking on a project with ISAPI.

The five MFC ISAPI classes form a wrapper for the API to make it easier to use:

- CHttpServer
- CHttpFilter
- CHttpServerContext
- CHttpFilterContext
- CHtmlStream

CH 10

Your application will have a server or a filter class (or both) that inherits from CHttpServer or CHttpFilter. These are like the classes in a normal application that inherit from CWinApp. Each DLL has only one instance of the class, and each server interaction with a client takes place through its own instance of the appropriate context class. (A DLL may contain both a server and a filter but, at most, one of each.) CHtmlStream is a helper class that describes a stream of HTML to be sent by a server to a client.

The ISAPI Extension Wizard is an application wizard that simplifies creating extensions and filters. To use this wizard, choose File, New, Project (as always) and choose Visual C++ Projects on the left side of the dialog box. Choose MFC ISAPI Extension DLL from the Templates list on the right side of the dialog box. Fill in the project name (Orders) and location, as shown in Figure 10.4, and click OK.

Figure 10.4
The ISAPI Extension Wizard is another kind of application wizard.

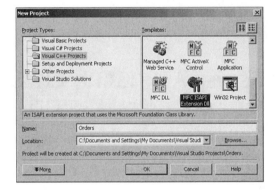

Creating a server extension is a one-step process. That step, which is also the first step for creating a filter, is shown in Figure 10.5. The names and descriptions for the filter and extension are based on the project name that you chose.

Figure 10.5
The first step in the ISAPI Extension Wizard process is to name the components of the DLL that you are creating.

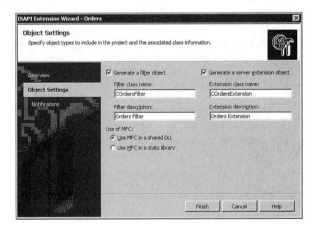

If you choose to create a filter, the Notifications tab is enabled and you can move to the second step for filters, shown in Figure 10.6. This list of parameters gives you an idea of the power of an ISAPI filter. You can monitor all incoming and outgoing requests and raw data, authenticate users, log traffic, and more.

Figure 10.6
The second step in the ISAPI Extension Wizard process is to set filter parameters.

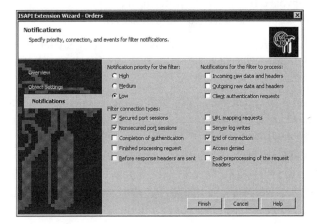

The Extension Wizard shows you a final confirmation screen, like the one in Figure 10.7, on the Overview tab. When you create a server and a filter at the same time, nine files are created for you, including source and headers for the class that inherits from CHttpServer and the class that inherits from CHttpFilter.

Figure 10.7
The ISAPI Extension Wizard process summarizes the settings that were chosen on the Overview tab.

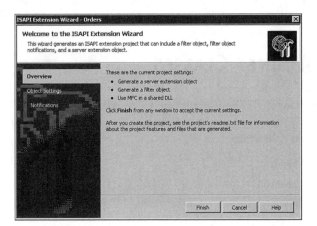

Writing a filter from this shell is quite simple. You have been provided with a stub function to react to each event for which notification is requested. For example, the filter class has a function called OnEndOfNetSession(), which is called when a client's session with this server is ending. You add code to this function to log, monitor, or otherwise react to this event.

When the filter is complete, you edit the Registry by hand so that the server will run your DLL.

To write an extension, add one or more functions to your DLL. Each function is passed a `CHttpContext` pointer, which can be used to gather information such as the user's IP address. If the function is invoked from an HTML form, additional parameters such as values of other fields on the form are also passed to the function.

The details of what the function does depends on the needs of your application. If you are implementing an online ordering system, the functions involved will be lengthy and complex. Other extensions will be simpler.

When the function is complete, place the DLL in the executable folder for the server— usually the folder where CGI programs are kept—and adjust your Web pages so that they include links to your DLL, like this:

```
Now you can <A HREF=http://www.company.com/exec/orders.dll> place an order</A>
online!
```

Visual Studio .NET includes a new tool, called ATL Server, to write powerful ISAPI filters and Web Services. You can read more about it in this chapter.

Adding the Internet to your applications is an exciting trend. It's going to make lots of work for programmers and create some powerful products that simplify the working life of anyone with an Internet connection. Just a few years ago, writing Internet applications meant getting your fingernails dirty with sockets programming, memorizing TCP/IP ports, and reading RFCs. The WinInet, MAPI, and ISAPI classes mean that today you can add amazing power to your application with just a few lines of code or by selecting a box on an application wizard dialog.

USING THE WININET CLASSES

MFC 4.2 introduced a number of new classes that eliminate the need to learn socket programming when your applications require access to standard Internet client services. Figure 10.8 shows the way these classes relate to each other. Collectively known as the WinInet classes, they are the following:

- `CInternetSession`
- `CInternetConnection`
- `CInternetFile`
- `CHttpConnection`
- `CHttpFile`
- `CGopherFile`
- `CFtpConnection`
- `CGopherConnection`

- CFileFind

- CFtpFileFind

- CGopherFileFind

- CGopherLocator

- CInternetException

Figure 10.8
The WinInet classes make writing Internet client programs easier.

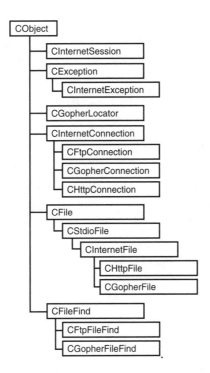

CObject
  - CInternetSession
  - CException
    - CInternetException
  - CGopherLocator
  - CInternetConnection
    - CFtpConnection
    - CGopherConnection
    - CHttpConnection
  - CFile
    - CStdioFile
      - CInternetFile
        - CHttpFile
        - CGopherFile
  - CFileFind
    - CFtpFileFind
    - CGopherFileFind

CH 10

> **Tip**
>
> These classes help you write Internet client applications, with which users interact directly. If you want to write server applications, which interact with client applications, you'll be interested in ISAPI, discussed in the next section.

First, your program establishes a session by creating a CInternetSession. Then, if you have a uniform resource locator (URL) to a Gopher, FTP, or Web (HTTP) resource, you can call that session's OpenURL() function to retrieve the resource as a read-only CInternetFile. Your application can read the file, using CStdioFile functions, and manipulate that data in whatever way you need.

If you don't have a URL or don't want to retrieve a read-only file, you proceed differently after establishing the session. Make a connection with a specific protocol by calling the session's GetFtpConnection(), GetGopherConnection(), or GetHttpConnection() functions, which return the appropriate connection object. You then call the connection's `OpenFile()` function. `CFtpConnection::OpenFile()` returns a `CInternetFile`; `CGopherConnection::OpenFile()` returns a `CGopherFile`; and `CHttpConnection::OpenFile()` returns a `CHttpFile`. The `CFileFind` class and its derived classes help you find the file you want to open.

This section works through a sample client program using WinInet classes to establish an Internet session and retrieve information.

> **Note**
>
> Though e-mail is a standard Internet application, you'll notice that the WinInet classes don't have any e-mail functionality. E-mail is handled by MAPI, instead. There is no support for Usenet news either, in the WinInet classes or elsewhere.

DESIGNING THE INTERNET QUERY APPLICATION

The sample application for this chapter, Query, demonstrates a number of the WinInet classes. It also serves a useful function: You can use it to learn more about the Internet presence of a company or organization. You don't need to learn about sockets or handle the details of Internet protocols to do this.

Imagine that you have someone's e-mail address `kate@gregcons.com`, for example and you'd like to know more about the domain (which in this example is gregcons.com). Perhaps you have a great idea for a domain name and want to know whether it's already taken. The Query application tries connecting to gregcons.com in a variety of ways and reports the results of those attempts to the user.

This application has a simple user interface. The only piece of information that the user needs to supply is the domain name to be queried, and there is no need to keep this information in a document. You might want a menu item called Query that brings up a dialog box in which users can specify the site name, but a better approach is to use a dialog-based application and incorporate a Query button into the dialog box.

A dialog-based application, as discussed in Chapter 2, "Building Your First Windows Application," has no document and no menu. The application displays a dialog box at all times; closing the dialog box closes the application. You build the dialog box for this application like any other, with Visual Studio.

To build this application's shell, choose File, New..., Project from within Visual Studio. Highlight MFC Application in the Templates list, name the application Query, and click OK. Choose Dialog Based on the Application Type tab of the MFC Application Wizard, as shown in Figure 10.9.

Figure 10.9
Choose a dialog-based application for Query.

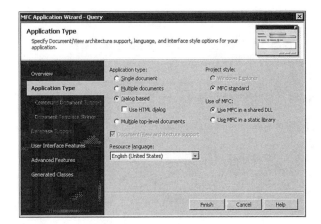

Accept all the defaults on the User Interface Features tab and move on to the Advanced Features tab. Choose no context-sensitive Help, no automation or ActiveX control support, and no sockets support, as shown in Figure 10.10. (This application won't be calling socket functions directly.) Check out the Overview tab to confirm your settings and click Finish to create the application.

Figure 10.10
This application doesn't need Help, automation, ActiveX controls, or sockets.

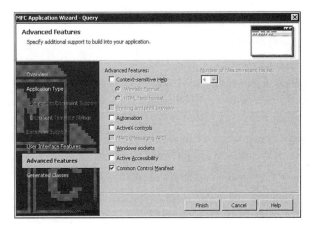

BUILDING THE QUERY DIALOG BOX

The MFC Application Wizard produces an empty dialog box for you to start with, as shown in Figure 10.11. To edit this dialog box, switch to the Resource view, expand the Query Resources, expand the Dialogs section, and double-click the IDD_QUERY_DIALOG resource. The following steps transform this dialog box into the interface for the Query application.

CH
10

Figure 10.11
The MFC Application Wizard generates an empty dialog box for you.

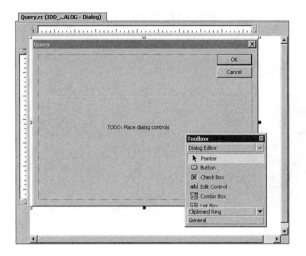

Tip

If working with dialog boxes is still new to you, be sure to read Chapter 3, "Interacting with Your Application."

1. Change the caption on the OK button to Query.
2. Change the caption on the Cancel button to Close.
3. Delete the TODO static text.
4. Grab a sizing handle on the right edge of the dialog box and stretch it so that the dialog box is 300 pixels wide or more. (The size of the currently selected item is in the lower right corner of the screen.)
5. At the top of the dialog box, add an edit box with the resource ID IDC_HOST. Stretch the edit box to make it as wide as possible.
6. Add a static label next to the edit box. Set the text to Site Name.
7. Grab a sizing handle along the bottom of the dialog box and stretch it so that the dialog box is 150 pixels high, or more.
8. Add another edit box and resize it to fill as much of the bottom part of the dialog box as possible.
9. Give this edit box the resource ID IDC_OUT.
10. On the Properties window for the edit box, set Multiline, Horizontal Scroll, Vertical Scroll, Border, and Read-Only options to True.

The finished dialog box and the Style properties of the large edit box should resemble Figure 10.12.

Figure 10.12
Build the Query user interface as a single dialog box.

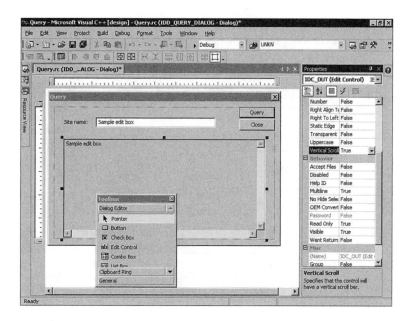

When the user clicks the Query button, the application should somehow query the site. The last step in the building of the interface is to connect the Query button to code. Three possible classes can catch the command the button click generates, but CQueryDlg is the logical choice because that class knows the host name. Follow these steps to make that connection:

1. Right-click the CQueryDlg class in the Class View window and choose Properties.

2. Click the Events button. Expand the IDOK node and select BN_CLICKED. This is the event that corresponds to the IDOK button being pushed.

3. Choose <Add> OnBnClickedOK from the drop-down box next to the BN_CLICKED element, as shown in Figure 10.13.

Figure 10.13
Add a function to handle a click on the Query button, still with the ID IDOK.

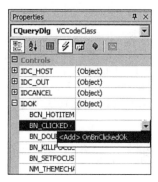

CH
10

4. Right-click the edit box IDC_HOST on the form and choose Add Variable.... Connect this control to a CString member variable of the dialog class called m_host, as shown in Figure 10.14.

Figure 10.14
Connect IDC_HOST to CQueryDlg: m_host.

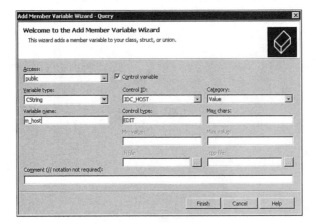

5. Connect IDC_OUT to m_out, also a CString.

Now all that remains is to write CQueryDlg::OnQuery(), which uses the value in m_host to produce lines of output for m_out.

QUERYING HTTP SITES

The first kind of connection to try when investigating a domain's Internet presence is HTTP, because so many sites have Web pages. The simplest way to make a connection using HTTP is to use the WinInet class CInternetSession and call its OpenURL() function. This returns a file, and you can display the first few lines of the file in m_out. First, add this line at the beginning of QueryDlg.cpp, after the inclusion statement for stdafx.h:

```
#include "afxinet.h"
```

This gives your code access to the WinInet classes. Because this application tries a number of URLs, add a function called TryURL() to CQueryDlg. It takes a CString parameter called URL and returns void. Right-click CQueryDlg in the Class View window and choose Add, Add Function to add TryURL() as a protected member function. The new function, TryURL(), is called from CQueryDlg::OnBnClicked(), as shown in Listing 10.3. Edit OnBnClicked() to add this code.

LISTING 10.3   QUERYDLG.CPP—CQueryDlg::OnBnClickedOK()

```
void CQueryDlg::OnBnClickedOK()
{
    const CString http = "http://";
```

LISTING 10.3   CONTINUED

```
    UpdateData(TRUE);
    m_out = "";
    UpdateData(FALSE);

    TryURL(http + m_host);

    TryURL(http + "www." + m_host);
}
```

The call to UpdateData(TRUE) fills m_host with the value that the user typed. The call to UpdateData(FALSE) fills the IDC_OUT read-only edit box with the newly cleared m_out. Then come two calls to TryURL(). If, for example, the user typed **microsoft.com**, the first call would try http://microsoft.com, and the second would try http://www.microsoft.com. TryURL() is shown in Listing 10.4.

LISTING 10.4   QUERYDLG.CPP—CQueryDlg::TryURL()

CH

10

```
void CQueryDlg::TryURL(CString URL)
{
    CInternetSession session;

    m_out += "Trying " + URL + "\r\n";
    UpdateData(FALSE);

    CInternetFile* file = NULL;
    try
    {
        //We know for sure this is an Internet file,
        //so the cast is safe
        file = (CInternetFile*) session.OpenURL(URL);
    }
    catch (CInternetException* pEx)
    {
        //if anything went wrong, just set file to NULL
        file = NULL;
        pEx->Delete();
    }
    if (file)
    {
        m_out += "Connection established. \r\n";
        CString line;

        for (int i=0; i < 20 && file->ReadString(line); i++)
        {
            m_out += line + "\r\n";
        }
        file->Close();
        delete file;
    }
    else
    {
```

LISTING 10.4   CONTINUED

```
        m_out += "No server found there. \r\n";
    }

    m_out += "----------------------\r\n";
    UpdateData(FALSE);
}
```

The remainder of this section presents this code again, a few lines at a time. First, establish an Internet session by constructing an instance of CInternetSession. There are a number of parameters to this constructor, but they all have default values that are fine for this application. The parameters follow:

- LPCTSTR pstrAgent. The name of your application. If NULL, it's filled in for you, using the name that you gave to AppWizard.

- DWORD dwContext. The context identifier for the operation. For synchronous sessions, this is not an important parameter.

- DWORD dwAccessType. The access type: INTERNET_OPEN_TYPE_PRECONFIG (default), INTERNET_OPEN_TYPE_DIRECT, or INTERNET_OPEN_TYPE_PROXY.

- LPCTSTR pstrProxyName. The name of your proxy, if access is INTERNET_OPEN_TYPE_PROXY.

- LPCTSTR pstrProxyBypass. A list of addresses to which connections are made directly rather than through the proxy server, if access is INTERNET_OPEN_TYPE_PROXY.

- DWORD dwFlags. Options that can be joined together with OR. The available options are INTERNET_FLAG_DONT_CACHE, INTERNET_FLAG_ASYNC, and INTERNET_FLAG_OFFLINE.

The dwAccessType parameter defaults to using the value in the Registry. Obviously, an application that insists on direct Internet access or proxy Internet access is less useful than one that enables users to configure that information. Making users set their Internet access type outside this program might be confusing, though. To set your default Internet access, double-click the My Computer icon on your desktop, then choose Control Panel, and then the Internet tool in the Control Panel. Choose the Connections tab (the version for Internet Explorer under Windows 2000 is shown in Figure 10.15) and complete the dialog box as appropriate for your setup. If you are using a different browser version, you might see a slightly different dialog, but you should still be able to choose your connection type:

- If you dial up to the Internet, add a connection and select when to dial the default connection.

- If you connect to the Internet through a proxy server, click the LAN Settings button, select the Use a Proxy Server check box, and identify your proxy addresses and ports.

- If you are connected directly to the Internet, leave the options blank.

Figure 10.15
Set your Internet connection settings once, and all applications can retrieve them from the Registry.

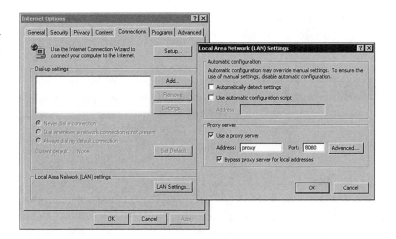

If you want to set up an asynchronous (nonblocking) session, for the reasons discussed in the "Using Windows Sockets" section earlier in this chapter, your options in dwFlags must include INTERNET_FLAG_ASYNC. In addition, you must call the member function EnableStatusCallback() to set up the callback function. When a request is made through the session—such as the call to OpenURL() that occurs later in TryURL()—and the response will not be immediate, a nonblocking session returns a pseudo error code, ERROR_IO_PENDING. When the response is ready, these sessions automatically invoke the callback function.

For this simple application, there is no need to enable the user to do other work or interact with the user interface while waiting for the session to respond, so the session is constructed as a blocking session and all the other default parameters are also used:

```
CInternetSession session;
```

Having constructed the session, TryURL() goes on to add a line to m_out that echoes the URL passed in as a parameter. The "\r\n" characters are return and newline, and they separate the lines added to m_out. UpdateData(FALSE) gets that onscreen:

```
m_out += "Trying " + URL + "\r\n";
    UpdateData(FALSE);
```

Next is a call to the session's OpenURL() member function. This function returns a pointer to one of several file types because the URL might have been to one of four protocols:

- file:// opens a file. The function constructs a CStdioFile and returns a pointer to it.
- ftp:// goes to an FTP site and returns a pointer to a CInternetFile object.
- gopher:// goes to a Gopher site and returns a pointer to a CGopherFile object.
- http:// goes to a World Wide Web site and returns a pointer to a CHttpFile object.

Cн

10

Because `CGopherFile` and `CHttpFile` both inherit from `CInternetFile`, and because you can be sure that `TryURL()` will not be passed a `file://` URL, it is safe to cast the returned pointer to a `CInternetFile`.

If the URL does not open, file is NULL, or `OpenURL()` throws an exception. Whereas in a normal application it would be a serious error if a URL didn't open, in this application you are making up URLs to see whether they work, and it's expected that some won't. As a result, you should catch these exceptions yourself and do just enough to prevent runtime errors. In this case, it's enough to make sure that file is NULL when an exception is thrown. To delete the exception and prevent memory leaks, call `CException::Delete()`, which safely deletes the exception. The block of code containing the call to `OpenURL()` is in Listing 10.5.

LISTING 10.5   QUERYDLG.CPP—`CQueryDlg::TryURL()`

```
CInternetFile* file = NULL;
try
{
    //We know for sure this is an Internet file,
    //so the cast is safe
    file = (CInternetFile*) session.OpenURL(URL);
}
catch (CInternetException* pEx)
{
    //if anything went wrong, just set file to NULL
    file = NULL;
    pEx->Delete();
}
```

If file is not NULL, this routine displays some of the Web page that was found. It first echoes another line to m_out. Then, in a `for` loop, the routine calls `CInternetFile::ReadString()` to fill the `CString` line with the characters in file up to the first \r\n, which are stripped off. This code simply tacks line (and another \r\n) onto m_out. If you would like to see more or less than the first 20 lines of the page, adjust the number in this `for` loop. When the first few lines have been read, `TryURL()` closes and deletes the file. That block of code is shown in Listing 10.6.

LISTING 10.6   QUERYDLG.CPP—`CQueryDlg::TryURL()`

```
if (file)
{
    m_out += "Connection established. \r\n";
    CString line;
```

LISTING 10.6 CONTINUED

```
        for (int i=0; i < 20 && file->ReadString(line); i++)
        {
            m_out += line + "\r\n";
        }
        file->Close();
        delete file;
    }
```

If the file could not be opened, a message to that effect is added to m_out:

```
    else
    {
        m_out += "No server found there. \r\n";
    }
```

Then, whether the file exists or not, a line of dashes is tacked on m_out to indicate the end of this attempt, and one last call to UpdateData(FALSE) puts the new u onscreen:

```
    m_out += "-----------------------\r\n";
    UpdateData(FALSE);
}
```

You can now build and run this application. If you enter **microsoft.com** in the text box and click Query, you'll discover that there are Web pages at both http://microsoft.com and http://www.microsoft.com. Figure 10.16 shows the results of that query.

Figure 10.16
Query can find
Microsoft's Web sites.

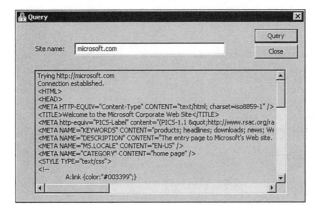

If Query doesn't find Web pages at either the domain name you provided or www. plus the domain name, it doesn't mean that the domain doesn't exist or even that the organization that owns the domain name doesn't have a Web page. It does make it less likely, however, that the organization both exists and has a Web page. If you see a stream of HTML, you know for certain that the organization exists and has a Web page. You might be able to read the HTML yourself, but even if you can't, you can now connect to the site with a Web browser such as Microsoft's Internet Explorer.

QUERYING FTP SITES

As part of a site name investigation, you should check whether there is an FTP site, too. Most FTP sites have names like ftp.company.com, though some older sites don't have names of that form. Checking for these sites isn't as simple as just calling TryURL(), again because TryURL() assumes that the URL leads to a file, and URLs such as ftp.greatidea.org lead to a list of files that cannot simply be opened and read. Rather than make TryURL() even more complicated, add a protected function to the class called TryFTPSite(CString host). (Right-click CQueryDlg in the Class View window and choose Add, Add Function... to add the function, which has a return type of void.)

TryFTPSite() has to establish a connection within the session, and if the connection is established, it has to get some information that can be added to m_out to show the user that the connection has been made. Getting a list of files is reasonably complex; because this is just an illustrative application, the simpler task of getting the name of the default FTP directory is the way to go. The code is in Listing 10.7.

LISTING 10.7   QUERYDLG.CPP—CQueryDlg::TryFTPSite()

```
void CQueryDlg::TryFTPSite(CString host)
{
    CInternetSession session;

    m_out += "Trying FTP site " + host + "\r\n";
    UpdateData(FALSE);

    CFtpConnection* connection = NULL;
    try
    {
        connection = session.GetFtpConnection(host);
    }
    catch (CInternetException* pEx)
    {
        //if anything went wrong, just set connection to NULL
        connection = NULL;
        pEx->Delete();
    }
    if (connection)
    {
        m_out += "Connection established. \r\n";
        CString line;

        connection->GetCurrentDirectory(line);
        m_out += "default directory is " + line + "\r\n";

        connection->Close();
        delete connection;
    }
    else
    {
        m_out += "No server found there. \r\n";
    }
```

LISTING 10.7   CONTINUED

```
    m_out += "----------------------\r\n";
    UpdateData(FALSE);
}
```

This code is very much like `TryURL()`, except that rather than open a file with `session.OpenURL()`, it opens an FTP connection with `session.GetFtpConnection()`. Again, exceptions are caught and essentially ignored, with the routine just making sure that the connection pointer isn't used. The call to `GetCurrentDirectory()` returns the directory on the remote site in which sessions start. The rest of the routine is just like `TryURL()`.

Add two lines at the end of `OnBnClickedOK()` to call this new function:

```
TryFTPSite(m_host);
TryFTPSite("ftp." + m_host);
```

Build the application and try it: Figure 10.17 shows Query finding no FTP site at microsoft.com and finding one at ftp.microsoft.com. The delay before results start to appear might be a little disconcerting. You can correct this by using asynchronous sockets or threading, so that early results can be added to the edit box while later results are still coming in over the wire. However, for a simple demonstration application like this, just wait patiently until the results appear. It might take several minutes, depending on network traffic between your site and Microsoft's, your line speed, and so on.

CH
10

Figure 10.17
Query finds one
Microsoft FTP site.

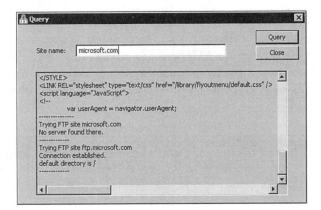

If Query doesn't find Web pages or FTP sites, perhaps this domain doesn't exist at all or doesn't have any Internet services other than e-mail. A few more investigative tricks are available, but they are beyond the scope of this chapter. E-mail and news protocols could be reached by stretching the WinInet classes a little more and using them to connect to the standard ports for these other services. You could also connect to some well-known Web search engines and submit queries by forming URLs according to the patterns those engines use. In this way, you could automate the sort of poking around on the Internet that most of us do when we're curious about a domain name or an organization.

ATL SERVER

As you can see in Chapter 21, "Creating an XML Web Service," it's easy to write a simple XML Web service. Visual Studio gives terrific support and enables you to quickly write code that any machine on the Internet can use, just by making a request to your Web server. But an XML Web service is like any other piece of software: There's more than one way to write one, and the way you choose depends on factors beyond just what's easiest. If you need outstanding power and speed, then—as always—you need C++. If you have a history as a COM developer, you're probably familiar with ATL's reputation as a tool to build fast, lightweight components and controls. That's the thinking behind ATL Server.

Have you ever thought about how ASP works? Developers write pages featuring a mixture of HTML and script (either JScript or VBScript) and name their files with an .asp extension. When a user with a browser requests the .asp page, the script runs on the server and the results are mixed in with the original HTML. Behind the scenes, an ISAPI filter (just like the ones you read about earlier in this chapter) intercepts the request for the file and executes the script in the file.

ASP has been wildly popular, even though it has performance issues and doesn't scale well. ASP.NET is a huge improvement on ASP and will be adopted by many Web developers. But if you want the ultimate in performance and scalability, you need the power of ISAPI and you need to develop in C++. ATL Server makes that simpler and easier than ever before. This section shows you how to do it.

When you use ATL Server to write an XML Web service, you get the fastest possible code, with none of the overhead of memory management or similar support from the .NET Framework. You should never use ATL Server to write a really simple Web service—it's like taking a sledgehammer to a flea. But to demonstrate how to use ATL to write a Web service, this section builds a very simple service called ATLCalculator with one method called Add.

> **Note**
>
> The basic concepts behind XML Web services are discussed at length in Chapter 21, "Creating an XML Web Service," and aren't repeated here.

THE ATL SERVER PROJECT WIZARD

To build a Web service yourself, start, as always, by opening Visual Studio .NET and choosing File, New, Project. On the left, choose Visual C++ Projects. On the right, choose ATL Server Web Service. Name the project ATLCalculator. The ATL Server Project Wizard appears.

Figure 10.18 shows the wizard's Project Settings tab. Leave these defaults unchanged. The wizard makes a handler and an ISAPI extension to route requests to handlers. You could combine these into a single DLL by selecting Generate Combined DLL for, in some cases, a slight performance improvement and easier deployment. This sample application self-deploys, because the Deployment Support box is checked, so it's OK to leave the Generate Combined DLL box unchecked.

Figure 10.18
Generate two DLLs and a deployment project.

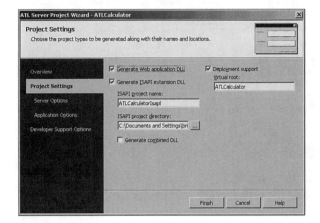

Figure 10.19 shows the wizard's Server Options tab. Here you could turn on caching for extra performance. This little sample doesn't need caching; just remember that it's there. In addition to caching, your XML Web service can use all the power of ASP.NET sessions—including sessions that are shared across server farms. This is useful if a client is likely to make repeated calls to your XML Web service and you want to keep some of the information that was passed in a server session. This sample application doesn't need sessions, so the defaults are fine on this tab.

Figure 10.19
Web services made with ATL Server can use caching and sessions with ease.

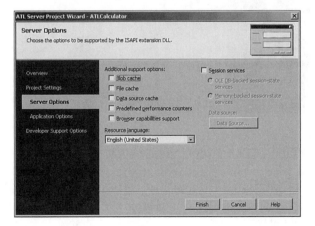

Figure 10.20 shows the Application Options tab of the wizard. You have no choice here: Create as Web Service is already selected, and it would be pointless to deselect it when you

are building an XML Web service. If you had just created an ATL Server project, this would be the tab where you could make it a Web service.

Figure 10.20
Confirm that your project is an XML Web service.

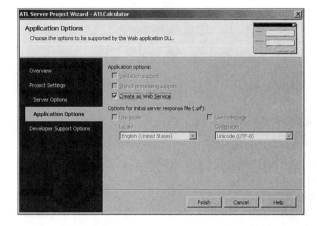

In Figure 10.21, you can see the Developer Support Options. There's no reason to suppress any of this help, so leave all the options selected. Click Finish to create the project.

Figure 10.21
The ATL Server Project Wizard can generate useful comments and more.

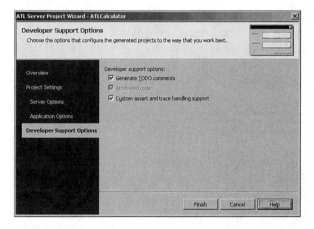

Two projects, ATLCalculator and ATLCalculatorISAPI, are created for you. The code is "classic C++," the same sort of code you would have written in Visual C++ 6, except that it has attributes (keywords in square brackets) as part of some of the definitions of classes and functions. These attributes direct the compiler to emit code for you, and they save you a tremendous amount of work.

ATLCalculator defines the actual service. Looking at it in the Class view, you'll see a namespace (identified with brace brackets) called ATLCalculatorService, and beneath that, a class called `CATLCalculatorService` and an interface called `IATLCalculatorService`. The interface defines one function, called `HelloWorld()`. If you double-click `IATLCalculatorService` in the Class view, you edit the definition, which looks like this:

```
__interface IATLCalculatorService
{
    // HelloWorld is a sample ATL Server web service method.  It shows how to
    // declare a web service method and its in-parameters and out-parameters
    [id(1)] HRESULT HelloWorld([in] BSTR bstrInput, [out, retval] BSTR *bstrOutput);
    // TODO: Add additional web service methods here
};
```

Here's the class that implements the interface:

```
class CATLCalculatorService :       public IATLCalculatorService
{
public:

// This is a sample web service method that shows how to use the
// soap_method attribute to expose a method as a web method
[ soap_method ]
HRESULT HelloWorld(/*[in]*/ BSTR bstrInput, /*[out, retval]*/ BSTR *bstrOutput)
{
    CComBSTR bstrOut(L"Hello ");
    bstrOut += bstrInput;
    bstrOut += L"!";
    *bstrOutput = bstrOut.Detach();

    return S_OK;
}
```

This code was generated for you to use as a sample. Finally, in ATLCalculator.htm, you see a list of the methods. Figure 10.22 shows you that page in Visual Studio .NET. You can also see the Class view in Figure 10.22, displaying the structure of the project.

Note

Unlike Web services written in Managed C++, the wizard doesn't generate a test page for you to run the Web service from a browser.

ATLCalculatorISAPI is a support project for the extension that will support the Web Services protocols such as SOAP.

ADDING A METHOD TO THE WEB SERVICE

Adding a method to your Web service is a two-step process: Add the method to the interface, then add an implementation of it to the class. Start with the interface: Right-click `IATLCalculatorService` in class view and choose Add, Add Method.

CH
10

Figure 10.22
The ATL Server Project Wizard generates the structure of a Web service, complete with a sample method and a page of HTML for documentation.

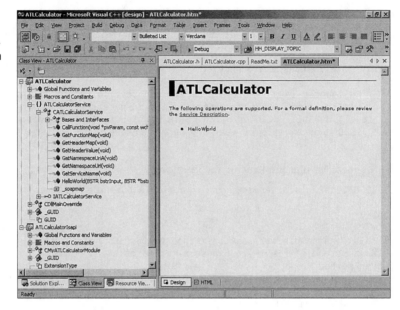

Enter **Add** for the Method Name. Then fill in the three parameters as follows:

- Select In for Parameter Attributes, choose DOUBLE for the Parameter Type, enter **x** for the Parameter Name, and click Add to add the parameter.

- Select In for Parameter Attributes, choose DOUBLE for the Parameter Type, enter **y** for the Parameter Name, and click Add to add the parameter.

- Choose DOUBLE* for the Parameter Type, which then enables you to select Out and Retval for the Parameter Attributes, enter **pResult** for the Parameter Name, and click Add to add the parameter.

Figure 10.23 shows the completed Add Method Wizard. Click Finish to add the method to the interface.

The Add Method Wizard adds this line to the interface definition:

```
[helpstring("method Add")] HRESULT Add([in] DOUBLE x, [in] DOUBLE y, [out,retval]
DOUBLE* pResult);
```

Copy the line down into the body of the class and edit it, then add the function body so it reads like this:

```
[ soap_method ]
HRESULT Add(/*[in]*/ DOUBLE x, /*[in]*/ DOUBLE y,/* [out,retval]*/ DOUBLE*
pResult)
{
    *pResult = x + y;
    return S_OK;
}
```

Figure 10.23
Add a method to the interface to add two numbers together.

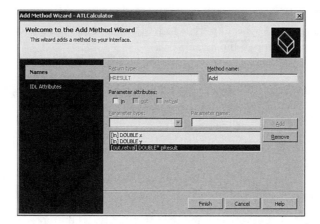

Strictly speaking, you don't need to repeat the keywords such as [in] before each of the function parameters. They are commented out here to ensure they don't confuse the compiler. But it's often helpful to developers to be reminded of the direction for each parameter.

The [soap_method] attribute is very important. It instructs the compiler to generate all the behind-the-scenes code that will make this into a Web-accessible method of the XML Web service. Not all functions added to the class are exposed over the Internet. You must request it with this attribute.

The code itself is trivial: it adds the two [in] parameters and puts the result in the memory to which pResult points. Then it returns S_OK, the HRESULT that indicates success.

After entering this code, build the project. Scroll through the output window and you'll see that the build process copies a number of files to a folder beneath the root of the local Webserver—c:\inetpub\wwwroot for most installations. It creates a folder called ATLCalculator there. Try opening a browser and entering **http://localhost/ ATLCalculator/ATLCalculator.htm**. You'll see the HTML file from the ATLCalculator project. Notice it wasn't updated automatically when you added the Add() method. You can also look at the .disco and .wsdl files for this Web service. More importantly, so can code that knows how to consume a Web service.

TESTING THE ATL SERVER WEB SERVICE

Using a Web service is nice and simple, whether the service is installed on the machine where you're developing or somewhere out on the Internet. If you wish, you can upload the contents of the c:\inetpub\wwwroot\ATLCalculator folder to another Web server. To ensure that the proper support files are in place, it would be best if the server had the .NET Framework installed. The instructions in this section assume you are testing on your development machine; change machine names if necessary.

Create an MFC dialog-based application called TestATLCalculator, as first described in Chapter 2. Change the Application Type to Dialog Based on the Application Type tab, and then click Finish to accept all the defaults.

Tip

> The instructions that follow assume you have experience creating and editing a dialog in the Resource View. If not, you can find more details on the process in Chapter 3, "Interacting with Your Application."

Open the IDD_TESTATLCALCULATOR_DIALOG dialog in the resource view, and edit it as follows:

- Remove the TODO static text and the OK and Cancel buttons.
- Add three edit boxes, all on the same horizontal line.
- Add a static text after the first edit box, and change its text to +.
- Add a button after the second edit box, and change its caption to =.
- Adjust the size of the dialog box to suit the controls.

The finished dialog should resemble Figure 10.24. Double-click the = button to add code that handles clicks on the button. A function called `CTestAtlCalculatorDlg::OnBnClickedButton1()` is generated, and the editor opens that code. As you can probably guess, clicking the button should invoke the Web service to add the two numbers together. So the first step is to add a Web Reference to the project that will enable Visual Studio .NET to consume the Web service.

Figure 10.24
Create a simple dialog box to test the Web service.

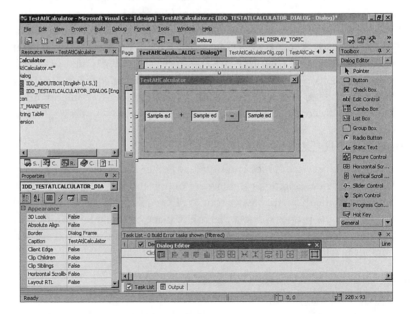

Choose Project, Add Web Reference. As in Figure 10.25, enter **http://localhost/ ATLCalculator/ATLCalculator.disco** for the Address, and press Enter. Visual Studio .NET loads the disco file that was generated for the ATLCalculator project and then copied to the ATLCalculator folder under the Web root. Click Add Reference to add this Web reference to your project.

Figure 10.25
Visual Studio .NET
can read DISCO files
to consume Web
services.

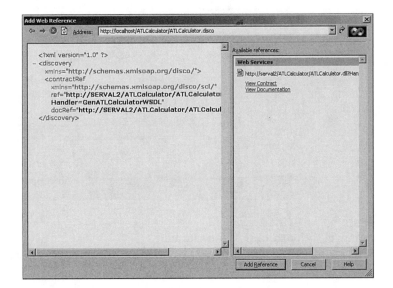

CH
10

A new entry appears in the Class View: a namespace called ATLCalculatorService. It contains a number of useful classes and maps, none of which you had to write. Figure 10.26 shows this namespace expanded—you should spot HelloWorld and Add in the names of the members of this namespace. To call the functions, you don't need to understand or change any of the code in this namespace; it's only a proxy for the real code in the ATLCalculator project.

The code that runs when a user clicks the = button uses the values that the user types into the first two edit boxes, and sets the value to be displayed in the third edit box. You must connect these controls to member variables of the dialog class before you can code the button-click handler. Right-click CTestAtlCalculatorDlg and choose Add, Add Variable. Set the Access to Private, and select the Control Variable check box. Select IDC_EDIT1 for the Control ID, and Value for the Category. Now you can enter **double** for the Variable Type and **x** for the Variable Name. Click Finish. Repeat these steps to connect IDC_EDIT2 to a double called **y** and IDC_EDIT3 to a double called **answer**.

At the top of the source file in which OnBnClickedButton1() is implemented, add this line:

```
#include "AtlCalculator.h"
```

Figure 10.26
Adding a Web
Reference generates a
namespace full of
useful proxies.

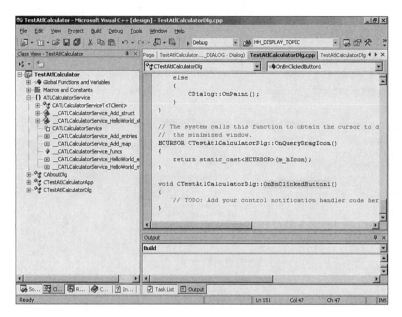

This brings in the proxy class definitions. Edit
CTestAtlCalculatorDlg::OnBnClickedButton1() so that it reads as in Listing 10.8.

LISTING 10.8   CTestAtlCalculatorDlg::OnBnClickedButton1()

```
void CTestAtlCalculatorDlg::OnBnClickedButton1()
{
    UpdateData(TRUE);
    ATLCalculatorService::CATLCalculatorService calc;
    calc.Add(x,y, &answer);
    UpdateData(FALSE);
}
```

The first line of OnBnClickedButton1() brings the values the user typed in the dialog box
into the member variables x, y, and answer. The last line uses the new values of these member variables to update the values to be displayed. In between is the actual work of processing the user's entries—and it's remarkably easy.

A class in the ATLCalculatorService namespace, CATLCalculatorService, represents the
Web service. To call methods of the Web service, just call methods of this proxy class. The
code in Listing 10.8 creates an instance of the proxy class, then calls the Add method.
Because the third parameter is a double*, it passes the address of answer rather than answer
itself. This enables Add() to change the value of answer.

That's how simple it is to use a Web service from ordinary, "classic" C++ code. The wrap-
pers and proxies that were generated for you rely on COM, so you need to make a small

change to another function to get COM initialized properly, and to clean up when the application is exiting. In the Class View, expand CTestAtlCalculatorApp and double-click InitInstance() to edit it. Most dialog-based applications respond differently when the dialog is dismissed with OK than when it is dismissed with Cancel. This one does not need to, so the code can be quite a bit simpler. Find and remove these lines:

```
INT_PTR nResponse = dlg.DoModal();
if (nResponse == IDOK)
{
   // TODO: Place code here to handle when the dialog is
   //  dismissed with OK
}
else if (nResponse == IDCANCEL)
{
   // TODO: Place code here to handle when the dialog is
   //  dismissed with Cancel
}
```

In their place, add this single line:

```
dlg.DoModal();
```

To activate COM support for this application, add this line at the very beginning of InitInstance():

```
::CoInitialize(NULL);
```

To clean up your COM work before returning from InitInstance(), add this line after the call to DoModal() and before the return statement:

```
   ::CoUninitialize();
```

Now, build the project again. Run it and enter numbers in the first two edit boxes, then click the = button. You'll get your answer, as in Figure 10.27, from your very own XML Web service.

Figure 10.27
An ordinary MFC application can use a Web service.

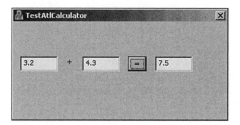

It's important to understand just how cross-platform XML Web services are. The MFC application created in this section can consume any XML Web service in the world, no matter in what language it was written or on what platform it runs. As long as you can point Visual Studio .NET at the DISCO file, you can consume the Web service. Similarly, code written in any language can consume the XML Web service written with ATL Server in this chapter, as long as the code is running on a machine that can find the Web service using the

Internet. The power is astonishing—and ATL Server makes it easily available to all C++ programmers, including those who aren't ready to move to the .NET platform yet.

FROM HERE

If you'd like to learn more about Internet protocols, port numbers, and what's happening when a client connects to a server, you might want to read Que's *Building Internet Applications with Visual C++*, 1995. The book was written for Visual C++ 2.0, and though all the applications in the book compile and run under later versions of MFC, the applications would be much shorter and easier to write now. Still, the insight into the way the protocols work is valuable.

The WinInet classes, too, can do much more than you've seen here. Query doesn't use them to retrieve real files over the Internet. Two of the WinInet sample applications included with Visual Studio do a fine job of showing how to retrieve files:

- FTPTREE builds a tree list of the files and directories on an FTP site.
- TEAR brings back a page of HTML from a Web site.

And of course, the whole .NET initiative is about Internet programming—a brand new kind of Internet programming. If you haven't read any of the .NET chapters in the second half of this book yet, now's the time to start! You've already seen how easy it is to create and use an XML Web service with "classic" C++—it's even easier with Managed C++.

Chapter 20, "Managed and Unmanaged C++," explains the differences between "classic" C++, like the MFC and Win32 programming in the first half of this book, and Managed C++, used to write .NET applications. Chapter 21, "Creating an XML Web Service," shows you how things work on the .NET side of Web services.

CHAPTER 11

DATABASE PROGRAMMING

In this chapter

WINDOWS DATABASE PROGRAMMING IN VISUAL C++

Without a doubt, databases are one of the most popular computer applications. Virtually every business uses databases to keep track of everything from its customer list to the company payroll. Unfortunately, there are many different types of database applications, each of which defines its own file layouts and rules. In the past, programming database applications was a nightmare because it was up to the programmer to figure out all the intricacies of accessing the different types of database files. As a Visual C++ developer, you have a somewhat simpler task because MFC includes classes built on the ODBC (Open Database Connectivity) and ADO (ActiveX Data Objects) systems.

Believe it or not, by using the MFC Application Wizard, you can create a simple database program without writing even a single line of C++ code. More complex tasks do require some programming, but not as much as you might think.

This chapter gives you an introduction to programming with Visual C++'s ODBC classes. You will also learn about the similarities and differences between ODBC and ADO. Along the way, you will create a database application that can not only display records in a database but also update, add, delete, sort, and filter records.

UNDERSTANDING DATABASE CONCEPTS

Before you can write database applications, you have to know a little about how databases work. Databases have come a long way since their invention, so there's much you can learn about them. This section provides a quick introduction to basic database concepts, and also describes the two main types of databases: flat and relational. It also introduces you to some important acronyms in database programming: SQL and ODBC.

USING THE FLAT DATABASE MODEL

Simply put, a database is a collection of records. Each record in the database is composed of fields, and each field contains information related to that specific record. For example, suppose you have an address database. In this database, you have one record for each person. Each record contains six fields: the person's name, street address, city, state, zip code, and phone number. A single record in your database might look like this:

NAME: Jane Customer
STREET: 16 Maple Drive
CITY: Indianapolis
STATE: IN
ZIP: 46290
PHONE: 800-555-1212

Your database will contain many records like this one, with each record containing information about a different person. To find a person's address or phone number, you search for the name. When you find the name, you also find all the information that's included in the record with the name.

This type of database system uses the flat database model. For home use or for small businesses, the simple flat database model can be a powerful tool. However, for large databases that must track dozens, or even hundreds, of fields of data, a flat database can lead to repetition and wasted space. Suppose you run a large department store and want to track some information about your employees, including their name, department, manager's name, and so on. If you have ten people in Sporting Goods, the name of the Sporting Goods manager is repeated in each of those ten records. When Sporting Goods hires a new manager, all ten records have to be updated. It would be much simpler if each employee record could be related to another database of departments and manager names.

USING THE RELATIONAL DATABASE MODEL

A relational database is like several flat databases linked together. Using a relational database, you can not only search for individual records, as you can with a flat database, but also relate one set of records to another. This enables you to store data much more efficiently. Each set of records in a relational database is called a table. The links are accomplished through keys, which are values that define a record. (For example, the employee ID might be the key to an employee table.)

The sample relational database that you use in this chapter was created using Microsoft Access. The database is a simple system for tracking employees, managers, and the departments for which they work. Figures 11.1, 11.2, and 11.3 show the tables: The Employees table contains information about each store employee; the DeptManagers table contains information about each store department's manager; and the Departments table contains information about the departments themselves. (This database is very simple and probably not usable in the real world.)

CH
11

Figure 11.1
The Employees table contains data fields for each store employee.

EmployeeID	EmployeeName	EmployeeRate	DeptID
236	Anderson, Maggie	8.95	COSMETICS
247	Anderson, Richard	6.53	MENSCLOTHING
242	Calbert, Susan	9.03	ENTERTAINMENT
250	Greene, Nancy	6.55	SPORTING
243	Hanley, Frank	7.25	HARDWARE
253	Harrison, Lenny	9.00	SPORTING
248	Jackson, Ken	5.75	MENSCLOTHING
246	Jenkins, Ted	8.92	HARDWARE
244	Johnson, Ed	7.10	HARDWARE
234	Johnson, Mary	7.35	COSMETICS
245	Kelly, Mick	7.10	HARDWARE
254	Littleton, Sarah	6.10	WOMENSCLOTHING
240	Nebbick, Lucy	5.90	ENTERTAINMENT
255	Olsen, Jane	6.88	WOMENSCLOTHING
241	Perry, Cal	5.36	ENTERTAINMENT
249	Peters, Sam	9.15	MENSCLOTHING
237	Sanford, Faith	6.55	ELECTRONICS
238	Smith, James	5.75	ELECTRONICS
251	Uley, Victor	6.78	SPORTING
235	White, Gail	6.22	COSMETICS
252	Wilson, Denny	6.20	SPORTING
239	Woods, Edward	10.65	ELECTRONICS
256	Yaslow, Meg	9.25	WOMENSCLOTHING
*	0		

Record: 1 of 23

Figure 11.2
The DeptManagers table contains information about each store department's manager.

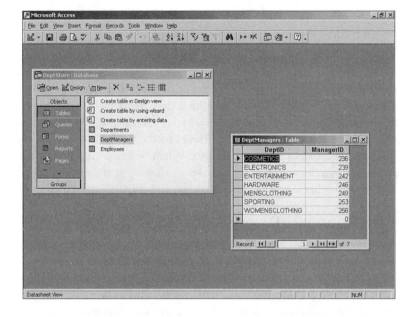

Figure 11.3
The Departments table contains data about each store department.

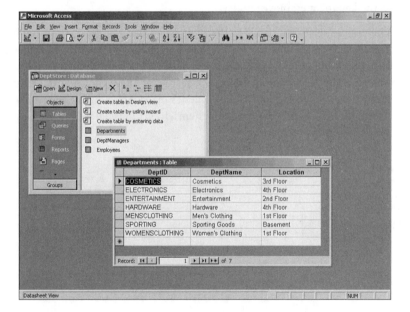

ACCESSING A DATABASE

To access relational databases, you must use some sort of database scripting language. The most commonly used database language is the Structured Query Language (SQL), which is used to manage not only databases on desktop computers but also huge databases used by banks, schools, corporations, and other institutions with sophisticated database needs. By using a language such as SQL, you can compare information in the various tables of a relational database and extract results made up of data fields from one or more tables combined.

> **Note**
>
> Most developers pronounce SQL as *sequel.*

Learning SQL, though, is a large task, one that is beyond the scope of this book (let alone this chapter). In fact, entire college-level courses are taught on the design, implementation, and manipulation of databases. Because there isn't space in this chapter to cover relational databases in any useful way, you will use the Employees table (refer to Figure 11.1) of the Department Store database in the sample database program you will soon develop. When you finish creating the application, you will have learned one way to update the tables of a relational database without knowing even a word of SQL. (Those of you who live and breathe SQL will enjoy the section later in this chapter, "SQL and the Enterprise Edition.")

THE VISUAL C++ ODBC CLASSES

When you create a database program with Visual C++'s MFC Application Wizard, you end up with an application that draws extensively on the various ODBC classes that have been incorporated into MFC. The most important of these classes are CDatabase, CRecordset, and CRecordView.

The MFC Application Wizard automatically generates the code needed to create an object of the CDatabase class. This object represents the connection between your application and the data source that you will be accessing. In most cases, using the CDatabase class in a program generated by the MFC Application Wizard is transparent to you, the programmer. All the details are handled by the framework.

The MFC Application Wizard also generates the code needed to create a CRecordset object for the application. The CRecordset object represents the actual data currently selected from the data source, and its member functions manipulate the data from the database.

Finally, the CRecordView object in your database program takes the place of the normal view window you're accustomed to using in applications generated by the MFC Application Wizard. A CRecordView window is like a dialog box that's being used as the application's display. This dialog box–type of window retains a connection to the application's CRecordset object, hustling data back and forth between the program, the window's controls, and the recordset. When you first create a new database application with the MFC Application Wizard, it's up to you to add edit controls to the CRecordView window. These edit controls must be bound to the database fields they represent so that the application framework knows where to display the data you want to view.

In the next section, you will see how these various database classes fit together as you build the Employee application step by step.

CREATING AN ODBC DATABASE PROGRAM

Although creating a simple ODBC database program is easy with Visual C++, you must complete a number of steps:

1. Register the database with the system.

2. Use the MFC Application Wizard to create the basic database application.

3. Add code to the basic application to implement features not automatically supported by the wizard.

In the following sections, you will see how to perform these steps as you create the Employee application, which enables you to add, delete, update, sort, and view records in the Employees table of the sample Department Store database.

REGISTERING THE DATABASE

Before you can create a database application, you must register the database that you want to access as a data source you can access through the ODBC driver. When your code uses the ODBC driver to work with the database, it will identify the database only by its Data Source Name (DSN). Follow these steps to create a Data Source Name (DSN) associated with the Department Store database:

1. Create a folder called Database on your hard disk and copy the file named DeptStore.mdb from this book's Web site to the new Database folder. If you don't have Web access, you can type the three tables into Microsoft Access. If you don't have Access, you can use a different database program, but you will have to connect to the data source for that program.

   The DeptStore.mdb file is a database created with Microsoft Access. You will use this database as the data source for the Employee application.

2. From the Windows Start menu, click Settings and then Control Panel. When the Control Panel dialog appears, double-click the Administrative Tools icon, and then double-click the Data Sources (ODBC) icon. (Depending on the version of Windows you are running, it may have a slightly different name—look for the letters ODBC.) The ODBC Data Source Administrator dialog box appears, as shown in Figure 11.4. Select the System DSN tab.

3. Click the Add button. The Create New Data Source dialog box appears. Select the Microsoft Access Driver from the list of drivers, as shown in Figure 11.5, and click Finish.

   The Microsoft Access Driver is now the ODBC driver that will be associated with the data source you create for the Employee application.

4. When the ODBC Microsoft Access Setup dialog box appears, enter **Department Store** in the Data Source Name text box and **Department Store Sample** in the Description text box, as shown in Figure 11.6.

Figure 11.4
Connecting a data source to your application starts with the ODBC Data Source Administrator.

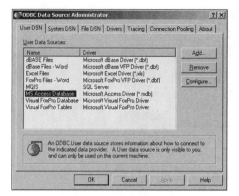

Figure 11.5
Creating a new data source is as simple as choosing Access from a list of drivers.

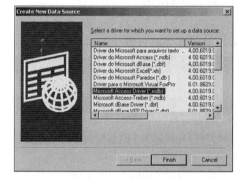

Figure 11.6
Name your data source whatever you like.

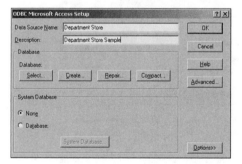

The Data Source Name is a way of identifying the specific data source you're creating. The Description field enables you to include more specific information about the data source.

5. Click the Select button. The Select Database file selector appears. Use the selector to locate and select the DeptStore.mdb file (see Figure 11.7).

6. Click OK to finalize the database selection and then, in the ODBC Microsoft Access Setup dialog box, click OK to finalize the data-source creation process. Finally, click OK in the ODBC Data Source Administrator dialog box and close the Control Panel.

Figure 11.7
Browse your way to
the .mdb file that
holds your data.

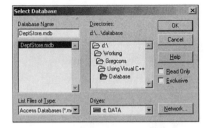

Your system is now set up to access the DeptStore.mdb database file with the Microsoft
Access ODBC driver using the DSN "Department Store."

CREATING THE BASIC EMPLOYEE APPLICATION

Now that you have created and registered your data source, create the basic Employee
application. The steps that follow lead you through this process. After you complete these
steps, you will have an application that can access and view the Employees table of the
Department Store database:

1. Select File, New, Project from Developer Studio's menu bar.

2. Select Visual C++ Projects on the left and MFC Application on the right, then type
   Employee in the Name edit box, as shown in Figure 11.8. Click OK. The MFC
   Application Wizard dialog box appears.

Figure 11.8
Create an ordinary
MFC application with
the MFC Application
Wizard.

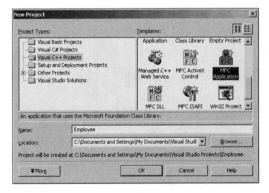

3. Select Single Document on the Application Type tab, as shown in Figure 11.9, to ensure
   that the Employee application doesn't allow more than one window to be open at a time.

4. On the Database Support tab, select the Database View Without File Support option
   and the ODBC option, as shown in Figure 11.10, so that the MFC Application Wizard
   will generate the classes you need to view the contents of a database. This application
   will not use any supplemental files other than the database, so it doesn't need file (serializing) support. Click the Data Source button to connect the application to the data
   source you set up earlier.

Figure 11.9
Create a single-document application.

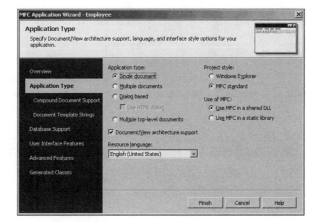

Figure 11.10
Arrange for a database view but no other file support.

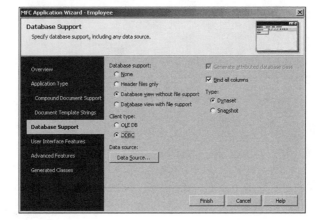

CH
11

5. In the Select Data Source dialog box, click the Machine Data Source tab and select the Department Store data source, as shown in Figure 11.11. Click OK. Leave the login name and password fields blank on the Login dialog and press OK.

6. In the Select Database Object dialog box, expand the Tables node and select the Employees table, as shown in Figure 11.12, and click OK.

    You've now associated the Employees table of the Department Store data source with the Employee application.

7. Accept the rest of the defaults and click the Overview tab. The result should look similar to Figure 11.13.

8. Click Finish and the MFC Application Wizard will create the basic Employee application.

Figure 11.11
Choose the
Department Store
data source.

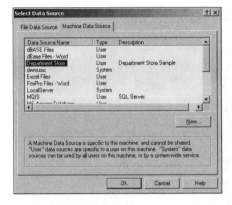

Figure 11.12
Select which table
from the data source
you want to use in
this application.

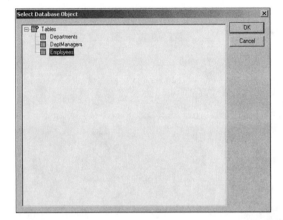

Figure 11.13
The Overview tab
summarizes the
choices made for this
database application.

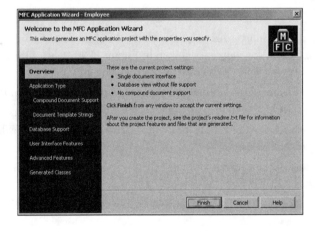

At this point, you can build the application by choosing Build, Build Solution. After the
program has compiled, choose Debug, Start to run the program. You can use the database

controls in the application's toolbar to navigate from one record in the Employees table to another. However, nothing appears in the window because you've yet to associate controls with the fields in the table that you want to view. You will do that in the following section. You will get one build error, and if you double-click that error in the Task list or Output window, here's what you'll see:

```
#error Security Issue: The connection string may contain a password
//The connection string below may contain plain text passwords and/or
//other sensitive information. Please remove the #error after reviewing
//the connection string for any security related issues. You may want to
//store the password in some other form or use a different user authentication.
```

Some data sources are protected by a password, and the simple connection string approach used here means the password will be kept in your source code: that's bad security. The #error statement was added to your code to make sure you looked into this and made a decision that's right for your project. Since there's no password on the Access file anyway, just remove or comment out the #error statement and build the project again.

CREATING THE DATABASE DISPLAY

The next step in creating the Employee database application is to modify the form that displays data in the application's window. Because this form is just a special type of dialog box, it's easy to modify with Visual Studio's Resource Editor, as you will discover while completing the following steps:

1. Choose View, Resource View to open the Resource View window and display the application's resources.

2. Open the resource tree by clicking + next to the Employee.rc resources folder. Then, open the Dialog resource folder the same way. Double-click the IDD_EMPLOYEE_FORM dialog box ID to open the dialog box into the Resource Editor, as shown in Figure 11.14.

3. Click the static string in the center of the dialog box to select it, and then press the Delete key to remove the string from the dialog box.

4. Use the dialog box editor's tools to create the dialog box, shown in Figure 11.15, by adding edit boxes and static labels. (Editing dialog boxes is introduced in Chapter 3, "Interacting with Your Application.") Give the edit boxes the following IDs: IDC_EMPLOYEE_ID, IDC_EMPLOYEE_NAME, IDC_EMPLOYEE_RATE, and IDC_EMPLOYEE_DEPT. Set the Read-Only property (found in the Properties window) of the IDC_EMPLOYEE_ID edit box to True.

CH
11

Figure 11.14
Open the dialog box in the Resource Editor.

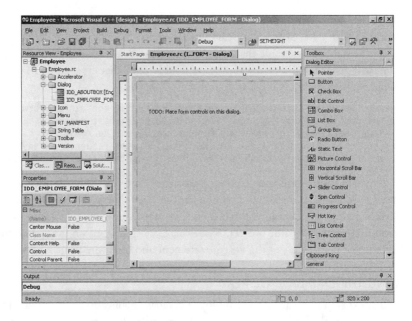

Figure 11.15
Create a dialog box to be used in your database form.

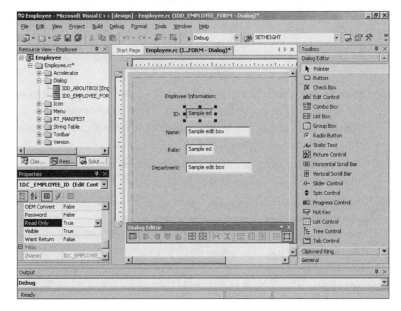

Each of these edit boxes represents a field of data in the database. The first edit box is read-only because it will hold the database's Primary Key, which should never be modified.

5. Associate the edit controls with member variables in the view class, CEmployeeView. In this case, the MFC Application Wizard has already provided a member variable; all you

have to do is connect that variable to the controls. The CEmployeeSet class is the connection between your application and the records in the Employees table in the database. It has member variables that tie directly to each of the records fields that are used to read from and write to the database table. However, the definition provided by the wizard must first be edited. In class view, double-click CEmployeeSet to edit the class definition. Find these lines:

```
long   m_EmployeeID;
CStringW       m_EmployeeName;
double m_EmployeeRate;
CStringW       m_DeptID;
```

Change CStringW to CString—the data exchange functions you're about to use don't work well with CStringW. Making this change means that you're relying on the ODBC drivers, rather than MFC, to handle Unicode for you. As long as your Access drivers are version 3.5 or higher, you're fine. The Access driver number is shown when you create your DSN—Figure 11.5 shows an Access driver version of 4.0.

6. Edit the CEmployeeView::DoDataExchange() function to resemble Listing 11.1.

LISTING 11.1   EMPLOYEEVIEW.CPP—CemployeeView::DoDataExchange()

```
void CEmployeeView::DoDataExchange(CDataExchange* pDX)
{
   DDX_Text(pDX, IDC_EMPLOYEE_ID, m_pSet->m_EmployeeID);
   DDX_Text(pDX, IDC_EMPLOYEE_NAME, m_pSet->m_EmployeeName);
   DDX_Text(pDX, IDC_EMPLOYEE_RATE, m_pSet->m_EmployeeRate);
   DDX_Text(pDX, IDC_EMPLOYEE_DEPT, m_pSet->m_DeptID);
   CRecordView::DoDataExchange(pDX);
}
```

CH

11

The code in Listing 11.1 associates each of the edit controls with members of the m_pSet variable by calling DDX functions. (DDX functions were covered in Chapter 3) The member variable m_pSet is a pointer to an instance of the CEmployeeSet class.

You've now created a data display form for the Employee application. Build and execute the program again, and you will see the window shown in Figure 11.16. Now the application displays the contents of records in the Employees database table. Use the database controls in the application's toolbar to navigate from one record in the Employees table to another.

After you've examined the database, try updating a record. To do this, simply change one field (except the employee ID, which is the table's Primary Key and can't be edited). When you move to another record, the application automatically updates the modified record. The commands in the application's Record menu also enable you to navigate through the records in the same manner as you do through the toolbar buttons.

Notice that you've created a sophisticated database-access program by writing hardly any C++ code—an amazing feat. Still, the Employee application is limited. For example, it can't add or delete records. As you may have guessed, that's the next piece of the database puzzle, which you will add.

Figure 11.16
The Employee application now displays data in its window.

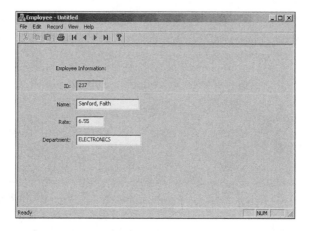

ADDING AND DELETING RECORDS

When you can add and delete records from a database table, you will have a full-featured program for manipulating a flat (that is, not a relational) database. In this case, the flat database is the Employees table of the Department Store relational database. Adding and deleting records in a database table is an easier process than you might believe, thanks to MFC's CRecordView and CRecordset classes, which provide all the member functions you need to accomplish these common database tasks. You need to add some menu items to the application, as first discussed in Chapter 6, "Building a Complete Application: ShowString." Follow these steps to include add and delete commands in the Employee application:

1. Open the Resource View window, open the Menu folder, and double-click the IDR_MAINFRAME menu ID. The Menu Editor appears, as shown in Figure 11.17.

2. Click the Record menu item to open it, click the blank menu item at the bottom of the menu, and then enter **&Add Record**, as shown in Figure 11.18 to set the caption.

3. In the new blank menu item below Add Record, add a delete command with the caption **&Delete Record**.

Next, you need to connect these commands to toolbar buttons, as first discussed in Chapter 7, "Status Bars, Toolbars, and Common Controls." Follow these steps:

1. In the Resource View window, open the Toolbar folder and then double-click the IDR_MAINFRAME ID. The application's toolbar appears in the Resource Editor.

2. Click the blank toolbar button to select it, and then use the editor's tools to draw a red plus on the button.

3. In the Properties Window, change the ID to ID_RECORD_ADDRECORD to connect this button to the menu, as shown in Figure 11.19.

Figure 11.17
Visual Studio's Menu
Editor is in the pane
on the right.

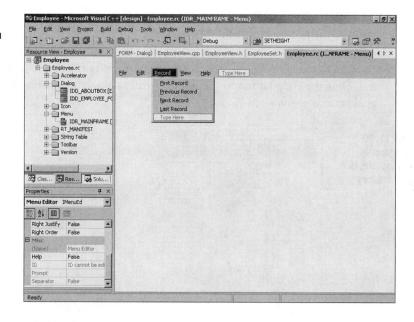

Figure 11.18
Add a menu item that
adds a record to the
Employees table.

Figure 11.19
Add a button and
connect it to the
menu item.

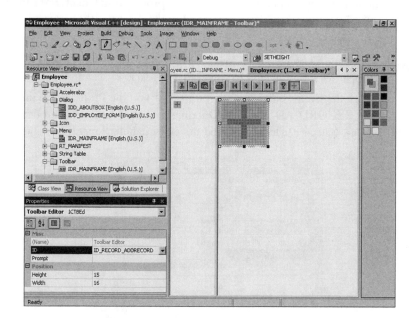

4. Select the blank button again and draw a red minus sign, giving the button the
   ID_RECORD_DELETERECORD ID.

5. Drag and drop the Add and Delete buttons to the left of the Help (question mark) button. Drag the Help button to the right to create a space between it and the newly created buttons as shown in Figure 11.20.

Figure 11.20
Grouping toolbar
buttons indicates to
the user that they
perform related
operations.

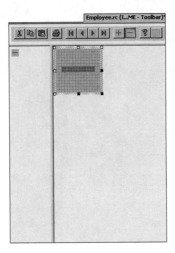

Now that you have added the menu items and the toolbar buttons, you need to arrange for
code to catch the command message sent when the user clicks the button or chooses the
menu item. Background information on this process is in Chapter 3, and in Chapter 6 and
Chapter 7. Because the view is connected to the database, the view will catch these messages. Follow these steps:

1. Open the Class View Window and right-click the CEmployeeView class. Choose
   Properties from the context menu that appears.

2. Click the Events button (the lightning bolt) on the Properties Window. Expand the
   ID_RECORD_ADDRECORD item, select the Command edit box, and then choose
   <Add> OnRecordAddrecord to add the event handler function, as shown in Figure 11.21.

Figure 11.21
Add a function to
handle the event.

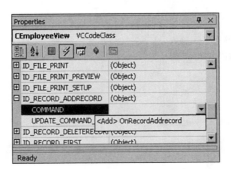

3. Add an event handler function for the ID_RECORD_DELETERECORD command in the same way.

4. Open the EmployeeView.h file by double-clicking CEmployeeView in the Class View window. In the Attributes section of the class's declaration, add the following lines:

```
protected:
  BOOL m_bAdding;
```

5. Double-click the CEmployeeView constructor in the Class View window to edit it, erase the TODO comment, and add this line at the bottom of the function:

```
m_bAdding = FALSE;
```

6. Double-click the OnRecordAddrecord() function and edit it so that it looks like Listing 11.2. (Explanations of the function code listings in these steps follow this section.)

LISTING 11.2   CEmployeeView::OnRecordAddrecord()

```
void CEmployeeView::OnRecordAddrecord(void)
{
    m_pSet->AddNew();
    m_pSet->m_EmployeeRate = 0.0f;
    m_pSet->m_EmployeeID = 0;
    m_bAdding = TRUE;
    CEdit* pCtrl = (CEdit*)GetDlgItem(IDC_EMPLOYEE_ID);
    int result = pCtrl->SetReadOnly(FALSE);
    UpdateData(FALSE);
}
```

CH
11

7. After adding a new record, when the user moves forward or backward in the recordset, you must ensure the database is correctly updated. To do this, you override the OnMove() function in the view. Right-click CEmployeeView in the Class View window and choose Properties. Click the Overrides button (the green lozenge,) select OnMove from the list on the left, and then choose <Add> OnMove from the adjacent drop-down box, as shown in Figure 11.22.

8. Edit the OnMove() function so that it has the code in Listing 11.3. (Explanations of the function code listings in these steps follow this section.)

LISTING 11.3   CEmployeeView::OnMove()

```
BOOL CEmployeeView::OnMove(UINT nIDMoveCommand)
{
    if (m_bAdding)
    {
        m_bAdding = FALSE;
        UpdateData(TRUE);
        if (m_pSet->CanUpdate())
            m_pSet->Update();
        m_pSet->Requery();
        UpdateData(FALSE);
        CEdit* pCtrl = (CEdit*)GetDlgItem(IDC_EMPLOYEE_ID);
        pCtrl->SetReadOnly(TRUE);
```

LISTING 11.3 CONTINUED

```
            return TRUE;
    }
    else
            return CRecordView::OnMove(nIDMoveCommand);
}
```

Figure 11.22
Override the
OnMove() function.

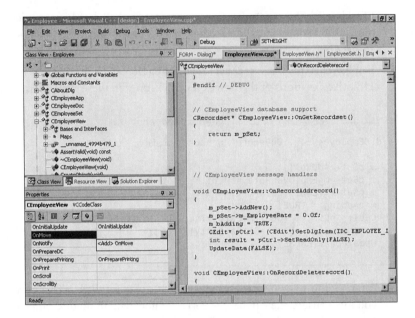

9. Double-click the OnRecordDeleterecord() function and edit it so that it looks like Listing 11.4. (Explanations of the function code listings in these steps follow this section.)

LISTING 11.4 CEmployeeView::OnRecordDelete()

```
void CEmployeeView::OnRecordDeleterecord(void)
{
        m_pSet->Delete();
        m_pSet->MoveNext();

        if (m_pSet->IsEOF())
            m_pSet->MoveLast();
        if (m_pSet->IsBOF())
            m_pSet->SetFieldNull(NULL);

        UpdateData(FALSE);
}
```

You've now modified the Employee application so that it can add and delete, as well as update, records. After compiling the application, run it by choosing Debug, Start, or by pressing F5. When you do, you see the Employee application's main window, which doesn't look any different than it did in the preceding section. Now, however, you can add new records by clicking the Add button on the toolbar (or by selecting the Record, Add Record command on the menu bar) and delete records by clicking the Delete button (or by clicking the Record, Delete Record command).

When you click the Add button, the application displays a blank record. Fill in the fields for the record; when you move to another record, the application automatically updates the database with the new record. To delete a record, just click the Delete button. The current record (the one on the screen) vanishes and is replaced by the next record in the database.

EXAMINING THE OnRecordAddrecord() FUNCTION

You might be wondering how the C++ code you added to the application works. OnRecordAddrecord() starts with a call to the AddNew() member function of CEmployeeSet, the class derived from CRecordset. This sets up a blank record for the user to fill in, but the new blank record doesn't appear on the screen until the view window's UpdateData() function is called. Before that happens, your code will set everything up so the update goes smoothly.

After the user has created a new record, the database needs to be updated. Because this add routine sets an indicator flag, m_bAdding, the move routine can determine whether the user is moving away from an ordinary database record or a newly added one.

When the user enters a new record, it should be possible to change the contents of the Employee ID field, which is currently set to read only. To change the read-only status of the control, the program first obtains a pointer to the control with GetDlgItem() and then calls the control's SetReadOnly() member function to set the read-only attribute to FALSE.

Finally, the call to UpdateData() displays the new blank record.

EXAMINING THE OnMove() FUNCTION

Now that the user has a blank record on the screen, it's a simple matter to fill in the edit controls with the necessary data. To add the new record to the database, the user must move to a new record, an action that forces a call to the view window's OnMove() member function. Normally, OnMove() does nothing more than display the next record. Your override saves new records as well.

When OnMove() is called, the first thing the program does is check the Boolean variable m_bAdding to see whether the user is in the process of adding a new record. If m_bAdding is FALSE, the body of the if statement is skipped and the else clause is executed. In the else clause, the program calls the base class (CRecordView) version of OnMove(), which simply moves to the next record.

CH
11

If m_bAdding is TRUE, the body of the if statement is executed. There, the program first resets the m_bAdding flag and then calls UpdateData() to transfer data out of the view window's controls and into the recordset class. A call to the recordset's CanUpdate() method determines whether it's okay to update the data source, after which a call to the recordset's Update() member function adds the new record to the data source.

To rebuild the recordset, the program must call the recordset's Requery() member function, and then a call to the view window's UpdateData() member function transfers new data to the window's controls. Finally, the program sets the Employee ID field back to read-only, with another call to GetDlgItem()and SetReadOnly().

EXAMINING THE OnRecordDeleterecord() FUNCTION

Deleting a record is simple. OnRecordDeleterecord() just calls the recordset's Delete() function. When the record is deleted, a call to the recordset's MoveNext() arranges for the record that follows to be displayed.

A problem might arise, though, when the deleted record is in the last position or when the deleted record is the only record in the recordset. A call to the recordset's IsEOF() function determines whether the recordset is at the end. If the call to IsEOF() returns TRUE, the recordset needs to be repositioned on the last record. The recordset's MoveLast() function takes care of this task.

When all records have been deleted from the recordset, the record pointer will be at the beginning of the set. The program can test for this situation by calling the recordset's IsBOF() function. If this function returns TRUE, the program sets the current record's fields to NULL.

Finally, the last task is to update the view window's display with another call to UpdateData().

SORTING AND FILTERING

In many cases when you're accessing a database, you want to change the order in which the records are presented, or you may even want to search for records that fit certain criteria. MFC's ODBC database classes enable you to *sort* a set of records on any field. You can also limit the records displayed to those whose fields contain given information, such as a specific name or ID. This latter operation is called *filtering*.

ADDING SORTING AND FILTERING

In this section, you will add sorting and filtering to the Employee application. Just follow these steps:

1. Add a Sort menu to the application's menu bar, as shown in Figure 11.23.
2. Use the Properties window to arrange for CEmployeeView to handle the four new sorting events. Figure 11.24 shows the resultant Properties window.

Figure 11.23
The Sort menu has four events for sorting the database.

Figure 11.24
After you add the four new functions, the Properties window looks like this.

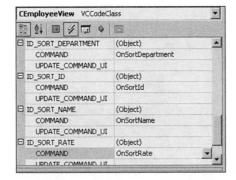

3. Add a Filter menu to the application's menu bar, as shown in Figure 11.25.

Figure 11.25
The Filter menu has four commands.

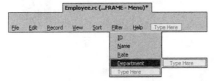

4. Use the Properties window to arrange for CEmployeeView to handle the four new filtering events.

5. Create a new dialog box by choosing Project, Add Resource, and double-clicking Dialog; then edit the dialog so that it resembles the dialog box shown in Figure 11.26. Give the edit control the ID IDC_FILTERVALUE. Give the entire dialog the ID IDD_FILTER.

6. Right-click the newly created dialog box in the editor and choose Add Class....

7. The MFC Class Wizard dialog box appears. In the Name box, type **CFilterDlg**; in the Base Class drop-down box choose CDialog; in the Dialog ID drop-down box choose IDD_FILTER. The resulting screen is shown in Figure 11.27. Click Finish to add the class.

8. Right-click the CFilterDlg class in the Class View window and choose Add, Add Variable... Connect the IDC_FILTERVALUE control, by Value, to a member control variable called m_filterValue (of type CString). Click the Finish button to add the variable.

Figure 11.26
Create a Filter dialog box.

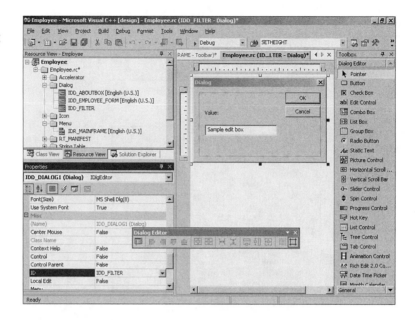

Figure 11.27
Create a dialog class for the Filter dialog box.

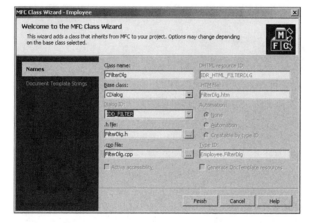

Now that the menus and dialogs have been created and connected to skeleton functions, it's time to add some code to those functions. Double-click `OnSortDepartment()` in the Class View window and edit it to look like Listing 11.5.

LISTING 11.5   CEmployeeView::OnSortDepartment()

```
void CEmployeeView::OnSortDepartment()
{
        m_pSet->Close();
        m_pSet->m_strSort = "DeptID";
        m_pSet->Open();
        UpdateData(FALSE);
}
```

Double-click `OnSortID()` in the Class View window and edit it to look like Listing 11.6.
Double-click `OnSortName()` in the Class View window and edit it to look like Listing
11.7. Double-click `OnSortRate()` in the Class View window and edit it to look like
Listing 11.8.

LISTING 11.6   CEmployeeView::OnSortId()

```
void CEmployeeView::OnSortId()
{
        m_pSet->Close();
        m_pSet->m_strSort = "EmployeeID";
        m_pSet->Open();
        UpdateData(FALSE);
}
```

LISTING 11.7   CEmployeeView::OnSortName()

```
void CEmployeeView::OnSortName()
{
        m_pSet->Close();
        m_pSet->m_strSort = "EmployeeName";
        m_pSet->Open();
        UpdateData(FALSE);
}
```

LISTING 11.8   CEmployeeView::OnSortRate()

```
void CEmployeeView::OnSortRate()
{
        m_pSet->Close();
        m_pSet->m_strSort = "EmployeeRate";
        m_pSet->Open();
        UpdateData(FALSE);
}
```

Сн

11

At the top of EmployeeView.cpp, add the following line after the other `#include` directives:

```
#include "FilterDlg.h"
```

Edit `OnFilterDepartment()`, `OnFilterID()`, `OnFilterName()`, and `OnFilterRate()`, so that
they match Listing 11.9.

LISTING 11.9   THE FOUR FILTERING FUNCTIONS

```
void CEmployeeView::OnFilterDepartment(void)
{
        DoFilter("DeptID");
}

void CEmployeeView::OnFilterId(void)
{
        DoFilter("EmployeeID");
}
```

LISTING 11.9 CONTINUED

```
void CEmployeeView::OnFilterName(void)
{
        DoFilter("EmployeeName");
}

void CEmployeeView::OnFilterRate(void)
{
        DoFilter("EmployeeRate");
}
```

All four functions call DoFilter(). You will write this function to filter the database records represented by the recordset class. Right-click CEmployeeView in the Class View window and choose Add, Add Function.... The Function Type is void, and the name is DoFilter. It takes one parameter, a CString named col. (You have to type **CString** yourself in the Parameter type box. Don't forget to click the Add button after you fill in the parameter information.) It's a protected member function because it's called only from other member functions of CEmployeeView. Click Finish to close the Add Member Function dialog box. Add the code from Listing 11.10.

LISTING 11.10 CEmployeeView::DoFilter()

```
void CEmployeeView::DoFilter(CString col)
{
    CFilterDlg dlg;
    int result = dlg.DoModal();

    if (result == IDOK)
    {
        CString str;
        if (col == "EmployeeRate")
            str = col + " = " + dlg.m_filterValue;
        else
            str = col + " = '" + dlg.m_filterValue + "'";

        m_pSet->Close();
        m_pSet->m_strFilter = str;
        m_pSet->Open();
        int recCount = m_pSet->GetRecordCount();

        if (recCount == 0)
        {
            MessageBox("No matching records.");
            m_pSet->Close();
            m_pSet->m_strFilter = "";
            m_pSet->Open();
        }

        UpdateData(FALSE);
    }

}
```

You've now added the capability to sort and filter records in the employee database. Build the application and run it. When you do, the application's main window appears, looking the same as before. Now, however, you can sort the records on any field, by selecting a field from the Sort menu. You can also filter the records by selecting a field from the Filter menu and then typing the filter string into the Filter dialog box that appears. You can tell how the records are sorted or filtered by moving through them one at a time. Try sorting by department or rate, for example. Then try filtering on one of the departments you saw scroll by.

EXAMINING THE `OnSortDept()` FUNCTION

All the sorting functions have the same structure. They close the recordset, set its `m_strSort` member variable, open it again, and then call `UpdateData()` to refresh the view with the values from the newly sorted recordset. You don't see any call to a member function that has Sort in its name. Then when does the sort happen? When the recordset is reopened.

A `CRecordset` object (or any object of a class derived from `CRecordset`, such as this program's `CEmployeeSet` object) uses a special string, called `m_strSort`, to determine how the records should be sorted. When the recordset is being created, the object checks this string and sorts the records accordingly.

EXAMINING THE `DoFilter()` FUNCTION

Whenever the user selects a command from the Filter menu, the framework calls the appropriate member function: `OnFilterDept()`, `OnFilterID()`, `OnFilterName()`, or `OnFilterRate()`. Each of these functions does nothing more than call the local member function `DoFilter()` with a string representing the field on which to filter.

`DoFilter()` displays the same dialog box, no matter which filter menu item was chosen, by creating an instance of the dialog box class and calling its `DoModal()` function.

If result doesn't equal IDOK, the user must have clicked Cancel. In that case, the entire `if` statement is skipped, and the `DoFilter()` function does nothing but return.

Inside the `if` statement, the function first creates the string that will be used to filter the database. Notice that if the user wants to filter by a string, such as the department ID, single quotes are added around the string. When filtering on a number, such as the Employee Rate, there are no single quotes.

Just as you set a string to sort the database, so, too, do you set a string to filter the database. In this case, the string is called `m_strFilter`. The string you use to filter the database must be in a form like this if you are filtering with a string criteria:

```
ColumnID = 'ColumnValue'
```

If the filtering criteria is numeric, the database filter string must be in a form like this:

```
ColumnID = ColumnValue
```

The column ID was provided to `DoFilter()` as a `CString` parameter, and the value was provided by the user. If, for example, the user chooses to filter by department and types

hardware in the filter value box, DoFilter() would set str to DeptID = 'hardware'. If the user was looking for all employees that have a rate of 6.50, DoFilter() would set str to EmployeeRate = 6.50.

With the string constructed, the program is ready to filter the database. As with sorting, the recordset must first be closed; then DoFilter() sets the recordset's filter string and reopens the recordset.

What happens when the given filter results in no records being selected? Good question. The DoFilter() function handles this by obtaining the number of records in the new recordset and comparing them to zero. If the recordset is empty, the program displays a message box telling the user of the problem. Then the program closes the recordset, resets the filter string to an empty string, and reopens the recordset. This restores the recordset to include all the records in the Employees table.

Finally, whether the filter results in a subset of records or the recordset has to be restored, the program must redisplay the data—by calling UpdateData(), as always.

CHOOSING BETWEEN ODBC AND ADO

In the preceding section, you read an introduction to Visual C++'s ODBC classes and how they're used in an AppWizard-generated application. When you're building a Visual C++ application, you could instead choose to use a set of COM objects that implement ADO (ActiveX Data Objects).

The main advantage of the ADO approach to database programming is performance. By taking more of the work onto yourself, you can create a faster application. The main disadvantage is that you have to do more of the work yourself. This isn't always a disadvantage, of course: if you don't want a stepping-through-the-records user interface like the one used in the Employee sample, you won't be upset when you don't get one written for you.

To work with the ADO objects, you need to write a COM application. Because that's a reasonably complex activity, the demonstration application for this section will be simple. Here's the design:

■ The sample uses the same DSN as the Employee application, presented earlier in this chapter.

■ The sample has a dialog interface with only one edit box, for entering an employee name. The dialog has one button.

■ When the button is clicked, the sample looks up the employee and changes the values of a set of static labels on the dialog to show the department and other information about the employee.

BUILDING THE ADOEMPLOYEE EXAMPLE

Building the ADOEmployee example starts with a new application, of course. Choose, File, New, Project, as always. Select C++ Projects on the left and MFC Application on the right. Name the project ADOEmployee and click OK.

The default MFC Application Wizard settings are almost exactly what is needed for this sample. On the Application Type tab, choose Dialog based, as shown in Figure 11.28. Click Finish to create your application.

Figure 11.28
Create a dialog-based application.

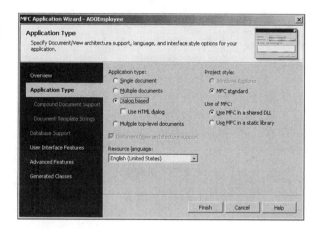

EDITING THE MAIN DIALOG BOX

> **Note**
>
> The instructions that follow assume you have experience creating and editing a dialog in the Resource View. If not, you can find more details on the process in Chapter 3, "Interacting with Your Application."

In the Resource View, double-click IDD_ADOEMPLOYEE_DIALOG to edit the main dialog of the application. Delete the static label with the TODO instruction. Click the OK button and choose View, Properties Window if it is not already displayed. Using the Properties Window, change the ID of the button to **ID_LOOKUP** and the caption to **Lookup**. Change the caption on the Cancel button to **Close**, but leave its ID unchanged.

Add an Edit Control and change its name to **IDC_LOOKUP_NAME**. Put a static label before it with the caption **Lookup Name:**. Move the Lookup and Close buttons down to the bottom right corner of the dialog box so that you can make the edit control wider.

Add four static controls, with captions of Name, Department, ID, and Rate, arranged verti-cally in the dialog. Next to each add an edit control, as shown in Figure 11.29. Widen the Name and Department edit controls because they are likely to contain longer strings. Lengthen the dialog box a bit if you need to.

Note

You will probably find the Align and Space Evenly choices on the Format menu useful as you work; select a number of controls and line them up neatly with these commands. The Test Dialog button (featuring a red exclamation mark) on the Dialog Editor toolbar lets you preview your dialog at any time.

Figure 11.29
Build a dialog box to look up employees in the database.

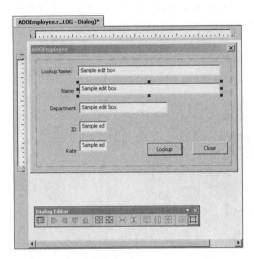

Make each of the four lower edit controls read only. For each one, click it, then find the Read Only property in the Properties Window. Drop down your choices of True or False and choose True. The background of the edit control changes to gray to remind you that the user will not be able to change the text displayed by this control. As you work through the edit controls, change their IDs to IDC_NAME, IDC_DEPT, IDC_ID, and IDC_RATE, respectively.

Right-click in the Name edit box and choose Add Variable to bring up the Add Member Variable Wizard. Select Private for the access, then select the Control check box to create a control variable. In the Category dropdown, select Value. This should change the variable type to CString automatically. Enter m_Name for the variable name. Make sure the Control ID is IDC_NAME. Figure 11.30 shows the completed wizard dialog. Click Finish to add the variable and connection to your class, then run the wizard again to connect IDC_DEPT to m_Dept, IDC_ID to m_ID, and IDC_RATE to m_Rate. (The type of m_Rate should be float, rather than CString like the others.) Finally, connect IDC_LOOKUP_NAME (the non-read-only edit box) to m_Lookup.

The last task to be completed with the dialog is to arrange for some of your code to run when the button is clicked. Double-click the Lookup button to add OnBnClickedLookup() to the class.

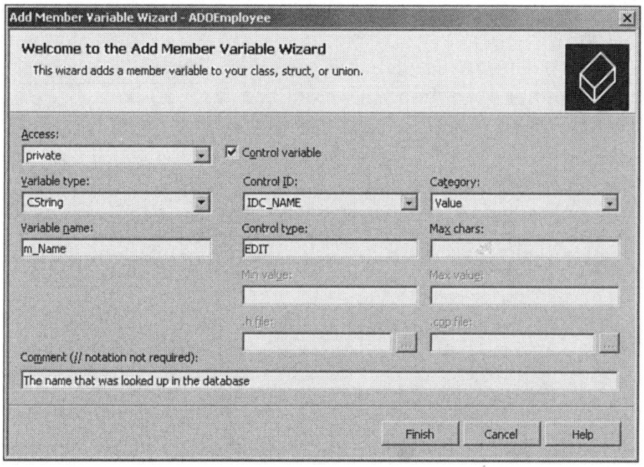

Figure 11.30
Connect each read-only edit box to a member variable.

ADDING ADO CODE TO YOUR APPLICATION SHELL

With the dialog complete, you can turn your attention to your code—specifically the header file, ADOEmployeeDlg.h, and the implementation file, ADOEmployeeDlg.cpp—for your application's dialog class.

Double-click `CADOEmployeeDlg` in the Class View window to edit the header file. At the top, after the line that starts `#pragma`, add this line:

```
#import "\Program Files\Common Files\System\ado\msado15.dll" no_namespace
rename("EOF", "EndOfFile")
```

> **Note**
>
> If you get any compilation errors that refer to this line, make sure the path to msado15.dll is correct for your machine. Don't move the DLL; change the `#import` directive if necessary.

This pre-processor instruction is a Visual C++ extension to C++ that dramatically simplifies working with COM components in Win32 programming. You can essentially think of the COM component as an object, and call its methods.

Before you can make any COM calls, you must initialize the COM library by calling `CoInitialize()`. The best place to do this is in the `InitInstance()` method of the application, CADOEmployeeApp. Use the Class View to navigate to this method and edit it, then add this line after the call to `AfxEnableControlContainer()`:

```
::CoInitialize(NULL);
```

The MFC Application Wizard has generated code here in InitInstance() to display the dialog, and has left places for code to handle the user pressing OK or Cancel. This application does nothing after the dialog closes, regardless of the button the user clicks to close, so replace these lines:

```
INT_PTR nResponse = dlg.DoModal();
if (nResponse == IDOK)
{
    // TODO: Place code here to handle when the dialog is
    //  dismissed with OK
}
else if (nResponse == IDCANCEL)
{
    // TODO: Place code here to handle when the dialog is
    //  dismissed with Cancel
}
```

With this single line:

```
dlg.DoModal();
```

After that line, and before the return statement, add this line to clean up COM:

```
::CoUninitialize();
```

All that remains is to write code that will look up names in the database when the Lookup button is clicked. Because you changed the ID of the Lookup button from IDOK to ID_LOOKUP, clicking it won't dismiss the dialog. You now edit the handler for the BN_CLICKED event so that it will look up an employee in the database and fill the read-only edit controls with the values for that employee. In Class View, navigate to CADoEmployeeDlg::OnBnClickedLookup() and edit it.

Listing 11.11 shows the code you should enter for this handler function. The details will be discussed shortly, but the overall structure of the handler is as follows:

1. Ensure the user has typed a name.
2. Create a connection to the database.
3. Create a recordset.
4. Open the connection to the database.
5. Open the recordset and use a SQL query to fill it.
6. Use the values from the recordset to set the edit box values, or display an error message.

All the ADO work is wrapped in a try block to handle any COM exceptions that might be thrown.

LISTING 11.11   CADOEmployeeDlg::OnBnClickedLookup()

```
void CLookupDlg::OnBnClickedLookup()
{
    this->UpdateData();

    if (m_Lookup == "")
    {
        AfxMessageBox("Please enter a name to look up.", MB_OK, 0);
        return;
    }
```

LISTING 11.11   CONTINUED

```
try
{
    _ConnectionPtr pConn = NULL;
    _RecordsetPtr pRS = NULL;
    _bstr_t sql;

    // create instances of the connection and recordset objects
    if (FAILED(pConn.CreateInstance(__uuidof(Connection))))
    {
        AfxMessageBox("Could not create instance of Connection",
            MB_OK | MB_ICONEXCLAMATION, 0);
        return;
    }

    if (FAILED(pRS.CreateInstance(__uuidof(Recordset))))
    {
        AfxMessageBox("Could not create instance of Recordset",
            MB_OK | MB_ICONEXCLAMATION, 0);
        return;
    }

    // open the connection to the database
    pConn->Open("Department Store", "", "", adConnectUnspecified);

    sql = "SELECT * FROM Employees WHERE EmployeeName LIKE '%"
            + m_Lookup + "%'";

    // look up the name
    pRS->Open(sql, pConn->GetConnectionString(),
        adOpenStatic, adLockReadOnly, adCmdText);

    if (!pRS->EndOfFile)
    {
        m_ID = pRS->GetFields()->GetItem("EmployeeID")->GetValue();
        m_Name = pRS->GetFields()->GetItem("EmployeeName")->GetValue();
        m_Rate = pRS->GetFields()->GetItem("EmployeeRate")->GetValue();
        m_Dept = pRS->GetFields()->GetItem("DeptID")->GetValue();

        this->UpdateData(FALSE);
    }
    else
    {
        AfxMessageBox("Employee could not be found.", MB_OK, 0);
    }

    // close the connection
    pConn->Close();
}
catch (_com_error &e) {
    CString msg;
    msg = "Error Description = ";
    msg.Append(e.Description());
    AfxMessageBox(msg, MB_OK | MB_ICONEXCLAMATION, 0);
}
}
```

CH
11

Key to understanding this code are the two smart pointer classes, _ConnectionPtr and _RecordsetPtr. Although they look exactly like pointers, they are not. The = operator and the -> operator have been overloaded so that what appears to be simple assignment or dereferencing statements are actually COM calls in disguise. For example, consider this block of code:

```
if (FAILED(pConn.CreateInstance(__uuidof(Connection))))
{
    AfxMessageBox("Could not create instance of Connection",
        MB_OK | MB_ICONEXCLAMATION, 0);
    return;
}
```

This creates a connection and sets values in the pConn smart pointer that can access the new connection. If CreateInstance returns an HRESULT of FAILED, an error message is shown to the user and the rest of the handler is skipped.

After you have a connection object, you can use it to open a connection to a DSN. After you have an open connection, you can run a query, putting the results into a recordset. The query here uses the SQL keyword LIKE and the % character to match on any part of the employee name. If a record is found, the calls to GetFields(), GetItem(), and GetValue() extract the value so that it can be put into the member variables you associated with the edit boxes. The call to UpdateData(FALSE), you should recall, updates the edit boxes from the member variables.

Note

This code shows only the first match from the recordset. If there were two employees with similar names, a more sophisticated application would show both, or encourage the user to search again. This application works well with a small database where the user will realize the name returned is not the desired one, and search again with more of the name.

After adding the code to CADoEmployeeDlg::OnBnClickedLookup(), build your application by choosing Build, Build, and then, after correcting any compilation errors, choose Debug, Start, to run it. Enter a first or last name that you know is in the Employees table, and click Lookup. The application should show you the details of your employee, as in Figure 11.31.

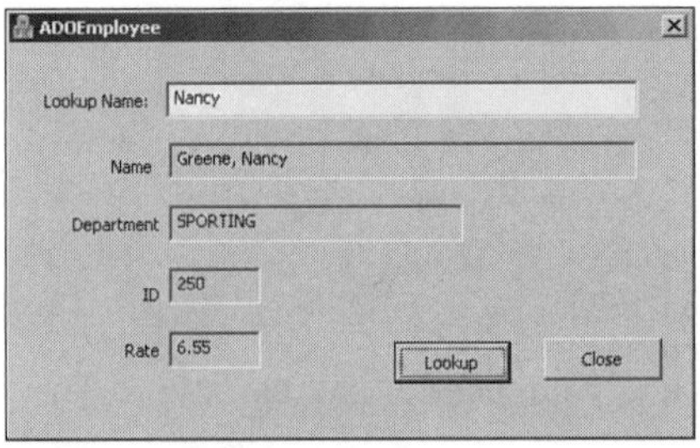

Figure 11.31
Simple ADO code can serve a useful purpose.

Understanding SQL

Structured Query Language (SQL) is a way to access databases, interactively or in a program, that is designed to read as though it were English. Most SQL statements are queries—requests for information from one or more databases—but it's also possible to use SQL to add, delete, and change information. As mentioned earlier in this chapter, SQL is an enormous topic. This section reviews the most important SQL commands so that even if you haven't used it before, you can understand these examples and see how powerful these tools can be.

SQL is used to access a relational database, which contains several tables. A table is made up of rows, and a row is made up of columns. Table 11.1 lists some names used in database research or in some other kinds of databases for tables, rows, and columns.

TABLE 11.1   DATABASE TERMINOLOGY

SQL	Also Known As
Table	Entity
Row	Record, Tuple
Column	Field, Attribute

Here's a sample SQL statement:

```
SELECT au_fname, au_lname FROM authors
```

It produces a list of authors' first and last names from a table called authors. (This table is included in the sample pubs database that comes with SQL Server, which you will be using in this chapter.) Here's a far more complicated SQL statement:

```
SELECT item, SUM(amount) total, AVG(amount) average FROM ledger
   WHERE action = 'PAID'
   GROUP BY item
having AVG(amount) > (SELECT avg(amount) FROM ledger
                     WHERE action = 'PAID')
```

A SQL statement is put together from keywords, table names, and column names. The keywords include the following:

- SELECT returns the specific column of the database. Secondary keywords, including FROM, WHERE, LIKE, NULL, and ORDER BY, restrict the search to certain records within each table.

- DELETE removes records. The secondary keyword WHERE specifies which records to delete.

- UPDATE changes the value of columns (specified with SET) in records specified with WHERE. It can be combined with a SELECT statement.

- INSERT inserts a new record into the database.

CH

11

- **COMMIT** saves any changes you have made to the database.
- **ROLLBACK** undoes all your changes back to the most recent **COMMIT**.
- **EXEC** calls a stored procedure.

Like C++, SQL supports two kinds of comments:

```
/* This comment has begin and end symbols */
— This is a from-here-to-end-of-line comment
```

WORKING WITH SQL DATABASES FROM C++

As you saw earlier in this chapter, an ODBC program that uses CDatabase and CRecordset can already access a SQL Server database or any database that supports SQL queries. What's more, with the ExecuteSQL function of CDatabase, you can execute any line of SQL from within your program. Most of the time, the line of SQL that you execute is a stored procedure—a collection of SQL statements stored with the database and designed to be executed on the fly by the database server.

There are lots of reasons not to hard-code your SQL into your C++ program. The three most compelling are

- Reuse
- Skill separation
- Maintainability

Many programmers accessing a SQL database from a C++ application are building on the work of other developers who have been building the database and its stored procedures for years. Copying those procedures into your code would be foolish indeed. Calling them from within your code lets you build slick user interfaces, simplify Internet access, or take advantage of the speed of C++, while retaining all the power of the stored procedures previously written.

Highly skilled professionals are always in demand, and sometimes the demand exceeds the supply. Many companies find it hard to recruit solid C++ programmers and equally as hard to recruit experienced database administrators who can learn the structure of a database and write in SQL. Imagine how difficult it would be to find a single individual who can do both—almost as difficult as having two developers work on the parts of the program that called SQL from C++. A much better approach is to have the C++ programmer to call well-documented SQL stored procedures and the SQL developer to build those stored procedures and keep the database running smoothly.

Separating the C++ and SQL parts of your application has another benefit: Changes to one might not affect the other. For example, a minor C++ change that doesn't involve the SQL compiles and links more quickly because the C++ part of the application is a little smaller without the SQL statements in it. Also, changes to the SQL stored procedure, if they don't involve the parameters to the function or the values it returns, take effect without requiring that the C++ program be compiled or linked.

There is a downside, however. It can be very difficult to track down problems when you are unsure whether they are in the C++ or the SQL part of your program. When one developer is doing both parts, learning two different tools and switching between them makes the job harder than it would be with a single tool. Also, the tools available for working with SQL lack many features that Visual C++ has offered C++ programmers.

Now, with the Enterprise Edition and Enterprise Architect Edition of Visual Studio, you can have the best of both worlds. You can separate your C++ and SQL for reuse and maintenance but use the editor, syntax coloring, and even the debugger from Visual Studio to work on your SQL stored procedures.

> **Caution**
>
> If you do not have the Enterprise Edition or Enterprise Architect Edition of Visual Studio .NET, you will probably not be able to complete the sample application in this section.

EXPLORING THE SAMPLE APPLICATION

To help you understand SQL programming and stored procedures, this chapter will build a sample application using a sample database that comes with SQL Server called pubs. It tracks the sales of books and the royalties paid to their authors. In this chapter you will write a new stored procedure and display the records returned by it in a simple record view dialog box. SQL Server should be up and running before you start to build the application.

CH

11

BUILDING THE APPLICATION SHELL

Open Visual Studio and create a new MFC Application called Publishing, as shown in Figure 11.32. Click OK to start the MFC Application Wizard.

Figure 11.32
Start the MFC Application Wizard in the usual way.

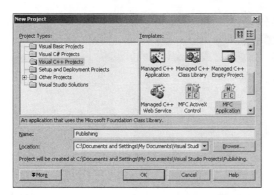

On the Application Type tab of the wizard, choose an SDI application. On the Database Support tab, choose the Database View Without File Support option and the ODBC option.

Next, set up the data source for your application. In previous examples, you saw how to create a DSN with the Control Panel; this section shows you how to create one directly from Visual Studio.

Click the Data Source button on the MFC Application Wizard to bring up the Select Data Source dialog, and then click the Machine Data Source tab, as shown in Figure 11.33. To create a new DSN, click the New button.

Figure 11.33
Create a new data source for this application.

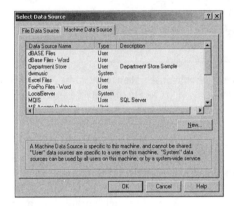

The Create New Data Source dialog box appears. Select the User Data Source option and click Next. Choose SQL Server as the driver for the connection, as shown in Figure 11.34, click Next, and then Finish.

Figure 11.34
Connect to a SQL Server.

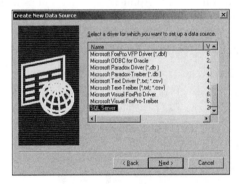

The Create a New Data Source to SQL Server dialog appears. Fill in a name and description for the data source, then drop down the Server box; choose your server or type its name. The special name (local) refers to your own machine. Figure 11.35 shows the completed dialog box for a test system with only the sample databases installed. The name of the data source name is vague, because as you'll see shortly it's going to identify the server rather than a particular database. Click Next.

Figure 11.35
Specify the server.

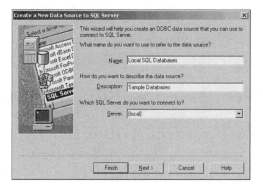

You can choose to connect to the server with NT authentication or SQL Server authentication. If you're not sure which to choose, talk to your system administrator. Because this sample was developed on a test machine, SQL Server authentication—with the default account of sa and no password—is acceptable. Figure 11.36 shows the completed dialog box. Click Next.

Figure 11.36
Security can be lax on test machines, but not in the real world.

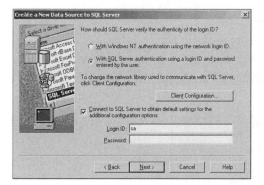

At this point, you choose whether to connect this data source name to a single database on the server, or to the server as a whole. If you want to associate this DSN with only one database, you would select the top check box and choose your database. For this sample application, leave the top check box deselected. In either case, leave the rest of the dialog box at the defaults, shown in Figure 11.37. Click Next.

Accept the defaults on the next dialog box, shown in Figure 11.38, and click Finish.

Figure 11.39 summarizes the settings from this connection process. It's a very good idea to test your connection before moving on. Click Test Data Source, and you should see something like Figure 11.40. If you don't, click Cancel to return to the final step of the process, and click Back until you are back to the step you need to adjust. Afterward, come forward again by clicking Next.

Figure 11.37
This DSN is connected to the entire server, not just one database.

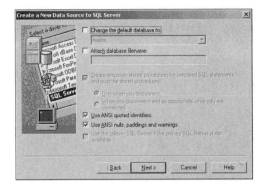

Figure 11.38
There is no need to change the regional settings, perform encryption, or log slow queries and driver statistics in this example.

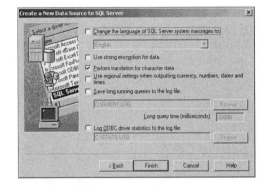

Figure 11.39
Confirm your choices for the ODBC SQL connection.

Now that you have created your data source, select it from the Select Data Source dialog and click OK. You are greeted by the SQL Server Login dialog box.

On the dialog box, click the Options button to show the expanded dialog shown in Figure 11.41. Choose pubs from the Database drop-down box and enter the ID and password at the top of the dialog box. Click OK.

Figure 11.40
Make sure your DSN
connects properly.

Figure 11.41
Connect to the sam-
ple pubs database.

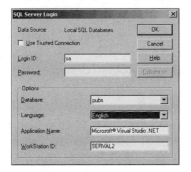

CH
11

The Select Database Object dialog box, shown in Figure 11.42, appears. Expand the Tables
node, then the dbo node. Select the authors, titleauthor, and titles tables, and then click OK.

Figure 11.42
Choose the authors,
titleauthors, and titles
tables.

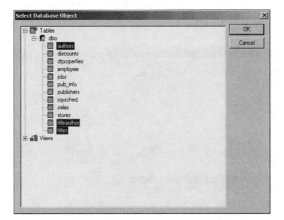

Finally, you return to the MFC Application Wizard. Click the Overview tab, shown in
Figure 11.43, to confirm your selections, and click Finish to create the project.

Figure 11.43
Confirm that your choices are correct before creating the project.

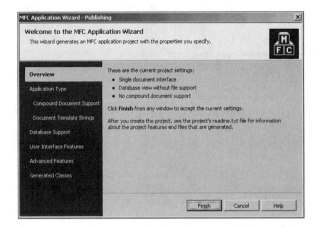

You have now completed a shell of an application that displays database values in a record view, much like the one discussed earlier in this chapter. Nothing you have done so far has been specific to the Enterprise Edition. That is about to change.

MAKING A DATA CONNECTION

The database tables you specified are connected to your record set, but they aren't available for use with the SQL features of the Enterprise Edition. You need to make a data connection to connect the database to your application. Follow these steps to make the connection:

1. Choose File, New, Project.
2. Expand the Other Projects item in the Project Types box and then select Database projects.
3. As shown in Figure 11.44, select a Database Project, name it PubDB, and select the Add to Solution radio button. Click OK.

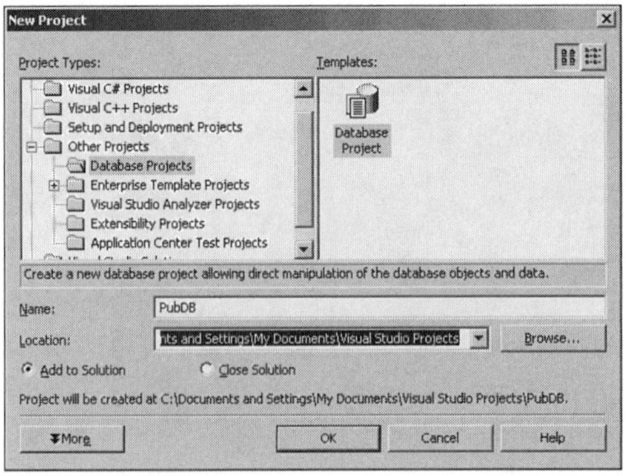

Figure 11.44
Create a subproject within this project.

4. The Data Link Properties dialog box appears. Open the Provider tab and choose the Microsoft OLE DB Provider for SQL Server item from the list box. Open the Connection tab and enter the server name, your user name and password, and the database that will be used (pubs in this case), as shown in Figure 11.45. Click OK to complete the data connection.

Figure 11.45
Connect to the database server.

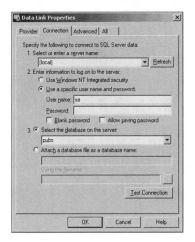

After creating the project, a new item appears in the Server Explorer window under the Data Connections node, as shown in Figure 11.46. It represents the data connection you created for the PubDB project. The data connection makes it easier to view objects in the database such as tables and procedures. You can also view table layouts and retrieve table data. For example, to see the layout of the authors table, expand the Tables node of the connection, then authors. To retrieve the data in the table, right-click authors, then choose Retrieve Data from Table.

If you expand the Database References node under the PubDB node in the Solution Explorer window, you will notice an item with the same name as your data connection. Database references are used to determine which data connection the scripts and queries in a database project use. By creating new database references, you can easily change which database your scripts and queries are using. This would be useful in a project with a test database and a production database. By creating database references for both, you could switch between them with a few mouse clicks.

To create a new database reference, right-click Database References, and then choose New Database Reference. To change the default database reference for the project, right-click the project name in the Solution Explorer window, choose Set Default Reference, and then select the reference you would like to use.

CH
11

Figure 11.46
The Data Connections node can show you the database structure and can display your data in the working area.

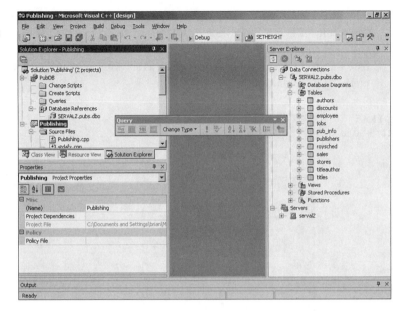

Also featured in Figure 11.46 is the Query toolbar (it's floating in the figure, but on your system it may also be docked near the top of the screen), with the following buttons:

- Show Diagram Pane toggles the Query Designer diagram pane (discussed in the next section).

- Show Grid Pane toggles the Query Designer grid pane (discussed in the next section).

- Show SQL Pane toggles the Query Designer SQL pane (discussed in the next section).

- Show Results Pane toggles the Query Designer results pane (discussed in the next section).

- Change Type creates a SELECT, INSERT, UPDATE, or DELETE query in the four panes of Query Designer, or enables you to create a new table.

- Run executes your SQL.

- Verify SQL Syntax checks the syntax of the SQL you have written.

- Sort Ascending displays records from the low value of a selected column to high.

- Sort Descending displays records from the high value of a selected column to low.

- Remove Filter shows all the records rather than only those that meet the filter specifications.

- Group By adds a GROUP BY condition to the query being built.

- Add Table creates a new table in the database.

WORKING WITH QUERY DESIGNER

When you double-click a table name, such as authors, in the Server Explorer window to display all the columns and all the records, you are actually executing a simple SQL query, as follows:

```
SELECT * FROM authors
```

The results of this query appear in the Results pane, which is the only one of the four Query Designer panes to be displayed, by default. This query was built for you by Query Designer and shows all the columns and records of the authors table. Figure 11.47 shows the four panes of Query Designer as they appear when you first make the data connection. To see all four panes, use the toolbar buttons to toggle them on. You can adjust the vertical size of each pane, but not the horizontal.

Figure 11.47
You can use the Query toolbar to view the different Query Designer panes.

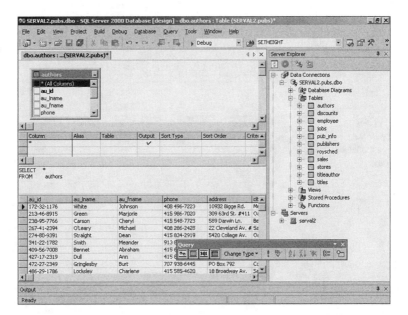

To change your query, select au_lname, au_fname, and phone in the Diagram pane (at the top of Figure 11.47). The values in the Results pane become gray to remind you that these aren't the results of the query you are now building. As you make these selections in the Diagram pane, the other panes update automatically, as shown in Figure 11.48.

Highlight phone in the Diagram pane and click the Sort Ascending button on the Query toolbar. This action produces results sorted by phone number. Click the Run button on the Query toolbar to execute the SQL that has been built for you. Figure 11.49 shows what you should see, including the new values in the Results pane.

Figure 11.48
You can build simple queries even if you don't know any SQL.

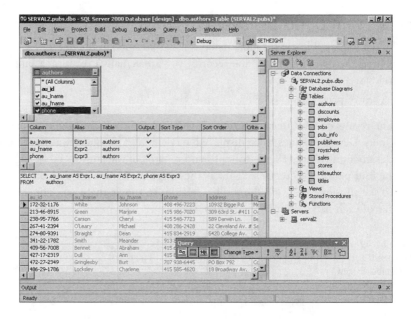

Figure 11.49
Running your SQL queries is a matter of a single click.

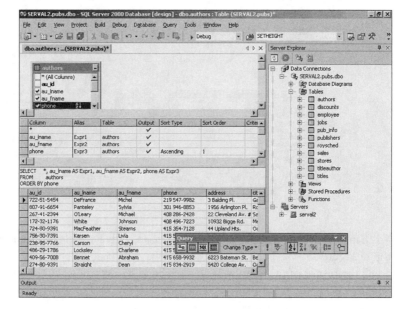

STORED PROCEDURES

The capability to create simple SQL queries quickly, even if your SQL skills aren't strong, is an amazing aspect of the Enterprise Edition. However, using stored procedures is where the real payoff of this software becomes apparent.

Collapse the Tables section in the Server Explorer window and expand the Stored Procedures section. This shows all the stored procedures that are kept in the database and are available for you to use. Double-click `reptq2` to display the procedure. One thing you probably notice immediately is the syntax coloring in the editor window. The colors are:

- Blue for keywords such as `PRINT` and `SELECT`
- Green for both styles of comment
- Black for other kinds of text

To run a stored procedure, choose Database, Run Stored Procedure; or right-click the stored procedure name in the Server Explorer window and choose Run Stored Procedure; or right-click in the editor and choose Run; or push Ctrl+E. The results appear in the Results pane of the Output window—don't confuse this with the Results pane of Query Designer. Figure 11.50 shows the Output window stretched very large to show some results of `reptq2`.

Figure 11.50
You can see the results of any stored procedure from within Developer Studio.

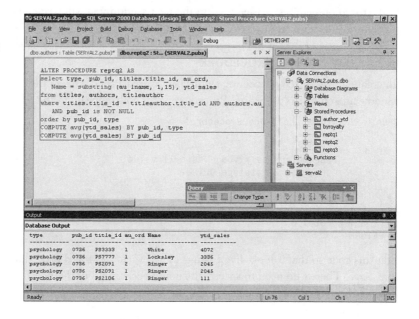

Some stored procedures take parameters. For example, double-click reptq3; its code looks like this:

```
ALTER PROCEDURE reptq3 @lolimit money, @hilimit money,
@type char(12)
AS
select pub_id, type, title_id, price
from titles
where price >@lolimit AND price <@hilimit AND type = @type OR type LIKE '%cook%'
order by pub_id, type
COMPUTE count(title_id) BY pub_id, type
```

This stored procedure takes three parameters: `lolimit`, `hilimit`, and `type`. If you run it, the dialog box shown in Figure 11.51 appears: Enter parameter values and click OK to run the procedure. See the results in the Output window.

Figure 11.51
Providing parameters to stored procedures is simple.

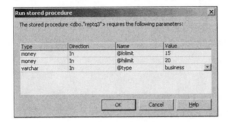

It might be nice if the type parameter were a drop-down box, enabling you to see all the type values in the table before submitting the query, rather than having to type the value yourself. That sort of capability is exactly what you can build into a C++ program that uses SQL stored procedures. To see how, in the next section you will write a new stored procedure and call it from your C++ program.

WRITING A NEW STORED PROCEDURE

To create a new stored procedure, right-click Stored Procedures in the Server Explorer window and choose New Stored Procedure. This code appears in the editor:

```
CREATE PROCEDURE dbo.StoredProcedure1
/*
   (
          @parameter1 datatype = default value,
          @parameter2 datatype OUTPUT
   )
*/
AS
   /* SET NOCOUNT ON */
   RETURN
```

Edit this code so that it looks like Listing 11.12. Save the stored procedure by choosing File, Save. There's no need to specify the name because it's in the first line. After the procedure has been saved, its name appears in the Server Explorer window.

LISTING 11.12   AUTHOR_YTD, THE NEW STORED PROCEDURE

```
CREATE PROCEDURE author_ytd @sales int
AS
SELECT authors.au_lname, authors.au_fname, titles.title, ytd_sales
   FROM authors, titles, titleauthor
   WHERE ytd_sales > @sales
      AND authors.au_id = titleauthor.au_id
      AND titleauthor.title_id = titles.title_id
ORDER BY ytd_sales DESC
```

This SQL code gathers information from three tables, using the au_id and title_id columns to connect authors to titles. It takes one parameter, sales, which is an integer value. Run the procedure to see the results immediately. Listing 11.13 shows the results, using 4000 as the value for sales.

LISTING 11.13   AUTHOR_YTD RESULTS (@SALES = 4000)

```
Running Stored Procedure dbo.author_ytd ( @sales = 4000 ).
au_lname        au_fname   title                                    ytd_sales
_____ ____     _____ ____ _____ _____ _____ _____ _____ _____    _____ ___

DeFrance        Michel     The Gourmet Microwave                        22246
Ringer          Anne       The Gourmet Microwave                        22246
Green           Marjorie   You Can Combat Computer Stress!              18722
Blotchet-Halls  Reginald   Fifty Years in Buckingham Palace Kitchens    15096
Carson          Cheryl     But Is It User Friendly?                      8780
Green           Marjorie   The Busy Executive's Database Guide           4095
Bennet          Abraham    The Busy Executive's Database Guide           4095
Straight        Dean       Straight Talk About Computers                 4095
Dull            Ann        Secrets of Silicon Valley                     4095
Hunter          Sheryl     Secrets of Silicon Valley                     4095
O'Leary         Michael    Sushi, Anyone?                                4095
Gringlesby      Burt       Sushi, Anyone?                                4095
Yokomoto        Akiko      Sushi, Anyone?                                4095
White           Johnson    Prolonged Data Deprivation: Four Case Studies 4072
No more results.
 (14 row(s) affected)
@RETURN_VALUE = 0
Finished running dbo.author_ytd.
```

CONNECTING THE STORED PROCEDURE TO C++ CODE

At the moment, you have an empty C++ application that uses a recordset and would display members of that recordset in a record view if you added fields to the dialog to do so. The recordset contains all the columns from the three tables (authors, titleauthor, and titles) that you specified during the MFC Application Wizard process. That's arranged by a function called CPublishingSet::GetDefaultSQL() that the MFC Application Wizard wrote for you. It looks like this:

```
CString CPublishingSet::GetDefaultSQL()
{
    return _T("[dbo].[authors],[dbo].[titleauthor],[dbo].[titles]");
}
```

You're going to change this default SQL so that it calls your stored procedure, which is now part of the pubs database. First, right-click the Publishing project in the Class View window and choose Set as StartUp Project. Expand CPublishingSet, and double-click GetDefaultSQL() to edit it. Replace the code with this:

```
CString CPublishingSet::GetDefaultSQL()
{
    return _T("{CALL author_ytd(4000)}");
}
```

CH

11

> **Note**
>
> Normally you would not hard-code the parameter value like this. Adding member variables to the class to hold parameters and passing them to the SQL is a topic you can explore in the online help when you are more familiar with the Enterprise Edition.

The records returned from this query go into your recordset. The query returns four columns (au_lname, au_fname, title, and ytd_sales), but the recordset is expecting far more than that. Follow these steps to delete the unnecessary variables:

1. Open PublishingSet.h by double-clicking it in the Solution Explorer window.
2. Remove all the member variable definitions except those for m_dboauthorsau_lname, m_dboauthorsau_fname, m_dbotitlestitle, m_dbotitlesytd_sales. The definitions look like this:

   ```
   CStringA        m_dboauthorsau_id;
   CStringA        m_dboauthorsau_lname;
   ...
   ```

3. Open PublishingSet.cpp as you did for PublishingSet.h.
4. The initialization for the deleted variables still exists in the class's constructor. Edit the constructor so it looks like Listing 11.14.

LISTING 11.14   CPublishingSet::CPublishingSet(): THE CLASS CONSTRUCTOR

```
CPublishingSet::CPublishingSet(CDatabase* pdb)
   : CRecordset(pdb)
{
   m_dboauthorsau_lname = "";
   m_dboauthorsau_fname = "";
   m_dbotitlestitle = "";
   m_dbotitlesytd_sales = 0;
   m_nFields = 4;
   m_nDefaultType = dynaset;
}
```

5. Edit CPublishingSet::DoFieldExchange() in PublishingSet.cpp to look like Listing 11.15. It is very important that the order in which the variables appear matches the order in which the fields are coming back from your stored procedure. Figure 11.52 shows DoFieldExchange() and the stored procedure together.

LISTING 11.15   CPublishingSet::DoFieldExchange()

```
void CPublishingSet::DoFieldExchange(CFieldExchange* pFX)
{
   pFX->SetFieldType(CFieldExchange::outputColumn);
// Macros such as RFX_Text() and RFX_Int() are dependent on the
// type of the member variable, not the type of the field in the database.
// ODBC will try to automatically convert the column value to the requested type
   RFX_Text(pFX, _T("[dbo].[authors].[au_lname]"), m_dboauthorsau_lname);
```

LISTING 11.15   CONTINUED

```
    RFX_Text(pFX, _T("[dbo].[authors].[au_fname]"), m_dboauthorsau_fname);
    RFX_Text(pFX, _T("[dbo].[titles].[title]"), m_dbotitlestitle);
    RFX_Long(pFX, _T("[dbo].[titles].[ytd_sales]"), m_dbotitlesytd_sales);
}
```

Figure 11.52
Make sure that the fields are in the same order in `DoFieldExchange()` as in your stored procedure.

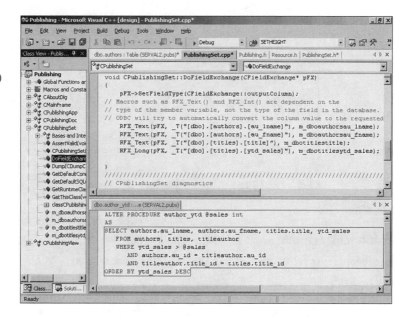

Your application can compile and run now, but until you edit the Record View dialog box, you won't be able to see the records and columns that another query returns. Editing the dialog box was covered earlier in this chapter and uses skills first demonstrated in Chapter 2, "Build Your First Windows Application," so the description here is brief.

Click the Resource View window, expand the resources, expand Dialogs, and double-click IDD_PUBLISHING_FORM. The MFC Application Wizard created this dialog box for you, but it has no controls yet. Delete the static text reminding you to add controls, and add four edit boxes and their labels so that the dialog resembles Figure 11.53. Use sensible resource IDs for the edit boxes, not the defaults provided by Visual Studio. Name them IDC_QUERY_LNAME, IDC_QUERY_FNAME, IDC_QUERY_TITLE, and IDC_QUERY_YTDSALES.

There is one task left: Connect these fields to member variables. Here's how to make that connection:

1. Open the file PublishingView.cpp.
2. As before, use the DDX functions to map the recordset variables to the dialog controls. Edit `CPublishingView::DoDataExchange()` to look like Listing 11.16.

CH
11

Figure 11.53
Edit your Record View
dialog box.

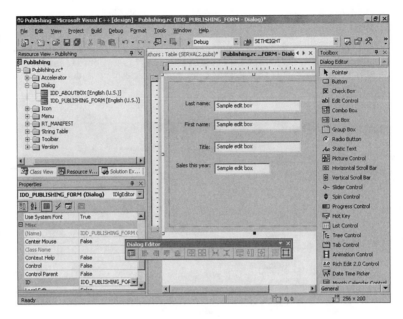

LISTING 11.16   CPublishingSet::DoDataExchange()

```
void CPublishingView::DoDataExchange(CDataExchange* pDX)
{
    CRecordView::DoDataExchange(pDX);
    DDX_Text(pDX, IDC_QUERY_LNAME, m_pSet->m_dboauthorsau_lname);
    DDX_Text(pDX, IDC_QUERY_FNAME, m_pSet->m_dboauthorsau_fname);
    DDX_Text(pDX, IDC_QUERY_TITLE, m_pSet->m_dbotitlestitle);
    DDX_Text(pDX, IDC_QUERY_YTDSALES, m_pSet->m_dbotitlesytd_sales);
}
```

Build your project and run it. You should see a record view like Figure 11.54 (you might have to go through the SQL login procedure again first), and if you scroll through the record view with the arrow buttons, you should see every author from the report in Listing 11.13.

Tip

Make sure you have saved the SQL stored procedure before you build. Because the stored procedures are in a subproject of Publishing, building Publishing does not trigger any saves in the subproject.

This application doesn't do much at the moment: It calls a stored procedure and neatly presents the results. With a little imagination, you can probably see how your SQL-based C++ programs can wrap stored procedures in user-friendly interfaces and how easy it is to develop and maintain these stored procedures by using Developer Studio. You can even debug your SQL by using the Developer Studio debugger.

Figure 11.54
Your application displays the results of the stored procedure's query.

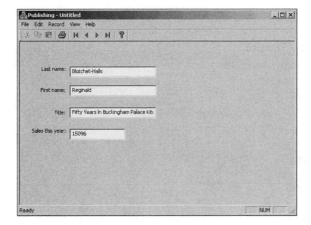

Working with Your Database

The Server Explorer window gives you full control over not only the contents of your SQL database but also its design. A raft of graphical tools makes it easy to see how the database works or to change any aspect of it.

Database Designer

Return to the Server Explorer window, right-click the authors table, and choose Design Table. With the Database Designer, shown in Figure 11.55, you can change the key column, adjust the width, apply constraints on valid values, and more.

Figure 11.55
The Database Designer lets you change any aspect of your database's design.

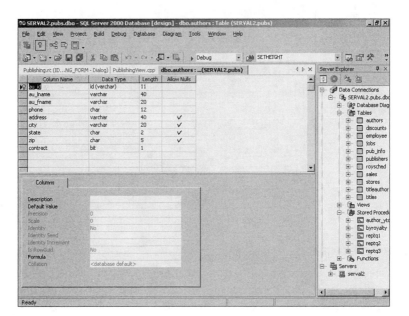

For example, to open the Property Pages dialog shown in Figure 11.58, click View, Property Pages while au_id is selected, and then click the Check Constraints tab. The constraint shown in Figure 11.56 means that au_id must be a 9-digit number. Clicking the Relationship tab, shown in Figure 11.57, shows that au_id is used to connect the authors table to the titleauthor table.

Figure 11.56
It's simple to specify column constraints.

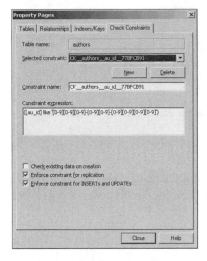

Figure 11.57
The Relationships tab makes it simple to see how tables are related.

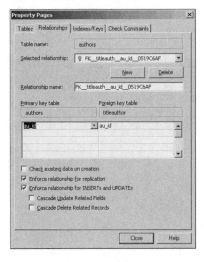

DATABASE DIAGRAMS

One of the easiest ways to quickly present information to people is with a diagram. Figure 11.58 shows a diagram that explains the relationships between the three tables used throughout this chapter. To create the same diagram yourself, follow these steps:

Figure 11.58
A picture is worth a thousand words when it's time to explain your database design.

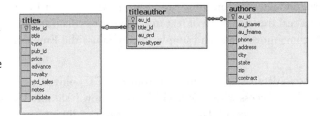

1. Right-click Database Diagrams in the Server Explorer window and choose New Diagram.
2. Use Ctrl+click to select the authors, titles, and titleauthor tables, and then click Add.
3. Click Close on the Add Table dialog.
4. Rearrange the tables so that their keys are aligned as in Figure 11.58.
5. Drag the links up or down until they run from one key to another, as they do in Figure 11.58.

If you want, you can save this diagram in the database. Just click the Save button on the standard toolbar and provide a name. The diagrams are available to any other developers who use the Enterprise Edition to access this database.

If you're a database developer, you probably can't wait to open your own database in the Database Designer and get to work. Be sure to take advantage of the many features on the Database Diagram toolbar. For example, you can add a note or explanation with the New Text Annotation button; this note can be moved wherever you want. The Table View drop-down button controls how much detail is shown for each table. The first option, Standard, shows all the details that were in the Design Table view. The second, Column Names, is the default in the diagram view. Keys shows only those columns that are keys, and Name Only shrinks the grid to a tiny column showing only the table's name. This is useful for diagrams representing the relationships of many tables or of tables from other projects. Custom applies a custom view that is created by choosing Modify Custom.

To change any design decision about these tables, open the context menu and choose Property Pages; then edit these properties as you did in the Database Designer. How's that for an easy way to design and administer a SQL database?

FROM HERE

Visual Studio .NET has a lot to offer a database programmer creating classic Windows applications. The starter MFC database applications can solve many business problems with a minimum of code. You can use ODBC or ADO to look up records in a database or to perform simple updates.

CH
11

For the SQL programmer, the Enterprise and Enterprise Architect Editions of Visual Studio.NET are a real treasure trove of features. Reporting, diagramming, design, and other complex tasks become more visual and simple when you use the Enterprise Edition's powerful capabilities.

If you're interested in database programming from a .NET point of view, skip ahead to Chapter 22, "Database Access with ADO.NET," to see how it's done. Visual Studio has excellent support for all aspects of database work, not just coding.

If you'd like to stick with classic Windows programming a little longer, I encourage you to go on to the next chapter, "Improving Your Application's Performance." You'll see how to prevent memory leaks, track down bugs, and prevent logic errors.

CHAPTER 12

IMPROVING YOUR APPLICATION'S PERFORMANCE

In this chapter

When developing a new application, developers must meet various challenges. You need your application to compile, to run without blowing up, and you must be sure that it does what you want it to do. On some projects, there is time to determine whether your application can run faster and use less memory, or whether you can have a smaller executable file. The performance improvement techniques discussed in this chapter can prevent your program from blowing up and eliminate the kind of "thinkos" that result in a program calculating or reporting the wrong numbers. These improvements are not merely final tweaks and touch-ups on a finished product.

You should form the habit of adding "an ounce of prevention" to your code as you write, as well as the habit of using the debugging capabilities that Visual Studio provides you to confirm what's going on in your program. If you save all your testing to the end, both the testing and the bug-fixing will be much harder than if you had been testing all along. Also, of course, any bug you manage to prevent will never have to be fixed at all!

PREVENTING ERRORS WITH ASSERT AND TRACE

The developers of Visual C++ did not invent the concepts of asserting and tracing. Other languages support these ideas, and they are taught in many computer science courses. What is exciting about the Visual C++ implementation of these concepts is the clear way in which your results are presented and the ease with which you can suppress ASSERT and TRACE statements in release versions of your application.

ASSERT: DETECTING LOGIC ERRORS

The ASSERT macro enables you to check a condition that you logically believe should always be TRUE. For example, imagine you are about to access an array like this:

```
array[i] = 5;
```

You want to be sure that the index, i, isn't less than zero or larger than the number of elements allocated for the array. Presumably you have already written code to calculate i, and if that code has been written properly, i must be between 0 and the array size. An ASSERT statement will verify that, as follows:

```
ASSERT( i > 0 && i < ARRAYSIZE)
```

Note

There is no semicolon (;) at the end of the line because ASSERT is a macro, not a function. Older C programs may call a function named assert(), but you should use the ASSERT macro because ASSERT disappears during a release build, as discussed later in this section.

You can check your own logic with ASSERT statements. They should never be used to check for user input errors or bad data in a file. Whenever the condition inside an ASSERT statement is FALSE, program execution halts with a message telling you which assertion failed.

At this point, you know you have a logic error, or a developer error, that you need to correct. Here's another example:

```
// Calling code must pass a non-null pointer
void ProcessObject( Foo * fooObject )
{
       ASSERT( fooObject )
       // process object
}
```

This code can de-reference the pointer in confidence, knowing execution will be halted if the pointer is NULL.

You probably already know that Visual Studio makes it simple to build debug and release versions of your programs. The debug version defines a constant, _DEBUG, and macros and other pre-processor code can check this constant to determine the build type. When _DEBUG isn't defined, the ASSERT macro does nothing. This means there is no speed constraint in the final code, as there would be if you added if statements yourself to test for logic errors. There is no need to go through your code, removing ASSERT statements when you release your application, and, in fact, it's better to leave them there to help the developers who work on version 2. They document your assumptions, and they'll be there when the debugging work starts again. ASSERT can't help you if there is a problem with the release version of your code because it is used to find logic and design errors before you release version 1.0 of your product.

TRACE: ISOLATING PROBLEM AREAS IN YOUR PROGRAM

As discussed in Chapter 13, "Debugging," the power of the Visual Studio debugger is considerable. You can step through your code one line at a time or run to a breakpoint, and you can see any of your variables' values in watch windows as you move through the code. This can be slow, however, and many developers use TRACE statements as a way of speeding up this process and zeroing in on the problem area. Then they turn to more traditional step-by-step debugging to isolate the bad code.

In the old days, isolating bad code meant adding lots of print statements to your program, which is problematic in a Windows application. Before you start to think up workarounds, such as printing to a file, relax. The TRACE macro does everything you want, and like ASSERT, it magically goes away in release builds.

There are several TRACE macros: TRACE, TRACE0, TRACE1, TRACE2, and TRACE3. The number suffix indicates the number of arguments, not counting the first, which is a simple string that works much like the format string in printf(). The different versions of TRACE were implemented to save data segment space.

When you generate an application with AppWizard, many ASSERT and TRACE statements are added for you. Here's a TRACE example:

```
if (!m_wndToolBar.Create(this)
    || !m_wndToolBar.LoadToolBar(IDR_MAINFRAME))
```

```
{
    TRACE0("Failed to create toolbar\n");
    return -1;       // fail to create
}
```

If the creation of the toolbar fails, this routine returns -1, which signals to the calling program that something is wrong. This happens in both debug and release builds. In debug builds, though, a trace output is sent to help the programmer understand what went wrong.

All the TRACE macros write to afxDump, which is usually the debug window, but can be set to stderr for console applications. The number suffix indicates the parametric argument count, and you use the parametric values within the string to indicate the passed data type—for example, to send a TRACE statement that includes the value of an integer variable:

```
TRACE1("Error Number: %d\n", -1 );
```

or to pass two arguments—maybe a string and an integer:

```
TRACE2("File Error %s, error number: %d\n", __FILE__, -1 );
```

The most difficult part of tracing is making it a habit. Sprinkle TRACE statements anywhere you return error values: before ASSERT statements and in areas where you are unsure that you constructed your code correctly. When confronted with unexpected behavior, add TRACE statements first so that you better understand what is going on before you start debugging.

ADDING DEBUG-ONLY FEATURES

If the idea of code that isn't included in a release build appeals to you, you may want to arrange for some of your own code to be included in debug builds but not in release builds. It's easy. Just wrap the code in a test of the _DEBUG constant, like this:

```
#ifdef _DEBUG
    // debug code here
#endif
```

In release builds, this code is not compiled at all.

All the settings and configurations of the compiler and linker are kept separately for debug and release builds and can be changed independently. For example, many developers use different compiler warning levels. To bump your warning level to 4 for debug builds only, follow these steps:

1. Switch to the Solution Explorer (choose View, Solution Explorer, if necessary) and click the solution (the root of the tree) to select it.

2. Choose View, Property Pages (the last item on the View menu), which opens the property pages for the solution. An example is shown in Figure 12.1.

Tip

If you get a message that no property page is available, you haven't selected the entire solution in Solution Explorer.

Figure 12.1

Project settings are all on the property pages for the entire solution.

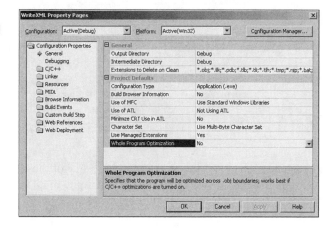

3. Choose Debug or Release from the drop-down list box at the upper left. If you choose All Configurations, you'll change debug and release settings simultaneously.

4. Click the C/C++ folder and the General item underneath it, then set the Warning Level to Level 4, as shown in Figure 12.2. The default is Level 3, which you will use for the release version (see Figure 12.3).

Figure 12.2

Warning levels can be set higher during development.

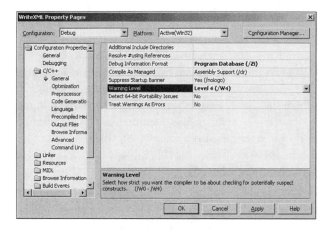

Figure 12.3
Warning levels are
usually lower in a
production release.

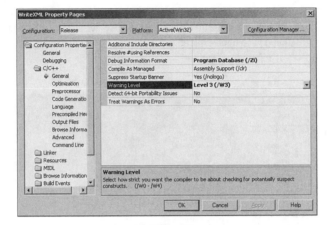

Warning level 4 generates a lot more errors than level 3. Some of those errors are likely to
come from code you didn't even write, such as MFC functions. You'll just have to ignore
those warnings.

SEALING MEMORY LEAKS

If you are working with .NET, memory leaks are not your problem—skip this section.
Seriously, one of the huge advantages of the .NET framework is garbage collection and
memory management. You won't have to worry about memory leaks. If you are mixing managed and unmanaged code, as described in Chapter 20, "Managed and Unmanaged Code,"
then you may have memory management issues. And if you're doing classic Win32 programming, the subject of the first half of this book, managing your application's memory is
your problem.

A memory leak can be the most pernicious of errors. Small leaks may not cause any execution errors in your program until it is run for an exceptionally long time or with a larger-
than-usual data file. Because most programmers test with tiny data files or run the program
for only a few minutes when they are experimenting with parts of it, memory leaks may not
reveal themselves in everyday testing. Alas, memory leaks may well reveal themselves to
your users when the program crashes or otherwise misbehaves.

COMMON CAUSES OF MEMORY LEAKS

What does it mean when your program has a memory leak? It means that your program
allocated memory and never released it. One very simple cause is calling new to allocate an
object or an array of objects on the heap and never calling delete. Another cause is changing the pointer kept in a variable without deleting the memory to which the pointer was
pointing. More subtle memory leaks arise when a class with a pointer as a member variable
calls new to assign the pointer, but doesn't have a copy constructor, assignment operator, or
destructor. Listing 12.1 illustrates some ways that memory leaks are caused.

LISTING 12.1 CAUSING MEMORY LEAKS

```
// simple pointer leaving scope
{
  int * one = new int;
  *one = 1;
} // one is out of scope now, and wasn't deleted

// mismatched new and delete: new uses delete and new[] uses delete[]
{
float * f = new float[10];
// use array
delete f; // Oops! Deleted f[0] correct version is delete [] f;
}

// pointer of new memory goes out of scope before delete
{
    const char * DeleteP = "Don't forget P";
    char * p = new char[strlen(DeleteP) + 1];
    strcpy( p, DeleteP );
} // scope ended before delete[]

class A
{
   public:
       int * pi;
}

A::A()
{
    pi = new int();
    *pi = 3;
}

// ..later on, some code using this class..

A firsta;    //allocates an int for first.pi to point to
A seconda;   //allocates another int for seconda.pi

seconda=firsta;

// will perform a bitwise (shallow) copy. Both objects
// have a pi that points to the first int allocated.
// The pointer to the second int allocated is gone
// forever.
```

These code fragments all represent ways in which memory can be allocated and the pointer to that memory lost before deallocation. After the pointer goes out of scope, you can't reclaim the memory, and no one else can use it, either. It's even worse when you consider exceptions, because if an exception is thrown, your flow of execution may leave a function before reaching the delete at the bottom of the code. Because destructors are called for objects that are going out of scope as the stack unwinds, you can prevent some of these problems by putting delete calls in destructors.

Like all bugs, the secret to dealing with memory leaks is to prevent them—or to detect them as soon as possible when they occur. You can develop some good habits to help you:

- If a class contains a pointer and allocates that pointer with new, be sure to code a destructor that deletes the memory. Also, code a copy constructor and an operator =.

- If a function will allocate memory and return something to let the calling program access that memory, it must return a pointer rather than a reference. You can't delete a reference.

- If a function will allocate memory and then delete it later in the same function, allocate the memory on the stack, if at all possible, so that you don't forget to delete it.

- Never change a pointer's value unless you have first deleted the object or array to which it was pointing. Never increment a pointer that was returned by new.

DEBUG new AND delete

MFC has a lot to offer the programmer who is looking for memory leaks. In debug builds, whenever you use new and delete, you are actually using special debug versions that track the filename and line number on which each allocation occurred and match up deletes with their news. If memory is left over as the program ends, you get a warning message in the output section, as shown in Figure 24.4.

Figure 24.4
Memory leaks are detected automatically in debug builds.

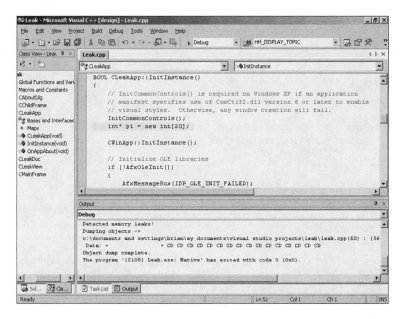

To see this for yourself, create an MFC Application called Leak, accepting all the defaults. In the InitInstance() function of the application class (CLeakApp in this example), add this line:

```
int* pi = new int[20];
```

Build a debug version of the application and run it by choosing Debug, Start. When the application comes up, just close it right away. You see output like that shown in Figure 12.4. Notice that the filename (Leak.cpp) and line number where the memory was allocated are provided in the error message. Double-click that line in the output window, and the editor window displays Leak.cpp with the cursor on line 50. (The coordinates in the lower right corner always remind you what line number you are on.) If you were writing a real application, you would now know what the problem is. Now you must determine where to fix it (more specifically, where to put the delete).

AUTOMATIC POINTERS

When a program executes within a particular scope, such as a function, all variables allocated in that function are allocated on the stack. The stack is a temporary storage space that shrinks and grows, like an accordion. The stack is used to store the current execution address before a function call, the arguments passed to the function, and the local function objects and variables.

When the function returns, the stack pointer is reset to that location where the prior execution point was stored. This makes the stack space after the reset location available to whatever else needs it, which means those elements allocated on the stack in the function are gone. This process is referred to as *stack unwinding*.

> **Note**
>
> Objects or variables defined with the keyword static are not allocated on the stack.

Stack unwinding also happens when an exception occurs. To reliably restore the program to its state before an exception occurred in the function, the stack is unwound. Stack-wise variables are gone, and the destructors for stack-wise objects are called. Unfortunately, the same is not true for dynamic objects (those allocated on the heap with the new operator). The handles (for example, pointers) are unwound, but the unwinding process doesn't call delete. This causes a memory leak.

In some cases, the solution is to add delete statements to the destructors of objects that you know will be destructed as part of the unwinding, so that they can use these pointers before they go out of scope. A more general approach is to replace simple pointers with a C++ class that can be used just like a pointer, but that contains a destructor that deletes any memory at the pointed location. Don't worry—you don't have to write such a class: One is included in the Standard Template Library, which comes with Visual C++. Listing 12.2 is a heavily edited version of the auto_ptr class definition, presented to demonstrate the key concepts.

CH

12

LISTING 12.2   A SCALED-DOWN VERSION OF THE auto_ptr CLASS

```cpp
// This class is not complete. Use the complete definition in
//the Standard Template Library.
 template <class T>
 class auto_ptr
```

LISTING 12.2   CONTINUED

```
{
public:
        auto_ptr( T *p = 0) : rep(p) {}
        // store pointer in the class
        ~auto_ptr(){ delete rep; }              // delete internal rep
        // include pointer conversion members
        inline T* operator->() const { return rep; }
        inline T& operator*() const { return *rep; }
  private:
        T * rep;
    };
```

The class has one member variable: a pointer to whatever type that you want a pointer to. It has a one-argument constructor to build an auto_ptr from an int* or a Truck* or any other pointer type. The destructor deletes the memory pointed to by the internal member variable. Finally, the class overrides -> and *, the dereferencing operators, so that dereferencing an auto_ptr feels just like dereferencing an ordinary pointer.

If there is some class C to which you want to make an automatic pointer called p, all you do is this:

```
auto_ptr<C> p(new C());
```

Now you can use p as though it were a C*—for example:

```
p->Method();   // calls C::Method()
```

You never have to delete the C object that p points to, even in the event of an exception, because p was allocated on the stack. When it goes out of scope, its destructor is called, and the destructor calls delete on the C object that was allocated in the new statement.

USING OPTIMIZATION TO MAKE EFFICIENT CODE

There was a time when programmers were expected to optimize their code themselves. Many a night was spent arguing about the order in which to test conditions, or about which variables should be registered or automatic storage. These days, compilers come with optimizers that can speed execution or shrink program size far beyond what a typical programmer can accomplish by hand.

Here's a simple example of how optimizers work. Imagine you have written a piece of code like this:

```
for (i=0;i<10;i++)
{
    y=2;
    x[i]=5;
}
for (i=0; i<10; i++)
{
    total += x[i];
}
```

Your code will run faster, with no effect on the final results, if you move the y=2 in front of the first loop. In addition, you can easily combine the two loops into a single loop. If you do that, it's faster to add 5 to the total each time than it is to calculate the address of x[i] to retrieve the value just stored in it. Really bright optimizers may even realize that the total can be calculated outside the loop as well. The revised code might look like this:

```
y=2;
for (i=0;i<10;i++)
{
    x[i]=5;
}
    total += 50;
```

Optimizers do far more than this, of course, but this example gives you an idea of what's going on behind the scenes. It's up to you whether the optimizer focuses on speed, occasionally at the expense of memory usage, or tries to minimize memory usage, perhaps at a slighter lower speed.

To set the optimization options for your project, select the solution in the Solution Explorer, then choose View, Property Pages. The property pages for the project, first shown in Figure 12.1, appear. Make sure you are looking at the Release settings. Click the C/C++ folder and select Optimization underneath that. Keep optimization turned off for debug builds, because the code in your source files and the code being executed won't match line for line, which only confuses you and the debugger. You should turn on Global Optimization for release builds, then choose the optimizations you prefer from the drop-down list at the bottom of the dialog, as shown in Figure 12.5.

Figure 12.5
Select the type of optimization you want.

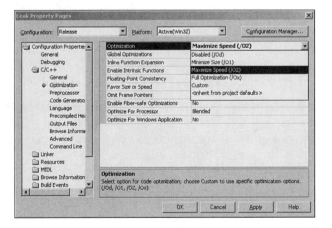

If you really know what you're doing, you can select from the list of individual optimizations on the property sheet. For now, it's enough of a boost just to turn optimization on.

FROM HERE

This chapter has covered some of the pitfalls that Win32 programmers can encounter as they develop, such as assumptions that turn out not to be true. It has also shown you how to avoid some of them by adjusting your settings or by using the code that has been written for you in MFC. Much of this advice is useful for those who develop managed applications for the .NET Framework, also.

To learn more about debugging your applications, read Chapter 13, "Debugging." To see how the .NET Framework manages your memory and prevents memory leaks, read Chapter 20, "Managed and Unmanaged C++."

DEBUGGING

In this chapter

THE IMPORTANCE OF DEBUGGING

Debugging is a vital part of programming. Whenever a program doesn't do what you expect, even if it doesn't blow up, you should still turn to the debugger to see what's really going on. Some of the philosophies and techniques of debugging have been explained elsewhere in this book, especially in Chapter 12, "Improving Your Application's Performance." This chapter concentrates on the nuts and bolts of how to use the debugger: the menus, toolbars, and windows that are not covered in Appendix C, "The Visual Studio User Interface, Menus, and Visual Studio." You'll learn what a breakpoint is, and how to set and use breakpoints while debugging your application. In addition, you'll learn how to use a handy utility called the ATL/MFC Trace Tool, and write a function that will provide debugging information to you when you need it.

DEBUGGING VOCABULARY: BREAKPOINTS AND RELATED CONCEPTS

Probably the most important word in debugging is *breakpoint*. A breakpoint is a spot in your program, a single line of code, where you would like to pause. Perhaps you are wondering how many times a loop is executed, whether control transfers inside a certain if statement, or whether a function is even called. Setting a breakpoint on a line makes execution stop when that line is about to be executed. At that point you may want the program to be off and running again, or you may want to move through your code a line or so at a time. You may want to know some of your variables' values, or to examine the call stack to see how control transferred to this point. Often, you'll spot the cause of a bug at a breakpoint and correct your code on the spot. The Visual Studio debugger has a lot of features, and it can be a challenge to decide how to look at your application. Throughout this chapter you can find tips and suggestions about where to place breakpoints and how to use them.

When it's time to move along, there are a number of ways you might like execution to resume:

- **Continue**. Execute to the next breakpoint or, if there are no more breakpoints, until the program completes.
- **Restart**. Start again from the beginning.
- **Step Over**. Execute only the next statement, and then pause again. If it is a function call, run the whole function and pause after returning from it.
- **Step Into**. Execute just the next statement, but if it is a function, go into it and pause before executing the first statement in the function.
- **Step Out**. Execute the rest of the current function and pause in the function that called this one.
- **Run to Cursor**. Start running and stop a few (or many) lines from here, where the cursor is positioned.

Most information made available to you by the debugger is in the form of new windows. These are discussed in the following sections.

DEBUGGING COMMANDS AND WINDOWS

Visual Studio has a powerful debugger with a rich interface. It includes menu items, toolbar buttons, and windows (output areas) that are used only when debugging.

MENU ITEMS

When you start debugging, new items appear on the Debug menu. From the Debug menu, you can choose:

- Windows, Breakpoints
- Windows, Running Documents
- Windows, Watch, Watch 1-4
- Windows, Autos
- Windows, Locals
- Windows, This
- Windows, Immediate
- Windows, Callstack
- Windows, Threads
- Windows, Modules
- Windows, Memory, Memory 1-4
- Windows, Disassembly
- Windows, Registers
- Continue
- Break All
- Stop Debugging
- Detach All
- Restart
- Apply Code Changes
- Processes...
- Exceptions...
- Step Into
- Step Over
- Step Out
- Quickwatch...
- New Breakpoint

CH
13

- Clear All Breakpoints
- Disable All Breakpoints
- Save Dump As

To understand these menu choices, you need to learn your way around the debug windows and understand what a breakpoint and a watch are. You'll see that in the sections that follow.

SETTING BREAKPOINTS

Probably the simplest way to set a breakpoint is to place the cursor on the line of code where you would like to pause. Then, toggle a breakpoint by pressing F9 or by clicking the Insert Breakpoint button on the Debug toolbar, which looks like an upraised hand. (You're supposed to think "Stop!") If you prefer, you can click the gray margin to the left of the line of code. A red dot appears in the margin to indicate you have placed a breakpoint here, as shown in Figure 13.1.

Figure 13.1
The F9 key toggles a breakpoint on the line containing the cursor.

> **Note**
>
> The application being debugged throughout this appendix is ShowString, as built in Chapter 6, "Building a Complete Application: ShowString."

Choosing Debug, Windows, Breakpoints displays a tabbed dialog box to set simple or conditional breakpoints. This is useful if you want to pause whenever a certain variable's value changes, for example. Searching through your code for lines that change that variable's value and setting breakpoints on them all is tiresome. Instead, choose Debug, New Breakpoint or click the New on mini-toolbar at the top of the Breakpoints window and open the Data tab on the New Breakpoint dialog box, shown in Figure 13.2. In the Variable field, enter the variable's name, and in the Context field enter the function's name, surrounded by braces, where the variable may be modified. When the value of the variable changes, a message box tells you why execution is pausing; then you can look at code and variables, as described in the following section.

Figure 13.2
You can arrange for
execution to pause
whenever a variable
or expression
changes value.

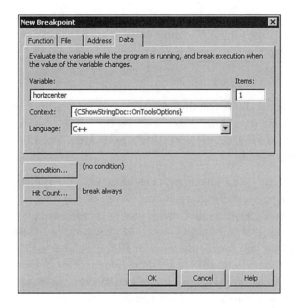

You can also set conditional breakpoints, such as break on a particular line when i exceeds 100, that spare you from mindlessly clicking Continue, Continue, Continue until you have been through a loop 100 times.

EXAMINING VARIABLE VALUES

When you set a breakpoint and debug the program, everything proceeds normally until the breakpoint line of code is about to execute. Then Visual Studio comes up on top of your application, with some extra windows in the display and a yellow arrow in the red margin dot that indicates your breakpoint, as shown in Figure 13.3. This shows you the line of code that is about to execute.

Figure 13.3
An arrow indicates
the line of code about
to execute.

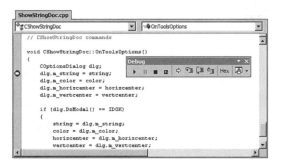

Move the mouse over a variable name, such as color or horizcenter. A DataTip appears, telling you the current value of this variable. You can check as many local variables as you want like this, then continue executing, and check them again. There are other ways, though, to examine variable values. The most popular are a QuickWatch, the Watch window, and the Locals window.

QUICKWATCH

The QuickWatch window shows you the value of a variable or expression in more detail than a DataTip. To bring up a QuickWatch, click on the variable (or move the cursor to it some other way) and choose Debug, QuickWatch, or click the QuickWatch button (a pair of glasses) on the Debug toolbar.

You're probably wondering why anyone uses this feature when DataTips can show you a variable's value without even clicking; it can even show you the value of simple expressions, such as dlg.m_horizcenter. With a quick watch you get a much more detailed view of a variable, as shown in Figure 13.4. In this example, a quick watch was set on the variable dlg. In the QuickWatch window you can see the value of all the member variables and base classes, both of which can be expanded to show even more information. You can also change a variable's value with this dialog box to give your application a chance to recover from horrible errors. A quick watch is easy to bring up, but you must dismiss it before you can continue with your debugging.

Figure 13.4
The QuickWatch dialog box evaluates expressions and gives detailed information on a variable.

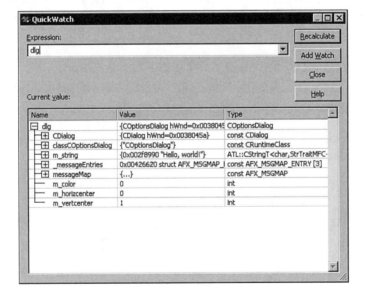

THE WATCH WINDOW

The watch window is much like a quick watch, but it shows only those values you add to it, and it stays available as your application runs.

Figure 13.5 shows a debug session after running forward a few lines from the original breakpoint (you'll see how to do this in the "Stepping Through Code" section later in this chapter). The Watch window has been undocked to show it more clearly, and two watches have been added: one for horizcenter and one for dlg. (An easy way to add a watch is to bring up the QuickWatch window for a dialog, then click Add Watch.) The program is paused immediately after the user clicks OK on the Options dialog, and in this case the user changed the string, the color, and both kinds of centering.

Figure 13.5
The Watch window makes it easy to know the values of all your variables.

The Watch window in Figure 13.5 shows the values of the two variables that were added to it. Horizcenter has been set to FALSE(0). The values under dlg correspond to those of its members. For example, m_string is "Hello, world!" because that was the value of the edit control when the dialog was submitted. (Dialogs, controls, and associating controls with member variables are discussed in Chapter 3, "Interacting with Your Application.")

THE LOCALS WINDOW

Also visible in Figure 13.5, on the lower left, is the Locals window. You don't add variables to this window: it shows all the variables that are local to the function that is executing. This window has a lot more information in it than the Watch window, which sometimes makes it harder to use. The local variable dlg and the pointer to the object for which this member function was invoked (this) are both in the Locals window in tree form: Click on a + to expand the tree and on a – to collapse it. In addition, the return value from DoModal(), 1, is displayed.

THE CALL STACK WINDOW

The Call Stack window is shown in Figure 13.6 and is one of the most useful tools in the debugger. It displays the path of execution of your application, and enables you to easily trace backward in that path. The Call Stack window lists, in order, the names of the functions that have been called as well as the names and values of the parameters that were passed to each one. Double-clicking on an entry in the Call Stack window shows you the point in the source code where the function was called.

The top entry in the call stack of Figure 13.6 is the function in which the line about to be executed is contained, CShowStringDoc::OnToolsOptions(). The second entry is the function that called this one, AfxDispatchCmdMsg(), which dispatches command messages. Chapter 3 introduces commands and messages and discusses the way that control passes to a message-handling function such as OnToolsOptions(). Here, the debugger gives proof of this process right before your eyes.

CH
13

Figure 13.6
The Call Stack window shows how execution reached this point in your application.

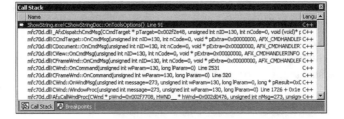

You may notice the number 130 recurring in a lot of the function calls. Select ShowString.rc in the Resource View window, then choose Edit, Resource Symbols, and you'll see that 130 means ID_TOOLS_OPTIONS, the resource ID associated with the menu item Tools, Options in ShowString (see Figure 13.7).

Figure 13.7
The number 130 corresponds to ID_TOOLS_OPTIONS.

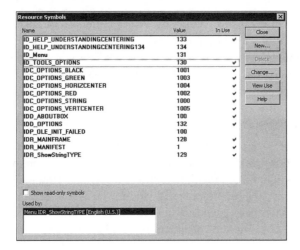

STEPPING THROUGH CODE

Double-clicking a function name in the call stack doesn't make any code execute; it simply gives you a chance to examine the local variables and code of the functions that called the function now executing. After you've looked at everything you want to look at, it's time to move on. Although the Debug menu includes options to Step Over, Step Into, and so on, most developers use the toolbar buttons or the keyboard shortcuts. (To see the Debug toolbar, refer to Figures 13.1, 13.3, and 13.5.) Pause your mouse over each button to see the command to which it is connected and a reminder of the keyboard shortcut. For example, the button showing an arrow going down into an indented paragraph is Step Into, and the shortcut key is F11.

As you move through code, the yellow arrow in the margin moves with you to show which line is about to execute. Whenever the program is paused, you can add or remove breakpoints, examine variables, or resume execution. These are the mechanics of debugging.

EDIT AND CONTINUE

Most developers are familiar with the cycle of debugging work. You build your project, you run it, and something unusual happens. You debug for a while to understand why. You find the bad code, change it, rebuild, rerun, and either find another bug or convince yourself that the application works. Sometimes you think you've fixed it, but you haven't. As your project grows, these rebuilds can take a very long time, and they break the rhythm of your work. It can also take a significant amount of time to run the application to the trouble spot each time. It's very boring to enter the same information every time on a dialog box, for example, trying to set up an error condition.

In Visual C++ .NET, in many cases you can keep right on debugging after making a code change—without rebuilding and without rerunning. This feature is called Edit and Continue and is sure to be a major time-saver.

To use Edit and Continue, you should start by confirming that it's enabled both for the product as a whole and for this specific project. Here's how:

1. Choose Tools, Options and click the Edit and Continue item under the Debugging tab.

2. Make sure that the check boxes Enable Edit and Continue, as well as Invoked by Debug Commands, are selected, as shown in Figure 13.8.

3. Select the project's name in the Solution Explorer window, then choose Project, Properties, and click the C/C++ tab.

4. Ensure that the Debug Information Format drop-down box contains Program Database for Edit and Continue. If not, drop the box down, select this option, as in Figure 13.9 (it's second to last on the list), and then rebuild the project after exiting the Project Settings dialog box.

Always check the project settings when you start a new project, to confirm that Edit and Continue is enabled.

Figure 13.8
Enable Edit and Continue on the Debugging tab of the Options dialog box.

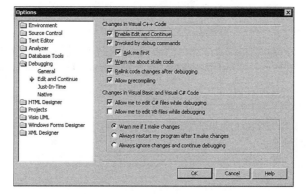

Figure 13.9
Your project must
generate Edit and
Continue information.

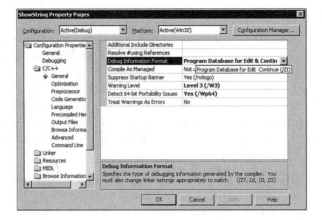

Now, debug as you always have, but don't automatically click Build after making a code change. Try to step to the next line. If it's not possible to continue without a build, you receive a line of output in the Build tab of the Output window telling you so and the familiar One or More Files Are Out of Date message box offering you a chance to rebuild your project. If it's possible to continue, you have saved a tremendous amount of time. Most simple code changes, such as changing the condition in an `if` or `for` statement or changing a variable's value, should work immediately. More complex changes require a rebuild. For example, you must rebuild after any one of these changes:

- Any change to a header file, including changing code in an inline function
- Changing a C++ class definition
- Changing a function prototype
- Changing the code in a global (nonmember) function or a static member function

Try it yourself:

1. Imagine that you can't remember why the string originally displayed by ShowString is black, and you'd like it to be red.

2. You suspect that the `OnNewDocument()` function is setting it, so you expand `CShowStringDoc` in the Class View window and double-click `OnNewDocument()`.

3. Place a breakpoint (F9) on this line:
   ```
   string = "Hello, world!";
   ```

4. Click Go (F5), or choose Debug, Start; ShowString runs, creates a new document, and stops at your breakpoint.

5. Change the next line of code to read as follows:
   ```
   color = 1;    //red
   ```

6. Click Continue again and the Edit and Continue dialog appears. Click Yes to accept the change and keep running the code. You can check the Never Show Me This Dialog Again box to always accept the changes.

7. Watch your output window and you can see that showstringdoc.cpp is recompiling. After a short wait, the familiar Hello, world! appears—in red. Your changes went into effect immediately.

When you finish your debugging session, it's a good idea to do a build because the changes used by Edit and Continue may be in memory only and not written out to your executable file.

MEMORY, REGISTERS, AND DISASSEMBLY

Three less important debug windows have not yet been mentioned: Memory, Registers, and Disassembly. These windows provide a level of detail rarely required in ordinary debugging. With each release of Visual C++, the number of circumstances that require these windows dwindles. For example, the Registers window used to be the only way to see the value returned from a function call. Now that same information is in the Variables window in a more accessible format.

THE MEMORY WINDOW

This window, illustrated in Figure 13.10, shows the hex values in every byte of the memory space from 0x00000000 to 0xFFFFFFFF. It's a very long list, which makes the dialog box hard to scroll through—use the Address box to enter an address that interests you. Typically, these addresses are copied (through the Clipboard, not by hand) from the Locals window. It is a handy way to look through a large array or to track down subtle platform-dependent problems.

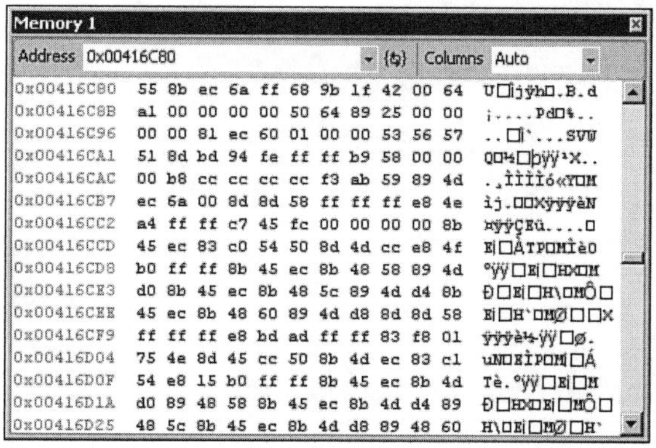

Figure 13.10
You can examine raw memory in the Memory window, though you'll rarely need to.

THE REGISTERS WINDOW

If you are debugging at the assembler level, it might be useful to examine the registers. Figure 13.11 shows the Registers window. This shot was taken at the same point of execution as Figure 13.5, and you can see that the EAX register contains the value 1, which is the return value from CDocument::OnNewDocument().

Figure 13.11
All the registers are available for examination.

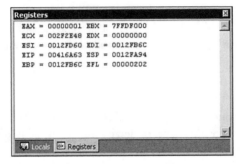

THE DISASSEMBLY WINDOW

By default, the Disassembly window comes up full screen, replacing the C++ code in the main working area. You can see the assembly language statements generated for your C++ code, shown in Figure 13.12. Debugging at the assembly level is beyond the scope of this book, though perhaps you might be curious to see the assembly code generated for parts of your program.

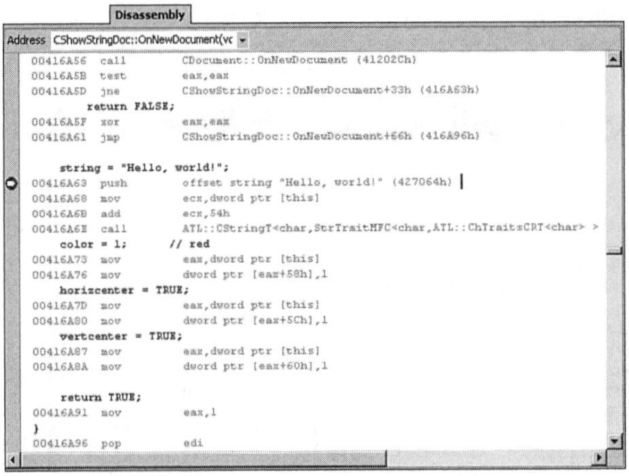

Figure 13.12
You can debug the assembler that was generated for you.

USING THE ATL/MFC TRACE TOOL

The ATL/MFC Trace Tool utility is a standalone application that can have an integrated menu item in Visual Studio. To run it, choose Tools, ATL/MFC Trace Tool. If the option is not there, you have to add it before you can use the tracer. To do this, choose Tools, External Tools. Click Add in the dialog box that appears. For the new entry, set the Title to ATL/MFC Trace Tool; set the command to the ATL/MFC Trace Tool executable (typically Common7\Tools\ AtlTraceTool.exe under the Microsoft Visual Studio. NET directory). Figure 13.13 shows the Trace Tool dialog that appears.

Figure 13.13
The ATL/MFC Trace Tool utility simplifies setting trace flags.

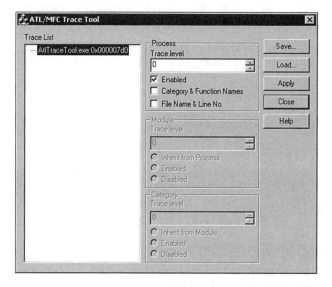

The ATL/MFC Trace Tool is an easy tool for setting trace flags that govern the kind of debug output you get. Try setting all the flags on and running ShowString; just start it up and shut it down. Turn off a few flags and see how the output changes.

With all the trace flags on, your application will be slow. Use the tracer to set only the ones you're interested in, while you're interested in them. It's much easier than changing a variable on the fly.

DEFINING A DUMP MEMBER FUNCTION

All MFC classes have a Dump() member function. When things go wrong, some error-handling code calls this function to show you the object's contents. You can write Dump() functions for your objects, too. Although you won't normally call these functions yourself, you could do so as part of your own error handling.

MFC classes inherit Dump() from CObject, where it is defined like this:

```
virtual void Dump(CDumpContext& dc ) const;
```

The keyword virtual suggests you should override the method in your derived classes, and const indicates that Dump() will not modify the object state.

CH

13

Like trace and assert statements, the Dump() member function disappears in a release build. This saves users seeing output they can't deal with and makes a smaller, faster release version for you. You have to make this happen yourself for any Dump() function you write, with conditional compilation, as discussed in the "Adding Debug-Only Features" section of Chapter 12.

The MFC Application Wizard generates a skeleton Dump() function in the classes it creates for you, but you may want to add support in your own MFC classes. In the header file, declare Dump() like this:

```
class CNewClass : public CObject
{
public:
    // other class stuff
    #ifdef _DEBUG
    virtual void Dump( CDumpContext& dc) const
    #endif
    // ...
};
```

In the implementation file, the definition, which includes a code body, might look like this:

```
#include "cnewclass.h"

#ifdef _DEBUG
void CNewClass::Dump( CDumpContext& dc ) const
{
    CObject::Dump( dc );      // Dump parent;
    // perhaps dump individual members, works like cout
    dc << "member: " << /* member here */ endl;
}
#endif
```

As you see in the code for the Dump() function, writing the code is much like writing to standard output with the cout object or serializing to an archive. You are provided with a CDumpContext object called dc, and you send text and values to that object with the << operator. If this is unfamiliar to you, read Chapter 5, "Printing and Saving."

AN EXAMPLE USING CDumpContext, CFile, AND axfDump

The sample application in this section uses the MFC debugging class CDumpContext and the global afxDump object. To run this application yourself, create a console application as described in Chapter 15, "Special Win32 Application Types," and create an empty C++ source file called Dump.cpp. Enter the code in Listing 13.1, build, and run a debug version of the project.

TROUBLESHOOTING

When you link a debug version of this product, or if you receive error messages that refer to _beginthreadex and _endthreadex, you need to change some settings. By default, console applications are single-threaded, but MFC is multithreaded. By including afx.h and bringing in MFC, this application is making itself incompatible with the single-threaded default. To fix this, you must change the Runtime Library to Multi-threaded Debug DLL, as described in Chapter 15. You should usually change the settings for release builds as well, but because the calls to Dump() aren't surrounded by tests of _DEBUG, this code won't be included in the release version anyway.

LISTING 13.1   DUMP.CPP—DEMONSTRATING THE MFC DEBUGGING CLASS CDumpContext AND THE OUTPUT CFile CODE

```cpp
#include <afx.h>
// _DEBUG defined for debug build

class CPeople : public CObject
{
public:
    // constructor
        CPeople( const char * name );
        // destructor
        virtual ~CPeople();
        #ifdef _DEBUG
            virtual void Dump(CDumpContext& dc) const;
        #endif
    private:
        CString * person;
    };

    // constructor
    CPeople::CPeople( const char * name) : person( new CString(name)) {}
    // destructor
    CPeople::~CPeople(){ delete person; }

#ifdef _DEBUG
    void CPeople::Dump( CDumpContext& dc ) const
    {
        CObject::Dump(dc);
        dc << person->GetBuffer( person->GetLength() + 1);
    }
#endif

int main()
    {
        CPeople person1("Kate Gregory");
        CPeople person2("Hans Hesse");


        // Use existing afxDump with virtual dump member function
        person1.Dump( afxDump );

        // Instantiate a CFile object
        CFile dumpFile("dumpout.txt", CFile::modeCreate |
            CFile::modeWrite);

        if( !dumpFile )
        {
            afxDump << "File open failed.";
        }
```

LISTING 13.1   CONTINUED

```
    else
    {
        // Dump with other CDumpContext
        CDumpContext context(&dumpFile);
        person2.Dump(context);
    }

    return 0;
}
```

This single file contains a class definition, all the code for the class member functions, and a main() function to run as a console application. Each part of the file is explained in the next few paragraphs. The class is a simple wrapper around a CString pointer, which allocates the CString with new in the constructor and deletes it in the destructor. It's so simple that it's actually useless for anything other than demonstrating the Dump() function.

First, the <afx.h> header file is included, which contains the CObject class definition and provides access to afxDump.

Next, this code defines the class CPeople derived from CObject. Notice the placement of the override of the virtual Dump() method and the conditional compiler wrap. (Any calls to Dump() should be wrapped in the same way, or that code will not compile in a release build.)

Following the constructor and destructor comes the code for CPeople::Dump(). Notice how it, too, is wrapped in conditional compiler directives. The call to CObject::Dump() takes advantage of the work done by the MFC programmers, dumping information all objects keep.

Finally, the main() function exercises this little class. It creates three instances of the CPeople class and dumps the first one.

For the second CPeople object, this code creates and opens a CFile object by passing a text string to the constructor. If the open succeeds, it creates a CDumpContextObject from the file and passes this context to Dump instead of the usual afxDump().

If you run this program, you'll see output like that shown in Figure 13.14. The file dumpout.txt will contain these lines:

```
a CObject at $ $0012FEB4
Hans Hesse
```

The first line of the output, to both the debug window and the file, came from CObject::Dump() and gives you the object type and the address. The second line is from your own code and is simply the CString kept within each CPeople.

Now that you've seen the basic tools of debugging in action, you're ready to put them to work in your own applications. You'll find errors quickly, understand other people's code, and see with your own eyes just how message-routing and other behind-the-scenes magic really occur. If you find yourself enjoying debugging, don't worry—no one else has to know!

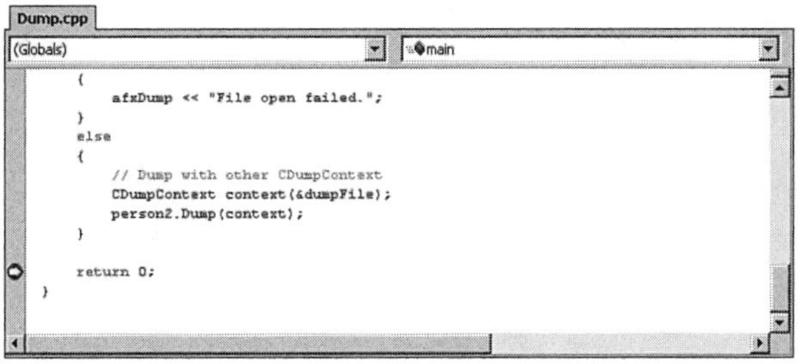

Figure 13.14
Using the afxDump context sends your output to the Debug window.

```
Dump.cpp
(Globals)                                        main
          {
                afxDump << "File open failed.";
          }
          else
          {
                // Dump with other CDumpContext
                CDumpContext context(&dumpFile);
                person2.Dump(context);
          }

          return 0;
          }
```

FROM HERE

The Visual Studio debugger is arguably the most useful of the tools that are integrated into the development environment. No amount of adding print statements or popping up message boxes can compete with the simplicity of simply pausing execution and examining variables. You can start simply, setting breakpoints and watching your code a step at a time. As you begin to realize the power of the debugger, try more features: Set a conditional breakpoint, or change a variable's value while your code is running. You'll soon develop a knack for finding trouble within your code as quickly as possible.

For more on preventing errors in your programs, be sure to read Chapter 12. You'll learn about memory leaks, and about using TRACE and ASSERT to monitor your application during debugging.

In the next chapter, "Multitasking with Windows Threads," you can see how to add more depth to your programming by taking advantage of threading. You can dramatically improve the performance of your applications by separating complex calculations into separate threads so that ordinary processing can continue.

sMULTITASKING WITH WINDOWS THREADS

In this chapter

UNDERSTANDING SIMPLE THREADS

With Windows 2000 (and other modern operating systems), you know that you can run several programs simultaneously. This capability is called *multitasking*. What you may not know is that many of today's operating systems also enable *threads*, which are separate processes that are not complete applications. A thread is a lot like a subprogram. An application can create several threads—several different flows of execution—and run them concurrently. Threads enable multitasking inside multitasking. In this chapter, you learn how to create and manage threads in your applications.

A thread is a path of execution through a program. In a multithreaded program, each thread has its own stack and operates independently of other threads running within the same program. MFC distinguishes between UI threads, which have a message pump and typically perform user interface tasks, and worker threads, which do not.

Note

Any application always has at least one thread, which is the program's primary or main thread. You can start and stop as many additional threads as you need, but the main thread keeps running as long as the application is active.

A thread is the smallest unit of execution, much smaller than a process. Generally each running application on your system is a process. If you start the same application (for example, Notepad) twice, there are two processes: one for each instance. It is possible for several instances of an application to share a single process: for example, if you choose File, New Window in Internet Explorer, two applications appear on your taskbar, and they share a process. The unfortunate consequence is that if one instance crashes, they all do.

To create a worker thread with MFC, all you have to do is write a function that you want to run parallel with the rest of your application. This is called a thread function. Then call `AfxBeginThread()` to start a thread that will execute your function. The function must take one parameter: an `LPVOID`. You can pass it a pointer to a structure or class, and cast the pointer back inside the function to effectively pass whatever you want to the function that the thread will execute. The function must return a `UINT` that indicates whether the work succeeded or not. The thread remains active as long as the thread function is executing: When the thread function exits, the thread is destroyed. A simple call to `AfxBeginThread()` looks like this:

```
AfxBeginThread(ProcName, param, priority);
```

In the preceding line, `ProcName` is the name of the thread function, `param` is any 32-bit value you want to pass to the thread, and `priority` is the thread's priority, which is represented by a number of predefined constants. Table 14.1 shows those constants and their descriptions, from lowest to highest priority.

TABLE 14.1   THREAD PRIORITY CONSTANTS

Constant	Description
THREAD_PRIORITY_IDLE	Sets a base priority of 1. For a REALTIME_PRIORITY_CLASS process, this sets a priority of 16.
THREAD_PRIORITY_LOWEST	Sets a priority two points below normal.
THREAD_PRIORITY_BELOW_NORMAL	Sets a priority one point lower than normal.
THREAD_PRIORITY_NORMAL	Sets normal priority.
THREAD_PRIORITY_ABOVE_NORMAL	Sets a priority one point higher than normal.
THREAD_PRIORITY_HIGHEST	Sets a priority two points above normal.
THREAD_PRIORITY_TIME_CRITICAL	Sets a base priority of 15. For a REALTIME_PRIORITY_CLASS process, this sets a priority of 31.

Note

A thread's priority determines how often the thread takes control of the system, relative to the other running threads. Generally, the higher the priority, the more running time the thread gets, which is why the value of THREAD_PRIORITY_TIME_CRITICAL is so high.

The call to AfxBeginThread() actually creates an instance of an MFC class called CWinThread. If you want to create a user-interface thread rather than a worker thread, you will work with CWinThread more closely. For most developers, the work to be spun off into a separate thread is more suited to a worker thread, so calling AfxBeginThread and ignoring the return value is appropriate.

To see a simple thread in action, build the Thread application as detailed in the following steps.

1. Create a new MFC Application Wizard-based project workspace called Thread, as shown in Figure 14.1.

Figure 14.1
Create a new MFC Application Wizard-based project workspace called Thread.

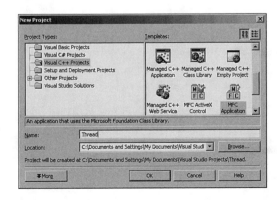

2. Give the new project the following settings in the MFC Application Wizard dialog boxes. The New Project Information dialog box then looks like Figure 14.2.

Figure 14.2
These are the MFC Application Wizard settings for the Thread project.

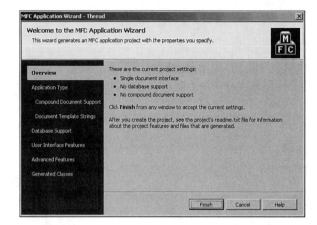

Application Type tab: Single document

Advanced Features tab: Turn off all options

Leave the rest of the options at their default values.

3. Use the resource editor to add a Thread menu to the application's IDR_MAINFRAME menu. Give the menu one command called Start Thread, and after selecting another item so that the command ID is assigned, click on the item again and enter a sensible prompt and ToolTip, as shown in Figure 14.3.

Figure 14.3
Add a Thread menu with a Start Thread command.

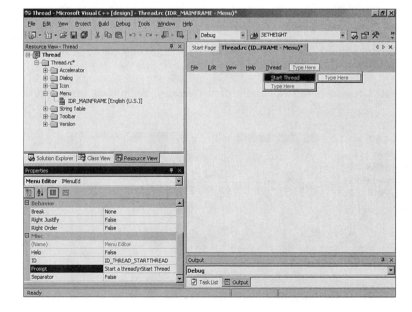

4. Use the Properties window to associate the ID_THREAD_STARTTHREAD command with the `OnThreadStartthread()` event handler function of `CThreadView`, as shown in Figure 14.4.

Figure 14.4
Add the
`OnThreadStart`
`thread()` message-
response function to
the view class.

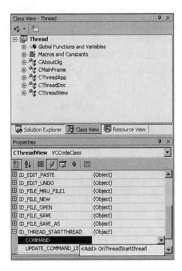

5. Add the following lines to the new `OnThreadStartthread()` function, replacing the TODO comment:

```
HWND hWnd = GetSafeHwnd();
AfxBeginThread(ThreadProc, hWnd, THREAD_PRIORITY_NORMAL);
```

This code calls a function you will write called `ThreadProc` within a worker thread of its own. Next, add `ThreadProc`, shown in Listing 14.1, to ThreadView.cpp, placing it right before the `OnThreadStartthread()` function. (Placing it there saves you having to declare it in advance.) Note that `ThreadProc()` is a global function and not a member function of the `CThreadView` class, even though it is in the view class's implementation file.

LISTING 14.1 THREADVIEW.CPP—ThreadProc()

```
UINT ThreadProc(LPVOID param)
{
    ::MessageBox((HWND)param, "Thread activated.", "Thread", MB_OK);

    return 0;
}
```

This threaded function doesn't do much; it just reports that it was started. The SDK function `MessageBox()` is very much like `AfxMessageBox()`, but because this isn't a member function of a class derived from `CWnd`, you can't use `AfxMessageBox()`.

CH
14

Tip

The double colons in front of a function name indicate a call to a global function, rather than a MFC class member function. For Windows programmers, this usually means an API or SDK call. For example, inside a MFC window class, you can call `MessageBox("Hi, There!")` to display `Hi, There!` to the user. This form of `MessageBox()` is a member function of the MFC window classes. To call the SDK version, you write something like **::MessageBox(0, "Hi, There!", "Message", MB_OK)**. Notice the colons in front of the function name and the additional arguments.

When you run the Thread program, the main window appears. Select the Thread, Start Thread command, and the system starts the thread represented by the `ThreadProc()` function and displays a message box, as shown in Figure 14.5.

Figure 14.5
The simple secondary thread in the Thread program displays a message box and then ends.

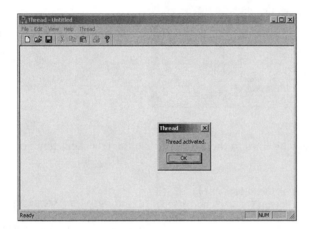

UNDERSTANDING THREAD COMMUNICATION

Usually, a secondary thread performs some sort of task for the main program, which implies that a channel of communication needs to exist between the program (which is also a thread) and its secondary threads. There are several ways to accomplish these communications tasks: with global variables, event objects, and messages. This section explores these thread-communication techniques.

COMMUNICATING WITH GLOBAL VARIABLES

Suppose you want your main program to be able to stop the thread. You need a way, then, to tell the thread when to stop. One method is to set up a global variable and then have the thread monitor the global variable for a value that signals the thread to end. Because the threads share the same address space, they have the same global variables. To see how this technique works, modify the Thread application as follows:

1. Use the Resource Editor to add a Stop Thread command to the application's Thread menu, as shown in Figure 14.6.

Figure 14.6
Add a Stop Thread
command to the
Thread menu.

2. Use the Properties window to associate the ID_THREAD_STOPTHREAD command with the OnThreadStopthread() event-handler function of CThreadView, as shown in Figure 14.7. Add the following line to the OnThreadStopthread() function, replacing the TODO comment as follows:

Figure 14.7
Add the
OnThreadStop
thread()
message-response
function.

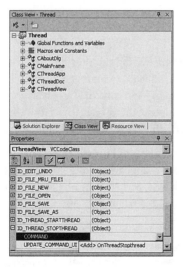

```
threadController = false;
```

This refers to a new global variable you are about to declare.

3. Add the following line to the top of the ThreadView.cpp file, right after the endif directive:

```
volatile bool threadController;
```

The volatile keyword means that you expect this variable will be changed from outside a thread that uses it. The keyword requests that the compiler not cache the variable in a register or in any way count on the value staying unchanged just because code in one thread doesn't seem to change it.

4. Add the following line to the OnStartthread() function, before the two lines you added earlier:

```
threadController = true;
```

By now, perhaps, you've guessed that the value of threadController determines whether the thread will continue. Replace the ThreadProc() function with the one shown in Listing 14.2.

LISTING 14.2   THE NEW ThreadProc() FUNCTION

```
UINT ThreadProc(LPVOID param)
{
    ::MessageBox((HWND)param, "Thread activated.", "Thread", MB_OK);

    while (threadController)
    {
        ;
    }

    ::MessageBox((HWND)param, "Thread stopped.", "Thread", MB_OK);

    return 0;
}
```

Now the thread first displays a message box, telling the user that the thread is starting. Then a while loop continues to check the threadController global variable, waiting for its value to change to false. Although this while loop is trivial, it is here that you would place the code that performs whatever task you want the thread to perform, making sure not to tie things up for too long before you recheck the value of threadController.

Try a test: Build and run the program, and choose Thread, Start Thread to start the secondary thread. When you do, a message box appears, telling you that the new thread was started. To stop the thread, select the Thread, Stop Thread command. Again, a message box appears, this time telling you that the thread is stopping.

Caution

Using global variables to communicate between threads is, to say the least, an unsophisticated approach to thread communication and can be a dangerous technique if you're not sure how C++ handles variables from an assembly-language level. Other thread-communication techniques are safer and more elegant.

COMMUNICATING WITH USER-DEFINED MESSAGES

Now you have a simple, albeit unsophisticated, method for communicating information from your main program to your thread. How about the reverse? That is, how can your thread communicate with the main program? The easiest method to accomplish this communication is to incorporate user-defined Windows messages into the program.

The first step is to define a user message, which you can do easily, like this:

```
const WM_USERMSG = WM_USER + 100;
```

The WM_USER constant, defined by Windows, holds the first available user-message number. Because other parts of your program may use some user messages for their own purposes, this line sets WM_USERMSG to WM_USER+100.

After defining the message, you call ::PostMessage() from the thread whenever you need to send the message to the main program. (Message handling was discussed in Chapter 3, "Interacting with Your Application." Sending your own messages enables you to take advantage of the message-handling facility built into MFC.) A typical call to ::PostMessage() might look like this:

```
::PostMessage((HWND)param, WM_USERMSG, 0, 0);
```

PostMessage()'s four arguments are the handle of the window to which the message should be sent, the message identifier, and the message's WPARAM and LPARAM parameters.

Modify the Thread application according to the next steps to implement posting user messages from a thread.

1. Add the following line to the top of the ThreadView.h header file, right before the beginning of the class declaration:
   ```
   const WM_THREADENDED = WM_USER + 100;
   ```

2. Still in the header file, add the following line after the declaration of the OnThreadStopthread() function:
   ```
   afx_msg LRESULT OnThreadended(WPARAM wParam, LPARAM lParam);
   ```

3. Switch to the ThreadView.cpp file and add the following line to the class's message map, making sure to place it right after the BEGIN_MESSAGE_MAP() macro:
   ```
   ON_MESSAGE(WM_THREADENDED, OnThreadended)
   ```

4. Replace the ThreadProc() function with the one shown in Listing 14.3.

LISTING 14.3 **THE MESSAGE-POSTING** ThreadProc()

```
UINT ThreadProc(LPVOID param)
{
    ::MessageBox((HWND)param, "Thread activated.", "Thread", MB_OK);

    while (threadController)
    {
        ;
    }

    ::PostMessage((HWND)param, WM_THREADENDED, 0, 0);

    return 0;
}
```

---

5. Add the function shown in Listing 14.4 to the end of the ThreadView.cpp file.

Сн
14

LISTING 14.4 CThreadView::OnThreadended()

```
LONG CThreadView::OnThreadended(WPARAM wParam, LPARAM lParam)
{
    AfxMessageBox("Thread ended.");
    return 0;
}
```

When you run the new version of the Thread program, select the Thread, Start Thread command to start the thread. When you do, a message box appears, telling you that the thread has started. To end the thread, select the Thread, Stop Thread command. Just as with the previous version of the program, a message box appears, telling you that the thread has ended.

Although this version of the Thread application seems to run identically to the preceding version, there's a subtle difference. Now the program displays the message box that signals the end of the thread in the main program rather than from inside the thread. The program can do this because when the user selects the Stop Thread command, the thread sends a WM_THREADENDED message to the main program. When the program receives that message, it displays the final message box.

COMMUNICATING WITH EVENT OBJECTS

A slightly more sophisticated method of signaling between threads is to use event objects, which under MFC are represented by the CEvent class, defined in afxmt.h, a header file full of MFC classes related to multithreaded programming. (The *mt* in afxmt stands for *multi-thread*.) An event object can be in one of two states: signaled and nonsignaled. Threads can watch for events to be signaled and so perform their operations at the appropriate time. Creating an event object is as easy as declaring a global variable, like this:

```
CEvent threadStart;
```

Although the CEvent constructor has a number of optional arguments, you can usually get away with creating the default object, as shown in the preceding line of code. On creation, the event object is automatically in its nonsignaled state. To signal the event, you call the event object's SetEvent() member function, like this:

```
threadStart.SetEvent();
```

After this line executes, the threadStart event object is in its signaled state. Your thread should be watching for this signal so that the thread knows it's okay to get to work. How does a thread watch for a signal? By calling the Windows API function, WaitForSingleObject():

```
::WaitForSingleObject(threadStart.m_hObject, INFINITE);
```

This function's two arguments are

- The handle of the event for which to check (stored in the event object's m_hObject data member).
- The length of time the function should wait for the event.

The predefined INFINITE constant tells WaitForSingleObject() not to return until the specified event is signaled. In other words, if you place the preceding line at the beginning of your thread, the system suspends the thread until the event is signaled. Even though you've started the thread execution, it's halted until whatever you need to happen happens. When your program is ready for the thread to perform its duty, you call the SetEvent() function, as previously described.

When the thread is no longer suspended, it can go about its business. However, if you want to signal the end of the thread from the main program, the thread must watch for another event to be signaled. The thread can do this by polling for the event. To poll for the event, you again call WaitForSingleObject(), only this time you give the function a wait time of 0, like this:

```
::WaitForSingleObject(threadend.m_hObject, 0);
```

In this case, if WaitForSingleObject() returns WAIT_OBJECT_0, the event has been signaled. Otherwise, the event is still in its nonsignaled state.

To better see how event objects work, follow these steps to further modify the Thread application:

1. Add the following line to the top of the ThreadView.cpp file, right after the line #include "ThreadView.h":
   ```
   #include ""afxmt.h""
   ```

2. Add thefollowing lines near the top of the ThreadView.cpp file, after the volatile bool threadController line that you placed there previously:
   ```
   CEvent threadStart;
   CEvent threadEnd;
   ```

3. Delete the volatile bool threadController line from the file.

4. Replace the ThreadProc() function with the one shown in Listing 14.5.

LISTING 14.5   YET ANOTHER ThreadProc()

```
UINT ThreadProc(LPVOID param)
{
    ::WaitForSingleObject(threadStart.m_hObject, INFINITE);
    ::MessageBox((HWND)param, "Thread activated.",
        "Thread", MB_OK);

    bool keepRunning = true;
    while (keepRunning)
    {
```

LISTING 14.5 CONTINUED

```
        int result =
            ::WaitForSingleObject(threadEnd.m_hObject, 0);
        if (result == WAIT_OBJECT_0)
            keepRunning = false;
    }

    ::PostMessage((HWND)param, WM_THREADENDED, 0, 0);

    return 0;
}
```

---

5. Replace all the code in the OnThreadStartthread() function with the following line:
   ```
   threadStart.SetEvent();
   ```

6. Replace the code in the OnThreadStopthread() function with the following line:
   ```
   threadEnd.SetEvent();
   ```

7. Use the Properties window to add an OnCreate() function to CThreadView that handles the WM_CREATE message, as shown in Figure 14.8.

Figure 14.8
Use the Properties window to add the OnCreate() function.

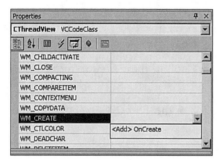

8. Add the following lines to the OnCreate() function, replacing the TODO comment:
   ```
   HWND hWnd = GetSafeHwnd();
   AfxBeginThread(ThreadProc, hWnd);
   ```

Again, this new version of the program seems to run just like the preceding version. However, the program is now using both event objects and user-defined Windows messages to communicate between the main program and the thread. No more messing with clunky global variables.

One big difference from previous versions of the program is that the secondary thread is begun in the OnCreate() function, which is called when the application first runs and creates the view. However, because the first line of the thread function is the call to WaitForSingleObject(), the thread immediately suspends execution and waits for the threadStart event to be signaled.

When the `threadStart` event object is signaled, the thread is free to display the message box and then enter its `while` loop, where it polls the `threadEnd` event object. The `while` loop continues to execute until `threadEnd` is signaled, at which time the thread sends the `WM_THREADENDED` message to the main program and exits. Because the thread is started in `OnCreate()`, after the thread ends, it can't be restarted.

USING THREAD SYNCHRONIZATION

Using multiple threads can lead to some interesting problems. For example, how do you prevent two threads from accessing the same data at the same time? What if, for example, one thread is in the middle of trying to update a data set when another thread tries to read that data? The second thread is almost certain to read corrupted data because only some of the data set will have been updated.

Trying to keep threads working together properly is called *thread synchronization*. Using event objects, about which you just learned, is a form of thread synchronization. This section examines critical sections, mutexes, and semaphores—thread synchronization objects that make your thread programming even safer.

USING CRITICAL SECTIONS

Using critical sections is an easy way to ensure that only one thread at a time can access a data set. When you use a critical section, you give your threads an object that they have to share. Whichever thread possesses the critical-section object has access to the guarded data. Other threads have to wait until the first thread releases the critical section, after which another thread can grab the critical section to access the data in turn.

Because the guarded data is represented by a single critical-section object, and because only one thread can own the critical section at any given time, the guarded data can never be accessed by more than a single thread at a time.

To create a critical-section object in a MFC program, you create an instance of the `CCriticalSection` class, like this:

```
CCriticalSection criticalSection;
```

Then, when program code is about to access the data that you want to protect, you call the critical-section object's `Lock()` member function, like this:

```
criticalSection.Lock();
```

If another thread doesn't already own the critical section, `Lock()` gives the object to the calling thread. That thread can then access the guarded data, after which it calls the critical-section object's `Unlock()` member function:

```
criticalSection.Unlock();
```

CH
14

Unlock() releases the ownership of the critical-section object so that another thread can grab it and access the guarded data.

The best way to implement something like critical sections is to build the data you want to protect into a thread-safe class. When you do this, you no longer have to worry about thread synchronization in the main program; the class handles it all for you. As an example, look at Listing 14.6, which is the header file for a thread-safe array class.

LISTING 14.6   COUNTARRAY.H—THE CCountArray CLASS HEADER FILE

```
#include "afxmt.h"

class CCountArray
{
private:
    int array[10];
    CCriticalSection criticalSection;

public:
    CCountArray() {};
    ~CCountArray() {};

    void SetArray(int value);
    void GetArray(int dstArray[10]);
};
```

The header file starts by including the MFC header file, afxmt.h, which gives the program access to the CCriticalSection class. Within the CCountArray class declaration, the file declares a 10-element integer array, which is the data that the critical section will guard, and declares the critical-section object, here called criticalSection. The CCountArray class's public member functions include the usual constructor and destructor, as well as functions for setting and reading the array. These latter two member functions must deal with the critical-section object because these functions access the array.

Listing 14.7 is the CCountArray class's implementation file. Notice that, in each member function, the class takes care of locking and unlocking the critical-section object. This means that any thread can call these member functions without worrying about thread syn-chronization. For example, if thread 1 calls SetArray(), the first thing SetArray() does is call criticalSection.Lock(), which gives the critical-section object to thread 1. The com-plete for loop then executes, without any fear of being interrupted by another thread. If thread 2 calls SetArray() or GetArray(), the call to criticalSection.Lock() suspends thread 2 until thread 1 releases the critical-section object, which it does when SetArray() finishes the for loop and executes the criticalSection.Unlock() line. Then the system wakes up thread 2 and gives it the critical-section object. In this way, all threads have to wait politely for their chance to access the guarded data.

LISTING 14.7 COUNTARRAY.CPP—The CCountArray **CLASS IMPLEMENTATION**
File#include "stdafx.h"

```
#include "CountArray.h"

void CCountArray::SetArray(int value)
{
    criticalSection.Lock();

    for (int x=0; x<10; ++x)
        array[x] = value;

    criticalSection.Unlock();
}

void CCountArray::GetArray(int dstArray[10])
{
    criticalSection.Lock();

    for (int x=0; x<10; ++x)
        dstArray[x] = array[x];

    criticalSection.Unlock();
}
```

Now that you've had a chance to see what a thread-safe class looks like, it's time to put the class to work. Perform the following steps, which modify the Thread application to test the CCountArray class:

1. Use the Project, Add Class command and add a new Generic C++ Class called CCountArray to the project, as shown in Figure 14.9. Enter the code from Listing 14.6 into the header file, CountArray.h, and enter the code from Listing 14.7 into the implementation file, CountArray.cpp.

Figure 14.9
Add the CCountArray class to the Thread project.

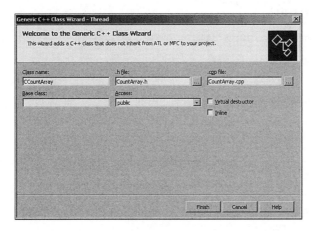

2. Switch to ThreadView.cpp and add the following line near the top of the file, after the line #include "afxmt.h", which you placed there previously:

```
#include "CountArray.h"
```

3. Add the following line near the top of the file, after the CEvent threadEnd line you placed there previously:

```
CCountArray countArray;
```

4. Delete the CEvent threadStart and CEvent threadEnd lines from the file.

5. Delete the lines ON_MESSAGE(WM_THREADENDED, OnThreadended), ON_COMMAND(ID_STOPTHREAD, OnThreadStopthread), and ON_WM_CREATE() from the message map.

6. Replace the ThreadProc() function with the thread functions shown in Listing 14.8.

LISTING 14.8   WriteThreadProc() **AND** ReadThreadProc()

```
UINT WriteThreadProc(LPVOID param)
{
    for(int x=0; x<10; ++x)
    {
        countArray.SetArray(x);
        ::Sleep(1000);
    }

    return 0;
}

UINT ReadThreadProc(LPVOID param)
{
    int array[10];

    for (int x=0; x<20; ++x)
    {
        countArray.GetArray(array);
        char str[50];
        str[0] = 0;
        for (int i=0; i<10; ++i)
        {
            int len = strlen(str);
            wsprintf(&str[len], "%d ", array[i]);
        }
        ::MessageBox((HWND)param, str, "Read Thread", MB_OK);
    }

    return 0;
}
```

8. Replace all the code in the OnThreadStartthread() function with the following lines:

```
HWND hWnd = GetSafeHwnd();
AfxBeginThread(WriteThreadProc, hWnd);
AfxBeginThread(ReadThreadProc, hWnd);
```

9. Delete the `OnThreadStopthread()`, `OnThreadended`, and `OnCreate()` functions from the file.

10. Switch to the ThreadView.h file and delete the line `const WM_THREADENDED = WM_USER + 100` from the listing.

11. Also, in ThreadView.h, delete the lines `afx_msg LRESULT OnThreadended(WPARAM wParam, LPARAM lParam)`, `afx_msg void OnThreadStopthread()`, and `afx_msg int OnCreate(LPCREATESTRUCT lpCreateStruct)` from the file.

12. Using the Resource Editor, remove the Stop Thread command from the Thread menu.

Now build and run the new version of the Thread application. When you do, the main window appears. Select the Thread, Start Thread command to get things hopping. The first thing you see is a message box (see Figure 14.10) displaying the current values in the guarded array. Each time you dismiss the message box, it reappears with the array's new contents. The message box reappears 20 times. The values listed in the message box depend on how often you dismiss the message box. The first thread writes new values into the array once a second, even as you're viewing the array's contents in the second thread.

Figure 14.10
This message box displays the current contents of the guarded array.

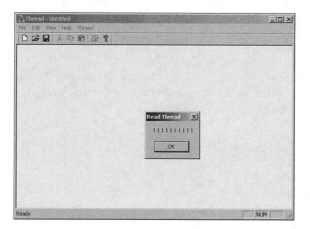

The important thing to notice is that at no time does the second thread interrupt when the first thread is changing the values in the array. You can tell that this is true because the array always contains 10 identical values. If the first thread were interrupted as it modified the array, the 10 values in the array would not be identical.

If you examine the source code carefully, you can see that the first thread, named `WriteThreadProc()`, calls the array class's `SetArray()` member function 10 times within a `for` loop. Each time through the loop, `SetArray()` gives the thread the critical-section object, changes the array contents to the passed number, and then takes the critical-section object away again. Note the call to the `Sleep()` function, which suspends the thread for the number of milliseconds given as the function's single argument.

The second thread, named ReadThreadProc(), also tries to access the same critical-section object to construct a display string of the values contained in the array. However, if WriteThreadProc() is currently trying to fill the array with new values, ReadThreadProc() has to wait. The inverse is also true. That is, WriteThreadProc() can't access the guarded data until it can regain ownership of the critical section from ReadThreadProc().

If you really want to prove that the critical-section object is working, remove the criticalSection.Unlock() line from the end of the CCountArray class's SetArray() member function. Then compile and run the program. This time when you start the threads, no message box appears. Why? Because WriteThreadProc() takes the critical-section object and never lets it go, which forces the system to suspend ReadThreadProc() forever (or at least until you exit the program).

USING MUTEXES

Mutexes are a lot like critical sections but a little more complicated because they enable safe sharing of resources, not only between threads in the same application, but also between threads of different applications or processes. Although synchronizing threads of different applications is beyond the scope of this book, you can get a little experience with mutexes by using them in place of critical sections.

Listing 14.9 is the CCountArray2 class's header file. Except for the new classname and the mutex object, this header file is identical to the original CountArray.h. Listing 14.10 is the modified class's implementation file. As you can see, the member functions look a lot different when they use mutexes rather than critical sections, even though both objects provide essentially the same type of services.

LISTING 14.9   CCOUNTARRAY2.H—THE CCountArray2 CLASS HEADER FILE

```
#include "afxmt.h"

class CCountArray2
{
private:
    int array[10];
    CMutex mutex;

public:
    CCountArray2() {};
    ~CCountArray2() {};

    void SetArray(int value);
    void GetArray(int dstArray[10]);
};
```

LISTING 14.10   COUNTARRAY2.CPP—THE CCountArray2 CLASS

```
Implementation File
#include "stdafx.h"
#include "CountArray2.h"
```

LISTING 14.10   CONTINUED

```
void CCountArray2::SetArray(int value)
{
    CSingleLock singleLock(&mutex);
    singleLock.Lock();

    for (int x=0; x<10; ++x)
        array[x] = value;
}

void CCountArray2::GetArray(int dstArray[10])
{
    CSingleLock singleLock(&mutex);
    singleLock.Lock();

    for (int x=0; x<10; ++x)
        dstArray[x] = array[x];
}
```

To access a mutex object, you must create a CSingleLock or CMultiLock object, which performs the actual access control. The CCountArray2 class uses CSingleLock objects because this class deals with only a single mutex. When the code is about to manipulate guarded resources (in this case, the array), you create a CSingleLock object, like this:

```
CSingleLock singleLock(&mutex);
```

The constructor's argument is a pointer to the thread-synchronization object that you want to control. Then, to gain access to the mutex, you call the CSingleLock object's Lock() member function:

```
singleLock.Lock();
```

If the mutex is unowned, the calling thread becomes the owner. If another thread already owns the mutex, the system suspends the calling thread until the mutex is released, at which time the waiting thread is awakened and takes control of the mutex.

To release the mutex, you call the CSingleLock object's Unlock() member function. However, if you create your CSingleLock object on the stack (rather than on the heap, using the new operator) as shown in Listing 14.10, you don't have to call Unlock() at all. When the function exits, the object goes out of scope, which causes its destructor to execute. The destructor automatically unlocks the object for you.

To try out the new CCountArray2 class in the Thread application, add new CountArray2.h and CountArray2.cpp files to the Thread project and then delete the original CountArray.h and CountArray.cpp files. Finally, in ThreadView.cpp, change all references to CCountArray to CCountArray2. Because all the thread synchronization is handled in the CCountArray2 class, no further changes are necessary to use mutexes instead of critical sections.

CH
14

USING SEMAPHORES

Although semaphores are used like critical sections and mutexes in an MFC program, they serve a slightly different function. Rather than enable only one thread to access a resource at a time, semaphores enable multiple threads to access a resource, but only to a point. That is, semaphores enable a maximum number of threads to access a resource simultaneously.

When you create the semaphore, you tell it how many threads should be allowed simultaneous access to the resource. Then, each time a thread grabs the resource, the semaphore decrements its internal counter. When the counter reaches 0, no further threads are allowed access to the guarded resource until another thread releases the resource, which increments the semaphore's counter.

You create a semaphore by supplying the initial count and the maximum count, like this:

```
CSemaphore Semaphore(2, 2);
```

In this section, you use a semaphore to create a thread-safe class. This is a class that looks after its own synchronization. It has a CSemaphore pointer as a member variable, and the CSemaphore object is created dynamically in the class's constructor, like this:

```
semaphore = new CSemaphore(2, 2);
```

After you have created the semaphore object, it's ready to start counting resource access. To implement the counting process, you first create a CSingleLock object (or CMultiLock, if you're dealing with multiple thread-synchronization objects), giving it a pointer to the semaphore you want to use, like this:

```
CSingleLock singleLock(semaphore);
```

Then, to decrement the semaphore's count, you call the CSingleLock object's Lock() member function:

```
singleLock.Lock();
```

At this point, the semaphore object has decremented its internal counter. This new count remains in effect until the semaphore object is released, which you can do explicitly by calling the object's Unlock() member function:

```
singleLock.Unlock();
```

Alternatively, if you've created the CSingleLock object locally on the stack, you can just let the object go out of scope, which not only automatically deletes the object but also releases the hold on the semaphore. In other words, both calling Unlock() and deleting the CSingleLock object increment the semaphore's counter, enabling a waiting thread to access the guarded resource.

Listing 14.11 is the header file for a class called CSomeResource. CSomeResource is a mostly useless class whose only purpose is to demonstrate the use of semaphores. The class has a single data member, which is a pointer to a CSemaphore object. The class also has a constructor and destructor, as well as a member function called UseResource(), which is where the semaphore will be used.

LISTING 14.11   SOMERESOURCE.H

```cpp
#include "afxmt.h"

class CSomeResource
{
private:
    CSemaphore* semaphore;

public:
    CSomeResource();
    ~CSomeResource();

    void UseResource();
};
```

Listing 14.12 shows the CSomeResource class's implementation file. You can see that the CSemaphore object is constructed dynamically in the class's constructor and deleted in the destructor. The UseResource() member function simulates accessing a resource: first it attains a count on the semaphore, and then it sleeps for five seconds, after which the hold on the semaphore is released when the function exits and the CSingleLock object goes out of scope.

LISTING 14.12   SOMERESOURCE.CPP

```cpp
#include "stdafx.h"
#include "SomeResource.h"

CSomeResource::CSomeResource()
{
    semaphore = new CSemaphore(2, 2);
}

CSomeResource::~CSomeResource()
{
    delete semaphore;
}

void CSomeResource::UseResource()
{
    CSingleLock singleLock(semaphore);
    singleLock.Lock();

    Sleep(5000);
}
```

If you modify the Thread application to use the CSomeResource object, you can watch semaphores at work. Follow these steps:

1. Delete any CountArray files that are still in the project. (In the Solution Explorer, click the file once to select it; then press Del to delete the file from the project.)

2. Create a new Generic C++ Class, as before, called CSomeResource. Leave the default file names of SomeResource.h and SomeResource.cpp.

3. Add the code from Listings 14.11 and 14.12 to these empty files.

4. Load ThreadView.cpp and replace the line #include "CountArray2.h" with the following:

```
#include "SomeResource.h"
```

5. Replace the line CCountArray2 countArray with the following:

```
CSomeResource someResource;
```

6. Replace the WriteThreadProc() and ReadThreadProc() functions with the functions shown in Listing 14.13.

LISTING 14.13   ThreadProc1(), ThreadProc2(), AND ThreadProc3()

```
UINT ThreadProc1(LPVOID param)
{
    someResource.UseResource();

    ::MessageBox((HWND)param,
        "Thread 1 had access.", "Thread 1", MB_OK);

    return 0;
}

UINT ThreadProc2(LPVOID param)
{
    someResource.UseResource();

    ::MessageBox((HWND)param,
        "Thread 2 had access.", "Thread 2", MB_OK);

    return 0;
}

UINT ThreadProc3(LPVOID param)
{
    someResource.UseResource();

    ::MessageBox((HWND)param,
        "Thread 3 had access.", "Thread 3", MB_OK);

    return 0;
}
```

7. Replace the code in the OnThreadStartthread() function with that shown in Listing 14.14.

LISTING 14.14 **NEW CODE FOR THE** `OnThreadStartthread()` **FUNCTION**

```
HWND hWnd = GetSafeHwnd();
AfxBeginThread(ThreadProc1, hWnd);
AfxBeginThread(ThreadProc2, hWnd);
AfxBeginThread(ThreadProc3, hWnd);
```

Now compile and run the new version of the Thread application. When the main window appears, select the Thread, Start Thread command. In about five seconds, two message boxes appear, informing you that thread 1 and thread 2 had access to the guarded resource. About five seconds after that, a third message box appears, telling you that thread 3 also had access to the resource. Thread 3 took five seconds longer because thread 1 and thread 2 grabbed control of the resource first. The semaphore is set to allow only two simultaneous resource accesses, so thread 3 had to wait for thread 1 or thread 2 to release its hold on the semaphore.

Note

Although the sample programs in this chapter have demonstrated using a single thread-synchronization object, you can have as many synchronization objects as you need in a single program. You can even use critical sections, mutexes, and semaphores all at once to protect different data sets and resources in different ways.

FROM HERE

For complex applications, threads offer the capability to maintain fast and efficient data processing. You no longer have to wait for one part of the program to finish its task before moving on to something else. For example, a spreadsheet application can use one thread to update the calculations while the main thread continues accepting entries from the user. Using threads, however, leads to some interesting problems, not the least of which is the need to control access to shared resources. Writing a threaded application requires thought and careful consideration of how the threads will be used and what resources they'll access.

If you're reading through the book in order, you've almost come to the end of the Windows programming chapters. Chapter 15, "Special Win32 Application Types," covers DLLs and console applications. Creating these types of applications is a task usually reserved for experienced Windows programmers, but not because they are hard to create. It's just that not all Windows programmers have discovered alternative application types. Explore a little.

CH

14

SPECIAL WIN32 APPLICATION TYPES

In this chapter

ADVANCED WIN32 PROGRAMMING TOPICS

A number of Win32 programming topics have not been covered elsewhere in this book, but are well known to experienced Visual C++ programmers. They are best explored after you have experience with Visual Studio, MFC, and C++ programming. This chapter covers just enough of them to show you how interesting these topics are, and to encourage you to explore them yourself in the months and years to come. In this chapter you will learn about:

- Console Applications
- Creating a Dynamic-Link Library
- Using a Dynamic-Link Library
- Sending Windows Messages and Commands
- Internationalization Issues
- Creating a Windows Service

CREATING CONSOLE APPLICATIONS

A console application looks very much like a DOS application, though it runs in a resizable window. It has a strictly character-based interface with cursor keys rather than mouse movement. You use the Console API and character-based I/O functions such as `printf()` and `scanf()`, or the C++ equivalents, `cout` and `cin`, to interact with the user.

Tip	Many Windows programmers had forgotten all about console applications until .NET came along. You'll see plenty of console applications written to the .NET framework in the second half of this book. This chapter uses the Win32 approach to console applications.

CREATING A CONSOLE EXECUTABLE

A console application is executed from the DOS command line or by choosing Start, Run and typing the full name (including the path) of the application. Console applications are among the easiest programs to create.

Let's walk through the few steps necessary to create a basic console application, and then explore some beneficial uses of creating these applications. The first console application you'll create in this chapter is a spin on the classic "Hello, World!" that Kernighan and Ritchie (the creators of C++'s ancestor C) created in the 1970s.

Open Visual Studio and follow these steps to create a console application:

1. Choose File, New, Project.
2. In the New Project box, choose Visual C++ Projects on the left and Win32 Project on the right. (If this isn't familiar, go back to Chapter 2, "Building Your First Windows Application.")
3. Name the project **HelloWorld** and set an appropriate folder for the project.
4. Click OK.
5. The Win32 Application Wizard appears. On the Application Settings tab of this wizard, you can customize your application. Choose Console Application as the Application Type.
6. Click Finish.

The project is created immediately with a very simple source file, holding the skeleton of a function for you to fill in.

If you have a textbook kicking around from some introductory C++ course you may have taken, you can find a Hello World sample there, or anywhere on the Web. Edit the file so that it looks like this:

```
// HelloWorld.cpp : Defines the entry point for the console application.
//

#include "stdafx.h"
#include <iostream.h>

int _tmain(int argc, _TCHAR* argv[])
{
    cout << "Hello from the console!" << endl;
    return 0;
}
```

> **Tip**
>
> When you write a function called `_tmain()`, the compiler actually creates either `main()` or `wmain()`, depending on your Unicode settings. When a console application runs, Windows calls one of these two functions: `wmain` (for wide main) for a Unicode application, and `main` for non-Unicode applications. Unicode is discussed later in this chapter, in the "International Software Development Issues" section.

Choose Debug, Start Without Debugging to compile, link, and execute the program. (A dialog asks you to confirm that you want to build the project before executing.) You should see a DOS box appear that resembles Figure 15.1. The line Press Any Key to Continue is generated by the system and gives you a chance to read your output before the DOS box disappears.

Tip

> If you just choose Debug, Start, then execution will not pause for you as just described.

Figure 15.1
Your application appears to be a DOS program.

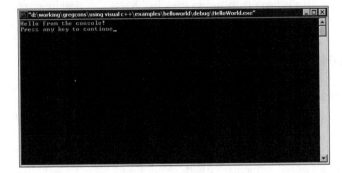

If you're sharp-eyed, you'll notice a warning message in your compiler output as you build this little application. It reads:

```
d:\Program Files\Microsoft Visual Studio. NET\Vc7\include\useoldio.h(21) : warning
C4995: '_OLD_IOSTREAMS_ARE_DEPRECATED': name was marked as #pragma deprecated
```

Warnings are relatively harmless. As you can see, the project still builds and runs. But the day may come, many releases of Visual Studio from now, when it will not. That's what "deprecated" means—it refers to a feature that is still OK today, but that programmers should get out of the habit of using.

The feature in question is the old iostream library provided in iostream.h and described in many introductory C++ textbooks. This library is moving into a namespace and the name of the include file is changing to one without a .h extension.

To eliminate the warning, change this line:

```
#include <iostream.h>
```

to this:

```
#include <iostream>
```

This brings in a slightly different library, one that sets up cout and the rest of the iostream members in a namespace. To save typing the full name, such as std::cout, whenever you use these members, add these lines:

```
using std::cout;
using std::endl;
```

Try building the project again. You should have no warnings now. What's more, the new code will still work even in future releases of Visual C++. Even though using <iostream.h> works, you should use <iostream> instead so that you won't run into trouble a few releases from now.

WRITING AN OBJECT-ORIENTED CONSOLE APPLICATION

The HelloWorld application is clearly C++ and would not compile in a C compiler, which doesn't support stream-based I/O with cout, but it's not object oriented—there's not an object in it. Replace the code in HelloWorld.cpp with the lines in Listing 15.1.

LISTING 15.1   HELLOWORLD.CPP—WITH OBJECTS

```
// HelloWorld.cpp
//

#include <stdafx.h>
#include <iostream>
#include <afx.h>

using std::cout;
using std::endl;

class Hello
{
private:
    CString message;

public:
    Hello();
    void display();
};

Hello::Hello()
{
    message = "Hello from the console!";
}

void Hello::display()
{
    cout << (const char*)message << endl;
}

int _tmain(int argc, _TCHAR* argv[])
{
    Hello hello;
    hello.display();

    return 0;

}
```

Now this is an object-oriented program, and what's more, it uses CString, an MFC class. To do so, it must include <afx.h>. If you build the project now, you will get linker error messages that refer to _beginthreadex and _endthreadex. By default, console applications are single-threaded, but MFC is multithreaded. By including afx.h and bringing in MFC, this application is making itself incompatible with the single-threaded default. When you created this project, there was an option on the Application Wizard to support MFC. You should select that option when you are creating new console applications that will use MFC.

To make existing console applications compatible with MFC, you have to change the project settings. Select the project name—HelloWorld in this case—in the Solution Explorer and then choose View, Property Pages. Expand the Configuration Properties and C/C++ tabs and select the Code Generation item under the C/C++ tab. In the drop-down box next to the label Runtime Library, choose Multi-Threaded Debug (/MTd). (The completed dialog box is shown in Figure 15.2.) Click OK and rebuild the project.

Figure 15.2
Make your console application multi-threaded so that it can use MFC.

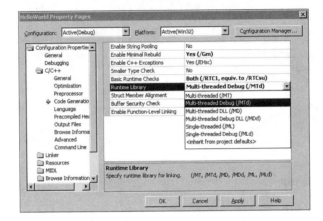

The output of this object-oriented program is just like that of the preceding program—it's just a sample. But you see that console applications can use MFC, be built around objects, and be quite small. They must have a function called _tmain(), and it is this function that is called by the operating system when you run the application.

SCAFFOLDING TO TEST ALGORITHMS

One important reason to build a console application these days is to *scaffold* small code fragments or single objects. A scaffold is a temporary framework around the code you want to test. (Some developers call this a *test harness*.) The simplest possible framework is a console application like the one you just built. In fact, you'll build a scaffold later in this chapter.

To scaffold an object or function, you should do the following:

1. Create a new console application just for the scaffolding process.
2. Add a function called _tmain() to the .CPP file you plan to scaffold.
3. Include the header file for the object or function to be tested.
4. Add code to _tmain() that exercises the function or object in a variety of test cases.

For example, the object-oriented console application you just saw exercised the display() method of the Hello class. If that class had other methods, they could also have been tested within the same _tmain() function.

Having followed those steps, you can now test the code thoroughly, focusing on only the performance characteristics and correctness of this small piece of your large project. Scaffolding holds true to the canon of software development that states, "Design in the large and program in the small."

By applying a scaffold to any algorithm, you are helping to ensure the accuracy in the small. Remember that additional benefits are involved, too: By placing the scaffold code directly into the module, you are clearly documenting that the code has been tested and how to use it. You make it available for further testing, debugging, or extending at a later date.

CREATING AND USING A 32-BIT DYNAMIC LINK LIBRARY

Dynamic link libraries (DLLs) are the backbone of the Windows operating systems. Windows uses Kernel32.dll, User32.dll, and Gdi32.dll to perform the vast majority of its work, and you can use them as well. The Visual C++ online help is a good source of information for these three DLLs.

A good tool for poking around in Windows applications is the DumpBin utility, usually found in \Program Files\Microsoft Visual Studio. NET\VC7\Bin. DumpBin is a command line program that shows you the imports and exports of executable files and dynamic link libraries. Listing 15.2 is an excerpted example of the output produced when using DumpBin to examine the executable file for Spy++, one of the utilities provided with Visual C++.

LISTING 15.2   OUTPUT FROM DUMPBIN

```
dumpbin -imports spyxx.exe
Microsoft (R) COFF/PE Dumper Version 7.00.9219
Copyright  Microsoft Corporation.  All rights reserved.


Dump of file spyxx.exe

File Type: EXECUTABLE IMAGE

  Section contains the following imports:

    SPYXXHK.DLL
                4018C0 Import Address Table
                44B458 Import Name Table
                     0 time date stamp
                     0 Index of first forwarder reference

                    A gfHookEnabled
                   27 gmsgOtherProcessData
                   2A gopd
                   2B gpidSpyxx
                    8 gcSubclass
                   10 ghhkRetHook
                    3 _SpyxxCallWndRetProc@12
                    E ghhkCallHook
                    2 _SpyxxCallWndProc@12
```

LISTING 15.2   CONTINUED

```
                           F ghhkMsgHook
                           4 _SpyxxGetMsgProc@12
                           6 gabMsgBuf
                           5 gaaClasses
                          2C gtidSpyxx
                           7 gcMsgPackets
                          29 goffWrite
                          28 goffRead
                           C gfOnWindows5x
                           B gfOnWindows4x
                           D gfOnWindows9x
                           9 gfEnableSubclass

        KERNEL32.dll
                      401080 Import Address Table
                      44AC18 Import Name Table
                           0 time date stamp
                           0 Index of first forwarder reference

                         22B LockResource
                         21D LoadResource
                          C4 FindResourceA
                         1C9 GlobalFree
                         1D4 GlobalUnlock
                         1CD GlobalLock
                         1C2 GlobalAlloc
                          21 CloseHandle
                          3D CreateFileA
                         346 WaitForSingleObject
                         2D1 SetEvent
                         23A MulDiv
                         148 GetLastError
                         2D6 SetFilePointer
                         284 ReleaseMutex
                         309 SizeofResource
                         28E ResetEvent
                         155 GetModuleHandleA
                          3A CreateEventA
                          49 CreateMutexA
                         357 WriteFile
                         1DA HeapAlloc
                         176 GetProcessHeap
                         1E0 HeapFree
                         1E4 HeapReAlloc
                         1E6 HeapSize
                         2E1 SetLastError
                          D5 FreeLibrary
                         379 lstrcpyA
                         174 GetProcAddress
                         218 LoadLibraryA
                         200 IsDBCSLeadByte
                         1CA GlobalGetAtomNameA
                         21E LocalAlloc
                         1B3 GetVersionExA
                         26A RaiseException
```

LISTING 15.2   CONTINUED

```
37F lstrlenA
1B2 GetVersion
34A WideCharToMultiByte
23B MultiByteToWideChar
1F2 InterlockedExchange
265 QueryPerformanceCounter
1A9 GetTickCount
122 GetCurrentThreadId
120 GetCurrentProcessId
30A Sleep
187 GetStartupInfoA
197 GetSystemTimeAsFileTime
 9B ExitProcess
```

```
USER32.dll
        401918 Import Address Table
        44B4B0 Import Name Table
             0 time date stamp
             0 Index of first forwarder reference

        10A GetDesktopWindow
        23C SetActiveWindow
         DA EnumWindows
         C7 EnumChildWindows
        1A2 IsIconic
        1AB IsZoomed
        1EB OffsetRect
        16F GetWindowPlacement
         F6 GetClassLongA
        178 GetWindowWord
        1A9 IsWindowUnicode
        186 InflateRect
        266 SetRectEmpty
        1B6 LoadIconA
        156 GetSysColor
        112 GetFocus
          7 AppendMenuA
         5D CreatePopupMenu
         B0 DrawFocusRect
         E5 FrameRect
        20F RegisterClassA
         5F CreateWindowExA
         FA GetClassWord
         98 DestroyWindow
        213 RegisterClipboardFormatA
        1D7 MessageBoxA
        283 SetWindowsHookExA
        2A7 UnhookWindowsHookEx
         F2 GetClassInfoA
        1F8 PostMessageA
         8D DefWindowProcA
         FE GetClipboardFormatNameA
        168 GetWindowDC
        108 GetDC
        223 ReleaseDC
```

Listing 15.2   Continued

```
        279 SetWindowLongA
        1B2 LoadCursorA
         FB GetClientRect
        222 ReleaseCapture
        2CE WindowFromPoint
        246 SetCursor
        23D SetCapture
         EF GetCapture
        2B4 UpdateWindow
         3F ClientToScreen
        166 GetWindow
        171 GetWindowRgn
        204 PtInRect
        141 GetParent
        18F InvalidateRect
        234 SendMessageA
        1A6 IsWindow
        237 SendMessageTimeoutA
        173 GetWindowTextA
         F8 GetClassNameA
        16A GetWindowLongA
        170 GetWindowRect
        177 GetWindowThreadProcessId
        2D1 wsprintfA
        11D GetKeyState
         DE FillRect
        1AA IsWindowVisible
        1B0 LoadBitmapA
        159 GetSystemMetrics
        27B SetWindowPlacement
          E BringWindowToTop
        250 SetForegroundWindow
        28B ShowWindow
        1A4 IsRectEmpty
        265 SetRect
         90 DeleteMenu
        158 GetSystemMenu
        273 SetTimer
        1AD KillTimer
        124 GetLastActivePopup
          2 AdjustWindowRectEx
        1F6 PeekMessageA
         9F DispatchMessageA
        2A3 TranslateMessage
         DB EqualRect
        1D2 MapWindowPoints
          1 AdjustWindowRect
        1D6 MessageBeep
        2AB UnpackDDElParam
        19A IsChild

   GDI32.dll

        401020 Import Address Table
        44ABB8 Import Name Table
```

LISTING 15.2   CONTINUED

```
                      0 time date stamp
                      0 Index of first forwarder reference

              194 GetObjectA
               12 BitBlt
               8F DeleteObject
               50 CreateSolidBrush
              1ED PtInRegion
               46 CreatePatternBrush
              1DA PatBlt
               47 CreatePen
              1A4 GetStockObject
              232 SetROP2
              1F3 Rectangle
               40 CreateHatchBrush
               ED FrameRgn
               4B CreateRectRgn
               3A CreateFontIndirectA
               DD ExtTextOutA
               27 CreateBitmap
              19B GetPixel
              16A GetDeviceCaps
              20B SelectObject
              1BB GetTextMetricsA
              1B3 GetTextExtentPoint32A
               2D CreateCompatibleDC

    ADVAPI32.dll
              401000 Import Address Table
              44AB98 Import Name Table
                   0 time date stamp
                   0 Index of first forwarder reference

              1CE RegCreateKeyA
              1E4 RegOpenKeyExA
              1CB RegCloseKey
              1E9 RegQueryInfoKeyA
              1EE RegQueryValueExA
              1FB RegSetValueExA
              1E3 RegOpenKeyA

    MFC70.DLL
              401148 Import Address Table
              44ACE0 Import Name Table
                   0 time date stamp
                   0 Index of first forwarder reference

                Ordinal   848
                Ordinal  5811
... 408 similar lines omitted ...
    MSVCR70.dll
              40180C Import Address Table
              44B3A4 Import Name Table
                   0 time date stamp
                   0 Index of first forwarder reference
```

LISTING 15.2 CONTINUED

```
            CC _c_exit
            FD _exit
            4F _XcptFilter
            CF _cexit
           298 exit
            AF _acmdln
            C4 _amsg_exit
            70 __getmainargs
           141 _initterm
            A1 __setusermatherr
           31F time
            84 __p__commode
            89 __p__fmode
            9E __set_app_type
            9D __security_error_handler
            10 ??1type_info@@UAE@XZ
            6D __dllonexit
           1BA _onexit
            34 ?terminate@@YAXXZ
            DD _controlfp
            F4 _except_handler3
           2C1 iscntrl
           323 toupper
           12F _getmbcp
           33A wcsrchr
           23B _wcsupr
           1AF _mbsstr
           304 sscanf
           192 _mbsicmp
           18B _mbschr
            CA _beginthread
            EE _endthread
           301 sprintf
           1C7 _purecall
           318 strtoul
           166 _itoa
           1F6 _splitpath
           18C _mbscmp
           2E7 memmove
            53 __CxxFrameHandler
           2AD free
           2E0 malloc
            BD _adjust_fdiv
           1E5 _setmbcp

MSVCI70.dll
           4017B4 Import Address Table
           44B34C Import Name Table
                0 time date stamp
                0 Index of first forwarder reference

              192 ?str@ostrstream@@QAEPADXZ
              163 ?rdbuf@ostrstream@@QBEPAVstrstreambuf@@XZ
              11F ?freeze@strstreambuf@@QAEXH@Z
              171 ?seekp@ostream@@QAEAAV1@J@Z
```

LISTING 15.2   CONTINUED

```
       8B  ??6ostream@@QAEAAV0@K@Z
       87  ??6ostream@@QAEAAV0@G@Z
      11B  ?flags@ios@@QBEJXZ
      1AC  ?width@ios@@QAEHH@Z
       85  ??6ostream@@QAEAAV0@E@Z
      11A  ?flags@ios@@QAEJJ@Z
       14  ??0ios@@IAE@XZ
       31  ??0ostrstream@@QAE@XZ
      118  ?fill@ios@@QAEDD@Z
      17B  ?setf@ios@@QAEJJ@Z
       47  ??1ios@@UAE@XZ
       50  ??1ostrstream@@UAE@XZ
       93  ??6ostream@@QAEAAV0@PBD@Z
       84  ??6ostream@@QAEAAV0@D@Z
       8A  ??6ostream@@QAEAAV0@J@Z
       89  ??6ostream@@QAEAAV0@I@Z
       88  ??6ostream@@QAEAAV0@H@Z

  Section contains the following delay load imports:

    vsansi.dll
             00000001 Characteristics
             0045F088 Address of HMODULE
             0045BE0C Import Address Table
             0044AA90 Import Name Table
             0044AAD4 Bound Import Name Table
             00000000 Unload Import Name Table
                    0 time date stamp

        004474D7                0 EnableWindow
        004474E1                0 SetDlgItemTextW
        004474EB                0 GetClassLongW

  Summary

        13000 .data
        10000 .rsrc
        4C000 .text
```

As you can see, the utility program Spy++ uses the C Runtime and Windows DLLs extensively.

You can call functions from the Windows DLLs in any of your programs, and more importantly, you can write DLLs of your own.

MAKING A 32-BIT DLL

There are several kinds of DLLs in Visual C++: some use MFC and some don't. Each kind of DLL has its own Application Wizard, as you will see shortly.

If you gather three or four functions into a DLL, your DLL exports those functions for other programs to use. Quite often a DLL also imports functions from other DLLs to get its work done.

IMPORTING AND EXPORTING FUNCTIONS

To designate a symbol as exportable, use the following syntax:

```
__declspec(dllexport) data_type var_name; // for variables
```

or

```
__declspec(dllexport) return_type func_name( [argument_list ] );
// for functions
```

Importing functions is almost identical: simply replace the keyword tokens, __declspec(dll-export) with __declspec(dllimport). The following example uses an actual function and variable to demonstrate the syntax this time:

```
__declspec(dllimport) int referenceCount;
__declspec(dllimport) void DiskFree( lpStr Drivepath );
```

> **Tip**
>
> Two underscores precede the keyword __declspec.

By convention, Microsoft uses a header file and a preprocessor macro to make the inclusion of DLL declarations much simpler. The technique requires that you make a preprocessor token using a unique token—the header filename works easily and requires very little in the way of memorization—and define a macro that replaces the token with the correct import or export statement. Thus, assuming a header file named Diskfree.h, the preprocessor macro in the header file would be as shown in Listing 15.3.

LISTING 15.3   DISKFREE.H

```
#ifndef __DISKFREE_H
#define __DISKFREE_H
#ifndef __DISKFREE__
#define __DISKFREELIB__ __declspec(dllimport)
#else
#define __DISKFREELIB__ __declspec(dllexport)
#endif
// Returns the amount of free space on drive number (e.g. 0 = A:, 1= B:,
// 2 = c:)
__DISKFREELIB__ unsigned long DiskFree( unsigned int drive );
#endif
```

By including the header file, you can let the preprocessor decide whether DiskFree is being imported or exported. Now you can share the header file for the DLL developer and the DLL user, and that means fewer maintenance headaches.

CREATING THE DISKFREE DLL

The DiskFree utility provides a simple way to determine the amount of free disk space for any given drive. The underlying functionality is the GetDiskFreeSpace() function found in Kernel32.dll.

To create a non-MFC DLL, choose File, New, Project, choose Visual C++ projects on the left and Win32 Project on the right, and enter **DiskFree** for the project name. Click OK and the Win32 Application Wizard dialog box appears. On the Application Settings tab, choose DLL as the Application Type and select the Empty project check box, as shown in Figure 15.3. Click Finish and your project will be created with no files in it.

Figure 15.3
Creating a non-MFC DLL project is a one-step process.

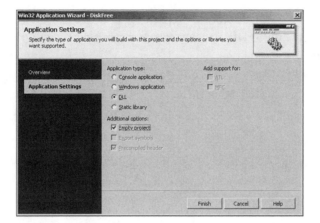

Add a C++ header file called DiskFree.h to the project and type in the code from Listing 15.3. Add a C++ source file called DiskFree.cpp and type in the code from Listing 15.4.

LISTING 15.4   DISKFREE.CPP

```cpp
#include <afx.h>          // needed for winbase to compile OK
#include <winbase.h>      // Declares kernel32 GetDiskFreeSpace
#define __DISKFREE__      // Define the token before including the library
#include "diskfree.h"
// Returns the amount of free space on drive number
// (e.g. 0 = A:, 1= B:, 2 = c:)
__DISKFREELIB__ unsigned long DiskFree( unsigned int drive )
{
    unsigned long bytesPerSector, sectorsPerCluster,
        freeClusters, totalClusters;
    char DrivePath[4] = { char( drive + 65 ), ':', '\\', '\0' };
    if( GetDiskFreeSpace( DrivePath, &sectorsPerCluster,
        &bytesPerSector, &freeClusters, &totalClusters ))
    {
        return sectorsPerCluster * bytesPerSector * freeClusters;
    }
    else
    {
        return 0;
    }
}
```

Now you can build the DLL. The next section shows you how to use 32-bit DLLs in general and how Windows finds DLLs on your system.

The most common use of a DLL is to provide extended, reusable functionality and to enable Windows to implicitly load the DLL. Topics that aren't discussed in this book, which you might want to explore for yourself, include the following:

- Dynamic versus static linking of MFC
- Implicit versus explicit DLL loading, which requires the use of LoadLibrary and FreeLibrary
- Multithreading DLLs
- Sharing data across DLL boundaries
- Calling conventions for DLLs that will be used by other languages (_stdcall, WINAPI, and so on)

In this chapter you are going to use a default compile of DiskFree, using an implicit DllMain (the compiler added one) and an implicit loading of the DLL, enabling Windows to manage loading and unloading the library.

USING 32-BIT DLLS

When your application loads a DLL, Windows searches for it, just as it does when you run an executable. First, the directory of the application loading the DLL is searched, then the current directory, the Windows\System directory for Windows 95 or 98, Winnt\System or Winnt\System32 for Windows NT or 2000, the Windows directory, and finally each directory specified in the path.

If you plan to have a DLL that many applications share, it's a good idea to put it in the System directory (Winnt\System or Windows\System) where it will be found easily. When one application installs an updated version of the DLL, all applications that use it will start to use the new one. If you prefer, you can copy the DLL to the same directory as the executable that uses it. You may end up with several copies of the DLL on your hard drive as a result. Some developers prefer to know that the DLL they are using will never be changed by anyone else, and consider a little wasted drive space a small price to pay for this reassurance.

USING A DLL

Implicitly loading and using a DLL is about as simple as using any other function. This is especially true if you created the header file as described in the "Creating the DiskFree DLL" section. When you compile your DLL, Microsoft Visual C++ creates a .LIB file. (So, DISKFREE.DLL has a DISKFREE.LIB created by the compiler.) The library (.LIB) file is used to resolve the load address of the DLL and specify the full pathname of the dynamic link library, and the header file provides the declaration.

All you have to do is include the header in the file that uses the DLL functionality and add the .LIB name to the project's Property Pages box, on the Input page of the Linker tab (see Figure 15.4), in the Additional Dependencies edit field.

Figure 15.4
Add your .LIB file to the project settings.

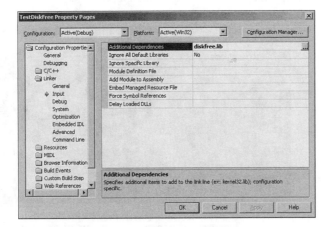

To test the DiskFree DLL, create a console application called TestDiskFree. Edit TestDiskFree.cppso so that it matches Listing 15.5.

LISTING 15.5   TESTDISKFREE.CPP

```cpp
// TestDiskFree.cpp : Defines the entry point for the console application.
//

#include "stdafx.h"
#include <iostream>
#include "diskfree.h"
#define CodeTrace(arg) \
     cout << #arg << endl;\
     arg

using std::cout;
using std::endl;

int _tmain(int argc, _TCHAR* argv[])
{
     CodeTrace( cout << DiskFree(2) << endl );
     return 0;
}
```

This code brings in the DLL by including DiskFree.h and then uses it. The CodeTrace macro simply prints out a line of code before executing it. All this application does is call the DiskFree() function to ask how much space is free on drive 2. Drive 0 is A:, drive 1 is B:, and drive 2 is C:.

Copy DiskFree.h to the TestDiskFree project folder. Copy DiskFree.dll and DiskFree.Lib to the TestDiskFree folder also. (You'll find them in DiskFree\Debug.) Change the project settings as just described to include the DiskFree.Lib file, and build the project. Build and execute the program, and you should see output like Figure 15.5.

Figure 15.5
Your little application calls the DLL.

According to TestDiskFree, the C: drive on the machine used for these samples has more than 3GB of free disk space. This number is correct.

Now you know how to write real functions in a DLL and use them yourself or make them available for others.

SENDING MESSAGES AND COMMANDS

As discussed in Chapter 3, "Interacting with Your Application," messages are the heart of Windows. Everything that happens in a Windows application happens because a message showed up to make it happen. When you move your mouse and click a button, a huge number of messages are generated, including WM_MOUSEMOVE for each movement of the mouse, WM_LBUTTONDOWN when the button goes down, WM_LBUTTONCLICK when the button is released, and higher-level, more abstract messages such as the WM_COMMAND message with the button's resource ID as one of its parameters. You can ignore the lower-level messages if you want; many programmers do.

What you may not know is that you can generate messages, too. Two functions generate messages: CWnd::SendMessage() and CWnd::PostMessage(). Each of these gets a message to an object that inherits from CWnd. An object that wants to send a message to a window using one of these functions must have a pointer to the window, and the window must be prepared to catch the message. A very common approach to this situation is to have a member variable in the sending object that stores a pointer to the window that will receive the message and another that stores the message to be sent:

```
CWnd* m_messagewindow;
UINT m_message;
```

Messages are represented by unsigned integers. They appear to have names only because names like WM_MOUSEMOVE are connected to integers with #define statements.

The sending class has a member function to set these member variables, typically very short:

```
void Sender::SetReceiveTarget(CWnd *window, UINT message)
{
    m_messagewindow = window;
    m_message = message;
}
```

When the sending class needs to get a message to the window, it calls SendMessage():

```
    m_messagewindow->SendMessage(m_message, wparam, lparam);
```

or PostMessage():

```
    m_messagewindow->PostMessage(m_message, wparam, lparam);
```

The difference between sending and posting a message is that SendMessage() does not return until the message has been handled by the window that received it, but PostMessage() just adds the message to the message queue and returns right away. If, for example, you build an object, pass that object's address as the lparam, and then delete the object, you should choose SendMessage() because you can't delete the object until you are sure that the message-handling code has finished with it. If you aren't passing pointers, you can probably use PostMessage() and enable the system to move on as soon as the message has been added to the queue.

The meaning of the wparam and lparam values depends on the message you are sending. If it is a defined system message such as WM_MOUSEMOVE, you can read the online documentation to learn what the parameters are. If, as is more likely, you are sending a message that you have invented, the meaning of the parameters is entirely up to you. You are the one who is inventing this message and writing the code to handle it when it arrives at the other window.

To invent a message, add a defining statement to the header file of the class that will catch it:

```
#define WM_HELLO WM_USER + 300
```

WM_USER is an unsigned integer that marks the start of the range of message numbers available for user-defined messages. In this release of MFC, its value is 0x4000, though you should not depend on that. User-defined messages have message numbers between WM_USER and 0x7FFF. When defining your own message, you need to come up with a good name for it (WM_HELLO is just an example) and a value to add to WM_USER. Each of your messages will have a different numerical value: for example this program might end up defining WM_GOODBYE as WM_USER + 301.

Then add a line to the message map, in both the header and source file. The source file message map might look like this:

```
BEGIN_MESSAGE_MAP(CMainFrame, CMDIFrameWnd)

    ON_MESSAGE(WM_HELLO, OnHello)
END_MESSAGE_MAP()
```

The entry between the macros catches the WM_HELLO message and arranges for the OnHello() function to be called. The header file message map might look like this:

```
// Generated message map functions
protected:

    afx_msg LRESULT OnHello(WPARAM wParam, LPARAM lParam);
    DECLARE_MESSAGE_MAP()
```

Then you add an implementation of OnHello() to the source file to complete the process.

INTERNATIONAL SOFTWARE DEVELOPMENT ISSUES

International boundaries are shrinking at incredible rates. As the Internet and other methods of cheap international software distribution continue to grow, so will the demand for components built by vendors worldwide. Even in-house software development will less frequently be able to ignore international markets. The rise in popularity of the Internet has expanded the reach of many developers into countries where languages other than English and character sets other than ASCII predominate. This means your applications should be able to communicate with users in languages other than English, and in characters sets other than the typical Western character set.

Microcomputers were invented in the United States, which explains why we have 8-bit character-based operating systems. There are only 26 letters in our alphabet and 10 digits, which leaves plenty of room (about 220 characters worth) for punctuation and other miscellaneous characters. But countries like Japan and China require a character set in the thousands.

Using Unicode is one way to tackle the character set problem. The Unicode standard was developed and is supported by a consortium of some of the biggest players in the international computing markets. Among these are Adobe, Aldus, Apple, Borland, Digital, IBM, Lotus, Microsoft, Novell, and Xerox. (For more information, check www.unicode.org.)

Unicode uses two bytes for each character, whereas ASCII uses only one. One byte (8 bits) can represent 2^8 or 256 characters. Two bytes (16 bits) can represent 65,536 characters. This is enough not just for one language, but for all the character sets in general use. For example, the Japanese character set, one of the largest, needs about 5,000 characters. Most require far less. The Unicode specification sets aside different ranges for different character sets and can cover almost every language on Earth in one universal code—a Unicode.

MFC has full Unicode support, with Unicode versions of almost every function. For example, consider the function CWnd::SetWindowText(). It takes a string and sets the title of the window, or the caption of a button, to that string. What kind of string it takes depends on whether you have Unicode support turned on in your application. In reality, two different functions set the window text—a Unicode version and a non-Unicode version—and in WINUSER.H, the block of code shown in Listing 15.6 changes the function name that you call to SetWindowTextA if you are not using Unicode or to SetWindowTextW if you are.

LISTING 15.6   MICROSOFT'S WINUSER.H IMPLEMENTING UNICODE SUPPORT

```
WINUSERAPI BOOL WINAPI SetWindowTextA(
    IN HWND hWnd,
    IN LPCSTR lpString);
WINUSERAPI BOOL WINAPI SetWindowTextW(
    IN HWND hWnd,
    IN LPCWSTR lpString);
#ifdef UNICODE
#define SetWindowText   SetWindowTextW
#else
#define SetWindowText   SetWindowTextA
#endif // !UNICODE
```

The difference between these two functions is the type of the second parameter: LPCSTR for the A version and LPCWSTR for the W (Wide) version.

If you are using Unicode, whenever you pass a literal string (such as "Hello") to a function, wrap it in the _T macro, like this:

```
pWnd->SetWindowText(_T("Hello"));
```

In fact, it's a really good habit to use the _T macros whenever you type a literal string. If you can deal with the annoyance of wrapping all text strings in _T macros, just like that, your application is Unicode-aware. When you prepare your Greek or Japanese version of the application, life will be much simpler.

CREATING A WINDOWS SERVICE

A Windows Service is an unusual kind of application. To start with, it doesn't have a user interface. Most Windows Services start themselves whenever you restart your computer, and continue to run the whole time your computer is up. For example, a Web server runs as a Windows Service.

If you have a project in mind that requires your code to react to something that happens, such as a file changing or a mail message arriving, then you probably want to write a service. Visual Basic and Visual C# programmers can't create a service unless they buy the Enterprise or Enterprise Architect editions of Visual Studio. But Visual C++ programmers can use ATL to create services quickly and easily.

Although a Windows Service doesn't have a user interface in the usual sense, you can interact with it. If you right-click the My Computer icon on your desktop and choose Manage,
you can see the Computer Management application shown in Figure 15.6. The Services section lists the Windows Services that are installed on your computer and shows their status.

Figure 15.6
Computer
management controls
Windows Services.

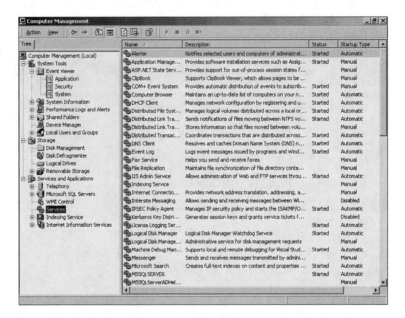

To create the Windows Service example in this chapter, use ATL, the Active Template
Library. ATL is discussed in more detail in Chapter 9, "Building COM+ Components with
ATL." Open Visual Studio and choose File, New, Project. On the left, choose Visual C++
Projects. On the right, choose ATL Project. Name the project DiskMonitor.

On the Application Settings tab of the ATL Project Wizard, select Service for the Server
Type. Uncheck the Attributed check box. The tab should look like Figure 15.7. Click
Finish.

Two projects are created for you within the solution. One is called DiskMonitor and the other
is called DiskMonitorPS. (PS stands for Proxy Stub.) This second project contains generated
code that makes it simpler for other code to use the service. You can safely ignore it.

In a file called DiskMonitor.cpp, you will find the definition of CDiskMonitorModule, which
was generated by the ATL Project Wizard. This workhorse class handles requests for your
service to start and stop. It uses a template defined in ATL called CAtlServiceModuleT. If
you expand this class in the Class View and drill down into the Base Classes and Interfaces
nodes, you will see that CDiskMonitorModule has a lot of functions already available to it.

Figure 15.7
Create a Service with
ATL Project Wizard.

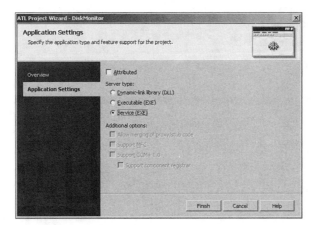

As part of this example, you'll be referring to a CDiskMonitorModule object in another piece of code. It is helpful to have the class definition in a header file of its own. A file called DiskMonitor.h has already been created, and contains generated code, so you can't put the class definition there. Instead, choose Project, Add New Item to add a C++ header file to the project called DiskMonitorClass.h. Move the class definition into that file. Add this line to DiskMonitor.cpp, after the include statements that are already present:

```
#include "DiskMonitorClass.h"
```

The actual work of this service is going to be performed by an ATL class. To add it to the project, choose Project, Add Class. On the right, choose ATL Simple Object. (To reduce the number of options shown on the right, expand the Visual C++ node on the left and select ATL.) Click Open to bring up the ATL Simple Object Wizard. Fill in **DiskReporter** as the short name, and the rest of the names are filled in for you. Click Finish to create the class.

At this point you can build the project to make sure you have not made any errors. Then select DiskMonitor in the Class View and choose Project, Properties. Click Debugging on the left. Fill in the Command Arguments as -Service, as shown in Figure 15.8. Now when you run the application, it registers the service, after which you can start the service from Computer Management.

Bring up Computer Management, and you should see DiskMonitor listed among the installed services. Right-click it and choose Start, as you see in Figure 15.9. Wait a little while, then right-click and choose Stop. You have created a service and made it available from Computer Management. This service can start and stop without errors.

When your service starts, Windows calls a method that ATL generated called ServiceMain(). Through a series of calls, eventually three methods of your class run: PreMessageLoop(), RunMessageLoop(), and PostMessageLoop(). Despite the word Loop in their names, these functions are not called repeatedly. Yet most services sit and wait for requests, and do things repeatedly. This functionality comes not from the way that Windows calls services, but rather from the code of the service itself.

Figure 15.8
Arrange for the service to be registered when you run it.

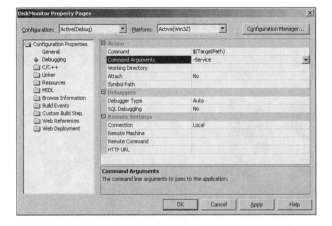

Figure 15.9
Start your service.

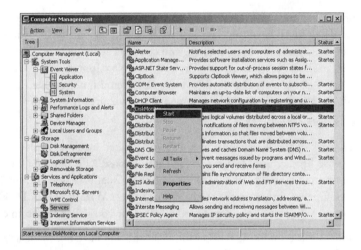

The best way to code an application that repeatedly waits, then reacts, is in a separate thread. The service can spin this thread in an override of `PreMessageLoop()`, and clean it up in an override of `PostMessageLoop()`. The function that the thread executes is a static member function of the `CDiskReporter` object you added to the project. A static member variable controls the thread execution.

Tip

Threading concepts are introduced in Chapter 14, "Multitasking with Windows Threads." If you'd like a little more insight into the code presented in this chapter, read that chapter to learn what a thread proc is, for example.

Here's what to do:

1. Double-click `CDiskReporter` in the Class View to edit the header file that includes the class definition. Add this line at the end of the class definition, after the keyword `pub-lic:` that is already there:

   ```
   static    bool m_bRunning;
   ```

2. Add this line to DiskReporter.cpp, after the include statements at the beginning of the file:

   ```
   bool CDiskReporter::m_bRunning = false;
   ```

   This allocates memory for the static variable that will control the thread execution.

3. Add a function to `CDiskReporter` by right-clicking the class name in Class View and choosing Add, Add Function. Fill in the Add Member Function Wizard as in Figure 15.10. The return type is `unsigned long`, the function name is `ThreadProc`, it takes a `void*` called p, and it is both public and static. Click Finish to create the function.

Figure 15.10
Add a `ThreadProc` function to `CDiskReporter`.

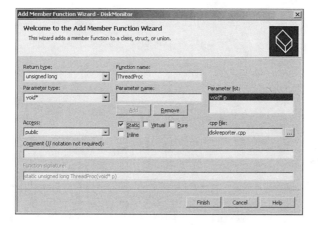

4. The wizard generates the function for you entirely in the .h file. Move the function body to the .cpp file. Edit the declaration in the .h file so it includes the `WINAPI` keyword, like this:

   ```
   static unsigned long WINAPI ThreadProc(void* p);
   ```

5. Edit the implementation, adding `WINAPI` and the class name, leaving the body of the function unwritten so that it reads like this:

   ```
   unsigned long WINAPI CDiskReporter::ThreadProc(void* p)
   {
       return 0;
   }
   ```

6. Build your application and correct any errors. If you get a message `Could not delete service`, then close Computer Management and build the application again.

Services can report to a user in a number of ways, even though they have no user interface. A service could write to an output file on the hard drive, for example. The best way to communicate, though, is through the Event Log. One section of the Event Log is specifically for messages from applications. The `CDiskMonitorModule` class that was generated for you has a `LogEvent()` method that adds messages to the Application Log. To call this method from `ThreadProc()`, take advantage of the void pointer argument and pass in the address of the `CDiskMonitorModule` object itself. You'll see this shortly.

Overriding `PreMessageLoop()` and `PostMessageLoop()` is quite simple. Here's how:

1. Select `CDiskMonitorModule` in the Class View. In the Properties Window, click the Overrides button (the green lozenge).

2. Click next to `PostMessageLoop` to drop down actions, and choose `<Add>` `PostMessageLoop`.

3. Click next to `PreMessageLoop` and choose `<Add>` `PreMessageLoop`, as in Figure 15.11.

Figure 15.11
Override
`PreMessageLoop()`
and
`PostMessageLoop()`.

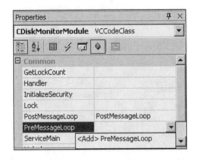

> **Caution**
>
> If Visual Studio adds these overrides to a new file called DiskMonitorClass.cpp, move them to DiskMonitor.cpp and remove DiskMonitorClass.cpp from the project.

4. Right-click `CDiskMonitorModule` in Class View and choose Add, Add Variable. Select Access to be private, enter **HANDLE** for the Variable Type, and enter **threadhandle** for the Variable Name. Click Finish to add the variable.

5. Add these three lines to `PreMessageLoop()`, replacing the TODO comment:

```
CDiskReporter::m_bRunning = true;
DWORD threadid;
threadhandle = CreateThread(NULL, 0, CDiskReporter::ThreadProc, this, 0,
➥&threadid);
```

This code sets the `m_bRunning` flag to `true`, and starts the thread, saving the handle in `threadhandle`.

6. Add these two lines to `PostMessageLoop()`, replacing the TODO comment:

```
CDiskReporter::m_bRunning = false;
WaitForSingleObject(threadhandle, 20000);
```

This code sets the `m_bRunning` flag to `false`, which should stop the thread. It waits until the thread stops, using the handle that was saved in the `threadhandle` member variable. The 20000 in this code indicates that `PostMessageLoop()` should wait up to 20 seconds for the thread to stop.

7. Add this line at the top of DiskMonitor.cpp, after the other include statements:

```
#include "DiskReporter.h"
```

8. Build the application to make sure there are no errors.

The call to `CreateThread()` in `PreMessageLoop()` passed `this` as the fourth parameter, which will be passed to `ThreadProc()` after the thread is created. Because `this` is a pointer to the `CDiskMonitorModule` object that is running the service, it will be very useful to `ThreadProc()`.

In the Class View, double-click `ThreadProc` under `CDiskReporter` to edit the code. Add these lines before the existing `return` statement:

```
CDiskMonitorModule* parent = (CDiskMonitorModule*) p;
parent->LogEvent(_T("thread has started"));
while (m_bRunning)
{
    parent->LogEvent(_T("thread is working"));
    Sleep(10000); // 10 seconds
}
```

This code goes into what appears to be an infinite loop. It uses the pointer that was passed to it to write an entry to the Application Log, and it sleeps for 10 seconds, then loops again. You've seen, though, that `PostMessageLoop()` will set `m_bRunning` to `false` to stop the thread. It's important that the call to `WaitForSingleObject()` at the end of `PostMessageLoop()` wait for at least as long as the `Sleep()` call here in `ThreadProc()`. That way `PostMessageLoop()` will still be waiting when `ThreadProc` wakes up, and everything will close down smoothly. Don't set the parameter to `Sleep()` too high, or you'll find your service very slow to respond when you stop it.

Add this include statement to DiskReporter.cpp, after the include statements at the top of the file:

```
#include "DiskMonitorClass.h"
```

Build the application, and run it once to register the server. Then open Computer Management and start the service. Still in Computer Management, open System Tools on the left, and Event Viewer below that. Click on Application and you should see a number of Application log messages, as in Figure 15.12. Wait twenty seconds or so, then refresh the window by pressing F5 to see more messages.

Figure 15.12
The service adds a new application log entry every ten seconds.

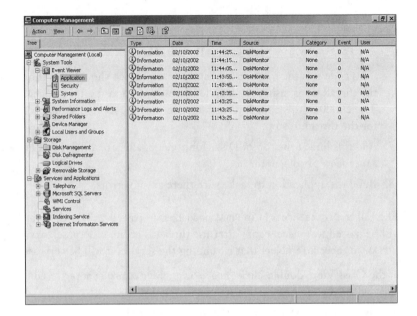

It's not very interesting to write the same message every ten seconds as this sample does. Why not adjust the service a little so that it actually reacts to your system? As an illustration, the service can use the DiskFree DLL developed earlier in this chapter. Follow these steps to change the service:

1. Copy diskfree.h and diskfree.lib from the TestDiskFree folder to the DiskMonitor folder. Copy diskfree.dll from the TestDiskFree folder to the DiskMonitor\Debug folder.

2. Add this line to DiskReporter.cpp, after the other include statements:

   ```
   #include "DiskFree.h"
   ```

3. Select DiskMonitor in the Class View and choose Project, Properties. Expand Linker on the left and click Input below it.

4. Add **diskfree.lib** on the line for Additional Dependencies. Click OK.

5. Change the call to LogEvent() inside the while loop in ThreadProc() to this:

   ```
   parent->LogEvent(_T("disk space is %d bytes"), DiskFree(2));
   ```

Build the application, and run it once to register it. Then start the service. View the Application Log, wait twenty seconds or so, then refresh to see some log entries from the service. Double-click one to read it, and make a note of the bytes of disk space reported at the end of the message. Now, with the service still running, do something to change this number: Empty the Recycle Bin, for example, or make a copy of a fairly large file. Wait about ten seconds, switch back to the Application Log, and read the latest log entry; it should report a different number. That's a service in action.

FROM HERE

It may sound strange to say that Windows programmers don't just develop Windows applications, but it's true. The special application types introduced in this chapter (console applications, DLLs, and services) aren't Windows applications, at least not exactly. Yet knowing how to create them is a mark of an advanced Windows programmer. As you've seen, the work involved in creating these special applications can be quite small. Yet many developers are intimidated by such tasks, and look for someone else to do them. Now that you know what's involved, you'll be ready when an opportunity arises.

If the idea of writing reusable code in a DLL intrigues you, but you'd rather write a component than a collection of functions, read Chapter 9, "Building COM+ Components with ATL." For more on threading, try Chapter 14, "Multitasking with Windows Threads."

This is the last chapter in the "classic Win32 programming" half of the book. If you're reading in order, it's time to get acquainted with .NET in the next chapter, "The Common Language Runtime."

CHAPTER 16

THE COMMON LANGUAGE RUNTIME

In this chapter

ARCHITECTURE OF .NET

All the .NET languages, including Managed C++, compile and link to a format that is not directly executable on your computer. Instead, they produce MSIL (Microsoft Intermediate Language)—a format designed to execute within a framework rather than natively on your PC. Your component is deployed as an *assembly*—a collection of executable MSIL and related *metadata* that explains the contents of your component. The framework doesn't interpret your MSIL; it compiles it using a Just-In-Time compiler, often referred to as a JIT. Your code actually runs inside the framework, as shown in Figure 16.1.

Figure 16.1
In .NET, your code compiles to intermediate language that executes inside a framework and uses the services of the framework.

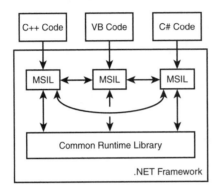

The framework within which these applications execute provides a number of services to you, the developer:

- Memory management—no more memory leaks!
- Type system conversions—no more BSTRs!
- Cross-language integration and inheritance
- Debugging and profiling
- Simpler access to other components—no more QueryInterface, AddRef, Release, or HRESULTs!

What's more, the framework can compile your MSIL to different native code on different platforms, taking advantage of performance differences from platform to platform and insulating you from many of the subtle and tricky deployment issues you would otherwise face. At the time I write this, the platforms involved are all different flavors of Windows—but that alone can present a significant programming challenge in some cases.

Finally, the framework comes with an enormous class library of services you are likely to need, from string manipulation and linked lists to manipulating XML, working with databases, and user authentication. This chapter introduces you to some of these very useful classes. There are no sample applications, though there are some short snippets of code. I expect you'll come back to this chapter after you have new .NET applications under your belt, to look for something that you know should be in the framework somewhere, but you just can't seem to find.

Because all the languages compile to MSIL, mixing and matching languages within an application is a snap. You choose whatever language is best for you. Of course, for most of you, that will be Visual C++. But whatever language you use, the entire Common Language Runtime is available to you, which saves you enormous amounts of time and energy.

THE SYSTEM NAMESPACE

All the classes of the Common Language Runtime are in a *namespace* called System, or one of the subnamespaces beneath it. To use a class in a namespace, you have two choices:

- Call the class by its full name (such as `System::Math`) whenever you're using it:

```
x = System::Math::PI / 4;
System::String* s = new System::String("hello");
```

- Add a `using` statement at the top of the file, then call the class by its name within the namespace:

```
using namespace System;
...
x = Math::PI / 4;
String* s = new String("hello");
```

The second choice is a better approach when you're going to be typing class names from the namespace a number of times, because it saves you typing the namespace name repeatedly.

Punctuation: . and ::

In most other .NET languages, the punctuation between the namespace name and the class name is a dot (.). For example, in both Visual Basic and C# a developer would type `System.Math.PI`. But in C++ it is a double colon (::), the scope resolution operator. In the documentation, if you see a reference to `System.Something`, you just need to change it to `System::Something` in your code. Use the scope resolution operator between namespace and subnamespace, namespace and class, or subnamespace and class.

As always, you use the dot between the name of an object and an ordinary function, and the scope resolution operator between the name of the class and a static function. In the previous examples, PI is a static member variable of the Math class. In other .NET languages, the punctuation between class or object name and function is always a dot, even when the function is static. This can make the documentation confusing. Most occurrences of . in the documentation should be changed to ::.

IntelliSense, the feature that pops up lists for you to choose from as you type, really helps with this confusion. If you type **"System."** into a file of C++ code, no list appears and the status bar reads:

IntelliSense: 'Could not resolve type for expression to the left of . or ->'

On the other hand, if you type **"System::"**, a list of namespaces and classes appears for you to choose from. If you use the lack of feedback from IntelliSense as an indicator that you have typed the wrong thing, you'll find working from the documentation a lot less confusing.

Whether you choose to add a using statement to your file or not, you must add a #using directive to the top of your source file. When you create a new .NET project, one of these directives is added for you automatically:

```
#using <mscorlib.dll>
```

This gives you access to all the classes that are directly under the System namespace, such as the System::Math class used in these examples. The documentation for the classes that are in subnamespaces of System includes a line like this one, from System::Xml.Document:

```
Assembly: System.XML.dll
```

This is a clue that you need to add this line to your file:

```
#using <System.XML.dll>
```

Don't worry about what seems to be extra dots in the file name, and don't change dots to :: here.

THE CORE CLASSES

The classes in the System namespace are ones you'll use in almost every .NET application. All the data types are represented, for example. Two classes in particular deserve special mention: System::Console and System::String.

System::Console

System::Console, called System.Console in the documentation, represents the screen and keyboard in a simple console application. After you add a using statement to your file so you don't have to type System:: every time, the Console class is simple to use. To write a line of text to the screen, you use the static function WriteLine():

```
Console::WriteLine("Calculations in Progress");
```

If you want to write text without a following line break, use the Write() function instead.

To read a line of text from the keyboard, first you should write out a line to prompt the user, then read the entire line into a System::String object with the static ReadLine() function:

```
Console::WriteLine("Enter a sentence:");
String* sentence = Console::ReadLine();
```

If you'd like to read in something more complicated than a single string, there really isn't any support for it within the Console class, nor the classes in the System::IO namespace covered later in this chapter. You can read it into a string and then use string member functions to separate it into the pieces you want.

If you want to write formatted output, there's an overload of WriteLine that's reminiscent of printf(), except that you don't have to tell the function the type of each parameter. For example:

```
Console::WriteLine("The time is {0} at this moment",
System::DateTime::Now.ToShortTimeString() );
```

You can write out a number of parameters at once. Use the placeholders, the things in brace brackets in the format string, to call for the parameter you want. As you can see, the count is zero-based. Here's an example:

```
Console::WriteLine("{0} lives at {1}", name, address);
```

System::String

The String class represents a string, like "Hello" or "Kate Gregory". That's familiar ground for any programmer. But working with .NET strings can be quite strange for an experienced C++ or MFC programmer. They are certainly very far removed from the arrays of characters that you may be used to working with.

If you've ever worked with the MFC class CString, you've probably written code like this:

```
CString message = "Value of x, ";
message += x;
message += "is over limit.";
```

You might guess that the .NET equivalent would be:

```
String* message = "Value of x, ";
message += x;
message += "is over limit.";
```

This just gets you a lot of strange compiler errors about illegal pointer arithmetic.

```
String* message = "Value of x, " + x + "is over limit.";
```

Compiling this line produces another error about pointer addition. Although there are ways around this, the bottom line is that you can't treat .NET strings like C++ or C strings at all.

So how do you build a string from several substrings, or from several pieces in general? If you want to build it so you can write it out, forget building the string, and use formatted output as described in the previous section. Or use the Format() method, which is reminiscent of sprintf(), or the Format() method of the old MFC class CString. But if you need to build a string in little bits and pieces, your best choice is a companion class called StringBuilder, from the System::Text namespace. You use a string builder like this:

```
String* name = "Kate";
System::Text::StringBuilder* sb = new System::Text::StringBuilder("Hello ");
sb->Append(name);
```

Using a string builder is more efficient than modifying a string as you go, because .NET strings actually can't be modified; instead, a whole new one is created with your changes, and the old one is cleaned up later. StringBuilder has all sorts of useful methods like Append(), Insert(), Remove(), and Replace() that you can use to work on your string. When it's ready, just pass the string builder object to anything that's expecting a string:

```
Console::WriteLine(sb);
```

The framework gets the built string from the string builder and passes it to the function for you.

The String class has its own useful methods too. Consider the problem mentioned earlier—reading something other than a single string from the keyboard. The easiest way for you to tackle the problem is to write code that reads the line of input into a string, then works with it. Here's a simple example:

```
Console::WriteLine("Enter three integers:");
String* input = Console::ReadLine();
String* numbers[] = input->Split(0);
int a1 = Convert::ToInt32(numbers[0]);
int a2 = Convert::ToInt32(numbers[1]);
int a3 = Convert::ToInt32(numbers[2]);
```

This code uses the Split() member function of the String class. It splits a String into an array of strings based on a separator character. If you pass in a null pointer (0), as in this example, it splits the string based on whitespace such as spaces or tabs, which is perfect for this situation. The ToInt32() method of the Convert class converts a String to an integer.

CLASSES FOR STANDARD PROGRAMMING TASKS

There are plenty of other useful classes in the System namespace. Some are covered elsewhere in this book. Almost every .NET developer is likely to use System::IO, System::Text, System::Collections, and System::Threading.

System::IO

Getting information from users and providing it to them is the sort of task that can be incredibly simple (like reading a string and echoing it back to the user) or far more complex. The most basic operations are in the Console class in the System namespace. More complicated tasks are in the System::IO namespace. This namespace includes 27 classes, as well as some structures and other related utilities. They handle tasks like:

- Reading and writing to a file
- Binary reads and writes (bytes or blocks of bytes)
- Creating, deleting, renaming, or moving files
- Working with directories

System::Text

In the same vein, the simplest string work can be tackled with just the String class from the System namespace. More complicated work involves the System::Text namespace. You've already seen System::Text::StringBuilder. Other classes in this namespace handle conversions between different types of text, such as Unicode and ASCII. The System::Text::RegularExpressions namespace lets you use regular expressions in string manipulations and elsewhere.

`System::Collections`

Another incredibly common programming task is holding on to a collection of objects. If you have just a few, you can use an array, like the array of `String` pointers in the code, to read three integers in one line of input. In fact, arrays in .NET are actually objects, instances of the `System::Array` class, which has some useful member functions of its own, such as `Copy()`. There are times when you want specific types of collections, though, and the `System::Collections` namespace has plenty of them. The provided collections include:

- **Stack.** A collection that stores objects in order. The object put in most recently is the first taken out again.

- **Queue.** A collection that stores objects in order. The first put in is the first taken out again.

- **Hashtable.** A collection that can be searched far more quickly than other types of collections, but takes up more space.

- **ArrayList.** An array that grows as elements are added to it.

- **SortedList.** A collection of two-part (key and value) items that can be accessed by key or in numerical order.

- **BitArray.** A very compact way to store an array of true/false flags.

One rather striking omission here is a linked list. You have to code your own if you need a linked or double-linked list.

`System::Threading`

Threading has been a difficult part of Windows programming from the very beginning. Chapter 14, "MultiTasking with Windows Threads," covers the basics of threading for Win32 programmers. It's quite a bit simpler in .NET. The vital classes for threading are in the `System::Threading` namespace. These include classes such as `Mutex`, `Thread`, and `ThreadPool`, which developers with experience in threaded applications will recognize instantly.

> **Tip**
>
> One of the bonus chapters for this book, "Advanced CLR Features," explains .NET threading in more detail. You'll find it at `http://www.usingvisualc.net`.

CLASSES FOR WEB APPLICATIONS

If you've ever coded a classic COM component that an ASP page uses, or worked in ASP directly, you're familiar with the objects that are available in that context, representing the request from the Web browser, the response that is sent back to the Web browser, and so on. These sorts of objects in the .NET framework are gathered together in the `System::Web` namespace.

Here you'll find a class called `HttpRequest` and another called `HttpResponse`—they represent the request from the browser and the response you are writing to send to the browser. A class called `HttpCookie` simplifies working with cookies. The `HttpUrl` class represents a URL, as described in the next section. A number of subnamespaces contain classes used in building a Web forms application or an XML Web service.

HttpUrl

The very useful `HttpUrl` class encapsulates a URL. You can construct one from a string, from another URL and a string, or from five strings and an integer if you want to put the URL together from its components. For example, you could create a URL like this:

```
System::Web::HttpUrl* url = new System::Web::HttpUrl(
    "http","msdn.microsoft.com", 80,
    "library/en-us/Dnvs700/html/ExpVSNETintro.asp",
    "frame=true",
    "expvsnetintro_topic2");
```

This would be equivalent to creating one like this:

```
System::Web::HttpUrl* url2 = new System::Web::HttpUrl(
    "http://msdn.microsoft.com:80/library/en-
us/Dnvs700/html/ExpVSNETintro.asp?frame=true#expvsnetintro_topic2");
```

These two URLs are equivalent, and identify a technical article on the Microsoft Web site.

SYSTEM::WEB SUBNAMESPACES

The `System::Web` namespace has several subnamespaces.

- `System::Web::Caching`
- `System::Web::Configuration`
- `System::Web::Hosting`
- `System::Web::Mail`
- `System::Web::Security`
- `System::Web::Services`
- `System::Web::SessionState`
- `System::Web::UI`
- `System::Web::Util`

Many of these subnamespaces have subnamespaces of their own that are not listed here, in the interests of space.

The Services subnamespace and its subnamespaces relate to Web Services, described in Chapter 21, "Creating an XML Web Service." You can learn about description and discovery in that chapter. The UI subnamespace and its subnamespaces relate to Web Forms, used to build intuitive user interfaces for your Web applications. You can see an example in Chapter 19, "Integrating with C#."

CLASSES FOR WORKING WITH DATA

Working with databases and working with XML are tasks that actually have quite a lot in common. If you want to store all the departments and employees in a company, for example, you could keep them in a small database, or you could write out a stream of XML and read it back later. To share this information between tiers in an application or between applications, you could exchange recordset objects if the two applications ran on the same platform, or you could exchange XML documents and be platform-independent.

Classes for working with databases are in the `System::Data` namespace.

For example, the `DataSet` class in `System::Data` represents an ADO dataset, like the recordsets or resultsets you may have used with other data access classes. This is the heart of the .NET data access technology. You can learn more about it in Chapter 24, "Database Access with ADO.NET."

It's easy to go back and forth from a table-column-row view of your data to an XML view with the `DataSet` class. As Figure 16.2 shows, a dataset has a collection of data tables (instances of the `DataTable` class of `System::Data`.) A data table has a collection of columns (instances of the `DataColumn` class of `System::Data`), or if you prefer you can use the collection of rows (instances of the `DataRow` class of `System::Data`.)

However, the very same object can also be used to fill those rows and columns from XML by creating an empty dataset and then calling its `ReadXML()` method. Or, if you have a dataset full of useful information, you can get it as XML by calling the dataset's `WriteXML()` method, thereby producing an XML document. This means that as far as your code is concerned, the data in your database is an XML document too. Figure 16.3 illustrates this concept.

CH

16

Figure 16.2
The classes of the
`System::Data`
namespace represent
parts of a database.

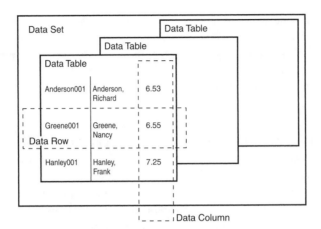

Figure 16.3
The classes of the
`System::Data`
namespace represent
parts of a database.

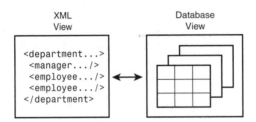

Several classes in the .NET framework help you work with your information in this dual way, including `System::Xml::XmlDataDocument`. Although it may feel a little strange at first to treat your data as both relational tables and a stream of XML, doing so can be incredibly convenient.

If your uses for XML go beyond getting information in and out of a database, you'll be pleased so see how much support for XML is in the .NET framework. You shouldn't be surprised, because .NET is built on XML. In addition to the XML support in the classes of the `System::Data` namespace, there are a number of XML namespaces:

- `System::Xml`
- `System::Xml::Serialization`
- `System::Xml::Schema`
- `System::Xsl`
- `System::XPath`

You can learn more about XML, and common programming tasks associated with XML, in Appendix B, "XML Review."

CLASSES FOR SECURITY

One of the huge advantages of the .NET framework is the infrastructure it provides. Some developers take shortcuts as they develop, leaving the hard parts until the core functionality is in place, and then skimp on those hard parts because of deadline pressure. Security, in my experience, is one of those aspects added in at the last minute on many projects, and foolish as it may seem, many projects skimp on security.

The solution to this is two-fold: make it easier to develop an application with security features, and make them part of the project from the beginning rather than saving them until the end. .NET developers gain tremendously from this approach to security, and so do the people who buy their software. You can learn more about .NET security in Chapter 24, "Security and Policies."

CH
16

The classes that the framework provides for securing your application are gathered into the System::Security namespace. For example, the SecurityManager class represents the "decision maker" provided by the framework to authorize specific actions. Your code, and code you call, checks with a security manager to see whether certain behaviors are allowed or not. You can't create an instance of this class, but the most useful functions are all static, so you can call them whether you have an instance or not.

Subnamespaces of System::Security hold related classes. These are:

- System::Security::Cryptography
- System::Security::Permissions
- System::Security::Policy
- System::Security::Principal

Just reading this list, you should start to realize how easy it's going to be to make your application more secure. For example, the System::Security::Cryptography namespace has a number of subnamespaces and a class called RSA_CSP. CSP stands for Cryptography Service Provider, so this class provides access to the RSA algorithm. It has methods such as LoadKey(), Encrypt(), and Decrypt(), which make encryption a lot simpler to implement within your applications.

TIPS FOR .NET-FRIENDLY CODE

As you'll see in the chapters that follow, when you write a .NET component, its methods may be called from any other .NET language. That means, among other things, you shouldn't use a parameter type or return type that doesn't exist in the other .NET languages. The System namespace implements a standard set of data types. Most of these have a native equivalent in the other .NET languages, but if there is no native equivalent, the developer can refer to them with the name from the System namespace. These types and their equivalents are presented in Table 16.1.

TABLE 16.1   FUNDAMENTAL DATA TYPES

C++ Built-In Type	.NET Framework Type	Comment
unsigned char	Byte	no equivalent in VB
signed char	SByte	
__wchar_t	Char	
short	Int16	16 bits
unsigned short	UInt16	no equivalent in VB
long	Int32	32 bits
unsigned long	UInt32	no equivalent in VB
__int64	Int64	VB and C# long, C++ equivalent is Microsoft-specific
unsigned __int64	UInt64	no equivalent in VB
float	Single	
double	Double	
Object*	Object	pointers in C++ are references elsewhere
bool	Boolean	

You can see by this table that Visual Basic does not support unsigned types, so avoid using them as parameter or return types in your .NET code. If you are working with a .NET function that takes or returns a System::Int64 (a long in C# or a Long in VB) you have to use the extension keyword __int64 for the C++ type. If you prefer, use System::Int64—they're equivalent.

As mentioned earlier in this chapter, a .NET string object is not at all like an array of characters. What's more, a .NET Char type is not like a C++ char; it's actually a wide character. The C++ extension wchar_t is the type that corresponds to System::Char and holds a single wide character.

The System namespace also makes available to C++ programmers a 96-bit decimal type called System::Decimal. Treat it as you do String: as a new fundamental type, courtesy of the framework. It was designed for financial calculations, where round-off errors must not occur, and provides 28 significant digits, holding numbers up to 79,228,162,514,264,337,593,543,950,335—whatever that is! More importantly, it holds fractions such as .25 as fractions, not as repeating decimals with a value close to the actual fraction. This dramatically improves accuracy.

FINDING THE OLD FAMILIARS

Here's a situation many new .NET developers find themselves in: You're about to start typing code and you realize you need to perform a simple and common activity, like finding a character in a string, or sending some output to the screen. You know how to do it with MFC, or the old C runtime functions, or even the Standard Template Library, and you just know there should be an equivalent in the .NET framework, but you can't find it.

INPUT AND OUTPUT

Reading from the keyboard and writing to the screen were discussed earlier in this chapter. To write to the screen with the C runtime, you used to code this sort of thing:

```
printf("hello there!\n");
printf("hello, %s!\n", name);
```

The C++ equivalent was:

```
cout << "hello there!" << endl;
cout <<"hello, " << name << '!' << endl;
```

In .NET, you do it like this:

```
Console::WriteLine("hello there!");
Console::WriteLine("hello, {0}!",name);
```

To read from the keyboard with the old C runtime functions you used scanf. In C++ it was cin, like this:

```
cin >> x >> y >> z;
```

Sample code presented earlier in this chapter shows how to read a line of input into a System::String object using Console::ReadLine and then parse the string yourself.

STRING MANIPULATION

In a program that didn't use MFC, you could work with C-style strings (arrays of characters), using functions such as strcat, strcpy, and so on. MFC was a big improvement, providing CString. But now you have to use System::String and learn the names of those useful functions all over again. Table 16.2 provides a handy summary.

TABLE 16.2   STRING FUNCTIONS

C Runtime	MFC CString	System::String
strcpy	operator=	operator=
strcat	operator+=	Append
strchr	Find	IndexOf
strcmp	operator == or Compare	Compare
strlen	GetLength()	Length
strtok	n/a	Split
[]	[] or GetAt()	Chars
sprintf	Format	Format
n/a	Left or Right or Mid	Substring

CH
16

If you've worked with strings in other languages, you'll appreciate `System::String` functions such as `PadLeft()`, `PadRight()`, `Remove()`, and `StartsWith()`. If those names aren't familiar to you, check the documentation. You may be able to do what you want with a single function call!

DATE AND TIME WORK

In MFC, you worked with time and date values with `CTime` or `CTimeSpan`. These have .NET equivalents, of course: `System::DateTime and System::TimeSpan`. The static member function `System::DateTime::Now()` returns the current date and time as a `DateTime` object. You can then use methods such as:

- **Day**: Returns the day of the month
- **Month**: 1 to 12
- **Year**: Four digits always
- **Hour**: 0 to 23
- **Minute**
- **Second**
- **DayOfWeek**: 0 means Sunday
- **ToString**: Creates a string based on the time and date, using a format string

The format string passed to `ToString()` is either a single character representing one of a number of "canned" formats, or a custom format string. The most useful canned formats include:

- **d**: A short date, such as 12/19/00
- **D**: A long date, such as Tuesday, December 19, 2000
- **f**: A full time and date, such as Tuesday, December 19, 2000 17:49
- **g**: A general time and date, such as 12/19/00 17:49
- **s**: A sortable time and date, such as 2000-12-19 17:49:03
- **t**: A short time, such as 17:49
- **T**: A long time, such as 17:49:03

If none of the canned formats are what you need, you can make your own by passing in strings such as `"MMMM d, yy"` for `"December 3, 02"` or whatever else you desire. You can find all the format strings in the online help.

If what you're looking for isn't a library class or method, but rather a menu item, toolbar button, or some other aspect of the user interface of Visual Studio, be sure to read Appendix D, "Upgrading From Visual C++ 6" to discover where the commands you used to use have gone.

FROM HERE

This chapter introduced you to the fundamentals of .NET programming. You've seen the architecture of .NET, learned your way around the System namespace a bit, and discovered some new ways to tackle familiar tasks. Now it's time to step into .NET programming for yourself.

In the next chapter, "Getting Started with .NET," you will see how to write a .NET application. You'll also write a .NET component, and another .NET application that uses the component. This lays the groundwork for Chapter 18, "Integrating with Visual Basic," and Chapter 19, "Integrating with C#," in which you use a C++ component from other languages, write components in other languages that inherit from a C++ component, and use those components from C++. The three chapters together form an excellent demonstration of the reality of cross-language development with .NET.

CH
16

CHAPTER 17

GETTING STARTED WITH .NET

In this chapter

YOUR FIRST .NET APPLICATION

Windows developers generally create Windows applications. Only some developers also created Windows components. In .NET things are different: you are likely to create both applications and components. In this chapter you will see how to write a simple application and a simple component, then go on to write an application that uses the component.

The structure of a .NET application is a little different from the Windows applications discussed so far in this book. If you've written a C++ application for Unix, or a Windows console application, you'll recognize the way it's laid out. The _tmain() function is called when you run your application. The code in that _tmain() function creates and uses objects, or calls functions provided by the Common Runtime Library. Learning your way around .NET means learning the Common Runtime Library, but you don't need to know all of it to get started.

To create a .NET application, you start as you would for a Win32 project: choose File, New, Project. The New project dialog box, shown in Figure 17.1, appears. Select Visual C++ projects on the left, then on the right side of the dialog, select Managed C++ Application. Name the project HelloWorld, and click OK to create it.

Figure 17.1
Create a Managed C++ application.

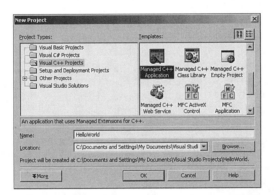

> **Tip**
>
> Be sure to create the project on a local drive, not a network share. By default, .NET applications cannot be run over a network share. Chapter 24, "Security and Policies," demonstrates how to arrange to run code from a trusted network share.

Expand the Class View, and you will see there are no classes in this project. You have a global function called _tmain(). Double-click the function in Class View to edit the code provided by the application wizard. Here's the code you were given:

```
// This is the main project file for VC++ application project
// generated using an Application Wizard.

#include "stdafx.h"
```

```
#using <mscorlib.dll>
#include <tchar.h>

using namespace System;

// This is the entry point for this application
int _tmain(void)
{
    // TODO: Please replace the sample code below with your own.
    Console::WriteLine(S"Hello World");
    return 0;
}
```

There are three interesting lines in this code: the #using statement, the using statement, and the call to WriteLine.

The #using statement is a new compiler directive. It serves a similar function to #include, providing a reference to code that has been implemented in another project. In a non-.NET application, to use code from another project you would have to #include the header file to keep the compiler happy, and then link with a .lib file or load the DLL while running to execute the code. The #using statement takes care of both tasks at once. The file mscorlib.dll includes not only executable code, but also information that the compiler can use to verify the functions you can call, the parameters those functions take, and so on.

The "using namespace" syntax is not new to .NET. Visual C++ has supported namespaces for several versions now. The many useful classes of the .NET framework are all in namespaces so that you can name your classes whatever you like without conflict. The _tmain() function that was generated for you uses the Console class. Without the namespace directive, you would have to call it by its full name, System::Console. (The scope resolution operator, ::, is used between the namespace name and the class name.)

The third interesting line is the call to WriteLine(), a static member function of the Console class. (The scope resolution operator is also used between the class name and the name of a static member function.) WriteLine() takes a string and writes it to "standard output." For most console applications, that's the screen.

Whenever I work with a console application like this one, I like to be sure it will pause at the end to give me a chance to read all the output. The easiest way to do that is to ask it to read something from the keyboard.

Using the text editor, add a line of code between the call to WriteLine() and the return statement:

```
Console::ReadLine();
```

Now build your project by choosing Build, Build.

The Output window in the lower left shows the result of your build. If all goes well, it should read like this:

```
------ Build started: Project: HelloWorld, Configuration: Debug Win32 ------

Compiling...
```

```
AssemblyInfo.cpp
HelloWorld.cpp
Generating Code...
Linking...

Build log was saved at "file://C:\Documents and Settings\kate\My Documents\Visual
Studio Projects\HelloWorld\Debug\BuildLog.htm"
HelloWorld - 0 error(s), 0 warning(s)


-------------------- Done --------------------

    Build: 1 succeeded, 0 failed, 0 skipped
```

If you have any errors, they appear in the output window. Fix them, and build the project again.

To run the project, choose Debug, Start. You should see a greeting, as shown in Figure 17.2. Notice that this console interface is character-based. Press Enter when you've looked at it as long as you care to; this satisfies the ReadLine() call and then the program finishes.

Figure 17.2
Your .NET application runs in a window that resembles a command prompt.

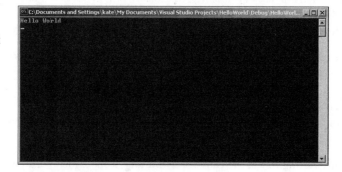

If you switch to the Solution View, you can see that in addition to the HelloWorld.cpp file you edited, your solution also contains a file called AssemblyInfo.cpp. This is where settings and attributes of the assembly are kept. When you build this project, you create an assembly, which is the .NET unit of execution. In later chapters, such as Chapter 24, you will see how attributes control the behavior of .NET assemblies.

YOUR FIRST .NET COMPONENT

As you've seen, a .NET application is quite simple to write. But the excitement in .NET is all about components. So why not try writing a component, and change the HelloWorld project to use a component?

A simple change to the current design would be to use a component to determine the string that is written to the screen when the HelloWorld application runs. Perhaps it could say "Good morning" or "Good afternoon," based on the time. It is enough for demonstration purposes if it just says something different from "Hello World".

You will create a component called `Greeter` with one method, `Greet()`, that returns "Hello from a component." After it's complete, you can change HelloWorld to use the `Greet()` method of the `Greeter` component.

Bring up a new copy of Visual Studio so that you can flip back and forth between `Greeter` and HelloWorld easily. In the new copy, choose File, New, Project. Select Visual C++ projects on the left. On the right, choose a Managed C++ Class Library, as in Figure 17.3. Call it `Greeter`.

Figure 17.3
To create a component, start with a Managed Class Library project.

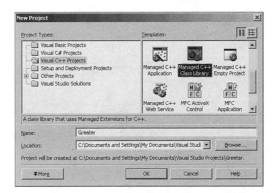

In Class View, double-click the `Class1` class to edit the .h file that was generated for you. Add this line before the namespace definition:

```
#using <mscorlib.dll>
```

As in the HelloWorld application, these lines make all the .NET framework code available to you, and enable you to refer to those classes simply by their names instead of with the System namespace specified each time.

While you are editing this class, change its name from `Class1` to `Greeter` by changing the class declaration so it reads like this:

```
public __gc class Greeter
```

To add the `Greet()` function to this component, right-click `Greeter` in the class view and choose Add, Add Function as shown in Figure 17.4.

The `Greet()` function should return a string that can be passed to `Console::WriteLine()`. The .NET class called String would seem to be perfect for this purpose. However, .NET types are managed types. Among other things, this means that the framework takes care of memory management for you, with the help of the garbage collector. As a result, you are not allowed to create an instance of a managed type on the stack. For example, this line of code will not compile:

```
String s;
```

Figure 17.4
Add a function to the
Greeter class.

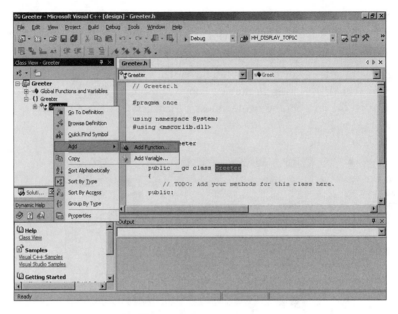

If you try it, you'll get this error:

```
error C3149: 'System::String' : illegal use of managed type 'System::String'; did
you forget a '*'?
```

Rather than a String, the Greet() function should return a String*, which is a pointer to a String. The framework manages the String object. Fill in the Add Member Function Wizard as shown in Figure 17.5. Enter the Return Type as **String***. (You have to type it yourself; it is not in the dropdown.) Enter the Function name as **Greet**. Ignore the parameter type that the wizard suggests, because there are no parameters. Leave the access as Public. Click Finish to add the function.

Figure 17.5
The function is called
Greet, and returns a
pointer to a .NET
String object.

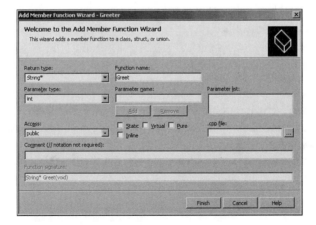

Edit Greeter.h so that the class definition looks like this:

```
public __gc class Greeter
{
public:
   String* Greet(void)
   {
         return S"Hello from a component";
   }
};
```

There are some extra keywords here that should be explained. On the class definition, note that you are not just defining a class. The keyword public here means that the class will be public—it will be available to other .NET components and applications. Because the plan is to use Greeter from within HelloWorld, it's good that the wizard made it generally accessible. The keyword __gc indicates that the class will be garbage collected; in other words, it will be a managed type.

Tip

You can learn more about garbage collection and managed types in Chapter 20, "Managed and Unmanaged C++."

The return statement uses the literal modifier S to build a .NET string from an ordinary quoted string. It's similar to writing 0L to mean a long literal with the value 0, even though 0 would fit into a short data type.

Build your component by choosing Build, Build Solution. Correct any typographical mistakes. A successful build creates your assembly as Greeter.dll.

Use the Windows Explorer to browse to the folder where you created the project. Look in the Debug folder, and you should see the DLL, as shown in Figure 17.6. If not, choose Tools, Folder Options from the folder menu in Windows 2000. (Choose View, Options in Windows NT.) On the View tab, make sure you are not hiding DLL files. Select the file, and with Ctrl+C, copy it. Now browse to the Debug folder of HelloWorld and paste a copy of the DLL into the folder. Perhaps you've heard about .NET and the simple "xcopy deploy?" This is what you've just done. By copying the DLL into the HelloWorld folder, you can use all the classes in it as easily as if they were part of the HelloWorld project. Chapter 24, shows how to make a component more globally available.

The changes to HelloWorld are not very extensive. Switch back to the Visual Studio instance where you are working on HelloWorld. The first thing to do is tell HelloWorld about Greeter. That information is all in the assembly, so you need to add only this line:

```
#using "Debug\Greeter.dll"
```

Put it directly after the #using that is already in HelloWorld.cpp. Build the project.

Figure 17.6
The component assembly appears to be a DLL, and is all contained within a single file.

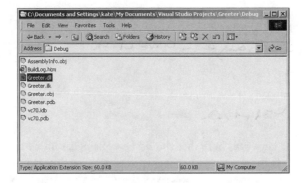

To call the `Greet()` function, you need an instance of the `Greeter` class. You can't just declare it, though, like this:

```
Greeter g;
```

`Greeter`, like `String`, is a managed type and you're not allowed to create instances on the stack in this way. Instead, use the `new` operator:

```
Greeter::Greeter* g = new Greeter::Greeter();
```

Notice the name of the component is not just `Greeter`, but `Greeter:: Greeter`. The component, `Greeter`, is contained in a namespace, also called `Greeter`. To use it, you call it by its full name, including the namespace. Add the preceding line at the beginning of the `_tmain()` method. Then type in this line:

```
Console::WriteLine(g->Greet() );
```

Remove the old call to `WriteLine()`. Build and run the application as you did before, and you should be greeted (see Figure 17.7) by your own component! Press Enter to let the application finish and exit.

If you've done any COM programming, or any other kind of component-based programming, what just happened may seem a bit too easy, as though you've skipped a step. But that's the whole point of .NET: calling a service offered by a component is as simple as calling a method of a class that is defined inside your project.

Figure 17.7
An application and a component can work together seamlessly.

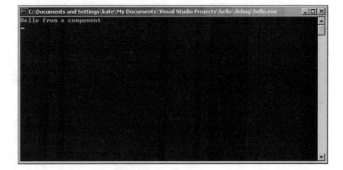

DESIGNING A USEFUL .NET COMPONENT

Saying hello is a traditional first application, and one that's easy to put together in Managed C++. The pattern you've just put together is one you can use time and time again. The component is in a DLL created as a Managed C++ Class Library project; it's used by an EXE created as a Managed C++ Application. You've seen how to make the DLL functions available to the EXE with a simple #using statement, and you've seen that the classes defined in that DLL are simple and easy to access.

But what about a component that's a bit more challenging? What about a component that could actually be used in a real application? In this section, you'll walk through the design decisions for a component that validates zip codes. In some future application, zip codes might be entered into a form (either a Web form or a WinForms application) or retrieved from a database, and this component could be used to confirm they are valid zip codes.

The rules for zip codes are pretty straightforward:

- Either 5 numbers, or 5 numbers, a dash, and 4 numbers are used in the code.
- No letters or punctuation other than the dash can be used, and only one dash.

CH
17

You might want to relax the rule about having a dash between the 5-digit part and the 4-digit part, perhaps to allow a space. You might also want to do something clever that cross-checks the state and the zip code. Those sorts of details can always be added later: these two rules will be just fine for demonstrating a useful .NET component.

To complete the design of the component, you need to give it a name, and give all its methods names and parameters. In addition, .NET methods have meaningful return values. If you've worked in COM before, you know that COM calls return an HRESULT that you can interpret to see whether the call worked. Any other return values you might want (such as the answer to a calculation) have to be sent back by changing the value of a parameter you passed in to the COM call. This makes COM programming a little awkward and uncomfortable for many developers. Not so in .NET! The methods you implement can return the answers they calculate. To indicate errors, methods throw .NET exceptions, which you can catch in the calling code.

It's tempting to design this component to throw an exception if one of the format rules is broken. However, throwing and catching an exception carries a performance penalty. One of my personal rules of thumb, for both C++ exceptions and .NET exceptions, is never to throw an exception for a predicatable user error. If the system is out of memory or the hard drive is full, an exception is the better way to go. You aren't expecting to run out of memory and it's wasteful to constantly check for it. User error, on the other hand, will always be with us.

A better approach, because user errors are expected, is to return a string. If the string is "OK", the zip code passed. If it's anything else, the zip code failed, and the string contains the error message. There are more efficient approaches than this, and approaches that work better in a multi-lingual application, but for your first useful component, this approach will do.

The component will be called ZipCheck. It will have one method, called Check(), that takes a String* and returns a String*.

Before you can begin coding, it's a good idea to know how you're going to accomplish your task. For example, what's a simple way to see whether a string contains only numbers? You could search for the character *a* in the string, and if that's not there, search for *b*, and so on, but that's going to be boring to type—and slow. Here's a neat shortcut: ask the compiler to convert the string to a number. Then convert the number back to a string. If it's the same as the original string, you can conclude there were no letters or punctuation, other than a decimal place, in the string. If you convert it to an integer and back, you also know there was no decimal place. There is a problem if the first digit of the string is zero—the conversion from number back to string would never add a leading zero. You can handle that by padding the converted string with some leading zeros before the comparison.

If the length of the string is five, and the conversion from string to number and back to string worked, you can confirm it's okay. If the length of the string is 10, you can split the string into the "first five" and "last four" and do this test on each part. Add a check for the character in between them, and your work is complete.

IMPLEMENTING A ZIP CODE FORMAT CHECKER

In the copy of Visual Studio you were using for Greeter, choose File, Close Solution. Then choose File, New, Project. Select Visual C++ projects on the left. On the right, choose a Managed C++ Class Library, as you did when creating Greeter. Call it ZipCheck.

Expand Class View, and double-click on the Class1 class. As before, add this line before the class definition:

```
#using <mscorlib.dll>
```

Change the name of the class to ZipCheck. Right-click on the ZipCheck class and choose Add, Add Function. Fill in the Add Function Wizard as shown in Figure 17.8, calling the

Figure 17.8
Add a Check function to the ZipCheck component.

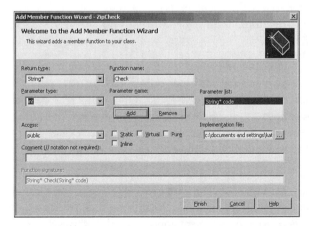

function Check with a return type of String* and a single parameter of type String* called code. Click the Add button immediately below the parameter name box to add the parameter to the function.

Listing 17.1 shows the code for the Check() function. It's quite complex, but the overall structure is like this:

```
String* Check(String* code)
{
        //set up variables
        switch (code->get_Length())
    {
    case 5:
            // deal with 5 digit string
        break;
    case 10:
            // deal with 5 and 4 digit string
    break;
    default:
            error =  S"invalid length";
    }
    return error;
}
```

LISTING 17.1   ZIPCHECK.H—Check()

```
String* Check(String* code)
{
    String* error = S"OK";
    Int32 number;
    String* compare;
    String* firstfive;
    String* lastfour;
    switch (code->get_Length())
    {
    case 5:
            number = Convert::ToInt32 (code);
            compare = number.ToString();
            compare->PadLeft(5,L'0');
            if (!code->Equals(compare))
            {
                    error =  S"Non numeric characters in 5 digit code";
            }
    break;
    case 10:
            firstfive = code->Substring(0,5);
            number = Convert::ToInt32 (firstfive);
            compare = number.ToString();
            compare = compare->PadLeft(5,L'0');
            if (!firstfive->Equals(compare))
                    error =   S"Non numeric characters in first 5 digits of zip+4
code";
            lastfour = code->Substring(6,4);
            number = Convert::ToInt32 (lastfour);
            compare = number.ToString();
            compare = compare->PadLeft(4,L'0');
```

LISTING 17.1   CONTINUED

```
            if (!lastfour->Equals(compare))
            {
                    error =  S"Non numeric characters in last 4 digits of zip+4 code
➡";
            }
            if (!code->Substring(5,1)->Equals(S"-"))
                    error =  S"Character between first 5 and last 4 is not -";
    break;
    default:
            error =  S"invalid length";
    }
    return error;
}
```

Rather than converting the string to a number, the .NET approach is to build a number from the string. The static `ToInt32()` function of the Convert class is used for this. To convert the number back to a string, use the structure's `ToString()` function. The String class has a useful `PadLeft` function that pads the string with leading zeroes, but you should know two things about it:

- It takes a wide character, so use the L literal modifier to send in the long version of '0'.

- It doesn't change the string itself, but returns a changed copy, which this code puts over the old version of the string.

Finally, to compare two strings you can't use the familiar == operator. After all, these are String pointers, and you'll just be comparing their addresses. Instead, you have to use the rather ugly approach shown here, calling the `Equals()` member function of one String* and passing it the other String* for a comparison.

Build the component and correct any typos, and you're ready to test it.

IMPLEMENTING A COMPONENT TEST HARNESS

Just as you tested Greeter by using the existing HelloWorld application to exercise Greeter's functionality, so too you can write a test harness for ZipCheck that will pass in various zip codes and see whether they are valid. A test harness is an application that doesn't have a purpose beyond testing a particular component. Typically it calls all the methods of the component and prints out some results.

Close whatever solutions you have open so that you have just one instance of Visual Studio running, with nothing open. Choose File, New, Project. On the New project dialog, select Visual C++ projects, and on the right side of the dialog, select Managed C++ Application. Name the project ZipTest, and click OK to create it.

After the #using directive that is already in place, add this one:

```
#using "Debug\ZipCheck.dll"
```

This would be a good time to copy ZipCheck.dll from the Debug folder under the ZipCheck project to the Debug folder under the ZipTest project. If necessary, create the Debug folder yourself.

Now add the code to exercise the method. I decided to test four zip codes:

- 46290-1097 is the zip code for Que Books in Indianapolis. It's an example of a zip+4 code.

- 20500 is the White House in Washington, DC. It's an example of a simple 5-digit zip.

- M5W 1E6 is a valid Canadian postal code that I expect to fail the validation as a zip code.

- 04112-0001 is a valid code with leading zeroes in both parts, to test the PadLeft() code.

The full code for _tmain() is shown in Listing 17.2. Just as HelloWorld created a Greeter* with a call to new, this code creates a ZipCheck* with a call to new, and uses that pointer repeatedly to validate a variety of codes. For each code, _tmain() echoes it to the console, then tests it and sends the error message to the console. The results are shown in Figure 17.9.

CH
17

LISTING 17.2   ZIPTEST.CPP—main()

```cpp
int _tmain(void)
{
   String* QueBooks = S"46290-1097";
   ZipCheck::ZipCheck* zip = new ZipCheck::ZipCheck();

   Console::Write("Checking ");
   Console::WriteLine(QueBooks);
   Console::WriteLine(zip->Check(QueBooks) );

   String* WhiteHouse = S"20500";

   Console::Write("Checking ");
   Console::WriteLine(WhiteHouse);
   Console::WriteLine(zip->Check(WhiteHouse) );

   String* BadCode= S"M5W 1E6"; // A valid Canadian Postal Code

   Console::Write("Checking ");
   Console::WriteLine(BadCode);
   Console::WriteLine(zip->Check(BadCode) );

   String* POBox1PortlandMaine= S"04112-0001"; //leading zeroes

   Console::Write("Checking ");
   Console::WriteLine(POBox1PortlandMaine);
   Console::WriteLine(zip->Check(POBox1PortlandMaine) );
   Console::ReadLine();

   return 0;

}
```

Figure 17.9
Test several different codes to be sure all the code is exercised by the test harness.

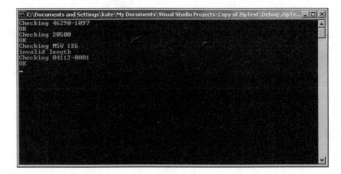

Build and run your version of ZipTest to be sure it works for you, too.

GENERALIZING THE ZIP CODE FORMAT CHECKER

One of the samples in ZipTest is a valid Canadian postal code. If you're writing a global e-commerce application, not all of your customers will have zip codes. Some will have postal codes in Canadian format, others in British format, and so on.

Several designs can handle this for you. One is to add more functions to ZipCheck called CheckCanadian(), CheckBritish(), and so on. The component gets larger and larger when you do so, and also gets a little harder to use.

Another design involves creating similar components, each with a function called Check, which knows the rules for other kinds of postal codes. The CanadaPostCheck component would know the rules for Canadian postal codes, for example. This is a more scalable solution; you install only those components you are likely to use. Changes to the rules in one country require you to reinstall only a single changed component.

These similar components can be created entirely independently, but because they will all have a Check function, they may well have some other aspects in common. It makes sense to use inheritance to maximize reuse. In the .NET world, using inheritance to extend components is as simple and easy as using it with classes in C++. You can even, as you'll see in upcoming chapters, inherit across languages!

I decided to call the base component, from which all the individual components will be derived, PostCodeCheck. ZipCheck will inherit from this base component. There is a function called Check() in the base component, which will be overridden in ZipCheck, and there is also a Test() method that returns true or false rather than a string. This method uses Check() and is implemented only in the base component, PostCodeCheck.

Here's how to build the new component. You'll find it simpler to have two instances of Visual Studio .NET open as you go through this process, to simplify copying code from one component to another. First, create a new project, a Managed C++ Library called PostCodeCheck. Change the name of the class from Class1 to PostCodeChecker. You could add a function using the wizards, but you can also do it by hand. Inside the class definition, add this code to PostCheckCode.h:

```
public:
   virtual String* Check(String* code)
   {
          String* error = S"OK";
          return error;
   }
```

Note that `Check()` is now a virtual function. This means that derived-class (such as ZipCheck) versions of it will be run whenever possible.

To demonstrate inheritance at work, and to make this component more useful when a text error message is not required, add this function to the class as well, right after `Check()`'s closing brace:

```
Boolean Test(String* code)
{
   Boolean ret = false;
   String* error = Check(code);
   if (error->Equals(S"OK"))
   {
          ret = true;
   }
   return ret;
}
```

This function returns a Boolean value: true or false. It doesn't contain any postal-code rules at all—the work is delegated to the `Check` function. Every component that inherits from PostCodeCheck will have a `Test` function and a `Check` function, and if the programmer for that component doesn't implement either function, the code here in the base class will be used.

Build PostCodeCheck to be sure you haven't made any typos, then copy the DLL from the Debug folder of PostCodeCheck to the Debug folder of ZipCheck. Now open ZipCheck (or switch to the Visual Studio in which ZipCheck is open) and make just a few small changes.

After the `#using` added originally by the wizard, add this line:

```
#using "Debug\PostCodeCheck.dll"
```

Post Check Code

This ensures that the .NET framework can find the implementation of the base class for ZipCheck. Next, change the first line of the class declaration slightly:

```
public __gc class ZipCheck : public PostCodeCheck::PostCodeChecker
```

This is the ordinary C++ syntax for inheriting, although you may not have seen a namespace used in the name of the base class before. It's certainly not how you'd inherit an interface or functionality in a classic COM application. But this is how simply it's done in .NET. That's all you have to do. Now build ZipCheck to be sure it still works.

To test the new component hierarchy, change ZipTest to use both the `Check()` function, which is implemented in ZipCheck, and the new `Test()` function, which is implemented only in PostCodeCheck. Start by copying both ZipCheck.dll and PostCodeCheck.dll into the Debug folder of ZipTest. Then add another `#using` statement into ZipTest, after the others:

```
#using "Debug\PostCodeCheck.dll"
```

Clear out some of the tests, and add a call to Test(), so that _tmain() looks like Listing 7.3.

LISTING 17.3   ZIPTEST.CPP—REVISED _Tmain()

```
int _tmain(void)
{
    String* QueBooks = S"46290-1097";
    ZipCheck::ZipCheck* zip = new ZipCheck::ZipCheck();

    Console::Write("Checking ");
    Console::WriteLine(QueBooks);
    Console::WriteLine(zip->Check(QueBooks) );

    if (zip->Test(QueBooks))
            Console::WriteLine(S"passed");
    else
            Console::WriteLine(S"failed");

    String* BadCode= S"M5W 1E6"; // A valid Canadian Postal Code

    Console::Write("Checking ");
    Console::WriteLine(BadCode);
    Console::WriteLine(zip->Check(BadCode) );

    if (zip->Test(BadCode))
            Console::WriteLine(S"passed");
    else
            Console::WriteLine(S"failed");

    Console::ReadLine();
    return 0;
}
```

Build and run the application, and you should see output like that shown in Figure 17.10, proving that both Check() and Test() work. Because the Check() in the base class always returns OK, you know the Check() from the derived class, ZipCheck, is being used both when ZipTest calls it directly and also when Test() calls it. That's because Check() is a virtual function in the base class.

Figure 17.10
Code from both the base class and the derived class can be called from the test harness.

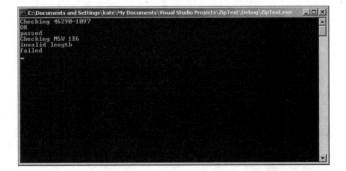

You'll be seeing ZipCheck and PostCodeCheck again in upcoming chapters. They form the start of a component hierarchy that can be used in a variety of contexts.

FROM HERE

This chapter introduced you to .NET programming and showed how to create a .NET application and a .NET component. It began a component hierarchy using a base component written in C++. The next chapter, "Integrating with Visual Basic," demonstrates writing a component in Visual Basic that inherits from this base C++ component. You'll see how easy it is to do cross-language development in Visual Studio .NET. This theme continues in Chapter 19, "Integrating with C#," which follows a similar pattern to Chapter 18, but uses C#, the new .NET programming language based on C++.

CH

17

INTEGRATING WITH VISUAL BASIC

In this chapter

USING A C++ COMPONENT FROM VISUAL BASIC

For many years, developers have been able to write programs in a mixture of languages, or create applications by combining parts that were written in different languages. It's a powerful and useful approach to software development. But it hasn't always been easy.

In Chapter 17 you created a .NET component in Visual C++ and then used that component in another Visual C++ application just as though it were an ordinary C++ class. In this chapter, you'll treat that very same component as though it were a Visual Basic class.

> **Note**
>
> As demonstrated in Appendix C, "The Visual Studio User Interface, Menus, and Visual Studio," you can adjust the look and feel of Visual Studio by choosing a *profile*. The illustrations throughout this book were taken while my copy of Visual Studio was using a Visual C++ Developer profile. That same profile was used in this chapter. If you're a Visual Basic developer, your screen layout may be a little different.

To create a Visual Basic application that can use the .NET component, start by choosing File, New, Project. Select Visual Basic Projects. As shown in Figure 18.1, select Windows Application and name the project VBZipTest.

Figure 18.1
Create a Windows application in Visual Basic.

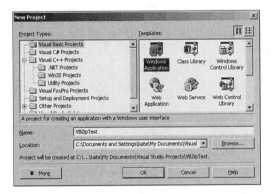

When you create a Windows application in Visual Basic, you are given a form to edit. Before you do so, you need to make the .NET component available to this project. Copy zipcheck.dll and postcodecheck.dll from the Debug folder under ZipCheck into the bin folder beneath the project folder that has just been created for VBZipTest.

Choose Project, Add Reference. Click the Browse button, double-click the bin folder, and you will see the two DLLs in the folder for this project, as shown in Figure 18.2. Select both of them and click Open. The References dialog for the project now shows both names at the bottom of the dialog, as shown in Figure 18.3. Click OK to add these references to the project. If you expand the References node under VBZipTest in the Solution view, you will see PostCodeCheck and ZipCheck listed as References for the project, as shown in Figure 18.4.

Figure 18.2
After you copy the DLLs to the project folder, they are available to be added as references.

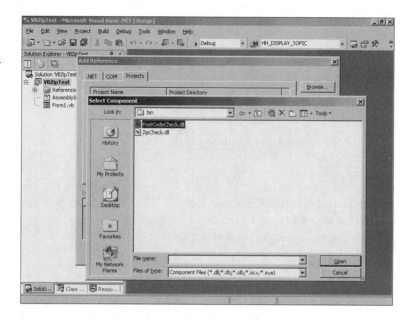

Figure 18.3
Confirm the references to be added.

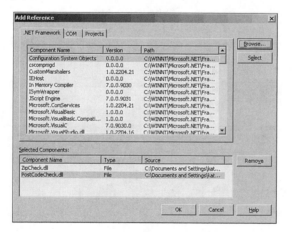

To build the form interface of this Windows application, you use the new WinForms functionality of Visual Studio .NET. WinForms is a library of components that you use to build a Windows user interface. For experienced Visual Basic developers, it looks very much like the way you have always built user interfaces.

Figure 18.4
The new references are shown in Solution Explorer.

Choose View, Toolbox to get a palette of interface components you can put on the form. If the Windows Forms section is not expanded, click it to expand it. Drag an textbox, a button, and a label onto the form. Click each in turn and use the Properties window at the lower left to adjust the following properties:

- The textbox name should be "code."
- The button name and text properties should both be "CheckZip."
- The label name should be "errormessage."

Arrange the user interface components as you see in Figure 18.5.

Figure 18.5
Create a simple user interface.

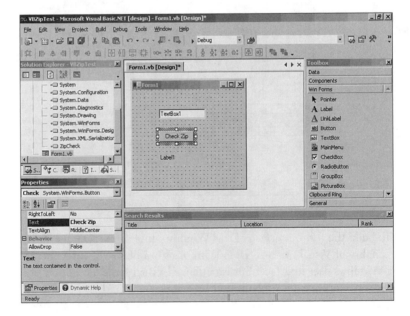

Double-click the button to edit the code that will run when it is clicked. Edit the `CheckZip_Click` subroutine that was generated for you so that it looks like this:

```
Protected Sub CheckZip_Click(ByVal sender As Object, ByVal e As System.EventArgs)

    Dim zip As New ZipCheck.ZipCheck()
    errormessage.Text = zip.Check(code.Text)

End Sub
```

As you type, notice how the auto-complete Intellisense offers you functions from the `ZipCheck` component, as in Figure 18.6. This code gets the `Text` property of the edit box and passes it to the `Check` method of the `ZipCheck` component. The string returned by `ZipCheck` is used to set the `Text` property of the label on the form.

Figure 18.6
After your component is known to Visual Studio, Intellisense reminds you of its functions.

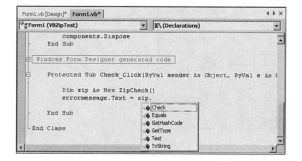

CH
18

If you build and run this application now, the initial values of the text box and label will not be very helpful. Scroll up in the code to the New sub (you may have to expand some code that is collapsed in the outlined view), and edit it so that it reads like this:

```
Public Sub New()
    MyBase.New()

    'This call is required by the Windows Form Designer.
    InitializeComponent()

    code.Text = "Enter a zip code"
    errormessage.Text = ""
End Sub
```

Build the project by choosing Build, Build Solution, then run it by choosing Debug, Start. The initial dialog, resembling Figure 18.7, will appear.

Enter a few codes. Figure 18.8 and 18.9 show a successful and a failed test. Close the form with the X in the upper right corner when you're finished testing.

Using a .NET component from Visual Basic is so simple, you're likely to forget that your Visual Basic application is running code that was written in Visual C++.

Figure 18.7
The application prompts for a postal code.

Figure 18.8
The label passes along the error message to the user.

Figure 18.9
You can try any string you like and pass it to ZipCheck.

EXTENDING A C++ COMPONENT IN VISUAL BASIC

The ZipCheck component that VBZipTest uses is part of a hierarchy. The base class of the hierarchy, PostCodeCheck, is written in Managed C++ and has two functions:

- Check(). Takes a String*. The base class version always returns OK. The expectation is that all derived classes will implement their own checks.

- Test(). Takes a String* and uses Check() to check it, then returns True or False. Derived classes are unlikely to override it.

One of the real "wow" moments for anyone meeting .NET for the first time has to be cross-language inheriting. Follow along and create a Visual Basic class that actually inherits from a class written in C++.

The class will be another .NET component in the PostCodeCheck hierarchy. This one will be called JapanCodeCheck and it will check that a string meets the rules for Japanese postal codes, which consist of three digits, a dash, and then four digits. For example, 107-8503 is the postal code of the Canadian embassy in Tokyo.

To create the component, start by opening a new copy of Visual Studio. Choose File, New, Project. Select Visual Basic Projects, and choose Class Library. Name the project JapanCodeCheck, as shown in Figure 18.10.

Figure 18.10
Create a Visual Basic Class Library project.

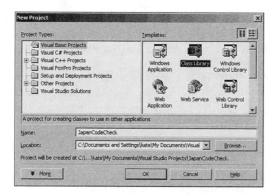

The project is created for you, along with an almost empty file. Copy PostCodeCheck.dll into the bin folder beneath the project folder and add a reference to it, just as you did when using ZipCheck from the VBZipTest project. In the code editor, which shows you Class1, find the lines like this:

```
Public Class Class1
```

This line defines the .NET component you are building. Edit it so it is two lines that read like this:

```
Public Class JapanCodeCheck
    Inherits PostCodeCheck.PostCodeChecker
```

This changes the name of the class and changes the base class to the postal code base component developed in Managed C++ as part of Chapter 17. Because you added the reference to postcodecheck.dll, PostCodeCheck.PostCodeChecker is one of the choices for a base class that is offered as you type this code.

Select JapanCodeCheck in Class view, and expand it. Expand Bases and Interfaces, then expand PostCodeChecker. You can see the functions that were defined in the base class (Figure 18.11). In this component, you are going to override the Check() function but not the Test() function.

The easiest way to override this function is to simply type the code into the editor. Add the code in Listing 18.1 after the inherits line and before the existing End Class line.

Figure 18.11
Class View shows the interface of the base class, which was written in Managed C++.

LISTING 18.1 JAPANCODECHECK.VB—Check()

```vb
Overrides Function Check(ByVal code As String) As String

        Dim errormessage As String = "OK"
        Dim number As Integer
        Dim compstring As String
        Dim firstthree As String
        Dim lastfour As String

    If code.Length = 8 Then
        firstthree = code.substring(0, 3)
        number = Convert.ToInt32(firstthree)
        compstring = Convert.ToString(number)
        Dim zero As Char = "0"
        compstring = compstring.PadLeft(3, zero)
        If firstthree <> compstring Then
            errormessage = "Non numeric characters in first 3 digits"
        End If

        lastfour = code.Substring(4, 4)
        number = Convert.ToInt32(lastfour)
        compstring = Convert.tostring(number)
        compstring = compstring.PadLeft(4, zero)
        If lastfour <> compstring Then
            errormessage = "Non numeric characters in last 4 digits"
        End If
        If code.Substring(3, 1) <> "-" Then
            errormessage = "Character between first 3 and last 4 is not -"
        End If
    Else
        errormessage = "invalid length"

    End If
    Return errormessage


    End Function
```

There are several important differences between this code and the code in Chapter 17 that tested a zip code. Of course, the valid format is slightly different, so you'll see different numbers passed to Substring() or PadLeft(), but that's to be expected. The language-specific differences are:

- What was a String* in Managed C++ is a String in Visual Basic. It's still managed and garbage-collected; it's just not treated as a pointer.

- The words *error* and *compare* are reserved words in Visual Basic, so the variables became errormessage and compstring.

- The conversions are done with the help of a Convert object rather than calling functions of the Int32 structure or the String class.

One other thing to note is the Overrides keyword in the first line of the function. This indicates to Visual Basic that this is an override of the Check() function from the base class. Without it, you will get an error message insisting that you add the keyword. This ensures that no one accidentally overrides a base class function and changes the behavior of a system.

Build the component and correct any typos or other errors.

To test the component, you can make a few changes to the VBZipTest project. Start by copying japancodecheck.dll from the bin folder under the JapanCodeCheck folder to the bin folder under the VBZipTest folder. Then switch back to the copy of Visual Studio in which you were working on VBZipTest. Add a reference to japancodecheck.dll.

Switch from editing code to working on the form by clicking the tab at the top labeled Form1.vb [Design]. Add another button to the form, and change the text and name properties to CheckJapan. Double-click it to edit the code. It's just as simple as the code for the CheckZip button:

```
    Private Sub CheckJapan_Click(ByVal sender As System.Object, ByVal e As
➥System.EventArgs) Handles CheckJapan.Click
        Dim japan As New JapanCodeCheck.JapanCodeCheck()
        errormessage.Text = japan.Check(code.Text)
End Sub
```

Build and run the revised VBZipTest and try testing a Japanese code, as shown in Figures 18.12 and 18.13.

Figure 18.12
Valid Japanese postal codes pass the test.

Figure 18.13
Valid zip codes are
not valid Japanese
postal codes.

USING A VISUAL BASIC COMPONENT FROM VISUAL C++

Let's complete the circle of cross-language development by using the Visual Basic component, JapanCodeCheck, from a Visual C++ application.

In the copy of Visual Studio where you are working on VBZipTest, Choose File, Close
Solution. Then choose File, New, Project. On the left, select Visual C++ Projects, and on
the right, choose a Managed C++ application. Call it JapanCodeTest, as shown in Figure
18.14. Build the project by choosing Build, Build Solution to create the Debug folder, then
copy postcodecheck.dll and japancodecheck.dll into the Debug folder under the
JapanCodeTest project folder.

Figure 18.14
Create a Managed
C++ application to
test the Visual Basic
component that
inherits code from a
Managed C++
component.

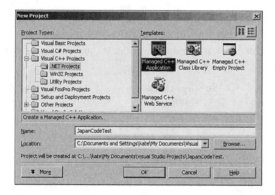

In the Class View, expand JapanCodeTest, then expand Global Functions And Variables.
Double-click _tmain() to edit JapanCodeTest.cpp. Add the following code before the
_tmain() function:

```
#using "Debug\PostCodeCheck.dll"
#using "Debug\JapanCodeCheck.dll"
```

As in previous managed C++ projects, these lines of code tell the .NET framework and
Visual Studio where to find the functions you'll be using from the component. It's equivalent to adding a reference in the Visual Basic project. You might be interested to note that

Add Reference does not appear on the Project menu while you're working on a Visual C++ project. You have to add the `#using` statement by hand.

With the references added, you can enter the code for `_tmain()`. You might want to copy and paste the `_tmain()` function from the Managed C++ project ZipTest, created in Chapter 17, to use as a starting point. Listing 18.2 shows how `_tmain()` should look:

LISTING 18.2   A TEST HARNESS FOR JAPANCODECHECK

```
int _tmain(void)
{
   String* Embassy = S"107-8503"; //Canadian Embassy in Tokyo
   JapanCodeCheck::JapanCodeCheck* japan = new JapanCodeCheck::JapanCodeCheck();

   Console::Write("Checking ");
   Console::WriteLine(Embassy);
   Console::WriteLine(japan->Check(Embassy) );

   if (japan->Test(Embassy))
         Console::WriteLine(S"passed");
   else
         Console::WriteLine(S"failed");

   String* BadCode= S"M5W 1E6"; // A valid Canadian Postal Code

   Console::Write("Checking ");
   Console::WriteLine(BadCode);
   Console::WriteLine(japan->Check(BadCode) );

   if (japan->Test(BadCode))
         Console::WriteLine(S"passed");
   else
         Console::WriteLine(S"failed");

   Console::ReadLine();
   return 0;

}
```

CH

18

Because JapanCodeCheck is in the JapanCodeCheck namespace, this code refers to it by its full name, using the scope resolution operator, ::, to separate the namespace name from the class name.

Figure 18.15 shows this code running. It's kind of fun to see the multiple languages in action: Managed C++ code in JapanCodeTest is calling Visual Basic code for `Check()`. Better still, Managed C++ code calls other Managed C++ for the base class version of `Test()`, which then calls the overriden version of `Check()` in Visual Basic. It all works together seamlessly. You don't have to know anything about the differences between the languages; you just use whatever language is right for you.

Figure 18.15
The Visual Basic component works perfectly from Managed C++.

FROM HERE

Cross-language development is an amazing concept. When I first heard of it, it seemed almost unbelievable. Yet when you do it, the process is so simple and ordinary that you almost don't notice what you're doing. Even cross-language inheritance doesn't appear spectacular. There's no special keyword to indicate you're using this feature, no switches or settings you need to adjust. But don't let that fool you, this is powerful stuff, and it's almost certainly going to change the way you develop software.

In the next chapter, "Integrating with C#," you'll see how to do in C# the things this chapter demonstrated for Visual Basic. You'll also see how to use Web forms to create an ASP.NET application in C#.

CHAPTER 19

INTEGRATING WITH C#

In this chapter

USING A C++ COMPONENT FROM C#

Every programming language has its strengths and weaknesses. One of the advantages of Managed C++ is that it's familiar to working C++ developers. Another is the total control: Developers turn on only the features they wish to use. C# is a simpler language, quicker to learn than C++ if you don't already know C++. The tradeoff is that you can write only managed code, and can't achieve the flexibility and control of C++. However, you don't need to make a choice between C++ and C#—you can use both.

In Chapter 17, "Getting Started with .NET," you created a .NET component in Visual C++ and then used that component in another Visual C++ application just as though it were an ordinary C++ class. In this chapter, you'll treat that very same component as though it were a C# class.

> **Note**
>
> As demonstrated in Appendix C, "The Visual Studio User Interface," you can adjust the look and feel of Visual Studio by choosing a *profile*. The illustrations throughout this book were taken while my copy of Visual Studio was using a Visual C++ Developer profile. That same profile was used in this chapter. If you're a C# developer, your screen layout may be a little different.

To create a C# application that can use the .NET component, start by choosing File, New, Project. Select C# Projects, as in Figure 19.1. Select Console Application and name the project CSZipTest.

Figure 19.1
Create a console application in C#.

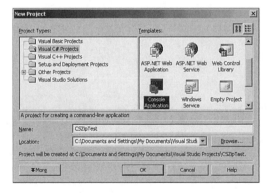

A class called Class1 is created for you, with a constructor that does nothing, and a Main() method, which is equivalent to the global main() function in the C++ ZipTest project. In C#, there are no global functions.

Before adding code to the Main() method of Class1, you should change the name of the class. You can see that the name appears several times in class1.cs, and is used for the name of the file as well. Rather than changing all these places by hand, let Visual Studio do it. (After all, it was Visual Studio that didn't ask what the class should be called before generating the code.) In Class View, expand the project and select Class1. In the Properties window, find the Name property and change it to ZipTest. Press Enter and, as Figure 19.2 shows, the change is made throughout your code, except for the file name.

Figure 19.2
Use the Properties Window to change a class's name, and Visual Studio ripples the name change throughout the project.

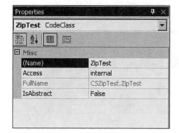

Now you're ready to add code to Main() that uses ZipCheck, the Managed C++ component created in Chapter 17. Start by making the .NET component available to this project: copy zipcheck.dll and postcodecheck.dll into the bin folder beneath the project folder that was just created for you. In Visual Studio, choose Project, Add Reference to bring up the Add Reference dialog. Click Browse on this dialog, browse into the bin folder, and you see the two DLLs, as shown in Figure 19.3. Select them both and click Open, and their names appear in the lower part of the Add Reference dialog, as shown in Figure 19.4. Click OK to add the references.

Figure 19.3
Select the DLLs in which ZipCheck and its base class are defined.

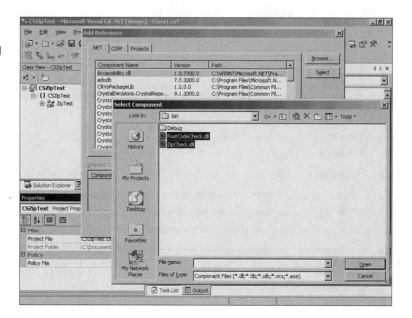

Figure 19.4
Confirm the two references to be added.

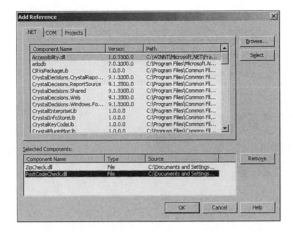

In the Solution Explorer, expand the References node. As Figure 19.5 illustrates, the two new references now appear.

Figure 19.5
ZipCheck and PostCodeCheck now appear as references for the C# project.

Listing 19.1 shows the code for the Main() method of the ZipTest class. It illustrates several important differences between Managed C++ and C#:

- What was a String* in Managed C++ is a string in C#. Pointer syntax isn't used, and the class name is all lowercase.

- The literal modifier S is not needed to change quoted strings into .NET strings.

- Calls to Console::WriteLine() in Managed C++ become calls to Console.WriteLine() in C#. Static class methods are called with a dot between the class name and the function name, rather than the scope resolution operator.

- The ZipCheck* in Managed C++ is just a ZipCheck, and calls to its methods are set off with a dot, not an arrow.

LISTING 19.1   CLASS1.CS—ZipTest.Main()

```
static void Main(string[] args)
{
        string QueBooks = "46290-1097";
        ZipCheck.ZipCheck zip = new ZipCheck.ZipCheck();

    Console.Write("Checking ");
    Console.WriteLine(QueBooks);
    Console.WriteLine(zip.Check(QueBooks) );

    string WhiteHouse = "20500";

    Console.Write("Checking ");
    Console.WriteLine(WhiteHouse);
    Console.WriteLine(zip.Check(WhiteHouse) );

    string BadCode= "M5W 1E6"; // A valid Canadian Postal Code

    Console.Write("Checking ");
    Console.WriteLine(BadCode);
    Console.WriteLine(zip.Check(BadCode) );

        string POBox1PortlandMaine= "04112-0001"; //leading zeroes

    Console.Write("Checking ");
    Console.WriteLine(POBox1PortlandMaine);
    Console.WriteLine(zip.Check(POBox1PortlandMaine) );
    Console.ReadLine();

}
```

Edit the CSZipTest code in class1.cs until it matches the code for Main() shown in Listing 19.1. Because this project has had references added to ZipCheck and PostCodeCheck, Intellisense provides a list of class members as you type, as shown in Figure 19.6. Check() is defined in ZipCheck and Test() is defined only in PostCodeCheck.

Build the project by choosing Build, Build Solution. Correct any typos, then run it by choosing Debug, Start. You should see output like that shown in Figure 19.7. Press Enter to allow the run to finish.

Although rewriting the test code in C# rather than C++ is a little tricky, there's really no work involved in using the Managed C++ component—after the references are added it feels just like using any other class.

USING A C++ COMPONENT FROM AN ASP.NET PAGE

Because a console application in C# is not very exciting, why not try a simple ASP.NET page that uses the Managed C++ component, ZipCheck? Separating business logic into reusable components is a great way to save programming time and effort.

Figure 19.6
Visual Studio knows the functions available in `ZipCheck` and its base class, `PostCodeCheck`.

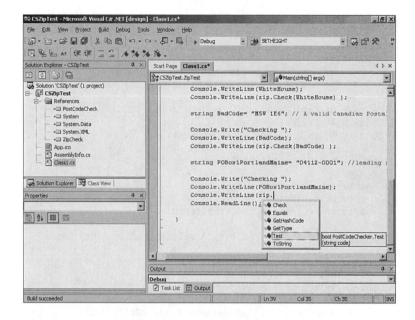

Figure 19.7
The output from the C# version of ZipTest is just like the Managed C++ output in Chapter 17.

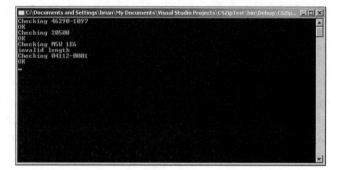

In Visual Studio .NET, close any solution you may have open and choose File, New, Project. As in Figure 19.8, select a C# project on the left, and an ASP.NET Web Application on the right. Fill in the location as `http://localhost/ASPZipTest`, which causes the project to be called ASPZipTest.

An empty ASP.NET page is opened for you in Design View, as you can see in Figure 19.9. If you've worked with ASP in the past, you probably think the thing to do is to use the buttons at the lower left of the editing area to switch to HTML View, and start typing in JavaScript or VBScript code. But ASP.NET introduces a new concept: The code can be in a separate file, and the code in that file can be written in any .NET language.

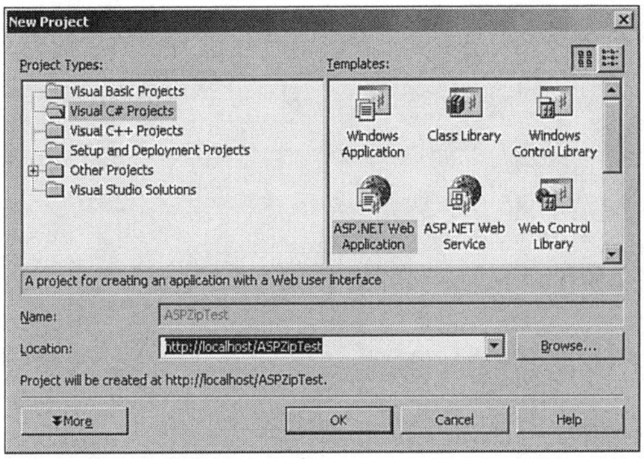

Figure 19.8
Create an ASP.NET
project in C#.

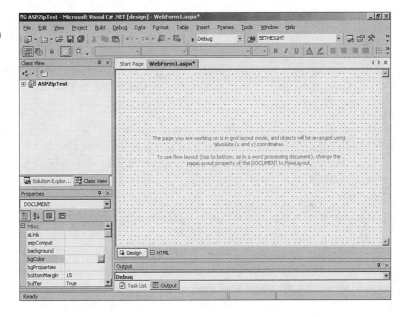

Figure 19.9
An ASP.NET web form
can be built easily in
Design View.

CH
19

Because this is a C# project, the skeleton code that was generated for you assumes the code-behind, as this separate file is called, is written in C#. This is indicated in the HTML for the page with this tag:

```
<%@ Page language="c#" Codebehind="WebForm1.aspx.cs"
AutoEventWireup="false" Inherits="ASPZipTest.WebForm1" %>
```

With Webform1.aspx open in Design View, choose View, Toolbox to bring up a collection of user-interface components you might add to your Web form. Drag a text box, a button, and a label onto the design surface. Use the Properties window to change the text of the button to Check Zip and to remove the Text property of Label that was assigned to the label. Your interface should resemble Figure 19.10.

Figure 19.10
Build a simple user interface.

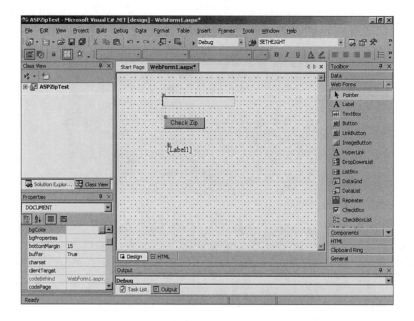

Double-click the Check Zip button to edit the code that runs when the button is clicked. As before, copy PostCodeCheck.dll and ZipCheck.dll from the Debug folder under ZipCheck to the bin folder under the c:\inetpub\wwwroot\ASPZipTest project folder. Add a reference to the ZipCheck project as before. With the reference in place, add these lines to the body of the function:

```
ZipCheck.ZipCheck zip = new ZipCheck.ZipCheck();
Label1.Text = zip.Check(TextBox1.Text);
```

This code creates an instance of the ZipCheck object from the ZipCheck namespace, then uses it to test the Text property of the TextBox on the Web form. The resulting message is put into the Text property of the Label on the Web form. In ASP.NET, working with HTML forms feels a lot like working with a Windows application—and you never have to type angle brackets!

Build the project and then run it by choosing Debug, Start. A new browser window appears and your Web page loads into it. Enter a zip code and click the button, and you can see the test results, as in Figure 19.11. Your ASP.NET application consumes your C++ "business logic" component almost without effort on your part. This is the promise of .NET in action.

Figure 19.11
Your ASP.NET page runs in a browser and uses your C++ component to test a zip code.

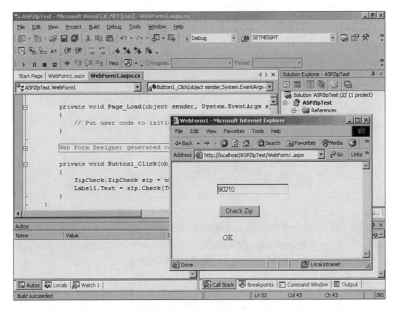

EXTENDING A C++ COMPONENT IN C#

The ZipCheck component that CSZipTest uses is part of a hierarchy. The base class of the hierarchy, PostCodeCheck, is written in Managed C++ and has two functions:

- Check(). Takes a String*. The base class version always returns OK. The expectation is that all derived classes will implement their own checks.

- Test(). Takes a String* and uses Check() to check it, then returns True or False. Derived classes are unlikely to override it.

One of the real "wow" moments for anyone meeting .NET for the first time has to be cross-language inheriting. Follow along and create a C# class that actually inherits from a class written in C++.

The class will be another .NET component in the PostCodeCheck hierarchy. This one will be called CanadaCodeCheck and it will check that a string meets the rules for Canadian postal codes, which follow the pattern LnL nLn, where L is a capital letter and n is a number. For example, K1P 5T1 is the postal code of the American embassy in Ottawa.

To build a component in C# that inherits from a component written in another language, start by opening another copy of Visual Studio. In this copy, choose File, New, Project. Select C# projects on the left and Class Library on the right. Name the project CanadaCodeCheck, as shown in Figure 19.12.

CH
19

Figure 19.12
Create a class library
project in C#.

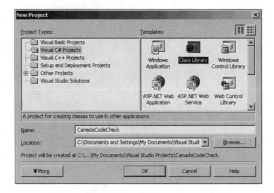

Change the name of the class from Class1 to CanadaCodeChecker by selecting it in Class
View, then scrolling in the Properties window until you find the Name property and changing
it. Find the line that declares this class, which currently reads:

```
public class CanadaCodeChecker
```

Change the line so that CanadaCodeCheck inherits from PostCodeChecker:

```
public class CanadaCodeChecker : PostCodeCheck.PostCodeChecker
```

You may notice a blue wavy line underneath the class name PostCodeCheck after you make
this change, as in Figure 19.13. PostCodeCheck hasn't been added to the references for this
project. Copy postcodecheck.dll to the bin folder beneath the project folder, then choose
Project, Add Reference. Click the Browse button, select the DLL, then click OK to confirm
adding the reference.

Figure 19.13
References are
checked on the fly
and if you forget to
add one, class names
are marked as errors.

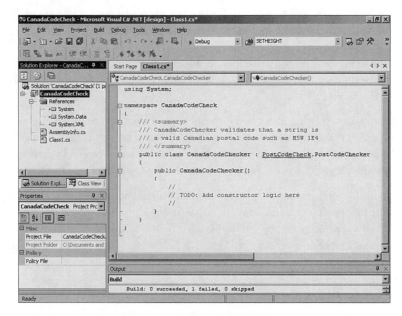

Between the braces that mark the beginning and end of the class definition, add the code for the Check() function shown in Listing 19.2 and build the project.

LISTING 19.2   CLASS1.CS—CanadaCodeChecker.Check()

```
public override string Check(String code)
{
    string error = "OK";
    if (code.Length != 7)
    {
        error = "Invalid length";
        return error;
    }
    for (int i = 0; i < code.Length; i++)
    {
        if (i == 0 || i == 2 || i == 5)
        {
            if (!Char.IsLetter(
                Convert.ToChar(code.Substring(i, 1))))
            {
                error = "Character " + i + " must be a letter";
            }
        }
        if (i == 1 || i == 4 || i == 6)
        {
            if (!Char.IsDigit(
                Convert.ToChar(code.Substring(i, 1))))
            {
                error = "Character " + i + " must be a numeric digit";
            }
        }
        if (i == 3)
        {
            if (code.Substring(i, 1) != " ")
            {
                error = "Character 3 must be a space";
            }
        }
    }
    return error;
}
```

Like the Visual Basic code presented in Chapter 18, "Integrating with Visual Basic," this code uses a Convert object, rather than FromString and ToString methods, to convert from strings—in this case to a single character. It also uses the Char structure from the System namespace. This structure isn't unique to C#; it's handy anywhere you want to explore the properties of a single character—in this case, whether that character is a letter or a digit.

Notice also the override keyword on the function definition. Without it, you will get a warning message that you are hiding the base class function. For this project, the message reads:

```
warning CS0114: 'CanadaCodeCheck.CanadaCodeCheck.Check(string)' hides inherited
member 'PostCodeCheck.Check(string)'. To make the current method override that
implementation, add the override keyword. Otherwise add the new keyword.
```

This is an interesting compromise between the C++ approach, which assumes you know what you're doing and doesn't even warn you when you override a function, and the Visual Basic approach, which insists on an `Overrides` keyword to ensure that no one accidentally overrides a base class function and changes the behavior of a system.

With the `override` keyword in place, build the component. Correct any typos or errors, and get ready to test it. A few changes to the `CSZipTest` project take care of the testing.

Find canadacodecheck.dll in the bin\Debug folder of the CanadaCodeCheck project folder. Copy it to the CSZipTest\bin folder. If you have two copies of Visual Studio open, return to the one in which you were working on `CSZipTest`. If not, open the `CSZipTest` solution now. Add a reference to `CanadaCodeCheck`.

Leave the beginning of `ZipTest.Main()` as it is, but change the last two blocks, which test M5W 1E6 and 04112-0001, so that the code reads like Listing 19.3.

LISTING 19.3   REPLACEMENT BLOCKS OF CODE FOR `CSZipTest`

```
CanadaCodeCheck.CanadaCodeChecker canada = new
➥CanadaCodeCheck.CanadaCodeChecker();
string GoodCode = "M5W 1E6"; // A valid Canadian Postal Code

Console.Write("Checking for Canada ");
Console.WriteLine(GoodCode);
Console.WriteLine(canada.Check(GoodCode) );

string POBox1PortlandMaine= "04112-0001"; //leading zeroes

Console.Write("Checking for Canada ");
Console.WriteLine(POBox1PortlandMaine);
Console.WriteLine(canada.Check(POBox1PortlandMaine) );
Console.ReadLine();
```

The changes here are:

- Use a `CanadaCodeChecker` object rather than the existing `ZipCheck` object.
- Name the Canadian postal code `GoodCode` rather than `BadCode`.
- Change the "Checking" reminder to clarify that the code is testing against the Canadian format.

Notice the name of the component is not just `CanadaCodeChecker`, but `CanadaCodeCheck.CanadaCodeChecker`. The component, `CanadaCodeCheck`, is contained in a namespace, also called `CanadaCodeCheck`. To use it, you call it by its full name, including the namespace. Build and run the project. You should see output that looks like Figure 19.14, which shows testing of the first two codes with `ZipCheck` and the last two with `CanadaCodeCheck`.

Figure 19.14
Valid zip codes are
not valid Canadian
postal codes.

USING A C# COMPONENT FROM C++

To complete the circle of cross-language development, you can use the C# component, `CanadaCodeCheck`, from a Visual C++ application.

Close the `CSZipTest` solution and choose File, New, Project. On the left, select Visual C++ Projects. On the right side, select a Managed C++ application. As in Figure 19.15, call it CanadaCodeTest.

Figure 19.15
Create a Managed
C++ application to
test the C#
component.

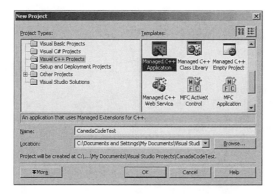

Build the project by choosing Build, Build to create the Debug folder, then copy postcodecheck.dll and canadacodecheck.dll into the Debug folder under the CanadaCodeTest project folder.

In the Class View, expand CanadaCodeTest, then expand Global Functions And Variables. Double-click `_tmain()` to edit CanadaCodeTest.cpp. Add this code before the `_tmain()` function:

```
#using "Debug\PostCodeCheck.dll"
#using "Debug\CanadaCodeCheck.dll"
```

As in other Managed C++ projects you've seen in this book, these lines of code tell the .NET framework and Visual Studio where to find the functions you'll be using from the component. It's equivalent to adding a reference in the C# project. You might be interested to note that Add Reference does not appear on the Project menu while you're working on a Visual C++ project. You have to add the #using statement by hand.

The code for _tmain() is very similar to the ZipTest code in Chapter 17 and the JapanCodeTest code in Chapter 18. It reads:

LISTING 19.4 CANADACODETEST.CPP—_tmain()

```cpp
int main(void)
{
   String* Embassy = S"K1P 5T1"; //US Embassy in Ottawa
   CanadaCodeCheck::CanadaCodeChecker* canada = new
►CanadaCodeCheck::CanadaCodeChecker();

   Console::Write("Checking ");
   Console::WriteLine(Embassy);
   Console::WriteLine(canada->Check(Embassy) );

   if (canada->Test(Embassy))
          Console::WriteLine(S"passed");
   else
          Console::WriteLine(S"failed");

   String* BadCode= S"90210"; // A valid Zip Code

   Console::Write("Checking ");
   Console::WriteLine(BadCode);
   Console::WriteLine(canada->Check(BadCode) );

   if (canada->Test(BadCode))
          Console::WriteLine(S"passed");
   else
          Console::WriteLine(S"failed");

   Console::ReadLine();
   return 0;

}
```

Because CanadaCodeChecker is in the CanadaCodeCheck namespace, this code refers to it by its full name, using the scope resolution operator, ::, to separate the namespace name from the class name.

Figure 19.16 shows this code running. It's kind of fun to see the multiple languages in action. Managed C++ code in CanadaCodeTest is calling C# code for Check(). Better still, Managed C++ code calls other Managed C++ for the base class version of Test(), which then calls the overridden version of Check() in C#. It all works together seamlessly. You don't have to know anything about the differences between the languages; you just use whatever language is right for you.

Figure 19.16
A Managed C++ uses the C# component flawlessly.

FROM HERE

When I am talking to people about .NET and what makes it so terrific to work with, cross-language development is always one of the first things I mention. The .NET base class libraries are available from all the .NET languages. You don't need to know what language they are written in to use them. You can bring the same freedom to your own projects, mixing and matching languages to serve your own needs.

The odd thing is that when you do it, the process is so simple and ordinary that you almost don't notice what you're doing. Even cross-language inheritance doesn't appear spectacular. There's no special keyword to indicate you're using this feature, no switches or settings you need to adjust. But don't let that fool you—this is powerful stuff, and it's almost certainly going to change the way you develop software.

CH
19

CHAPTER 20

MANAGED AND UNMANAGED C++

In this chapter

C++ SUPPORTS BOTH MANAGED AND UNMANAGED PROGRAMMING

Visual Studio .NET equalizes the programming languages it supports more than any other release of Visual Studio. There was a time when certain features were only for C++ programmers, and others were only for Visual Basic programmers, but those days are gone. Well, almost gone. A few little C++-only features remain. In Chapter 10, "Internet Programming," you meet ATL Server, a C++-only part of .NET.

As discussed in the Introduction, the first half of this book covers "classic Win32 programming"—programming just as you used to do in Visual C++ before .NET was released. All that old code can still be compiled in Visual Studio and doesn't have to be converted or ported in any way. That's not true with other programming languages— Visual Studio doesn't support "classic Visual Basic," for example.

The second half of this book is about Visual C++ .NET programming—programming with all the power of the Common Language Runtime libraries, with memory management taken care of for you, with the amazing cross-language inheritance, inter-language interoperability, and breathtakingly easy Web Service creation.

If you hadn't noticed yet, take a look: Visual C++ programming before .NET is very, very different from Visual C++ after .NET. You can't just write any old C++ class and then write a Visual Basic class that inherits from it. You can't take some code that's busy doing its own memory management and suddenly expect the .NET framework to start doing that management for you—especially if that legacy code uses `malloc` and `delete` to manage memory used by non-objects.

This chapter is all about the differences between managed code (essentially, .NET-compatible code) and unmanaged (classic) code. You can write whichever you prefer; you can even mix and match the two in a single application. After all, if C++ had a motto, it would be "You're the programmer, so go ahead and try it."

WHAT IS MANAGED CODE?

You decide whether a class you write is a managed class or not. (All the classes in the Common Language Runtime are managed.) There are three kinds of managed classes in Visual C++ .NET:

- Garbage-collected classes
- Value classes
- Managed interface classes

Most managed classes are garbage-collected classes. To declare a class to be garbage-collected (and therefore managed), declare it like this:

```
__gc class Employee
{
  // class content goes here
};
```

GARBAGE COLLECTION: MEMORY MANAGEMENT

The keyword __gc (it starts with two underscores) indicates that your class is a garbage-collected class; its memory usage is the framework's responsibility, not yours. Notice that the default, if you don't specify __gc, is the same C++ behavior that has always existed.

Managed Extensions

Perhaps you remember a rule of thumb from when you first learned C++ that, even though underscores are valid anywhere in a variable name, you shouldn't start a variable name with an underscore. C++ compiler vendors may add extra keywords to their implementation of the language, and they've agreed that these keywords will always start with at least one underscore. If you avoid starting your variable names with underscores, you will never run into a conflict with a vendor-specific keyword.

These vendor-specific keywords are called *extensions*, because they are a mechanism for compiler vendors to extend the language. The new keywords discussed in this chapter, including __gc, __property, __box, and __value, are collectively called Managed Extensions for C++.

Here's an illustration of what it means to say that the class's memory is managed by the framework, not by you. If Employee is an ordinary class, you work with it like this:

```
// fragment of a larger program
Employee * pe = new Employee(); // could pass parameters to constructor
//
//   ... use various methods of Employee instance
//
delete pe;
// program continues
```

You allocate the memory for an instance of Employee, indirectly, by using the new operator, which allocates memory and calls the constructor. And when you don't need the instance any more, you make that memory available for other allocations by using the delete operator, which calls the destructor and frees the memory.

If you forget to use the delete operator, you have a *memory leak*. In Chapter 12, "Improving Your Application's Performance," you can learn more about memory management by hand. It can be really hard work.

By contrast, if your class is garbage-collected, the memory management is not your problem. Your code looks like this, instead:

```
// fragment of a larger program
Employee * pe = new Employee(); // could pass parameters to constructor
//
//   ... use various methods of Employee instance
//
// program continues
```

You don't delete the pointer when you're finished with the instance. When your pointer goes out of scope, if no other pointer is around and pointing to the instance, then the instance may be cleaned up. On the other hand, it may not—if your program has not allocated a lot of memory, the garbage collector may never run. Most of the time, you don't care. As long as your program doesn't grind to a halt for lack of memory, that's all that matters.

If you need your destructor to run for some reason, there are a few ways to arrange for it. Perhaps it closes a file or releases some resource other than memory. You can call the destructor directly:

```
pe->~Employee();
```

You can set the pointer to 0 (or NULL), which is a strong clue to the garbage collector that you are finished with the instance, and then trigger garbage collection:

```
pe = 0;
GC::Collect();
```

You can also delete the pointer yourself, which calls the destructor and sets the pointer to 0 for you:

```
delete pe;
```

However, before engaging in this sort of coding, you should imagine a VB or C# programmer using your class. They are unlikely to be comfortable with any of these approaches. Probably the best thing to do is to add some appropriately-named cleanup method, such as `CloseFiles()` or `ReleaseLocks()`, and hope that programmers remember to call it. Although that may seem like a step backward, remember that if the instance was allocated with `new`, you always had to hope that programmers remembered to use `delete`.

A Pointer to a Managed Object Is Not a Pointer to an Umanaged Object

The CLR libraries are full of useful classes and methods. `System::Collections::Stack`, for example, represents a simple stack, with methods such as `Push()` and `Pop()`. If you would like to have a stack of `Employee` instances, then `Employee` needs to be a garbage-collected class. And rather than a stack of instances, you'll keep a stack of pointers to `Employee` instances.

(The other languages in Visual Studio .NET, and the documentation, refer to them as references, but in C++ they are pointers.) Why does your class have to be garbage-collected to pass an instance of it (or a pointer to an instance of it) to a framework method? These methods expect one or more pointers to garbage-collected instances. Sometimes, when you pass a method something other than what it expects, there's no problem: the compiler just generates a cast for you. But there is no cast between "classic" and garbage-collected object pointers. They are just too different.

The most important thing about a pointer to an instance of a garbage-collected class is that the numerical value of the pointer may change at any time. If the garbage collector is tidying up, it may move the instance. When it does so, it changes all the pointers so that they point to the new location. As a result, you cannot do any kind of pointer arithmetic or pointer manipulation (incrementing or decrementing) with a pointer to a managed object.

BOXING A CLASSIC POINTER

Say you have a simple piece of information that you are not keeping in a garbage-collected class:

```
int i = 3;
```

Now perhaps you would like to pass this to one of the overloads of System::Console::WriteLine(). One overload takes a format string (reminiscent of the format strings in printf, though differently formatted) and a pointer to an instance of a garbage-collected class. You might try it like this:

```
System::Console::WriteLine("i is {0}",i);
```

That gets you a compiler error message:

```
error C2665: 'System::Console::WriteLine' : none of the 18 overloads can convert
parameter 2 from type 'int'
        could be 'void System::Console::WriteLine(System::String __gc
*,System::Object __gc *)'
```

A natural conclusion here is to think "Ah, it needs a pointer," and to try again:

```
System::Console::WriteLine("i is {0}", &i);
```

This just gets you essentially the same error message, only now it can't convert from int*.

The solution is to *box* the integer. This creates a temporary instance of a garbage-collected class, puts the integer in it, and gives you a pointer to the instance. You can pass this pointer to code that expects such a pointer:

```
System::Console::WriteLine("i is {0}",__box(i));
```

This works beautifully, and opens the functionality of the framework classes to every data type, including the fundamental types such as integers.

PINNING A MANAGED POINTER

Sometimes your problem is the other way around. You may have a function, already written, that expects a pointer of some sort. If this is legacy code, it doesn't expect a pointer that can move around; it expects a classic pointer to an unmanaged object. Even a pointer to an integer member variable of a managed object can be moved by the garbage collector when it moves the entire instance of the object.

Consider the simple managed class in Listing 20.1.

LISTING 20.1 A SIMPLE MANAGED CLASS

```
__gc class Sample
{
public:
```

LISTING 20.1 CONTINUED

```
    int a;
    int b;
    Sample(int x, int y)
    {
        a = x;
        b = y;
    }
    void Report()
    {
        Console::WriteLine("a is {0} and b is {1}",__box(a),__box(b));
    }
};
```

You might argue about whether it's a good idea for the member variables a and b to be public, but bear with me for a moment. Consider this simple function, perhaps one that was written in an earlier version of Visual C++:

```
void Equalize(int* a, int* b)
{
    int avg = (*a + *b)/2 ;
    *a = avg;
    *b = avg;
}
```

Say that you want to use this Equalize() function on the two member variables of an instance of this Sample class:

```
Sample* s = new Sample(2,4);
s->Report();

Equalize(&(s->a),&(s->b));
s->Report();
```

This code won't compile. The error is:

```
error C2664: 'Equalize' : cannot convert parameter 1 from 'int __gc *' to 'int *'
        Cannot convert a managed type to an unmanaged type
```

Though they are both pointers, the pointer to a garbage-collected type cannot be converted to a pointer to an unmanaged type. What you can do is *pin* the pointer. This creates another pointer you can pass to the function, and ensures that the garbage collector will not move the instance (in this case, s) for the life of the pinned pointer. Here's how it's done:

```
int __pin* pa = &(s->a);
int __pin* pb = &(s->b);
Equalize(pa,pb);
```

The two new pointers, pa and pb, are pointers to unmanaged types, so they can be passed to Equalize(). They point to the location in the memory where the member variables of s are kept, and the garbage collector will not move (unpin) the instance, s, until pa and pb go out of scope.

You can unpin the instance sooner by deliberately setting pa and pb to 0, a null pointer, like this:

```
pa=0;
pb=0;
```

CAN ALL CLASSES BE GARBAGE-COLLECTED CLASSES?

Making your class a garbage-collected class is not always as simple as adding the __gc keyword to the definition. There are some restrictions on the way you can define your class if you want it to be garbage-collected, and some restrictions on the way you use it, too.

Some of these restrictions apply to all three kinds of managed classes, and some only to garbage-collected classes.

A MANAGED CLASS CANNOT INHERIT FROM AN UNMANAGED CLASS

Consider the class in Listing 20.2, a slight variation on the Sample class introduced earlier in this chapter.

LISTING 20.2   A GARBAGE-COLLECTED CLASS THAT USES INHERITANCE

```
class A
{
protected:
   int a;
};

class B
{
protected:
   int b;
};
__gc class Sample: public A, public B
{
public:
   Sample(int x, int y)
   {
        a = x;
        b = y;
   }
   void Report()
   {
        Console::WriteLine("a is {0} and b is {1}",__box(a),__box(b));
   }

};
```

This looks like perfectly good C++. And it would be, if it weren't for that __gc extension keyword in the definition of Sample. If you type this in and try to compile it, you'll be told:

```
error C3253: 'A' : a managed class cannot derive from an unmanaged class
error C3253: 'B' : a managed class cannot derive from an unmanaged class
```

To fix the problem, make the base class managed if possible, or leave the Sample class unmanaged.

GARBAGE-COLLECTED CLASSES CANNOT USE MULTIPLE INHERITANCE

If you try to fix the sample code in Listing 20.2 by putting the __gc keyword in each of the class definitions (for A and B), you get this error:

```
error C2890: 'Sample' : managed class can only have one non-interface superclass
```

Most C++ programmers never use multiple inheritance. If you're such a programmer, it's no great loss to give it up. If you have working code that uses multiple inheritance, it's best to leave it as unmanaged and access it from new managed code. You'll see how to do that shortly.

You can, if you wish, inherit from as many managed interfaces as you need to. These are discussed later in this chapter, in the "Managed Interfaces" section.

ADDITIONAL RESTRICTIONS ON MANAGED AND GARBAGE-COLLECTED CLASSES

Managed classes have some other restrictions:

- You cannot use the friend keyword to give another class access to the private members of a managed class.
- No member variable of the class can be an instance of an unmanaged class (unless all the member functions of the unmanaged class are static).

In addition, garbage-collected classes have further restrictions:

- You cannot override operator & or operator new.
- You cannot implement a copy constructor.

At first glance, these may seem restrictive. But remember that the reason you usually write a copy constructor is that your destructor does something destructive, such as freeing memory. A garbage-collected class probably has no destructor at all, and therefore has no need for a specialized copy constructor.

When it is time for you to use a garbage-collected class, you'll notice one restriction right away. You aren't allowed to create instances of a garbage-collected class on the stack, like this:

```
Sample s(2,4);
s.Report();
```

If you try, you'll get this error:

```
error C3149: 'Sample' : illegal use of managed type 'Sample'; did you forget a
'*'?
```

All instances of a garbage-collected class must be created on the heap, like this:

```
Sample* s = new Sample(2,4);
```

This is what gives the instance to the garbage collector to manage. The numerical value of s (which is the address in memory of the Sample instance) may vary—but who cares? You surely don't. That is the point when you are using garbage-collected types.

VALUE TYPES

Many programmers feel uncomfortable when they are told they cannot create instances of a garbage-collected class on the stack. There are a number of advantages, in "classic" C++, to creating an object on the stack:

- The object is destructed for you when it goes out of scope.
- The overhead of allocating on the stack is slightly less than allocating on the heap.
- The heap can get fragmented (and therefore you will have a performance hit) if you allocate and free a lot of short-lived objects.

In Managed C++ (in other words, C++ with Managed Extensions), the garbage collector takes care of destructing the object for you. It can also de-fragment the heap. But the garbage collector introduces overhead of its own, of course, and the allocation cost difference between the stack and the heap remains. So, for certain kinds of objects, it may be a better choice to use a value class rather than a garbage-collected class.

The fundamental types, such as int, are referred to as *value types*, because they are allocated on the stack. You can define a simple class of yours to be a value class. You can also do the same for a struct. If your class mainly exists to hold a few small member variables, and doesn't have a complicated lifetime, it's a good candidate to be a value class.

Listing 20.3 redefines Sample to be a value class.

LISTING 20.3   A VALUE CLASS

```
__value class Sample
{
public:
   int a;
   int b;
   Sample(int x, int y)
   {
        a = x;
        b = y;
   }
   void Report()
   {
        Console::WriteLine("a is {0} and b is {1}",__box(a),__box(b));
   }
};
```

CH
20

To create and use an instance of Sample, you must allocate it on the stack, not the heap:

```
Sample s(2,4);
s.Report();
```

These value classes are still managed, but they're not garbage-collected. All the restrictions of managed classes listed earlier apply to value classes. In addition:

- You cannot implement a copy constructor.
- A value class cannot inherit from a garbage-collected class, or another value class, or an unmanaged class. It can inherit from any number of managed interfaces.
- A value class cannot have virtual methods other than those it inherits (and possibly overrides) from System::ValueType.
- No class may inherit from a value class.
- A value class cannot be labeled abstract with the __abstract keyword.

The best candidates for value classes are small classes whose objects don't exist for long and aren't passed around from method to method (thus creating a lot of references to them in different pieces of code).

Tip

> If you've been reading or hearing about Visual Studio.NET already, you may have heard that structs are value types and classes are reference types, or that structs are on the stack and objects are on the heap. Those statements apply to C#. In C++, you're in charge—you can allocate instances of value types (classes or structs) on the stack and instances of garbage-collected types (classes or structs) on the heap.

Another advantage of value classes is that instances are essentially never uninitialized. When you allocate an instance of Sample on the stack, you can pass parameters to the constructor. But if you do not, the member variables are initialized to zero for you. This is true even if you wrote a constructor that takes arguments, and didn't write a constructor that doesn't take arguments. Look at these two lines of code:

```
Sample s2;
s2.Report();
```

When this code runs, it will report:

```
a is 0 and b is 0
```

Because the Sample class is managed, the members are initialized automatically.

Managed Interfaces

Think of a managed interface as a representation of a COM interface. The __interface keyword enforces a number of restrictions on a class, and the __gc keyword adds a few more. Classes that meet these restrictions can be used as extra base classes for garbage-collected classes, which provides a useful (and generally safe) form of multiple inheritance in Managed C++.

Declaring a Managed Interface

If you want to write your own interface, here's an example:

```
__gc __interface ISomething
{
   void UsefulMethod();
};
```

Notice the double dose of extension keywords: you mark your interfaces with both __gc and __interface. It's traditional to start interface names with *I*, and though this isn't enforced by the compiler, I strongly recommend you stick to the convention. Managed interfaces are subject to all the restrictions already listed for managed classes, and in addition:

- All members of the interface must be public.

- An interface cannot have any member variables. (If you have used Java interfaces, you might think you can have static member variables, but you cannot.)

- The interface cannot implement any of its methods. (They must all be pure virtual.)

- The interface cannot have a constructor or destructor.

- The interface cannot overload any operators.

- The interface can inherit only from other managed interfaces.

Using the __interface keyword changes the defaults for the class. Ordinary C++ classes have a default access of private. Consider this class:

```
class Point
{
private:
   int x;
   int y;
};
```

This definition could have also been written like this:

```
class Point
{
   int x;
   int y;
};
```

The default access is private. But the default access for an interface is public.

In an ordinary C++ class, a function (or method) is non-virtual unless you mark it as virtual. If you don't intend to implement a virtual function, you must indicate this with the slightly obscure notation =0 after the definition of the class, like this:

```
virtual void SomeFunction(int a, int b) =0 ;
```

But when you mark a class as an interface, all methods are assumed to be pure virtual. These two defaults mean that the ISomething interface defined earlier could also have been written this way:

```
__gc __interface ISomething
{
public:
   virtual void UsefulMethod()=0;
};
```

CH
20

The slightly shorter notation is convenient, but when you see that __interface keyword remember what it does to the usual defaults in a class declaration.

INHERITING FROM A MANAGED INTERFACE

If a garbage-collected class inherits from a managed interface, it has to implement all the methods of the interface. Code that expects a pointer to an instance of the interface easily accepts a pointer to a class derived from the interface. In this way the compiler gives you type-safety when you are working with interfaces. It's very convenient.

Here's an example: Imagine a bank account. You probably have one. Maybe you earn interest on the money you keep in this account. Most saving accounts give you interest. And perhaps a statement is mailed to you each month, or perhaps you update your passbook when you go into the branch. How can you represent that in code?

I would start with a CAccount class to hold everything that accounts have in common, like a balance. Every account has an owner, too, and a log of transactions. Then I would create subclasses, also called derived classes, that inherit from CAccount. We could start with CSavingAccount and CStatementSavingAccount. But rather than just add methods to these classes any old way, I would define some interfaces: IStatement for bank accounts that print statements, IPassbook for those that print passbooks, and IInterestEarning for those that earn interest. Listing 20.4 shows the base classes and interfaces in the system.

LISTING 20.4   BASE CLASSES AND INTERFACES FOR THE BANK EXAMPLE

```
__gc __interface IPassbook
{
   void Print();
};


__gc __interface IStatement
{
   void Print();
};

__gc __interface IInterestEarning
{
   void IncreaseBalanceByInterest();
};

__gc class CAccount
{
 // whatever is common to all kinds
 // of bank accounts: balance, owner, etc
protected:
   int balance; //in pennies to avoid rounding errors
};
```

The interfaces just define a method. (In a real system, they would probably define several related methods.) Implementation of these methods is left for the classes that inherit from the interfaces. Listing 20.5 presents a drastically simplified version of CSavingAccount.

Listing 20.5 Possible Implementation of CSavingAccount

```
__gc class CSavingAccount: public CAccount, public IPassbook, public
➥IInterestEarning
{
public:
   void Print()
   {
          Console::WriteLine("passbook: balance is {0} pennies", __box(balance));
          // a real saving account would go through the transaction
          // log and print (passbook style) all unprinted transactions,
          // then mark them printed
   }
   void IncreaseBalanceByInterest()
   {
          balance += 100;   //$1 a month interest no matter what
          // a real saving account would go through the transaction
          // log and determine the monthly or daily interest and
          // increase the balance by that amount
   }
private:
   // other member variables and functions go here
};
```

This class inherits from one garbage-collected class and two managed interfaces. It implements all the methods of each interface. Listing 20.6 presents a really simple CStatementSavingAccount:

Listing 20.6 Possible Implementation of CStatementSavingAccount

```
class CStatementSavingAccount: public CAccount, public IStatement, public
➥IInterestEarning
{
public:
   void Print()
   {
          Console::WriteLine("statement: balance is {0} pennies", __box(balance));
          // a real statement account would go through the transaction
          // log and print (statement style) all transactions this period,
          // then update the "last statement printed" date
   }
   void IncreaseBalanceByInterest()
   {
          balance += 100;   //$1 a month interest no matter what
          // a real saving account would go through the transaction
          // log and determine the monthly or daily interest and
          // increase the balance by that amount
   }
private:
   // other member variables and functions go here
};
```

CH

20

Having defined and implemented the two kinds of accounts, I can write a simple main() that exercises them, a program often called a "test harness" because it is only for testing the code in a class, or occasionally a few related classes. An example is presented in Listing 20.7.

LISTING 20.7   TEST HARNESS FOR BANKING EXAMPLE

```cpp
int main(void)
{

    CSavingAccount* save = new CSavingAccount();
    save->Print();
    save->IncreaseBalanceByInterest();
    save->Print();

    Console::WriteLine("-------------");

    CStatementSavingAccount* statement = new CStatementSavingAccount();
    statement->Print();
    statement->IncreaseBalanceByInterest();
    statement->Print();

    return 0;

}
```

This code will compile and run, and as you might expect, it produces this output:

```
passbook: balance is 0 pennies
passbook: balance is 100 pennies
-------------
statement: balance is 0 pennies
statement: balance is 100 pennies
```

That's not terribly exciting, and it doesn't demonstrate the true power of interface programming. So consider this global function:

```cpp
void CreditInterest(IInterestEarning* i)
{
    i->IncreaseBalanceByInterest();
}
```

This code doesn't know anything about bank accounts, saving accounts, CSavingAccount, or CStatementSavingAccount. It just knows about IInterestEarning. Yet you can pass a pointer to either of these accounts to this function:

```cpp
CreditInterest(save);
CreditInterest(statement);
```

You can imagine creating some sort of collection of all kinds of accounts, all of which inherit from IInterestEarning, and passing them one at a time to this function. Because IInterestEarning is a C++ base class of the account classes, the compiler itself verifies that this is an appropriate parameter to pass to the function. Similarly, you could pass all kinds of accounts that inherit from IStatement to a function that runs once a month and prints everyone's statements. That's how interface programming makes life simpler, and programs more maintainable.

PROPERTIES

Managed classes have one other feature you may wish to use: properties. You have probably written classes like the one in Listing 20.8.

LISTING 20.8   A CLASS WITH SIMPLE Get AND Set METHODS

```
class Employee
{
private:
   int salary; //dollars
   // remaining member variables
public:
   int getSalary() {return salary;}
   void setSalary(int s)
      {salary = s;}
   // remaining public methods
};
```

Even if you would write slightly more complicated code for setSalary(), with some kind of error checking, the basic concept is the same: a private variable with public get and set functions. Not every variable is treated like this, of course: the bank balance in the previous example shouldn't be settable from outside, but should instead be changed by various business operations such as deposits and withdrawals. But many classes follow this "get and set" paradigm.

The good thing about this, of course, is encapsulation. I am free to add error checking to either the get or the set method after my system is partially built or in a follow-on phase. I can even change the type of the variable and just adjust the code to reflect the change. Encapsulation is a great thing, and no wise programmer will give it up.

The downside is the way your code looks when you're using get and set functions. If I have a pointer to an instance of the Employee class, e, and I wish to give that employee a $5,000 raise, here's the code:

```
e->setSalary(e->getSalary() + 5000);
```

That works, but it's not exactly pretty. But in the .NET framework, I can have my cake and eat it too. I just change my definition of Employee slightly, as shown in Listing 20.9.

LISTING 20.9   PROPERTIES IN A MANAGED CLASS

```
__gc class Employee
{
private:
   int salary; //dollars
   // remaining member variables
public:
   __property int get_Salary()
      {return salary;}
```

LISTING 20.9   CONTINUED

```
    __property void set_Salary(int s)
        {salary = s;}
    // remaining public methods
};
```

Now the class has a `Salary` property. It's directly tied to the `salary` member variable, but there's no requirement that it should be, and in fact the name of the property cannot be exactly the same as the name of a member variable, which is why for Employee the property name (which appears after the get_ and set_ of the function names) is `Salary` and the member variable is `salary`.

To use the property, you write code that treats it like a public member variable:

```
e->Salary = 10000;
e->Salary = e->Salary + 5000;
```

You can use any of the familiar C++ operators with a property:

```
e->Salary += 5000;
```

Yet behind the scenes, your `get` and `set` functions, with all their attendant error checking, are being called. You get all the benefits of encapsulation, yet your code is as easy to read as if all your member variables were public.

MIXING MANAGED AND UNMANAGED CODE

Now that you've seen the advantages of managed classes, you're probably ready to resolve that all your new development will use them. But what about all your existing code? Can you just stick a __gc in front of all your class declarations and recompile? It's pretty unlikely. Some of your classes may not meet the restrictions listed in this chapter for managed classes. You may not want to find every place that allocates an object on the stack and change it to allocate the garbage-collected class with `new`, then change every line that used the object with '.' to dereference the object pointer with '->'. It's a lot of work.

If you're working on a project with many unmanaged classes, does that mean you can never use any of the great .NET framework resources? No, it doesn't.

ACTIVATING .NET SUPPORT

When you create a .NET project, you get these two lines at the top of your source file:

```
#using <mscorlib.dll>
using namespace System;
```

There's nothing to stop you from putting these two lines in any source file you are working on. You won't get what you want, though, unless you also turn on the .NET compiler switch, /CLR, to indicate that you want your project to be managed. That's done for you automatically when you create a .NET project. To see the setting (or to set it in a non-managed project), follow these steps:

1. Switch to Class View or the Solution Explorer by clicking the appropriate tab on the project workspace, or choose View, Solution Explorer, or View, Class View.

2. Click on the name of the entire solution.

3. Choose View, Property Pages. This is the last item on the menu. Don't get sidetracked by the Properties Window menu item.

4. The Property page appears. You should be on the General page, directly below the Configuration Properties folder. If not, expand Configuration Properties if necessary, and click on General.

5. Set the Use Managed Extensions property to Yes.

6. Click OK to accept the change.

After you have set the compiler switch, you must add the #using line to your source files. This makes the Common Language Runtime library available to you. You don't have to add the second line (using namespace System) if you don't want to—you can just call all the System classes by their full names if you prefer.

IDENTIFYING UNMANAGED CODE

Managed code and managed types are slightly different things. Managed code compiles to Intermediate Language (MSIL) and runs under the CLR. Unmanaged code does not. Deciding whether to use managed or unmanaged code is a separate decision from deciding whether a class is a managed (garbage-collected, value, or interface) class or not. You can write managed code that works entirely with unmanaged types. After you have turned on the /CLR compiler switch, all the code in your project is assumed to be managed.

To work with unmanaged types from managed code, you can declare a class with the __nogc keyword, to indicate that it is not garbage collected. However, the member functions of such a class will be managed code, and will, for example, generate all the overhead of the garbage collector to manage the memory they use.

It's more usual to just "drop out" of managed code for a while, using a pragma for this purpose:

```
#pragma unmanaged
// unmanaged code goes here
#pragma managed
//back to managed code again
```

You can use this technique to mix old and new code in the same file, which is really quite extraordinary. You'll get plenty of practice boxing and pinning, and you'll probably have to write a wrapper class or two, but no other language can mix and match in this way, and if you need it, you need it.

If your old and new code are going to be in different files, though, there's a better approach. Wrap up your old objects as COM components. Write your new stuff as .NET objects. They can talk to each other just fine: the .NET code thinks of COM components as .NET objects, as discussed in Chapter 23, "COM Interop."

CH
20

FROM HERE

Whichever way you go, remember that you don't have to abandon (or port) all your old legacy code just to get access to the .NET goodies. And if there's nothing in .NET you want, no problem! You can still write ordinary, "classic" Windows32 code using Visual Studio .NET. That's what the whole first half of this book was about. For more on .NET and what it offers you in addition to garbage collection and no more memory leaks, stay in this half of the book because there's lots more to discover.

CHAPTER 21

CREATING AN XML WEB SERVICE

In this chapter

XML WEB SERVICE

XML Web services are the heart of Microsoft .NET. They represent the ultimate in distributed components: components that you access over the Web, though they might be located anywhere in the world. With the support for XML Web services built into Visual Studio, you can write a Web service in Visual C++, C#, Visual Basic .NET, or any other .NET language. But C++ programmers have access to another tool as well—ATL Server. This chapter explores managed Web services only. ATL Server is covered in Chapter 10, "Internet Programming."

WHAT SHOULD AN XML WEB SERVICE OFFER?

An XML Web service does not a have a user interface—it is code for other applications to call. Think of it as similar to a COM component that offers services to other components. One service might have a number of different methods that all relate in some way. For example, a doctor's office might offer a Web service that

- Indicates whether a given block of time is available or fully booked.
- Indicates whether a specific doctor is scheduled to be in the office on a specific day.
- Provides the next available block of time, given the requested length of the block.

Another Web service from the same office might, after verifying a user's identity, allow an application to

- Book an appointment for the user.
- Confirm an appointment for the user.
- Cancel or reschedule an appointment for the user.

Whatever visual aspects you might imagine around these queries and requests come from the application that consumes the Web service: the Web service itself does not provide, for example, a clickable calendar. An application designed for a large screen and a high-bandwith connection will have a very different user interface from one designed for a cell phone; both rely on the Web service for access to the booking system at the doctor's office, but they display that information very differently.

When choosing the methods that you will offer, it's best to avoid a "chatty" model, where the application requests information one piece at a time. Connections over the Internet are likely to be a bottleneck, and because each request and response carries a certain amount of overhead, you'd like as much real information in there as possible. So, for example, if your Web service offers information about training classes, don't use a method that returns the title, another that returns the price, and a third that returns the length of the course; instead return all this information at once and have the requesting application present it to the user.

DESIGNING THE SAMPLE WEB SERVICE

A Web service that handles all the booking for a doctor's office is too complex to present in a single chapter. What's more, it uses techniques such as database access that you might not yet be ready to use. So I'm going to choose some really simple functionalities:

- The service can add any two numbers together.
- The service can multiply any two numbers.

Although it doesn't seem likely that this functionality is going to rely on the raw power and speed of C++, at least it's not "Hello World" again. And it will show you how to implement two different methods as part of the same Web service.

The service itself will be called Calculate. The methods will be called Add and Multiply. Each will take two floating point numbers and return a floating point number.

IMPLEMENTING THE SAMPLE WEB SERVICE

Not surprisingly, Visual Studio .NET has a wizard to help you create a Web service. Before you get started, make sure you have IIS running on your development machine. Your Web service is going to need a Web server to run on. Choose File, New, Project to get started. Choose .NET Projects and then, on the left, select Managed C++ Web Service, as shown in Figure 21.1. Name the project Calculator.

Figure 21.1
Create a Managed C++ Web service project.

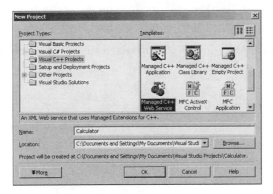

Click the ClassView tab and expand the Calculator node. You see a class called `Class1`: double-click it and you see the class definition reproduced in Listing 21.1.

LISTING 21.1   GENERATED CODE FOR A WEB SERVICE

CH
21

```
// Calculator.h

#pragma once

#using <System.Web.Services.dll>
```

LISTING 21.1 CONTINUED

```
using namespace System;
using namespace System::Web;
using namespace System::Web::Services;

namespace Calculator
{
    public __gc
        class Class1 : public WebService
    {

    public:
        // WEB SERVICE EXAMPLE
        // The HelloWorld() example service returns the string "Hello, World!".
        // To test this web service, ensure that the .asmx file in the
deployment path is
        // set as your Debug HTTP URL, in project properties.
        // and press F5.

        [System::Web::Services::WebMethod]
        String __gc* HelloWorld();

        // TODO: Add the methods of your Web Service here

    };
}
```

The [System::Web::Services::WebMethod] attribute on the HelloWorld () declaration is what makes the method available to the Internet as whole from within your Web service.

Expand Class1 in ClassView and double-click the HelloWorld method to edit the code. The wizard generates the code in Listing 21.2 for you.

LISTING 21.2 GENERATED CODE FOR A WEB SERVICE

```
#include "stdafx.h"
#include "Calculator.h"
#include "Global.asax.h"

namespace Calculator
{
    // WEB SERVICE EXAMPLE
    // The HelloWorld() example service returns the string "Hello, World!".
    // To test this web service, ensure that the .asmx file in the deployment path
is
    // set as your Debug HTTP URL, in project properties.
    // and press F5.

     String __gc* Class1::HelloWorld()
     {
```

LISTING 21.2   CONTINUED

```
        // TODO: Add the implementation of your Web Service here

        return S"Hello World!";

    }

};
```

Rename Class1 by opening the Properties pane, clicking Class1, and changing the Name property to Calc. The tree in ClassView changes right away. Switch to Solution Explorer and double-click Calculator.asmx, which is the file you view in the browser to run your Web service. Find this line:

```
<%@ WebService Class=Calculator.Class1 %>
```

Change it to read like this:

```
<%@ WebService Class=Calculator.Calc %>
```

Now remove the HelloWorld() method from the .h and .cpp files, and add the Add and Multiply methods. Your class definition, in Calculator.h, should look like Listing 21.3.

LISTING 21.3   CLASS DEFINITION FOR CALCULATOR

```
// Calculator.h

#pragma once

namespace Calculator
{

    __gc class Calc {

    public:
        [System::Web::Services::WebMethod]
        double Add(double x, double y);

        [System::Web::Services::WebMethod]
        double Multiply(double x, double y);

    };
}
```

Your class implementation, in Calculator.cpp, should look like this:

LISTING 21.4   IMPLEMENTATION FOR CALCULATOR

```
#include "stdafx.h"
#include "Calculator.h"
#include "Global.asax.h"

namespace Calculator
{
```

CH

21

LISTING 21.4   CONTINUED

```
double Calc::Add(double x, double y)
    {
            return x + y;
    }
double Calc::Multiply(double x, double y)
    {
            return x * y;
    }

};
```

Build the solution by choosing Build, Build Solution. If you watch your output as the build progresses, you will see messages from the compiler and the linker, but then that familiar output is followed by something like Listing 21.5. All the files that are necessary to test and deploy your XML Web service are copied to a folder where IIS can serve them over the Internet. As you can see, there's a tremendous amount of work being done for you. Not all of it is needed for such a simple service, but when you go to write a real service, you'll be pleased to have such simple deployment.

LISTING 21.5   BUILD OUTPUT FOR WEB SERVICE

```
Deploying the web files...
Copied file from c:\Documents and Settings\My Documents\Visual Studio
Projects\Calculator\Calculator.asmx to
c:\inetpub\wwwroot\Calculator\Calculator.asmx
Copied file from c:\Documents and Settings\My Documents\Visual Studio
Projects\Calculator\Calculator.vsdisco to
c:\inetpub\wwwroot\Calculator\Calculator.vsdisco
Copied file from c:\Documents and Settings\My Documents\Visual Studio
Projects\Calculator\Web.config to c:\inetpub\wwwroot\Calculator\Web.config
Copied file from c:\Documents and Settings\My Documents\Visual Studio
Projects\Calculator\Global.asax to c:\inetpub\wwwroot\Calculator\Global.asax
Copied file from c:\Documents and Settings\My Documents\Visual Studio
Projects\Calculator\Debug\Calculator.dll to
c:\inetpub\wwwroot\Calculator\bin\Calculator.dll
Copied file from c:\Documents and Settings\My Documents\Visual Studio
Projects\Calculator\Debug\Calculator.pdb to
c:\inetpub\wwwroot\Calculator\bin\Calculator.pdb

Build log was saved at "file://c:\Documents and Settings\My Documents\Visual
Studio Projects\Calculator\Debug\BuildLog.htm"
Calculator - 0 error(s), 0 warning(s)


-------------------- Done --------------------

    Build: 1 succeeded, 0 failed, 0 skipped
```

TESTING THE SAMPLE WEB SERVICE

After the service is built, it should be tested. The deployment process created a folder on the default Web site of the target machine called Calculator, and added a file called Calculator.disco and another called Calculator.asmx to that folder. Open a Web browser and type in the URL to the asmx file (on most machines `http://localhost/Calculator/Calculator.asmx` will work; if you use a proxy server or if localhost doesn't seem to work for you, use your machine name or IP address instead) and you should see a machine-generated description of your service, like the one in Figure 21.2.

Figure 21.2
The deployment process creates a descriptive Web page.

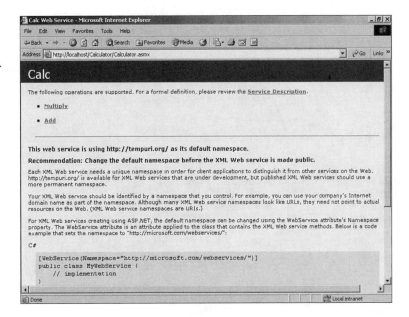

Visual Studio generated all the information on the Web page for you, because the `[System::Web::Services::WebMethod]` attribute is on the `Add()` and `Multiply()` methods. But this page doesn't just describe your methods; it gives you a chance to test them. Click the `Add()` method and another Web page will load, as in Figure 21.3. Here you can see a pair of edit boxes labeled x and y where you can enter parameter values. I entered 1 and 2, clicked Invoke, and got the result shown in Figure 21.4. Although XML may not be beautiful to human eyes, it's easy for code to read, and your Web service correctly returns the sum of the two numbers, wrapped in XML.

Note

Web services rely heavily on XML to exchange information and to describe themselves. If you aren't as familiar with XML as you should be, read Appendix B, "XML Review." You need to understand XML structure to read the examples presented throughout this chapter.

CH
21

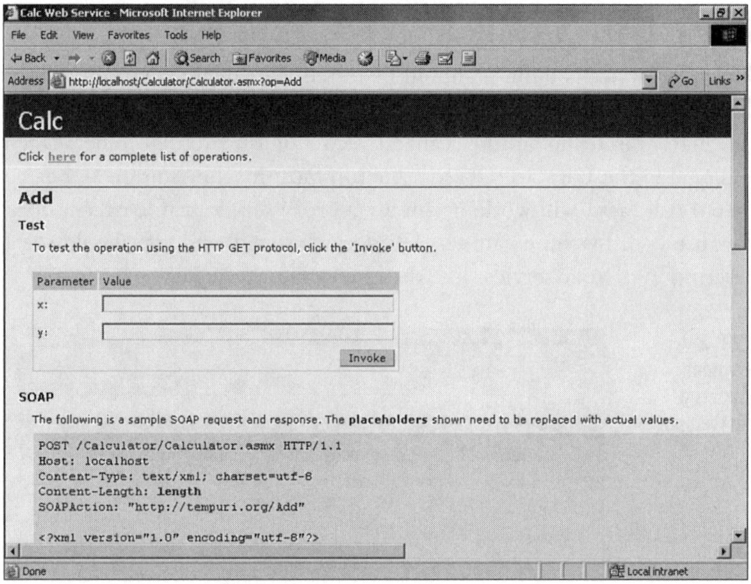

Figure 21.3
You can test your
Web service's
methods in a
browser.

Figure 21.4
You can run your
Web service over the
Web, and get XML
output.

WEB SERVICES DESCRIPTION LANGUAGE

Flip back to the Web page from which you can test your methods, and enter strings such as
hello and **world**, rather than floating point numbers, for the two parameters. Click Invoke,
and instead of nice XML-wrapped output, you'll see something like Listing 21.6. You're
using this component at runtime, and if you pass a parameter of the wrong type, there's no
compiler to warn you in advance. A runtime exception is generated instead.

LISTING 21.6   TYPE CONVERSION ERRORS

```
System.ArgumentException: Cannot convert hello to System.Double.
Parameter name: type ---> System.FormatException: Input string was not in a
correct format.
    at System.Number.ParseDouble(String s, NumberStyles style, NumberFormatInfo
info)
    at System.Double.Parse(String s, NumberStyles style, IFormatProvider provider)
    at System.Convert.ToDouble(String value, IFormatProvider provider)
    at System.String.System.IConvertible.ToDouble(IFormatProvider provider)
    at System.Convert.ChangeType(Object value, Type conversionType, IFormatProvider
provider)
```

LISTING 21.6   CONTINUED

```
  at System.Web.Services.Protocols.ScalarFormatter.FromString(String value, Type
type)
  --- End of inner exception stack trace ---
  at System.Web.Services.Protocols.ScalarFormatter.FromString(String value, Type
type)
  at
System.Web.Services.Protocols.ValueCollectionParameterReader.Read(NameValueCollect
ion collection)
  at System.Web.Services.Protocols.UrlParameterReader.Read(HttpRequest request)
  at System.Web.Services.Protocols.HttpServerProtocol.ReadParameters()
  at System.Web.Services.Protocols.WebServiceHandler.Invoke()
  at System.Web.Services.Protocols.WebServiceHandler.CoreProcessRequest()
```

This is a circumstance you would like to avoid whenever possible. Before code calls your Web service, it should know what parameters the Web service takes and their types. This information is available, in a format called WSDL (Web Services Description Language,) from the same Web server that offers the Web service. On the Calculator.asmx page, there is a link to the Service Description in WSDL. Follow the link and you will see a page of XML like Listing 21.7. Your output will have your own Web server named, of course.

LISTING 21.7   WSDL FOR THE CALCULATOR WEB SERVICE

```xml
<?xml version="1.0" encoding="utf-8" ?>
<definitions xmlns:http="http://schemas.xmlsoap.org/wsdl/http/"
xmlns:soap="http://schemas.xmlsoap.org/wsdl/soap/"
xmlns:s="http://www.w3.org/2001/XMLSchema" xmlns:s0="http://tempuri.org/"
xmlns:soapenc="http://schemas.xmlsoap.org/soap/encoding/"
xmlns:tm="http://microsoft.com/wsdl/mime/textMatching/"
xmlns:mime="http://schemas.xmlsoap.org/wsdl/mime/"
targetNamespace="http://tempuri.org/" xmlns="http://schemas.xmlsoap.org/wsdl/">
<types>
        <s:schema elementFormDefault="qualified"
targetNamespace="http://tempuri.org/">
            <s:element name="Add">
                <s:complexType>
                    <s:sequence>
                        <s:element minOccurs="1" maxOccurs="1" name="x"
type="s:double" />
                        <s:element minOccurs="1" maxOccurs="1" name="y"
type="s:double" />
                    </s:sequence>
                </s:complexType>
            </s:element>
            <s:element name="AddResponse">
                <s:complexType>
                    <s:sequence>
                        <s:element minOccurs="1" maxOccurs="1" name="AddResult"
type="s:double" />
                    </s:sequence>
                </s:complexType>
            </s:element>
            <s:element name="Multiply">
```

CH
21

LISTING 21.7   CONTINUED

```
                    <s:complexType>
                        <s:sequence>
                            <s:element minOccurs="1" maxOccurs="1" name="x"
type="s:double" />
                            <s:element minOccurs="1" maxOccurs="1" name="y"
type="s:double" />
                        </s:sequence>
                    </s:complexType>
                </s:element>
                <s:element name="MultiplyResponse">
                    <s:complexType>
                        <s:sequence>
                            <s:element minOccurs="1" maxOccurs="1"
name="MultiplyResult" type="s:double" />
                        </s:sequence>
                    </s:complexType>
                </s:element>
                <s:element name="double" type="s:double" />
            </s:schema>
        </types>
        <message name="AddSoapIn">
            <part name="parameters" element="s0:Add" />
        </message>
        <message name="AddSoapOut">
            <part name="parameters" element="s0:AddResponse" />
        </message>
        <message name="MultiplySoapIn">
            <part name="parameters" element="s0:Multiply" />
        </message>
        <message name="MultiplySoapOut">
            <part name="parameters" element="s0:MultiplyResponse" />
        </message>
        <message name="AddHttpGetIn">
            <part name="x" type="s:string" />
            <part name="y" type="s:string" />
        </message>
        <message name="AddHttpGetOut">
            <part name="Body" element="s0:double" />
        </message>
        <message name="MultiplyHttpGetIn">
            <part name="x" type="s:string" />
            <part name="y" type="s:string" />
        </message>
        <message name="MultiplyHttpGetOut">
            <part name="Body" element="s0:double" />
        </message>
        <message name="AddHttpPostIn">
            <part name="x" type="s:string" />
            <part name="y" type="s:string" />
        </message>
        <message name="AddHttpPostOut">
            <part name="Body" element="s0:double" />
        </message>
        <message name="MultiplyHttpPostIn">
            <part name="x" type="s:string" />
```

LISTING 21.7   CONTINUED

```
            <part name="y" type="s:string" />
    </message>
    <message name="MultiplyHttpPostOut">
            <part name="Body" element="s0:double" />
    </message>
    <portType name="CalcSoap">
        <operation name="Add">
            <input message="s0:AddSoapIn" />
            <output message="s0:AddSoapOut" />
        </operation>
        <operation name="Multiply">
            <input message="s0:MultiplySoapIn" />
            <output message="s0:MultiplySoapOut" />
        </operation>
    </portType>
    <portType name="CalcHttpGet">
        <operation name="Add">
            <input message="s0:AddHttpGetIn" />
            <output message="s0:AddHttpGetOut" />
        </operation>
        <operation name="Multiply">
            <input message="s0:MultiplyHttpGetIn" />
            <output message="s0:MultiplyHttpGetOut" />
        </operation>
    </portType>
    <portType name="CalcHttpPost">
        <operation name="Add">
            <input message="s0:AddHttpPostIn" />
            <output message="s0:AddHttpPostOut" />
        </operation>
        <operation name="Multiply">
            <input message="s0:MultiplyHttpPostIn" />
            <output message="s0:MultiplyHttpPostOut" />
        </operation>
    </portType>
    <binding name="CalcSoap" type="s0:CalcSoap">
        <soap:binding transport="http://schemas.xmlsoap.org/soap/http"
style="document" />
        <operation name="Add">
            <soap:operation soapAction="http://tempuri.org/Add" style="document"
/>
            <input>
                <soap:body use="literal" />
            </input>
            <output>
                <soap:body use="literal" />
            </output>
        </operation>
        <operation name="Multiply">
            <soap:operation soapAction="http://tempuri.org/Multiply"
style="document" />
            <input>
                <soap:body use="literal" />
            </input>
            <output>
```

CH
21

LISTING 21.7 CONTINUED

```
                <soap:body use="literal" />
            </output>
        </operation>
    </binding>
    <binding name="CalcHttpGet" type="s0:CalcHttpGet">
        <http:binding verb="GET" />
        <operation name="Add">
            <http:operation location="/Add" />
            <input>
                <http:urlEncoded />
            </input>
            <output>
                <mime:mimeXml part="Body" />
            </output>
        </operation>
        <operation name="Multiply">
            <http:operation location="/Multiply" />
            <input>
                <http:urlEncoded />
            </input>
            <output>
                <mime:mimeXml part="Body" />
            </output>
        </operation>
    </binding>
    <binding name="CalcHttpPost" type="s0:CalcHttpPost">
        <http:binding verb="POST" />
        <operation name="Add">
            <http:operation location="/Add" />
            <input>
                <mime:content type="application/x-www-form-urlencoded" />
            </input>
            <output>
                <mime:mimeXml part="Body" />
            </output>
        </operation>
        <operation name="Multiply">
            <http:operation location="/Multiply" />
            <input>
                <mime:content type="application/x-www-form-urlencoded" />
            </input>
            <output>
                <mime:mimeXml part="Body" />
            </output>
        </operation>
    </binding>
    <service name="Calc">
        <port name="CalcSoap" binding="s0:CalcSoap">
            <soap:address location="http://localhost/Calculator/Calculator.asmx"
/>
        </port>
        <port name="CalcHttpGet" binding="s0:CalcHttpGet">
            <http:address location="http://localhost/Calculator/Calculator.asmx"
/>
```

LISTING 21.7   CONTINUED

```
        </port>
        <port name="CalcHttpPost" binding="s0:CalcHttpPost">
            <http:address location="http://localhost/Calculator/Calculator.asmx"
/>
        </port>
    </service>
</definitions>
```

This WSDL file starts with a `<types>` element, followed by 12 `<message>` elements. Each presents slight variations on the same information: this Web service has a method called `Add` and a method called `Multiply`, and each method takes two parameters, x and y, each of type `double`, and returns a `double`. The `<portType>`, `<binding>`, and `<service>` elements list the URLs to be used when actually running the XML Web service.

While a human can read WSDL, it's obviously not meant for us. It's meant for software to consume. And one product that knows how to use it is right in front of you: Visual Studio .NET.

CONSUMING A WEB SERVICE FROM CODE

Writing an application that uses an XML Web service is made much easier by the support for Web services in Visual Studio. In this section you'll see for yourself how to do it. Close the Visual Studio solution in which you built the Calculator Web service. Choose File, New, Projects, and choose a Managed C++ application. Call it Consumer. In ClassView, expand the Consumer project and the Global functions under it, then double-click the `_tmain()` function to edit it.

To make the Web service you built earlier available to this project, choose Project, Add Web Reference. The Add Web Reference dialog box, shown in Figure 21.5, appears. At the bottom of the left-hand pane is a link to Web References on Local Server. Click the link. Visual Studio will explore the local Web server looking for XML Web services, then show you a list like the one in Figure 21.6.

Click the link to `http://localhost/Calculator/Calculator.vsdisco` and you'll see something like Figure 21.7. In many cases the information shown here will be enough to confirm that you have found the correct XML Web service. If you're unsure, click the View Documentation link, and as Figure 21.8 shows, the same Web page you loaded in the browser to test the Web service is displayed in the Add Web Reference dialog box. After you're sure you've found the correct service, click the Add Reference button at the bottom of the dialog box to add a reference to the Calculator Web service to your Consumer project.

Figure 21.5
Visual Studio can consume XML Web services after you locate the reference.

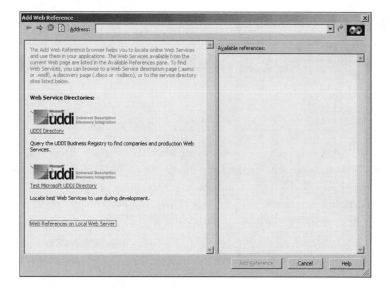

Figure 21.6
List the XML Web services on your server.

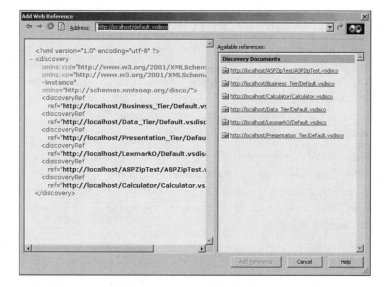

Visual Studio generates a proxy class that represents the component and adds it to your project. This class is called Calc. A header file is generated for you that makes the methods of the XML Web service available. To use the Calc class, you must include the WebService.h header file in your code.

In Consumer.cpp, before the definition of main() starts, add this line:

```
#include "WebService.h"
```

Figure 21.7
A discovery file can lead to documentation or a WSDL contract.

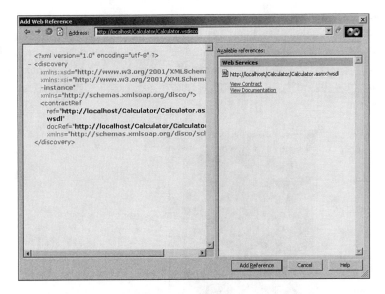

Figure 21.8
A discovery file can lead to documentation or a WSDL contract.

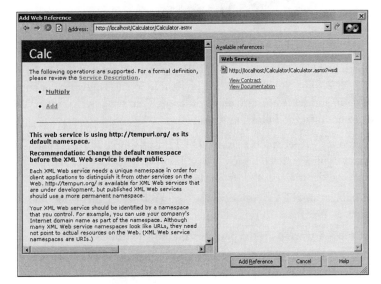

In the body of _tmain(), remove the TODO comment and add this code, editing the call to WriteLine:

```
double answer;
Calc* calc = new Calc();
answer = calc->Add(1,2);
Console::WriteLine(answer);
Console::ReadLine();
return 0;
```

Cн
21

Build the application, correct any typing errors, and run it by choosing Debug, Start. You should see something like Figure 21.9. It's just the number 3 in a console output box, but it proves that your Managed C++ application went to the Web server, ran a WebMethod of an XML Web service, got back an answer all wrapped up in XML, and extracted the number from inside the XML for you to print on the screen—all without any special coding on your part.

Figure 21.9
Your application can use an XML Web service without a lot of coding.

It's worth looking at that again. XML Web services are based on open standards such as HTTP, XML, and SOAP. They can be written in any language, on any platform or operating system, and served out by many different Web servers. To run a Web service, code needs to perform the following steps:

1. Choose whether to do a simple HTTP get, simple HTTP post, SOAP get, or SOAP post. Typically this decision is based on the types of information being sent to the method or received back from the method.

2. Establish an HTTP connection to the Web server that offers the XML Web service, such as localhost in this example.

3. If necessary, wrap up the parameters to the method call in XML.

4. Send a properly formatted get or post request to the Web server, followed by the parameters or XML-wrapped parameters.

5. Read the response from the Web server.

6. Unwrap the response from the XML around it.

7. Convert the response to the type required (such as float in this example).

This list doesn't even include the work that code is expected to perform to determine the name of the Web service, its methods, and the parameters and return types of the methods. Now let me remind you of the code you had to write to get those seven or more steps accomplished:

```
Calc* calc = new Calc();
answer = calc->Add(1,2);
```

All the plumbing work is done for you behind the scenes by code from the .NET Framework and the Base Class Library. You just work with the proxy class that represents the XML Web service as though it were an ordinary C++ class. It's so simple, you might not even notice what an amazing thing is going on.

DISCO AND UDDI

Visual Studio was able to compile your calls to the Calculator Web service because the WSDL file describes the service in detail—including the Web methods it offers and the parameters they take. But when you added the Web reference, you didn't browse directly to the WSDL file, but rather to the Visual Studio DISCO file, Calculator.vsdisco. Discovery of a Web service has to come before a detailed list of the functionality of that service, and DISCO files enable discovery of Web services across the Internet. They are part of UDDI (Universal Discovery, Description, and Integration).

DISCO files contain links to more information about a service. The file generated for Calculator contained relative links to the Calculator.asmx file on the same site, but imagine a DISCO file on a third-party site that contained absolute links from that site to the Web server that actually hosted Calculator, or perhaps some genuinely useful service such as bookings for a doctor's office, or reserving books at a library.

You can find a repository of DISCO files at `http://www.uddi.org`. You or your software can use them to find useful Web services that someone else has already written. As always, the quickest way to get code is to reuse it, and UDDI makes that possible. And when you write a terrific XML Web service that everyone's going to want to use, be sure to add it to the repository for everyone to find!

FROM HERE

In this chapter, you saw how simple it is to create an XML Web service in Managed C++. If you write such a service, and spread the word that it is on your server, code from all over the Internet can run your XML Web service. That code might be written in one of the .NET languages, but it doesn't have to be. XML Web services are built on open standards and can be consumed from Java applications, from applications written in C or Perl and running on Unix, or from almost any combination of language, operating system, and Web server.

This chapter also showed you that the simplest way to consume a Web service is from another Managed C++ application; calling the methods of the XML Web service is just like calling the methods of an ordinary C++ class. You can consume any XML Web service in this way; all you need to do is browse to the DISCO and WSDL files on the server that offers the service. It might be written in Java, or Python, or some language you've never heard of, and it doesn't matter at all. From your code, using the XML Web service is as simple as using any C++ object. This is why XML Web services are going to change the way software is made.

If you're reading the .NET part of this book in order, you're probably noticing that a lot of tasks that used to be really difficult are now really simple—as simple as using an ordinary C++ class. You can see more of that in action in Chapter 22, "Database Access with ADO.NET" and Chapter 23, "COM Interop."

DATABASE ACCESS WITH ADO.NET

In this chapter

GETTING STARTED WITH ADO.NET

Chapter 11, "Database Programming," introduced a number of important database concepts and demonstrated several Win32 database applications. In this chapter you'll see a .NET spin on those same concepts, and see how to build .NET applications that use ADO.NET to access a database. To keep things as simple as possible, these sample applications will use the same sample database as that used in Chapter 11, DeptStore.mdb. You might want to read Chapter 11 before this chapter, just to learn your way around that database sample.

The heart of ADO.NET is the dataset class, System::Data::Dataset. It represents a snapshot of a subset of a database and holds several tables at once. The related classes System::Data::DataTable, System::Data::DataColumn, and System::Data::DataRow enable you to reach parts of a dataset with ease. Figure 22.1 shows how these classes are related.

Figure 22.1
The ADO.NET dataset represents several tables from a database.

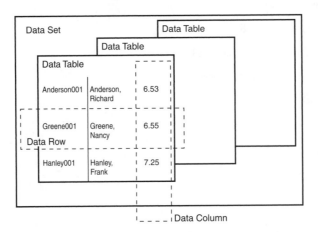

The dataset class represents the database to your code. You can fill it from the database, then close your connection and just work with the dataset. You can build a dataset at your leisure from user input, then connect to the database and use the dataset to update it.

A DATA ACCESS COMPONENT

In Chapter 11, one of the sample applications was a form-based program that allowed you to enter an employee name and "look up" that employee in the database. In this chapter the sample application does the same thing. To add a slight twist to what you've already seen, the application is a .NET object that is used by an ASP.NET page.

The class is called Employee and is wrapped in a namespace called EmployeeData. It has a RetrieveData() method that returns a pointer to a DataSet object so that the ASP.NET page can work with the data that was retrieved.

CREATING THE SKELETON OF THE CLASS

To create the .NET object, start by creating a new project. Choose File, New, Project, and choose Managed C++ Class Library. Call the project EmployeeData. In Class View, change the classname from Class1 to Employee and add two private variables, both String*, called m_Connection and m_Query.

The member variable m_Connection holds the connection string, which is used to connect to the database. In some designs, the connection information is hardcoded into the component. In general, you will build more portable applications if the connection string is passed in. When it's hardcoded, you have to recompile your application if anything about the database changes. That can be really annoying.

Now, how will that variable get set? The easiest approach is probably to build a constructor that takes a string. That way no one can use this class without setting the connection string first. Add a constructor to the class definition and add code for it inline. The class should look like Listing 22.1 so far.

LISTING 22.1   Employee CLASS WITH CONNECTION STRING

```
// Employee.h

#pragma once

namespace EmployeeData
{
   public __gc class Employee
   {
   private:
          String* m_Query;
          String* m_Connection;
   public:
          Employee(String* connection)
          {
                  m_Connection = connection;
          }
   };
}
```

CODING RetrieveData()

When the RetrieveData() method runs, a connection is made and a query is executed. How will the string for this query be set? As a starting point, just hard-code it in the constructor:

```
Employee(String* connection)
{
   m_Connection = connection;
   m_Query = "SELECT * FROM Employees";
}
```

Now add that RetrieveData() method. It doesn't take any parameters and it returns a DataSet*. You implement it in the .cpp file rather than inline in the header file. Start by adding a line to the class declaring the member function, right after the declaration and implementation of the constructor:

```
DataSet* RetrieveData();
```

Use Solution Explorer to edit EmployeeData.cpp and add a stub for this method:

```
DataSet* EmployeeData::Employee::RetrieveData()
{
    DataSet* ds = new DataSet("Employees");
    return ds;
}
```

Notice the full name of the method. Both the namespace name and the classname precede the function name. This stub just creates a dataset and returns a pointer to it. It will do for a start.

The code as it stands right now will not compile, because it uses names from the `System::Data` namespace without using their full names, and it doesn't add the requisite assembly reference. At the top of EmployeeData.h, immediately before the `namespace EmployeeData` line, add these lines:

```
#using <System.dll>
#using <System.Data.dll>
#using <System.Xml.dll>
using namespace System::Data;
using namespace System::Xml;
```

At the top of EmployeeData.cpp, add these lines after the existing `#include` statements:

```
#using <System.Data.dll>
using namespace System::Data;
```

If you didn't know what DLL to name here, the online help for `System::Data::DataSet` mentions the assembly in which the class is found. At this point you should be able to build the project by choosing Build, Build or pressing F7. Correct any compile errors before continuing.

RETRIEVING DATA

Filling in the `RetrieveData()` method is quite straightforward. Here are the steps it follows:

1. Use the connection string to create a connection.
2. Open the connection.
3. Create an adapter.
4. Use the query string to put a command into the adapter.
5. Use the adapter to fill the dataset.
6. Close the connection.

Because this is managed code and all the objects created are on the managed heap, there's no cleanup code to speak of. After you've closed the connection you can just return from the function and know that the command, adapter, and other temporary variables will be tidied up for you. The completed function looks like Listing 22.2.

LISTING 22.2 Employee::RetrieveData()

```
DataSet* EmployeeData::Employee::RetrieveData()
{
    DataSet* ds = new DataSet("Employees");
    OleDbConnection* conn = new OleDbConnection(m_Connection);
    conn->Open();

    OleDbDataAdapter* adapter = new OleDbDataAdapter();
    adapter->SelectCommand = new OleDbCommand(m_Query, conn);

    try
    {
        adapter->Fill(ds);
    }
    catch (OleDbException* e)
    {
        Console::WriteLine("OleDbException caught while filling the dataset");
        Console::WriteLine(e->Message);
    }
    conn->Close();

    return ds;
}
```

You have to add another using statement at the top of Employee.cpp:

```
using namespace System::Data::OleDb;
```

Try building the code again at this point and correct any errors.

BUILDING THE ASP.NET PAGE

The Employee class isn't really complete yet; it only retrieves all records. But it's usable enough, so why not build an ASP.NET page to give it a workout? The visual designer for Web Forms doesn't generate C++ code, so this page will be written in C#; it's the ASP.NET-supported language that's closest to C++.

In Visual Studio, with your EmployeeData project open, choose File, New, Project. Select C# on the left and ASP.NET Web Application on the right. Make sure that the Add to Solution radio button is selected. Enter the Location as http://localhost/EmployeeUI. Figure 22.2 shows your choice. Click Open to create the page.

The project is created for you and added to the solution. A number of files are created within the project. In Solution Explorer, double-click WebForm1.aspx to open it in Design mode. Choose View, Toolbox to display a palette of controls you can add to the page. The Web Forms tab should be showing, as in Figure 22.3.

Figure 22.2
Create a C# project for your user interface.

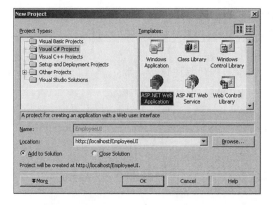

Figure 22.3
The Web Forms controls in the Toolbox are used to build the user interface.

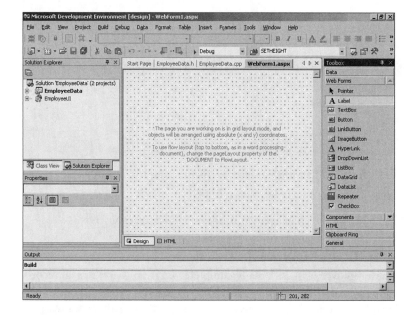

Add a label before the text box and change the Text property to **Enter the name, or partial name, of an employee to look up:**. Add another label before that one and set the text to **Department Store Employee Database**. Expand the Font property, and set Bold to True and Size to Large.

Click the text box and use the Properties window to change the ID to Criteria. This field will hold the criteria you plan to pass to the database to use in the query. Click the button and change the text property to `Retrieve Data`. Figure 22.4 shows how the Web page should look. Double-click the button to edit the code that runs when it is clicked. You'll notice that this code opens in a different file, WebForm1.aspx.cs. This file is called the *code behind file* for the ASP.NET page.

Figure 22.4
Build an ASP.NET
user interface.

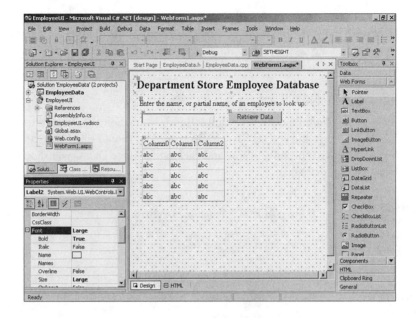

ADDING SCRIPT TO THE PAGE

This ASP.NET page is full of controls that are processed on the server. What it needs now
is some server-side script to run when the Retrieve Data button is clicked. The script should
look at the contents of the text field and use that to restrict the employees that are retrieved,
but because that capability is not in the component yet, this first version of `Button1Click()`
ignores the text field and just retrieves all the employees.

Edit the `Button1_Click()` method that was generated for you so that it reads like this:

```
private void Button1_Click(object sender, System.EventArgs e)
{
        String path = "D:\\Working\\Gregcons\\Using Visual
➡C++\\Database\\deptstore.mdb";
    EmployeeData.Employee emp = new EmployeeData.Employee(
            "Provider=Microsoft.Jet.OLEDB.4.0;Data Source="+path);
    DataSet ds = emp.RetrieveData();
    DataGrid1.DataSource = ds;
    DataGrid1.DataBind();
}
```

Tip

Because this is C#, the full name of the Employee class is `EmployeeData.Employee`,
rather than `EmployeeData::Employee`, as it would be in C++. Also, you are using a
String reference rather than a String* as you would in Managed C++. For more on the
differences between C++ and C#, see Chapter 19, "Integrating with C#."

Be sure to change the path to the database to match the location where you've copied DeptStore.mdb. For this code to work, the script needs to know how to find the Employee class. Choose Project, Add Reference. Click on the Project tab and select the EmployeeData line. Click OK to confirm the reference.

TESTING THE ASP.NET PAGE

Build your solution by choosing Build, Build. In the Solution Explorer, right-click WebForm1.aspx and choose View in Browser. You should see the entry screen as shown in Figure 22.5. Try entering a name and clicking Retrieve Data—you should see results that look like Figure 22.6.

Figure 22.5
Test your ASP.NET page from within Visual Studio.

Figure 22.6
The Data Grid control presents the contents of your DataSet automatically.

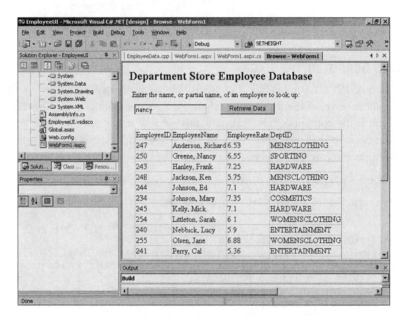

It doesn't matter what you type in the text field, because the script ignores the text field at the moment. You should see a list of employees with their names, IDs, departments, and rates.

How did that happen? There are so few lines of code in Button1_Click()—in fact, only five lines. The first line builds a connection string that represents the DeptStore.mdb database. The second line creates an instance of the Employee class that was written earlier in this chapter. The third calls the RetrieveData() method of that class, which returns a dataset.

The fourth gives the dataset to the data grid to display, and the final line in the routine tells the data grid that all the data has been sourced, so the grid can be displayed. That's it! Your ASP.NET application relies on two pieces of existing code: the `Employee` object that knows how to get information from the department store database, and the `DataGrid` control that is supplied with the .NET framework and knows how to display a data set.

> **Note**
>
> Did you notice that C# code in `Button1_Click()` called Managed C++ code in RetrieveData()? Cross-language development is a seamless reality in .NET.

FILTERING ON EMPLOYEE NAME

To filter on the employee's name, you have to modify the component. It is still open in Visual Studio, so in Class View, right-click the `Employee` class and choose Add, Add Function. Figure 22.7 shows the Add Member Function Wizard dialog filled out with a void return type, the name FilterEmployee, and the single parameter, a `String*` called name. Click Finish after filling out the dialog. The declaration is added to the class definition in EmployeeData.h and a stub is added to EmployeeData.cpp for you.

Figure 22.7
Add a function to narrow your query a little.

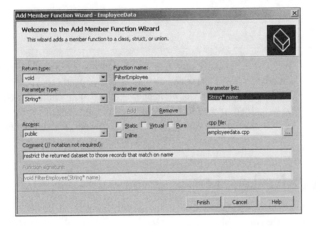

All this function needs to do is change the query string. Using a `StringBuilder` makes it simple to build a query string around the name that was passed in. Here's how the function looks:

```
void EmployeeData::Employee::FilterEmployee(String* name)
{
    System::Text::StringBuilder* sb =
        new System::Text::StringBuilder(
            S"SELECT * FROM Employees WHERE EmployeeName LIKE '%");
    sb->Append(name);
    sb->Append(S"%'");
    m_Query = sb->ToString();
}
```

If you're typing this yourself, pay close attention to single and double quotes. Double quotes surround the strings passed to the `StringBuilder` constructor and the final call to `Append()`. The constructor parameter ends with a single quote and a percent sign–these are delimiters used in the SQL query. The parameter to `Append()` ends with a percent sign and a single quote.

Now change the ASP.NET page so it uses what's in the text box and calls this function. Switch over to WebForm1.aspx.cs and after the line that creates the `Employee` object, add this line:

```
emp.FilterEmployee(Criteria.Text);
```

Build the project, then view the page in the browser again. Enter a partial name and you should see that employee's database entry, as shown in Figure 22.8.

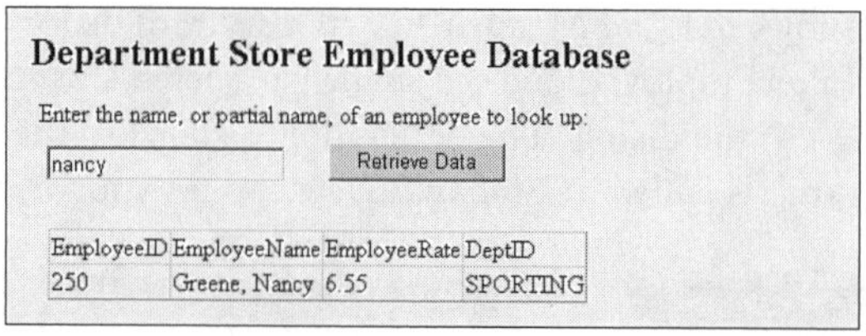

Figure 22.8
Look up employees by name or partial name.

Department Store Employee Database

Enter the name, or partial name, of an employee to look up:

nancy	Retrieve Data

EmployeeID	EmployeeName	EmployeeRate	DeptID
250	Greene, Nancy	6.55	SPORTING

The `DataGrid` control can do far more than you see in this little sample. Try playing around with the properties a little to adjust its appearance. Click the links to Auto Format or Property Builder that appear at the bottom of the Properties window when the `DataGrid` is selected, and do a little experimenting. It's worth the diversion into C# from time to time when you gain access to convenience like this.

USING A DataRelation

The sample application in the last section used a very simple SQL SELECT statement to find employees. It used only one table from the database and simply went through the dataset by rows. In this section, you'll see how to build an application that tackles a task normally handled with a SQL JOIN. Rather than dealing with an ASP.NET page and server-side controls, this is a simple console application.

CREATING THE PROJECT

Start by creating a new project: choose File, New, Project. Create a Managed C++ application called Relation. In this sample all the work happens within the `_tmain()` function. The structure of `_tmain()` looks like this:

1. Open a connection to the database.
2. Create a `DataSet` and associated `DataTable` objects, and fill them.

3. Create the `DataRelation` objects and add them to the `DataSet`.

4. Close the connection.

5. Write out the employees and prompt the user to choose one.

6. Use the relations to find the employee's manager.

7. Write out the manager's name.

Each of these steps is explored in the sections that follow. But before you can begin to add code to the project, you need to add references to the required assemblies and namespaces. Add these lines to replace the line that brings in the System namespace:

```
#using <System.dll>
#using <System.data.dll>
#using <System.Xml.dll>

using namespace System;
using namespace System::Data;
using namespace System::Data::OleDb;
```

Build the project to ensure you have no typing errors before continuing. Remove the TODO comment and the line that writes out "Hello World".

OPEN A CONNECTION TO THE DATABASE

Opening the connection to the database is quite simple: Build a connection string, then open a connection. If the file isn't found, an exception will be thrown, so it's a good idea to wrap the whole thing in a `try` block, as shown in Listing 22.3. Edit `_tmain()` so the code in Listing 22.3 appears immediately before the existing `return` statement.

LISTING 22.3   OPENING A CONNECTION TO THE DATABASE

```
OleDbConnection* conn;
try
{
    String* connectionstring = "Provider=Microsoft.Jet.OLEDB.4.0;Data
➥Source=deptstore.mdb;";
    conn = new OleDbConnection(connectionstring);
    conn->Open();
}
catch(OleDbException* e)
{
    Console::WriteLine("OleDbException caught");
    Console::WriteLine(e->get_Message());
}
conn->Close();
Console::ReadLine();
```

Copy the DeptStore.mdb file into the project folder, then build and run the project to confirm that the connection can be opened successfully.

CREATE AND FILL DataSet AND DataTable OBJECTS

The DataSet object in this sample is not filled from a simple query. Instead, DataTable objects are added to it, and the tables are filled from queries. Start by creating the objects themselves. Add this code before the try block:

```
DataSet* deptStore = new DataSet("DepartmentStore");
DataTable* depts = new DataTable("Departments");
DataTable* employees = new DataTable("Employees");
DataTable* managers = new DataTable("DeptManagers");
```

Next, create a query and adapter to fill each table. Add this code inside the try block, right after the call to Open():

```
String* query;
OleDbDataAdapter* adapter = new OleDbDataAdapter();
```

Use these to fill the DataTable for the departments:

```
query = "SELECT * FROM Departments";
adapter->SelectCommand = new OleDbCommand(query, conn);
adapter->Fill(depts);
deptStore->get_Tables()->Add(depts);
```

Copy this block twice, changing the query, the name of the DataTable that is passed to Fill() and to Add()—use each of the data tables in turn.

In the Employees table, the EmployeeID is the primary key. Some code a little later in this section is going to use the primary key to search the table, so you need to set this key in the DataTable object. After the block that fills the employees DataTable, add these lines:

```
DataColumn* keys __gc[] = new DataColumn* __gc[1];
keys[0] = employees->get_Columns()->get_Item("EmployeeID");
employees->set_PrimaryKey(keys);
```

The rather unusual __gc[] syntax is used to create managed arrays, so the first line declares a managed array that can hold one pointer to a DataColumn. The second line creates that pointer by asking the employees DataTable object for the EmployeeID column. The third line sets that column as the primary key.

CREATE RELATIONS

The key to this sample is the relations between the tables. You may recall that the layout is as follows:

- The Departments table has three fields: DeptID, DeptName, and Location.
- The Employees table has four fields: EmployeeID, EmployeeName, Rate, and DeptID.
- The DeptManagers table has two fields: ManagerID and DeptID.

The DeptID field is the link among these three tables. In addition, the ManagerID in the DeptManagers table corresponds to some EmployeeID entries in the Employees table.

However, the Access database does not contain any indication of these links. Traditionally you would establish the links with a join, perhaps in a SQL statement like this:

```
SELECT * from Employees, Departments WHERE Employees.DeptID=Departments.DeptID
```

It can be repetitive to specify conditions like this over and over again, so it's more efficient to set up a relation between the tables in your dataset. Add this code at the end of the try block:

```
DataRelation* mngr_dept = new DataRelation("Manager_To_Dept",
    managers->get_Columns()->get_Item("DeptID"),
    depts->get_Columns()->get_Item("DeptID"));
deptStore->get_Relations()->Add(mngr_dept);

DataRelation* dept_emp = new DataRelation("Dept_to_Employee",
    depts->get_Columns()->get_Item("DeptID"),
    employees->get_Columns()->get_Item("DeptID"));
deptStore->get_Relations()->Add(dept_emp);

DataRelation* emp_mngr = new DataRelation("Employee to Manager",
    employees->get_Columns()->get_Item("EmployeeID"),
    managers->get_Columns()->get_Item("ManagerID"));
deptStore->get_Relations()->Add(emp_mngr);
```

This creates the two relations and adds each to the data set.

CLOSE THE CONNECTION

The ADO.NET approach to data access is a disconnected approach. After you've filled your tables, you don't need the database connection anymore. Closing it frees resources for other applications that might need to access the database. A call to Close() has already been added after the catch block, so you don't need to add any code for this step.

PROMPT FOR A USER

Continue to add code to _tmain(), carrying on after the catch block and immediately after the call to Close(). Add these lines:

```
int empCount = employees->get_Rows()->get_Count();

Console::WriteLine("Find a Manager");
Console::WriteLine("");
Console::WriteLine("Employees:");
for (int i = 0; i < empCount; i++)
{
        Console::Write(employees->get_Rows()->get_Item(i)-
➥>get_Item("EmployeeID"));
    Console::Write(" ");
    Console::Write(employees->get_Rows()->get_Item(i)->get_Item("EmployeeName"));
    Console::WriteLine("");
}

int empNum;
try
{
```

```
        Console::Write("Enter the number of an employee: ");
        empNum = Convert::ToInt32(Console::ReadLine());
        if (empNum < 0) throw new FormatException();
}
catch(FormatException*)
{
        Console::WriteLine("Invalid choice");
}
```

This code writes out all the employees, one at a time, using the rows of the data table. It serves as a handy example of the uses of a data table. The user is then prompted to enter a number, and the string the user types is converted to an integer. Build this code and run it—you should see all the employees, and be prompted to choose one. Try entering a string that is not a number, or a negative number, to see the error message you coded.

USE RELATIONS TO FIND A MANAGER

After the user has chosen an employee, you need to look up the manager. Add this code at the bottom of the second try block, after the line that checks empNum is in range:

```
DataRow* emp = employees->get_Rows()->Find(__box(empNum));
DataRow* mgr = emp->GetParentRow("Dept_to_Employee")->
    GetParentRow("Manager_to_Dept")->
    GetParentRow("Employee to Manager");
```

This saves the selected employee. Then a single statement that spans three lines goes from the selected employee through one relation to that employee's department, through another relation to that department's manager, and finally through a third from the manager's ID back to the manager's name.

WRITE OUT THE MANAGER'S NAME

Still at the bottom of the second try block, add these last few lines of code to get the manager's name from the data row and write it to the console:

```
Console::WriteLine("");
Console::Write("The manager for ");
Console::Write(emp->get_Item("EmployeeName"));
Console::Write(" is:   ");
Console::Write(mgr->get_Item("EmployeeName"));
Console::WriteLine("");
```

All this code is in the try block so that it is skipped if the user enters an invalid employee index. Build and run the application now. You should see output like Figure 22.9 when you choose an employee index that is in range.

Using relations is as simple as that. Save yourself a lot of repetitive typing, and get your database connections closed as early as possible, by using data sets to their fullest, and not just as though they were traditional recordsets.

Figure 22.9
Relations let you combine information from several tables.

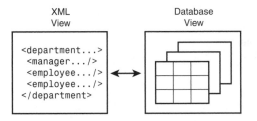

CH
22

GETTING XML FROM A DATABASE

A `DataSet` object is not only a collection of tables, each with rows and columns. You can also think of it as an XML document, and work with it as though it were XML. Figure 22.10 illustrates this.

Figure 22.10
A `DataSet` can be thought of as tables or as XML at the same time.

```
XML                          Database
View                         View

<department...>
 <manager.../>
 <employee.../>  ←→
 <employee.../>
</department>
```

To see how quickly you can create XML from a database, create a new Managed C++ application called WriteXML. Add these `#using` and `using` statements at the top, replacing the `using namespace System;` line:

```
#using <mscorlib.dll>
#using <System.dll>
#using <System.Data.dll>
#using <System.Xml.dll>

using namespace System;
using namespace System::Data;
using namespace System::Data::OleDb;
using namespace System::Xml;
using namespace System::IO;
```

The body of the `_tmain()` function is shown in Listing 22.6. Enter this code in place of the body of `_tmain()` that was provided, and build the project. Copy the DeptStore.mdb file into this project folder, and run the application.

LISTING 22.6   A main() FUNCTION TO EXTRACT DATA AND WRITE IT AS XML

```
OleDbConnection* conn;
DataSet* employees = new DataSet("EmployeeList");
try
{
    String* connectionstring = "Provider=Microsoft.Jet.OLEDB.4.0;Data
➥Source=deptstore.mdb;";
    conn = new OleDbConnection(connectionstring);
    conn->Open();
    String* query;
    query = "SELECT * FROM Employees";
    OleDbDataAdapter* adapter = new OleDbDataAdapter();
    adapter->SelectCommand = new OleDbCommand(query, conn);
    adapter->Fill(employees);
    conn->Close();
}
catch(OleDbException* e)
{
    Console::WriteLine("OleDbException caught");
    Console::WriteLine(e->get_Message());
}
conn->Close();

FileStream* xmlFile;
try
{
    xmlFile = new FileStream("db.xml",
            FileMode::Create,
            FileAccess::Write);
}
catch(...)
{
    Console::WriteLine("Could not create XML file.");
    return -1;
}
XmlTextWriter* writer = new XmlTextWriter(xmlFile,
    new System::Text::UTF8Encoding(true));
writer->set_Formatting(Formatting::Indented);
writer->WriteStartDocument();
employees->WriteXml(writer);

return 0;
```

After you run the sample application, the file db.xml should contain XML built from the contents of the employee table. Here's an excerpt:

```
<?xml version="1.0" encoding="utf-8"?>
<EmployeeList>
  <Table>
    <EmployeeID>247</EmployeeID>
    <EmployeeName>Anderson, Richard</EmployeeName>
    <EmployeeRate>6.53</EmployeeRate>
    <DeptID>MENSCLOTHING</DeptID>
  </Table>
  <Table>
    <EmployeeID>250</EmployeeID>
```

```
    <EmployeeName>Greene, Nancy</EmployeeName>
    <EmployeeRate>6.55</EmployeeRate>
    <DeptID>SPORTING</DeptID>
  </Table></EmployeeList>
```

Notice the surrounding tag name, EmployeeList. This comes from the string passed to the DataSet constructor at the top of main(). The other tag names come from the schema of the database itself. This code is all very straightforward—the only complicated part is writing to a file. If you wanted to get all the tables from the database at once, you could create individual DataTable objects and add them to the DataSet object as you saw in the Relation example earlier in this chapter, then have the DataSet object write out its XML.

FILLING A DATABASE FROM XML

The same simplicity comes into play when you use an XML file to fill a data table. To see it at work, create a new Managed C++ application called ReadXML. As before, add these lines in place of the using namespace System; line:

```
#using <mscorlib.dll>
#using <System.dll>
#using <System.Data.dll>
#using <System.Xml.dll>

using namespace System;
using namespace System::Data;
using namespace System::Data::OleDb;
using namespace System::Xml;
using namespace System::IO;
```

Listing 22.7 contains the body of the main() function to read a file of XML and use it to update the database. Enter this code in place of the body of main() that was provided, and then build the project.

LISTING 22.7   A main() FUNCTION TO FILL A DATABASE FROM A FILE OF XML

```
DataSet* deptStore = new DataSet("DepartmentStore");
OleDbConnection* conn;
FileStream* xmlFile;
try
{
    xmlFile = new FileStream("db.xml",
            FileMode::Open,
            FileAccess::Read);

    XmlTextReader* reader = new XmlTextReader(xmlFile);
        deptStore->ReadXml(reader, XmlReadMode::InferSchema);

    // write the loaded data to the database
    String* connectionstring = "Provider=Microsoft.Jet.OLEDB.4.0;Data
➥Source=deptstore.mdb;";
    conn = new OleDbConnection(connectionstring);
    conn->Open();
```

LISTING 22.7 A main() FUNCTION TO FILL A DATABASE FROM A FILE OF XML

```
    OleDbDataAdapter* adapter = new OleDbDataAdapter();
        adapter->SelectCommand = new OleDbCommand("SELECT * FROM Employees", conn);
    OleDbCommandBuilder* CB = new OleDbCommandBuilder(adapter);
    adapter->Update(deptStore, "Employees");

    Console::WriteLine("The database was filled successfully.");
}
catch(IOException* ioe)
{
    Console::WriteLine("Could not open XML file.");
    Console::WriteLine(ioe->get_Message());
}
catch(Exception*  e)
{
    Console::WriteLine("The database could not be filled.");
    Console::WriteLine(e->get_Message());
}
conn->Close();
Console::ReadLine();
return 0;
```

Copy the DeptStore.mdb file into this project folder. You'll need an XML file for the update. Here's one that will do:

```xml
<?xml version="1.0" encoding="utf-8"?>
<EmployeeList>
  <Employees>
    <EmployeeID>301</EmployeeID>
    <EmployeeName>Smith, John</EmployeeName>
    <EmployeeRate>7.02</EmployeeRate>
    <DeptID>MENSCLOTHING</DeptID>
  </Employees>
  <Employees>
    <EmployeeID>302</EmployeeID>
    <EmployeeName>Lee, Alice</EmployeeName>
    <EmployeeRate>7.55</EmployeeRate>
    <DeptID>SPORTING</DeptID>
  </Employees>
</EmployeeList>
```

It's important that none of the EmployeeID values in this XML file are already in use in the database. An exception is thrown if you try to add a record with a non-unique key. Save this file as db.xml in the project folder and then run the application. After the application has run, double-click DeptStore.mdb to open it in Access. You should see two new records in the Employees table, as in Figure 22.11.

Figure 22.11
Two new employees
have been added to
the table.

EmployeeID	EmployeeName	EmployeeRate	DeptID
236	Anderson, Maggie	8.95	COSMETICS
247	Anderson, Richard	6.53	MENSCLOTHING
242	Calbert, Susan	9.03	ENTERTAINMENT
250	Greene, Nancy	6.55	SPORTING
243	Hanley, Frank	7.25	HARDWARE
253	Harrison, Lenny	9.00	SPORTING
248	Jackson, Ken	5.75	MENSCLOTHING
246	Jenkins, Ted	8.92	HARDWARE
244	Johnson, Ed	7.10	HARDWARE
234	Johnson, Mary	7.35	COSMETICS
245	Kelly, Mick	7.10	HARDWARE
254	Littleton, Sarah	6.10	WOMENSCLOTHING
240	Nebbick, Lucy	5.90	ENTERTAINMENT
255	Olsen, Jane	6.88	WOMENSCLOTHING
241	Perry, Cal	5.36	ENTERTAINMENT
249	Peters, Sam	9.15	MENSCLOTHING
237	Sanford, Faith	6.55	ELECTRONICS
238	Smith, James	5.75	ELECTRONICS
251	Uley, Victor	6.78	SPORTING
235	White, Gail	6.22	COSMETICS
252	Wilson, Denny	6.20	SPORTING
239	Woods, Edward	10.65	ELECTRONICS

FROM HERE

Database programming in .NET is really quite different from classic Windows database programming. Probably the most important difference is that most ADO.NET applications work with a disconnected data set rather than staying connected throughout the manipulation of the data. Relations and keys are kept in the data set itself, so there's no need to go back to the database to filter records, search on the primary key, or even to join tables.

The sample applications in this chapter showed you how to create a library component—typically part of a data access layer—that works with a data source, and a user-interface component that displays the information in a data set. Almost as an aside, the ASP.NET sample also demonstrates cross-language development and the power of the data grid. If you'd like to see more cross-language development, be sure to read Chapter 18, "Integrating with Visual Basic," and Chapter 19, "Integrating with C#," which also feature more ASP.NET samples.

Many powerful interconnections exist between data and XML. Relational data can be expressed well in XML, so it makes sense for conversions between the two to be simple. The samples in this chapter showed how to extract XML from a database or use XML to fill a database. For more on XML support in Visual Studio .NET, be sure to read Appendix B, "XML Review."

CHAPTER 23

COM INTEROP

In this chapter

USING A COM COMPONENT FROM A .NET APPLICATION

One of the most amazing things about .NET is the way you can leverage the code and components you already have. Essentially, a .NET object is a COM component and a COM component is a .NET object. The behind-the-scenes work that makes them substitutable is referred to as COM *interop*, short for interoperability. If you've written a COM object and want to use it from a .NET application, COM interop makes that incredibly easy. If you're working on a COM application and want to use a .NET object, COM interop makes that incredibly easy, too. In fact, believe it or not, it's actually easier to use a COM component from a .NET application than from a class COM application!

In Chapter 9, "Building COM+ Components with ATL," you saw how to build a simple COM component that validates a phone number, and built a test harness that used the COM component. That component was compiled into a DLL called PhoneFormat.dll, which was described in a type library called _PhoneFormat.tlb. Such an arrangement is standard for COM components: executable code in one file, metadata that describes the code in another. Another arrangement puts the type library inside the DLL along with the executable.

Many .NET components compile into a file with a .dll extension, but the content and layout of that file are completely different from the "classic COM" DLL that was created for PhoneFormat. The .NET dll file is completely self-contained. It contains MSIL that can run in the runtime as well as all the metadata that describes the component completely.

Figure 23.1 illustrates this fundamental difference in the way that DLL files are laid out for COM-format DLLs and .NET-format DLLs.

Figure 23.1
Classic COM and .NET use very different file formats.

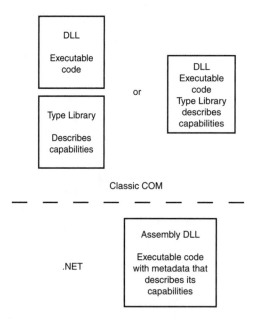

To use the component in a .NET application, you need to create a .NET-style .dll file that describes the component and provides access to it. There's a utility called tlbimp.exe that does just that, as shown in Figure 23.2. The name is short for "type lib import" and it's used to import a type library, from a .tlb file or a COM DLL, into the .NET world. It creates a wrapper or proxy DLL that a .NET application can treat like any other .NET object. Whenever a call is made into this wrapper DLL, it's just passed along to the COM DLL for actual processing.

Figure 23.2
The tlbimp utility can build .NET-format DLLs from classic COM-type libraries.

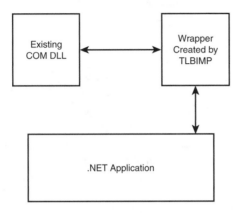

CH
23

To use the PhoneFormat component from a .NET application, start by creating a folder called PhoneInterop. Copy _PhoneFormat.tlb from the PhoneFormat project folder to this new folder. Open a command prompt and navigate to this folder, then issue this command:

```
tlbimp _PhoneFormat.tlb
```

You will notice that PhoneFormat.dll has materialized in this directory. This is a DLL in the .NET format with metadata describing the PhoneFormat functionality, and simple wrapper functions that invoke methods of the original DLL. Because it has the same name as your old COM-format DLL, they can't be in the same folder.

Note

If you are developing the .NET code and the classic COM code on different machines, you need to register the classic COM DLL, just as in the old all-COM world. After you copy the COM-format DLL to your .NET machine, in a command prompt, change directories to the folder that contains the COM-format PhoneFormat.dll and issue this command:

```
regsvr32 phoneformat.dll
```

If your .NET work is on the same machine as your COM work, the DLL was already registered when you compiled it, so leave it where it is and let COM find it.

That's all it takes to make your COM DLL usable by a .NET application! To try it out, create a new console application in C++ (a managed C++ application) called PhoneTestInterop, as in Figure 23.3.

Figure 23.3
Create a Managed C++ application to test the COM DLL in .NET.

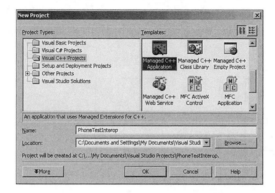

You get a skeleton _tmain() function, as usual, created for you when you create the project. Add this line with the other using statements, before _tmain() begins:

```
#using "Debug\PhoneFormat.dll"
```

Now creating an instance of your COM object is as simple as creating an ordinary C++ object. Edit _tmain() so it looks like Listing 23.1

LISTING 23.1   USING A COM COMPONENT FROM .NET

```
int _tmain(void)
{
   PhoneFormat::CPhoneNumberClass* validator = new
➡PhoneFormat::CPhoneNumberClass();
   Console::WriteLine(S"Enter a phone number, please:");
   String* number = Console::ReadLine();
   String* errormessage;
   unsigned char errorcode;
   validator->ValidatePhoneNumber(number, &errorcode, &errormessage);
   Console::Write("Code: {0} ", __box(errorcode));
   Console::WriteLine(" Message: {0}", errormessage);

    return 0;
}
```

Listing 23.1 uses full names, such as PhoneFormat::CPhoneNumberClass, to demonstrate more clearly where everything comes from. You can add a using statement before _tmain() if you wish, to lessen your typing. Adding the #using statement just references your assembly; it doesn't automatically bring in your namespace.

If you compare this test harness code to that in Chapter 9, you'll notice that it's actually simpler to use a COM object from a .NET application than from a "classic COM" application—no more BSTRs, calls to W2A, or other confusing conversion issues. The .NET framework takes care of all that for you.

Copy the .NET-format PhoneFormat.dll from the PhoneInterop folder to a new folder called Debug within the PhoneTestInterop project folder, then build your project. Run it, and try entering some valid and invalid phone numbers. To steal a phrase from the .NET developers, it just works! Figure 23.4 shows some sample output.

Figure 23.4
A .NET console application can reuse code from a COM component.

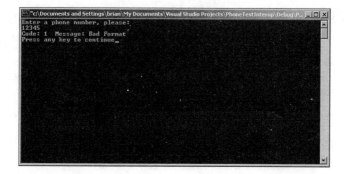

EXTENDING A COM COMPONENT IN .NET

The ease and simplicity of COM interop is great news for everyone who has existing COM objects. You won't need to port them to the .NET world; you can just use them from your .NET applications. The vision is clear: a COM component is a .NET object. But are there limits to that? For example, a .NET object can be used as a base class for another .NET object. Chapter 18, "Integrating with Visual Basic," and Chapter 19, "Integrating with C#," demonstrate how simple it is to extend a .NET object to add functionality, even in another .NET language. Can you extend COM components in the same way? Believe it or not, you can!

In Visual Studio, close any solution you may have open. Create a new managed C++ application called PhoneTestInheritance, as shown in Figure 23.5. This application extends the COM component and uses the resulting .NET object in a simple test.

Figure 23.5
Create a managed C++ application to extend the COM component in .NET.

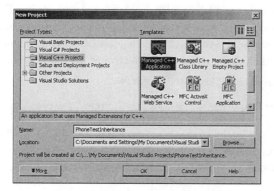

At the top of PhoneTestInheritance.cpp, after the other #using and #include statements, add this line:

```
#using "Debug\PhoneFormat.dll"
```

This statement makes the PhoneFormat component available, as before. Remember to copy that DLL into the Debug directory of this new project. Now, before the _tmain function, add the class shown in Listing 23.2.

LISTING 23.2   A .NET OBJECT THAT INHERITS FROM A COM COMPONENT

```
__gc class ShortPhoneValidator: public PhoneFormat::CPhoneNumberClass
{
public:
    void ValidateShortPhoneNumber(String* number, unsigned char* pError, String**
➥pErrorString)
    {
            Regex* regexp = new Regex("[0-9][0-9][0-9]-[0-9][0-9][0-9][0-9]" ); //
➥555-1212
            MatchCollection* mc = regexp->Matches(number);

            if (mc->Count > 0 && number->Length == 8)
            {
                    *pError = 0;
                    *pErrorString = S"OK";

            }
            else
            {
                    *pError = 1;
                    *pErrorString = S"Bad Format";
            }

    }
};
```

This class inherits from PhoneFormat::CPhoneNumberClass, the class within the COM component that actually implements the ValidatePhoneNumber() method. It inherits ValidatePhoneNumber() unchanged and adds a function, ValidateShortPhoneNumber(), that has slightly different rules.

The COM component uses the ATL regular expressions classes. A .NET application doesn't normally use ATL, but don't worry: the Common Language Runtime has a powerful set of regular expression classes in the System::Text::RegularExpressions namespace. To simplify the code that follows, add a using statement at the top of the file with the others:

```
using namespace System::Text::RegularExpressions;
```

Add this reference as well to bring in the code for the regular expression classes:

```
#using <System.dll>
```

If you could read the original code for ValidatePhoneNumber(), you should be able to read ValidateShortPhoneNumber() too. In fact, it's a lot easier to read, because .NET makes working with strings so much easier than it is in COM. Experienced COM programmers are generally delighted to stop using BSTRs and HRESULTs.

Now all you need is some test code in _tmain() that exercises this new class. Edit _tmain() so it looks like Listing 23.3.

LISTING 23.3 TESTING THE NEW .NET OBJECT

```cpp
int _tmain(void)
{
   ShortPhoneValidator* shortvalidator = new ShortPhoneValidator();
   Console::WriteLine(S"Enter a phone number, please:");
   String* number = Console::ReadLine();
   String* errormessage;
   unsigned char errorcode;
   Console::WriteLine("Checking long format:");
   shortvalidator->ValidatePhoneNumber(number, &errorcode, &errormessage);
   Console::Write("Code: {0} ", __box(errorcode));
   Console::WriteLine(" Message: {0}", errormessage);

   Console::WriteLine("Checking short format:");
   shortvalidator->ValidateShortPhoneNumber(number, &errorcode, &errormessage);
   Console::Write("Code: {0} ", __box(errorcode));
   Console::WriteLine(" Message: {0}", errormessage);

   return 0;
}
```

Listing 23.3 uses both the ValidatePhoneNumber() and ValidateShortPhoneNumber() methods, using an instance of ShortPhoneValidator. Even though the base class method, ValidatePhoneNumber(), is actually implemented in a COM component, you can't see any difference in the way the methods are used here in _tmain(). That's the beauty of COM interop—it's seamless. Figure 23.6 shows some output from this application, mixing strings generated by a COM component with those generated by a .NET object.

Figure 23.6
You can add functionality to existing COM components as easily as if they were .NET objects.

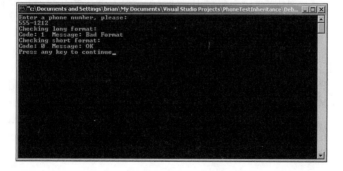

USING A .NET OBJECT AS A COM COMPONENT

COM interop doesn't just bring COM components into the .NET world—it brings .NET objects into classic COM applications as well. Of course, the .NET format DLL or EXE file that holds the assembly for the .NET object is not in a format that the COM code is expecting. COM wants a type library, and you can get one quite simply, by using the tlbexp utility. The name is short for *type library export*. Figure 23.7 demonstrates the role of tlbexp. A .NET assembly is used to create a COM-format DLL and a .tlb file. After creating the type library, you need to add something to the Registry so that COM can find the assembly; you take care of this with a utility called regasm.exe—short for *register assembly*.

Figure 23.7
The tlbexp utility can build COM type libraries from .NET-format DLLs.

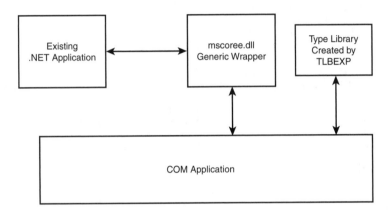

You don't need to generate a custom wrapper DLL for each component. Instead, mscoree.dll can wrap any .NET object to use as a COM component.

> **Tip**
>
> A working name for what became .NET was COR: Common Object Runtime. You'll see those letters appear from time to time in file names such as mscorlib.dll, the file all .NET applications bring in with a `#using` statement. The EE in mscoree.dll stands for execution engine.

In this section, you'll see how to use Greeter, the .NET component that was created in Chapter 17, "Getting Started with .NET." If you didn't follow along and create that component, you should do so now. To use Greeter from a classic COM application, you need to make a tiny change to the way it is implemented. You need to add an interface to the component to simplify accessing it from COM. After the namespace statement, and before the declaration of the Greeter class, add these lines:

```
public __gc __interface IGreet
{
public:
  String* Greet(void);
};
```

This simply declares the interface that `Greeter` will implement. Change the declaration of the `Greeter` class to look like this:

```
public __gc class Greeter : public IGreet
```

This line of code tells the compiler that the `Greeter` object inherits from `IGreet`. Because `IGreet` doesn't contain any method implementations, the compiler expects those methods to be implemented in `Greeter`. There's only one method, actually, and it's already implemented, so that's not a problem. Build your project to be sure you have no errors.

> **Note**
>
> If you wish, you may open the old HelloWorld project that was used in Chapter 17 to test `Greeter` and confirm that it works without changes. Adding this interface hasn't changed the way .NET applications see this object.

CH
23

Open a command prompt and change directories to the Debug folder under the Greeter folder. Issue this command:

```
>"c:\Program Files\Microsoft Visual Studio .NET\FrameworkSDK\Bin\tlbexp.exe "
➡greeter.dll
```

> **Tip**
>
> If you installed Visual Studio to a different folder, adjust this path accordingly.

Your .NET object is ready to use as a COM component. You will copy the .tlb file shortly, after you've created a project where you can copy it.

In a new instance of Visual Studio, choose File, New, Project to bring up the New Project dialog. Select Visual C++ projects on the left, and MFC Application on the right. Name the application COMGreeter as in Figure 23.8.

Figure 23.8
Create an MFC application to use the .NET object.

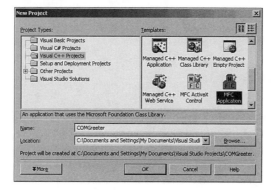

On the Application Type tab of the MFC Application Wizard, select Dialog Based. The other defaults are all okay for this application, so after flipping through the other tabs for a quick look, click Finish.

In the ResourceView, double-click IDD_COMGREETER_DIALOG to edit the main dialog of the application. Delete the static label with the TODO instruction. Click the OK button and choose View, Properties Window if it is not already displayed. Using the Properties window, change the ID of the button to ID_GREET and the caption to Say Hello. Change the caption on the Cancel button to Close, but leave its ID unchanged.

Click in the background of the dialog (away from all the controls) to select the dialog itself, then drag the bottom of the dialog upward to make a smaller dialog box. The completed dialog box should resemble Figure 23.9.

Figure 23.9
Build a simple dialog to exercise the Greet() method.

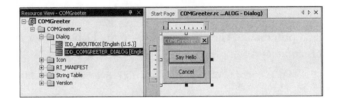

Now you just need to write code that calls Greet() when the user clicks the Say Hello button. Double-click the Say Hello button on the dialog box and you are switched to editing the function that handles the click on the button.

When the button is clicked, the test code calls the Greet() method of the Greeter component. It uses the DLL and type library prepared earlier.

Open the source code for CCOMGreeterDlg, and scroll to the top of the file. After the #include statements that are already there, add this line:

```
#import "Debug\greeter.tlb"
```

Edit OnBnClickedGreet() so that it looks like this:

```
void CCOMGreeterDlg::OnBnClickedGreet()
{
   Greeter::IGreetPtr greet("Greeter.Greeter");
   AfxMessageBox(greet->Greet());
}
```

Thanks to the #import directive, creating an instance of the .NET object and calling its methods looks just like creating an ordinary C++ object. If you were wondering how to decide what name to use for the smart pointer's type, it's the namespace of the .NET object (a namespace statement was generated for you in the Greeter project) followed by the name of the interface with Ptr added onto the end—Greeter::IGreetPtr in this case. What you pass into the constructor is the ProgID of the class: the namespace, a dot, then the name of the class in which you implemented the interface—Greeter.Greeter in this case.

Build the project at this point to make sure you don't have any errors, but it's not quite ready to run. Ignore any errors about not being able to find your type library—you haven't copied it yet. Building the project is a simple way to create the Debug directory where you will copy the type library and DLL.

Copy the .tlb file that was created for you, greeter.tlb, from the Debug directory of Greeter to the Debug directory of this project. Also copy greeter.dll to the Debug directory of this project. Open a command prompt and change directories to the Debug folder of this project, then issue this command:

```
regasm greeter.dll
```

> **Tip**
>
> The regasm command is in the .NET Framework directory, typically C:\WINDOWS\ Microsoft.NET\Framework\v1.0.3705 or something similar. You can add this directory to your path or enter the full path and name of the command.

Now the DLL and type library are ready to use. However, this little MFC dialog-based application isn't properly COM-aware, so you have a few code changes to make.

In the Class View, expand CCOMGreeterApp and double-click InitInstance to edit it. Most dialog-based applications respond differently when the dialog is dismissed with OK than when it is dismissed with Cancel. This one does not need to, so the code can be quite a bit simpler. Find and remove these lines:

```
INT_PTR nResponse = dlg.DoModal();
if (nResponse == IDOK)
{
   // TODO: Place code here to handle when the dialog is
   //  dismissed with OK
}
else if (nResponse == IDCANCEL)
{
   // TODO: Place code here to handle when the dialog is
   //  dismissed with Cancel
}
```

In their place, add this single line:

```
dlg.DoModal();
```

(Because you changed the ID of the Say Hello button from IDOK to ID_GREET, clicking it won't dismiss the dialog.) To activate COM support for this application, add this line at the very beginning of InitInstance():

```
::CoInitialize(NULL);
```

To clean up your COM work before returning from InitInstance(), add this line after the call to DoModal() and before the return statement:

```
   ::CoUninitialize();
```

Now, build the project again, and it's ready to run. Click the button, and as you see in Figure 23.10, you'll be greeted by the .NET component.

Figure 23.10
This string came from
a .NET object.

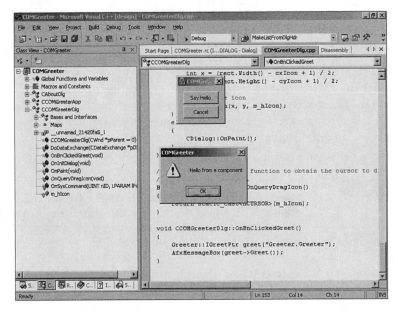

FROM HERE

Developers are excited about Visual Studio .NET, the power of the libraries, the way the tools generate so much of the code for you, and all the cool things you can do in the .NET world. But developers with a substantial amount of existing code are a little worried about maintaining that code. Nobody wants to port their code if there's no reason to do so. With COM interop, you don't need to. Your COM and .NET applications can communicate seamlessly.

The chances are good that you'll use Managed C++ and the .NET libraries to create new projects, just because of all the time and effort they save. Knowing you can continue to use all your COM components makes that transition a lot easier. If you have existing code that isn't a COM component, it's a lot quicker to wrap it up into a COM component than to try to port it to .NET and translate all your MFC or SDK calls to the .NET equivalents.

For more on COM development with ATL, read Chapter 9, "Building COM+ Components with ATL." If you've never built a .NET object before, you can learn how to do it in Chapter 17, "Getting Started with .NET." The next chapter, "Security and Policies," explains the way that the .NET Framework can protect your system from malicious code.

CHAPTER 24

SECURITY AND POLICIES

In this chapter

Making Applications More Secure

For too many developers, security is something left until the end of a project. During development, passwords are left off everything, and toward the end of a project they are added. This approach often falters when it becomes clear that some early design decisions have left the system less secure than it needs to be.

Developing with .NET will make your applications more secure even if you ignore security. Your applications are more secure from start to finish. For example:

- Managed code is less vulnerable to certain kinds of attacks than unmanaged code.
- By default, code from a machine accessed over a network (even your office LAN) is not allowed to perform certain operations that might cause damage on your machine.
- End-users cannot give permission for code to execute in a browser as they can today. Instead, downloaded code must meet local security requirements.

This chapter cannot cover all aspects of developing secure applications. It does, however, introduce the .NET security model and the basics of working with that model.

The .NET Security Model Is Consistent

Whether you're writing a Windows application, console application, ASP.NET application, Web Service, a control that will be downloaded and hosted in a Web browser, a control to be used in a Windows application, or any other kind of .NET application, the security model is the same.

Throughout the time that your code is running, it attempts a variety of actions: It tries to read from or write to the file system, to download information through the Internet, or to connect to SQL Server, for example. The framework can determine whether or not a particular action will be allowed in three ways:

- Where did this code come from?
- Who is running this code?
- What authority has been built into this code by its developers?

The various things your code might try to do involve requesting *code access permissions*.

Code Access Permissions

As your application goes about its work, it triggers requests against the .NET runtime whenever it tries to access any potentially protected resource or perform a potentially protected operation. The protected actions include the following:

- Displaying a user interface to the user and accepting input from the user
- Showing the user a file dialog, and retrieving the name of the chosen file

- Reading from or writing to files on the local hard drive
- Reading from or writing to files in a special protected area called isolated storage
- Printing
- Using OLE DB to access a database
- Using SQL to access a database
- Reading or changing Registry values
- Reading or writing an environment variable
- Reading or writing to the event log
- Looking at or changing a performance counter
- Accessing services
- Communicating over a socket
- Accessing the Web or serving out responses over the Web
- Looking up a domain name to get an IP address
- Accessing MSMQ message queues
- Interacting with Active Directory
- Using .NET reflection to discover information about an object's type
- Bypassing parts of the security system, for example by calling unmanaged code

You can see that this is a very detailed list. An application might be allowed to write files to the hard drive, but not to change any Registry values, for example. The administrative effort involved in assigning permissions this detailed to every piece of code that might run would be significant. This is a problem, because when administrators feel that security is too much work, they tend to over-assign permissions just so that code can work. This can introduce serious security vulnerabilities. To prevent this problem, .NET uses a default set of permissions that many administrators can use without changing. These permission sets are described in the next section.

PERMISSION SETS AND CODE GROUPS

When you install the .NET framework or Visual Studio .NET on your computer, you are also installing a default set of security rules. Specifically, four *permission sets* and eight *code groups* are created, with each code group assigned into a permission set. These are:

Permissions Sets	Code Groups	Function/Comments
Full Trust	My Computer zone ECMA Strong Name	Applications in this set are not restricted by code access security.

CH
24

Permissions Sets	Code Groups	Function/Comments
Local Intranet	Local Intranet code group	Applications in this set can access only a few environment variables, can read only from the network share where the code originated, cannot write files or access the Registry, can connect to the Web site from which it came, and can have a user interface. The code is often said to be "sandboxed": It can run, but can't cause any harm.
Internet	Internet code Trusted zone	Applications in this set can't access environment variables or the Registry, can't access files on the hard drive (but have limited access to the more restrictive isolated storage) and must use special user-interface windows called SafeTopLevelWindows, which are clearly labeled and cannot be mistaken for system dialogs. This set is more dramatically sandboxed than the Local Intranet permission set.
Nothing	All Code Restricted Zone	Applications in this set can't do anything; they are denied all the accesses and operations listed earlier.

Imagine a user points a Web browser to a Web page that includes a .NET control, identified with an `<object>` tag. If the browser is Internet Explorer 5.5 and above, and the user is running the .NET framework, the control is downloaded and starts to execute. No security dialog appears to ask the user's permission. But if that control tries to do anything damaging, such as writing a local file, the .NET runtime prevents it from doing so. In this way you get the best of both worlds: no annoying security dialogs, and no back-of-the-mind worry that the code you just authorized might do something unpleasant.

HOW TO RUN A .NET APPLICATION OVER A NETWORK SHARE

Try this: In Visual Studio.NET, choose File, New, Project. Select Visual C++ projects on the left, then Managed C++ Application on the right. Name the project Hello, and in the Location box, enter a path that leads to a folder on a network share, as in Figure 24.1. Click OK, and before the application is created, you'll receive a warning like the one in Figure 24.2. Click OK to keep going.

Build the application, then run it by choosing Debug, Start. You'll run headlong into an exception, shown in Figure 24.3—a PolicyException that is thrown before your code even starts to run. "Required permissions cannot be acquired," you're told—in other words, in the default configuration of the .NET framework, the dirt-simple Hello World console application can't run from a network share. Because so many installations blindly accept defaults without thinking about it, this is much better than having the default be wide open.

Figure 24.1
Create an application on a network share.

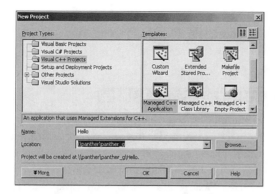

Figure 24.2
Visual Studio.NET warns when you might be restricted by security rules.

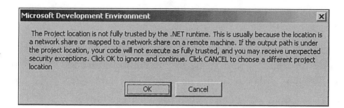

Figure 24.3
Running Hello World over a network share triggers a security exception.

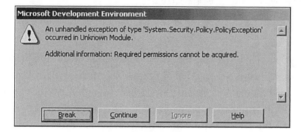

You can overcome these security restrictions in several ways. One is to change the rules so that intranet applications can do whatever they request permission to do. But that's rarely the best approach. It's far better to adjust the permission for a specific assembly or a specific folder on a network share. You can use a command-line tool called the Code Access Security Policy tool, CASPol, to do this.

Open a command prompt, and issue a command like this:

```
>caspol -addgroup 1.2 -url
➥"file://computername/sharename/path/to/development/Hello/*" Everything
```

In place of *computername*, enter the name of the computer on which the share is located. In place of *sharename*, enter the name of the shared drive. In place of *path/to/development/*, enter the actual path to the project folder.

After entering this command, you will be prompted about whether you want to change security policy. Press Y to confirm your decision. Now try running the Hello application again and it should work perfectly.

ISOLATED AND SHARED ASSEMBLIES

Many things are very different under .NET than under "classic" Windows programming. One of the important differences concerns sharing of code—specifically of DLLs—throughout a single computer. From the early days of DOS and the PATH environment variable allowing a command to be issued from any folder, to the present-day C:\WINNT\SYSTEM32 with hundreds of DLLs used by almost every application on the system, developers are used to code that is shared, not isolated.

DLL HELL

If you've been programming as long as I have, you remember when DLLs first arrived on the scene. What a great idea they seemed! You could reuse code and share it between two applications. If one module changed, you could just install a new DLL and the next time the application ran, it would get the new code. You've seen this in action if you've ever played one of the Solitaire variants that come with the different versions of Windows: They all use cards.dll to draw the backs and faces of cards.

The flip side of this, of course, is what's come to be known as *DLL Hell*. Sooner or later it happens to all of us. You write an application, deploy it to a number of desktops, and feel pretty good about yourself. Then one day the phone rings: Your application has stopped working. A little investigation reveals that the user has recently installed something new and seemingly unrelated. Maybe a new version of Internet Explorer—that packs a huge number of DLLs—or some little application you've never heard of. Whatever was installed, it copied a new version of some DLL or another onto the user's hard drive—and now your application doesn't have the functionality it was relying on.

In .NET, that's all different. Application isolation is the default. Whatever DLLs your application needs are in its own folder, typically a folder called bin—for binary files such as assemblies. Other applications may have copies of those very same assemblies in their folders, but that's irrelevant. And if one of those other applications gets upgraded, and the assembly in that other folder gets changed, that has no effect on your application at all. There's still a nice safe untouched copy of the assembly tucked away in your application's own bin folder. No more DLL Hell.

This is the story behind what's being called *xcopy deployment*, too. Because multiple applications aren't sharing a single copy of the DLL, there's no need to use a central repository like the Registry to make sure everyone knows where to find that single copy. So you don't need an Install program that registers the DLL, or anything like that. Just put the assemblies in the bin folder and away you go.

The Global Assembly Cache

So, you can prevent DLL Hell with application isolation, each application having its own copy of its own DLLs. For most of us, the story stops there. Hard drives are big. Having several copies of a few particularly popular DLLs is not a hardship. But in a few special cases, you need several applications to share a common code base, and it's vital that updating the assembly for one application will simultaneously update it for all the applications involved. For these unusual situations, you do have access to something called the *global assembly cache*. It's a place where assemblies can be accessed by all applications, and where a number of other restrictions are imposed on assemblies.

Tip

The global assembly cache is often referred to as the gac, pronounced "gack."

Use the global assembly cache only when you need to put an assembly some place where all applications get the new version at the same instant. As you've seen in earlier chapters, you can use an assembly simply by copying it around or specifying a relative path from one project folder that leads to the assembly's DLL file. Chapter 18, "Integrating with Visual Basic," and Chapter 19, "Integrating with C#," show assemblies being used by other projects. Some developers assume that because COM relies on the Registry, you should use the global assembly cache for COM interop, but as Chapter 23, "COM Interop," demonstrates, that is certainly not necessary. The decision to use the gac is not one to be taken lightly.

The simplest way to view your assembly cache is to use Windows Explorer to browse to it. A clever little Windows extension makes it look like a folder on your machine. It's the Assembly folder of your Windows directory (C:\WINNT or C:\Windows, for example.) Figure 24.4 shows a view of the cache on a development machine. You can right-click any assembly and choose Properties to see a little more detail about it. Because it's kept beneath the Windows directory, if your system administrator has added security to the Windows directory, this will be a secured folder—not all users will be able to add assemblies or delete them, for example.

To add an assembly to the cache while you're developing, you can simply drag and drop the DLL or EXE to this Windows Explorer window and it will be added. But there's a catch: Before an assembly can be added to the cache, it must have a *strong name*. If you just drag and drop any old DLL or EXE you happen to have on your system into the cache, you'll get an error like that in Figure 24.5.

After your development is complete, you should use the Windows Installer to copy your assembly to the gac. Dragging and dropping is a simple approach for use in development, but it's missing some of the safeguards that you'll get by using the Installer.

Figure 24.4
The global assembly cache holds assemblies that many different applications can use.

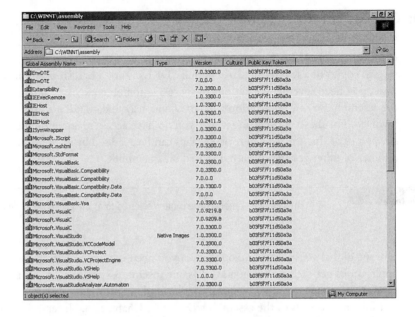

Figure 24.5
DLLs that do not have a strong name can't be dropped into the cache.

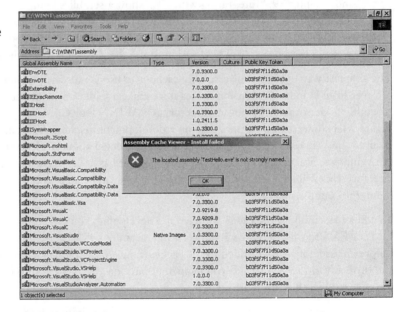

STRONGLY NAMED ASSEMBLIES

A strong name is a name generated for an assembly from several components:

- The simple name, such as ChartEngine
- The version number

- The culture (localization) information
- A public key provided by the developer
- A digital signature

Because these components are combined into a single name, strong names must be unique. If another developer has an assembly called ChartEngine, that developer will have a different key than you do, so the strong name will be different. When you release a new version of ChartEngine, the version number will be updated, so the strong name will also change. In this way the global assembly cache can hold many assemblies with the same name and distinguish among them. In addition, code can insist on only a particular version of an assembly.

What's more, no one can change an assembly after it has been delivered. If someone does, the strong name will no longer match the assembly's digital signature. In this way you can be confident that the assembly you are using is the assembly that the code publisher shipped.

Note

Strongly named assemblies are not allowed to reference assemblies that are not also strongly named, because simply named assemblies do not have the same assurances about versioning and other changes since installation.

Creating a Strong Name for an Assembly

Before you can assign a strong name to your assembly, you must have a key pair—a private and public key you can use for signing. There's a tool called sn that generates these. It's usually in the c:\Program Files\Microsoft Visual Studio .NET\FrameworkSDK\Bin folder. If that's not on your path, you have to type the full path to the command. To generate a key pair called chartdeveloper, for example, open a command prompt and issue this command:

```
> sn -k chartdeveloper.snk
```

This will create the key pair in the folder where you issued the command. From there you must move the file (chartdeveloper.snk in this example) to the appropriate spot inside your project folder, and adjust your project to use the key pair. In this section you will see how to give a strong name to a very simple assembly.

Create a Managed C++ Class Library called Hello, and edit Hello.h to look like Listing 24.1.

Listing 24.1 A Very Simple Component

```
#pragma once

using namespace System;

namespace Hello
{
```

CH
24

LISTING 24.1   CONTINUED

```
public __gc class Hello
{
public:

        String* Morning()
        {
                return S"Good Morning";
        }
};
}
```

Use Solution Explorer to open AssemblyInfo.cpp and scroll to the bottom, where you'll find these lines:

```
[assembly:AssemblyDelaySignAttribute(false)];
[assembly:AssemblyKeyFileAttribute("")];
[assembly:AssemblyKeyNameAttribute("")];
```

Change the `AssemblyKeyFileAttribute` so that it indicates the strong key file you created with sn.exe:

```
[assembly:AssemblyKeyFileAttribute("chartdeveloper.snk")];
```

Move the chartdeveloper.snk file from the folder where you created it to the Hello project folder, then build the application. If the key file is in the wrong folder, the project won't build.

USING AN ASSEMBLY FROM THE GLOBAL ASSEMBLY CACHE

If you look in the Debug folder of the Hello project, you will see Hello.dll, the assembly you just built. Drag a copy into the Assembly folder and you've just added it to the global assembly cache.

As you should know, before you can use an assembly in another project you must add a reference to it. There is, however, no way to add a reference to an assembly that is in the global assembly cache. (This capability may be added in a future release of Visual Studio .NET.) So while you are developing the project that will use your globally cached assembly, work with a copy of the assembly's DLL file, just as you would if the assembly were not in the global assembly cache. This ensures that the compiler knows all the namespaces and types in the assembly, and provides Intellisense support for you as you develop. You can build and test your application using this local copy of the assembly. Then when you deploy your assembly—your single DLL—do not copy the other assembly to the deployment location. When the .NET framework goes looking for the referenced assembly and doesn't find it in the same folder as your assembly, guess where it looks next? The global assembly cache. Mission accomplished.

USER-BASED AND ROLE-BASED SECURITY

Earlier in this chapter you saw that .NET prevents code from performing certain operations, based on aspects of the code itself, such as the location from which it was loaded.

Code loaded from a network share or an intranet cannot perform certain operations. This provides good protection for your system from code that was written elsewhere and downloaded to your machine.

There are other kinds of security requirements. Perhaps you have an application that works with sensitive financial data. Whether or not that application is allowed to open certain files, for example, might depend on who is running the application. Under certain circumstances you might even want an application run by a user to be enabled to open a file that the user would not ordinarily be allowed to open. User-based security in .NET is used to handle this level of security.

Answering the question "who is running this application?" is not as simple as you might first think. In some cases, you want to restrict activities to specific individual users. In others, you might want to create roles, such as Manager, and restrict activities to those roles. This makes it simpler to deal with the comings and goings of individual users and employees. Classes in the `System::Security::Principal` namespace encapsulate some important concepts and rules in this area.

The `WindowsIdentity` class represents the Windows user who is running the application. Member functions such as `IsAnonymous()` and `IsGuest()` let you discover quite a bit about the user. You can even use `get_Name()` to get the Windows logon name for this user. The `WindowsPrincipal` class represents a principal, a slightly more abstract version of an identity, similar to a group. You can use member functions such as `IsInRole()` to learn more about a principal. `IsInRole()` is heavily overloaded, taking an integer, a string, or a `WindowsBuiltInRole` enumeration. These include `AccountOperator`, `Administrator`, `Guest`, and `User`. In addition, you can define your own roles and check against them.

More useful than checking to see who is running this code is insisting that only certain users or roles are allowed to run it. Although you could use these classes, perform some simple tests, and perhaps throw an exception if the wrong user is running, it's much easier to do it with attributes. Listing 24.2 is a simple component that defines a function that can be run by only an administrator:

CH

24

LISTING 24.2   DEMANDING A SPECIFIC ROLE

```
using namespace System;
using namespace System::Security::Permissions;

namespace Hello
{
   [PrincipalPermissionAttribute(SecurityAction::Demand, Role = "Administrator")]
   public __gc class Hello
   {
   public:
           String* Morning()
           {
                   return S"Good Morning";
           }
   };
}
```

SECURITY FROM THE COMPILER

No discussion of security in .NET would be complete without a review of the secure aspects of .NET itself. When you write managed code and let .NET manage memory, you gain security benefits. Many of the unwieldy or buggy aspects of traditional Windows programming are also security vulnerabilities.

A classic example concerns applications that accept requests over the Internet in the form of a string. Typically, the string is expected to be at most a few hundred characters long. A decade ago, many Unix-based Internet sites started to disable the `finger` command because it was implemented in a way that left it vulnerable when a very long string was sent in the request. If a malicious user sent a string thousands of characters long, and chose those characters carefully, the extra characters would end up overwriting the code that was executing, which would allow the malicious user to send code along to be executed on the remote computer. Similar logic was behind the 2001 Nimda virus that exploited Microsoft Index Server—another Internet service that accepts a string.

Under the .NET Framework, such attacks cannot happen. If the input is too long for the space allotted, it doesn't just overflow its boundaries into nearby memory. Because memory is managed for you by the .NET Framework, a number of memory-based attacks simply cannot happen to a .NET application.

Managed .NET applications are more strongly typed than applications created with traditional programming tools. They have runtime checks on memory usage, array boundaries, and much more. This eliminates not only bugs, but also security vulnerabilities. That sets a firm foundation on which to build. The next layer of protection is the .NET security system itself, with concepts such as code-access security and user-based security. Finally, the default security settings installed with the .NET Framework and with Visual Studio .NET are very tight, so that absent-minded users and administrators who never change their settings will have safe and secure machines.

Don't forget to continue this line of thought into the other work you do. For example, if your code accesses a database, you should have a password on that database. Never deploy a solution using the default passwords or no passwords at all. Don't even upload a test version of a database to an Internet-connected server without strong passwords in place. An attacker can learn your database structure while you're testing, and be in a position to use some other attacks later based on knowledge of field and table names, for example.

FROM HERE

In this chapter, you've seen how the .NET Framework supports security. Because .NET applications run in the Framework, they can be prevented from taking actions that might wreak havoc on your computer, such as changing the Registry or updating a database. If you know what you're doing, you can grant permissions to selected applications, while still enjoying the Framework's protection for the other applications you run.

The .NET libraries include a number of classes related to security. What's more, attributed programming makes it simple (almost trivial) to request that your code be handled in a specific way—for example, that only an Adminstrator can run it.

This chapter is the last of the .NET chapters in this book. The Appendices that follow are for reference. If you haven't tried your hand at .NET programming yet, Chapter 17, "Getting Started with .NET," is a good jumping-off point. After you've created the sample application from that chapter, try your hand at avoiding DLL Hell by using Chapter 17's component in the sample applications of Chapter 18, "Integrating with Visual Basic," or Chapter 19, "Integrating with C#."

CH
24

WINDOWS PROGRAMMING REVIEW AND A LOOK INSIDE CWnd

In this appendix

PROGRAMMING FOR WINDOWS

The Microsoft Foundation Classes were written for one purpose: to make Windows programming easier by providing classes with methods and data that handle tasks common to all Windows programs. The classes that are in MFC are designed to be useful to a Windows programmer specifically.

> **Note**
>
> If you're a .NET programmer, you don't use MFC; you use the .NET Common Language Runtime class library instead. It's covered in Chapter 16, "The Common Language Runtime."

The methods within each MFC class perform tasks that Windows programmers often need to perform. Many of the classes have a close correspondence to structures and window classes, in the old Windows sense of the word *class*. Many of the methods correspond closely to API (Application Programming Interface) functions already familiar to old-time Windows programmers, who often refer to them as the Windows SDK or as SDK functions.

If you've programmed for Windows in C, you know that the word *class* was used to describe a window long before C++ programming came to Windows. A window class is vital to any Windows C program. A standard structure holds the data that describes this window class, and the operating system provides a number of standard window classes. A programmer usually builds a new window class for each program and registers it by calling an API function, RegisterClass(). Windows that appear onscreen can then be created, based on that class, by calling another API function, CreateWindow(). MFC makes Windows programming much easier by encapsulating the Windows API inside easy-to-use classes.

A C-STYLE WINDOW CLASS

The WNDCLASS structure, which describes the window class, is equivalent to the WNDCLASSA structure, which looks like Listing A.1.

LISTING A.1   WNDCLASSA STRUCTURE FROM WINUSER.H

```
typedef struct tagWNDCLASSA {
    UINT        style;
    WNDPROC     lpfnWndProc;
    int         cbClsExtra;
    int         cbWndExtra;
    HINSTANCE   hInstance;
    HICON       hIcon;
    HCURSOR     hCursor;
    HBRUSH      hbrBackground;
    LPCSTR      lpszMenuName;
    LPCSTR      lpszClassName;
} WNDCLASSA, *PWNDCLASSA, NEAR *NPWNDCLASSA, FAR *LPWNDCLASSA;
```

WINUSER.H sets up two very similar window class structures: WNDCLASSA for programs that use normal strings and WNDCLASSW for Unicode programs.

Tip

WINUSER.H is code supplied with Visual Studio. It's typically in the folder \Program Files\ Microsoft Visual Studio .NET\Vc7\PlatformSDK\Include.

If you were creating a Windows program in C, you would need to fill a WNDCLASS structure. The members of the WNDCLASS structure are as follows:

- style. A number made by combining standard styles, represented with constants like CS_GLOBALCLASS or CS_OWNDC, with the bitwise OR operator (|). A perfectly good class can be registered with a style value of 0; the other styles are for exceptions to normal procedure.

- lpfnWndProc. A pointer to a function that is the Windows Procedure (generally called the WindProc) for the class. Refer to Chapter 3, "Interacting with Your Application," for a discussion of this function.

- cbClsExtra. The number of extra bytes to add to the window class. It's usually 0, but C programmers may sometimes build a window class with extra data in it.

- cbWndExtra. The number of extra bytes to add to each instance of the window, usually 0.

- hInstance. A handle to an instance of an application, the running program that is registering this window class. For now, think of this as a way for the window class to reach the application that uses it.

- hIcon. An icon to be drawn when the window is minimized. Typically, this is set with a call to another API function, LoadIcon().

- hCursor. The cursor that displays when the mouse is over the screen window associated with this window class. Typically, this is set with a call to the API function LoadCursor().

- hbrBackground. The brush to be used for painting the window background. The API call to GetStockObject() is the usual way to set this variable.

- lpszMenuName. A long pointer to a string that is zero terminated and contains the name of the menu for the window class.

- lpszClassName. The name for this window class, to be used by CreateWindow(), when a window (an instance of the window class) is created. You make up a name.

WINDOW CREATION

If you've never written a Windows program before, having to fill out a WNDCLASS structure might intimidate you. This is the first step, though, in Windows programming in C. However, you can always find simple sample programs to copy, like the one in Listing A.2.

Listing A.2   Filling a WNDCLASS Structure and Registering a Windows Class

```
WNDCLASS wcInit;

wcInit.style = 0;
wcInit.lpfnWndProc = (WNDPROC)MainWndProc;
wcInit.cbClsExtra = 0;
wcInit.cbWndExtra = 0;
wcInit.hInstance = hInstance;
wcInit.hIcon = LoadIcon (hInstance, MAKEINTRESOURCE(ID_ICON));
wcInit.hCursor = LoadCursor (NULL, IDC_ARROW);
wcInit.hbrBackground = GetStockObject (WHITE_BRUSH);
wcInit.lpszMenuName = "DEMO";
wcInit.lpszClassName ="NewWClass";

return (RegisterClass (&wcInit));
```

Hungarian Notation

You might wonder what kind of variable name lpszClassName is or why it's wcInit and not just Init. Microsoft programmers use a variable naming convention called Hungarian Notation. It is so named because a Hungarian programmer named Charles Simonyi popularized it at Microsoft (and probably because at first glance, the variable names seem to be written in another language).

In Hungarian Notation, the variable is given a descriptive name, such as Count or ClassName, that starts with a capital letter. If it is a multiword name, each word is capitalized. Then, before the descriptive name, letters are added to indicate the variable type—for example, nCount for an integer or bFlag for a Boolean (TRUE or FALSE) variable. In this way, the programmer should never forget a variable type or do something foolish such as pass a signed variable to a function that is expecting an unsigned value.

The style has gained widespread popularity, although some people hate it. If you long for the good old days of arguing where to put the braces, or better still whether to call them brace, face, or squiggle brackets, but can't find anyone to rehash those old wars anymore, you can probably find somebody to argue about Hungarian Notation instead. The arguments in favor boil down to "you catch yourself making stupid mistakes," and the arguments against it to "it's ugly and hard to read." The practical truth is that the structures used by the API and the classes defined in MFC all use Hungarian Notation, so you might as well get used to it. You'll probably find yourself doing it for your own variables, too. The prefixes are as follows:

Prefix	Variable Type	Comment
a	Array	
b	Boolean	
d	Double	
h	Handle	
i	Integer	"index into"
l	Long	
lp	Long pointer to	
lpfn	Long pointer to function	
m_	Member variable	
n	Integer	"number of"
p	Pointer to	

Prefix	Variable Type	Comment
s	String	
sz	Zero-terminated string	
u	Unsigned integer	
C	Class	

Many people add their own type conventions to variable names; the wc in wcInit, for example, stands for window class.

Interestingly enough, Hungarian notation is falling out of favor in the world of .NET. You'll still meet plenty of Hungarian notation in the MFC code and in Windows programs, but you'll probably see less of it elsewhere over the next few years.

Filling the wcInit structure and calling RegisterClass is standard stuff: the code in Listing A.2 registers a class called NewWClass with a menu called DEMO and a WindProc called MainWndProc. Everything else about it is ordinary to an experienced Windows C programmer. After registering the class, when those old-time Windows programmers wanted to create a window onscreen, almost without effort they popped out some code like Listing A.3.

LISTING A.3   CREATING A WINDOW ONSCREEN

```
HWND hWnd;
hInst = hInstance;
hWnd = CreateWindow (
    "NewWClass",
    "Demo 1",
    WS_OVERLAPPEDWINDOW,
    CW_USEDEFAULT,
    CW_USEDEFAULT,
    CW_USEDEFAULT,
    CW_USEDEFAULT,
    NULL,
    NULL,
    hInstance,
    NULL);

if (! hWnd)
    return (FALSE);

ShowWindow (hWnd, nCmdShow);
UpdateWindow (hWnd);
```

This code calls CreateWindow(), then ShowWindow() and UpdateWindow(). The parameters to the API function CreateWindow() are as follows:

- lpClassName. A pointer to the classname that was used in the RegisterClass() call.
- lpWindowName. The window name. You make this up.
- dwStyle. The window style, made by combining #define constants with the | operator. For a primary application window like this one, WS_OVERLAPPEDWINDOW is standard.

- x. The window's horizontal position. CW_USEDEFAULT enables the operating system to calculate sensible defaults, based on the user's screen settings.

- y. The window's vertical position. CW_USEDEFAULT enables the operating system to calculate sensible defaults, based on the user's screen settings.

- nWidth. The window's width. CW_USEDEFAULT enables the operating system to calculate sensible defaults, based on the user's screen settings.

- nHeight. The window's height. CW_USEDEFAULT enables the operating system to calculate sensible defaults, based on the user's screen settings.

- hWndParent. The handle of the parent or owner window. (Some windows are created by other windows, which own them.) NULL means that there is no parent to this window.

- hMenu. The handle to a menu or child-window identifier; in other words, a window owned by this window. NULL means that there are no children.

- hInstance. The handle of the application instance that is creating this window.

- lpParam. A pointer to any extra parameters. None are needed in this example.

CreateWindow() returns a window handle—it seems everybody calls window handles hWnd—that is used in the rest of the standard code. If it's NULL, the window creation failed. If the handle returned has any non-NULL value, the creation succeeded and the handle is passed to ShowWindow() and UpdateWindow(), which together draw the actual window onscreen.

Handles

A handle is more than just a pointer. Windows programs refer to resources such as windows, icons, cursors, and so on, with a handle. Behind the scenes there is a handle table that tracks the resource's address as well as information about the resource type. It's called a handle because a program uses it as a way to "get hold of" a resource. Handles are typically passed to functions that need to use resources and are returned from functions that allocate resources.

There are a number of basic handle types: HWND for a window handle, HICON for an icon handle, and so on. No matter what kind of handle is used, remember that it's a way to reach a resource so that you can use the resource.

ENCAPSULATING THE WINDOWS API

API functions create and manipulate windows onscreen, handle drawing, connect programs to Help files, facilitate threading, manage memory, and much more. When these functions are encapsulated into MFC classes, your programs can accomplish these same basic Windows tasks, with less work on your part.

There are literally thousands of API functions, and it can take six months to a year to get a good handle on the API, so this book doesn't attempt to present a mini-tutorial on the API. In the "Programming for Windows" section earlier in this chapter, you were reminded about two API functions: RegisterClass() and CreateWindow(). These illustrate what was difficult about C Windows programming with the API and how the MFC classes make it easier. Documentation on the API functions is available on MSDN, which comes with Visual C++.

INSIDE CWnd

CWndis an enormously important MFC class. Roughly a third of all the MFC classes use it as a base class—classes such as CDialog, CEditView, CButton, and many more. It serves as a wrapper for the old-style window class and the API functions that create and manipulate window classes. For example, the only public member variable is m_hWnd, the member variable that stores the window handle. This variable is set by the member function CWnd::Create() and used by almost all the other member functions when they call their associated API functions.

You might think that the call to the API function CreateWindow() would be handled automatically in the CWnd constructor, CWnd::CWnd, so that when the constructor is called to initialize a CWnd object, the corresponding window on the screen is created. This would save you, the programmer, a good deal of effort because you can't forget to call a constructor. In fact, that's not what Microsoft has chosen to do. The constructor looks like this:

```
CWnd::CWnd()
{
 AFX_ZERO_INIT_OBJECT(CCmdTarget);
}
```

AFX_ZERO_INIT_OBJECT is just a macro, expanded by the C++ compiler's preprocessor, that uses the C function memset to zero out every byte of every member variable in the object, like this:

```
#define AFX_ZERO_INIT_OBJECT(base_class)
➡ memset(((base_class*)this)+1, 0, sizeof(*this)
➡ - sizeof(class base_class));
```

The reason why Microsoft chose not to call CreateWindow() in the constructor is that constructors can't return a value. If something goes wrong with the window creation, there are no elegant or neat ways to deal with it. Instead, the constructor does almost nothing, a step that essentially can't fail, and the call to CreateWindow() is done from within the member function CWnd::Create() or the closely related CWnd::CreateEx(), which looks like the one in Listing A.4.

Many SDK and CWnd functions have names ending in *Ex*. It's short for *extended*, and it's a relic of the time when the developers writing the SDK or MFC realized they should have had more parameters to a particular method—Create(), for example. Rather than change the signature of Create() and break existing code, they added another method, CreateEx(), with the extra parameters, and relied on the rest of us to choose the appropriate method to call.

LISTING A.4   CWnd::CreateEx() FROM WINCORE.CPP

```cpp
BOOL CWnd::CreateEx(DWORD dwExStyle, LPCTSTR lpszClassName,
 LPCTSTR lpszWindowName, DWORD dwStyle,
 int x, int y, int nWidth, int nHeight,
 HWND hWndParent, HMENU nIDorHMenu, LPVOID lpParam)
{
 // allow modification of several common create parameters
 CREATESTRUCT cs;
 cs.dwExStyle = dwExStyle;
 cs.lpszClass = lpszClassName;
 cs.lpszName = lpszWindowName;
 cs.style = dwStyle;
 cs.x = x;
 cs.y = y;
 cs.cx = nWidth;
 cs.cy = nHeight;
 cs.hwndParent = hWndParent;
 cs.hMenu = nIDorHMenu;
 cs.hInstance = AfxGetInstanceHandle();
 cs.lpCreateParams = lpParam;

 if (!PreCreateWindow(cs))
 {
 PostNcDestroy();
 return FALSE;
 }

 AfxHookWindowCreate(this);
 HWND hWnd = ::CreateWindowEx(cs.dwExStyle, cs.lpszClass,
 cs.lpszName, cs.style, cs.x, cs.y, cs.cx, cs.cy,
 cs.hwndParent, cs.hMenu, cs.hInstance, cs.lpCreateParams);

#ifdef _DEBUG
 if (hWnd == NULL)
 {
 TRACE1("Warning: Window creation failed: Â
 GetLastError returns 0x%8.8X\n",
 GetLastError());
 }
#endif

 if (!AfxUnhookWindowCreate())
 PostNcDestroy();
 // cleanup if CreateWindowEx fails too soon

 if (hWnd == NULL)
 return FALSE;
 ASSERT(hWnd == m_hWnd); // should have been set in send msg hook
 return TRUE;
}
```

WINCORE.CPP is code supplied with Visual Studio. It's typically in the folder \Program Files\Microsoft Visual Studio .NET\Vc7\atlmfc\src\mfc.

This sets up a CREATESTRUCT structure very much like a WNDCLASS and fills it with the parameters that were passed to CreateEx(). It calls PreCreateWindow, AfxHookWindowCreate(), ::CreateWindow(), and AfxUnhookWindowCreate() before checking hWnd and returning.

The AFX prefix on many useful MFC functions dates back to the days when Microsoft's internal name for its class library was Application Framework. The :: in the call to CreateWindow identifies it as an API function, sometimes referred to as an SDK function in this context. The other functions are member functions of CWnd that set up the window for you.

On the face of it, there doesn't seem to be any effort saved here. You declare an instance of some CWnd object, call its Create() function, and have to pass just as many parameters as you did in the old C way of doing things. What's the point? Well, CWnd is really a class from which to inherit. Things become much simpler in the derived classes. Take CButton, for example, which is a class that encapsulates the concept of a button on a dialog box. A button is just a tiny window, but its behavior is constrained. For example, the user can't resize a button. Its Create() member function looks like this:

```
BOOL CButton::Create(LPCTSTR lpszCaption, DWORD dwStyle,
 const RECT& rect, CWnd* pParentWnd, UINT nID)
{
 CWnd* pWnd = this;
 return pWnd->Create(_T("BUTTON"), lpszCaption, dwStyle, rect, pParentWnd, nID);
}
```

That amounts to a lot fewer parameters. If you want a button, you create a button and let the class hierarchy fill in the rest.

GETTING A HANDLE ON ALL THESE MFC CLASSES

There are more than 200 MFC classes. Why so many? What do they do? How can any normal human keep track of them and know which one to use for what? Good questions—questions that take a large portion of this book to answer. The first part of this book presents the most commonly used MFC classes. This section looks at some of the more important base classes.

CObject

Figure A.1 shows a high-level overview of the inheritance tree for the classes in MFC. Only a handful of MFC classes do not inherit from CObject. CObject contains the basic functionality that all the MFC classes (and most of the new classes you create) are sure to need, such as persistence support and diagnostic output. As well, classes derived from CObject can be contained in the MFC container classes, such as CObArray and CobList.

Figure A.1
Almost all the classes in MFC inherit from `CObject`.

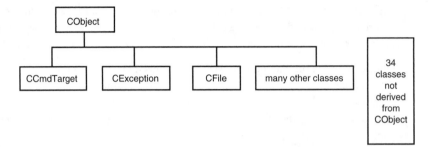

CCmdTarget

Some of the classes that inherit from `CObject`, such as `CFile` and `CException`, and their derived classes don't need to interact directly with the user and the operating system through messages and commands. All the classes that do need to receive messages and commands inherit from `CCmdTarget`. Figure A.2 shows a bird's-eye view of `CCmdTarget`'s derived classes, generally called command targets.

Figure A.2
Any class that will receive a command must inherit from `CCmdTarget`.

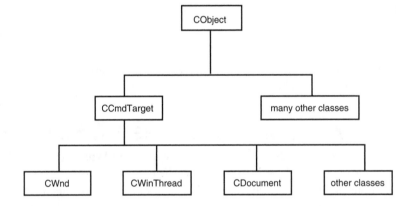

CWnd

As already mentioned, `CWnd` is an extremely important class. Only classes derived from `CWnd` can receive messages; threads and documents can receive commands but not messages.

> **Tip**
>
> Chapter 3 explores the distinction between commands and messages. Chapter 4, "Displaying Information," explains documents, and Chapter 14, "Multitasking with Windows Threads," explains threads.

CWnd provides window-oriented functionality, such as calls to CreateWindow and DestroyWindow, functions to handle painting the window onscreen, processing messages, talking to the Clipboard, and much more—almost 250 member functions in all. Only a handful of these need to be overridden in derived classes. Figure A.3 shows the classes that inherit from CWnd; there are so many control classes that to list them all would clutter up the diagram, so they are lumped together as control classes.

Figure A.3
Any class that will receive a message must inherit from CWnd, which provides lots of window-related functions.

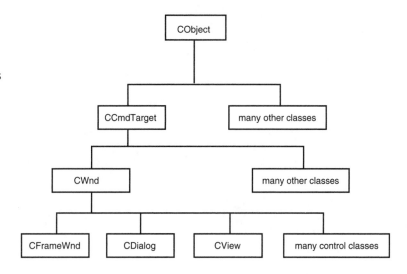

ALL THOSE OTHER CLASSES

So far you've seen ten classes in these three figures. What about the other 200+? You'll meet them in context throughout the book. If there's a specific class you're wondering about, check the index. Check the online help, too, because every class is documented there. Also, don't forget that the full source for MFC is included with every copy of Visual C++. Reading the source is a hard way to figure out how a class works, but sometimes you need that level of detail.

XML Review

In this appendix

WHAT IS XML?

XML is an exciting technological development. The entire .NET initiative is held together by—one might even say built around—XML. If you're working with XML every day, you know why that is and what it has to offer. But if you never heard of XML until you installed a copy of Visual Studio .NET, you may be wondering what all the excitement is about.

EXtensible Markup Language, or XML, is a notation, a way of writing down information. It's highly structured, and it follows rules. That makes it ideal for software to generate and to read. At the same time, XML documents are plain text ASCII files that you could read and write with Notepad. That makes XML easy for programmers to check, which reduces errors in programs that use XML to communicate. (Using Notepad is certainly not a scalable technique, but it speeds development and debugging dramatically.)

Here's a sample piece of XML:

```
<department id="MENSCLOTHING" name="Men's Clothing">
   <manager id="249" name="Peters, Sam" />
   <employee id="247" name="Anderson, Richard" rate="6.53" />
   <employee id="248" name="Jackson, Ken" rate="5.75" />
</department>
```

Tip

If you recognize this data, it's from the sample database in Chapter 11, "Database Programming."

At first glance, XML looks a lot like HTML, and they do have a lot in common:

- Both feature < and > characters, called angle brackets.
- Both feature tags, such as the <department> tag in this example. XML tags are more formally called *elements*.
- Both use matching start and end tags, such as <department> and </department> in this example.
- Both have attributes on tags, such as the rate attribute on the employee tag.
- Both permit tags inside other tags, such as the <employee> and <manager> tags that are between <department> and </department>.

There are some important differences, though, between XML and HTML. If you're familiar with HTML, these may trip you up: XML is a lot stricter than HTML. Specifically:

- XML is case sensitive: `<department>` and `<Department>` are definitely not the same thing.

- XML insists on quotes around attribute values. In HTML you could get away with `<A HREF=details.htm>` but in XML this would be an error. `<A HREF="details.htm">` works just fine.

- XML requires that all tags be closed. They might have a closing tag like the `</department>` shown earlier, or be closed "on-the-spot" with the extra `/` you see in the `manager` and `employee` tags, right before the final angle bracket of the tag. This symbol closes the tag right away. Without it, the XML has an error.

The example XML you've seen is well formed. Well-formed XML follows all the rules such as closing tags, using quotes around attributes, and more. You can find all the rules for well-formed XML at `http://www.w3.org/TR/REC-xml`, the XML 1.0 specification.

The rules that define a well-formed XML document are not optional. Any software that processes XML rejects XML that is not well formed. Some software rejects it more graciously than others, so when an XML-aware application does something really unexpected, be sure to check that the XML it's receiving is well formed.

APP
B

CREATING, EDITING, AND CHECKING XML

Because XML is plain ASCII, you can open it in Notepad if you wish. Figure B.1 shows the example from earlier in this chapter being edited in Notepad. You can also open XML files in Internet Explorer, which provides a collapsible tree view on your data, as you can see in Figure B.2. Unfortunately, you can't edit XML with Internet Explorer; you can only look at it.

Figure B.1
You can edit XML in Notepad.

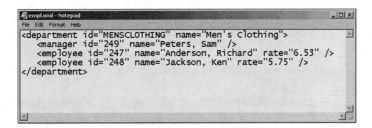

Figure B.2
You can display (but not edit) XML in Internet Explorer.

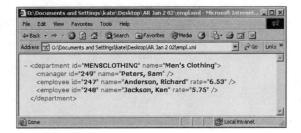

Because you're a Visual C++ developer, you have a terrific XML editor available to you: Visual Studio. Figure B.3 shows empl.xml being edited in Visual Studio. Notice the syntax coloring. That alone makes it a much better editor than Notepad. But look at the bottom of the editing area and note that you have a tabbed view on the file. Figure B.3 is of the XML view. Click the Data tab and to see something like Figure B.4. This data view of your XML file enables you to add elements as though you were editing a database. Switch back to the XML view to see that Visual Studio generated the appropriate elements for you.

Figure B.3
Visual Studio is a fine XML editor.

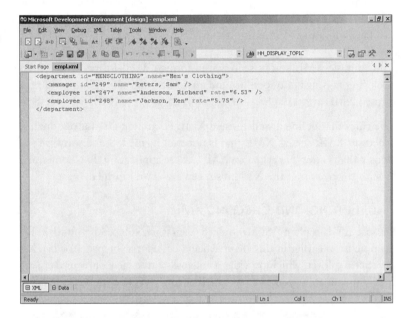

Figure B.4
With Visual Studio's Data View, you can edit XML just as you can database records.

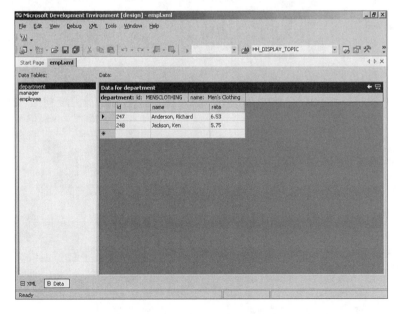

Visual Studio can also be used to edit schemas, and to generate schemas from sample XML. You'll see this in action later in this chapter, in the "Visual Studio Support for DTDs and Schemas" section.

Visual Studio may well be the only XML editor you need. If you'd like more XML-specific features, look into XML Spy (you can download a trial version at www.xmlspy.com.) It's the most popular XML editor, and the one I use myself when working with XSLT (covered later in this chapter.) For everything else, I use Visual Studio.

WORKING WITH XML IN .NET

A variety of classes in the System.Xml namespace represent an XML document. The simplest is XmlDocument. Listing B.1 shows a .NET application that just loads a file of XML into an XMLDocument instance.

LISTING B.1   WORKING WITH XMLDocument

```
// This is the main project file for VC++ application project
// generated using an Application Wizard.

#include "stdafx.h"

#using <mscorlib.dll>
#include <tchar.h>
#using <System.Xml.dll>

using namespace System;
using namespace System::Xml;

// This is the entry point for this application
int _tmain(void)
{
   XmlDocument* doc = new XmlDocument();
   doc->Load("empl.xml");
   Console::WriteLine("Loaded XML OK");
     return 0;
}
```

Tip

The code in Listing B.1 has an extra #using line. Without this line your code will not compile or run. This makes the classes of the System.Xml namespace available to you.

If the XML you read in (department.xml in Listing B.1) is not well formed, this code stops with a runtime exception, like this:

```
Exception occurred: System.Xml.XmlException: Unexpected token.  Expected 'EndTag'.
   at System.Xml.XmlTextReader.Read()
   at System.Xml.XmlLoader.LoadChildren(XmlNode parent)
   at System.Xml.XmlLoader.ReadCurrentNode()
```

```
    at System.Xml.XmlLoader.ReadCurrentNode()
    at System.Xml.XmlLoader.LoadChildren(XmlNode parent)
    at System.Xml.XmlLoader.ReadCurrentNode()
    at System.Xml.XmlLoader.ReadCurrentNode()
    at System.Xml.XmlLoader.LoadChildren(XmlNode parent)
    at System.Xml.XmlLoader.Load(XmlDocument doc, XmlNode root, XmlReader reader,
➡Boolean preserveWhitespace)
    at System.Xml.XmlDocument.Load(XmlReader reader)
    at System.Xml.XmlDocument.Load(String filename)
    at main() in c:\documents and settings\kate\my documents\visual studio
➡projects\xml\xml.cpp:line 15
```

You might prefer to catch that exception and write out a message. Listing B.2 shows the revised main().

LISTING B.2   CATCHING XML EXCEPTIONS

```
int _tmain(void)
{
   try
   {
   XmlDocument* doc = new XmlDocument();
   doc->Load("department.xml");
   Console::WriteLine("Loaded XML OK");
   }
   catch (Exception* e)
   {
           Console::WriteLine("load problem");
           Console::WriteLine(e->Message);
   }
     return 0;
}
```

Now when you provide XML to the application that is not well formed, you get more readable output, like this:

```
load problem
Unexpected token.  Expected 'EndTag'.
```

WORKING WITH XML IN A WIN32 APPLICATION

Listing B.3 shows a simple console application that loads an XML file into an object, using COM to access the MSXML4 component.

Note

If the DLL used in this sample, msxml4.dll, is not installed on your system, you can get a copy from http://msdn.microsoft.com/downloads/sample.asp?url=/ MSDN-FILES/027/001/766/msdncompositedoc.xml.

LISTING B.3   LOADING XML IN A WIN32 APPLICATION

```cpp
#include "stdafx.h"

#import "msxml4.dll"
using namespace MSXML2;

#include <iostream>
using std::cout;
using std::endl;


int _tmain(int argc, char* argv[])
{
   CoInitialize(NULL);
   {//extra braces for scope only

        MSXML2::IXMLDOMDocumentPtr xmlDoc("MSXML2.DOMDocument.4.0");
        xmlDoc->async = false;
        bool ret = xmlDoc->load("empl.xml");

        if ( ret)
        {
               cout << "Document loaded ok." << endl;
        }
        else
        {
               cout << "load problem" << endl;
        }
   }
   CoUninitialize();
   return 0;
}
```

APP

B

> **Note**
>
> You can learn more about console applications in Chapter 15, "Special Win32 Application Types." You can learn more about working with COM components in Chapter 9, "Building COM+ Components with ATL."

This code creates an XML document object, instructs the object not to return from the load() call until parsing is complete, and loads the XML into it. (To test and run it yourself, put empl.xml into the project folder.) If the document is well formed, load() returns true. If it's not well formed, load() returns false.

DEFINING DATA STRUCTURE

One of the real delights of using XML is that you can write your own set of rules, over and above the well-formed rules, and software enforces these rules for you with little or no programming on your part. Having the rules kept not in code, but in a separate rules file, saves you a lot of work, and ensures that the rules will be checked. Even better, you may be able to use a design (and rules) developed by somebody else, and save yourself even more work.

What kind of rules would you want to enforce about XML? For example, you could make a rule that every department has exactly one manager. An XML document that met this rule would be called valid, and one that did not would be invalid. Although a document is either well formed or not, a document is valid against a specific set of rules. The same document can be valid against one set of rules (perhaps one in which managers are optional) and invalid against another set.

Arithmetic makes a useful analogy here. Say I present you with an equation like this:

```
1 + - 2 - = 5 + = 7
```

Is this equation correct? You are likely to answer that it isn't even an equation. It's gibberish and there's no way to tell whether it's arithmetically correct or not. This is like XML that is not well-formed: no one can understand it at all.

Now consider this equation:

```
1 + 1 = 10
```

This is well formed. It follows the rules of arithmetic grammar. Is it correct? Most people would say it is not; that 1 + 1 is equal to 2. This equation is invalid according to our usual rules of arithmetic. Interestingly enough, though, this equation is actually correct if you are working in base 2, or binary, arithmetic. In arithmetic, as in XML, whether something is valid or not depends on the rules against which it is being tested.

You can write your rules in several formats: the two most important are the Document Type Definition, or DTD, and the schema.

DTD

The first widely adopted mechanism for writing the rules of an XML document was the DTD. With a DTD you can specify such things as:

- What elements (tags) will be in an XML document
- Which other elements each element can contain
- What attributes each element has, and what kind of attribute each is

For example, you can mark an attribute as optional (called IMPLIED in a DTD) or required. Listing B.4 shows the DTD for the department example.

LISTING B.4   A SAMPLE DTD

```
<?xml version="1.0" encoding="UTF-8"?>
<!ELEMENT department (manager, employee*) >
<!ATTLIST   department
```

LISTING B.4   CONTINUED

```
        id CDATA #REQUIRED
        name CDATA   #REQUIRED
>


<!ELEMENT manager EMPTY>
<!ATTLIST   manager
        id CDATA #REQUIRED
        name CDATA   #REQUIRED
>

<!ELEMENT employee EMPTY>
<!ATTLIST    employee
        id CDATA   #REQUIRED
        name CDATA #REQUIRED
        rate CDATA #REQUIRED
>
```

The first ELEMENT entry in this DTD specifies that a department element contains exactly one manager element and any number of employee elements. (The * symbol means "zero to infinity of.") Because no other elements are listed as part of the department ELEMENT entry, no other elements are allowed inside a department element. Both the manager and employee elements are defined as EMPTY, which means they cannot contain other elements.

The first ATTLIST entry in the DTD defines the attributes on a department element. The entry shown here means that a department element has an id attribute and a name attribute. Both are ordinary text (character data) and both are required. Similarly, a manager has an id and a name, and an employee has an id, a name, and a rate.

As you can see, DTDs are not easy to read. They were designed for software—not people—to use. A wide variety of tools exist to generate DTDs for you and to validate XML against a DTD.

To indicate inside a document or stream of XML that it follows the rules of a certain DTD, you add a DOCTYPE element at the start of your XML. Listing B.5 shows an example featuring the department example again:

LISTING B.5   XML THAT USES A DTD

```
<?xml version="1.0" encoding="UTF-8"?>
<!DOCTYPE department SYSTEM "department.dtd">
<department id="MENSCLOTHING" name="Men's Clothing">
    <manager id="249" name="Peters, Sam"/>
    <employee id="247" name="Anderson, Richard" rate="6.53"/>
    <employee id="248" name="Jackson, Ken" rate="5.75"/>
</department>
```

DOCTYPE elements can be tricky: you must use the same name in your DOCTYPE as you are using for the single element the entire rest of the document can reduce to — in this case, the word "department." The SYSTEM keyword indicates the DTD is on the same computer as the XML file. You could also use the PUBLIC keyword and provide a URL to a DTD written by somebody else: a vendor, client, or industrial association might provide you with a DTD that describes an XML document you exchange with others.

The XmlDocument class in the first .NET code sample in this chapter (Listing B.1) doesn't validate XML. To load and validate XML, you must use a reader class: XmlValidatingReader, to be specific. The body of main() thus becomes as shown in Listing B.6.

LISTING B.6   USING XmlValidatingReader

```
try
{
    XmlDocument* doc = new XmlDocument();
    XmlTextReader* tr = new XmlTextReader("department with DTD.xml");
    XmlValidatingReader* reader = new XmlValidatingReader(tr);
    doc->Load(reader);
    Console::WriteLine("Loaded XML OK");
}
catch (Exception* e)
{
    Console::WriteLine("load problem");
    Console::WriteLine(e->Message);
}
return 0;
```

If the document is valid, all is well. You can edit the document to something invalid, like Listing B.7.

LISTING B.7   DELIBERATELY INVALID XML

```
<?xml version="1.0" encoding="UTF-8"?>
<!DOCTYPE department SYSTEM "department.dtd">
<department id="MENSCLOTHING" name="Men's Clothing">
    <manager id="249" name="Peters, Sam" />
    <employee id="247" name="Anderson, Richard" rate="6.53" />
    <employee id="248" name="Jackson, Ken" rate="5.75" />
    <bad>this tag doesn't belong</bad>
</department>
```

If you re-run your application now, you'll get an error message:

```
load problem
Element 'department' has invalid content. Expected 'employee'. An error occurred
at file:///c:/Documents and Settings/kate/My Documents/Visual Studio
Projects/Xml2/department with DTD.xml(7, 5).
```

Just as the .NET code needed to use a different object to validate XML while loading it, the Win32 code needs a slight change, too. Nonvalidating parsers can get through XML more quickly than validating ones, so you have to ask specially to get a validating parser. Only one line of code has to change. Find the line that instantiates the parser:

```
MSXML2::IXMLDOMDocumentPtr xmlDoc("MSXML2.DOMDocument.4.0");
```

Change the type of pointer (the COM interface) you will use with this object:

```
MSXML2::IXMLDOMDocument2Ptr xmlDoc("MSXML2.DOMDocument.4.0");
```

Everything else remains unchanged. Because you are using a validating parser, if you try to load well-formed but invalid XML, you get a "load problem" message.

SCHEMAS

The rules that a DTD can enforce are fairly limited. You can insist that every `employee` element have a `rate` attribute, for example. Consider this `employee` element:

```
<employee id="247" name="Anderson, Richard" rate="varies" />
```

In some systems, this might be an acceptable entry for an employee's rate. If you write code that puts the values from the XML straight into a database, and the database is expecting numerical values, you get a runtime error of some sort when this element is processed. A DTD can't stipulate that an element's content or an attribute's value meet any conditions other than the existing ones. (One exception is the `enumerated` attribute, which must have one value from a pre-set list of values, but that wouldn't be helpful in the case of an employee's name or hourly rate.)

You can see that it would be useful to write rules that govern the actual content inside some XML. For example, that an employee's rate be a positive number, or that an employee's name be a string of no more than 40 characters. This was the motivation behind the development of XML Schemas: to provide far more control over the definition of a valid XML document.

Another advantage Schemas have over DTDs is that they are XML. That means you can edit them with any XML editor, including Visual Studio. There are plenty of tools to convert back and forth between DTDs and Schemas, as well.

Caution

XML Schemas went through quite a number of changes during development. Older tools may support older versions. As well, the name "Schemas" may be applied to more than one notation for describing the structure of an XML document. Check that the tool you plan to use supports W3C Schemas.

Listing B.8 presents a schema for the department example that enforces the same rules as the DTD shown earlier:

LISTING B.8   SCHEMA FOR DEPARTMENT SAMPLE

```
<?xml version="1.0" encoding="UTF-8"?>
<xsd:schema xmlns:xsd="http://www.w3.org/2000/10/XMLSchema"
elementFormDefault="qualified">
   <xsd:element name="department">
      <xsd:complexType>
         <xsd:sequence>
            <xsd:element name="manager">
               <xsd:complexType>
                  <xsd:attribute name="id" type="xsd:string" use="required"/>
                  <xsd:attribute name="name" type="xsd:string" use="required"/>
               </xsd:complexType>
            </xsd:element>
            <xsd:element name="employee" minOccurs="0" maxOccurs="unbounded">
               <xsd:complexType>
                  <xsd:attribute name="id" type="xsd:string" use="required"/>
                  <xsd:attribute name="name" type="xsd:string" use="required"/>
                  <xsd:attribute name="rate" type="xsd:string" use="required"/>
               </xsd:complexType>
            </xsd:element>
         </xsd:sequence>
         <xsd:attribute name="id" type="xsd:string" use="required"/>
         <xsd:attribute name="name" type="xsd:string" use="required"/>
      </xsd:complexType>
   </xsd:element>
</xsd:schema>
```

This is itself a piece of XML. Each element in this piece of XML has a name that starts with xsd:—this is a naming scheme that uses XML namespaces. If you're familiar with C++ namespaces (and you can't do much .NET work in C++ without noticing namespaces) then you know as much as you need to know about XML namespaces.

This schema says that a department element holds a *sequence* of other elements—that the order of those elements matters. It goes on to say that there is to be exactly one manager element, and it lists the attributes of the manager element, and any number (minimum occurrences is zero and maximum occurrences is unbounded) of employee elements. It lists the attributes of the employee element. Finally, it lists the attributes of the department element, after the sequence is complete.

Most developers find Schemas easier to read than DTDs. But the real fun begins when you start to restrict the content of the XML document using the extra functionality of Schemas. Insisting that the employee's rate be a number is as simple as changing xsd:string to xsd:float in the attribute definition.

As with DTDs, you need to indicate inside a document or stream of XML that it follows the rules of a certain Schema. Rather than adding a DOCTYPE element at the start of your XML, you put an attribute on the enclosing element. Here's an example featuring the department example again:

```
<?xml version="1.0" encoding="UTF-8"?>
<department xmlns ="empl.xsd" id="MENSCLOTHING"
   name="Men's Clothing">
   <manager id="249" name="Peters, Sam"/>
   <employee id="247" name="Anderson, Richard" rate="6.53"/>
   <employee id="248" name="Jackson, Ken" rate="5.75"/>
</department>
```

The attribute is the location of the Schema.

The code for validating against a Schema is no different than for validating against a DTD—all you need is an object (a .NET framework class for your .NET project, and a COM object for your Win32 project) that supports validating against the latest W3C schema specification.

VISUAL STUDIO SUPPORT FOR DTDS AND SCHEMAS

Visual Studio is a nice XML editor: You get syntax coloring, and the Data view can make your editing a lot less trouble. But the XML support in Visual Studio goes far beyond that to include schema generation, visual schema editing, and IntelliSense while editing XML.

GENERATING SCHEMAS WITH VISUAL STUDIO

As you can see from the explanation of schemas earlier in this chapter, they are really no fun to write by hand. So imagine how much work you can save by getting Visual Studio to generate schemas for you from sample XML. Figure B.5 shows the context menu that appears when you right-click the editing surface while you edit XML.

Figure B.5
Generating a schema from sample XML is as simple as right-clicking.

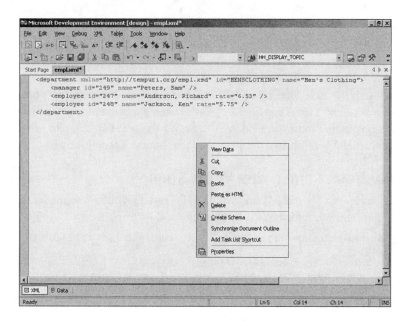

When you right-click and choose Create Schema, Visual Studio goes through the file of sample XML you are editing and infers the relationships and data types that are probably in your schema. For example, the employee elements in empl.xml all have a name attribute, so the schema includes this as one of its rules. Figure B.6 shows a visual representation of the generated schema. You can use the XML tab at the bottom of the visual editing area to edit the XML for the schema, or if you prefer you can edit it visually, changing the data type of an element, for example.

Figure B.6
Visual Studio generates schemas and provides visual editing.

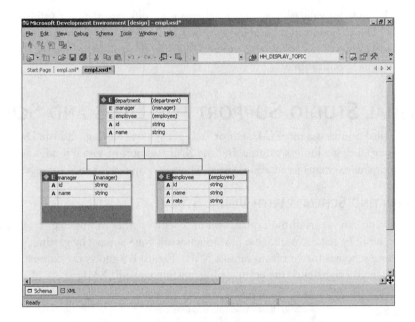

I encourage you to play around a bit with the visual schema editing and the schema generation in Visual Studio. For example, if you choose View, Server Explorer, you can browse through databases that are installed on your servers. Try dragging a database table onto this schema editing view. Figure B.7 shows a schema generated from such a drag-and-drop. The data types that were specified in SQL Server (such as DateTime for ord_date) are used in the generated XML schema. This can save you hours of repetitive work.

SCHEMA-AWARE EDITING WITH VISUAL STUDIO

If you open a file of XML in Visual Studio and generate a schema for it, the schema location is automatically added to the XML file, like this:

```
<department xmlns="http://tempuri.org/empl.xsd" id="MENSCLOTHING" name="Men's
Clothing">
    <manager id="249" name="Peters, Sam" />
    <employee id="247" name="Anderson, Richard" rate="6.53" />
    <employee id="248" name="Jackson, Ken" rate="5.75" />
</department>
```

Figure B.7
Visual Studio generates XML schemas from database tables automatically.

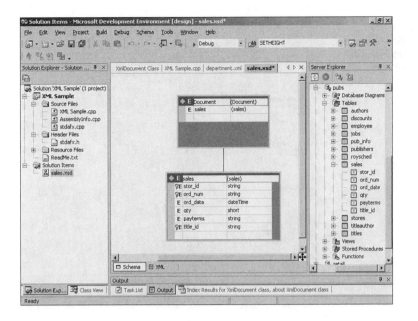

When a file of XML has an associated schema, editing with Visual Studio is dramatically different from editing with Notepad. IntelliSense reads the schema and gives you statement completion for XML. Figure B.8 shows the drop-down that appears when you type an opening angle bracket in a file of XML that has a schema associated with it. Press Tab to accept the suggestion. IntelliSense also enters your closing tag, and suggests attributes, as in Figure B.9.

Figure B.8
Visual Studio suggests XML tags when you edit an XML file that has a schema.

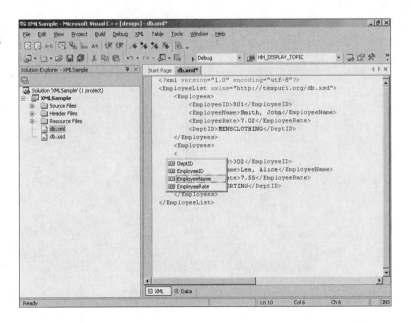

Figure B.9
IntelliSense suggests
XML attributes while
you edit a tag.

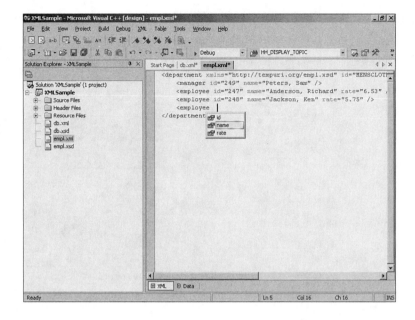

If you type XML that is not well formed or not valid, you'll get a visual indication of your error, just as you get wiggly underlines in code to indicate compiler errors before you compile. Hold your mouse over the underlined piece of XML, and a ErrorTip like the one in Figure B.10 tells you what's wrong.

Figure B.10
Find out about errors
while you're still
editing.

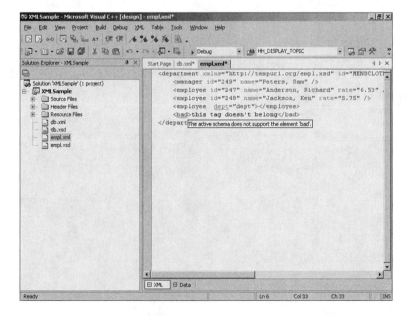

WHAT CAN XML BE USED FOR?

XML is ideal for any situation where information needs to cross a boundary. Some of these situations are more obvious than others. Consider:

- Business information, such as an invoice, being sent from one company to another.
- Small quantities of information, such as a configuration file, being saved at one moment and loaded again later.
- Information that was gathered by business-logic parts of your application, perhaps in the middle tier, being passed to the presentation layer of the same application.
- Information being transferred from one platform to another, perhaps from a Linux system to a Windows system.
- Information being transferred from one application to another, such as from WordPerfect to Word, or from Oracle to SQL Server.

All this information crosses a boundary, whether real (such as when the machines are in different buildings) or imagined (such as the process boundary when information passes from application to application on the same machine). And in all these examples, and many more, XML makes the boundary far easier to cross.

EXCHANGING INFORMATION BETWEEN COMPANIES

There are lots of ways to send an invoice to a customer. The tried-and-true way is to have your software print an invoice on paper, which you put in an envelope and entrust to the postal system. A few days later (maybe a lot of days later) it arrives at your customer's location, and the first thing that happens to it is that someone re-types all that information into another piece of software. Although this feels like a tremendous waste of time and effort, it has the advantage of working. You don't need to know what software your customer uses, and they don't need to change what they use to accommodate you, and still information comes out of your software and into your customer's software.

Another approach is to use EDI, Electronic Data Interchange. This set of technologies has been around for many years. The drawbacks are that it's expensive, that it relies on a proprietary connection that works only with specific software, and that it is seemingly impossible to navigate without a consultant. For big firms with a large volume of information to exchange, it may still be worth it. For smaller exchanges, such as one invoice a month, it's probably a lot less work to retype paper invoices than to implement EDI.

Of course, you can exchange information electronically without using EDI. For example, you can type your invoice into a Word or Excel document and email it to your customer. Then you can type it into your accounting software while your customers are typing into theirs. It sounds funny, but it's actually quite a popular solution. If your accounting software can export Word or Excel files, or if you can copy-and-paste between your accounting software and whatever format you like to email in, you can save a little time on retyping.

If you email that customer an XML document, you can really start to save time on both ends. Get your accounting software (or Excel) to export the document for you. (If you're a really small shop, you can always type the document from scratch in Notepad.) Email it to the client. The client imports it into Excel, or the accounting program, or the mind-bendingly expensive financial management package. Or opens it in Notepad. It doesn't matter: XML is fast becoming the universal import format. So, just as with the tried-and-true paper invoices, you don't need to know what software your customer uses, and nobody has to change software to exchange information electronically.

KEEPING CONFIGURATION INFORMATION IN A FILE

The boundaries of time are just as tricky to cross as those of space. Think about the challenges for Win32 programmers in saving and loading a file, as discussed in Chapter 5, "Printing and Saving." How can you test loading a file when you don't have any saved files to load? If you write your saving and loading code, then save something and load it again and it comes back wrong, is the bug in the saving or loading code? How can you tell?

When you save plain text files, you can generate them by hand while you test loading. You can look at them in Notepad or Visual Studio while you test saving. Life is just a lot simpler. But it's boring and repetitive work trying to parse a plain text file, and nobody likes to reinvent the wheel.

XML parsers and processors are all around you. Microsoft provides a fine one as a COM component that you can use from any code you wish. You can also find lots of XML support (reading it, manipulating it, and generating it) in the CLR libraries. So saving a stream of XML is a really nice solution to a number of serialization problems. Your geekier users will probably edit the configuration file themselves in Notepad rather than using the tool you provide, but you should consider that a feature too—they like that sort of thing.

One drawback to XML, though, is that it's verbose. If you are saving a large document, this can really matter. A single byte in a binary file can hold a number up to 255. If you change that file to plain text, you need three bytes to hold the characters '2', '5', and '5'. Then imagine going to an XML format and representing the same information as:

```
<NumberofItems>255</NumberofItems>
```

Now you need 36 characters to hold this information! This kind of inflation might be significant if your save document is already large. But for something small, such as a configuration file, the inflation from a few hundred bytes to a few thousand really doesn't matter. The gain in readability and ease of programming is well worth it.

PASSING INFORMATION BETWEEN TIERS

Although a lot of magazine covers, Web sites, and general hoopla have been devoted to XML as a way to exchange information between organizations or applications, a lot less has been said about XML between tiers of a multi-tiered application. Yet in many ways this is the easiest way to start benefiting from XML right away. You don't have to agree on a data exchange format with a trading partner, or adopt a shared DTD or schema. You just design the architecture of your next system so that XML is the information that passes between layers.

Here's the way it works in many such applications: the business objects collaborate to fill a DOM tree with XML. Perhaps they get it from a database application such as SQL Server 2000 that can provide XML in response to a query. Perhaps they build it with calls to CLR methods that generate XML. After the XML is created, it's passed back to the next tier. In many XML-enabled Web applications, for example, an ASP page gets XML from a COM or .NET component. Then the XML can be transformed into HTML with just a few lines of XSLT code, and returned to the Presentation layer (perhaps a Web browser) to be shown to the user. You can even transform the same XML with different templates to produce HTML that's customized for the capabilities of the browser making the request.

APP

B

> **Note**
>
> You'll learn more about XSLT a little later in this chapter.

The advantage of using XML between tiers is that it really disconnects the tiers. The goal of tier separation is to reduce the number of skills that each person requires. For example, if your ASP page rummages around in the database with SQL SELECT statements and then emits some HTML mixed with some information from the database, the person who codes that page needs to be good at a great number of things:

- The language in which the ASP page is written, typically JScript or VBScript
- The ASP objects and programming model
- SQL Syntax and the layout of the database used in this application
- HTML
- Aesthetics of page design and of presenting information to the user effectively

That's a lot to expect one person to know! Yet because all the code is mixed up together in one HTML page, it could be a nightmare for more than one person to work on that one file.

When you move to a multi-tier application, you can separate the skills involved. Your ASP programmer just writes code to get XML from the business objects and transform them to HTML. Your XSLT programmer concentrates on HTML, page design, and presenting information. Your business object programmer just worries about getting the information out of the database, not about organizing or presenting it. Even if all three of those people are the same person—you—at least you don't have to keep track of everything at the same time.

EXCHANGING INFORMATION BETWEEN PLATFORMS

Have you ever emailed a Word document to a devoted Linux user, who promptly emailed back reminding you that not everyone has Word? Have you ever been sent an ordinary text file from a Mac user and found it came out all on one really long line when you edited it in Notepad? XML solves a lot of these problems by being platform independent. XML doesn't care about line breaks, or whitespace, and that means it doesn't break when moved from platform to platform. And because most XML editors can display one tag per line, or neaten up your line breaks, you don't care either.

EXCHANGING INFORMATION BETWEEN APPLICATIONS

If you had a WordPerfect document to read, and only Word to read it with, what would you do? Open it in Word, that's what; Word does a reasonable job of converting between the two formats. But what if someone sent you a document in some other obscure word processing format, and Word couldn't open it? If it was me, I would probably write back and ask if the obscure word-processing application could export to a Word format. If the answer was no, I'd probably run through a list of formats Word can import and convert, to see whether the obscure thing could export to any of them. I once converted an ancient old database format by having it export to Lotus 1-2-3 format, which I could import into Excel and save as an ordinary Excel file, which I could then import into Access. Really!

Already many new versions of applications can import XML and export XML. As time goes by, more and more applications will gain this capability. After all, if you're writing a new productivity app, would you rather write code to import from ten different formats, or just from XML? This universal import/export capacity makes XML a huge timesaver for application developers.

You may wonder whether the format in which one application exports a word processing file matches the format in which another wants to import it. Probably not. But—and this is where the value of XML starts to show—it doesn't matter! If one of the two firms involved (or any other third party) writes an XSLT template to transform from one format to the other, the problem is solved. It can even be automated!

WHAT IS XSLT?

XSLT stands for eXtensible Stylesheet Language Transformations. Don't confuse it with just plain XSL, discussed in the next section. XSLT is used to transform XML from one layout (DTD or schema) to another.

For example, consider this XML:

```
<Dept LookUp="MENSCLOTHING" FullName="Men's Clothing">
    <Manager LookUp="249">Peters, Sam</Manager>
    <Employee LookUp="247" rate="6.53">Anderson, Richard" </Employee>
    <Employee LookUp="248" rate="5.75">Jackson, Ken></Employee>
</Dept>
```

This contains the same names, rates, and IDs as the XML you've been seeing throughout this chapter, but it's laid out in a very different way. You can think of the first way as the export from one application, and the second way as the import into another. They don't match, but they are related. You could probably write some code to change one into the other, looking for the string department and changing it into Dept, for example.

This is what XSLT does. You write a template that explains how to transform one layout into the other, and then use an application that knows how to transform XML layouts, often called an XSLT engine. XML editors such as XML Spy can act as an XSLT engine, and so can the XML component from Microsoft.

TRANSFORMING XML TO XML

Listing B.9 presents the XSLT to transform from the <department> XML to the <Dept> XML:

LISTING B.9   TRANSFORMING XML FROM ONE LAYOUT TO ANOTHER

```
<?xml version="1.0" encoding="UTF-8"?>
<xsl:stylesheet version="1.0" xmlns:xsl="http://www.w3.org/1999/XSL/Transform">
   <xsl:output method="xml" version="1.0" encoding="UTF-8" indent="yes"/>
   <xsl:template match="department">
   <Dept>
      <xsl:attribute name="LookUp"><xsl:value-of select="@id"/></xsl:attribute>
      <xsl:attribute name="FullName"><xsl:value-of
select="@name"/></xsl:attribute>
      <Manager>
         <xsl:attribute name="LookUp"><xsl:value-of
select="manager/@id"/></xsl:attribute>
         <xsl:value-of select="manager/@name"/>
      </Manager>
      <xsl:apply-templates select="employee"/>
   </Dept>
   </xsl:template>

   <xsl:template match="employee">
      <Employee>
         <xsl:attribute name="LookUp"><xsl:value-of select="@id"/></xsl:attribute>
         <xsl:attribute name="rate"><xsl:value-of select="@rate"/></xsl:attribute>
         <xsl:value-of select="@name"/>
      </Employee>
   </xsl:template>
</xsl:stylesheet>
```

This stylesheet is XML. It has a mixture of two kinds of elements: those that start xsl: and those that do not. The ones that start xsl: are XSLT instructions. This example uses the key building blocks of XSLT:

- xsl:template defines a template and provides instructions on how to handle a specific element in the input. This sample has a template for a department element and another template for an employee element. The match attribute on the xsl:template element indicates which input elements it transforms.

- xsl:attribute adds an attribute to an output element. This example writes out a Dept element and then adds the LookUp and FullName attributes to it with xsl:attribute elements.

- xsl:value-of transfers content from the input XML document to the output XML document. The select attribute gives the path to the source of the value. An @ in this path indicates an attribute.

- xsl:apply-templates triggers another template to be applied. In this example the employee template is applied from inside the department template.

The paths shown in the select attributes on the xsl:value-of elements are relative to the piece of XML being processed. The first four xsl:value-of elements in this sample are in the department template, so the paths are from the department element. The first finds the ID attribute (the @ sign, pronounced "at," is supposed to make you think "attribute") of the department element. The second finds the name attribute of the department element. The third finds a manager element inside the department element, and then the ID attribute of that manager element. The fourth finds the manager element again, and the name attribute of that element.

These paths can be far more complex, incorporating test conditions such as finding employees whose rate is over 6.00, or the last employee, but if you want to see how those sorts of tricks are done, you'll need an XSLT reference book, not a quick review chapter.

To transform XML in a .NET application, you use the XslTransform class in the System::Xml::Xsl namespace. So start by adding another using statement at the top of your source file:

```
using namespace System::Xml::Xsl;
```

After loading the XML into your XmlDocument, add these lines to transform it and write it to the console:

```
XslTransform* xslt = new XslTransform();
xslt->Load("department to Dept.xsl");

XmlWriter* writer = new XmlTextWriter(Console::Out);
xslt->Transform(new DocumentNavigator(doc),0,writer);
```

This code just creates an XslTransform object and loads the XSLT into it. Then it creates an XmlWriter associated with the console, and passes it into the Transform() method, along with a DocumentNavigator created from the XmlDocument. The middle parameter, 0 in this sample code, is for a namespace parameter, but it's not used in this release of the .NET framework. Just pass 0 for a null pointer.

In a Win32 application, you follow the same steps to transform your document as you do in the .NET application: load the XML into one object, load the XSLT into another, and apply the transform. What's different here is that you use the same object type to hold both the XML and the XSLT. Listing B.10 presents the lines to add to the main() of the Win32 example:

LISTING B.10   TRANSFORMING XML IN WIN32 PROGRAMMING

```
IXMLDOMDocumentPtr xsltDoc("MSXML2.DOMDocument");
xsltDoc->async = false;
ret = xsltDoc->load("department to Dept.xsl");

_bstr_t transformed = xmlDoc->transformNode(xsltDoc);
char* printable = transformed;
cout <<  printable << endl;
```

There's a small trick here, because the transformNode() method returns a BSTR. The easiest way from a BSTR to a char* is through the helper class _bstr_t, which wraps a BSTR and provides a conversion to char*, so that you can print the XML on cout.

TRANSFORMING XML TO XHTML

In an earlier section about multi-tiered Web applications, I suggested XML could be transformed to HTML, which is then sent to a Web browser for display. To be strictly accurate, it's transformed to XHTML. This is HTML that meets all those nitpicky XML rules. Browsers still display it just as though it were ordinary HTML, but you have to remember the nitpicky rules while you're writing your XSLT. For example, if you want to use a <BR> tag in your HTML, you must actually use either
 (the close-on-the-spot style) or
</BR> (opening and then closing the tag.)

In Listing B.11 you will find some XSLT that transforms the department XML to HTML.

LISTING B.11   TRANSFORMING XML TO XHTML

```
<?xml version="1.0" encoding="UTF-8"?>
<xsl:stylesheet version="1.0" xmlns:xsl="http://www.w3.org/1999/XSL/Transform">
   <xsl:output method="html" version="1.0" encoding="UTF-8" indent="yes"/>
   <xsl:template match="department">
   <html>
   <head><title>Department Listing</title></head>
   <body>
   <h1>Department: <xsl:value-of select="@id"/> - <xsl:value-of
select="@name"/></h1>
           <h2>Manager: <xsl:value-of select="manager/@name"/></h2>
           <ul>
           <xsl:apply-templates select="employee"/>
           </ul>
   </body>
   </html>
   </xsl:template>
   <xsl:template match="employee">
           <li><xsl:value-of select="@name"/> $<xsl:value-of select="@rate"/></li>
   </xsl:template>
</xsl:stylesheet>
```

As you can see, this is a combination of familiar HTML tags, such as <h1> or <li>, with XSLT elements just like those used in the XML-to-XML example. When an XSLT engine is used to transform the department XML with this XSLT, it produces the XHTML in Listing B.12.

LISTING B.12   XHTML FROM XSLT

```
<html>
   <head>
      <META http-equiv="Content-Type" content="text/html; charset=UTF-16">
      <title>Department Listing</title>
   </head>
   <body>
      <h1>Department: MENSCLOTHING - Men's Clothing</h1>
      <h2>Manager: Peters, Sam</h2>
      <ul>
         <li>Anderson, Richard $6.53</li>
         <li>Jackson, Ken $5.75</li>
      </ul>
   </body>
</html>
```

Figure B.11 shows this HTML displayed in a browser. This is bare-bones simple; a talented HTML artist could create a marvelously complex page, and just edit the XSLT to work with the original HTML. The programmer who got this information out of the database wouldn't need to change a thing.

Figure B.11
This HTML was created from a file of XML.

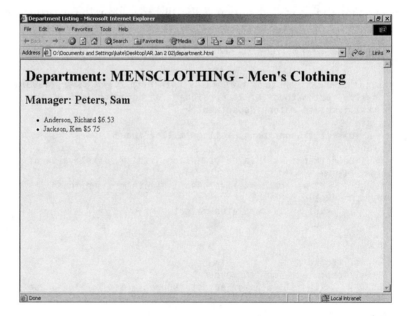

From a code point of view, transforming to HTML is no different than transforming to HTML. Load the XML, load the XSLT, and then do the transformation.

WHAT IS XSL?

XSLT solves a number of important problems by transforming XML into another layout of XML or into XHTML. But it can't be used to generate a Word file, or a PDF, or a Postscript file. You could use XSLT to make HTML and then use some other utility to translate that, but HTML is not a good formatting tool—it doesn't give designers the control they demand.

Instead, you can use XSL—eXtensible Stylesheet Language. You can use XSL to describe in a generic way how you would like a piece of content formatted—say Times Roman, 10 point, black on white. Companion pieces of software called *drivers* can produce Postscript, PDF files, or whatever other kind of output you need. An XSL file describes how to display an XML document, without regard to what you are going to display it with.

That's quite a technical challenge, and it wasn't completed until some time after XSLT became generally supported. Learning XSL is beyond the scope of this chapter; if you're curious, a good place to start learning it on your own is `http://www.w3.org/Style/XSL/`, which features tutorials and reference materials along with the latest news about XSL and related specifications, including XSLT.

WHAT DOES THE FUTURE HOLD FOR XML AND RELATED TECHNOLOGIES?

XML is, among other things, a standard. It's controlled by a standards body, the World Wide Web Consortium, generally referred to as W3C. Most vendors add features to their XML-enabled products only when the W3C committee or committees approves a change to XML or to one of the related technologies such as SOAP, XSL, XSLT, XLink, or XPath. (One notable exception is Microsoft, which tends to implement based on early drafts of standards and may add features that are not part of any standard.)

Technologies typically change quite slowly when they are controlled by a standards body. XML has moved incredibly quickly in that context. The very first draft of the XML specification was in 1996, and it became a Recommendation (the closest thing W3C has to a standard) in February 1998. It has since been revised once, in October 2000. The core of XML itself can thus be considered stable—the use of angle brackets, the rules about quotes around attributes, the definition of well-formed, and the like.

From the beginning, DTDs were suggested as a way to describe the structure of an XML document. They were already in use to describe, for example, different versions of HTML. In January 1998 a submission was made to W3C suggesting another way to describe that structure, and using the name *XML Schema*. By May 2001, "Schema" was a W3C Recommendation, though it had undergone some very significant changes in those three years. The status of "Recommendation" means that future changes should be fairly minor.

XML technologies that have reached the status of Recommendation include XML itself and XML Schema, and the following related technologies:

- **XML Linking Language (formerly XLink).** A notation to form links between XML documents in the same spirit as those between HTML documents.
- **XML Namespaces.** A notation to distinguish between elements with the same common name by placing them in different namespaces.
- **XHTML 1.1.** The variant of HTML that obeys all the rules of well-formed XML.

Some XML technologies are not yet Recommendations. This means that they could undergo important changes before they stabilize. The relevant technologies are:

- **Xpath.** The syntax used in the "match" and "select" clauses you saw in the XSLT examples, and many other places, to instruct a processor which piece of an input file you wish to use.
- **XML Query (formerly XQuery).** Technologies to search XML documents as easily as any other data store. Relies heavily on XPath.
- **XML Pointer Language (formerly XPointer).** A way to specify a fragment of an XML document. It too is based on XPath.
- **Canonical XML and XML Signature.** Technologies that deal with the difficulty of determining whether two XML documents are the same or different, given that whitespace is irrelevant, that order may or may not be relevant according to the DTD or schema being used, and that documents can be very long and complex.

For most XML developers, the time of the most turbulent transitions has passed. As more and more tools support schemas, and schemas have stopped changing, you can develop in confidence, knowing that future developments will not break your code. But keep an eye on www.w3.org/XML to see what other new technologies are coming down the pipe.

THE VISUAL STUDIO USER INTERFACE, MENUS, AND VISUAL STUDIO

In this appendix

VISUAL STUDIO: AN INTEGRATED DEVELOPMENT ENVIRONMENT

When you buy Microsoft Visual C++ .NET, you actually get Microsoft Visual Studio .NET with the Visual C++ .NET component activated. Visual Studio is far more than just a compiler, and you have far more to learn than you may think. The interface is very visual, which means that many possibilities greet you when you first run Visual Studio.

Microsoft Visual C++ .NET is one component of the Microsoft Visual Studio .NET. The capabilities of this one piece of software are astonishing. It is called an integrated development environment (IDE) because within a single tool, you can perform the following:

- Generate starter applications without writing code.
- View a project several different ways.
- Edit source and include files.
- Connect to external resources, such as databases.
- Build the visual interface (menus and dialog boxes) of your application.
- Compile and link.
- Debug an application while it runs.

Visual C++ is, technically speaking, just one component of Visual Studio. You can buy, for example, Microsoft's Visual Basic .NET compiler and use it in Visual Studio as well. You can even buy a language from a vendor other than Microsoft, and use it in Visual Studio too. Figure C.1 shows Perl being debugged in Visual Studio.

Figure C.1
Visual Studio can support any number of languages—not all sold by Microsoft.

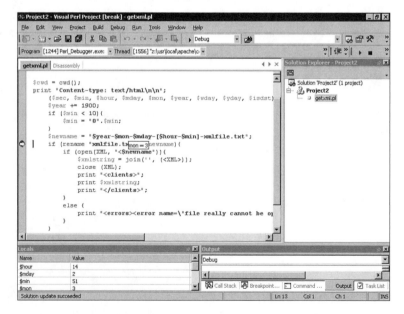

CHOOSING A VIEW

The user interface of Visual Studio encourages you to move from view to view in your project, looking at your resources, classes, and files. The main screen is divided into panes that you can resize to suit your own needs. Many shortcut menus, reached by right-clicking different places on the screen, simplify common tasks.

If you are familiar with the window layout in Visual C++ 6, you may be surprised when you first run Visual Studio. You can restore a "Visual C++ 6" look, and I recommend that you do. To do so, click My Profile from the Start Page and change the profile to Visual C++ Developer, as shown in Figure C.2. All the figures in this book were taken with the Visual C++ Developer profile selected.

Figure C.2
Visual Studio.NET supports several developer profiles. Choose Visual C++.

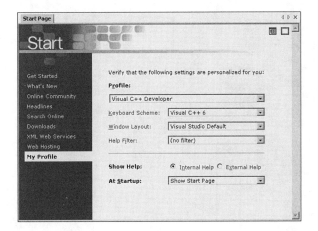

With Visual C++, you work on a single application as a *solution*, which contains one or more *projects*. A project is a collection of files: source, headers, resources, settings, and configuration information. Visual Studio is designed to enable you to work on all aspects of a single solution at once. You create a new application by creating a new project. When you want to work on your application, open the solution (a file with the extension .SLN) rather than each code file independently. The interface of Visual Studio, shown in Figure C.3, is designed to work with a solution and is divided into several zones.

To minimize the clutter on screen, you can set certain windows to be *fly-outs*. A fly-out window is displayed as an icon and a label when the user is working on another area of the screen, and it "flies out" when the user hovers over the icon, as shown in Figure C.4. (You can see the icon and label for dynamic help at the far left of Figure C.3, earlier.)

The zones that make up the Visual Studio interface are as follows:

- **Across the top**. This zone includes menus and toolbars. These are discussed in the second half of this appendix.
- **On the left**. This zone includes the view windows, such as the Class View window and the Solution Explorer.

- **On the right**. This is your main working area where you edit files.
- **Across the bottom**. This area includes the output window and status bar.

Figure C.3
The Visual Studio interface presents a lot of information. The Class View window is on the left.

Figure C.4
The Dynamic Help window is set as a fly-out window to minimize clutter.

Other than the menu bar, you can move any of the toolbars or windows anywhere you like. You can float them on the screen, dock them to the sides, or dock them to other windows. Visual Studio enables you to customize your development environment to suit your development needs and personal preferences.

Open Visual Studio and try to resize the panes and follow along as functions are described in this appendix. If you want an application to follow along with, you can build a very simple one as described in Chapter 2, "Building Your First Windows Application," or Chapter 17, "Getting Started with .NET."

The View windows determine which way you look at your project and what is in the main working area: code or resources (menus, icons, and dialog boxes). Each view is discussed in detail in a separate section in this appendix, as follows:

- The Resource View window is discussed in the "Looking at Interface Elements" section.

- The Class View window is discussed in the "Looking at Your Code, Arranged by Class" section.

- The Solution Explorer window is discussed in the "Looking at Your Code, Arranged by File" section.

Visual Studio uses three different files to keep track of all the information about your solution. The main solution file, with an .SLN extension, contains the names of all the projects in the solution, what directories they are in, compiler and linker options, and other information required by everyone who may work on the project. There is also a project file, with a .VCPROJ extension, for each project within the solution. The solution user options file, with an .SUO extension, contains all your personal settings for Visual Studio—colors, fonts, toolbars, which files are open and how their windows are sized and located, breakpoints from your most recent debugging session, and so on. If someone else is going to work on your solution, you give that person a copy of the main solution file and project files but not the user options file. Do not try to edit this file.

To open the solution, open the main solution file. The other files are opened automatically.

LOOKING AT INTERFACE ELEMENTS

After you've opened or created a solution, opening the Resource View window (by choosing View, Resource View) opens an expandable and collapsible outline of the visual elements of your program: accelerators, dialog boxes, icons, menus, the string table, toolbars, and version information. These resources define the way users interact with your program. Chapter 3, "Interacting with Your Application;" Chapter 6, "Building a Complete Application: ShowString;" and Chapter 7, "Status Bars, Toolbars, and Common Controls" cover the work involved in creating and editing these resources. The next few sections cover the way in which you can look at completed resources.

Tip

Open one of the projects that you've already built, or a sample project from Visual C++, and follow along as functions are described in this section. ShowString, the sample application from Chapter 6, is a good choice because it uses most of the features described in this section.

ACCELERATORS

Accelerators associate key combinations with menu items. Figure C.5 shows an accelerator resource. The MFC Application Wizard generated all but one of the accelerator combinations in the figure. These are made for you when you create a new application. You can add accelerators for specific menu items, if necessary. In Figure C.5, the ID_TOOLS_OPTIONS accelerator was added as part of the sample.

Figure C.5
Accelerators associate key combinations with menu items.

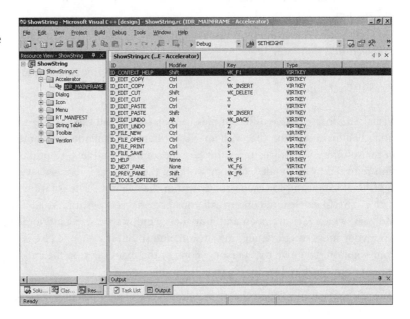

DIALOG BOXES

Your application receives information from users through dialog boxes. When a dialog resource is being displayed in the main working area, as in Figure C.6, a toolbox is displayed, either docked or floating over the working area. (If it's not displayed, choose View, Toolbox to display it.) Each small icon on the toolbox represents a control (edit box, list box, button, and so on) that can be inserted onto your dialog box. Choose View, Properties, and the Dialog Properties box shown in Figure C.6 is displayed. Here the behavior of a control or of the whole dialog box can be controlled.

This method of editing dialog boxes is one of the reasons for the name Visual C++. In this product, if you want a button to be a little lower on a dialog box, you click it with the mouse, drag it to the new position, and release the mouse button. Similarly, if you want the dialog box larger or smaller, grab a corner or edge and drag it to the new size, like any other sizable window. Before Visual C++ was released, the process involved coding and pixel counting and took many minutes rather than just a few seconds. This visual approach to dialog box building made Windows programming accessible to many more programmers.

Figure C.6
Dialog boxes receive information from the user.

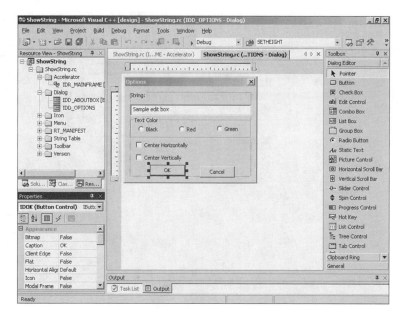

ICONS

Icons are small bitmaps that represent your program or its documents. For example, when a program is minimized, an icon is used to represent it. A larger version of that icon is used to represent both the program and its documents within an Explorer window. When an MDI window is minimized within your application, the minimized window is represented by an icon. Figure C.7 shows the default icon provided by the MFC Application Wizard for minimized MDI windows. One of your first tasks after building any application is to replace this with an icon that more clearly represents the work your program performs.

An icon is a 32×32 pixel bitmap that can be edited with any number of drawing tools, including the simple bitmap editor included in Visual Studio. The interface is very similar to Microsoft Paint or Microsoft Paintbrush in Zoom mode. You can draw one pixel at a time by clicking, or you can click and drag to draw lines in freehand mode. You can work on the small or zoomed versions of the icon and see the effects at once in both places.

MENUS

With menus, users can tell your program what to do. Keyboard shortcuts (accelerators) are linked to menu items, as are toolbar buttons. The MFC Application Wizard creates the standard menus for a new application, and you edit those and create new ones in this view. You use the Properties window to connect menu items to functions within your code. Figure C.8 shows a menu displayed in the Menu Editor. Choose View, Properties Window to display the properties for the menu item. Every menu item has the following three basic components:

Figure C.7
Icons represent your application and its documents.

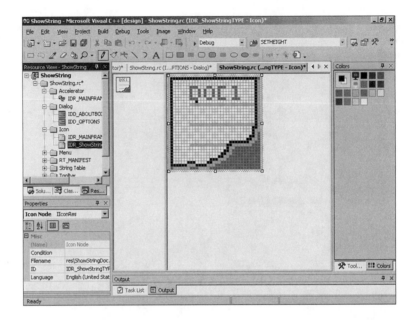

Figure C.8
Your application receives commands through menus. You create and edit the menus in Visual Studio itself.

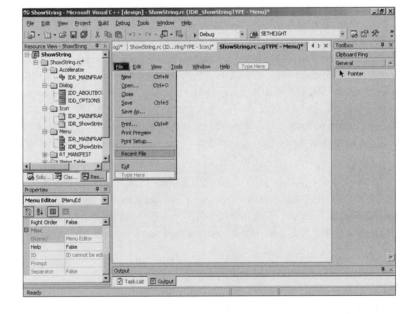

- **Resource ID**. This uniquely identifies this menu item. Accelerators and toolbar buttons are linked to resource IDs. The convention is to build the ID from the menu choices that lead to the item. For example, the resource ID for the New item on the File menu is ID_FILE_NEW.

- **Caption**. This is the text that appears for a menu choice. For example, the caption for the New item on the File menu is &New\tCtrl+N. The & means that the N is to appear underlined, and the menu item can be selected by typing N when the menu is displayed. The \t is a tab, and the Ctrl+N is the accelerator for this menu item, as defined in Figure C.5.

- **Prompt**. A prompt appears in the status bar when the highlight is on the menu item or the cursor is over the associated toolbar button. For File, New, the prompt is Create a new document\nNew. Only the portion before the newline (\n) is displayed in the status bar. The second part of the prompt, New, is the text for the ToolTip that appears if the user pauses the mouse over a toolbar button with this resource ID. The framework of Visual C++ and MFC provides all this functionality for you automatically.

THE STRING TABLE

The string table is a list of strings within your application. Many strings, such as the static text on dialog boxes or the prompts for menu items, can be accessed in far simpler ways than through the string table, but some are reached only through it. For example, you can keep a default name or value in the string table and change it without recompiling any code, though the resources have to be compiled and the project linked. Each of these could be hard-coded into the program, but then changes would require a full recompile.

Figure C.9 shows the string table for a sample application. To change a string, open the String Table and double-click an ID, a Value, or a Caption, and type in the new value.

Figure C.9
The string table stores all the prompts and text in your application.

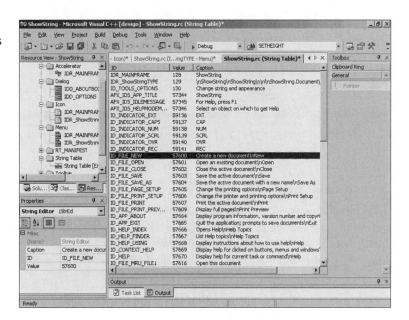

TOOLBARS

Toolbars are the lines of small buttons typically located directly underneath the menus of an application. Each button is linked to a menu item, and its appearance depends on the state of the menu item. If a menu item is grayed, the corresponding toolbar button is grayed as well. If a menu item is checked, the corresponding toolbar button is typically drawn as a pushed-in button. In this way, toolbar buttons serve as indicators as well as mechanisms for giving commands to the application.

A toolbar button has two parts: a bitmap of the button and a resource ID. When a user clicks the button, it is just as though the menu item with the same resource ID was chosen. Figure C.10 shows a typical toolbar and the properties of the File, New button on that toolbar. In this view, you can change the resource ID of any button and edit the bitmap with the same tools used to edit icons.

Figure C.10
Toolbar buttons are associated with menu items through a resource ID.

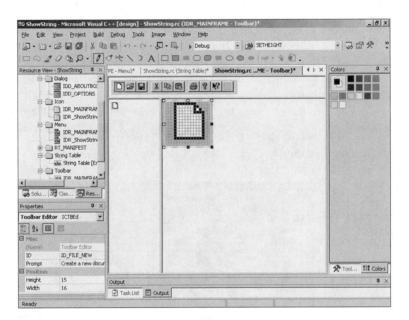

VERSION INFORMATION

Good installation programs use the version information resource when installing your application on a user's machine. For example, if a user is installing an application that has already been installed, the installation program may not have to copy as many files. It may alert the user if an old version is being installed over a new version, and so on.

When you create an application with the MFC Application Wizard, version information like that in Figure C.11 is generated for you automatically. Before attempting to change any of it, make sure you understand how installation programs use it.

Figure C.11
Version information is used by install programs.

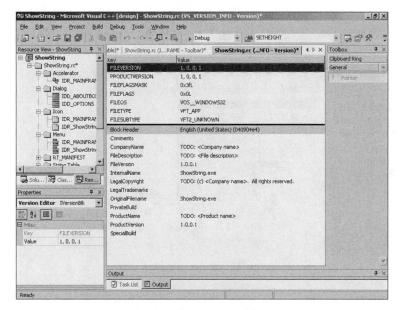

LOOKING AT YOUR CODE, ARRANGED BY CLASS

The Class View window shows the classes in your application. Under each class, the member variables and functions are shown, as demonstrated in Figure C.12. Member functions are shown first with a purple icon next to them, followed by member variables with a turquoise icon. Protected members have a key next to the icon, whereas private members have a padlock.

Figure C.12
The Class View window shows the functions and variables in each class in your application.

Double-clicking a function name opens the source for that function in the main working area, as shown in Figure C.12. Double-clicking a variable name opens the file in which the variable is declared.

Right-clicking a classname opens a shortcut menu, shown in Figure C.13, with these items:

Figure C.13
Common commands related to classes are on the Class View window shortcut menu for a class.

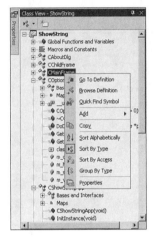

- **Go to Definition**. Opens the header (.h) file at the definition of this class.
- **Browse Definition**. Opens the Object Browser with the selected class highlighted.
- **Quick Find Symbol**. Finds all symbols (class names, function names, and so on) matching the classname. Using this command on the CMainFrame class finds the CMainFrame class declaration and the CMainFrame constructor.
- **Add, Add Function**. Opens the Add Member Function Wizard shown in Figure C.14. This adds a declaration of the function to the header file, and the stub of a definition to the source file.

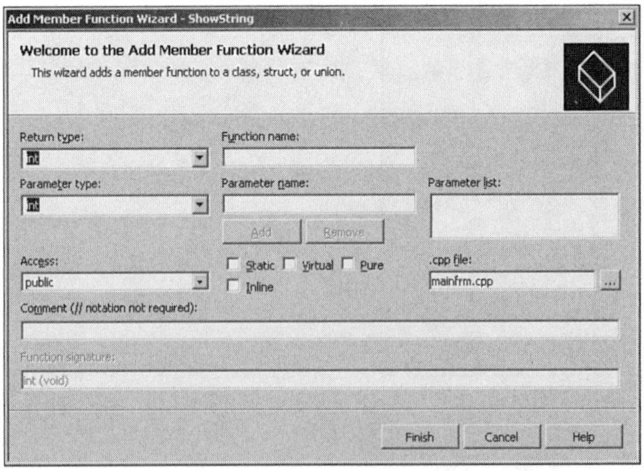

Figure C.14
Never again forget to add part of a function declaration or definition when you use the Add Member Function Wizard.

■ **Add, Add Variable**. Opens the Add Member Variable Wizard shown in Figure C.15. This adds a declaration of the variable to the header file.

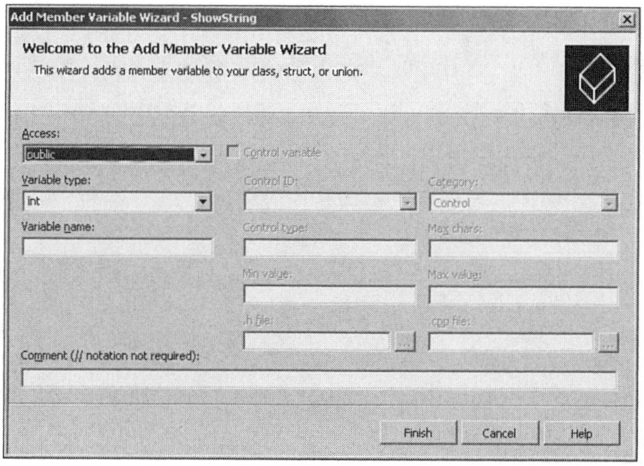

Figure C.15
Simplify adding member variables with this wizard.

■ **Add Solution to Source Control**. Enables you to use a source control program, such as Visual SourceSafe, to track modifications to the solution.

■ **Copy**. Copies the name of the class onto the Clipboard so that it can be pasted elsewhere.

■ **Sort Alphabetically**. Displays the sub-nodes of the class in the Class View window (the member function nodes, member variable nodes, the Maps node, and the Bases and Interfaces node) in alphabetical order.

■ **Sort by Type**. Displays the sub-nodes of the class ordered by type. First member functions, then member variables, and so on are displayed.

■ **Sort by Access**. Displays the sub-nodes of the class in the order of first non-code elements, then, public members, private members, and lastly protected members.

■ **Group by Type**. Groups the member functions into a single sub-folder and the member variables into another sub-folder.

■ **Properties**. Displays the Properties window for the class, which contains plenty of useful information.

Tip

Menu items that appear on a toolbar have their toolbar icon next to them on the menu. Make note of the icon; the next time you want to choose that item, perhaps you can use a toolbar instead.

Right-clicking the name of a member function opens a substantial shortcut menu, with the following menu items:

- **Go to Definition**. Opens the file in which the function is defined, and highlights that point in the file.

- **Go to Declaration**. Opens the file in which the function is declared, and highlights that point in the file.

- **Browse Definition**. Opens the Object Browser with the selected function highlighted.

- **Quick Find Symbol**. Finds all symbols matching the function name, and displays them in the Find Symbol Results window.

- **Add Solution to Source Control**. Enables you to use a source control program, such as Visual SourceSafe, to control modifications to the solution.

- **Copy**. Copies the name of the function onto the Clipboard so that it can be pasted elsewhere.

- **Sort Alphabetically**. Displays the sub-nodes of the class in the Class View window (the member function nodes, member variable nodes, the Maps node, and the Bases and Interfaces node) in alphabetical order.

- **Sort by Type**. Displays the sub-nodes of the class ordered by type. First member functions, then member variables, and so on are displayed.

- **Sort by Access**. Displays the sub-nodes of the class in the order of first non-code elements, then public members, private members, and lastly protected members.

- **Group by Type**. Groups the member functions into a single sub-folder and the member variables into another sub-folder.

- **Properties**. Displays the Properties window for the function.

Right-clicking the name of a member variable opens a shortcut menu with fewer menu items. The items are as follows:

- **Go to Definition**. Opens the file in which the variable is defined, and highlights that point in the file.

- **Browse Definition**. Opens the Object Browser with the selected variable highlighted.

- **Quick Find Symbol**. Finds all symbols matching the variable name, and displays them in the Find Symbol Results window.

- **Add Solution to Source Control**. Enables you to use a source control program, such as Visual SourceSafe, to track modifications to the solution.

- **Copy**. Copies the full name of the variable on to the Clipboard, so that it can be pasted elsewhere.

- **Sort Alphabetically**. Displays the sub-nodes of the class in the Class View window (the member function nodes, member variable nodes, the Maps node, and the Bases and Interfaces node) in alphabetical order.

- **Sort by Type**. Displays the sub-nodes of the class ordered by type. First member functions, then member variables, and so on are displayed.

- **Sort by Access**. Displays the sub-nodes of the class in the order of first non-code elements, then public members, private members, and lastly protected members.

- **Group by Type**. Groups the member functions into a single sub-folder and the member variables into another sub-folder.

- **Properties**. Displays the Properties window for the variable.

When the main working area is displaying a source or header file, you can edit your code as described in the later section "Editing Your Code."

LOOKING AT YOUR CODE, ARRANGED BY FILE

The Solution Explorer is much like the Class View window in that you can display and edit source and header files (see Figure C.16). However, it gives you access to parts of your file that are outside class definitions and makes it easy to open non-code files such as resources and plain text.

Figure C.16
The Solution Explorer displays a list of the files that make up your solution.

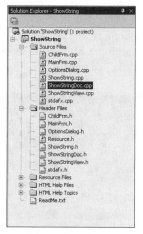

The Solution Explorer window contains a tree view of the source files in your project. The default categories used are Source Files, Header Files, Resource Files, Help Files (if your project has Help) and External Dependencies. You can add your own categories by right-clicking a project name, or an existing folder name, then choosing Add, New Folder from the context menu. You can now add new files to this folder, or drag existing ones into it.

If you would like to specify that a folder should contain only certain types of files, you can add a filter to the folder. Bring up the Properties window by right-clicking the folder and choosing Properties. In the Filter field of the Properties window enter the extensions of the files that you would like to place in the folder. Each extension should be in the format .ABC, and semicolons should separate multiple extensions. Figure C.17 shows a new folder, called XML files, that will contain XML-related files.

Figure C.17
In the Solution Explorer, you can use filters to specify what types of files should go in each folder.

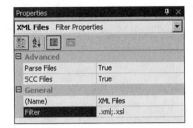

Double-clicking a file name displays that file in the main working area. You can then edit the file (even if it isn't a source or header file) as described in the later section "Editing Your Code."

OTHER USEFUL WINDOWS

Several other miscellaneous windows display useful information. These windows are not shown by default, but can be shown by choosing View, Other Windows, and the name of the window. By default, most of the windows appear on the bottom of the screen as tabs along the bottom of a parent window (although there is no reason they have to stay there,) while others appear as regular windows in the working area or fly-outs on the sides of the screen, as shown in Figure C.18.

Figure C.18
Plenty of useful information is available to you in other Visual Studio windows.

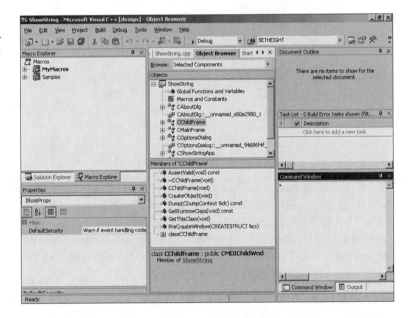

There are nine such windows:

- **Macro Explorer**. The Macro Explorer enables you to run your own macros, or those supplied with Visual Studio. You can also create new macros. Double-clicking a macro in the Macro Explorer runs that macro. Double-clicking a macro module launches the macro IDE, where you can add, delete, and edit macros. Macros are written in Visual Basic and use objects from the Visual Studio object model. The best way to learn how to produce macros is through examining the included samples and the help files.

- **Object Browser**. This window is displayed as a regular window within the working area; you can easily switch between the Object Browser window and any other window you may be working in. With the Object Browser, you navigate through a tree view of all the elements in your project. However, most of this functionality can be found in the Class View window. The real power comes from being able to browse other projects or components. By choosing Selected Components from the Browse drop-down box, then choosing Customize, you can add components, either .NET or COM, to the Object Browser window and view the elements that are contained within. The Object Browser is a very simple, yet powerful way to understand the function of a project or component.

- **Task List**. This window maintains a "to-do" list for your solution. Tasks can be added or deleted either by the user or by the Visual Studio environment. For example, when you build your project, if you have compiler or linker errors Visual Studio adds tasks reminding you to correct them. You can set a task to completed or not completed. Tasks are a great way of reminding yourself of work to be done, or a bug that needs fixing. You can also customize the Task List window by choosing View, Show Tasks, and the view you would like for the window.

- **Command Window**. This window is a simple command-line interface to the Visual Studio environment. Nearly every action in the Visual Studio environment can be run from the Command Window. The Command Window also includes an auto-complete feature and a history feature that enables you to cycle through past commands with the up and down arrow keys. The Command Window is useful for quickly running commands that otherwise would only be accessible through nested menus or dialog boxes.

- **Output**. Displays the results of compiling and linking.

- **Find Results 1**. Displays the results of the Find in Files search, discussed later in this chapter.

- **Find Results 2**. An alternative display window for Find in Files results so that you can preserve earlier results.

- **Find Symbol Results**. Displays the results of the Find Symbol and Quick Find Symbol commands. Double-clicking an entry opens the file in which the symbol is referenced within the working area, and highlights the symbol. Furthermore, if you have Browse Information enabled for your project, you can view the Browse Information for each entry.

- **Favorites**. Displays your Internet Explorer Favorites window. You can navigate and manage your Favorites, and open Web resources within Visual Studio.

APP

C

EDITING YOUR CODE

For most people, editing code is the most important task you do in a development environment. If you've used any other editor or word processor before, you can handle the basics of the Visual Studio editor right away. You should be able to type in code, fix your mistakes, and move around in source or header files by using the basic Windows techniques you would expect to be able to use. Because this is a programmer's editor, there are some nice features you should know about.

BASIC TYPING AND EDITING

To add text to a file, click where you want the text to go and start typing. By default, the editor is in Insert mode, which means your new text pushes the old text over. To switch to Overstrike mode, press the Insert key. Now your text types over the text that is already there. The OVR indicator on the status bar reminds you that you are in Overstrike mode. Pressing Insert again puts you back in Insert mode. Move around in the file by clicking with the mouse or use the cursor keys. To move a page or more at a time, use the Page Up and Page Down keys or the scrollbar at the right side of the main working area.

When you are editing several files at once, they are all on top of each other, accessed by tabs across the top of the working area. Clicking a window's tab displays it in the main working area. You can display several windows at the once by using a vertical or horizontal tab group. Right-click a tab and choose New Vertical Tab Group or New Horizontal Tab Group to create a tab group. Horizontal tab groups stretch windows across the width of the working area, one above the other, whereas vertical tab groups stretch windows across the height of the working area, one next the other. You can drag tabs from one tab group to another and create new tab groups using the method already described. Figure C.19 shows three horizontal tab groups.

Figure C.19
Your files are tabbed windows, so you can switch between them quickly, and edit several at once, side by side.

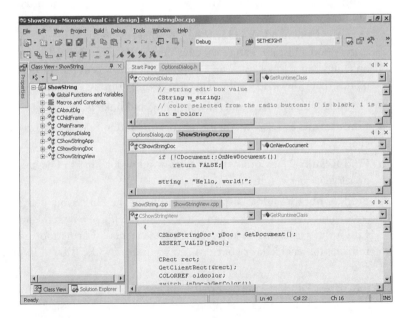

Tip

If you are used to the Visual Studio 6 interface, you can switch to the MDI (Multiple Document Interface) by choosing Tools, Options, then, in the Environment, General tab, selecting the MDI environment radio button, as in Figure C.20. You have to close and re-open Visual Studio for the change to take effect. Figure C.21 shows code being edited, MDI-style.

Figure C.20
You can select MDI windows if you prefer them to tabbed windows.

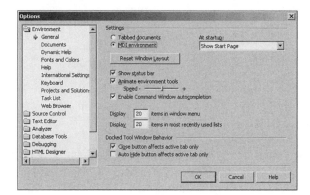

Figure C.21
MDI windows are familiar to those who used Visual C++ 6.

OUTLINING

New in the editor for Visual Studio.NET is code outlining. This can save tremendous amounts of time scrolling around in your code looking for things. Figure C.22 shows code being edited as an outline.

Figure C.22
An outline view of your code makes understanding the structure much easier.

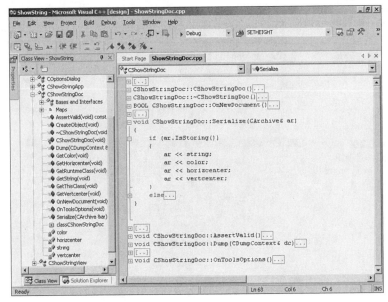

As you can see in the figure, code is collapsed into an outline structure. You can expand any node by clicking on the + to the left of it. You can collapse an expanded node by clicking the –. A number of options on the Edit, Outlining menu, discussed a little later in this chapter, give you fine control over outlining behavior.

By default, outlining is not turned on for Visual C++ developers. You can turn it on file by file. Choose Edit, Outlining, Collapse to Definitions. The nodes in your outline are based on:

- Brace brackets, such as those that surround the body of a function, a class definition, or a block statement after an if, while, or for.

- Comment blocks, whether defined with /* */ or //.

You can create your own node by selecting several lines with the mouse and choose Edit, Outlining, Hide Selection. You can then expand and collapse this section at will.

If you find the outlining annoying, you can turn it off by choosing Edit, Outlining, Stop Outlining.

WORKING WITH BLOCKS OF TEXT

Much of the time, you will want to perform an action on a block of text within the editor. First, select the block by clicking at one end of it and, holding the mouse button down, moving the mouse to the other end of the block, then releasing the mouse button. This should be familiar from many other Windows applications. Not surprisingly, at this point you can copy or cut the block to the Clipboard, replace it with text you type, replace it with the current contents of the Clipboard, or delete it.

> **Tip**
>
> To select columns of text, as shown in Figure C.23, hold down the Alt key as you select the block.

Figure C.23
Selecting columns makes fixing indents much simpler. Hold down the Alt key as you select the block.

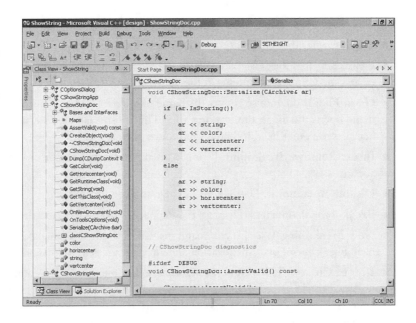

SYNTAX COLORING

You may have noticed the color scheme used to present your code. Visual Studio highlights the elements of your code with syntax coloring. By default, your code is black, with comments in green and keywords (reserved words in C++ such as `public`, `private`, `new`, or `int`) in blue. You can also arrange for special colors for strings, numbers, or operators (such as + and -) if you want, using the Environment, Fonts and Colors tab of the Options dialog box, reached by choosing Tools, Options.

Syntax coloring can help you spot silly mistakes. If you forget to close a C-style comment, the huge swath of green in your file points out the problem right away. If you type **inr** where you meant to type **int**, the **inr** isn't blue, and that alerts you to a mistyped keyword. This means you can prevent most compiler errors before you even compile.

> **Tip**
>
> If you build Web pages and still use Notepad from time to time so that you can see the tags, you're in for a pleasant surprise. Open an HTML file in Visual Studio and see HTML syntax coloring in action. You'll never go back to Notepad.

SHORTCUT MENU

Many of the actions you are likely to perform are available on the shortcut menu that appears when you right-click within a file you are editing. The items on that menu are as follows:

- **Cut**. Cuts the selected text to the Clipboard.
- **Copy**. Copies the selected text to the Clipboard.
- **Paste**. Replaces the selected text with the Clipboard contents, or if no text is selected, inserts the Clipboard contents at the cursor.
- **Open File**. If the mouse is over the name of a file in an `#include` statement, this command opens the file in the working area. This is especially useful for header files because you don't need to know what folder they are in.
- **Insert/Remove Breakpoint**. Inserts a breakpoint at the cursor or removes one that is already there.
- **Disable Breakpoint**. Disables an existing breakpoint.
- **Breakpoint Properties**. Displays the Properties page for an existing breakpoint.
- **New Breakpoint**. Use this command instead of the Insert Breakpoint command to have finer control over the location and circumstances of a breakpoint.
- **Run to Cursor**. Builds and executes your solution (assuming no build errors), and breaks at the location of the cursor. If the line the cursor is on is not a valid line on which to break, execution breaks at the nearest valid line.
- **Add/Remove Task List Shortcut**. Adds a task with the text of the current line to the Task List, or removes the Task if it already exists.
- **List Members**. Lists the member variables and functions of the object under the cursor.
- **Parameter Info**. Pops up a tip to remind you the parameters a function takes.
- **Complete Word**. "Wakes up" AutoComplete to help with a variable or function name that is partially typed.
- **Quick Info**. Pops up a tip to remind you of the type of a variable or function.
- **Go to Definition**. Opens the file where the item under the cursor is defined (header for a variable, source for a function) and positions the cursor at the definition of the item.
- **Go to Declaration**. Opens the file where the item under the cursor is declared and positions the cursor at the declaration of the item.
- **Go to Reference**. Positions the cursor at the next reference to the variable or function whose name is under the cursor.
- **Synchronize View Class**. Opens the Class View window and highlights the item under the cursor, expanding nodes as necessary.

- **Outlining, Hide Selection**. Outlines the currently selected text into a tree node that can be expanded or collapsed.

- **Outlining, Toggle Outlining Expansion**. If the text under the cursor is outlined and collapsed, it is expanded; if the text is outlined and expanded, it is collapsed.

- **Outlining, Toggle All Outlining**. Switches between collapsing all outlined text and expanding all outlined text.

- **Outlining, Stop Outlining**. Removes outlining for all outlined text in the file.

- **Outlining, Stop Hiding Current**. Removes outlining, if present, from the text under the cursor.

- **Outlining, Collapse to Definitions**. Outlines function definitions and other miscellaneous text into collapsible nodes.

- **Move File Into Project**. Enables you to add a file that is not already in the solution into a specific project. This is often used when you drag files into the working area from Explorer or another application.

- **Check In/Out**. If you're using Visual Source Safe, either submits the changes to a file back into the source control database, or marks the file as being edited by you.

Not all the items are enabled, or displayed, at once. For example, Check In/Check Out is enabled only when the solution has been added to source control. Furthermore, some commands simply don't work, depending on the location of the cursor. The Visual Studio user interface is heavily context-sensitive. It presents you with options that are applicable to the current situation. All these actions have menu and toolbar equivalents and are discussed more fully later in this chapter.

LEARNING THE MENU SYSTEM

Visual Studio has many menus. Some commands are three or four levels deep under the menu structure. In most cases, there are far quicker ways to accomplish the same task, but for a new user, the menus offer an easier way to learn because you can rely on reading the menu items as opposed to memorizing shortcuts. The Visual Studio menu bar has nine menus, as follows:

- **File**. For actions related to entire files, such as opening, closing, and printing.

- **Edit**. For copying, cutting, pasting, searching, and moving about.

- **View**. For changing the appearance of Visual Studio, including toolbars and subwindows such as the Solution Explorer window.

- **Project**. For dealing with your entire project.

- **Build**. For compiling, linking, and deploying your solution.

- **Debug**. For debugging your solution.

- **Tools**. For customizing Visual Studio and accessing standalone utilities.

- **Window**. To change which window is maximized or has focus.

- **Help**. To access the exhaustive Help system.

The following section presents each Visual Studio menu in turn and mentions keyboard shortcuts and toolbar buttons where they exist.

USING THE FILE MENU

The File menu, shown in Figure C.24, collects most of the commands that affect entire files or the entire solution.

Figure C.24
The File menu has actions for files, such as Open, Close, and Print.

NEW

This cascading menu lists the different items that can be created; these include:

- **Project... (Ctrl+Shift+N)**. This command opens the New Project dialog box, shown in Figure C.25. This dialog box allows you to add many different types to an existing solution, or create a new solution for the project.

- **File... (Ctrl+N)**. Opens the New File dialog. New files are not automatically added to a project, but you can do so using the shortcut menu described earlier in this chapter.

- **Blank Solution...** Opens the New Project dialog with the Blank Solution template selected as well as the option to close the current solution.

OPEN

This cascading menu enables you to open several different items, including:

- **Project... (Ctrl+Shift+O)**. Displays the Open Project dialog box. From this dialog you can open any Visual Studio solution or project. The file type defaults to All Project Files, which includes, but is not limited to, solutions, projects from all templates, and old Visual C++ projects and workspaces. You can use a more selective filter by choosing the appropriate item from the Files of Type drop-down box.

- **Project From Web**... Enables you to open a project at a given URL.

- **File**... **(Ctrl+O)**. Choosing this item opens the Open File dialog box, as shown in Figure C.26. (It's the standard Windows File Open dialog box, so it should be familiar.) The file type defaults to Visual C++ Files, if you have set your profile as Visual C++ developer or are working on a Visual C++ project, with extensions related to developing in C++, such as .CPP, .H, .RC, or .IDL. By clicking the drop-down box, you can open almost any kind of file, including text files and executables.

- **File From Web**... Enables you to open a file at a given URL.

Figure C.25
The New Project box contains numerous templates for you to use as a starting point for your application.

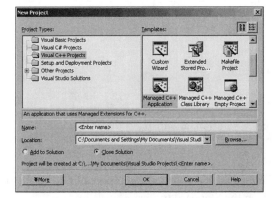

Figure C.26
The familiar Open dialog box is used to open a variety of file types.

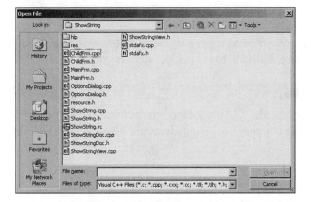

Tip

Don't forget the list of recently opened files and projects farther down the File menu. That can save a lot of typing or clicking.

APP
C

CLOSE

Choosing the File, Close item closes the file that has focus; if no file has focus, the item is grayed. You can also close a file by clicking the Cancel button, depicted by an X, in the top-right corner.

ADD NEW ITEM… (CTRL+SHIFT+A)

Similar to the File, New, File… command, but automatically adds the file to the active project.

ADD EXISTING ITEM… (SHIFT+ALT+A)

Similar to the File, Open, File… command, but automatically adds the file to the active project.

OPEN SOLUTION…

Use this item to open a solution.

CLOSE SOLUTION

Closes the currently opened solution, and displays the Start Page.

SAVE (CTRL+S)

Use this item to save the file that has focus at the moment; if no file has focus, the item is grayed. A Save button is on the Standard toolbar as well.

SAVE AS

Use this item to save a file and change its name at the same time. It saves the file that has focus at the moment; if no file has focus, the item is grayed.

ADVANCED SAVE OPTIONS…

Enables you to change the character encoding and line ending conventions used when your files are saved. This command is extremely useful if you are working on multiple platforms.

SAVE ALL

This item saves all the files that are currently open. All files are saved just before a compile and when the application is closed, but if you aren't compiling very often and are making a lot of changes, it's a good idea to save all your files every 15 minutes or so. (You can do it less often if the idea of losing that amount of work doesn't bother you.)

CHECK IN/OUT…

If your solution is using a source control program, such as Visual Source Safe, you can flag the current file as being editing by you, or if you have the file checked out, you can resubmit it to the source control database.

SOURCE CONTROL

This cascading menu lists the options available to you relating to your source control. The following are the options when you control source code revisions with Visual Source Safe:

- Open Project from Source Control...
- Add Project to Source Control...
- Exclude File from Source Control
- Change Source Control...
- Get Latest Version
- Get...
- Check Out...
- Check In
- Undo Check Out...
- History...
- Share...
- Compare Versions...
- Properties...
- Source Control Manager...
- Refresh Status

APP

C

PAGE SETUP...

This item opens the Page Setup dialog box, shown in Figure C.27. Here you specify the margins—left, right, top, and bottom—as well as the orientation of the print-out.

Figure C.27
Use the Page Setup dialog box to lay out your printed pages the way you want.

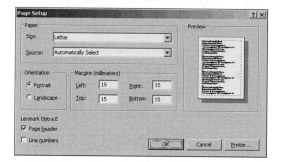

FILE PRINT... (CTRL+P)

Choosing this item prints the file with focus according to your Page Setup settings. (The item is grayed if no file has focus.) The Print dialog box, shown in Figure C.28, has you confirm the printer on which you want to print. If you have some text highlighted, the

Selection radio button is enabled. Choosing it enables you to print just the selected text; otherwise, only the All and Pages radio buttons are enabled.

Figure C.28
The Print dialog box confirms your choice to print a file.

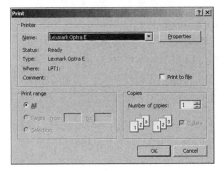

RECENT FILES AND RECENT PROJECTS

The RecentFiles and Projects items, between Print and Exit, each lead to a cascading menu. The items on the secondary menus are the names of files and projects that have been opened most recently. You can set the number of entries in this list in the Options dialog on the Environment tab. These are real time-savers if you work on several projects at once. Whenever you want to open a file, before you click that toolbar button and prepare to point and click your way to the file, think first whether it might be on the File menu. Menus aren't always the slower way to go.

FILE EXIT

Probably the most familiar Windows menu item of all, this closes Visual Studio. You can also click the X in the top right corner or double-click what used to be the System menu in the top left. If you have made changes without saving, you get a chance to save each file on your way out.

EDIT

The Edit menu, shown in Figure C.29, collects actions related to changing text in a source file.

UNDO (CTRL+Z)

The Undo item reverses whatever you just did. Most operations, like text edits and deleting text, can be undone. When Undo is disabled, it is an indication that nothing needs to be undone or you cannot undo the last operation.

An Undo button appears on the Standard toolbar. Clicking the arrow next to the button displays a stack (reverse order list from most recent to least recent) of operations that can be undone. You must select a contiguous range of undo items that includes the first, second, and so on. You cannot pick and choose.

Figure C.29
The Edit menu holds items that change the text in a file.

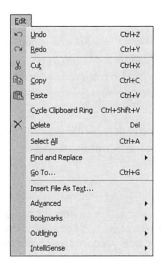

REDO (CTRL+Y)

As you undo actions, the name given to the operations moves from the Undo to the Redo list. (Redo is next to Undo on the toolbar.) If you undo a little too much, choose Edit, Redo to un-undo them (if that makes sense).

CUT (CTRL+X)

This item cuts the currently highlighted text to the Clipboard. That means a copy of it goes to the Clipboard, and the text itself is deleted from your file. The Cut button (represented as scissors) is on the Standard toolbar.

COPY (CTRL+C)

Editing buttons on the toolbar are grouped next to the scissors (Cut). Edit, Copy copies the currently selected text or item to the Windows Clipboard.

PASTE (CTRL+V)

Choosing this item copies the Clipboard contents at the cursor or replaces the highlighted text with the Clipboard contents if any text is highlighted. The Paste item and button are disabled if there is nothing in the Clipboard in a format appropriate for pasting to the focus window. In addition to text, you can copy and paste menu items, dialog box items, and other resources. The Paste button is on the Standard toolbar.

CYCLE CLIPBOARD RING (CTRL+SHIFT+V)

The Clipboard Ring enables you to cut or copy several pieces of data and then paste them separately elsewhere. This command pastes the next item in the Ring (the previous item that was copied) at the cursor location.

DELETE (DEL)

Edit, Delete clears the selected text or item. If what you deleted is undeletable, the Undo button is enabled, and the last operation is added to the Undo button combo box. Deleted material does not go to the Clipboard and cannot be retrieved except by undoing the delete.

SELECT ALL (CTRL+A)

This item selects everything in the file with focus that can be selected. For example, if a text file has focus, the entire file is selected. If a dialog box in the dialog box editor has focus, every control on it is selected.

Tip

To select many items on a dialog box, you can click the first item and then Ctrl+click each remaining item. It is often faster to use Edit, Select All to select everything and then Ctrl+click to deselect the few items you do not want highlighted.

FIND AND REPLACE, FIND (CTRL+F)

The Find dialog box shown in Figure C.30 enables you to search for text within the file that currently has focus. Enter a word or phrase into the Find What edit box. The following checkboxes set the options for the search:

- **Match Case**. If this is checked, *Chapter* in the Find What box matches only *Chapter*, not *chapter* or *CHAPTER*. Uppercase and lowercase must match.
- **Match Whole Word**. If this is checked, *table* in the Find What box matches only *table*, not *suitable* or *tables*.
- **Search Hidden Text**. Normally text that has been outlined and collapsed is not searched. Choosing this option forces a search inside the collapsed text.
- **Search Up**. Choose this option if you would like to search upward through the file; otherwise the search proceeds down through the file.
- **Use: Regular Expression**. The Find What box is treated as a regular expression if the Use option box is checked and this item is chosen in the neighboring drop-down box.
- **Use: Wildcards**. Wildcards, such as *, can be used in the Find What box when the Use option box is checked and this item is chosen in the neighboring drop-down box.
- **Search Current Document**. Limits the search to file that currently has focus.
- **Search All Open Documents**. Expands your search to all the documents you have open at the moment.
- **Only: Current Block**. Searches the current block of text, indicated by the location of the cursor. This could be a function, comment block, or other similar items.

Figure C.30
The Find dialog box is used to find a string within the file that has focus.

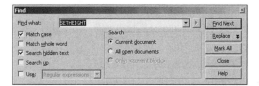

APP

C

Tip

If you highlight a block of text before selecting Edit, Find and Replace, Find, that text is put into the Find What box for you. If no text is highlighted, the word or identifier under the cursor is put into the Find What box.

A typical use for the Find dialog box is to enter some text and click the Find Next button until you find the precise occurrence of the text for which you are searching. You may want to combine the Find feature with bookmarks (discussed a little later in this section) and put a bookmark on each line that has an occurrence of the string. Click the Mark All button in the Find dialog box to add temporary, unnamed bookmarks on match lines; they are indicated with a blue oval in the margin.

A Find edit box appears on the Standard toolbar. Enter the text you want to search for in the box and press Enter to search forward. Regular expressions are used if you have turned on that option in the Find dialog box. To repeat a search, click in the Search box and press Enter. You may wish to add the Find Next or Find Previous buttons to the Standard toolbar using the Tools, Customize menu item described later in this chapter.

Regular Expressions

Many of the find and replace operations within Visual Studio can be made more powerful with regular expressions. For example, if you want to search for a string only at the end of a line, or one of several similar strings, you can do so by constructing an appropriate regular expression, entering it in the Find dialog box, and instructing Visual Studio to use regular expressions for the search. A regular expression is some text combined with special characters that represent things that can't be typed, such as "the end of a line" or "any number" or "three capital letters."

When regular expressions are being used, some characters give up their usual meaning and instead stand in for one or more other characters. Regular expressions in Visual Studio are built from ordinary characters mixed in with these special entries, shown in Table C.1.

You don't have to type these in if you have trouble remembering them. Next to the Find What box is an arrowhead pointing to the right. Click there to open a shortcut menu of all these fields, and click any one of them to insert it into the Find What box. (You need to be able to read these symbols to understand what expression you are building, and there's no arrowhead on the toolbar's Find box.) Remember to select the Regular Expressions box so that these regular expressions are evaluated properly.

Here are some examples of regular expressions:

* `^test$` matches only *test* alone on a line.
* `doc[1234]` matches *doc1*, *doc2*, *doc3*, or *doc4* but not *doc5*.
* `doc[1-4]` matches the same strings as `doc[1234]` but requires less typing.

- doc[^56] matches *doca*, *doc1*, and anything else that starts with *doc* and is not *doc5* or *doc6*.
- H\~ello matches *Hillo* and *Hxllo* (and lots more) but not *Hello*. H[^e]llo has the same effect.
- [xy]z matches *xz* and *yz*.
- New *York matches *New York* but also *NewYork* and *New York*.
- New +York matches *New York* and *New York* but not *NewYork*.
- New.*k matches *Newk*, *Newark*, and *New York*, plus lots more.
- \:n matches *0.123*, *234*, and *23.45* (among others) but not *-1C*.
- World$ matches *World* at the end of a line, but World\$ matches only *World$* anywhere on a line.

TABLE C.1   REGULAR EXPRESSION ENTRIES

Entry	Matches
^	Start of the line.
$	End of the line.
.	Any single character.
[]	Any one of the characters within the brackets (use - for a range, ^ for "except").
\~	Anything except the character that follows next.
*	Zero or more of the next character.
+	One or more of the next character.
{ }	Doesn't match specially, but saves part of the match string to be used in the replacement string. Up to nine portions can be tagged like this.
[]	Either of the characters within the [].
\:a	A single letter or number.
\:b	Whitespace (tabs or spaces).
\:c	A single letter.
\:d	A single numerical digit.
\:n	An unsigned number.
\:z	An unsigned integer.
\:h	A hexadecimal number.
\:i	A string of characters that meets the rules for C++ identifiers (starts with a letter, number, or underscore).
\:w	A string of letters only.
\:q	A quoted string surrounded by double or single quotes.
\	Removes the special meaning from the character that follows.

FIND AND REPLACE, REPLACE (CTRL+H)

This item opens the Replace dialog box, shown in Figure C.31. It is very similar to the Find dialog box but is used to replace the found text with new text. Enter one string into the Find What edit box and the replacement string into the Replace With edit box. The three check boxes—Regular Expression, Match Case, and Match Whole Word Only—have the same meaning as on the Find dialog box (discussed in the previous section). The Replace In radio buttons enable you to restrict the search-and-replace operation to a block of highlighted text, if you prefer. To see the next match before you agree to replace it, click Find Next. To replace the next match or the match you have just found, click Replace. If you are confident that there won't be any false matches, you can click Replace All to do the rest of the file all at once. (If you realize after you click Replace All that you were wrong, there is always Edit, Undo.)

Figure C.31
The Replace dialog box is used to replace one string with another.

FIND AND REPLACE, FIND IN FILES (CTRL+SHIFT+F)

This useful command searches for a word or phrase within a large number of files at once. In its simplest form, shown in Figure C.32, you enter a word or phrase into the Find What edit box, restrict the search to certain types of files in the File Types box, and choose the folder within which to conduct the search in the Look In drop-down box. The following checkboxes in the bottom half of the dialog box set the options for the search:

Figure C.32
The simplest Find In Files approach searches for a string within a folder and its subfolders.

- **Match Case**. If this is checked, *Chapter* in the Find What box matches only *Chapter*, not *chapter* or *CHAPTER*. Uppercase and lowercase must match.

- **Match Whole Word Only**. If this is checked, *table* in the Find What box matches only *table*, not *suitable* or *tables*.

- **Use: Regular Expression**. The Find What box is treated as a regular expression (see the sidebar "Regular Expressions") if the Use box is checked and this item is chosen in the neighboring drop-down box.

- **Use: Wildcards**. Allows the use of wildcards in the Find What box if the Use box is checked and this item is chosen in the neighboring drop-down box.

- **Look in Subfolders**. Work through all the subfolders of the chosen folder if this is checked.

- **Display in Find 2**. Sends the results to the Find Results 2 window, so as not to wipe out the results of an earlier search.

- **Display File Names Only**. The output of the Find in Files command typically lists names of the files that matched the criteria as well as some of the text surrounding the matching criteria. When this box is checked, only the file names are listed.

If you highlight a block of text before selecting Find in Files, that text is put into the Find What box for you. If no text is highlighted, the word or identifier under the cursor is put into the Find What box.

The results of the Find in Files command appear in the Find Results 1 window (unless you ask for window 2); the output window will be visible after this operation if it was not already. You can resize this window as you do any other window, by holding the mouse over the border until it becomes a sizing cursor, and you can scroll around within the window in the usual way. Double-clicking a filename in the output list opens that file with the cursor on the line where the match was found.

FIND AND REPLACE, REPLACE IN FILES (CTRL+SHIFT+H)

This command searches for a word or phrase within a large number of files at once and replaces it with another word or phrase. This command is somewhat like a combination of the Replace command and the Find in Files command. The Replace in Files dialog contains the following options:

- **Match Case**. If this is checked, *Chapter* in the Find What box matches only *Chapter*, not *chapter* or *CHAPTER*. Uppercase and lowercase must match.

- **Match Whole Word Only**. If this is checked, *table* in the Find What box matches only *table*, not *suitable* or *tables*.

- **Use: Regular Expression**. The Find What box is treated as a regular expression (see the sidebar "Regular Expressions") if the Use box is checked and this item is chosen in the neighboring drop-down box.

- **Use: Wildcards**. Allows the use of wildcards in the Find What box if the Use box is checked and this item is chosen in the neighboring drop-down box.

- **Keep Modified Files Open After Replace All**. If this box is checked, any files that were modified are opened in the working area so that you can inspect the changes that have been done.

- **Look in Subfolders**. Work through all the subfolders of the chosen folder if this is checked.

- **Display in Find 2**. Sends the results to the Find Results 2 window, so as not to wipe out the results of an earlier find or replace command.

EDIT FIND AND REPLACE, FIND SYMBOL (CTRL+SHIFT+H)

This command searches for a specified symbol-items such classes, structures, namespaces, functions, and variables—within a specified scope. The scope can be the active project, or user-defined. You can look for symbols in any component (.NET or COM) that has been registered in the system or has a type library file. The following options are available on the Find Symbol dialog, shown in Figure C.33:

- **Match Whole Word Only**. If this is selected, *table* in the Find What box matches only *table*, not *suitable* or *tables*.

- **Match Prefix**. If this option is selected, the value in the Find What box is considered to be the prefix of the symbol. For example, if the value of the Find What box is *alpha*, and this option is selected, a class called `alphaChar` and a function `alphaToNum()` would match, but not `num_to_alpha()`.

- **Match Substring**. If this option is selected, any symbol that contains the value in the Find What box will be matched. For example, if the value of the Find What box is *alpha*, and this option is selected, a class called `alphaChar` and a function `alphaToNum()` would match, as would `num_to_alpha()`.

APP

C

Figure C.33
The Find Symbol command enables you to search not only within your own projects but also in components registered on your system.

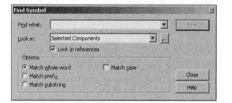

GO TO LINE (CTRL+G)

The Go to Line dialog box (see Figure C.34) gets you quickly to a particular line number.

Figure C.34
The Go to Line dialog box moves you around within your project.

INSERT FILE AS TEXT

This item inserts the complete contents of a file into the currently active file.

ADVANCED

Choosing this item opens a cascading menu with the following items:

- **Format Selection (Ctrl+K, Ctrl+F).** This item adjusts the indenting of a selection using the same rules that apply when you are entering code.
- **Tabify Selection.** Converts spaces to tabs.
- **Untabify Selection.** Converts tabs to spaces.
- **Make Uppercase (Ctrl+Shift+U).** Converts the selected text to capital letters.
- **Make Lowercase (Ctrl+U).** Converts the selected text to lowercase letters.
- **Delete Horizontal White Space (Ctrl+K, Ctrl+\).** Deletes any whitespace characters, not including newline characters, from the selected text.
- **View White Space (Ctrl+R, Ctrl+W).** Inserts small placeholder characters (. for space and >> for tab) to show all the whitespace in your document.
- **Word Wrap (Ctrl+R, Ctrl+R).** Wraps any text that goes off the edge of the screen to the next line.
- **Incremental Search (Ctrl+I).** This is a faster search than opening the Find dialog box discussed earlier. You enter your search string directly on the status bar. As you type each letter, Visual Studio finds the string you have built so far. For example, in a header file, if you choose Edit, Advanced, Incremental Search and then type **p**, the cursor jumps to the first instance of the letter *p*, probably in the keyword `public`. If you then type **r**, the cursor jumps to the first *pr*, probably in the keyword `protected`. This can save you typing the entire word you are looking for.
- **Comment Selection (Ctrl+K, Ctrl+C).** Adds comment symbols (//) to the start of every line in the selection.
- **Uncomment Selection (Ctrl+K, Ctrl+U).** Removes any // symbols that occur within the selection.
- **Increase Line Indent.** Adds an extra tab at the beginning of the line.
- **Decrease Line Indent.** Removes a tab from the beginning of the line (if at least one exists).

BOOKMARKS

Choosing this item opens a cascading menu with the following items:

- **Toggle Bookmark (Ctrl+K, Ctrl+K).** Adds a bookmark to the line of the cursor if one is not already there; otherwise removes the bookmark on the line of the cursor.
- **Next Bookmark (Ctrl+K, Ctrl+N).** Jumps to the next bookmark in the file (relative to the cursor's position).
- **Previous Bookmark (Ctrl+K, Ctrl+P).** Jumps to the previous bookmark in the file (relative to the cursor's position).

- **Clear Bookmarks (Ctrl+K, Ctrl+L)**. Removes all bookmarks from the file.
- **Add Task List Shortcut (Ctrl+K, Ctrl+H)**. Adds a shortcut to the Task List at the line of the cursor.

OUTLINING

Choosing this item opens a cascading menu with the following items:

- **Hide Selection**. Outlines the currently selected text into a tree node that can be expanded or collapsed.
- **Outlining Expansion**. If the text under the cursor is outlined and collapsed, it will be expanded; if the text is outlined and expanded, it will be collapsed.
- **Toggle All Outlining**. Switches between collapsing all outlined text and expanding all outlined text.
- **Stop Outlining**. Removes outlining for all outlined text in the file.
- **Stop Hiding Current**. Removes outlining, if present, from the text under the cursor.
- **Collapse to Definitions**. Outlines function definitions and other miscellaneous text into collapsible nodes.

INTELLISENSE

Intellisense gives you context-sensitive information about your code. Choosing this item leads to a cascading menu with the following options:

- **List members (Ctrl+J)**. Lists the member variables and functions of the object under the cursor.
- **Parameter Info (Ctrl+Shift+Space)**. Pops up a tip to remind you the parameters a function takes.
- **Complete Word (Ctrl+K, Ctrl+I)**. "Wakes up" AutoComplete to help with a variable or function name that is partially typed.
- **Quick Info (Alt+Right Arrow)**. Pops up a tip to remind you of the type of a variable or function.

RESOURCE INCLUDES

Choosing this item opens the Resource Includes dialog box. It is unusual for you to need to change this generated material. In the rare cases where the resource.h file generated for you is not quite what you need, you can add extra lines with this dialog box. This item is available when the focus is in the Resource View window.

RESOURCE SYMBOLS

This item opens the Resource Symbols dialog box. It displays the resource IDs, such as ID_EDIT_COPY, used in your application. The large list box at the top of the dialog box

APP
C

lists resource IDs, and the smaller box below it reminds you where this resource is used—on a menu, in an accelerator, in the string table, and so on. The buttons along the right side are used to make changes. Click New to create a new resource ID, Delete to delete this resource ID (if it's not in use), Change to change the ID (if it's in use by only one resource), and View Use to open the resource (menu, string table, and so on) that is highlighted in the lower list. This item is available when the focus is in the Resource View window.

ADD RESOURCE

Displays the Add Resource dialog box. See the same command under the Project menu for a complete description.

USING THE VIEW MENU

The View menu, shown in Figure C.35, collects actions that are related to the appearance of Visual Studio—which windows are open, what toolbars are visible, and so on.

Figure C.35
The View menu controls the appearance of Visual Studio.

OPEN

Opens the file that is selected in the Solution Explorer window.

OPEN WITH

Opens the file that is selected in the Solution Explorer window with a specified program, rather than the Visual Studio default. This can be used to open an XML Schema in a text editor rather than the XML Schema Editor for quick editing.

SOLUTION EXPLORER (CTRL+ALT+L)

This command displays the Solution Explorer window, shown in Figure C.36. This window displays a tree-view of all the files that make up your projects and solutions. You learn how to use the Solution Explorer window starting in Chapter 3.

Figure C.36
The Solution Explorer window shows the files that make up your solution.

CLASS VIEW (CTRL+ALT+C)

This command displays the Class View window, shown in Figure C.37. The Class View window displays a detailed tree view of all the user-defined types within your solution. You learn how to use the Class View window starting in Chapter 3.

SERVER EXPLORER (CTRL+ALT+S)

This command displays the Server Explorer window, shown in Figure C.38. The Server Explorer enables you to access and manage resources such as servers and data connections. The Server Explorer window is covered in more detail in Chapter 11, "Database Programming."

RESOURCE VIEW (CTRL+ALT+E)

This command displays the Resource window, shown in Figure C.39. This window displays a tree view of all the resources that are used in your solution. You learn how to use the Resource View window starting in Chapter 3.

APP

C

Figure C.37
The Class View window makes it easy to navigate around your solution.

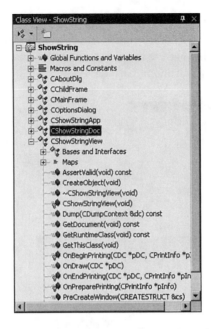

Figure C.38
The Server Explorer window makes it easy to access remove servers and data connections.

PROPERTIES WINDOW (ALT+ENTER)

This command displays the Properties window, shown in the lower left of Figure C.40. The Properties window is the central hub of information in the Visual Studio environment. The contents of the window are based on what item currently has focus: for example, if it is a class in the Class View window, then information pertinent to the class is displayed. You learn how to use the Properties window starting in Chapter 3. The Properties window, for the most part, has replaced the ClassWizard from Visual C++ 6.0.

Figure C.39
The Resource View window displays a list of the resources used by your solution.

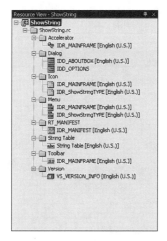

Figure C.40
The Properties window can be used to access massive amounts of information about your solution, and to simplify many actions.

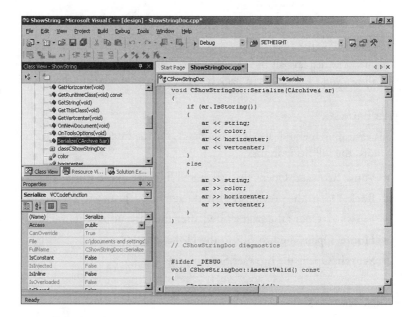

TOOLBOX (CTRL+ALT+X)

This command displays the Toolbox, shown in Figure C.41. The Toolbox contains different tools based on the context of the current focus. The Toolbox is typically used while editing dialog boxes, but can also be used for other chores, such as accessing specific items in the Clipboard Ring.

APP

C

Figure C.41
The Toolbox can be used in many situations, not just editing dialog boxes.

PENDING CHECKINS

This window displays all the files that have been checked out of a source control program, and allows you to check them back in and assign comments to the modifications.

WEB BROWSER

This cascading menu deals with commands for the integrated Visual Studio Web browser. It contains the following items:

- **Show Browser**. Opens the integrated browser in the working area.
- **Back**. Opens the previously visited page in the browser, if it is open.
- **Forward**. Opens the page visited after the current page in the browser, if it is open.
- **Home**. Opens the browser to the Home page.
- **Search**. Opens the browser Search page.

OTHER WINDOWS

This cascading menu shows a list of windows that contain valuable information, described earlier in this chapter. It contains the following items:

- Macro Explorer
- Object Browser
- Document Outline
- Task List
- Command Window
- Output

- Find Results 1
- Find Results 2
- Find Symbol Results
- Favorites

SHOW TASKS

This cascading menu enables you to navigate the Task List window. It contains the following items:

- Previous View
- All
- Next Task
- Previous Task
- Comment
- Build Errors
- User
- Shortcut
- Policy
- Current File
- Checked
- Unchecked

TOOLBARS

This cascading menu enables you to add and remove toolbars from the display. It contains all the toolbars provided by Visual Studio (see the "Toolbars" section for more information) so you can customize them to maximize your efficiency.

FULL SCREEN (SHIFT+ALT+ENTER)

This item hides all the toolbars, menus, Output window, and Project Workspace window, giving you the entire screen as the main working area. One small toolbar appears, whose only button is Toggle Full Screen. Click that button or press the Esc key to restore the menus, toolbars, and windows.

NAVIGATE BACKWARD (CTRL+-)

Jumps to the previously visited location (using the Navigation toolbar or Bookmark/Task navigation options) in the file.

APP

C

NAVIGATE FORWARD (CTRL+SHIFT+-)

Undoes a Navigate Backward command by jumping to the subsequently visited location in the file.

PROPERTY PAGES

This item is available only if the item that has focus has Property Pages associated with it. Its most important use is for compiler and development environment settings, as shown in Figure C.42. Click the project or solution name in Solution Explorer, then choose this menu item.

Figure C.42
The Property Pages dialog for a source file enables you to modify more uncommon options.

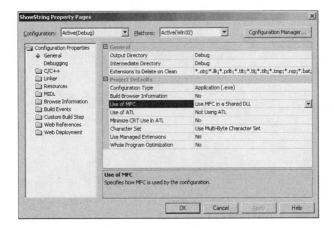

PROJECT

The Project menu, shown in Figure C.43, holds items associated with project maintenance. The items in this menu are listed in the following sections.

Figure C.43
The Project menu simplifies project maintenance.

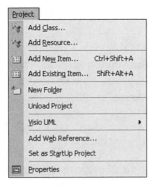

ADD CLASS

Use this item to add a class to your project. When you choose this item, the Add Class dialog box shown in Figure C.44 appears. From this dialog you can chose from a large variety of templates on which to base your class. After having chosen a template, the appropriate Class Wizard is displayed, such as the MFC Class Wizard shown in Figure C.45.

Figure C.44
The Add Class dialog box has a large number of templates that save you time.

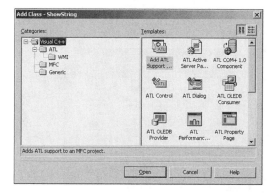

Figure C.45
Class Wizards help you customize the class templates.

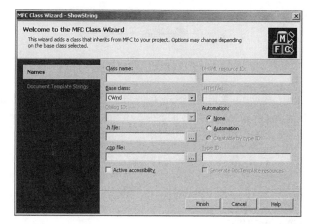

ADD RESOURCE

Use this item to add a new resource to your project. The Add Resource dialog box, shown in Figure C.46, appears. Choose the type of resource to be added and click New.

ADD NEW ITEM

Add New Item displays the Add New Item dialog box, shown in Figure C.47, which enables you to add a new file, selected from a large range of types, to the current project.

Figure C.46
Using the Add Resource dialog box is the easiest way to add resources to your project.

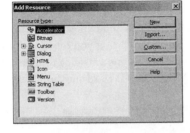

Figure C.47
You can choose from a large variety of files to add to your projects.

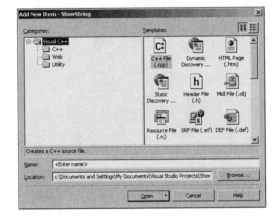

ADD EXISTING ITEM

Add existing item displays the Add Existing Item dialog box. Use this command to add an existing file to the current project. This is especially useful when you are reusing code from another project.

NEW FOLDER

New Folder adds a new folder to the project directory.

VISIO UML, REVERSE ENGINEER

If you have the Enterprise Architect Edition of Visual Studio .NET you can create UML (Unified Modeling Language) diagrams based on your projects.

PROJECT ADD WEB REFERENCE

This command displays the Add Web Reference dialog box, shown in Figure C.48, which enables your project to easily consume a Web Service. Web Services are one of the center-pieces of Visual Studio .NET and are covered in greater detail in Chapter 21, "Creating an XML Web Service."

Figure C.48
The Add Web Reference dialog box makes it easy to find and consume Web Services.

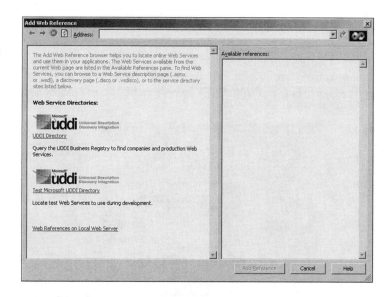

PROJECT BUILD ORDER

If you have several projects in your solution, this item sets the order in which the projects are built.

SET AS STARTUP PROJECT

If you have several projects in your solution, this item sets which project is run when the solution is executed.

PROJECT DEPENDENCIES

This item enables you to make one project dependent on another so that when one project is changed, its dependents are rebuilt.

PROJECT PROPERTIES

This item replaces the Project Settings item from Visual C++ 6.0. It opens the Property Pages for the current project.

Tip

If you are used to Visual C++ 6.0, you may have been frustrated when you could not find the Project Settings option; for this item to appear on the menu, you must have the name of the project selected in the Solution Explorer window or the Class View window.

APP
C

The Project Property Pages contains nine tabs and two miscellaneous pages, as follows:

- **General**. This page, shown in Figure C.49, shows the settings that determine the location of your project's files as well as other defaults used by your project. From this tab you can change many of the choices you made in the in MFC Application Wizard, such as the choice between using MFC in a shared DLL or as static library.

Figure C.49
The General tab of the Project Property Pages governs where files are kept and other project defaults.

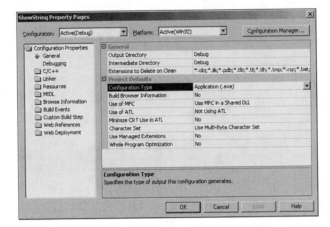

- **Debug**. These settings are discussed in Chapter 13, "Debugging."
- **C/C++**. These are your compiler settings. Figure C.50 shows the General page. The Additional Include Directories field on the General page, and the Optimization field on the Optimization page, are two of the more useful fields under this tab. This tab is discussed in more detail in Chapter 12, "Improving Your Application's Performance."

Figure C.50
The C/C++ tab of the Project Property Pages governs compiler settings in ten categories, starting with General.

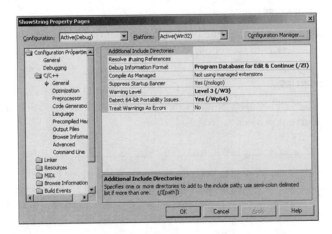

- **Linker**. This tab controls linker options, which you are unlikely to need to change. However, remember that if you are using external libraries, you must add the files to the Additional Dependencies field on the Input page. The settings are divided into eight categories; the General category is shown in Figure C.51.

Figure C.51
The Linker tab of the Project Property Pages governs linker settings in eight categories, starting with General.

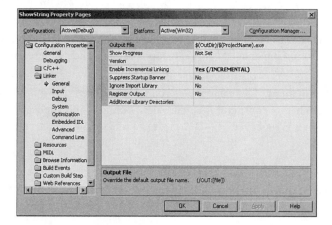

- **Resources**. This tab, shown in Figure C.52, is used to change the language in which you are working. This tab enables you to change which resources are compiled into your application, and other resource settings.

Figure C.52
The Resources tab of the Project Settings dialog box governs resources settings, including language.

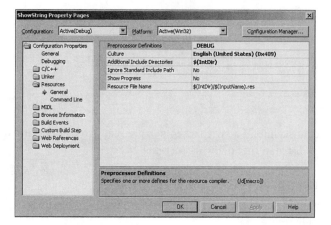

- **MIDL**. This tab is used by programmers who are building a type library (TLB), typically when using ATL. ATL is described in greater detail in Chapter 9, "Building COM+ Components with ATL."

- **Browse Information**. This tab controls the Browse Info (.BSC) file used for Go to Definition, Go to Declaration, and similar menu items. If you never use these, your links will be quicker if you don't generate browse information. If you want browse information, set the Enable Browse Information field of the Browse Information page under the C/C++ tab to the appropriate value.

- **Build Events**. These settings enable you to add your own steps to be performed as part of every build process.

- **Custom Build Step**. Enables you to perform a customized build on certain input files.

- **Web References**. This tab contains settings for managing Web references in your project. Such settings include whether to use Managed C++ Extensions (see Chapter 20, "Managed and Unmanaged C++," for more details) when generating the Web proxy code.

- **Web Deployment**. This tab enables you to customize how your application is deployed. This is very useful if you are developing a Web application that must be deployed to a Web server.

BUILD

The Build menu, shown in Figure C.53, holds all the actions associated with compiling and running your application.

Figure C.53
The Build menu is used to compile, link, and execute your application.

The Build menu is a hub of activity when you are ready to compile and debug. The Build menu items are listed in the following sections.

BUILD SOLUTION (F7)

This item compiles all the changed files in the project and then links them. The Build toolbar has a Build button.

REBUILD SOLUTION

This item compiles all files in the project, even those that have not been changed since the last build, and then links them. There are times when a typical build misses a file that should be recompiled; using this item corrects the problem.

CLEAN SOLUTION

This item deletes all the intermediate and output files so that your project directory contains only source files.

BATCH BUILD

Typically a project contains at least two configurations: Debug and Release. Usually you work with the Debug configuration—changing, building, testing, and changing the project again until it is ready to be released—and then you build a Release version. If you ever need to build several configurations at once, use this menu item to open the Batch Build dialog box shown in Figure C.54. Choose Build to compile only changed files and Rebuild to compile all files. If the compiles are successful, links follow. Choose Clean to delete intermediate and output files, leaving only source files.

Figure C.54
The Batch Build dialog box builds several configurations of your project at once.

APP

C

CONFIGURATION MANAGER

The Configuration Manager dialog box, shown in Figure C.55, sets which of your configurations is active (typically Debug and Release). The Build commands build the active configuration.

Figure C.55
The Configuration Manager dialog box sets the default configuration.

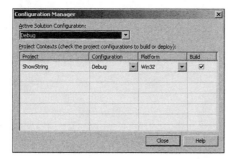

COMPILE (CTRL+F7)

Choosing this item compiles the file with focus. This is a very useful thing to do when you are expecting to find errors or warnings, such as the first time you compile after a lot of changes. For example, if a header file that is included in many source files contains an error, a typical build produces error messages related to that header file over and over again as each source file is compiled. If there are warnings in one of your source files, a typical build links the project, but you might prefer to stop and correct the warnings. The Build toolbar has a Compile button, represented by a stack of papers with an arrow pointing downward.

DEBUG

The Debug menu, shown in Figure C.56, contains many commands and tools that help you execute and debug your applications. The menu consists of the items in the following section. See Chapter 13, for more information on this topic.

Figure C.56
The Debug menu contains commands you use while debugging.

WINDOWS

This cascading menu lists the windows that help with debugging. Note that many more items will appear on this menu when the application is in the process of being debugged. The following items appear on the menu:

- Breakpoints
- Running Documents
- Watch
- Autos
- Locals
- This
- Immediate
- Call Stack
- Threads
- Modules
- Memory

- Disassembly
- Registers

START (F5)

Start begins the application, building if necessary.

START WITHOUT DEBUGGING (CTRL+F5)

This starts the application, building if necessary, but does not run the debugger.

CONTINUE (F5)

Continue restarts an application that has stopped during debugging.

BREAK ALL (CTRL+ALT+BREAK)

Break all breaks execution at the current statement, within or outside the project.

STOP DEBUGGING (SHIFT+F5)

Stop debugging stops the application and the debugger.

DETACH ALL

Detach all detaches the application from any processes to which it has been attached.

RESTART (CTRL+SHIFT+F5)

Restart restarts the application and the debugger at the beginning of the application.

APPLY CODE CHANGES (ALT+F10)

Apply Code Changes applies any changes to the code that have been made while the debugger is running, and re-executes the application.

PROCESSES

Processes displays the Processes dialog box. From this dialog box, you can attach and detach processes to and from your application, as well as terminate its execution.

EXCEPTIONS

Exceptions displays the Exceptions dialog box. This dialog box enables you monitor the exceptions your application throws, and determine what action should be taken if a handled or unhandled exception is thrown.

STEP INTO

As Chapter 13 discusses in more detail, you can execute your code a line at a time. This menu item is used to step into an executing function.

STEP OVER

When executing your code a line at a time, Steps Over enables you to step over a function call rather than into it, so that debugging continues at the line after the function call.

STEP OUT

When executing a line of code at a time, Step Out runs the application until the flow of control leaves this function, and resumes debugging on the line after the one that called the current function.

QUICKWATCH

Quickwatch sets a quick watch, described in Chapter 13 on the variable that is selected.

NEW BREAKPOINT

New Breakpoint sets a breakpoint as described in Chapter 13.

CLEAR ALL BREAKPOINTS

Clear All Breakpoints clears all breakpoints you have set.

TOOLS

The Tools menu, shown in Figure C.57, simplifies access to add-in tools and holds some odds-and-ends leftover commands that don't fit on any other menu.

Figure C.57
The Tools menu organizes add-in tools.

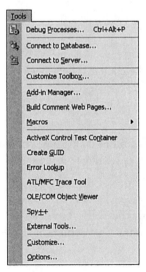

DEBUG PROCESSES

Choosing this item is the same as Debug, Processes, discussed earlier.

CONNECT TO DATABASE

Choosing this item brings up the Data Link Properties dialog, shown in Figure C.58, so that you can connect to a database server. It also activates the Server Explorer window, described earlier and covered in more detail in Chapter 11.

Figure C.58
Connecting to a database is simple.

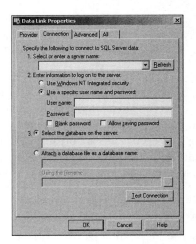

CUSTOMIZE TOOLBOX

Choosing this item brings up the Customize Toolbox dialog, shown in Figure C.59. Here you can add ActiveX controls and components to your application. They appear on the Toolbox that is used when you edit dialogs and other visual resources.

Figure C.59
You can add components to your project.

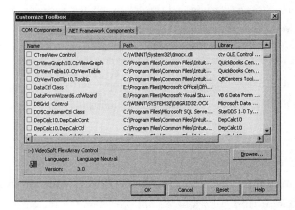

ADD-IN MANAGER

Add-ins are extensions to Visual Studio that you write yourself or obtain from a third party. Some parts of the Visual Studio documentation call them *automation objects*, because they are used to automate Visual Studio. They differ from macros because they are written in one of the Visual Studio languages (Visual Basic, C#, or Visual C++) and can do anything that can be done in code.

BUILD COMMENT WEB PAGES

Choosing this item generates HTML pages that can be customized to describe your code. It describes the parts of your project. If you were working in C#, it would also include specially formatted comments from your code itself.

MACROS

A macro is essentially a sequence of keystrokes you intend to do over and over. In previous editions of Visual Studio, they were available to Visual C++ programmers only, but now macros are available throughout Visual Studio. Macros are organized into *modules*, which can hold multiple related *commands*. Several related macros can be gathered together into a *macro project*. The items under Tools, Macro facilitate writing, using, and managing macros. They are:

- **Run Temporary Macro**. After recording a temporary macro, this item runs it.
- **Record Temporary Macro**. Starts saving your keystrokes and building a temporary unnamed macro. While you are recording, an extra toolbar with Pause, Stop, and Cancel buttons appears. A Stop Recording entry is added to the Tools, Macro menu as well.
- **Save Temporary Macro**. After you record a temporary macro, this item enables you to save it so that it can be used repeatedly or shared among projects. You can also edit it after saving it.
- **Cancel Record**. Stops recording and throws away what has been recorded so far.
- **Macro Explorer**. Opens another window on the left, where the Solution Explorer, Class View, and so on appear. You can run and edit macros from this window, shown in Figure C.60.
- **Macros IDE**. Opens another window for editing macros.
- **Load Macro Project**. Opens a project that contains macros you have previously created.
- **Unload Macro Project**. Closes a macro project.
- **New Macro Project**. Starts the process of creating a macro project of your own.
- **New Macro Module**. Adds a macro module to the currently selected macro project.
- **New Macro Command**. Adds a new empty command to the current module for you to edit.
- **Run Macro**. Runs the selected macro.
- **Edit**. Edits the selected macro in the Macro IDE.

Figure C.60
The Macro Explorer box is the nerve center for editing and using macros.

ACCESSORY TOOLS

A number of tools are added to the Tools menu when you install Visual C++, and you can add more tools yourself. By default the tools that are added are:

- **ActiveX Control Test Container**. For testing ActiveX controls

- **Create GUID**. An important utility for some COM developers.

- **Error Lookup**. A handy utility that takes error codes, especially COM HRESULTs, and translates them into English.

- **MFC/ATL Trace Tool**. When an MFC or ATL application is running, this tool displays information about the modules that are executing.

- **OLE/COM Object Viewer**. Shows all the COM objects installed on your machine and some of their properties.

- **Spy++**. Displays all the windows on your machine at the moment and some information about them. This can be very useful if a window is displaying outside the visible area, for example. You can also spy on processes and threads, and watch messages go from window to window.

- **External Tools**. Enables you to manage this list of tools yourself, as shown in Figure C.61.

Figure C.61
You can add tools to the menu, or remove them.

CUSTOMIZE

Choosing this option opens the Customize dialog box. The Commands pane of that dialog box is shown in Figure C.62 with the File buttons showing. The buttons and commands on the right correspond to items on the File menu, and if you would like one of those items on any toolbar, drag it from the dialog box to the appropriate place on the toolbar and release it. The list box on the left side of the Toolbar tab enables you to choose other menus, each with a collection of toolbar buttons and commands you can drag to any toolbar. Remember that the menu bar is also a toolbar to which you can drag buttons, if you want. You can use the Keyboard button to change the keyboard shortcuts for commands or add shortcuts for commands without them.

Figure C.62
The Commands pane of the Customize dialog box enables you to build your own toolbars.

The Toolbars pane, shown in Figure C.63, can be used to control which toolbars are displayed. Most developers prefer to right-click any toolbar, then select toolbars they would like to add or remove, one at a time.

Figure C.63
Using the Toolbars tab of the Customize dialog box is one way to turn a toolbar on or off.

The Options tab, shown in Figure C.64, takes care of some bits and pieces related to tools. You can suppress ToolTips if they annoy you or turn on larger toolbar buttons if you have the space for them. (The toolbars in the background of Figure C.64 have large buttons.)

Figure C.64

The Options tab of the Customize dialog box controls toolbar and menu appearance.

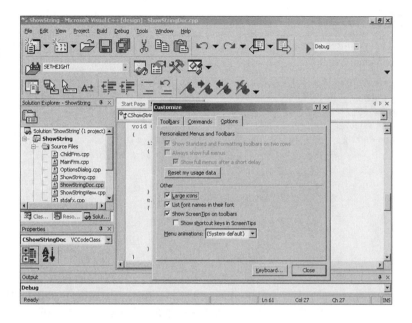

OPTIONS

This item gathers up a great number of settings and options that relate to Visual Studio itself. For example, Figure C.65 shows the General item under the Text Editor tab of the Options dialog box. If there is a feature of Visual Studio you don't like, you can almost certainly change it within this large dialog box.

Figure C.65

The Text Editor tab of the Options dialog box is where you change editor settings.

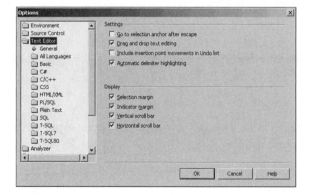

Tip

Earlier versions of Visual C++ had a Directories section of the Options dialog that set the locations where the compiler and linker would look for header files and libraries. In Visual Studio .NET, you set those locations on the Property Pages for the solution. Click on the entire solution in Solution Explorer, then choose View, Property Pages.

WINDOW

The Window menu, shown in Figure C.66, controls the windows in the main working area of Visual Studio.

Figure C.66
The Window menu controls the windows in the main working area.

NEW WINDOW

Choosing this item opens another window containing the same source file as the window with focus. The first window's title bar is changed, with :1 added after the filename; in the new window, :2 is added after the filename. Changes made in one window are immediately reflected in the other. The windows can be scrolled, sized, and closed independently.

SPLIT

Choosing this window splits the active window across the center, horizontally. You can drag the boundary about in the usual way if it is not in the right place. Drag the boundary to the very top or bottom and it will disappear.

DOCKABLE

This menu item governs whether the window with focus is a docking view. It is disabled when the main working area has focus.

FLOATING

Floating makes the dockable window (output pane, solution explorer, and so on) with focus a floating (non-docked) window.

HIDE

This item hides the dockable window with focus.

AUTO-HIDE

Auto-hide sets the dockable window with focus to auto-hide. It will "fly-out" when the mouse hovers over it, and hide on a side of the screen otherwise.

AUTO-HIDE ALL

Auto-hide all sets all dockable windows to auto-hide.

NEW HORIZONTAL TAB GROUP

This item sts up a horizontal split that enables you to view different files at once. The section "Basic Typing and Editing" earlier in this chapter explains tab groups.

NEW VERTICAL TAB GROUP

This item sets up a vertical split that enables you to view different files at once.

CLOSE ALL DOCUMENTS

Choosing this item closes all the windows in the main working area. If you have any unsaved changes, you are asked whether to save them.

OPEN WINDOWS

The bottom section of this menu lists the windows in the main working area so that you can move among them even when they are maximized. If there are more than nine open windows, only the first nine are listed. The rest can be reached by choosing Window, Windows.

APP
C

WINDOWS

This item opens the Windows dialog box, shown in Figure C.67. From here you can close, save, or activate any window.

Figure C.67
The Windows dialog box allows access to any window in the main working area.

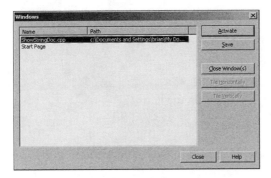

HELP

The Help system for Visual Studio is integrated into the IDE. Choosing items on this menu, shown in Figure C.68, either activates a window on the left or changes what is displayed in the main working area.

Figure C.68
The Help menu is
your doorway to the
help system.

DYNAMIC HELP

Activates a window on the left, below the Solution Explorer and Class View, with links to topics that may be relevant to what you appear to be doing. It can slow performance, so if you never use it, close it.

CONTENTS

Contents activates the Table of Contents window on the left.

INDEX

Index activates the Index window on the left.

SEARCH

Search activates the Search window on the left.

INDEX RESULTS

Index Results displays the output window (across the bottom) with index results after you have closed it.

SEARCH RESULTS

Search Results redisplays the output window (across the bottom) with search results after you have closed it.

EDIT FILTERS

This advanced item enables you to change the meaning of the filters you can set on the Index, Contents, and Search windows.

PREVIOUS TOPIC

When available, this moves you back one item in the table of contents.

NEXT TOPIC

When available, this moves you forward one item in the table of contents.

SYNC CONTENTS

Sync Contents activates the Table of Contents window and scrolls it to the item you are looking at. Useful after a search when you want to explore related topics.

SHOW START PAGE

Show Start Page activates the Start Page. Useful if you want to set your profile, as discussed at the start of this chapter, or open a recent project.

CHECK FOR UPDATES

Check for Updates connects to a Microsoft server to see whether a service pack or update is available for Visual Studio. If so, you can install it over the internet.

TECHNICAL SUPPORT

Technical Support brings up a page with links to technical support information.

HELP ON HELP

Help on Help provides explanations and links for those new to the Visual Studio Help system.

ABOUT MICROSOFT VISUAL C++

About Microsoft Visual C++ shows your version number and licensing information, including the specific sub-products you have installed.

TOOLBARS

After you are familiar with the sorts of actions you are likely to request of Visual Studio, the toolbars save you a lot of time. Instead of choosing File, Open, which takes two clicks and a mouse move, it is simpler to just click the Open button on the toolbar. This product, however, has 30 toolbars plus a menu bar, and that means a lot of little icons to learn. In this section, you will see some popular toolbars and which menu items the buttons correspond to.

Figure C.69 shows some of the more commonly used toolbars that are available in Visual Studio. The quickest way to turn several toolbars on and off is with the Toolbars dialog box, discussed earlier. Any of these toolbars can dock against any of the four edges of the working area, as shown in Figure C.70. To move a docked toolbar, drag it by the wrinkle—the

APP
C

dotted vertical bar at the far right or top. You move an undocked toolbar like any other window. When it nears the edge of the main working area, the shape change shows you it will dock. Docked toolbars take up less room, but can be harder to read. Take some time to experiment moving toolbars around until you find a configuration that suits you.

Figure C.69
Visual Studio has 30 toolbars. Six of the most commonly-used are shown here floating.

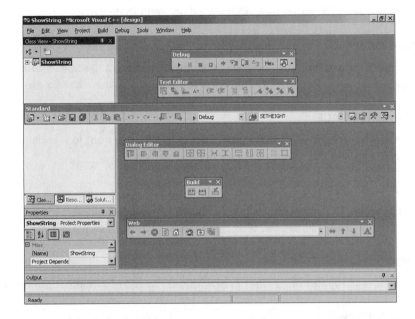

Figure C.70
Visual Studio toolbars can dock against any edge.

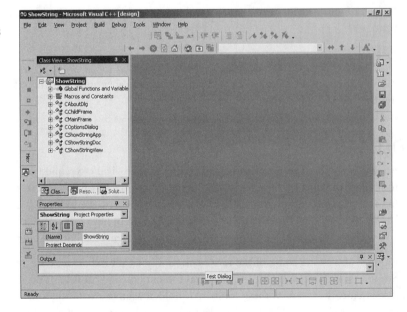

STANDARD TOOLBAR

Probably the most important toolbar is the Standard toolbar. It helps you maintain and edit text and files in your workspace. Table C.2 names each Standard tool button and its equivalent menu operation. For a full description of what each button does, refer to the section earlier in this chapter for the corresponding menu item.

TABLE C.2 STANDARD TOOLBAR BUTTONS AND EQUIVALENT MENU OPERATIONS

Button Name	Menu Equivalent
New Project	File, New, Project
Add New Item	File, Add New Item
Open	File, Open
Save	File, Save
Save All	File, Save All
Cut	Edit, Cut
Copy	Edit, Copy
Paste	Edit, Paste
Undo	Edit, Undo
Redo	Edit, Redo
Navigate Backward	View, Navigate Backward
Navigate Forward	View, Navigate Forward
Start	Debug, Start
Solution Configurations	Choose your active configuration
Find in Files	Edit, Find in Files
Find	Edit, Find
Solution Explorer	View, Solution Explorer
Properties Window	View, Properties Window
Toolbox	View, Toolbox
Class View	View, Class View

USING OTHER TOOLBARS

You can display any or all of the toolbars, add and remove buttons to them, and generally make Visual Studio into a product that works the way you work. Experiment and see what simplifies your software development effort.

UPGRADING FROM VISUAL C++ 6

In this appendix

MAKING VISUAL STUDIO .NET RESEMBLE VISUAL C++ 6

If you were a Visual C++ 6 user and you've just installed Visual Studio .NET, you've probably been thrown for a loop. The two products look very different, as Figures D.1 and D.2 show. Your first impression may be something like "What on earth happened to my favorite development tool!" The menus are different too, and at first glance you may have no idea how to perform once-familiar tasks.

In this appendix, you'll get yourself on slightly more solid ground. First, you'll learn how to restore much of the familiar Visual C++ look and feel, including menu items and keyboard shortcuts. Many of Visual Studio's features have been renamed, so this appendix explains the new terminology in use. There's a quick tour of the visual changes, and directions to some commands that have moved from their old menu locations. You'll learn your way around the new and improved Class View window, and see how to get along without good old Class Wizard. You'll also meet some features that you may recognize from Visual Basic 6, which have been integrated into Visual Studio for developers to use in all languages.

The first thing you should do is to change your *user profile* to that of a Visual C++ developer. As Figure D.3 shows, that's going to bring the interface much closer to what you're used to seeing. On the Start page that is displayed whenever you start Visual Studio, click My Profile. As shown in Figure D.4, identify yourself as a Visual C++ developer and your interface will become more familiar. All the illustrations in this chapter and throughout the book were taken with a Visual C++ profile.

Figure D.1
Visual C++ 6 has an interface many developers know well.

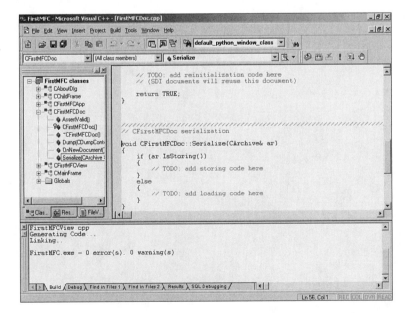

Figure D.2
Visual Studio .NET looks very different from Visual C++ 6.

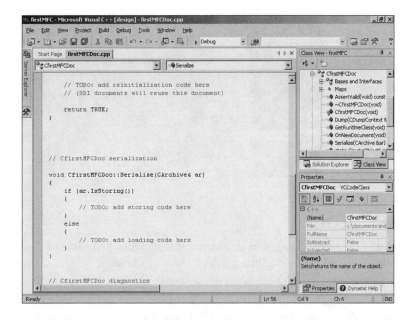

Figure D.3
Visual Studio .NET can be configured to look more like Visual C++ 6.

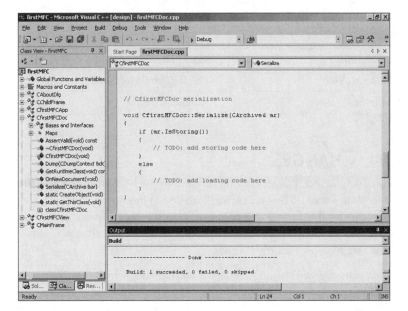

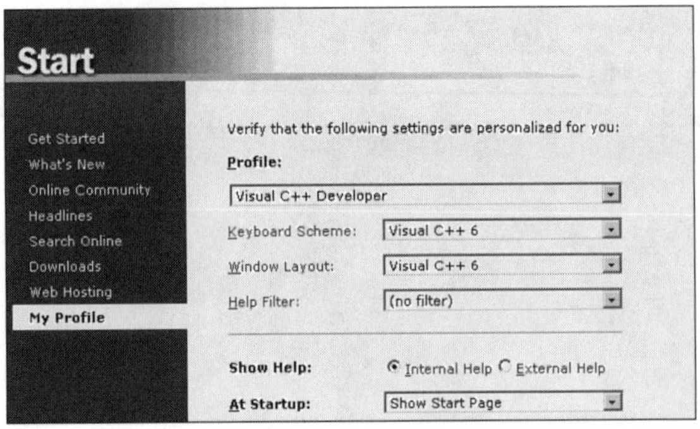

Figure D.4
Set your profile to
Visual C++ developer
to change the inter-
face.

TERMINOLOGY

Some words have changed, which means that you may find some of the instructions in this book or the online help a little harder to follow. The underlying concepts are not different, just the names. Table D.1 offers a quick translation.

TABLE D.1   NEW NAMES FOR USER INTERFACE COMPONENTS IN VISUAL STUDIO

Visual C++ 6 Word	Visual Studio .NET Word
Workspace	Solution
ClassView	The Class View window
ResourceView	The Resource View window
FileView	Solution Explorer

VISUAL CHANGES

Visual Studio .NET is an exciting product with a lot of new functionality. If you're using it to do things you did before, such as building Windows applications, you may be frustrated by not being able to find things that you know must be in the product somewhere. The visual changes to the product are mostly superficial, and after you've located your missing item, you'll be back on track again.

The primary visual changes are to the editing area, which now uses tabbed rather than MDI windows, and provides code outlining—a very neat feature. Help has changed, as it does with every release, and there's a handy Start page that makes it simple to create a new project or open an old one.

TABBED WINDOWS

By default, documents in the main working area are displayed as tabbed windows. This makes it easy to switch from window to window, including Help topics and your code. Figure D.5 shows this tab arrangement. It may feel a little odd at first, but it does simplify many aspects of coding. You can see at a glance which files you have open. As well, any file that has changed but has not been saved features the familiar * after its name on the tab itself, whether it has focus or not. Look at Figure D.6 and spot which files have unsaved changes.

Figure D.5
Documents you are editing are displayed as tabbed windows.

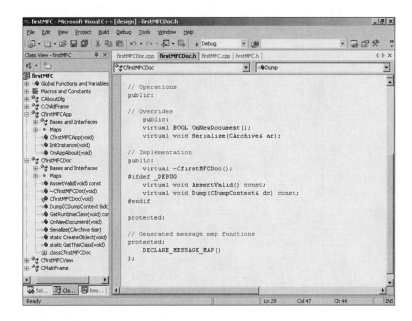

Figure D.6
It's easy to see which files are not yet saved.

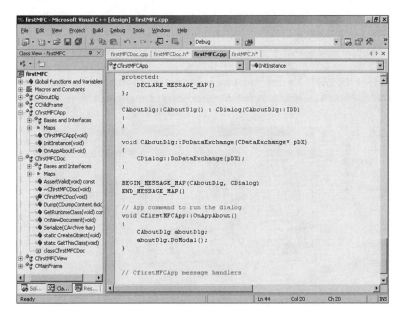

If you want to see two files side by side, set up a vertical tab group. Right-click the tab for one of the files and from the shortcut menu that appears, choose New Vertical Tab Group. After the group is created, you can move files from group to group by clicking and dragging them by their tabs. Figure D.7 shows a pair of vertical tab groups. You can also create horizontal groups if you wish. If you close the only file in a tab group, or drag it to another group, the now-empty group disappears.

Figure D.7
To see files side by side, set up a vertical tab group.

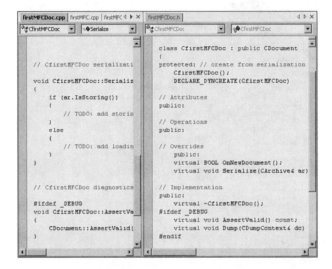

If you really can't stand the tabbed windows, it is possible to switch back to the MDI interface. I recommend that you spend a day or so using the tabbed windows before you give up, because they increase most developers' productivity. To switch to MDI, choose Tools, Options, to bring up the Options dialog. Select the General section under Environment, and set the MDI Environment radio button, as shown in Figure D.8. You'll have to close and re-open Visual Studio for the change to take effect.

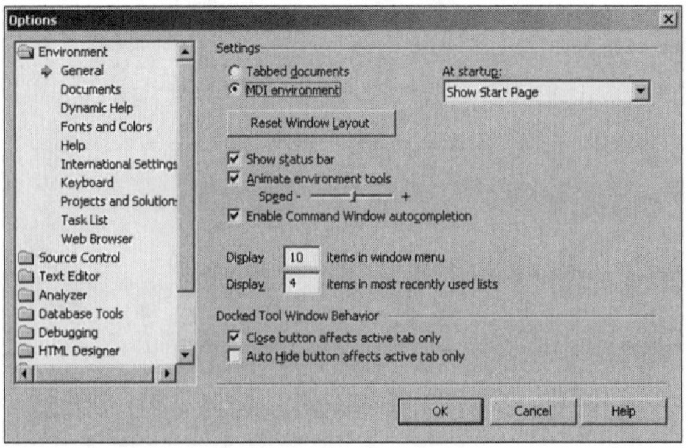

Figure D.8
You can switch back to the MDI interface, but give tabbed windows a chance first.

HELP

Help is displayed within Visual Studio, as shown in Figure D.9, which shows a Help topic on the Intellisense feature as just another tabbed window inside Visual Studio. If you've been using Visual C++ for many versions now, you're probably smiling, because Help moves back and forth from version to version. Visual Studio now displays HTML internally, so you get all the advantages of HTML, such as including pictures and following links, without having to switch to a separate product. The Contents, Index, and Search windows are on the left with the Class View window and Solution Explorer. Each can be "reawakened" with the appropriate choice from the Help menu; for example, Help, Contents displays the Contents window.

Figure D.9
A Help topic is just another tab among your tabbed windows.

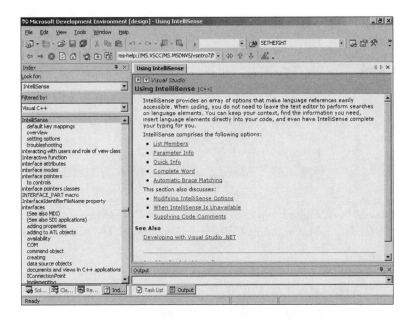

APP

D

Dynamic Help is also provided. Figure D.10 shows Dynamic Help at work. Like Intellisense, it tracks what you're doing and offers links to topics that might be relevant. In Figure D.10, the cursor in the working area is on the else line, so the topics offered include the C++ if-else construct. Dynamic Help can hurt the performance of the Integrated Development Environment a little, so if you never pay any attention to what it's suggesting, you should probably close the window to get zippier performance.

OUTLINING

If you open a project that someone else has been working on, you might find that outlining has been turned on, as in Figure D.11. If you've ever used Microsoft Word in Outline View, you'll have no trouble working with outlined code. Click a + to expand collapsed code, and click a - to collapse some code.

Figure D.10
Dynamic Help (at the lower left) adjusts to match what you're doing.

Figure D.11
Built-in outlining enables you to collapse or expand blocks of code and comments.

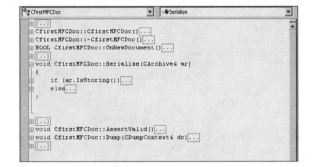

By default, outlining is not turned on for Visual C++ developers. You can turn it on file by file. Choose Edit, Outlining, Collapse to Definitions. The nodes in your outline are based on:

- **Brace brackets**, such as those that surround the body of a function, a class definition, or a block statement after an `if`, `while`, or `for`.

- **Comment blocks**, whether defined with `/* */` or `//`.

You can create your own node by selecting several lines with the mouse and choosing Edit, Outlining, Hide Selection. You can then expand and collapse this section at will.

If you find the outlining annoying, you can turn it off by choosing Edit, Outlining, Stop Outlining.

START PAGE

When Visual Studio starts, it opens a Start Page (Figure D.12) every time. From here you are only one click away from some of the most common tasks for a Visual C++ programmer:

Figure D.12
The Start Page makes common tasks simple.

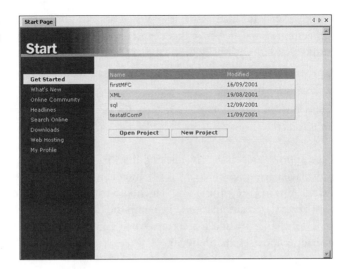

- Open a project you were working on recently. Notice that the list reminds you when you worked on each project last. These same projects are available to you under File, Recent Projects.
- Read the many What's New topics by clicking on What's New. You'll find plenty of information relevant to Visual C++ 6 users who are moving to Visual Studio .NET, as Figure D.13 shows. Note that the information is presented in tabbed windows, and that you can filter by language.

Figure D.13
Extensive What's New coverage simplifies upgrading.

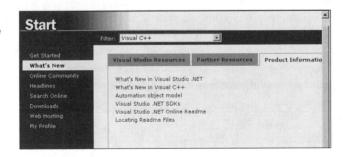

- Get a clickable list of Microsoft newsgroups for discussing Visual Studio .NET by clicking Online Community.
- Get recent news from Microsoft by clicking Headlines. Notice that a Web browser is integrated into Visual Studio .NET so that you don't have to switch between two products.
- Search MSDN online by clicking Search Online. It's generally faster to search your own CD or DVD of MSDN first, but the online version may have more recent information.

- Change your settings for many aspects of Visual Studio .NET at once by clicking My Profile. As demonstrated earlier in this chapter, you can change the appearance of Visual Studio .NET dramatically by changing your profile.

- Open an existing project (beyond just the most recent that are shown to you) by clicking Open Existing Project.

- Create a new project by clicking Create New Project. This is quicker than choosing File, New, Project.

If the Start Page annoys you, close it by clicking the x in the upper right corner. If you never want it to be displayed again, go to your profile and change the drop-down box at the bottom of the dialog. Also in your profile you can choose to automatically load the project you worked on most recently, to automatically bring up the Open Project or New Project dialogs, or to perform no extra automatic steps when you open Visual Studio. If you want the Start page back, choose Help, Show Start Page.

FINDING FAMILIAR COMMANDS

One of the frustrations for anyone who moves from one version of a product to another is finding things you were in the habit of using. Menus get rearranged; dialogs get renamed; options get moved from one dialog to another. The switch from Visual C++ 6 to Visual C++ .NET is no exception.

START

In Visual C++ 6, the Debug menu appeared only while you were debugging. When your program wasn't running, a Build menu appeared instead. The theory was that you don't need to build your application while it's running, and you don't need any of the debug commands while it's not running. That leaves one problem: where to put the commands to start debugging. They ended up, slightly illogically, on the Build menu. You would choose Build, Start Debug, and a cascading menu would appear with choices such as Go or Step Into.

In Visual Studio .NET, the Debug menu is always displayed. As a result, these commands have been moved from the Build menu to the Debug menu. Go is now called Start and the toolbar symbol has been changed from a downward-pointing arrow next to a page of code to a rightward-pointing triangle reminiscent of the Play button on a tape recorder or VCR.

PROJECT SETTINGS

Say you've just received an error message that a header file wasn't found, and you want to add another directory to the list of those searched for header files. Or perhaps you have a linker error about a missing library. Maybe you want to change your warning level, or fiddle with your optimization settings. In Visual C++ 6, you took care of all these things in a single place: You chose Project, Settings and up came a tabbed dialog box with all the settings for your particular project.

Well, Visual Studio .NET still has a Project menu, but there's no Settings choice on it. In fact, the chances are that no matter what you click, you won't find the command that brings up the dialog you need. That's because you need to select the right thing before heading to the menus.

In Solution Explorer (the window on the left that looks a lot like File View,) click the name of the project. (If Solution Explorer isn't visible, choose View, Solution Explorer.) Now choose the Project menu and a Properties item is on it. Choose that and you bring up the Property Pages for your project, as in Figure D.14.

Tip

You could also choose View, Property Pages (at the bottom of the view menu—don't confuse it with View, Properties) when the project is selected in Solution Explorer. That brings up the same dialog. Or select the project name in Class View (the root of the tree) and choose Project, Properties or View, Property Pages.

Figure D.14
The Property Pages dialog replaces the old Project Settings dialog box.

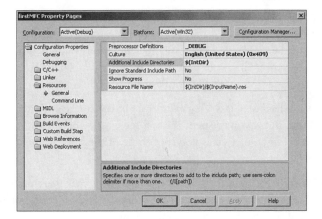

If you click the solution rather than the project, you get a different, and less useful, Property Pages dialog for the solution. As Figure D.15 shows, this dialog is more about the relationships of the projects in a solution than about any individual project.

Figure D.15
There is a Property Pages dialog for the overall solution as well.

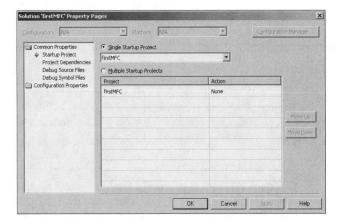

WHAT HAPPENED TO CLASSVIEW?

In Visual C++ 6, there was ClassView. It was a really useful way to see your classes. Double-click a member variable, and you'd find yourself editing the file that declared the variable, scrolled to the right line. Double-click a member function, and you'd be editing the code for that function. A powerful set of context menus put many common tasks, such as Add Member Variable or Add Member Function, just a few clicks away.

Visual Studio .NET has the Class View window. On the surface, it's not very different from good old ClassView. But if you've spent the last few years working in Visual C++, you'll find a little smile of relief on your face as you spot some of the improvements to be found in this new view.

The most obvious difference in the Class View window is that there are more nodes under each class. It's easy to find macros and constants, base classes, message maps, and other parts of your class, in addition to the methods and variables.

MACROS AND CONSTANTS

Just under Global Functions and Variables, there's a new node: Macros and Constants. It contains (not surprisingly) macros and constants. From all over your project these little definitions are gathered into this node for easy access. Figure D.16 shows the expanded node. Double-click any macro or constant to edit the file in which it is defined. For a number of these constants, it's enough to know that they are defined at all, so just looking at the list will tell you what you need to know.

BASES AND INTERFACES

Every class in the Class View window has a new node under it: Bases and Interfaces. For example, in Figure D.17, the class CFirstMFCDocument inherits from CDocument, so CDocument is listed under Bases and Interfaces. If you expand it, you can see all the nodes under

CDocument that you see under any other class in the Class View window, including Bases and Interfaces. This makes it easy to browse through an inheritance hierarchy and look at or edit code from a base class or an implemented interface.

Figure D.16
The Macros and Constants node will save you a lot of searching.

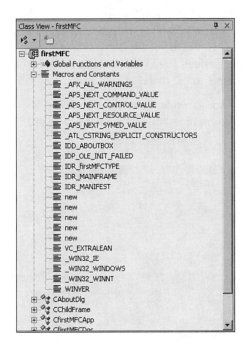

Figure D.17
The Bases and Interfaces node makes browsing through an inheritance hierarchy a lot easier.

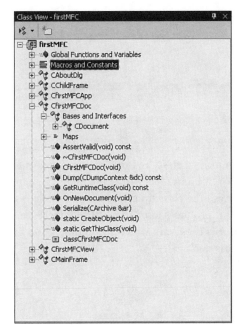

MAPS

In Visual C++ 6, the way to get to your message maps was not obvious. I used to double-click a randomly chosen member function to edit the implementation file, then scroll up looking for the message map. And just my luck, I'd click a function that was implemented inline in the class definition, so that would open the header file. Grrr. Alternatively, I'd switch to FileView and double-click the file name, but that was inconvenient too. If you didn't mind running everything through ClassWizard, fine, but I'm an edit-the-code person at times and it wasn't always simple to get there.

In Visual Studio .NET there's another node under every class: the Maps node. It shows you the maps (message maps, connection maps, dispatch maps, and so on) for this class, as shown in Figure D.18. Double-click one to edit the code.

Figure D.18
The Maps node makes short work of finding message (or other) maps to edit them.

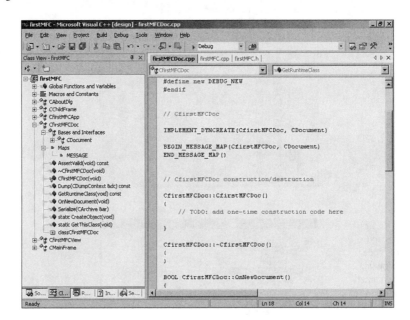

ENUMERATIONS

If you define an enumeration outside a class, an extra node appears at the same level as the classes in your project, as shown in Figure D.19. If you define an enumeration inside a class, the extra node appears underneath the class. In either case the node is named with the enumeration name, and expanding it produces a list of all the enumeration's elements. Double-clicking one of the elements opens the file in which the enumeration is defined and scrolls to the spot where that element is declared.

Figure D.19
Enumerations are
added to a node of
their own.

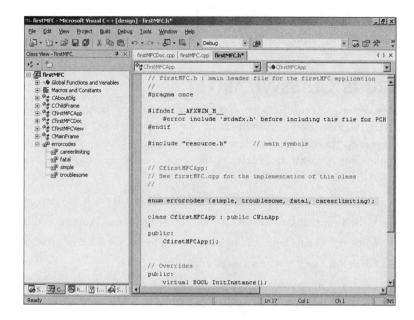

SORTING THE CLASS VIEW WINDOW

By default, the nodes under a class are shown in this order:

- Bases and Interfaces
- Enumerations in alphabetical order
- The class name if the object can be viewed in the object browser
- Member variables in alphabetical order
- Member functions in alphabetical order

At the top of the Class View window is a small toolbar with two buttons: Sort and New Folder. The Sort button is actually a drop-down, which enables you to sort Class View nodes in a number of ways:

- **Sort alphabetically**. Sorts everything according to the letter it starts with, mixing member variables and member functions with other nodes such as Maps.
- **Sort by type**. The default behavior as just described.
- **Sort by access**. Very similar to the default behavior, in that the primary sort is by type, but within each type (for example, member variables) the elements are presented as public first, then private, then protected. Within each access, elements are presented alphabetically.
- **Group by type**. Creates an expandable and collapsible node called variables and another called functions. Elements are listed alphabetically within each node.

App

D

The New Folder button creates a folder that you can use to organize a large project. Ignore it while you're getting used to all the changes in the Class View window.

WHERE IS CLASSWIZARD?

ClassWizard is gone. To catch a message or event, you use the Properties window. This is covered in more detail in a number of chapters in the first half of this book, especially Chapter 3, "Interacting with Your Application," and Chapter 6, "Building a Complete Application: ShowString." Here are the steps to catch a command or command update in a nutshell:

1. In the Class View window, select the class that will catch the message.

2. If the Properties window is not visible, choose View, Properties Window.

3. Click the Events button (a lightning bolt) to display a list of message IDs.

4. Click the + next to the message you want to catch.

5. Click either COMMAND or COMMAND_UI and a drop-down appears to the left.

6. Click the drop-down and select Add <Function Name> as shown in Figure D.20.

Figure D.20
The Properties window provides much of Class Wizard's functionality.

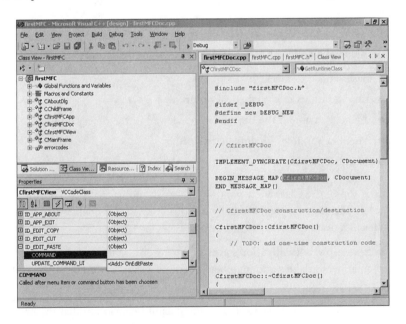

7. Use the Class View window to navigate to the function you just added, and edit it to add code.

The procedure is the same for ordinary messages (such as notifications) except that you click the Messages button rather than the Events button on the Properties Window toolbar. Finally, available overrides are listed if you click the green lozenge Overrides button.

Plenty of other wizards are still hiding behind the visual interface. Try right-clicking in the Class View window and adding a function or variable, and you'll find yourself in pretty familiar territory, at least conceptually. The facelift these wizards have undergone is not so radical that you won't know how to use them.

IS THIS VISUAL BASIC?

Visual C++ 6 and Visual Basic 6 had very different user interfaces. Visual Studio .NET can resemble either product, or look quite different, but underneath it's all one product. The same features are available to you regardless of the language you are using, with just a few exceptions. As a result, some features that have been in Visual Basic for a long time are now available to Visual C++ programmers. You can arrange to break execution whenever an exception is thrown, reverse-engineer UML diagrams from your code with Visio, and scroll around within a code file by choosing a function name from a drop-down bar at the top of the code editing area.

BREAK ON EXCEPTIONS

On the Debug menu, there is an Exceptions menu item. If you choose this item, the Exceptions dialog, shown in Figure D.21, appears. If you've worked in Visual Basic before, you'll recognize it. If this is new to you, take a minute to look around the dialog. Expand the categories and you'll see which exceptions might occur in your project. Without setting a breakpoint, you can arrange for the debugger to break execution when a C++ exception, a .NET Common Language Runtime exception, or another runtime error occurs. You can choose to break on all exceptions or just unhandled ones.

Figure D.21
It's simple now to break whenever an exception is thrown.

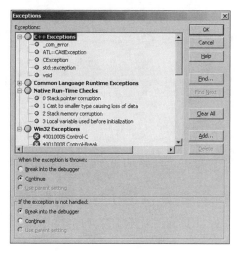

REVERSE ENGINEER

If you have Microsoft Visio installed on your system, the Project menu includes a cascading submenu called Visio UML. Among other things, you can reverse engineer a diagram (see Figure D.22) from your code. This can save a tremendous amount of time. For example, you might be asked to maintain a system that was developed by someone else. A diagram of the relationships among the classes in the system is a terrific starting point. Alternatively, you might have made a number of minor changes to your system (such as changing the naming convention for member variables) that require time-consuming updates to your design documents. Obviously, large design changes are made in the diagrams themselves first and then in code, but small changes may be done in code only—and they may leave the diagrams invalid. Generating new diagrams from the code itself updates your design documentation almost painlessly.

> **Tip**
>
> When reverse-engineering a C++ project, be sure you generate browse information, because the browse file is used to create the diagram. Bring up the Properties page for the project, as described earlier in this chapter, and in the General section under Configuration Properties, make sure that Build Browser Information is set to Yes.

Figure D.22
A picture is worth a thousand words—or a thousand lines of code?

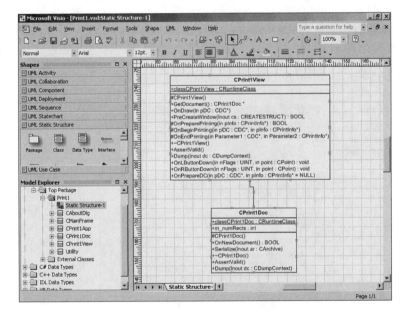

CLASSBAR

When you are editing code, a toolbar appears at the top of the working area, immediately below the tabs with the file names. The left-most drop-down box in this toolbar lists the classes that are defined in this file. The rightmost lists functions in the class, as in Figure

D.23. Grayed entries are not defined in this file; full-color entries are. If a grayed entry is selected it does nothing; if a full-color entry is selected it scrolls the code to the start of that function.

Figure D.23
Reach a specific place in your code quickly with ClassBar.

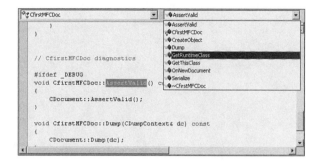

INDEX

How can we make this index more useful? E-mail us at indexes@quepublishing.com.

How can we make this index more useful? E-mail us at indexes@quepublishing.com.

www.usingvisualc.net